AMERICAN
METAPHYSICAL
RELIGION

"A lucid tour through the Wild West of American-style spirituality. Pontiac drives us through landscapes peopled by odd characters that some have deemed 'mad, bad, and dangerous to know' but whose burning arrows have ignited things in our psyches whether we knew it or not. I was constantly delighted by the new, luminous insights into characters and events that I thought I knew everything about but clearly didn't."

ALAN RICHARDSON,
AUTHOR OF *ALEISTER CROWLEY AND DION FORTUNE*

"Scholarly yet eminently readable, this is a must for the bookshelf of any reader interested in the sociology of religion, the history of psychical development, and the psychology of sacred feeling. Highly recommended."

TOD DAVIES, AUTHOR OF *THE HISTORY OF
ARCADIA* VISIONARY FICTION SERIES

"Ronnie Pontiac does his readers an inestimable service, surveying and summarizing an immense amount of academic material. Pontiac makes a strong argument that America has always had a religious consciousness, separation of church and state notwithstanding. Thomas Edison, William James, Timothy Leary, Carlos Castaneda, and Terence McKenna are only some of the figures Pontiac takes on in this detailed, thorough, and readable account of the often wildly disparate beliefs held by that 'one nation under God.'"

GARY LACHMAN, AUTHOR OF *THE RETURN OF HOLY RUSSIA*

"Ronnie Pontiac's book is a full engagement with these deep currents and a wild map of the ocean they form. The reader sets the book down with a sense of the endless nature of those waters but also with the conviction that, below the waves, 'America' is fundamentally an esoteric idea and a mystical ideal and always has been."

JEFFREY J. KRIPAL, AUTHOR OF *THE SUPERHUMANITIES:
HISTORICAL PRECEDENTS, MORAL OBJECTIONS, NEW REALITIES*

"The most fascinating book I have read in decades. Hollywood may have written its own history of cowboys and cattle, but kindly allow Ronnie Pontiac to enchant you with a different story. This is an especially long book, over 600 pages, but the work never loses pace, not a word is wasted, every sentence is packed with information. An illuminating journey into the eternal spiritual quest of human nature set free in a new land."

NAOMI OZANIEC, AUTHOR OF *BECOMING A GARMENT OF ISIS*

"This book is much closer to the mainstream psyche than academics would have us believe. Ronnie Pontiac's book is a lively, engaging, thoughtful, and insightful introduction to this dazzling world."

RICHARD SMOLEY, AUTHOR OF *A THEOLOGY OF LOVE*

"Pontiac's ambitious and inclusive book is an important contribution to our understanding of the culturally and philosophically diverse influences that have, from the very beginning, impacted the character of American spiritual thought and experience. This book is a critical project that shows us the contours and multitudes of cultural and historical influence that converge to produce a uniquely American esotericism."

AMY HALE, AUTHOR OF *ITHELL COLQUHOUN*

"I couldn't put this book down. It's a storybook concerning a multi-formed religion that lies just below the surface of American awareness yet plays a significant part in the beliefs and inspirations that characterize our psyche. Its 'metaphysical' ideas reach everyone, from presidents to heads of corporations as well as major figures in the arts and sciences and the average citizen. We can see them as people struggling to make sense of life, the world, and other realities. Prepare to be amazed."

MARY K. GREER, AUTHOR OF *WOMEN OF THE GOLDEN DAWN*

"Permanently unseats the lingering myth that the United States is (or was) an exclusively Christian nation. Read this book: I guarantee you will encounter a character who helps you locate your own lineage in the tangled skein of American metaphysical religion."

THEA WIRSCHING, AUTHOR OF *THE AMERICAN RENAISSANCE TAROT*

"Especially valuable for me is the groundbreaking discussion of the Platonic enthusiasts Thomas Moore Johnson, Alexander Wilder, and Hiram K. Jones. Well researched, relevant, and revelatory."

K. PAUL JOHNSON, AUTHOR OF *EDGAR CAYCE IN CONTEXT*

AMERICAN METAPHYSICAL RELIGION

*Esoteric and Mystical Traditions
of the New World*

RONNIE PONTIAC

Inner Traditions
Rochester, Vermont

Inner Traditions
One Park Street
Rochester, Vermont 05767
www.InnerTraditions.com

Text stock is SFI certified

Cataloging-in-Publication Data for this title is available from the Library of Congress

ISBN 978-1-64411-558-9 (print)
ISBN 978-1-64411-559-6 (ebook)

Printed and bound in the United States by Lake Book Manufacturing, LLC
The text stock is SFI certified. The Sustainable Forestry Initiative. program
promotes sustainable forest management.

10 9 8 7 6 5 4 3 2 1

Text design and layout by Priscilla Haris Baker
This book was typeset in Garamond Premier Pro with Americanus and Gill Sans
used as display typefaces

To send correspondence to the author of this book, mail a first-class letter to the
author c/o Inner Traditions • Bear & Company, One Park Street, Rochester, VT
05767, and we will forward the communication.

To Tamra, I seal the amazing adventures we shared that became this book with a quote from Petronius Arbiter, to echo your words to me on that sacred night:

Serva me, servabo te.

—◁o▷—

In a "secular" society the search for the sacred refuses to go away.

CATHERINE ALBANESE

There are indeed millions of Christians in the United States, but most Americans who think that they are Christians truly are something else, intensely religious but devout in the American Religion, a faith that is old among us, and that comes in many guises and disguises, and that overdetermines much of our national life.

HAROLD BLOOM

In modern academic research, "esotericism" is no more than a convenient label to cover a large collection of claims of knowledge that have been rejected as illegitimate "nonsense" or "superstition" by academics since the period of the Enlightenment but deserve to be studied seriously and without prejudice. Whether any of them is true or not is wholly irrelevant to that project.

WOUTER HANEGRAAFF

I am often struck by the dangerous narcissism fostered by spiritual rhetoric that pays so much attention to individual self-improvement and so little to the practice of love within the context of community.

BELL HOOKS

Although it is said that it is impossible to be disturbed by anything upon reaching enlightenment, I could not help but cry upon bidding farewell to a loved one.

KŌBŌ-DAISHI

But it does me no injury for my neighbor to say there are twenty gods, or no god. It neither picks my pocket nor breaks my leg.

THOMAS JEFFERSON

Imagination is usually regarded as a synonym for the unreal. Yet is true imagination healthful and real, no more likely to mislead than the coarser senses. Indeed, the power of imagination makes us infinite.

JOHN MUIR

Contents

◄O►

Acknowledgments

THIS BOOK WOULD NOT EXIST without the help of many collaborators, especially Tamra Lucid, to whom it is dedicated. Without the kindness of Manly Palmer Hall I never would have started the research that ultimately became this book. K. Paul Johnson has provided encouragement, resources, and detailed editorial advice. I am also grateful to the late Norman Arthur Johnson for convincing me to finish what I started. Kimberly Cooper Nichols was the first editor to post the essays that became several of these chapters, and Bookforum's blog *Omnivore* featured one. Tod Davies provided early encouragement and essential advice throughout. Edie Shapiro provided invaluable edits and contributions. Thea Wirsching gave crucial new perspectives when the content overwhelmed me. For encouragement, advice, resources, quotations, and other contributions I am grateful to Normandi Ellis, Jon Graham, Jay Bregman, Sasha Chaitow, Gary Lachman, Matt Marble, Adam McClean, Mary K. Greer, Isis Aquarian, David Metcalfe, Kate McCallum, Steven A. Ross, Jon Larson, Joe Linus, Renée Heitman, Vadim Putzu, and Patrick Reeves.

INTRODUCTION

A Heritage We Didn't Know We Had

IN THE QUIET of the Philosophical Research Society Library, surrounded by shelves of rare esoteric books, I found myself at a dead end. On that day the library was closed to visitors. The librarian and her assistants were busy upstairs. Manly Hall, a venerable mystic, sat at his desk holding a tome a few inches from his face. Meanwhile his secretary Edith, a white-haired World War II veteran, patiently waited for the next sentence of his dictation. Outside, the southern California sun ruled all with heat and glare. I had searched every shelf. I had asked the librarian, the assistants, and the old man himself, but to no avail. Trips to the libraries of Occidental College, UCLA, USC, and Loyola Marymount fared no better.

It all began when I first saw a large leather-bound volume inside the library vault where my job gave me access to Mr. Hall's alchemical manuscripts and other rarities of rogue philosophy and religion through the ages. I opened it carefully. To my surprise it contained the first issues of a newspaper called the *Platonist*. I gently turned the fragile pages. I found translations of ancient Greek philosophical and religious texts, but also the work of the famous French occultist Eliphas Levi, rendered into English by Abner Doubleday, a retired general who fired the first shot in defense of Ft. Sumter at the beginning of the Civil War. Later Doubleday became vice president of the Theosophical Society. In 1907 the Mills Commission declared that he had invented the game of baseball, but historians beg to differ.

Strange enough that any newspaper should be devoted to that

kind of content, but even stranger that it was published in St. Louis, Missouri, in 1881—the year Wyatt Earp and his brothers battled Ike Clanton and his cowboys at the gunfight at the O.K. Corral. While the legendary cattle drives continued, St. Louis was becoming notorious for terrible smog caused by coal-burning factories. How in the world, I wondered, and why in the world, had this newspaper come to life at such a seemingly inhospitable time and place?

Eventually I found a little book called *Platonism in the Midwest* by Paul R. Anderson, published by Temple University Press in 1963. Some of my questions were answered. I gained a sense of the man behind the *Platonist,* but so many mysteries remained. As online search tools opened vast archives of academic work, I began looking for papers and books in my areas of interest. To my surprise I found a trickle of new research that with the arrival of the new millennium became a flood. A revolution in academia had opened the way for a new generation of scholars to explore and document what had been neglected and dismissed.

Unfortunately for amateur enthusiasts such as myself, these new books are prohibitively expensive, and people who do not move in academic circles could live their entire lives without any access to them, probably never knowing they exist. Since I have been fortunate to have friends in academia I hope this book will serve as a bridge, bringing some of the latest research to people who would like to know about it, making accessible the hard work of these historians. Consider the bibliography of this book an invitation to exploration. Request them at your library if you want all the details.

Please understand, I am not an academic. I am not attempting to prove that American Metaphysical Religion is anything more than a catchall metaphor for the esoteric beliefs and practices that have found a home in the melting pot of America. Think of me instead as your tour guide to the rough-and-tumble world of spirituality American-style. Far more questions will be raised than answered. We will consider not only wild tales of metaphysical leaders and communities, scandals and gossip, but also many neglected gems of thought and action that sincere seekers may find inspiring.

This book is an introduction to four centuries of America's metaphysical saints, grifters, misfits, revolutionaries, visionaries, eccentrics, and some important thinkers who were far ahead of their time. In some ways this is a guidebook to all the different ways spirituality can be used to cheat people, but we also find examples of the inexplicable and genuine.

It's no surprise that the people who came to America to make a life, or who were brought here against their will, would have the daring to not only experiment with the occult but also to weave together their own approaches to spirituality. However, for generations well-meaning religiously motivated scholars deliberately ignored this rich, detailed, and influential history, including the fact that the majority of Founding Fathers, mostly Deists and Freemasons, had little respect for the superstitious factions of Christianity most eager to claim them.

Several centuries of denominational historians, scholars of Christian and Jewish history, were mostly interested in prominent people and the fates of institutions. They were eventually replaced by historians who were considered more liberal because they glanced at fundamentalists and Pentecostals. But the metaphysical tradition was kept alive by rogue scholars. In the various metaphysical organizations populated by enthusiasts, books survived that academia had wished into the cornfield. Finally, in the 1990s, professional researchers began exploring metaphysical religion. But it would take until the twenty-first century for the occult to become a legitimate subject of study for a new generation of historians and the academic presses that publish them. "Many of the studies of new religions have been polemical, apologetic, or inaccessible to the general reader," Sarah M. Pike wrote in *New Age and Pagan Religions in America* (2004). "The field has often been polarized between scholars who are critical of new religions and those who are more sympathetic to them. . ."

American Metaphysical Religion has been treated as pseudo-religion, yet its influence is substantial. As Patrick Reeves wrote in personal correspondence of 2021 used by his permission, "Is it marginal or mainstream (or mainstream but we've been deluded into thinking it's marginal)?" He also reminds us that religions don't fit the categories scholars give them: "I think of definitions on religion not as something we discover but lenses we put on reality to make sense of it."

Many well-educated people argue that the subject of this book doesn't exist. At best they will allow American Metaphysical Religion (AMR) as an umbrella phrase for the collection of superstitions. However, some scholars believe that AMR is a real religion lacking only unifying institutions, and perhaps better for the lack of them. A few wonder if it might eventually evolve a new religion. All three of these perspectives on AMR have merit. Perhaps time will reveal its true definition, or it may remain a mysterious but ubiquitous influence for centuries, as it has since the earliest days of colonization.

However, we might consider the example of the Imperial Romans, who wrote about Christianity as a disorganized underground of bizarre cults. No Holy Bible existed then. Gnostic sects had at least a dozen gospels of their own; at least another dozen gospels would be lost. Some Christians believed in reincarnation. Others worshipped a Christian goddess, Sophia, the personification of pious wisdom. Some expected the world to end any day. Others thought the world a never-created and never-ending testing place for souls. Despite differences of beliefs, practices, and ethics all were forms of Christianity. Despite its chaotic countercultural beginnings, as Christianity matured it evolved empires.

A characteristic quality of AMR is its relentless optimism, which contributed greatly to American exceptionalism. This world can be so beautiful. Sunrises and sunsets paint the sky. Mosslike malachite grows in copper. An adored cat purrs contentedly. A lover smiles. A child's innocent laughter rings like the chime of silver bells under the clear sky of a Sunday afternoon. And yet everything in this world that inspires wonder and appreciation can be, has been, and is exploited. We puny creatures with our cosmic minds have already foreseen the sun's fate and that of our home world. Keep moving! That sign is everywhere in our universe.

And yet, American Metaphysical Religion reminds us, at times life can seem like paradise. If so shouldn't we study how to make that happen more often or, even better, perpetually? The world may be full of suffering but it's the responsibility of each of us to do everything we can to make our own little world a heaven. Throughout history such utopian ideas have been for the most part met with ridicule. But American Metaphysical Religion has never given up on this belief in a more perfect world, or at least a more prosperous and joyous life for believers.

While ambition and survival are common motives in the lives we are about to explore, most of these innovators hoped to heal the sick, enlighten the ignorant, and liberate the oppressed. Even the most fraudulent seemed to think they were doing some good, like a discredited medium pointing out that at least the grief-stricken were comforted. They all appreciated and made use of the opportunities for learning and action that freedom provides, as they attempted to understand the meaning of life and the purpose for which it exists. They didn't just write about it. Most tried out their theories in their own lives, among their friends, and a few with large groups of followers. Most of these grand experiments are little known today. Their obscurity is not necessarily a measure of their value.

As for the influence of what we're calling American Metaphysical Religion it goes far and wide in the United States. For example, America's beloved poet Emily Dickinson studied Rosicrucianism, Theosophy, and alchemy. She was deeply interested in Spiritualism. "Spirit pen" was her nickname for her favorite writing instrument. One of Emily's favorite books was *Zanoni,* by the British occultist Lord Bulwer-Lytton, a novel about an encounter with a Rosicrucian. Zanoni, Missouri, is an unincorporated town located in Ozark County. The post office and a watermill are all that's left of this community founded in 1898 and named after Bulwer-Lytton's book. Allegedly the town inspired an unincorporated community in Gloucester County, Virginia, to also name itself Zanoni.

William James, the father of American psychology, and the first to offer a psychology class, put his reputation as a scientist and a professor at Harvard University on the line when he, and other great intellects with as much to lose, including Alexander Graham Bell, formed the American Society for Psychical Research in 1884. Investigating poltergeists, haunted houses, psychic mediums, they found no proof of the supernatural until William James met a medium named Mrs. Piper.

As James explained in his report on her, "If you wish to upset the law that all crows are black, you mustn't seek to show that no crows are; it is enough if you prove one single crow to be white. My own white crow is Mrs. Piper. I cannot resist the conviction that knowledge appears which she has never gained by the waking use of her eyes and ears and wits. What the source of this knowledge may be I know not, and have not the glimmer of an explanatory suggestion to make; but from admitting the fact of such knowledge I can see no escape."

Leonora Piper was a housewife from Boston. Many tested her after James dubbed her his white crow, but no one ever caught her committing fraud. The more tests she passed, the higher the demand and the fees for her psychic services became. Some skeptics argued that like most of her ilk she was adept at fishing, reading body language, and other techniques of fraudulent mind readers.

Stories about her failures circulated. She told one client he would soon find a wife and would have children, but he never did. Another client had been told his son had died in Mexico. He refused to accept it, convincing himself his son had been kidnapped. Mrs. Piper concurred, describing the asylum where he was being held and the name of the crazed doctor behind the kidnapping. Investigations revealed no asylum, no doctor, and the accuracy of the death as reported by the authorities.

Mrs. Piper was also unable to distinguish sincere clients from skeptics testing her skills. Those tests she often failed. How could Uncle Louie be standing in spirit right behind his beloved nephew when he was actually a thousand miles away on a boat headed for Europe? Even more suspect, how could she not know that Uncle Louie was a made-up character?

Then there were the questions about Mrs. Piper's controls, the spirits that communicated through her, such as the French physician who could not understand French. A control named Moses predicted a great war would happen soon. The Russians and French would go to war against the British. The Germans would stay out of it. So many mistakes in one prophecy.

We hope Mrs. Piper was equally wrong about the fate of Madame Blavatsky, whom she described as winding up "in the deepest part of hell." Mrs. Piper is our first but not our last example of this ambiguous combination of genuine inexplicable experiences, such as William James described, and mistaken assertions. But was what James experienced really inexplicable? A maid in the James household was friends with a maid in Mrs. Piper's house. She may have been the source of Mrs. Piper's knowledge about the life of William James. Was the friendship between the maids unknown to James? Were both maids willing accomplices? Could his maid have known the details that Mrs. Piper related to James? As promised, we are left with more questions than answers.

As for Mrs. Piper, later in life she announced she never thought she was actually speaking to spirits. She considered her controls aspects of her own subconscious. She thought that what she had done was perhaps telepathy rather than channeling. Later the same year she issued a less decisive comment. She really didn't know how to explain what had happened to her. She couldn't be certain that it had nothing to do with spirits.

So many of the stories we will encounter in this chronicle of American Metaphysical Religion culminate in these dead ends where the street signs are all question marks. Is this book nothing but a guide to black crows? I believe we may have a white crow, or several, but we can never completely remove the shadow of doubt. But we can keep in mind a famous statement William James made about the nature of consciousness. In his classic *The Varieties of Religious Experience,* he wrote: "One conclusion was forced upon my mind at that time, and my impression of its truth has ever since remained unshaken. It is our normal waking consciousness, rational consciousness as we call it, is but one special type of consciousness, whilst all about it, parted from it by the flimsiest of screens, there lie potential forms of consciousness entirely different. We may go through life without suspecting their existence; but apply the requisite stimulus, and at a touch they are there in all their completeness, definite types of mentality which probably somewhere have their field of application and adaptation. No account of the universe in its totality can be final which leaves these other forms of consciousness quite discarded" (James 1936).

1

Ingredients for the
Melting Pot

*The American presents a strange picture, a European with
Negro behavior and an Indian soul. He shares the fate of
all usurpers of foreign soil.*

CARL JUNG

THIS BOOK IS NOT A DEFENSE of cultural appropriation, although
it contains many examples of it. There's no denying that American
Metaphysical Religion has thrived on appropriation. Where most religions seek to keep their beliefs and practices pure, uncontaminated by
foreign influences, in America the cross-pollination of esoteric traditions has always been popular. Throughout most of history an American
with an interest in metaphysics would know their way around the
Jewish Kabbalah, the theurgy of the Neoplatonists, the poets of Persian
Sufism, and the sutras of Buddhism. Most of them argued that religions
are something true wrapped in something false. The false comes from
the place and time when the religion was born. Peculiarities of custom
and accidents of language make it seem that all religions are different.
But the truth at the core is common to all spiritual traditions, because
it is the human condition.

Let's begin with an overview. American Metaphysical Religion is
so mysterious it may not even exist, or it may be one of the largest and
most traditional religious communities in the United States—it just

doesn't know it is. It's a community without self-awareness. The members think they are more or less alone, oddballs, delegated to the fringe. But that couldn't be further from the truth, and the proof is in this book. Even before it had a name America was fascinated by the *occult, pagan, metaphysical, mystical,* whichever inadequate *word* we choose for what academics are beginning to call American Metaphysical Religion.

In this chronicle of rebellious and individualized spirituality we encounter outright criminals, inexplicable combinations of apparent miracles and fraud, sincere fanatics, ironic endings, and worthy efforts that fell out of step with changing times. All of them were inspired by the idea that they could help to shape the world, as opposed to merely fitting into it. Let's begin with a look at the kinds of ingredients that the world has thrown into the melting pot that is American Metaphysical Religion.

Despite their dubious history psychic readings are a billion-dollar industry today. Perhaps you know someone who claims to have received a message from beyond? Nearly one in three Americans believe they have experienced some form of communication with the dead. As late as the early 1980s subjects like mediumship and reincarnation were rarely seen in mass media; forty years later, psychics allegedly relaying messages from the great beyond have popular TV shows and YouTube channels.

Americans have always explored the mysteries of conversing with the departed. In Colonial Pennsylvania while prominent Quakers tried to convince members of their own denomination to give up divination by geomancy, palmistry, and astrology, they were themselves experimenting with not just communication with the dead but also, like their brethren back home in England, inspired by the New Testament, a few tried to raise the dead. Even less experimental Quakers owed much to the great German mystic Jakob Böhme, the Kabbalah, and Rosicrucian and alchemical undercurrents. Spiritual healing was a constant theme.

A hundred years later in 1839 several young women of the Shaker community were walking in a field when above their heads they heard what they described as beautiful singing. Back home they danced around their rooms, according to witnesses, "under the influence of a power not their own." They fell into trances and were lifted onto beds where they gave messages from the dead. Like Edgar Cayce, they were hailed as sleeping prophets. They called them then what we call them now, spirit mediums.

Ever read your horoscope? Do you have a friend or relative who frequently provides you with the latest astrological predictions for your sign? The gentlemen farmers of the Virginia Colony studied the stars for more than reckoning the best time for planting. Some believed that astrology provided the truest navigation of life, and the best hope for avoiding trouble. Genesis 1:14 provided justification: "And God said, 'Let there be lights in the firmament of the heaven to divide the day from the night; and let them be for signs.'" The astrology of agriculture circulated widely in popular almanacs, but also by word of mouth, taught by family matriarchs and patriarchs, many of whom could not read books but could read the stars.

These Virginians, descendants of royalists rewarded by the crown, gambled not only for fun, but to divine the current state of their luck. They worried over dreams and omens, visited fortune-tellers, and employed cunning folk to control weather. They carved ancient signs of protection on their houses. William Byrd, member of the Virginia Council of State, is said to have practiced the conjuring of magical angelic power and to have freely discussed it with his friends.

Perhaps you know someone who collects four-leaf clovers or some other lucky charm they wouldn't be without? The same concept of mysterious protection has inspired the Pennsylvania Dutch to paint hex signs on not only barns but homes in America since around 1700. As well as being beautiful, these mystical symbols are said to block the influence of evil.

Have you ever known someone who practices sympathetic magic? Perhaps someone who wears a rose quartz crystal or other love charm. Many Americans have adopted the Latinx tradition of putting folded money in your shoe for financial good luck in the new year. Some Kentuckians still believe, as did their ancestors, that carrying three pennies in your pocket is lucky. Among the hill people of early colonial Kentucky, farmers planted, cultivated, and harvested according to lunar phases and the moon's zodiac placement. A baby born with an equal number of folds on each leg meant the next baby would be a girl. Their knowledge of their terrain must have appeared magical. They watched how the wasps built their nests in spring to predict the weather. The first tick found on a child had magical importance. If a parent wanted a child to be a hard worker the tick was crushed with a shovel. If the parent wanted the child to have a beautiful singing voice the tick was crushed with a bell or banjo.

As we explore American Metaphysical Religion we'll find many contradictions—for example, the story of a Puritan magistrate who condemned women as witches but had close friends who were alchemists and astrologers. There have been times when the ideas and symbols of American Metaphysical Religion flourished, but also times when it was suppressed and censored. The following is one of many absurd examples of this pushback by traditional religion.

Generations of farmers had made the state of Missouri prosperous. In 1924, in recognition of that fact, a new statue of Ceres, the ancient Roman goddess of agriculture, crowned the state capitol. Almost a hundred years later in 2019, a Christian politician argued that Ceres should be banished from public property as "a false god." Meanwhile, Instagram is a springtime bloom of young witches, tarot readers, and astrologers. Novices offer photos of their first attempts at altars for the perusal of their communities on YouTube, TikTok, and in Facebook groups private and public. Esoteric books so rare that not so long ago only the wealthiest and luckiest could obtain them are now easily downloaded as PDFs. However, there is no proof that statues of pagan gods on government buildings are responsible for these developments.

If the reader will forgive the all too obvious metaphor, American Metaphysical Religion is like a soup, all the individual ingredients are there, but they are not as they were and together they become something quite different from what they were apart. From the first, America was a vibrant blend of every faith, from every place.

Kidnapped and enslaved Africans brought with them their spiritual practices and beliefs, their natural and supernatural cures, and their intoxicating rhythms. African religion was an early transplant to

America. In 1680 the Anglican minister Morgan Godwyn complained of spirit possession among enslaved people, who drummed and danced in rituals for rain. The hoodoo that would become so familiar in the American South was already being practiced as dog teeth, feathers, broken bottles, and egg shells were gathered for use in spells. Almost 150 years later the notorious dances at Congo Square in New Orleans gave birth to the rhythms of jazz, rock and roll, and hip hop, three characteristically American art forms.

The resistance to slavery and its ideology by enslaved people began with preservation of their spiritual traditions. West African beliefs and practices influenced not only American Metaphysical Religion but also American Christianity, transforming church traditions that had long banned dancing, as Southern churches came to life with music that demanded dance. Eventually, individual practitioners found ways to turn this heritage into a business model that continues to this day.

In his 1970 book *High Sheriff of the Low Country*, J. E. McTeer wrote about a famous lineage of American voodoo. "Dr. Buzzard, beyond any doubt, was the king of the Root Doctors. He inherited his 'mantle' or stock of powers from his father, who was an extremely powerful practitioner in his own right. But, Dr. Buzzard, whose real name was Stepheney Robinson, brought the art to a fine point of perfection. He was tall, thin, and about fifty years of age at the peak of his power. His dealings were far reaching, and the effects of his roots and spells were felt in many states. He could always be recognized by his purple or green tinted sunglasses, the traditional badge of the Root Doctor, which also conveniently blocked a man's view of his eyes and thoughts." After Robinson died a succession of others took up the identity of Dr. Buzzard, including Ernest Bratton who in the late 1980s promoted his home video *Voo Doo, Hoo Doo, You Do* on *Late Night with David Letterman*. In 2022 yet another "Famous Doc Buzzard" appeared in an ad in the back of the *National Enquirer*.

The impact goes far beyond religious practices. In African culture we find the origin of the American preoccupation with coolness. Robert Farris Thompson's eloquent description of Yoruba culture is also the heart and soul of American cool. Thompson wrote: "Like character, coolness ought to be internalized as a governing principle for a person to merit the high praise, 'His heart is cool.' In becoming sophisticated, a Yoruba adept learns to differentiate between forms of spiritual coolness. . . . So heavily charged is this concept with ideas of beauty and correctness that a fine carnelian bead or a passage of exciting drumming may be praised as 'cool.' . . . To the degree that we live generously and discreetly, exhibiting grace under pressure, our appearance and our acts gradually assume virtual royal power . . . we find the confidence to cope with all kinds of situations . . . mystic coolness" (Thompson 2011).

Indigenous Americans suffered and still suffer terrible injustices, from the intentional pandemics caused by infected blankets that decimated the Indigenous population to the order to use lethal force if necessary against the peaceful Water Protectors at Standing Rock. But America's religious love of the wilderness and the spiritual connection some Americans feel with nature was not inspired by the Pilgrims who feared wild places. Indigenous Americans are not the only people with a long history of using sacred smoke, but when most Americans burn sage to clear the atmosphere they believe they are following an Indigenous tradition that also inspires Americans of every race to have vision quests, sweat lodges, and shamanic journeys. The exploitation of Indigenous American spiritual beliefs and practices by non-Indigenous teachers seeking fame and riches began long before the New Age movement where it reached a peak.

In the second decade of the twenty-first century the concept of *Wetiko* has returned. As Indigenous writer Jack D. Forbes wrote in his book *Columbus and Other Cannibals: The Wetiko Disease of Exploitation, Imperialism, and Terrorism:* "for several thousands of years human beings have suffered from a plague. The Algonquin and other Indigenous First Nations identified the mental illness of the white man, upon his arrival to their native homelands, as 'Wetiko,' literally translated as cannibalism: the consuming of another's life for one's own private purpose or profit. Brutality knows no boundaries. Greed knows no limits. Perversion knows no borders. This is the disease of the consuming of other creatures' lives and possessions. This disease is the greatest epidemic sickness known to man." In 2022 at a workshop hosted by East West Bookshop, a metaphysical store favored by Silicon Valley, founded before there was a Silicon Valley, techies pondered ways to address the burden of their inheritance of Wetiko.

Mexican American culture contributed the increasingly popular festival of the Day of the Dead. This colorful celebration of family captured the imagination of Americans, some of whom were inspired to create their own altars with family pictures, while many more adopted skeletal face makeup and fiesta costumes for the more traditional American holiday Halloween. *Botanica* shops have flourished in American cities for decades. There a statue, herbs, or a candle spell addressed to a saint can be purchased. Consultations are available—with more powerful rituals for those who can afford them. Some may have preyed on the fears of innocents, but many earned stalwart reputations as the place to go for those who couldn't afford modern medical or psychological treatments. Through the shops, and many of the local markets, or *mercados,* which also carry magical items, Americans have become acquainted with *brujeria,* and the witches that practice it. More recently Santa Muerte or Saint Death's influence has grown, as she attracts devotees far outside the world of cartels where her worship was revived. Google maps provides ratings and directions to shrines and temples devoted to Santa Muerte, now the fastest growing new religious movement in 2022, mostly in Los Angeles, but also in Tucson, Houston, Chicago, Miami, and New York.

Jewish immigrants brought the mystical Kabbalah, which arrived in America early. In 1688 a Quaker leader wrote to a disciple about what he called "the mystical theology of the Jews." Meanwhile a Puritan minister concocted a theology that a generation or two later led to the conversion of a Jew in Boston. From that convert came the first book about the Kabbalah written and published in America. In the latter half of the 1700s Ezra Stiles, a president of Yale College, was inspired by that book to study the Kabbalah. He found a teacher, the Palestinian Rabbi Raphael Hayyim Isaac Carregal, a wandering teacher who had lived in Constantinople, Curaçao, Hebron, London, and Jamaica, and who was then spending a year in the British colonies of North America. In 1781 Stiles gave a speech at Yale in which he argued that the Kabbalah should be taught at all the Protestant colleges in the United States. He and Benjamin Franklin enjoyed conversations about the Kabbalah.

Yoga from India had a profound influence on spirituality in America. Beginning with Swami Vivekananda's first visit to America in 1893, as we shall see, yoga and the beliefs of Hinduism captured the American imagination. Paramahansa Yogananda was so popular in 1926 he gave a seven-day series of lectures at Carnegie Hall. His paperbacks could be found in hippie crash pads and New Age communities alike, and having influenced several generations, continue to be relevant. Swami Prabhavananda founded the Vedanta Society of Southern California in Los Angeles in 1930. His student Christopher Isherwood wrote books about his teacher and what he had learned, but he is more famous for his memoir about his earlier life in Berlin, which inspired the movie *Cabaret*. The Beatles made Maharishi Mahesh Yogi famous, so he toured the United States, establishing centers for teaching meditation. And what are we to make of Yogi Ramacharaka, who was actually a lawyer named William Atkinson who suffered a nervous breakdown? We'll be seeing more of him later.

The French brought tarot cards, the dramatic Freemasonry of the Grand Orient de France, and the books of Eliphas Levi, the magus of nineteenth-century Paris. Levi had a profound influence on the Hermetic Order of the Golden Dawn, Aleister Crowley, Helena Blavatsky, and Manly Hall, among many others. For example, American master of horror H. P. Lovecraft name-dropped Eliphas Levi twice in his book *The Case of Charles Dexter Ward*. Levi was also an important influence on Albert Pike, a mountain man of a Freemason, and author of the most influential book in Scottish Rite Masonry, *Morals and Dogma;* a book said to be inspired by Levi's *The History of Magic*.

Morals and Dogma does resemble Levi's chronicle of masters, and so do the esoteric timelines offered by Blavatsky, Manly Hall, Édouard Schuré, and so many other occult writers. In all of them we find the natural philosophers Agrippa and Paracelsus, the Neoplatonists, the Jewish and Egyptian mysteries, and echoes of the wisdom of the ancient temples Greece, India, and Persia. Pike organized this heritage into a series of ritualized experiences and studies that would help to elevate the soul step by step within a supportive community. However, Pike was also a Confederate general. *Morals and Dogma* includes a disturbing paragraph about the proper attitude for those who owned enslaved people. He advocated caring for them as a master would for an apprentice, but the practice of slavery he did not question. Protesters during the Black Lives Matter marches of summer 2020 toppled his statue in Washington, D.C.

Inspired by questionable sources including a notorious hoaxster, in his book *Satan, Prince of this World* (1959), William Carr portrayed Pike as a Satanist and the architect of world wars that occurred decades after he died, which along with water fluoridation were an Illuminati plot to eliminate religions and kill millions. Carr wrote of a letter by Pike to an Italian revolutionary about a plan to unleash atheism and nihilism, but the letter was proven a fraud. Folklorist Bill Ellis calls Carr "the most influential source in creating the American Illuminati demonology."

Early Dutch and German immigrants brought America the Rosicrucian vision of an enlightened new world, the Hermetic medicine of Paracelsus, and the Christian theosophy of Jakob Böhme. The British, Irish, and Scottish brought alleged author of the Shakespeare plays Sir Francis Bacon, as well as the less dramatic forms of Freemasonry, a fascination with ghosts and elementals, a preoccupation with Elizabethan angelic magic, and also the freedom loving Hellfire Club, which counted among its members Benjamin Franklin.

Immigrants from Sweden contributed the writings of scientist and philosopher Emanuel Swedenborg. His scientific discoveries are impressive, including advances in the understanding of the cerebral cortex, cerebrospinal fluid, the pituitary gland, metallurgy, and the nebular hypothesis in astronomy. But he also wrote detailed descriptions of the inhabitants and societies of other planets and dimensions, including heaven and hell, garnered from his visions, and from conversations he claimed to have had with spirits. In Swedenborg's heaven, happily married couples combine to become one angel in the afterlife in the ultimate ecstasy of spiritual union.

Swedenborg reported that no soul is thrown into hell by God.

Swedenborg assures us a loving god would never do that. Souls jump into hell of their own free will because it's where they feel most at home. They are not damned forever. If they can learn to love, they can be saved. Swedenborg's conception of hell has never been more timely. The chief emotions of the damned are outrage at receiving no support, and gloating when seeing others suffer the same fate. Does that make social media a portal of hell?

Swedenborg's writing influenced generations of Americans, including the most famous American medium until Edgar Cayce, Andrew Jackson Davis. With a journal entry on March 31, 1848, Davis announced the commencement of America's fascination with Spiritualism: "About daylight this morning, I heard a voice tender and strong, saying, 'Brother, the good work has begun. A living demonstration is born!'" A reprehensible husband and father who abandoned his family at the whim of the spirits, Davis nevertheless had great influence on American Metaphysical Religion by way of his books, especially his six-volume encyclopedia *The Great Harmonia*. Aside from being an author, he also practiced magnetic healing. His followers called him the John the Baptist of Spiritualism. Rumors abounded that President Lincoln consulted him more than once. But his books are filled with scientific errors, and why exactly did he feel compelled to lie about how many books he had read? He claimed the only book he ever read was the Holy Bible. Was he trying to cover up his plagiarism? Davis was frequently plagiarized himself, but then his popularity made even Edgar Allan Poe jealous.

Japan gave America Zen, karate, the tea ceremony, Shinto, and Judo. The Chinese, many of them brought here to work on the railroads, contributed to American Metaphysical Religion the influential oracle the Book of Changes, or Yi Jing, also known as the I Ching, the spiritual martial art of kung fu, and the philosophy of Daoism. After the invasion of 1950, the Chinese occupation of Tibet exiled Tibetan teachers to new homes all around the world. Communities have grown and flourished over the years. In downtown Los Angeles there is a temple devoted to Tibetan Bon, the hybrid of Buddhism and shamanism. There an initiated Bon priest brings the traditional teachings to a new world of students. The current Dalai Lama, whose predecessors were mysterious legends, is a bestselling author and worldwide celebrity. Publishers like Shambhala and Snow Lion have brought rare texts to readers who would otherwise have had no chance to learn from them. We now have books about the Tibetan Book of the Dead written by, or in collaboration with, Tibetan masters of high attainment.

Masonic groups who adopted some of the trappings of Islam were often dedicated to supporting local communities, and the pomp and fashion were meant in good fun, but the lodges did acquire more from Islam than fez hats and costumes with ceremonial scimitars. Many American Freemasons considered themselves akin to Sufis. They considered Sufism the Freemasonry of the Eastern world.

Iranian spirituality has had a profound influence on American Metaphysical Religion. The Persian poet Rumi, considered by many the greatest of the many great Sufi poets, gained a wide audience during the New Age in the 1980s, with numerous translations and studies, popular and academic. Through the prism of Nietzsche's *Thus Spoke Zarathustra,* American outsider artists like Jim Morrison of the Doors absorbed the Persian worldview of existence as a battle between light and dark. In his book *The American Religion,* Harold Bloom (1992) described religious experience in twentieth-century America as "a return to Zoroastrian origins."

Bloom is in some ways emblematic of American Metaphysical Religion, a field of study he helped create. Until the 1980s very few scholars had studied esoteric subjects. Not many books explored that part of American history. Religious and cultural prejudices dismissed all beliefs outside the major religions as superstition. Raised in the Orthodox Jewish faith in the Bronx, Bloom grew up to spend six decades as an English professor at Yale University. His first book, *Shelley's Mythmaking,* showed no patience for the reigning generation of literary critics who had allowed their faith in Christianity to distort their understanding of Shelley's poetry. Bloom's next book, a similar defense of the poet and Golden Dawn mystic W. B. Yeats was published by Oxford University Press. In the late 1960s, Bloom focused his studies on Freud, but also Ralph Waldo Emerson, the Hermetic tradition, and the Kabbalah. He saw the tremendous influence they had on not only American literature but Western culture.

In 1992 Bloom published his classic *The American Religion: The Emergence of the Post-Christian Nation,* where he argued that Christianity in America has more in common with gnosticism than it does with traditional churches it inhabits. Bloom considered himself a gnostic, but he didn't adhere to a strict definition of the word. In 1996 Bloom published *Omens of the Millennium: The Gnosis of Angels, Dreams, and Resurrection,* where he examined New Age beliefs, correlated them to their historical origins, and argued that the New Age is a revival of gnostic and Persian spirituality. With the mysterious Orphics of ancient Greece in mind Bloom described the emerging American religion as "California Orphism." Both are characterized by personalized practices, respect for nature, musical rituals, and probable belief in reincarnation, just a few of the similarities.

"While Bloom's perception of the American Religion could be said to have opened the way, he was hardly a liberal. He complained eloquently about what he called the School of Resentment, by which he meant multiculturalists, feminists, Marxists, neoconservatives, and others whom he saw as betraying literature's essential purpose," as the *New York Times* explained in his obituary. The *Times* of London obit pulled no punches: "In 21st-century academia nobody is less fashionable than Harold Bloom, the great American literary critic who died on Monday at the age of 89. Vain, self-mythologising and a furious opponent of the political correctness that has swept through American universities since the early 1990s, a special place awaits him in the dustbin of history marked 'dead white males.'" This obit goes on to say that today's educational institutions have much to learn from Bloom, especially his reverence for great art. But Bloom was not writing for academics, as his million-dollar publishing advances proved.

2

A Map of the Tour

WE BEGAN WITH AN ORIENTATION to get us started. First "A Heritage We Didn't Know We Had," then a quick but detailed list of "Ingredients for the Melting Pot." Next we will consider two major themes of American Metaphysical Religion. In a chapter titled "When East Meets West" we'll explore examples of the influence on America of Eastern esoteric traditions like Zen, Tibetan Buddhism, and Sufism. At times the influence was so strong some Western esoterics condemned interest in Asian wisdom as a threat to the survival of the West's own heritage of traditions.

The second major theme we'll consider is "American Metaphysical Christianity." Metaphysics and Christianity have coexisted uncomfortably, to put it mildly, for generations in America. For most of American history Christianity was the outward face, and esoteric traditions the inward preoccupation, of national spirituality. American Christianity has been profoundly influenced and many denominations now resemble New Thought more than Original Sin.

"Turtle Island" is one of the names of the North American continent used by Indigenous tribes. In this chapter we will take a long look at America in its pristine glory while we explore the spirituality that was here before Europeans arrived. We'll track the arrival of the first Europeans from the Spanish debacle to the French and Dutch traders. We'll see a side of the Pilgrims that most histories of America have swept under the rug.

"Thomas Harriot: America's First 'Evil' Genius" will give us a look at the English side of colonization but also at the superstitions that considered science the work of the devil. And yet, Harriot's long list of exploitable natural resources in America, often accompanied by the portentous refrain "we took it and ate it" foreshadowed twentieth-century consumer culture.

"The Pagan Pilgrim" introduces us to Thomas Morton, a man of many firsts. He was the first man banned in Boston. He was the first American foreclosed on by a company. He was the first American to publish a fart joke, and the first American to publish a dick joke. He was the first American accused of being a traitor. He's the first bad neighbor throwing a wild party in recorded American history. He also erected the first maypole in America, arousing the ire of the Pilgrims. His trading post became a model of peaceful coexistence. It took so much business away from the Pilgrims they became resentful. Morton had some caustic nicknames for the Pilgrims enshrined in the American imagination by Disney. Eventually they used force to destroy the maypole, the trading post, and Morton.

John Winthrop Jr., who helped form the state of Connecticut, was also an alchemical doctor who had purchased most of the famous Elizabethan occultist and astrologer John Dee's library. Winthrop Jr.'s experiments and the experiments of his friends mark the beginning of modern science, but with one foot in the esoteric worlds of astrology and Rosicrucianism. They called themselves the Intelligencers. Through their letters to each other the world would learn of many wonders. "The Intelligencers and the Fifth Moon of Jupiter" explores their beliefs, their relationships, the facts behind cultivated legends, and inspiring tales of brave seekers after truth working for the betterment of life for all.

Although Frances Wright was born in the United Kingdom she fell in love with America from the moment she first learned of it as a child. She urgently searched through every book with a map she could find hoping that the United States would still be there. A young heiress, she visited America with her sister, daring to travel as two single women. Frances found her idealism validated, by sailors eager to talk about the Constitution and farmers contemplating Aristotle, until she reached a state with legal slavery. She did not understand how Americans could allow slavery to continue. Her friends included Thomas Jefferson and the Marquis de Lafayette. She became a popular speaker praised by Walt Whitman. But Americans turned on her. She became notorious as "The Red Harlot." She eventually put her inheritance into an ill-fated experiment to lift people out of slavery. She later lived in squalor with her husband and child in France. When she attempted to claim the stage again she was not even considered a curiosity. As we shall see, her grandsons contributed to the spiritual life of New York City.

"The Uncivil War" reveals a split in the American psyche that continues to this day. In the North, mediumship was not only popular, it claimed scientific validation. To religious Southerners the dedication of Northerners to not only necromancy but industrialization was proof of the influence of Satan on the Yankees.

Thanks to the *Platonist* we are able to visit a party for Plato's birthday organized by a club of mostly women, devoted to study, who lived a short carriage ride away from the prairie. Finding out how and why this chimerical periodical existed led me to Alexander Wilder and Thomas Moore Johnson. Their stories are told in "The Platonist on the Sunset Strip." Wilder was a rogue scholar, a pioneer of holistic medicine, and editor of Blavatsky's classic *Isis Unveiled*. Johnson was a two-time mayor and two-time town prosecutor who not only published the *Platonist* but also became deeply involved with the Theosophical Society and the Hermetic Brotherhood of Luxor, which we explore in the next chapter "The Secrets of the Hermetic Brotherhood of Luxor."

Come along with a German tourist to explore California and its psychics at the beginning of the twentieth century. "Willy Reichel's Psychic Adventure Tour" reveals a world of wonder and of inexplicable experiences like the manifestation of the spirit of a friend of his who had passed on. The spirit wore the correct uniform and spoke to Reichel in the correct German dialect about personal family matters. How could a medium in San Francisco have been able to fake every detail and then, as we shall see, do the same in a completely different language for a room full of people from around the world?

The grandsons of the Red Harlot take center stage in "Pagan Christianity of the Early Twentieth Century." They both ran churches, but very differently. The older brother William collaborated on programs with Martha Graham, Kahlil Gibran, Isadora Duncan, and Frank Lloyd Wright. In 1921 William wrote that afternoon services at his parish of St. Mark's would feature consideration of "Vedantism, Parseeism, Bahaism, Buddhism, Taoism, Confucianism, Shintoism, ancient Roman religion, ancient Greek religion, Chaldean religion, Egyptian religion, Mithraism, etc." William's younger brother Kenneth self-published obscure Neoplatonist translations with strangely vaude-villian ads in the front and back. In his church a small museum pro-vided proof of slavery in New York City, a reminder to deniers. Yet, despite their common interests the brothers do not appear to have ever gotten along.

"Scandalous Psychic Adventures of the Roaring Twenties" begins with the psychic who channeled a Chinese spirit who solved a prob-lem involving an obscure ancient dialect while speaking it to a professor who was one of perhaps five people in the world who could understand it. It ends with the bitter feud between Houdini and the Witch of Lime Street. The witch was notorious for nude or near-nude séances. Houdini went so far as to cheat in order to discredit her, according to the man who claimed to have helped.

In "American Metaphysical Religion in the Twentieth Century," we'll explore important themes that continue to be relevant, including the Reincarnation Renaissance, the Tarot Renaissance, the Astrology Renaissance, the art of the Southwestern Transcendentalists, the mid-century cosmic jazz of Vincent Lopez, the private interests of two very different writers, J. D. Salinger and William Safire, and the mystical fas-cism of Nazi Germany and their American admirers the Silver Legion, which had connections to the I AM movement, which had connections to the Violet Flame.

Our tour continues with "Prayer Wheel for the Bodhi Tree Bookstore," which tells the story of one of the most famous metaphysi-cal bookstores of all time. A landmark of the New Age, the Bodhi Tree flourished for decades but then succumbed to gentrification and the ease and thrift of buying books from amazon.com. Esoteric scholar Gary Lachman, a manager and friend of the owners, contributes a remi-niscence of the store.

A broad view of important themes of our time, "American Metaphysical Religion in the Twenty-First Century" looks at Apocalyptic Politics, Digital Sigils, Electronic Mediumship, Psychedelic Salvation, Evoking Queer Power, Evolving Female Power, and the Sekhmet Revival, one example among many of ancient deities who have gained exponentially in popularity.

In "Esoteric Architecture of Washington, D.C.," we explore the popular idea that buildings and landmarks in the nation's capital reveal a secret message or are part of some plan. Where is the line drawn between conspiracy and inspiration or imitation? There is no doubt that esoteric symbols can be found in many monuments of D.C., but what did they mean to the people who chose them?

3

When East Meets West

WE BEGIN WITH A LOOK at the immense influence of the Near and Far East upon American spirituality. Rather than quoting statistics, such as plotting immigration data against the adoption of nontraditional spirituality, we introduce the approach that will characterize most of this book. By telling the stories of the lives of carefully chosen examples, we can illuminate the obvious and subtle issues of a particular aspect of American Metaphysical Religion.

In the early days of the colonies and the country, the influence of Eastern traditions on Americans was limited to books. As the railroads crossed the continent here and there an American might encounter Buddhism among the Chinese workers. Madame Blavatsky and other popular writers of the 1880s claimed to transmit wisdom from masters in Egypt, India, and Tibet. But the inauguration of America's popular fascination with Eastern wisdom began in earnest when the charismatic Swami Vivekananda represented India at the Parliament of the World's Religions in Chicago in 1892.

Vivekananda lectured to thousands, touring between Chicago and New York City, where in 1894 he founded the first Vedanta Society in the United States. He continued touring through 1902, starting another center in Los Angeles, but exhaustion finally took its toll. After recuperating he gave free lectures and private lessons at the center in New York. In his wake a tsunami of swamis followed. Los Angeles in particular became a magnet for them.

America's readiness to adopt Asian traditions, from yoga to Buddhism, belies the difficulties that have occurred in the clash of such distinct cultures. In 1889 the classic esoteric book *The Light of Egypt* was published. The preface states that the book is intended to counter "the strenuous efforts now being systematically put forth to poison the budding spirituality of the Western mind, and to fasten upon its mediumistic mentality, the subtle, delusive dogmas of Karma and Re-incarnation, as taught by the sacerdotalisms of the decaying Orient."

But other Americans deeply embraced what they called Oriental Wisdom, completely transforming their lives, and the lives of those they taught, or otherwise influenced, sometimes with nothing more than a picture of a white man in an improbable yoga pose on the cover of a popular magazine in the 1930s. As Philip Deslippe wrote in *The Swami Circuit* (2018): "early American yoga was not physical or postural, but primarily mental and magical. Early American yoga was not centered on books or specific figures, but rather upon an active and widespread network of traveling teachers who gave tiered levels of instruction through public lectures, private classes, and dyadic relationships. Teachers of yoga were overwhelmingly of a type—educated, cultured, and professionally savvy—and students were largely female, affluent, and invested in American metaphysical religion."

One American family in particular had several members whose experiences were shocking to their peers, but who nevertheless pioneered new approaches to spirituality in America. Ora Ray Baker was born in Albuquerque, New Mexico, in 1892 to a prominent California family who were not only wealthy but powerful—among her relations was a senator. But her most famous relative was her second cousin, Mary Baker Eddy, the founder of Christian Science. Mary Baker Eddy's evolution from invalid to what Mark Twain called the "monarch" of Christian Science made her the most powerful woman in the United States. Twain was envious and spiteful about her massive success. In 1906 thirty thousand of her followers joined her in Boston for the dedication of the expanded, and magnificent by any measure, Mother Church. In her eighties Eddy said she was dying not because of old age but because of the deadly thoughts of the press who were expecting her death, and the death wishes of the leaders of her own Church of Christian Science, who were too eager to get her out of the way so they could run the profitable international organization themselves. At its peak around 1971 almost two thousand churches were operating worldwide. Today they number themselves at around 1,700.

When Ora's parents died, her older half brother, Pierre Bernard, became her guardian. Pierre was becoming famous, too, as a master of hatha yoga. He and his brother Glen had met a tantric yogi, a Syrian Bengali by the name of Sylvais Hamati, in of all places, Lincoln, Nebraska, toward the end of the 1880s. Both brothers devoted themselves to yoga but in very different ways. While Glen approached yoga with respectful devotion, Pierre didn't mind earning money by entertaining people with his skills. For example, in 1898 he gave a demonstration of his alleged yogic powers in San Francisco. As physicians surrounded him Pierre assumed the Kali mudra, the pose of death. A doctor poked a large needle through Pierre's earlobe, cheek, upper lip, and nostril, but Pierre had no reaction.

By 1905 Pierre taught tantric sexual techniques and hypnotism in San Francisco, but Portland, Seattle, and Tacoma have also laid claim to being the place where Pierre started the Tantrik Order of America around 1906. Eventually there were Tantrik centers in other cities, including Chicago, Philadelphia, New York, and Cleveland. Pierre was almost singlehandedly responsible for America's oversexed interpretation of tantra.

In the shadows of Mary Baker Eddy and Pierre Bernard, Ora sought for her own understanding of spirituality. She found not only that, but the love of her life, when she met Inayat Khan, founder of the Sufi Order in the West, a Muslim from Northern India, and the great-great-grandson of the revered Tipu Sultan, the Tiger of Mysore, who courageously resisted British rule.

To begin his mission Inayat sailed to America in 1910, which happened to be the year Mary Baker Eddy died. As a master musician he planned to use music to teach Sufi mysteries, as in Persia and India. But America was still decades away from Ravi Shankar at Woodstock, so Americans showed no interest in his musical skills or his wisdom. This surprised Inayat, as did the pace and brusqueness of life in New York City near the beginning of the twentieth century, but he persisted until he found appreciative listeners for both his music and his lectures at Columbia University. Other universities then invited him. He crossed the continent entertaining and enlightening eager listeners all the way to San Francisco, where Ora was in the audience. She was an eighteen-year-old girl, but given her family history she was hardly an ordinary teenager. He was thirty years old.

It's possible that Pierre hired Khan to give Ora a music lesson, but he did not expect them to fall in love. When Ora announced that they planned to marry, Pierre forbade it. He based his entire life on Eastern practices but when a master of them captured his half sister's heart, well, Pierre wasn't willing to go that far when it came to respect for foreign wisdom. Not only that, but Pierre was embroiled in a scandal of his own. Two teenage girls accused him of kidnapping them because he wouldn't let them leave his house. One of the girls reported that Pierre had her take off all her clothes then put his hand on her breast so he could check her heartbeat.

Neighbors reported ladies arriving at late hours wearing all their jewels, and the unseemly cries of women in the night. The charges were dropped but salacious headlines appeared, like this one from Colorado's *Herald Democrat* December 19, 1911: "Shocked by Guru Orgy: 'Oom the Omnipotent' Taught Gross Immorality Under Cloak of Sanskrit College." Pierre was now calling himself Om the Omnipotent. However, he was also on his way to having the best collection of Sanskrit books and manuscripts in America.

Ora and Khan refused to say goodbye when Khan left America bound for London. Their unhappiness apart continued until one day Ora was straightening up Pierre's desk. She found a letter from Khan with his address in London. Ora traveled alone out of the United States, across the Atlantic, and right to Khan's side. They married immediately. Ora took the name Ameena Begum, meaning roughly "honest married woman." Then they settled near Paris in a house given to them as a gift by an admirer. They started a family and a school. Khan influenced the music of the French composer Debussy.

Ora and Khan had two daughters and two sons. One of their sons became a respected Sufi teacher like his father. One of their daughters was the legendary spy Noor-un-Nissa Inayat Khan. An expert in wireless code transmission, she exchanged messages with the allies from Nazi-occupied France until she was captured. After enduring long-term imprisonment and torture, Noor became a Night and Fog prisoner, which meant she had been disappeared into the shackles of a windowless room. An SS man beat her before shooting her in the head. The last word she spoke is said to have been *liberty*. She was posthumously awarded two prestigious medals, the British George Cross, and a French Croix de Guerre with silver star. Khan did not live to see it. He broke Ameena's heart when he died in 1927, only forty-five years old.

As her own death approached in the late 1940s, Ameena composed a collection of 101 poems called *A Rosary of One Hundred and One Beads*. Forty-seven of the poems were lost during World War II, but the surviving poems were finally published in 1998. They could be described as musings inspired by the teaching, and the loss, of her beloved husband, and also reflections on her experiences as a loving mother of extraordinary children. She did not long survive her war-hero daughter.

As for Ameena's half brother Pierre, he was gifted a house, too, but his was a bit grander: a thirty-room mansion on a seventy-two-acre estate in Nyack, New York. Despite the scandal, Pierre had remained popular with the monied ladies of New York City, earning extra cash on the side as a matchmaker. Ida Rolf, founder of the physical therapy named after her, was one of his students.

Pierre met his own match when he married Blanche de Vries, the first woman to own a yoga studio. She was famous in New York City for her sensual dances inspired by choreography from the Near and Far East. At eighty years old she still taught classes. Blanche seems to have settled Pierre down. He involved himself in more reputable businesses, such as dog tracks. But irony aside, Pierre also earned money from an airport, baseball stadiums, and in 1931 he was president of the State Bank of Pearl River.

While Pierre's quietly yogic brother Glen never approved of his brother's adventures, Glen's son Theos, which means "god" in Greek, found his uncle Pierre to be just what the doctor ordered. Born in

Pasadena, California, in 1908, when his parent's marriage failed not long after his birth, his mother took Theos home to her family in Tombstone, Arizona.

On a cold day in 1927 several of his fellow students at University of Arizona threw Theos into a fountain as part of his hazing. He became so sick with pneumonia he had to return home. His long recuperation gave him time to read his mother's books on yoga and Eastern philosophy. The references to "immortal energy" captured his imagination, but nowhere in his mother's library could he find any information about how to experience that.

By 1932 Theos was in Los Angeles working as an intern with a law degree at the beginning of what promised to be a respectable career. That summer he got a job as a court clerk. There he serendipitously ran into his father Glen, who became his yoga teacher. Theos told no one about the reunion or the lessons he received. Even when he wrote his memoir he invented a guru instead of telling the truth. Glen convinced Theos to go back to the University of Arizona to study psychology and philosophy, so Theos left Los Angeles and his budding legal career for two years of learning about historical perspectives on human nature.

Like many perennial college students Theos ran out of money when his mother ran out of patience. She may not have known about her ex-husband's influence on her son, but she did know that being a lawyer was a much better paying job than being a philosopher. Trying to figure a way out of his predicament Theos leafed through a copy of *Fortune* magazine. There he saw for the first time his uncle Pierre. Theos took a trip to meet his uncle. He received a warm welcome, and not only from Pierre. Theos quickly fell in love with Dr. Viola Vertheim.

Viola was an extraordinary woman. Her brother was a well-known investment banker. But Viola was a pioneer in the world of psychiatry at a time when approved techniques for dealing with psychological issues included metrazol convulsion therapy, which involved the injection of a powerful stimulant that induced convulsions and coma, and which was sometimes fatal. In contrast, Viola focused on the ways that the life of a community and the life of an individual intersect. Throughout her career Viola supported civil rights and fought against violence and poverty in cities. She considered these issues important to mental health. A famous advocate of adoption, she helped open the way for the adoption of children of color and of children with special needs.

Theos and Viola married in 1934. With Pierre's help Theos resumed his studies, but now instead of University of Arizona, he was attending Columbia. In 1936, to celebrate his son's master of the arts degree, Glen took Theos and Viola on a trip to India. The honeymoon became something else when after several months of travel Theos declined to join his bride and his father on the journey home. Instead, he journeyed to Kashmir, to Ceylon, to every corner of India in search of gurus. He met a lama in Calcutta with whom he spent a year studying the language of Tibet. At last his request to visit Tibet was granted by the British authorities.

During his three months in Tibet, Theos learned about tantric yoga from teachers born to the tradition, and he started what would become an impressive collection of Tibetan books and other artifacts. He left UC–Berkeley mandalas, paintings, bronze statues, wood-block prints, hats, robes, ritual tools such as singing bowls and symbolic thunderbolts of enlightenment.

But what Theos became best known for were the more than eleven thousand photographs and twenty thousand feet of film he took of Tibet. He returned home in 1937 and declared himself a lama, as he put it, "initiated into the age-old religious rites of Tibetan Buddhism—the first white man ever to live in the lamaseries and cities of Tibet." Theos must have been quite a student to earn in one year the title lama, which requires twenty-five years of practice. He considered himself, and may well have been, an emissary from Tibet.

Theos wrote about his adventures in a series of syndicated newspaper articles the accuracy of which his biographer and others have questioned. In his search for more stories to tell he told his father's stories as if they were his own. The articles led to radio broadcasts and public lectures. A publisher quickly rushed out his first book, *Penthouse of the Gods*. At this point Viola realized she had married more than she had bargained for. The eager student from the West she had fallen in love with was now a Tibetan lama building a career as a guru and travel writer. Divorce allowed them both to pursue their individual missions.

Theos remained popular through the end of the 1930s, especially the photographs of him in Tibetan costume, or contorted in a difficult yoga pose. Theos was a ruggedly handsome man with an impressive physique. The magazine *Family Circle* gave him five cover stories, the perfect introduction for his quickly produced second book, *Heaven Lies Within Us,* a hatha yoga manual disguised as a memoir. In 1939 Theos opened the American Institute of Yoga. While the world was at war in the early 1940s Theos earned a Ph.D. at Columbia. In his dissertation he cast himself as a scholar but also a practitioner. He explained why he was assigned certain asanas, comparing them to prescriptions. He discussed breathing exercises, the meaning of certain hand gestures, and purification rituals and practices.

In 1942 Theos married Ganna Walska, a mediocre opera singer whose career had been bankrolled by her wealthy elderly husband. Orson Welles claimed that she was an inspiration to his masterpiece *Citizen Kane.* Ganna may not have been that great a singer but she had a knack for marrying wealthy men. Four out of her six husbands were rich. By the time Theos became her sixth husband Ganna's wealth had accumulated into a vast estate.

Together Theos and Ganna bought a nearly forty-acre property in one of California's most exclusive communities, Montecito, near Santa Barbara. They named it Tibetland. Theos hoped that Tibetan monks and lamas would visit California, perhaps even relocating, but the war made travel impossible. In 1943 Theo's dissertation became his third book, *Hatha Yoga: The Report of a Personal Experience.* It included photos of Theos demonstrating the techniques he wrote about. Experts on yoga have praised it as the first really accurate book on yogic practices in English. By 1946 Ganna decided she preferred life without Theos. She divorced him but had to pay $1,500 in alimony. Ganna rechristened her estate Lotusland. An enthusiastic gardener, she made the grounds into a botanical garden that remains an attraction to this day.

After the war ended, Theos got married again. This time to Helen Graham Park. Park was an associate of Cornelius Vander Starr, founder of AIG, a famous philanthropist and international insurance tycoon with a special interest in China. Park was also an internationally recognized architect. She had been studying Buddhism, Jung, and the healing practices of Tibetans, Hindus, Persians, and the Chinese.

Theos and Helen traveled to the Ki monastery in Tibet on a honeymoon perhaps only they could enjoy, searching for obscure manuscripts. Unfortunately, Theos found himself in the middle of the Partition of India. In the violence between Hindus and Muslims when parts of Punjab were in the midst of becoming Pakistan, Theos and his Tibetan friend were shot dead. Their bodies were dumped in the river, never to be recovered.

Helen continued their work. In 1984 the Helen Graham Park Foundation opened in Miami, Florida. There the copious notes of her lifelong researches can be consulted, as well as the collection of books and other resources she accumulated with and without Theos. The foundation hosts events such as a conversation between a psychotherapist and a Tibetan lama.

The plan Theos had to bring Tibetan teachers to America was realized in a much less gracious way when the Chinese invasion of Tibet caused lineage carriers to relocate all over the world. With the advent of publishers like Snow Lion and Shambhala rare texts of Buddhist wisdom became available at bookstores. Tibetan Buddhist art and ritual implements became popular at New Age gift shops.

"Coffee shops, where poet performers read aloud, painted on walls, discussed Jung, Zen, the I Ching, Kafka, the pleasures of pot and red wine," Peter Plagens (1974) wrote of the Beats in his book *Sunshine Muse*. Beat culture's combination of Eastern wisdom, especially Buddhist, with the moving storytelling and beautiful prose and poetry of writers like Jack Kerouac, Gary Snyder, and Allen Ginsberg, inspired the spiritual revolution of the 1960s that flourished in the 1970s, and achieved wide awareness during the New Age in the 1980s.

For Ora, Pierre, Glen, Theos, and Helen Eastern practices and beliefs became a way of life. But the student is not the only one transformed as Asian traditions interact with American culture. Teachers are also faced with unfamiliar contexts that can lead to trouble. Consider for example Roshi Taizan Maezumi, the master who brought the White

Plum lineage of Zen Buddhism to sunny Southern California around 1960. Over the next thirty-five years he became founding teacher of Yokoji-Zen Mountain Center and the Zen Center of Los Angeles, also known as Buddha Essence Temple. He helped people from all walks of life realize that, as he put it, "all of us are equally absolute, equally precious, equally splendid, wherever we are at this moment."

In 1983 the roshi admitted he had an alcohol problem, and that he had cheated on his wife with several of his female students. He checked into the Betty Ford Center for rehabilitation. The Zen Center, which had been a busy hub of Buddhist scholarship and practice, became quiet. The emptiness the students had been striving for now filled the rooms of the two-story Colonial Revival bungalow, a private home on a quiet street in Koreatown converted into a *zendo*.

Christianity, of course, has plenty of examples of renegade behavior by priests. In the second decade of the twenty-first century ads appeared on television and online advising victims of molestation by clergy to contact particular law firms specializing in such cases. Sex scandals afflict American churches regularly.

Zen has its share of masters who indulged in physical pleasures, like the great poet Ikkyu, who at age seventy realized that sexual passion is the great path to enlightenment. Zen monks and geishas were known to enjoy each other's company. Did the pleasures of the City of Angels, the sunshine, the approachable women, the neighborhood liquor store, seduce the roshi? Or did his perfectly traditional Zen passions cause unexpected consequences in a society where even the most liberal are conflicted by puritan conditioning. The community fractured. Taizan could not return. There would be no forgiveness. After a night out drinking, while visiting family in Japan, Taizan drowned in a bathtub.

The Zen Center continues, thanks to the lineage the roshi established. The current abbot emeritus and head teacher Wendy Egyoku Nakao Roshi was born in Hawaii. In 1978 she began living at the Zen Center. Twenty-one years later she became abbot. She set out to bring something new to American Zen. For example, she gave dharma transmission to Merle Kodo Boyd, the first African American woman to receive it. The severity of tradition she tempered with an approach more welcoming to families. When she retired to work on developing a complete curriculum for the Zen Center she appointed a Caucasian woman, Deborah Faith-Mind Thoresen, as the center's fourth abbot. Nakao coauthored, with Roshi Eve Marko, a volume of modern koans: *The Book of Householder Koans: Waking Up in the Land of Attachments,* published in 2020.

Ironically, Taizan's drinking and dallying with women, which ruined the community, was traditional, while the feminism of the fourth abbot is viewed by conservative lineages as a radical departure from the norm. In the rejection that followed the revelation of Taizan's weaknesses, do we see nothing more than the influence of Western culture? Or is the reorganization of privilege in a world of greater equality evolving at the Zen Center, with the blessings of a master who knew when it was time to step away?

America's ambiguous relationship with Eastern wisdom continues as demonstrated by the state of Alabama. In May of 2021 the governor of Alabama signed a bill that ended a twenty-seven-year ban against yoga being taught in schools, but only in a very restricted way: "School personnel may not use any techniques that involve hypnosis, the induction of a dissociative mental state, guided imagery, meditation, or any aspect of Eastern philosophy and religious training in which meditation and contemplation are joined with physical exercises to facilitate the development of body-mind-spirit." Furthermore, "Chanting, mantras, mudras, use of mandalas, induction of hypnotic states, guided imagery, and *namaste* greetings shall be expressly prohibited."

4

American Metaphysical Christianity

ON HER WEBSITE a Christian prophetess reveals secrets of heaven. The dinosaurs are so tame you can ride them. There's an amusement park with a roller coaster called "The Rush." Those who live in heaven "take turns staying in each other's mansions." Of the four hundred who offered questions for the prophetess to answer over a hundred asked the same one: Do our pets join us in heaven? Yes, they do. Sports are the same yet different in heaven. "Each team has a place on the scoreboard, but all the points go to Jesus." As for clothes, each resident has "a gown of Salvation and a robe of Righteousness for corporate or united gatherings," and also "a wardrobe of many different tunic tops and pants." There's an ice cream parlor in heaven, "the scoops are huge." She has over a hundred thousand followers on Facebook. Near the end of February 2021 she live-streamed a prayer to encourage Donald Trump to take back the presidency. As she prayed she used a staff, a tree branch, like the handle of a witch's broom, to pound on the ground, emphasizing words like *declare* and *destiny*. With her pink hair and American flag shawl she has the appearance of a grandmother reminiscing about the first Woodstock concert.

When most of us think of American religion, we think of evangelicals preaching in sleek modern megachurches, ministers in neighborhood pulpits, choirs in southern Baptist congregations, or somber Catholic ceremonies. Most Americans believe America is a Christian nation, founded by Christians.

American Christianity opposes American Metaphysical Religion as a source of contamination from which Christians can never quite free themselves. From the Force in the *Star Wars* movies to fashionable young witches in TV shows, from newspaper horoscopes to bestselling novels and comic books, AMR is impossible to completely avoid.

American Metaphysical Religion has had a strong influence on American Christianity. In modern Christian America, for the majority of believers, sin is no longer the original and unavoidable pain of life as understood by early Christians. Suffering, Mother Theresa's path to salvation, never quite caught on in America where pain is believed to be a navigational warning to help the traveler get back on the God-ordained road to good health and prosperity. This is the so-called prosperity gospel, for the most part, the religion of televangelism.

Christians of earlier eras struggled with the certainty that because of Original Sin they were damned at birth. If they could attract the grace of God with their faith, charity, and patient suffering, they might hope to escape to heaven. Calvinists believed the fate of human beings even after death to be preordained no matter how well they lived.

But to Americans devastated by the Civil War, sin was the absence of lost loved ones, and séances were salvation. Today sin is understood by many American Christians as a lack of faith that leads to the lack of material wealth, which provides not only enhanced opportunities and quality of life, but also proof of divine approval. Many American evangelical leaders profited greatly by telling their followers that if they are poor that is evidence they have not donated enough to the church.

The so-called occult and Christianity are generally understood to be utterly opposed, and yet there is a long history of cultures grafting pagan magical beliefs into Christian settings. In the voodoo, Santeria, Lucumi, and brujeria communities Christian saints can coexist beside ancient African and other Indigenous gods and spirits. The secrecy of these practices makes it hard to estimate devotees but they are certainly in the millions. Still struggling with legality in the U.S., and widely opposed due to rituals involving animal sacrifice, these communities arouse considerable suspicion among monotheists. Yet tolerance has broken out here and there in ways that may promise a more cooperative and respectful relationship between these very different communities. In 2002 Timothy Freke and Peter Gandy published *Jesus and the Lost Goddess: The Secret Teachings of the Original Christians*. They argue that Sophia was the Great Goddess of Christianity, and that Jesus was a goddess worshipper or even consort. In surviving Gnostic writings, they explain, can be found proof that the female half of Christian spirituality was eliminated by patriarchies with political and economic agendas. Today a website offers "Christian I Ching" interpretations illustrated by quotes from the Bible. There are a number of tarot-inspired decks designed for Christians, including Mary, Queen of Angels Oracle; the Saints Deck; and Loving Words from Jesus.

AMR has never been shy about appropriating whatever it likes from traditional religions. While Jesus remains important in most versions of AMR, among many New Agers and certain schools of the occult, the focus is on the "Christ energy" and "the white light of the Christ." Numerous mediums have claimed, and continue to claim, that they channel any and all saints, apostles, and quite often none other than Jesus Christ himself. But the relationship between Christianity and Spiritualism has always been difficult. After all, for most denominations trance channeling is nothing less than necromancy, trafficking with the dead. In return, Spiritualists have not always been respectful of organized religions.

For example, in 1892 the Oriental Publishing Company of Philadelphia released *Antiquity Unveiled*. The cover features a golden sun in the left upper corner. Golden rays surround a disk inscribed "LIGHT OF TRUTH." The author is not listed on the title page, but the casual browser may presume that the genial-looking elderly white man with a beard who signed his name J. M. Roberts was the author, or more correctly, the editor, since the full title of the book is *Antiquity Unveiled: Ancient Voices from the Spirit Realms Proving Christianity to be of Heathen Origin*. He also wrote a book called *Apollonius of Tyana Identified as the Christian Jesus*.

The introduction to *Antiquity Unveiled* explains that Roberts was the son of a senator. When a medium channeled convincing messages from his deceased father, Roberts became one of many abolitionists who embraced Spiritualism. *Antiquity Unveiled* is a six-hundred-page Who's Who of deceased historical figures. They all chimed in to reveal the fraudulent origins of Christianity.

Contributors included the church father Origen, the alchemist and astronomer Albertus Magnus, the Roman historian Tacitus, the Neoplatonists Plotinus, Iamblichus, and Porphyry, the Persian prophet Zoroaster, the Roman Emperor Vespasian, and twelve pages more of small print listing the contributing spirits, many of them Romans or early church figures of lesser historical importance. Paracelsus did not show up; however, one of his students did. A veritable convention of notable spirits, including Jewish high priests and rabbis, and prominent Christians like Pope Innocent III and Clement of Alexandria, all dedicated to the conversion of Christians into Spiritualists.

The author's preoccupation with Apollonius of Tyana was apparently shared by the spirits as the subject comes up over two hundred times. Whether written by spirits or an incarnate author, the book is very learned. The argument that Apollonius of Tyana was a Nazarene and that his story was stolen to create the myth of Jesus Christ, is supported by exploration of the Chaldean language, the teachings of Pythagoras, historians of the ancient world, and Essene, Druid, and Hindu doctrine. The book includes a fanciful portrait of "Apollonius the Nazarene." Toward the end of the book, there's another illustration. Laughing Catholic clergy throw books into a fire. Are they demonstrating why they are the enemy, or are they celebrating their redemption from the lies of the church?

The argument that Apollonius was Jesus may not be convincing from the perspective of modern scholarship, but along the way, to explain the identity of each spirit, Roberts provides interesting quotes from the works of church fathers and from historians of the ancient world. He also includes his own notes, comments, and reactions to the revelations of the ancient spirits.

The spirit of Emperor Vespasian reports that Apollonius was with him in Jerusalem and acted as channel for Vespasian's ancestors. Apuleius, author of the first novel, *The Golden Ass,* regrets having once said that Apollonius was the reincarnation of Buddha. In the afterlife

Apuleius learned that Apollonius had been a medium who channeled Buddha, to help keep Buddhism alive.

The spirit of Iamblichus tells us that he was a follower of Ammonius Saccas, the teacher of Plotinus. Ammonius it seems had written a sacred book about the journey of the sun through the twelve signs of the zodiac. The book had been intended only for the few. But it got into the wrong hands, and with minor changes became what we call the New Testament. The spirit of Plotinus offers Buddhist doctrine as the origin of much of what is considered Christian. The spirit of St. Germain, a bishop, not the famous occultist, said that he was "anxious and willing to rectify the mortal errors of my life." So he explained from the beyond that Jesus Christ was an elaboration on the myth of Krishna. According to the ancient spirits Christianity, like AMR, borrowed from other religions freely in the creation of its myth, doctrine, and practice.

Antiquity Unveiled belongs in the same category as *Anacalypsis: An Attempt to Draw Aside the Veil of Isis,* Blavatsky's *Isis Unveiled,* Antoine Fabre d'Olivet's *The Hebraic Tongue Restored,* and other majestic creations of the imagination seeking a unifying meaning in history. These marvelous books may have had too many roots in questionable and dated scholarship, and the conclusions regarding history that they put forth may not have stood the test of time, but they are delightful explorations of the art of speculation. If *Antiquity Unveiled* was a work of fiction, it might be a masterpiece of Pessoa proportions, though the Portuguese literary genius took the trouble to make his pseudonyms write differently, since each had a unique style. In *Antiquity Unveiled,* all the spirits seem to express themselves in the same way.

But there have been happier hybrids of Christianity and Spiritualism. For example, the Reverend Edward A. Monroe. The most extraordinary psychic I've met, Ed was a retired police department mechanic. Late in life he was initiated as a shaman by the Tiwa tribe of the Taos Pueblo. He specialized in medical mediumship, and I can attest to his accuracy and to the effectiveness of his often folksy cures. I have found no reference to him or his work online. No one wrote a book about Ed, although Jess Stearn, one of Edgar Cayce's better known biographers, had planned to do so. Ed had no organization of students. His cassette tapes were copied and traded among groups of grateful clients, many of them Christian retirees in southern and Sunbelt states. Ed's mission began after he retired from the LAPD, when he prayed to be made useful in the Chapel of the Holy Cross, among the red rocks of Sedona.

Ed would recline in a chair and induce his trance listening to bagpipes playing "Amazing Grace" on a cassette recorder. The spirit that spoke through him had a deep Scottish brogue. Jock, as he called himself, had a saying that could be a motto for American Metaphysical Religion, "We don't much care what you believe as long you believe in something." This was not a cynical dismissal of dogma and practice, but rather the idea that when a human being believes in something more than the material world certain qualities can develop, and more assistance can be provided from beyond. A closed-off soul simply cannot be reached. There must be some openness that allows for connection. The words given to the details of making and keeping that connection are the idiosyncrasies of time and place. We are urged to find what works best for us.

Steven A. Ross, Ph.D., is president and cofounder of World Research Foundation, a global resource for people who want to understand illness and how to cure it. The foundation offers collected research on allopathic treatments alongside alternative healing methods ancient and modern. Dr. Ross was a key consultant when the City of Los Angeles sued the state of California for aerial application of pesticide without the city's approval. One of his greatest services has been providing accredited continuing education for physicians through classes and lectures at hospitals and medical networks.

Ross worked with Ed and Jock for many years. He knows a surgeon who innovated a new technique thanks to Jock, who appropriately enough claimed to have been a regimental surgeon for the Scottish Black Watch in his most recent life. Ross also knows an astronomer working with information Jock gave him. Jock had Ross index four thousand readings, ten thousand questions, and twelve thousand past lives, every single one distinct, including a reading during which Jock explains that the Ed and Jock experiment was not about publicizing mediumship but about tracking the effects of the readings on individuals as they influenced others over the long arc of time. Ross reports that everything Jock told him in 1973 about his future has taken place.

In personal correspondences of 2021 used with his permission, Ross shared five examples of Jock's accuracy, one of them personal. Ross's father woke up once with a terribly swollen left leg. He had to be taken to the hospital in an ambulance. There two doctors disagreed. One blamed an insect bite and the other a problem with circulation. The leg got worse as the doctors tried to decide what therapeutic approach to take because no bite mark could be found. That day a friend of Dr. Ross had a reading. A question was asked about the dire situation. Only the hospital address and room number were provided. Jock first mentioned the disagreement between the doctors. Then he predicted they would find the spider bite and all would be well. The doctors soon discovered the bite and proceeded to treat the leg.

On another occasion a woman entered the anonymous storefront office Ed had in Van Nuys, California. Ross describes what he heard on the cassette tape recording of the session: "The tape begins with Jock saying, 'People come for many reasons to visit the Ol' Scotty, but this would be a first. Now you have two contraptions in your purse today. You won't need the recorder since we will provide you a copy of your sessions today. You most certainly will not need the weapon that you've brought.' Then on the tape you hear a thud when her purse hits the ground. Later she admits that she was with the fraud group of the Van Nuys division of the LAPD and she was checking to see if Ed was a crooked fortune-teller."

A woman was diagnosed with a likely fatal condition that would have to be treated surgically immediately. Turning to Jock in her denial and desperation she received the message that her problems were due to certain vertebrae having moved out of place. He then listed how far and in which direction for each vertebrae. He advised her to take her reading to a good chiropractor then play him the directions provided. The astonished chiropractor confirmed the accuracy of the measurements, made the necessary adjustments, and her condition greatly improved. With further treatment she regained her health.

Once a psychiatrist who believed the whole thing was an act and a symptom of Ed's serious mental illness booked a reading. But he was dumbfounded when Jock began the reading by asking if the good doctor would like to know the reason for his erectile dysfunction? After much stammering and throat-clearing the psychiatrist settled down and listened carefully.

Then there was the child who appeared to be perfectly normal according to the tests but who would not communicate with anyone or anything. Jock explained that this was the first incarnation of this soul and so the soul had no previous experiences to draw upon. Jock also correctly pointed out that the child's only occupation was drawing pictures of planets.

I spoke with two other witnesses to Jock's accuracy. A young woman was suffering abdominal pains. Advised to have exploratory surgery she turned to Ed for advice. Jock told her she had a deep fear of pregnancy. That she had blocked her femininity. He advised her to take bubble baths and paint her toes. She should also choose from the most dependable birth control methods and use them without fail. An appointment was made to acquire birth control. A bubble bath was taken. The pain stopped. She followed through on Jock's advice and the pain never returned.

Another young woman's life changed for the better when Jock told her that her medical problems were the result of too much wine and cheese, which she should not have except on rare occasions. The dietary change cured her ills. He also described to her a career she would have in the future. It involved technology unlike anything she had heard of before. It sounded like science fiction or fantasy. She forgot Jock's prediction until she found him in the pages of an early manuscript of this book. Having become an expert at immersive media, mixed reality, virtual reality, full dome productions, and new media technology platforms, she realized that Jock's prediction finally made sense.

By reporting these unusual events I do not advocate that medical treatment should always be avoided, or that all alternative methods of healing are effective for everyone. These hearsay cures were appropriate for specific individuals at a certain time and place. Jock advised many people to see physicians.

Several of Ed's clients were told that in past lives they knew Jesus. But this was no mere imitation of Edgar Cayce. Ed described Jesus as strong and swarthy, the kind of man who could survive in the desert. Most of the vignettes are quick incidents. A girl at a well who saw a miracle and ran away "as if scalded" when Jesus offered to teach her about how he had done it. Another fellow had a sandal-shaped birthmark on his rear. He had earned a kick from the savior himself—a little reminder from back in the day about moneylending in the temple. What makes the reading special is that the client did not mention the birthmark. Instead, Jock inquired as to why he was not asking about it.

Ed is a good example of the Christian side of Spiritualism but there is also a mystical and hermetic Christian tradition within American Metaphysical Religion. Most American alchemists and astrologers were Christians. But the occult was usually considered a private matter, an exclusive club, a privilege demanding discretion. The word *occult* literally means "secret." The border between the occult and Christianity has always been obscure in America. A rather quiet and reclusive woman did a great deal to illuminate this border and remove its stigma. She became an important influence on New Age occultists and mystical Christians alike.

Corinne Heline was born in Atlanta, Georgia, in 1882, a member of the Duke family, among the most aristocratic of the Old South. The inheritance she received when she turned sixteen allowed her to pay for the self-publishing of the twenty-eight books she would author. Her education in classical and religious studies complemented her sensitivity. Her lifelong study of ancient initiations gave her work a dimension beyond her frequent biblical references.

To understand Heline, we must first consider Mount Ecclesia in Oceanside, California, the international headquarters and spiritual temple of the Rosicrucian Fellowship, an organization founded in 1909 by Danish American Carl Louis von Grasshoff, better known by his pen name, Max Heindel.

In 1903 Heindel came to Los Angeles looking for work. Lectures by C. W. Leadbeater inspired him to join the Theosophical Society of Los Angeles, where he served as vice president from 1904 through

1905. Theosophy led him into the study of astrology and the practice of vegetarianism. Working too hard, but not earning enough to support himself, let alone the woman he had fallen in love with who would soon become his wife, in 1905 Heindel's health broke down and he became bedridden for months. The doctors predicted his death at any moment, but he recovered. He claimed that during his convalescence he had been studying in the invisible realms where he had found a new commitment to helping people. This led to two years of lecturing, which led to more time in the hospital. But he recovered more quickly this time and resumed his lecture tours.

In 1907 Heindel visited Berlin to attend lectures by Rudolf Steiner. He was deeply impressed by Steiner, but also convinced that Steiner would never reach a significant American audience; Steiner simply did not speak their language. Perhaps that is why Heindel's books borrow generously from Steiner's. Heindel may have seen his task as translation but he claimed a different source for his teachings.

Depressed that he had wasted his time visiting Berlin, Heindel felt he should have been lecturing, especially given the limitation on his life expectancy. Then, we are told, he was visited by an Elder Brother of the Rosicrucian Order, of the inner worlds, founded in 1313 by twelve Elder Brothers and an adept.

Seventeenth-century Rosicrucian Michael Maier described the origins of Rosicrucianism as "Egyptian, Brahmanic, derived from the Mysteries of Eleusis and Samothrace, the Magi of Persia, the Pythagoreans, and the Arabs." One could argue that Rosicrucianism functioned as an early prototype of American Metaphysical Religion given the way it drew from such diverse sources. In fact, Maier's idea of the utopia America could be, inspired four of the people involved in the plan for the first Virginia Colony, including the treasurer, the future treasurer, a lawyer, and a committee member.

Heindel claimed to have received instructions on how to visit the Temple of the Rose Cross, an invisible edifice of etheric energy on the border of Germany and Bohemia. Visiting this location in his own etheric body, Heindel claimed direct communication with the invisible order. Heindel also received teachings that became his most popular and influential book *The Rosicrucian Cosmo-Conception,* published in 1909. Like Blavatsky, apparently neither Heindel nor the Rosicrucians who taught him were shy about their belief in Caucasian superiority over the Semitic and African shades of humanity. These were not overt racists—they did not make a point of racism, except in their theories about evolution.

In 1910 one of these elders, known as "The Teacher," gave Heindel a vision of what would become the Temple of the Rose Cross. Heindel tried to explain the nature of the vision in various ways, calling it telepathy, picture consciousness, and "Jupiter consciousness."

Heindel and his wife searched the southern coast of California for the site, but they could not find the place he had seen in the vision. Until, one day in 1911, they set out from their home in Santa Monica, with horse and buggy, to visit the Franciscan Mission of San Luis Rey de Francia, founded in 1798 by Junipero Serra himself. On the way they found the place that matched the vision. Even better, it had a for-sale sign. Heindel bought the forty-acre property and named it Mount Ecclesia. On its dedication day months later, Heindel and seven friends planted a white cross then Mrs. Heindel planted a rose bush that would grow to vine around it. Everyone took a turn to pray while pouring water on it.

From the summer of 1914 onward the Rosicrucian Fellowship gave spiritual healings at services. It took nine years to open the Healing Temple that would enshrine the traditional Rosicrucian edict to heal the sick free of charge. Unfortunately, Heindel didn't live to see it completed, he died in 1919. His wife Augusta lived another thirty years, during which she devoted herself to her mission of beautifying Oceanside, California. Manly Palmer Hall expressed gratitude for Augusta's generosity and support when he first began his career.

Hall and his mother enjoyed visiting Mount Ecclesia on holidays. Impressed by Hall's commitment to esoteric wisdom, by his good manners, and his apparent understanding of her husband's complicated books, Augusta and her community taught Hall astrology; he later became well known for his astrological books and lectures. They also taught him everything he needed to know about the art of printing books and pamphlets, from typesetting to binding. Hall began calling Augusta "mother." There's little doubt that not only her community but also her reputation among Rosicrucians and Theosophists greatly benefited the beginning of his career. But Augusta didn't approve of Manly's interest in hypnosis and Hollywood. She became dubious of him when he ignored her advice.

Perhaps hypnosis did get Hall into trouble. It's not surprising that he was drawn to the movie business. He had friends who were movie stars. His ill-fated relationship with cinema began in the late 1930s with *When Were You Born,* a noir murder mystery starring Anna May Wong about a detective who uses astrology to solve crimes. He came up with the story, narrated it, and appeared in the introduction, during which he shows us a book by Mother Shipton, the sixteenth-century English prophetess, while listing her accomplished prophecies. With a hint of a smile he relays Mother Shipton's once shocking prediction that women would one day wear short hair and trousers. Then, for three long minutes Hall introduces key characteristics of each sign of the zodiac. Finally, he vouches for it as a science. It's a strange way to start a feature film even one that is a monument to expository dialogue, but his next appearance on film was even cheesier.

In 1940 Hall appeared in the trailer for *Black Friday,* the Boris Karloff horror flick. Newspaper headlines declared Lugosi to be the first actor ever to perform on camera while hypnotized. Hall, mysteriously now a doctor, though he was then neither a Ph.D. nor a physician, is shown hypnotizing Bela Lugosi "to give reality to" the scene in which Lugosi's gangster character suffers an attack of claustrophobia when locked in the closet where he will die. Hall looks gaunt and downright creepy. Strangely, he doesn't sit or stand in front of Lugosi to hypnotize him. He sits behind him making mesmeric passes at the back of Lugosi's neck that resemble come hither gestures. When I was his assistant and asked him about these films, he didn't volunteer much information and he assured me no copies, to his relief, were likely ever to be found. Little did he know that they would one day be as near as YouTube. Augusta Heindel had tried to warn him.

Hall published his own take on Christianity in 1951 in his book *The*

Mystical Christ: Religion as a Personal Spiritual Experience, volume 2 of his trilogy *How to Understand Your Bible.* Hall's metaphysical interpretation of the New Testament doubts the accuracy of the four gospels. Hall was always respectful toward the various denominations and often lectured and wrote on Christian topics, but reserved his greatest enthusiasm for the Neoplatonists, Daoists, and Buddhists. Fascinated by the occult in his youth, he matured into a writer and speaker with a talent for distilling arcane wisdom into practical observations about how to live a meaningful life while enjoying greater well-being. He gained his wisdom from officiating over decades of christenings, weddings, hospital visits, funerals, and counseling about everything from marriage problems to eliminating ghosts and preparing for death. As his assistant I had the privilege of attending a few of these sessions.

On Christmas Day in 1938 the Rosicrucian Fellowship dedicated a sanitarium building where patients could stay for extended treatment. With its own printing press, the fellowship has been successful, printing hundreds of books and pamphlets, including the astrological ephemeris, or guide to the daily positions of the planets, astrologers have depended on for decades.

An article by Edward Sifuentes in the *San Diego Union-Tribune* on July 1, 2016, is titled "Rosicrucian Fellowship Boosts Security." Sifuentes quotes the general secretary, "gang members and taggers were coming in at night to write graffiti on buildings and cause other damage. Transients, including some with criminal histories, were setting up camps behind the property." Donations dried up during an economy that forced many to work more than one job. Most folks don't have time for esoteric studies. Then came the pandemic. Despite the problem of buildings requiring millions of dollars of retrofitting mandated by the state, the Rosicrucian Fellowship continues Max Heindel's tradition of taking no money for healing, education, or membership. They point out that Mount Ecclesia has always gotten by on a patchwork of legacies, donations, book sales, room rentals, and cafeteria purchases.

In the early days of Mount Ecclesia, Max Heindel became Corinne Heline's teacher. There she met her second husband Theodore, who handled the many details of getting her books published, including

Occult Anatomy and the Bible, Tarot and the Bible, Color & Music in the New Age, and *Magic Gardens.*

As a small child, Heline often left her Methodist Sunday school to cross the street so she could admire and commune with the statue of Mary in a Catholic church. A Theosophist neighbor by the name of Mrs. Little allowed Corinne to borrow one of her occult books each time she visited. Then Mrs. Little gave Corinne the book that would change her life, *The Rosicrucian Cosmo-Conception* by Max Heindel.

Corinne was only sixteen years old when her mother died. Her generous inheritance did nothing to comfort her grief. Then her mother appeared to her. Happy in what she called the Higher Worlds, she urged Corinne to cheer up her despondent father. She also told Corinne about an old trunk where she had hidden Christmas money. Corinne found the money and bought herself a present, the Bible she would use for her New Age Bible interpretations.

Corinne married her first husband when she was twenty-nine years old, but he only lived nine more years. So the widow moved to California where she introduced herself to Heindel. Recognizing her intelligence and devotion to the mysteries, and perhaps impressed by her wealth, Heindel accepted her as a student. She studied with him for five years. He urged her to compile her New Age biblical interpretations in a book, but she remained skeptical. Three years after his death, she had a vision of Mary who, with a kiss on Corinne's cheek, assigned her the job of interpreting the Bible for the Aquarian Age.

Theodore Heline was a Shakespearean actor who became an author and lecturer on Rosicrucian subjects, editor and founder of the *New Age Interpreter,* publisher of *New Age Press,* and editor of *Rays of the Rose Cross,* the official journal of the Rosicrucian Fellowship. Theodore and Corinne were friends for a long time before they finally married in 1938, when they were both fifty-six years old. They moved to Los Angeles three years later, where they bought a house on a hill and named it Madonna Crest. The trees and flowers in the beautiful garden were all dedicated to Mary, which didn't seem to bother the nature spirits Corinne believed lived in the trees.

At Madonna Crest Corinne found her ideal work environment.

But she and her husband were also charmed by the New Age Bible and Philosophy Center in Santa Monica, an early midcentury California bungalow converted from a home into a library and lecture space. While the world was at war in Europe and Asia, the Helines became popular ministers. Theodore lectured occasionally in Santa Monica and at the Rosicrucian Fellowship. Lectures by Corinne were less frequent special events, but she did speak at every Christmas Eve service. People were charmed by her reminiscences of Max Heindel. She would also talk about the past life when she knew Jesus and Mary.

Theodore planted seeds for the 1980s New Age with his New Age Press headquartered in La Canada in the 1960s, but he shuffled off his mortal coil unexpectedly in 1971. He had written many books and pamphlets, and published many more. He wrote *The Archetype Unveiled: A Study of the Sound Patterns Formed by the Creative Word; Romeo and Juliet: The Occult in Shakespeare; The Neo-American: Building a New Race;* and published posthumously in 1973 *America's Destiny: A New Order of the Ages,* with chapters on the Great Seal, the Law of Thirteen, and Topping the Pyramid. It's interesting to note that Manly Hall published his *America's Assignment with Destiny* that summer. But Hall's book focused on the Aztecs, the Maya, the Inca, Indigenous American shamans, German mystics, and Latin American patriots. Of course, Hall had already published his influential *The Secret Destiny of America* in 1944.

Corinne continued to write books including *Temples of Music and Healing,* which she declared would become common in the future. Her favorite composer was Wagner. She lectured all over America on the esoteric meaning of his operas. Visits to Corinne meant listening to Wagner, and Wagner provided the soundtrack for the seasonal sacred festivals Corinne celebrated at Madonna Crest. Her book *Magic Gardens* is a charming exploration of the mission all flowers and their guardian angels hold dear, reminding human beings of heavenly beauty.

Corinne was seventy-two years old when she completed the seventh volume of her *New Age Bible Interpretation.* She lived another twenty-one years. The last book she wrote was the posthumously published *Blessed Virgin Mary: Her Life and Mission,* in which she wrote: "Mary, the ideal embodiment of womanhood and motherhood, belongs to all the world. The Blessed Mary is a master Initiate, the highest that ever came to earth wearing a feminine body. Hers was a sublime and a unique mission. Because of her spiritual attainment she was chosen to be the mother of the Holy Master Jesus. After she had fulfilled this role she took upon herself the mission of working for the upliftment of all women in the world. Her devotion to this cause will not cease until all women attain to a status equal in influence to that of man, the world over."

The year Corinne Heline was born, Oscar Wilde toured America giving lectures; Thomas Edison provided electricity for one square mile of Lower Manhattan; and Jesse James was shot in the back of the head. In 1975, the year Corinne died, VHS tapes were introduced, revolutionizing home movies and the pornography industry. Queen released their legendary *A Night at the Opera* album. *Jaws* was the movie of that summer.

Esoteric commentary on the Bible can only go so far. For a real revolution in the image of Jesus Christ, a new gospel can take further liberties. As a boy, Levi Dowling of Bellville, Ohio, had three separate visions of a shining white city he would someday build. At the age of thirteen, he followed in the footsteps of his father, becoming a Church of Christ preacher among pioneers. Levi was born in a log cabin. The opponent in Levi's first public debate, at age thirteen, was a pious Presbyterian elder who argued for the everlasting punishment of the wicked. Dowling argued against it. He never changed his belief that eternal damnation is false doctrine. He became a recognized preacher by the time he turned sixteen. Two years later he became pastor of a humble church. He got married and soon had a son.

Then the U.S. Army drafted Levi to fight in the Civil War. But his superiors recognized his skills, so they made him a captain, and perhaps the youngest chaplain in the service. When Levi's wife and son came to him to celebrate the end of the war just before he was mustered out, they both died in the smallpox epidemic. His son died three days before they were to go home. His wife died on the day Levi received his military discharge. He took their bodies home. Not long after, he preached at President Lincoln's funeral service to Union troops in Illinois.

After the war Dowling spent two years studying at Northwestern

Christian University in Indianapolis. His older brother William preached there while they both continued to work for the advancement of the Church of Christ. Levi also ventured into publishing. He worked with two legendary hymnodists by the names of George Root and Philip Bliss to create *The Crown of Sunday School Songs,* a popular songbook. The brothers published children's Sunday school newspapers, first in Indianapolis, then Chicago, with print runs of more than a hundred thousand a week. In 1867 Levi and William published the *Morning Watch,* a weekly newspaper suitable for Sunday schools. Settling in St. Louis, William kept the publishing business going for another thirty years.

William and Levi didn't only publish, they promoted. The brothers preached at churches, encouraging them to have Sunday school classes not only for children but also adults. They trained the teachers. They demonstrated classes at all age levels. They could, of course, provide standardized lessons, hymnals, and all necessary educational materials. It must not have been an easy life for his second wife, Kate. He soon gave it up.

Perhaps in response to the shocking deaths of his first wife and son, Levi next studied homeopathic medicine at a college in Chicago. At the Homeopathic Medical College of Missouri, in St. Louis, Levi earned a Ph.D. For a short time he taught chemistry and toxicology there. The marriage with Kate didn't last. He waited a long time to officially divorce her, until he was eager to marry his third wife, Eva.

But Levi didn't change his missionary ways. He was no longer selling the theory and practice of Sunday schools. Now he traveled all around the Midwest preaching and organizing communities in support of prohibition. Wherever Levi preached, he also offered healing. He became so popular in Topeka he filled the large tabernacle every night for two months. No other Christian event in Kansas had achieved such success. At night he preached. During the day he visited the sick. Eva worked with him, a nurse to the sick and a deacon to the distressed. They traveled together on this mission for two years. Three years after their son Leo was born, Levi and Eva settled down in Fort Wayne, Indiana, with the new century, the 1900s, only five years away.

In Fort Wayne, Levi became Dr. Dowling. He not only claimed to be a dermatologist, he could cure the flu and allergies, depression, stomach problems, and serious respiratory ailments. He also had a new treatment for moles that would remove them and any risk they may have posed. Levi and Eva still belonged to a church, but Levi was also a member of the Fort Wayne Occult Science Society. By then Levi had encountered the hidden masters of Theosophy, who gave him a mission. He would organize councils. At meetings they would wear white robes. This wasn't a KKK revival, however. These white robes were about bringing peace to the world. Articles in journals followed, appealing to Theosophists, Spiritualists, and practitioners of New Thought alike. Soon Levi's writing overtook his medical practice.

Three years after the twentieth century began, Eva and Levi moved to Los Angeles. Los Angeles has attracted and incubated generations of metaphysicians. Of all places, it seemed to them the most likely to fulfill Blavatsky's prediction that human evolution will soon birth a new race on the West Coast of North America. In Los Angeles Levi practiced homeopathic medicine, gave lectures on the Kabbalah, and published magazines and books. He also came to believe that he could reveal the lost truth about Jesus Christ.

Levi's medical practice and his lectures, which often included quotes from Eliphas Levi, took place in his home. There Dowling reigned as national seer and national hierophant of the Aquarian Commonwealth. The fledgling organization was not only inspired by the occult but also by socialism, as members were pledged to help each other. Eva was given the title national scribe. Three well-known mediums were among the founders, including a famous medium named James Peebles. His participation lent Levi Dowling credibility not only in the Spiritualist community, but among Theosophists. Peebles had worked with Blavatsky and Olcott in the early days of the Theosophical Society.

Levi wrote a book called *Biopneuma,* a lesson course in "the true science of the Great Breath." William Atkinson, under his pseudonym Yogi Ramacharaka, had published in 1904 the perpetually popular *Science of Breath,* which perhaps inspired Levi to present his own version. *Biopneuma* advocated for a strict code of conduct. No smoking. No impure sexuality. No alcohol. No drugs. No foul language. No bad temper. And no tight clothing. Instead we are told to will properly, think forcefully, and breathe deeply. Every day should include outdoor exercise and bathing. Keep regular hours for all activities, including two hours of meditation daily. Chew food thoroughly, at least twenty times for each bite. As for the term *Biopneuma,* or life breath, for Levi it meant the Holy Spirit.

The sex magic or tantric element Levi added to these other practices had nothing to do with erotic fervor. As we shall see, a recurring theme in American Metaphysical Religion is the preoccupation with proper procreation for the betterment of the species. With the right devotions, proper preparations, conducted at the right astrological day and hour, with the correct degree of reverence, love, gratitude, and intention, the best possible soul could be attracted for incarnation in one's family, community, and nation.

Magical sexuality fascinated many American metaphysicians from Paschal Beverly Randolph through Pierre Bernard, with many less famous teachers in between, for example, Delmar Deforest Bryant, who was better known by his pseudonym, Adiramled the alchemical author. This mystical name was actually an anagram of his name combined with his wife's name. Adiramled was also the name of Delmar's monthly newsletter and his publishing company. *The Light of Life or the Mastery of Death* was published in 1911 by Sun Center Publishing Company. The subject is regeneration, of the body and the soul.

In a response to a letter written to him by a reader named Juliet Rublee, Delmar wrote a two-page reply on the first day of June 1922. First he wrote about the breathing exercises of yoga. Then he commented on kundalini, and sexuality as an occult path. He explained, "the breathing exercises were not put in the lessons, for if the sexual practice there indicated is carried out right there is no need of them. The sexual practice is SURE to raise the seed.—the time of greatest desire on the part of the female—should be utilized for a full expression.—Now there you have the secret," but "I do not think that regeneration will be attained except through a counter-parted man and woman." The letter ends with a pushy sales pitch for a fig plantation project.

Juliet Barrett Rublee, the recipient of Delmar's letter, was an heiress to a fortune made from her family's tar and roofing supplies company.

Rublee produced a feature motion picture, *Flame of Mexico;* a silent movie that may be the first American film shot entirely south of the border. Rublee was not only a suffragist, she was the principal financial backer of Margaret Sanger's mission to make birth control accessible. Rublee also led a treasure hunt, a diving expedition in the Mediterranean. We are left to wonder what she may have thought of Delmar's secret.

In October of 1904 the *Los Angeles Herald* newspaper featured a story with the title "Founder and Seer of New Sect Would Build Holy City by Sea." The subtitle was, "Buys Large Tract of Land Near Redondo and Sells Lots." Here is the complete article:

Levi Dowling, abbaguru [father-teacher] of the Gnostics, expects to build on 800 acres near Redondo his Mount-Carmel-by-the-Sea. The doctor did not explain whether in his visions he had seen Hermosa and Redondo or the tract of land which he has purchased and which until lately has been given over to the growth of sand burrs, barley, and wheat, but the city will spring up, for there has been a well sunk and many lots have been sold. A temple of the sun is to be the first building erected, then is to come the polytechnic institute and the university buildings, and then after that the vision has it that there will rise into the California ethereal blue, the temple of resplendent light.

Since February 4 the doctor has been in the city and lately took up his residence at 1364 Figueroa Street [between Pico and Venice], where he lives with his family, wife and son. Here the visions keep on coming, and in his study on the second floor he looks into the great beyond, gets counsel and consolation, and arranges plans and specifications for the buildings that are to be erected near the sea.

In a queer combination of astrology, astronomy, Christianity, Hindu philosophy, and occultism, Dr. Dowling stands at the head of the Gnostics, and with a following of several hundreds hopes to found in place where he has purchased ground a community so ideal in the characters which compose it that in the end the whole world will be drawn into his Brotherhood of Universal Peace. The doctor does not foretell at what date this is to take place, but says that he knows. He does say, however, that within the next ten years the whole world will be thrown into an international complication which will bring about a war such as has never occurred in the history of man.

There is a silver lining to the darkest cloud, however, and in the end eternal peace will reign, with all disputes settled by arbitration. Before this comes about, however, one-third of the male population of the globe will have perished in the struggle. The Russian-Japanese war is not to come to a settlement until the dove of peace settles down over the land.

Forty years ago, while in the wilds of Indiana, where he was preaching in behalf of the Disciples' church, abbaguru (then plain Levi Dowling) had a vision, in which a voice said, "Levi, you shall be connected with the building of the White City of the Mystic Initiates and the Temple of Resplendent Light where the mountains dip into the sea." Over near Redondo the mountains dip and here will rise the walls of the city. Two hundred lots have been platted and over $22,000 worth of the property has been sold, the money obtained in this way going to the improvement of the land. The head officers hope to see many homes in course of erection within the next few months.

The Temple of the Sun is to be of brick, erected at a cost of $30,000 and the twelve buildings surrounding it in the ten-acre park that has been set aside are to cost between $4,000 and $5,000 each. Built as the modern sanitarium of today, these buildings are to be used for that purpose, and the advertising which is being sent out and which speaks of Los Angeles County under the name of Beulah Land calls attention to the fact that here the sickly may find rest and eventually health. Twelve physicians and healers are to have this work in charge, but are to use no drugs.

Six families are already here from Grand Rapids, where the doctor proselyted for some time, and a number of families are expected to follow before the advent of winter. The order of the Gnostics is made up of twelve sees, named after various precious gems and having for their headquarters those buildings named in the terms of the zodiac.

Abbaguru is of the imperial see, his wife is hierarch of the Chalcedonian see, and the only son officiates as Mercury and runs errands for his mother. Dr. Dowling says that he receives no regular salary, and that when the full number of sees are completed he will cease securing new members and go to teaching in the university which is to be erected. "Whenever $50 is needed it comes; whenever $100 is necessary it appears," said the doctor yesterday morning. He was in need of a little ready money Wednesday night, and at the session of the Jasper see he was presented with $50, which came as the proceeds of a fair which had been held. There were about fifty present at the session of the see, and the company was made up of well-dressed, well educated people. It is expected that many of these will go to the Carmel-by-the-Sea tract and erect their homes. The abbaguru has a first-class library of volumes on Hindu and Indian philosophy, astrology, and the occult sciences, but says that he has not read one of them, his understanding of the laws of the order having come from visions.

Despite its condescending tone the article proves that Levi prophesied correctly about the devastating war looming just ahead. World War I erupted "within the next ten years." But he was wrong about that war ending all wars, though many shared his delusion. He was also wrong about the success of his holy city.

He attempted a less ambitious venture in the summer of 1910. The Aquarian Commonwealth planned to start a commune. But this would be more than a commune, it would be an investment including stock ownership in the Etiwanda Vineyards in the San Gabriel Valley. But once again too few investors volunteered to join the experiment.

The Aquarian College of Teachers and Healers opened at the start of 1911. Students had access to weekly lectures, correspondence courses, and a course of instruction leading to two rather odd degrees. On the title page of *The Aquarian Gospel* Eva's name is followed by A.Ph.D. She was a doctor of Aquarian philosophy. The college also offered the A.H.M., or master of Aquarian healing degree. The famous psychic James Peebles, among others, joined the Dowlings to teach classes there.

That spring the First Aquarian Congress of North America convened in Levi's house. Officers were selected. Resolutions passed. A fundraising campaign began. The June issue of *Aquarian Age Magazine* announced that thanks to a generous donation from wealthy patrons "Levi had retreated to Catalina Island, where reading the Akashic Records would be easier." The gospels of Enoch and Melchizedek would soon be available.

But Levi went to Chicago before going to Catalina Island. He wanted to supervise the printing of the new edition of *The Aquarian Gospel*. Driving himself too hard at work, and on the road over the Rocky Mountains, he lost his health. Not long after his return from the trip, riding a train in South Pasadena, he collapsed and died with Eva and Leo at his side.

The Aquarian Congress convened on the same day as Levi's funeral. They elected Eva to take her husband's place. They declared her new name would be Leva. In the immediate aftermath of Levi's death, Peebles took an executive position and wrote for the *Aquarian New Age Magazine*. A month later he left the commonwealth. Perhaps he realized that however good Eva's intentions were, she would not be able to sustain the community her charismatic husband had built. Peebles moved on politely, pleading that he had too much work of his own to attend to. The Aquarian Commonwealth became only memories.

Eva and Leo lived together in the house that had been the headquarters of the Aquarian Congress. The house she had bought with Levi before he went Aquarian. Twelve years after Levi had died Eva fell ill and followed her husband into the great beyond. Leo inherited the house and the copyrights of *The Aquarian Gospel,* and his father's other books. Leo administered his father's copyrights until the end of his life in the summer of 1974. Levi's dream of an Aquarian Age and gospel were only beginning the powerful arc of their influence. Many writers credit Levi with being the first to popularize the idea of an Age of Aquarius.

The Aquarian Gospel was copyrighted in 1908, the year that *The Count of Monte Cristo* became the first film made in Hollywood. Published in 1909 by mail order, the first edition was soon sold out. No one knows why former Wyoming congressman Henry Coffeen participated in the copyright. He wrote the introduction for the first edition but that was left out of future printings, probably because of Coffeen's close ties with C. W. Leadbeater, who was embroiled in a scandal at the time. From the 1911 edition onward the introduction is by the publisher, Eva Dowling. She tells the story of the mysterious Levi transcribing in the wee hours of the night. She discourages interest in his life. He was merely a channel.

According to *The Aquarian Gospel,* Jesus visited Egypt, Assyria, Greece, Persia, India, and Tibet. In each of these civilizations of advanced learning Jesus was tested. He learned and he taught. They all came to know him as the divine chosen one, the Christ. That was the source of the teaching and the illumination that Jesus brought back to his people suffering under the domination of Rome. Jesus worked hard to make himself worthy to receive the Christ, the christening, the anointing of a truly holy human being. Jesus was a vessel.

There are some big differences between *The Aquarian Gospel* and the biblical gospels. In *The Aquarian Gospel* reincarnation is the reflex of justice. Those who seem to prosper when they do evil will reap the results of their sins in a future life. Encased in matter, human beings forget God. We live many lives on the way to remembering. When we fully remember then we too shall be christened. In fact, that is the destiny of us all, because no one is ever abandoned by God.

Unfortunately, the book contains numerous mistakes. There's one in the opening sentence where Herod Antipas is confused with his father Herod the Great. Another historical problem is a meeting between Jesus and the Chinese sage Meng-Ste. History does not record any philosopher by that name. There is a Chinese sage Meng-Tse however, though he lived three centuries earlier. Also, Jesus visits the grand Persian city of Persepolis, but Alexander had destroyed it three centuries before Jesus was born.

True believers have argued that Meng-Tse was an ascended master, so he met Jesus in his etheric body. Persepolis, of course, had been destroyed only physically. Its etheric form and inhabitants continued to exist, like the Invisible Temple of the Rosicrucians. But Jesus visiting Lahore is harder to explain, as that city would be built at least a hundred years later. Then there's Jesus visiting a Buddhist temple in Lhasa five hundred or more years before Buddhism reached Tibet. Still, those errors could be explained away as all too human. These kinds of mistakes, we are told, are typical in channeling, since imperfect human beings can distort what they receive. Perhaps the city was not Lahore. Perhaps Meng-Ste was not Meng-Tse, but another Chinese sage forgotten by history.

Levi claimed to have written down the truth about Jesus from the Akashic Records, but *The Aquarian Gospel* did not exactly come out of thin air. In 1887 Nicolas Notovitch published *The Unknown Life of Jesus Christ: By the Discoverer of the Manuscript*. Notovitch argued that during the eighteen mysterious years the Bible is silent about, Jesus had traveled the world. *The Aquarian Gospel* covers much the same ground, but it is written and published with a numbered chapter and verse layout meant to resemble the Bible. It reads like a rediscovered gospel. Blavatsky's influence is obvious; Levi borrows terminology, and a racist theory of human evolution, from *The Secret Doctrine*. He is firmly in the tradition of American mediums who have been offering corrections of the gospels since the beginning of Spiritualism in the nineteenth century. Peebles went so far as to reduce Jesus to nothing more than a medium.

It's not surprising that *The Aquarian Gospel* inspired the creation of the Aquarian Christine Church Universal, Inc. However, it is surprising that it greatly influenced the Moorish Science Temple of America and so, indirectly, contributed to the existence of the Nation of Islam.

A predominately African American movement born in 1913 in Newark, New Jersey, Moorish Science grew quickly because of the Great Migration of African Americans from the South to the North and Midwest in the late 1920s. By the 1930s around thirty thousand people were members, ten thousand of them in Chicago alone, with big congregations in Philadelphia and Detroit.

The founder of Moorish Science dubbed himself Noble Drew Ali. He told his followers that in his travels in search of wisdom he had encountered a high priest of the Egyptian mysteries, who revealed Drew to be the reincarnation of not only Jesus and Muhammad, but also the Buddha. From this mysterious teacher Ali received the missing section of the Holy Koran.

The Moorish Science Temple of America's *Circle Seven Koran* has a red numeral seven in a blue circle on the cover. The first nineteen chapters are copied from *The Aquarian Gospel*. The next twenty-five chapters were lifted from *Unto Thee I Grant,* by the mysterious Sri

Ramatherio, a publication of the Ancient and Mystic Order of the Rosy Cross. Ali wrote the last four chapters himself.

The Moorish Science community strategy involved supporting local businesses and building relationships with distinguished people who could help provide opportunities for the community. But in 1929 when the business manager of Chicago's Temple No. 1 declared himself a Grand Sheik, and took a significant portion of the community with him, he was stabbed to death in the Unity Hall of the Moorish Science Temple in Chicago. Ali was out of town at the time but the police arrested him anyway. Not long after his release from jail Ali died at home at the age of forty-three. His death certificate said he died from severe respiratory illness, but nobody remembered seeing him cough.

The Moorish Science Convention had once attracted thousands of participants, but by 2007 only a couple of hundred mostly elderly members attended. Groups splintered off as ambitious leaders attempted to take Ali's place over the years, including several who claimed to be his reincarnations. One of the splinter groups evolved into the Nation of Islam, though they long denied the connection, until 2014 when Louis Farrakhan acknowledged Ali's contributions.

In the summer of 1937, with the world on the verge of WW2, two titans of American Metaphysical Religion were already fighting a war of words. Manly Palmer Hall had publicly criticized the Ancient Mystical Order of the Rosy Cross. Hall accused the group's founder H. Spencer Lewis of "misinterpretation and impostures," of glamorizing and distorting Rosicrucian ideas.

Lewis, nearing the end of his life in 1939, published in his popular journal the *Rosicrucian Forum* a scathing response, "Mr. Hall and a hundred more like him making the same statements across the country could not do any real serious injury to AMORC unless they went far enough to indulge in incriminating charges which they happily evade doing." That's a peculiar and rather vague statement at the end there. Lewis next advised his flock to avoid the popular lecturer, because he doesn't offer "any real knowledge or any real help."

Lewis further condemned Hall for lecturing about black magic. "When any individual pretends to lecture on such a theme with sincerity, he must be either self-deceived or is attempting to deceive his audience. Furthermore, by claiming that black magic ever existed, let alone existing in the present day, he is contributing to the fear complexes, the sufferings, the anguish, and the heartaches of many individuals who do not understand."

Antiquus Mysticusque Ordo Rosæ Crucis, the Ancient and Mystical Order Rose Cross (AMORC), or simply the Rosicrucian Order, is known as the largest Rosicrucian organization in the world, claiming seventeen Grand Lodges. The more humble Grand Lodges administer to Greece, Denmark, or Croatia. The grander lodges have titles like the Grand Lodge of North and South America; the Grand Lodge of Europe, Africa, and the Middle East; and the Grand Lodge of Australia, New Zealand, and Asia. There are Grand Lodges in Japan, Poland, Russia, Slovakia, Romania, and Norway.

The founder of this successful organization arose from humble beginnings. H. Spencer Lewis was born in Frenchtown, New Jersey, his mother an immigrant German teacher, and his father an advertising artist. As a precocious teenager he joined a group of researchers investigating mediums. They exposed more than fifty frauds.

At age twenty he was elected president of the newly formed New York Institute for Psychical Research, which became focused on Rosicrucian studies. Lewis gave up smoking and drinking alcohol. Among the officers were poet and New Thought author Ella Wheeler Wilcox and Lutheran minister Isaac Funk of *Funk and Wagnalls Dictionary* fame. Funk suffered ridicule for his defense of discredited Spiritualist mediums. Wilcox had the distinction of being associated with both of America's most famous twentieth-century Rosicrucians, Lewis and Max Heindel. After her husband of more than thirty years died, having promised to communicate from the beyond, Wilcox suffered for weeks without receiving any message.

Wilcox later wrote in her autobiography *The Worlds and I*, published in 1918,

> In talking with Max Heindel, the leader of the Rosicrucian
> Philosophy in California, he made very clear to me the effect of

intense grief. Mr. Heindel assured me that I would come in touch with the spirit of my husband when I learned to control my sorrow. I replied that it seemed strange to me that an omnipotent God could not send a flash of his light into a suffering soul to bring it conviction when most needed. Did you ever stand beside a clear pool of water, asked Mr. Heindel, and see the trees and skies repeated therein? And did you ever cast a stone into that pool and see it clouded and turmoiled, so it gave no reflection? Yet the skies and trees were waiting above to be reflected when the waters grew calm. So God and your husband's spirit wait to show themselves to you when the turbulence of sorrow is quieted.

The book is vague about whether a message was received before publication. She gives the impression it was not. The epilogue condemns Ouija boards as dangerous because spirits of lower stages of development might intrude on the proceedings causing mischief with their bad advice. Like Yogi Ramacharaka in his *The Life Beyond Death,* Wilcox tells readers not to bother the deceased. She asks if we would annoy a friend who had been sent away to an important diplomatic assignment with requests for what amounts to trivial reassurance. To live in faith is better than seeking signs. With faith in the afterlife, and appropriate devotion and development the lucky few earn the ability to become consciously aware of the great beyond.

Following in the grand tradition of Americans since the days of John Winthrop Jr. and the Intelligencers in the early colonies, in 1909 Lewis took a trip to Europe in search of the Rosicrucians. Unlike the other seekers who returned disappointed Lewis claimed to have not only found them in Toulouse, France, but to have been initiated by them. They gave him North America as his territory for the foundation of a new branch of the order.

Was this all a vision? Or had Lewis met an actual Rosicrucian order, perhaps tied to Masonry, or a secret society with a long local heritage? The most popular perspective on the mystery was that immortal adepts, or initiates, had accomplished for Rosicrucianism what Blavatsky's Masters of Ancient Wisdom had done for the Theosophical Society.

Enlightened beings had intervened for the benefit of humanity. Harvey Spencer Lewis was their representative in America.

His partner in this enterprise was May Banks-Stacy. Lewis claimed Oliver Cromwell as her ancestor. She descended from the first Rosicrucians to settle in America, in the seventeenth century in what would become Pennsylvania, and she was an initiate of the Rosicrucians of the East, India specifically. She gave to him the original papers of the order since its establishment in the New World. However May did not sign the AMORC charter. No one has ever found evidence of her membership. The research of David Rocks, published in the journal *Theosophical History* in 1996, revealed that May was a widow with sons in military service. She moved between relatives all her life, always on the edge of abject poverty. She never had the means to visit India, nor is there the slightest evidence that she had.

In 1915 AMORC was born. It would become such a success that Lewis was able to design and construct Rosicrucian Park, including an auditorium, a library, the Rosicrucian Egyptian Museum, a planetarium, an alchemical laboratory, and offices. The lush grounds and buildings have become a sort of private park for San Jose, and a tourist attraction.

The story of the Rosicrucian Egyptian Museum started in 1915 when Lewis fancied a small antique statuette of Sekhmet, the ancient Egyptian lioness goddess we'll be taking a deeper look at later. Lewis placed it on his desk so he could look at it every day. In the 1920s AMORC gave support to the Egypt Exploration Society for their excavations in the city of the Pharaoh Akhenaten. Lewis then led a tour through Egypt. He explained his plan for a collection of antiquities in San Jose. Donations of money and artifacts made possible the construction of the museum building with its distinctive ancient Egyptian style.

In New York City in 1916 Lewis allegedly transmuted zinc into gold to demonstrate the principles of alchemy. The invitation-only audience included AMORC grand masters, select members of the organization, and one scientist and journalist. The scientist told those present that Lewis had made gold.

In 1921 Lewis received an official charter from Theodor Reuss, founder of the O.T.O. Lewis became an honorary member. He was now a representative of the O.T.O. Sovereign Sanctuary. O.T.O. could have been mistaken for an ancient order connected to the Templars, although it was the creation of a small group of European occultists including Franz Hartmann in the first decade of the twentieth century.

In 1929, the year the Great Depression began, Lewis published *The Mystical Life of Jesus,* plagiarizing chapters from *The Aquarian Gospel of Jesus the Christ.* Lewis argued that Jesus did not die on the cross. When he swooned on the cross it was mistaken for death. The subject of transfiguration was discussed at the AMORC conclave of 1931. If surviving mimeographed notes are accurate, the event included instruction on climate control and levitation.

Rosicrucian Principles for Home and Business, another book by Lewis, published in 1935, has a chapter on attracting money, and another about affirmations. It's either a strange interpretation of Rosicrucian principles or a strained application of them to goals earlier Rosicrucians would have considered trivial. But the book nevertheless gave hope and comfort to its readers, along with helpful advice about living a more mindful life.

AMORC claims that Lewis was a "secret partner of Big Business in America." We are told that Arthur Stilwell, the founder of Port Arthur, Texas, considered Lewis the most impactful ally of free enterprise. Walt Disney and Gene Roddenberry are mentioned as AMORC members who studied the courses. But what conclusions are we to draw from these vague facts dropped like hints? For some they become fodder for conspiracy theories.

Mexican muralist painter Diego Rivera was one of the founders of AMORC's lodge in Mexico City. He painted Quetzalcoatl for the temple in the 1920s. But in 1954 Rivera told the Mexican Communist Party that his membership had been nothing more than infiltration of a capitalist organization. He described AMORC as "essentially materialist."

According to AMORC its lineage begins with Mystery Schools created by the pharaohs Thutmose III and Hatshepsut. Since history's first monotheist the Pharaoh Akhenaten and Queen Nefertiti were initiated in those mystery schools, AMORC claims them as members, along with Napoleon, da Vinci, and a list of historical celebrities.

His verbal scuffle with Manly Hall wasn't the only feud Lewis became involved in. Reuben Swinburne Clymer represented a rival American Rosicrucian organization as grand master of the Fraternitas Rosae Crucis, founded by the notorious Paschal Beverly Randolph, whom we'll later consider in more detail. Clymer claimed Lewis plagiarized the AMORC lessons. We've seen that Lewis did plagiarize the *Aquarian Gospel* for one of his books. Clymer alleged that Lewis and his family bought their homes and paid their bills using AMORC money.

In a self-described "brochure" of 130 pages titled *An Exposé of the Imperator of A.M.O.R.C.: His pilfering charlatanism and his connections with Aleister Crowley the Black Magician,* Clymer criticized Lewis for advertising sacred mysteries on radio and in magazine ads. A letter exists in which Crowley tries to convince Lewis to join A∴A∴, his organization for spreading the Law of Thelema. Lewis did not join, but Clymer accused Crowley and Lewis of scheming together to turn AMORC into a black magic cult teaching sex magic. After all, AMORC had an alliance with O.T.O, which did teach a form of sex magic in its higher grades. However, the source for those theories and practices appears to have been none other than Clymer's own teacher Randolph.

Clymer also accused Lewis of cooking up schemes to continuously ask his followers for more money. The Rosicrucian Egyptian museum Clymer dismissed as a laughingstock compared to real museums. Using company funds to pay the bills wasn't an unusual practice among metaphysicians and preachers alike, but can we trust Clymer? In his biography of Randolph he claimed that other members of his Rosicrucian order included Randolph's dear friends Abe Lincoln, the French emperor Napoleon III, and perhaps most mysteriously, since Randolph was a man of color, the Confederate general and Freemason Albert Pike. We have no evidence of such friendships.

Lewis never let the accusations stop him. Whatever he may have been siphoning off for himself and his family, AMORC was unusually successful for a metaphysical organization. As Lewis wrote in *Mental Poisoning,* "Thus we, as individuals, can become the victims of our own poisonous thoughts, but we cannot become the victims of the poisonous thoughts of another."

AMORC survived the loss of its founder in 1939 and continued to flourish, though rocked by scandal in 1990 when the board of directors accused an Imperator of embezzlement. Several years of expensive legal troubles followed until the charges were dismissed and the Imperator resigned.

In Sweden, in the summer of 2001, less than a month before the September 11 terrorist attacks, AMORC released a fourth Rosicrucian manifesto, the *Positio Fraternitatis Rosæ Crucis*. The book's fond wishes for a peaceful humanity and a more hopeful future lead to a call for the establishment of a Rosicrucian Utopia. In a world where so many live in fear of their governments, calls for one world government have an ominous quality that lends credence to conspiracy theories about malevolent elites.

Walt Disney's membership in AMORC is a popular tale among such theorists. An organization of well-intentioned people was reimagined as a diabolical secret society dominating politics and media. Mail order correspondence courses that rehashed the basic principles of American Metaphysical Religion in the glamour of conspiracy became "powerful secrets" that allowed initiates like Napoleon, Roddenberry, and Disney to achieve great success. Their imaginations and their approaches to life may have been improved by the distillations of wisdom that all such courses provide. But AMORC and the other Rosicrucian organizations spend their time on their studies, attending lectures and discussion groups, volunteer service, and lunch served on paper plates. When they talk about one world government, they mean a utopia of the enlightened not a theocratic dictatorship. In the summer of 2004 the Rosicrucian World Peace Conference was held in San Jose. Over two thousand Rosicrucians from seventy countries attended.

In his journal the *Equinox*, Aleister Crowley wrote a mock obituary for A. E. Waite, the verbose but trailblazing esoteric scholar, author of many classics including *The Brotherhood of the Rosy Cross* and *The Real History of the Rosicrucians*. Crowley gave it the title "Dead Waite." Waite (1923) had this to say about American Rosicrucian organizations: "It would serve no useful purpose to enlarge upon later foundations, like that of Dr. R. Swinburne Clymer, who seems to have assumed the mantle laid down by Randolph, or Max Heindel's Rosicrucian

Fellowship of California. They represent individual enterprises which have no roots in the past."

Of course, that isn't exactly true. Much of the wisdom taught by AMORC does come from the past. Waite no doubt meant that AMORC has no connection in terms of an actual lineage of handed-down tradition. We might compare Lewis to Sun Bear, taking traditions from different tribes and making something similar. In a sense all these branded versions of American Metaphysical Religion, with their correspondence courses and administrative hierarchies, are merely different ways of packaging the same content. All three Rosicrucian organizations consider themselves Christian, yet they traffic in astrology, Kabbalah, and theories about the lost continent of Atlantis.

We cannot move on from American Metaphysical Christianity until we have mentioned its notorious adversary, Satanism. Historical records and current endeavors are abundant and easily available so we will pause here only long enough to point out that Satanism and the prosperity gospel have in common the conviction that a particular moral alignment can bring worldly rewards. Satanism satirizes the characters, rules, and rituals of Christianity, and holds opposite views about many moral issues, so we seldom think of it as Christian. Could Satan be a caricature of Jesus embodying all the sins projected by Christians on the Jewish people? The popularity of blue-eyed blond and Caucasian Jesus in illustrations for the devoted speaks to the collective desire to provide the savior with a more comfortable ethnicity. Some recent Satanic groups have looked to the ancient Egyptian god Set for a different model of Satan, still red, and a lover of liars, but no longer tied to the universe of Christianity. Kronos has been offered as another prototype, perhaps helped along by his portrayal in Hollywood blockbusters as a horned red titan rising from the fiery recesses of the Earth. However, the ancient Greeks depicted Kronos as a dignified, bearded old man with a sickle. He's familiar to us as Father Time. But such contradictions happen only when we mistake metaphor for fact. Beyond the words and images a truth exists for those who have experienced it.

5

Turtle Island

BEFORE WE EXPLORE in greater detail this curated collection of the communities and personalities of American Metaphysical Religion it will be helpful to establish context. Some of the richest spiritual heritage available to Americans belongs to the tribes of these lands. Turtle Island is a common name for America, preferred by many Indigenous people, since it predates the arrival of Columbus.

Many imagine America began with the Pilgrims, but our shared spiritual history begins much earlier. According to the current consensus, fourteen thousand years before European colonists arrived, Paleolithic tribes came here hunting mammoths, mastodons, and caribou, from generation to generation, slowly crossing the continent. They followed their prey in seasonal migrations through lichen-rich spruce forests. As the Ice Age declined, and the mastodon died out, the hunters applied their skills to smaller game: moose, deer, and elk. By around 8000 BCE they established regular camping spots in what we now call New England, then a great pine forest. At first, families gathered at these sites, then small communities of several families.

By 6000 BCE villages were forming near bays, lakes, and rivers teeming with fish. Instead of following the migration of their prey, the people could survive on fish until the herds returned. A thousand years later, millstones were used for grinding grain, tools became more specialized. A thousand years after that, as pine trees disappeared, forests of oaks and hemlocks sheltered flowers, birds, animals, and other species we would recognize in all the rich variety the abundant new environment could provide at the close of the Ice Age.

Populations grew around the coast where great migrations of fish flourished in the warming waters. Seal hunting and shellfish gathering provided not only food, but also new skills, tools, and adornment. By 2500 BCE sophisticated assemblies for catching fish were built. One survives to this day: 65,000 wooden stakes driven into a riverbed. Inserting brush between the stakes made a net to catch even the strongest fish. Villages of circular lodges, replete with a ceremonial lodge, left burial mounds that showed great respect for the dead. It took fifteen hundred more years for agriculture, and especially squash, beans, and corn cultivation, to arrive from the south. But by 300 CE tribal warriors were smoking tobacco out of neatly carved soapstone pipes that would not look out of place in a glass case in a cannabis dispensary in California.

To talk about Indigenous American culture as if it were similar from coast to coast is impossible. Over 550 languages were spoken and many had a variety of dialects as different from each other as Los Angeles English is from the dialect of the Scottish Highlands. Religious beliefs, political organizations, family traditions, and every other aspect of life widely differed. Not all tribes lived in sustainable harmony with nature; the Mississippian culture, for example, developed urban centers that were doomed by the amount of resources they consumed. However, it can be said that in contrast to the colonists, Indigenous cultures considered the natural world sacred. Nature was neither fallen nor cursed. Living a good life depended on living in harmony with it. Hunter and harvester both said prayers of apology and gratitude when taking the life of an animal or a plant. The four directions were honored, and since every ritual was intended to restore lost harmony, all began with prayers to the East, West, South, and North. Power could be found in the correspondences and resemblances of everything in the world, and everything deserved respect, not only for having meaning, but also for having consciousness. As Black Elk would say around the time Elvis Presley was getting started, a message from the Great Spirit could come from a messenger as small as an ant. Nothing in nature was without spiritual essence; even a stone must have a soul.

AMERICA'S FIRST CITY

Archaeologists have found Mississippian sites, circa 150–750 CE, along the Florida Gulf Coast and in the valleys of Alabama and Georgia. The Mississippian culture split into at least seventeen of the Indigenous nations still with us, from the Rockies to the eastern seaboard. Probably around 800 CE but perhaps as early as 1200 BCE, they settled across the river from what is now St. Louis. In the early 1100s CE the inhabitants built a two-mile stockade around their city, with guard towers every seventy feet. Within a hundred years the city was larger than London or Paris at the time. At the peak of its population it housed an estimated forty thousand in a complex of plazas and 120 earthen mounds covering six square miles. The great mound covers fourteen acres, rises a hundred feet, and was topped by a five-thousand-square-foot building fifty feet tall.

Woodhenge, a circle of posts used to mark the solstices and equinoxes, stood to the west of the great mound. Archaeologists also discovered the remains of a copper workshop, and evidence of what may have been ritual human sacrifice. The executed may have been meant to follow some celebrated leader into the afterlife. Rulers lived in wooden houses on platforms atop the mounds. Their favorite ornaments were made of seashells they traded for with tribes a thousand miles away.

Farms surrounding the city supplied it with corn, beans, squash, pumpkin, and the other necessities of daily life. The complex was abandoned a hundred years before Columbus arrived. Resources in the area may have been depleted, or an urban disease may have broken out. The population scattered to live as hunters and gatherers. Later they began to breed horses brought by the Europeans, and to hunt buffalo on the great plains.

Just as the European colonists were travelers to the farthest edge of their known world, so too were these tribes the descendants of several waves of migrations that traveled not only across the Bering Strait, but also all the way across the North American continent to its farthest edge. But their way of life would be lost in just a few generations. By the late fifteenth century, English, French, and Portuguese explorers were arriving in America hoping to find the kind of incredible wealth the Spanish had exploited farther south. Fishing crews, especially English and French, used the beaches of North America to dry their summer catches. By the time the first English settlements were attempted, there was already almost a century of interaction with Europeans.

LIFE BEFORE EUROPEANS

How did the Algonquins live before the Europeans arrived? Spring began when green shoots sprouted and the wild geese returned. This was the time to repair fishing gear and prepare canoes. By late March smelt arrived, so many you could scoop them out of the water bare handed. By April spawning sturgeon and salmon provided most of the food while fields were sown. In early May ocean cod and freshwater trout, striped bass, and flounder were added to the feast along with scallops, clams, crabs, oysters, and mussels gathered by the women and children, who also snared ducks and collected their eggs. They tapped the sugar maples for syrup. Every year the Algonquins would burn away the thick bramble of the woods. This not only made travel easier but made animals more visible for hunters; one Pilgrim said a deer could be seen from four miles away. Burning the underbrush also encouraged the growth of grass, berries, and other delicacies loved by prey.

Spring was for freshwater fishing in streams. The men fished by day, using weirs and nets, funneling the fish to the place where they would be most vulnerable. Beans spiraled up the corn stalks, fertilizing the soil with nitrogen, while melons growing on the ground below helped preserve moisture. Tradition told of a crow that came from the west bearing a corn kernel and a bean. In appreciation the hunters never killed crows. Some tribes built small, covered platforms where a man would wait to scare the birds away from the crops. Others trained hawks to scare crows. While most fields were gardens, some colonists reported several hundred cultivated acres of white, red, yellow, and blue corn. But the corn did not grow easily, and the Algonquins would often remind the colonists that not only did they have to be taught how to grow it, but their results were always inferior. One reason for this was that the

English simply couldn't resist the urge to neatly divide their crops, thus missing out on the synergy enjoyed by Algonquin fields.

The English attitude can best be understood by considering the changes in the definitions of two words. Today *natural* has mostly positive connotations, while *artificial* is often viewed with suspicion. For the English colonists and their relatives back home, *natural* meant rude and undeveloped, while *artificial* was a compliment, indicating that human artifice had improved on nature.

In the summer women carefully weeded gardens of corn, beans, squash, cucumbers, Jerusalem artichokes, pumpkins, sunflowers, and gourds. When the soil was exhausted, every decade or so, the tribe would move to another location, where they would fell trees to make new gardens. Men had their own gardens, too, where they tended tobacco. The following chapter about Thomas Harriot contains his account of how very important tobacco was to Indigenous culture.

In July and August children gathered cranberries, raspberries, strawberries, blueberries, blackberries, and grapes. Men hunted deer, moose, ducks, geese, swans, and turkeys. When passenger pigeons in huge flocks that blocked out the sun arrived, women and children would knock them off their perches with a long stick, like abundant fruit on a mature tree. The women, along with all their other duties, would find time to locate clay banks for their baked pottery. The men tended their snares and their traps, including dead falls of precariously balanced tree trunks piled with rocks so heavy they could kill a bear.

Summer was for fishing in the sea. During the day they hunted seals, porpoises, walruses, and whales. Night fishing by torchlight, they speared the fish attracted by the glow. Summer was also a time of gathering for celebration. Stick ball, lacrosse, running races, stone throwing, archery contests, dance competitions, were all performed before appreciative audiences, including a game comparable to soccer, but the field, a sandy beach, was a mile long and the game took two days to play. Tripping an opponent was allowed in England at the time, but not among the tribes. Some of our most iconic American foods came from these tribes. Popcorn, Johnnycakes, snow cones (the cone was bark, the snow was sweetened with maple sugar and syrup), baked beans, hominy, succotash, and clambakes were all inventions of the New England tribes. They had infant formula if a mother had no milk, and "no cakes" as they called a simple pounded parched corn cake. Four days' worth could be kept easily in a small pouch tied to a hunter's belt to be mixed with water whenever needed.

In the fall, as the leaves turned red and gold, firewood was stacked. Bird flocks were hunted as they resumed migration. Wild nuts, acorns, and wild herbs were gathered. Corn ripened and some was stored for the harsh winter months. The big harvest came in September, and the abundance was boiled, dried, and sacked. Inside the village stockade, pits five feet deep and five feet in diameter, lined with clay and bark, were filled with containers of reeds, silk grass, dried tree bark, wild hemp, sun-dried berries, smoked meat, walnuts, and acorns.

In winter the tribe gathered for two main deer drives. Large groups of several hundred hunters cooperated to chase a herd of deer into a funnel of fences where hunters stood ready. Fishing through holes chipped in the ice provided extra food. This was a quiet time spent with family. Women cured furs, making them into clothes and blankets. Men carved holes into lucky stones to wear as reminders of spiritual experiences. Winter was a time of feast or famine. When meat was served the band might eat ten times in a day, and then fast until the next successful hunt. Winter ended with a healthful one-hour steam for the entire tribe, followed by a cold plunge into a lake or stream, a health regimen popular throughout America's history of alternative healing.

The earliest Thanksgiving on the continent was not the much celebrated feast of the Pilgrims we observe yearly. Many tribes had Thanksgiving ceremonies. The Seneca tribe of the Iroquois League performed their Thanksgiving ritual for all important events except deaths. Before the assembled tribe the story was told of how the Creator invented all the good things of this world with forethought for the well-being of his human creations. Herbs to be used as medicine, and the moon to give light in the night, all these promises were fulfilled. As the story was told the order and harmony of the world was revealed. Gratitude was given, including quiet prayer before every meal whether alone or together.

A Roman Catholic observer in Maryland noted that the first corn, or first fruits of hunting or fishing, were prayed over by an old shaman, who would take a portion, burn half, then eat the other half; only then would the tribe partake. While some English writers reported tribal feasts of ravenous eating, saving nothing for the future, when tribes were invited to eat with the colonists they mirrored their manners, not only eating polite portions, but waiting for their hosts to sit down before beginning their meals.

Festivals of dancing, singing, and feasting were held in early spring, late summer, and midwinter, and for turning points in the human life cycle, with ceremonies of naming, puberty, marriage, and death. Special festivals of ritual were held during times of sickness, famine, drought, or war. But individuals were known to create personal ceremonies. One colonist tells of a woman who having suffered many hardships and the deaths of close relatives chose a day and place where she spoke of her troubles, declared her intent to have a prosperous future, danced, gave away gifts to the poor, and received a new name. In this example we are are not far from American Metaphysical Religion's belief in self-reinvention as rebirth.

LIFE BEFORE EUROPEANS: RELATIONSHIPS

Unfortunately the only historical records we have regarding Indigenous socialization were written by European observers who were biased not only by their own religious dictates but by their deep-seated fear of their new surroundings. However some writers would seem to be more faithful to honest reporting than others. According to English reports sexual freedom, including homosexuality, was allowed before marriage among some Indigenous American tribes. Most writers noted that Indigenous women behaved more modestly than their European counterparts. Unmarried Algonquin women could sleep with any unmarried Algonquin men, but to become pregnant outside marriage was a disgrace. Fortunately, the Algonquin women knew what herbs to take, a stark contrast with the Puritans who could only condemn what they considered promiscuity and infanticide.

The opposing opinions on the abortion issue that so deeply divide America existed at the very root of the country, at first contact between the tribes and the colonists. We cannot doubt that this argument only added to the Puritan sense of moral authority. On the other hand, many tribes had no word for rape. While Europeans sold captive women and children into slavery, the Iroquois adopted them into families who had lost loved ones to war. Enemy warriors however were treated otherwise, as we'll see later.

Iroquois is a French corruption of a word for "snake". Haudenosaunee, or People of the Longhouse, is their name for themselves in their own language. The French called them the Iroquois Confederacy while the English knew them as the League of Five Nations. We will continue to use Iroquois in this book as it remains much more familiar.

Generations of American academics argued that we have no proof the Founding Fathers considered the government of the Iroquois when designing their own, but in 1998 Bruce Johansen's book *Debating Democracy: Native American Legacy of Freedom* detailed "the unacknowledged influence of Native American thought on modern American government," and the forces in academia and elsewhere opposed to admitting it. The Founding Fathers, especially Benjamin Franklin and Thomas Jefferson, were well aware of the example of the Iroquois, as Indigenous tradition has long held. "It would be a very strange thing, if six Nations of ignorant savages should be capable of forming a Scheme for such a Union . . . and yet that a like union should be impracticable for ten or a Dozen English Colonies," Benjamin Franklin wrote in a letter in 1751 that can be found on the U.S. government's website *founders.archive*. This contradictory racist comment dismisses the Iroquois as primitives, while endorsing imitation of their union.

The Founding Fathers ignored a key aspect of Iroquois culture: Iroquois women were property owners. Hereditary leadership passed not through fathers but through mothers. Women owned dwellings, horses, and farmland, and a wife's property prior to marriage remained exclusively her own. Newlywed couples lived with the wife's family. Divorce was as easy as asking a bad husband to leave the home and take his possessions with him, but one English writer reported that he knew many Indigenous couples who had been married two, three, even four decades.

A few English writers alleged that prostitution, the trade of goods for sexual favors, was rarely practiced. Reports conflict regarding the fidelity of spouses. All writers agree loyalty was cherished, but some say philandering was acceptable, while others insist adultery was severely punished. Perhaps it depended on the tribe, or the writer. Polygamy was available to chiefs, but even they usually had one wife, though some had several. However, as tribes broke down due to disease and warfare it became more common for powerful chiefs to take many wives, solidifying alliances between tribes. The tribes were puzzled when told that the king of England had no wife. They wondered how anything got done in his household.

English observations on gender relations among the tribes emphasized that the men seemed lazy while the women did all the work. On the other hand, Indigenous people thought English women were lazy and were scandalized that male colonists worked the fields without their women. Writers portrayed Indigenous women living lives as little better than beasts of burden, while their men hunted, then lounged, smoking like British gentlemen. The truth was more complex. Women did most of the planting, cared for the crops, and harvested. They preserved and prepared food. They built houses, and when the tribe moved they carried the poles and woven mats from which their dwellings were built. These woven mats provided such excellent insulation from rain and sleet the colonists would steal them when they couldn't barter for them.

When men fished they tossed their catch on the bank and the women gathered and prepared the fish. When men hunted, women dragged the kill to the place where they would make it into food, skins, rope, and tools. With great care the women kept the hearth fire; if it went out that was a bad omen. But men were known to help with the crops. Men cleared the fields, which would be planted then harvested by the gathered tribe. Tribal chiefs made their own bows and arrows, shoes, and clothes, as well as planting and hunting for themselves. Many writers commented on how hardy Indigenous women were. One testified he had seen a new mother with her four-day-old baby strapped to her back digging clams out of the ice for her husband. The English also failed to notice that the women owned the corn they grew and the houses they carried. Menstrual huts provided segregated sanctuary for women, who preferred to give birth in solitude.

Many English writers commented on the affection shown by Indigenous families. They noticed how quiet their tenderly cared for children were. They criticized the way the aged back home in England were treated in comparison to the respect and consideration shown to tribal elders. Indigenous fathers doted on their children and hated to be separated from them. Their adopted fathers regarded colonist children, captured by the tribes and raised within their families, with just as much affection. This made all the more heinous the colonist strategy, advocated by John Smith, of kidnapping their children to make the tribes compliant to colonist demands.

Indigenous children were bathed in concoctions that were said to make them nearly impervious to any kind of weather. Buried up to their necks in snow they learned how to ignore the cold. By age two boys began training with bows and arrows. English writers praised the superior health and physical powers of the Indigenous people. Until the devastation wrought by European diseases, the tribes had lived without the scourges that made life miserable back home in Europe, like gout and the common cold. Their sensory perceptions astonished the colonists. Thomas Morton, the Pagan Pilgrim, wrote of an Indigenous man with eyesight so sharp he sighted a ship at sea two hours before any Englishman could. Morton also tells of a hunter who could tell fresh deer tracks from old by sight and smell.

In oral traditions written down by historians and folklorists at the beginning of the nineteenth century we find records of advice given from fathers to sons that provide a unique glimpse of the Indigenous worldview. Fasting and gifts of tobacco are the means to gain favor from the spirits the creator put in charge of giving blessings. These spirits of the waters, of the sky, of animals, and of plants give wisdom and power to those who earn their respect.

To have no spirit helping you was to live a bad life. Even one spirit could guide a man through life's "narrow passages," multiplying the goods things of life and preventing suffering. To live in harmony with nature was to live a trouble-free life, a life blessed by good timing and good sense, one of the foundational beliefs of American Metaphysical Religion. Why fasting? Of course, food could not always be counted on. By fasting a man could learn to go without, allowing his family to have more. Fasting also produced trance states, including a heightened sense of awareness; it naturally inspired meditation, and a contemplative state of mind.

Fathers also told their sons to learn all the medicines. Medicines were mostly herbal, but they could also be methods of gaining shamanic power. Medicine could heal the sick, reduce hunger or cause it, induce a man to run after women, or a woman to fall in love. Medicine included the knowledge of how to prepare a field with signs that would keep out intruders, and to prepare war paint, which contained power of the spirits of water, so that every enemy arrow or bullet would miss, and victory was assured. But to die at war was best. Men were told not to listen to their women who would try to keep them home safe from battle. To die in battle meant to die conscious. To then have the power to consciously choose whether to be reborn as a man, a mighty stag, or a walker on the light, as birds were known. Spirits, birds, and animals were to be communicated with by singing, chanting, and prayers. They were not inferior; they were other. To be alive together on the earth was a bond between all beings, and a gift of responsibility from the ancestors and the Creator.

The morality taught was not so different from Christian ethics. Feed the hungry, always share your food or your food becomes poisonous. Show gratitude for all you receive from the earth. Treat your wife with kindness for the earth is your grandmother and sees all, and if you are cruel she will cause you to live a life of suffering and early death. Be good to your children. Get along with everyone. Take care of old people and learn from them. When you share your war stories don't exaggerate, be humble. Don't be jealous or your sisters will be, too, and your wife will become annoyed and leave you. Keep your word and guard your honor. Don't ask a second question until the first has been fully answered. Give to the poor. Learn which plants heal the sick, so you can heal yourself and your own family, and be asked to heal others.

While Indigenous people could be said to own the tools they made, their snares and weirs, and the prey caught by them, they were also obligated to share their possessions and their food for the good of the tribe. The Indigenous reputation for stealing began early when European visitors misunderstood the ritual of reciprocal gift giving. The Indigenous people gave gifts and when the Europeans didn't give them gifts in return they took what they considered to be of equal value. Colonists, on the other hand, frequently used force to take whatever they needed.

Among the tribes, orphans and widows were cared for, no one was reduced to begging for their survival. Meanwhile, the city of London would soon be shipping off starving street children to the colonies. Among the tribes, strangers were welcomed by chiefs, given shelter and food, and entertained according to their station. Indigenous people were known to go far out of their way, and to face danger, to rescue and return home hapless colonists dying in the wilderness.

Some English writers exaggerated wars among the tribes, based on evidence as trivial as after-dinner shows commemorating battles. The usually dependable Roger Williams testified that their warfare was much less bloody than war in Europe, with very few casualties, perhaps twenty in a pitched battle. Another observer wrote that in seven years they might lose only seven men. Rattles of various sizes and primitive flutes along with shouting and singing were used to frighten off the enemy. When John Smith tried to get corn from them they refused him. When Smith's party tried to take the corn by force, they were met by several dozen Indigenous men painted red, black, and white who charged them with an idol made of skins stuffed with moss, hung with chains and copper. They expected to chase the English away with a loud display of spiritual force, but the colonists fired their guns, frightening the men into dropping the fetish. To get it back they offered a canoe stuffed with corn, venison, and turkey.

Most battles ended with a few wounds, or one of the forces running out of arrows. Even the most concentrated Indigenous attacks on the colonists would not be followed by more attacks until annihilation. The tribes were accustomed to their enemies withdrawing. They expected that after being soundly defeated the English would leave. Wars were not fought for land. They were fought to abduct women and children to be incorporated into the tribe, because their work was the most important kind of wealth. War could be avoided by giving objects of value to the aggrieved in cases of revenge, and even by gambling and games. A player might lose everything he owned but he would accept the outcome. Thunder stones, pieces of crystal, or perhaps meteorite dug from the ground under lightning-struck trees, were considered the ultimate good luck charms for gamblers. Hubhub, for example, was played with peach pits painted white on one side and black on the other. When the pits were tossed into a shallow basket the player would have to guess how many of each color would show.

As the colonists sought to learn tribal languages the Indigenous people helped to teach them. Many Europeans developed the mistaken opinion that Indigenous languages were simple, lacking fine distinctions, but the truth was that the colonists were deliberately being taught a dumbed-down dialect. Observant colonists noticed that even those among them who were said to be fluent in an Indigenous language had no idea what was being said when members of the tribe were speaking among themselves.

Roger Williams was an exception to that rule. He understood the subtlety and detail of these languages. He noted five words for soul, and the belief that the principal seat of the soul in the body was the brain. One word for soul was related to their word for sleep, because the soul was most active in dreams. Another word for soul was related to their word for the image of a clear reflection. The great American linguist Edward Sapir described Algonquin words as "tiny imagist poems."

SOUL LIBERTY AND THE FIRST FOUNDING FATHER

Indigenous people watching Christians pray with eyes turned to the heavens asked politely whether this was moon worship, or sun worship, then laughed quietly. Meanwhile, the English wondered what it could mean when hundreds of Indigenous men stamped on the ground, then beat sticks on stones, then beat the stones on the ground while looking around as if expecting some imminent arrival.

To talk about the spiritual beliefs of the tribes of New England we must first understand a certain Puritan writer. But Roger Williams was a Puritan a bit different from the sort that colonized Plymouth. He arrived with his wife, Mary, in America in 1631. He was immediately invited to become assistant minister, presiding over a Boston church while its minister returned to England to fetch his wife. Roger created quite a stir when he turned down the position, explaining that the civil authorities should have no right to punish religious infractions, and that every colonist should have freedom of conscience to pursue religion as he or she saw fit. His invitation to preach in Salem was blocked by Boston. He was allowed to enlighten Plymouth, but became disenchanted. For one thing, he wanted to see a stricter separation between church and state.

Roger Williams faced trial in Boston, and his writings were burned. His attempts to set up a colony reflecting his beliefs, and those of his followers, were fought until at last he sojourned far from the beaten path and bargained with the tribes themselves for the land that would become known as Rhode Island. With twelve friends he established the town of Providence. This colony of heresy was considered a threat, but when the Pequot War broke out, the powers that be had to rely on the intelligence provided by Williams and his followers, and many lives were saved because Roger convinced his friends, the Narragansett tribe, not to join in the attack.

For thirty years the colonies of Massachusetts, Connecticut, and Plymouth had tried to undermine and destroy Providence and the Narragansett tribe. Finally, in 1643, they formed the United Colonies military alliance to purify America by wiping out the heretics. That same year Williams published his book *A Key into the Language of America,* printed by the great Protestant poet John Milton's publisher. The book was a great success in England. When Williams returned there to seek legal protection for Providence, to the dismay of the other colonies he got it.

Williams was disgusted by the religious wars ravaging Europe and his homeland. He blamed them on the use of government to impose religion. He declared that civic authority should have no right to prosecute over religious dogma. The towns that had sprung up around Providence eventually joined in the formation of Rhode Island, which became a sanctuary for Jews, Quakers, Baptists, and all round pegs who could not fit the square holes of American Puritan society. His contemporaries thought him something like an anarchist and believed his ideas could lead only to disaster. They were equally chagrined that he not only declared the Indigenous people as good as any Europeans, but worse still, once he had learned their language and their customs, he refused to try to convert them to Christianity.

Williams was the most trusted Englishman among the tribes. However, when they fought the rebellion known as King Philip's War to eliminate all the colonists in 1676, one hundred years before the birth of the United States of America, Providence and Roger's own house were burned. The story is told that Roger marched right up to the warriors and demanded to know why they had burned to ashes a home so many of them had been sheltered in. He was told that the times were strange and that God was angry at the English for their many injustices. Williams guided the rebuilding of Providence over the next dozen years before this defender of what he called "soul liberty" died peacefully in his bed.

According to Williams, the tribes had words for themselves as a collective people, as tribes, and as individuals, but they had no word for stranger until the Europeans arrived. The Europeans came from a culture where the stranger was a fearful and long-held concept, back beyond the Romans, with their contempt and eventual terror of barbarians, to ancient Egypt and their dreaded god Set, a god of liars and strangers, perhaps the first prototype for the Christian Satan. The tribes had viewed all people as part of one great family of human beings, but the Europeans had a long tradition of fearing people across borders, and within them.

The Indigenous people differed from the Europeans in another crucial way. In tribal culture, for example, the sun itself was a living being, a nonhuman person, a conscious god pouring blessings of light and warmth upon the world. They believed consciousness created form, not the other way around. All things in the world, animals, plants, stones, were respected as conscious beings. The Indigenous view of all nature as the interplay of conscious beings (rather than lifeless matter), was dismissed by critics of twentieth-century art and literature as "the pathetic fallacy."

For the Europeans, with their monotheistic God, and their hierarchical Bible promising them all living things as their bounty, the world was not a cosmic dance of living forces. Plants and animals lacked souls. The sun was merely there to serve humans, as was everything else in the world. Since incarnation was caused by sin the world itself was a sinful place, where beauty was a snare, and eternal suffering must lurk behind every temporary joy. Even today this perspective persists as certain schools of modern Christians advocate using up all natural resources before the divinely appointed end of the world.

Though he had many deep discussions with Indigenous people about their spirituality, Roger Williams refused to attend their rituals, because he considered any religion other than his own the work of the devil. For the same reason he would not attend Anglican or Catholic rituals. But he did write of the great feasts of the Narragansetts that might involve a thousand people, who would be given not only food but gifts of every kind, accompanied by rituals so strenuous the shamans, glistening with perspiration, would sometimes faint. Some burned their worldly goods in bonfires during these feasts of thanksgiving, and believed this sacrifice kept them free of diseases and other curses that troubled the Europeans. Since trading with the newcomers had made some tribes unusually wealthy this return to the more modest ways of the past may have been understood as a way of restoring balance and harmony to their world.

Here is perhaps the most famous paragraph by Roger Williams on Indigenous beliefs: "There is a general Custom amongst them, at the apprehension of any Excellency in Men, Women, Birds, Beasts, Fish, etc to cry out Manittou, that is, it is a God, thus if they see one man excel others in wisdom, valor, strength, activity, etc they cry out Manittou, a

God: and therefore when they talk amongst themselves of the English ships, and great buildings, of the plowing their fields, and especially of books and letters they will end thus: Manitowock. They are gods. Cummanitoo, you are a god, etc" (Williams 1643).

The tribes so loved to receive news of current events that a colonist who could update them in their own language was declared *manitou*. Among the Dutch colonists this was spelled *menetoo,* and they explained it as applying to anything that was beyond human skill and power. *Wonderful* has been offered as a translation but is perhaps too meek a word. Manitou might be compared to classic Southern California surfer slang: a wave, or a song, or any special moment might be described as "godly," but *manitou* was no mere adjective for emotional appreciation. Like the Iroquois word *orenda, manitou* referred to a supernatural voltage of sacred or magical power, power that is local and personal, not omnipresent, specific not omnipotent, like a spirit shining through matter. The sensitive orenda of a hunted animal who escaped a skilled hunter was said to have foiled the hunter's orenda. But the term was also applied to something unexpected, surprising, or uncanny, because unknown. Indigenous America was filled with spirits that could be known by seeing them, hearing them, feeling them emotionally, dreaming of them, and by the signs and results they provided.

WHEN SPIRITUAL WORLDS COLLIDE

While Williams remains an essential source for understanding Indigenous American spirituality in dialogue with European spirituality, modern scholarship has given us a much more comprehensive view.

Shamans could be roughly divided into two classes, those whose responsibility was healing and worship, and others who provided military and spiritual leadership. Thomas Harriot, about whom we'll hear more soon, noted that their ability to predict the future, or report the location of enemies or prey, was so accurate he considered their skills the work of the devil. They could bring rain during droughts. They were called to find lost or stolen people or objects. Many of their skills were the same as those of the cunning men and women back home in

England, witches in all but name, tolerated by the common folk and nobility for their useful skills.

Indigenous shamans knew how to communicate with the gods. Some were said to have the power to not only bring rain but to move the sun. They could visit the spirit world, usually in dreams, and return with crucial information. They knew how to summon and banish spirits. They shared a language known only to other shamans. Their hairstyles and other adornments of office, such as a cloak of quilted rabbit fur, made them readily recognizable. The colonists reported that *Cheepi* and other gods and spirits were said to directly materialize in their rituals. Then again Cotton Mather reported the materialization of an angel in his own study.

Sometimes instead of seeing apparitions, shamans heard voices that guided them. The shamanic tradition has some close parallels with what became trance channeling, a popular practice of American Metaphysical Religion. Shamans who exhausted themselves dancing around the flame, striking themselves to inspire greater effort, consuming intoxicants, would at last fall into a trance. As they lay on the ground senseless, the chiefs would ask them questions and receive answers.

The brightest, strongest boys were chosen for shamanic training. Fasting and lack of sleep were augmented by hallucinogenic concoctions, some of which included white hellebore. They beat their shins with sticks, according to one European author, forcing them to run through brambles in the cold, making them tough; the exhaustion and stress contributed to the power of their visions.

Shamans could treat individuals or convene a family or entire tribe for ritual healing. For the ritual of a great chief a thousand might attend. Williams reports that the shamans conjured and threatened illness out of the victim's body. The belief that divine powers live in the human body, in the pulse, heart, and breath, allowed the shamans to communicate with these powers, sucking out bad spirits, imitating the sounds of various animals, hitting their own arms, chests, thighs, even frothing at the mouth in the delirium of the ritual. Stroking the skin with their hands or a rattle, sprinkling the body with water, they would chant. Fresh or powdered herbal applications were applied to wounds sucked free of poison. Roger Williams admitted the cures were often effective, but of course believed they were provided by the devil.

Shamans received generous gifts for their cures, and Williams criticized them for it because Indigenous people were forced to save up so they could afford the services of their greedy doctors. He pointed out that the poor received less lavish treatments and seemed to succumb to their illnesses much more often. He did not however mention the same state of affairs among the Europeans back home. Williams believed Christian ministers should not accept salaries and that healing performed by the power of Christ should always be free, one of his points of agreement with the Rosicrucian manifestos that had been circulating around the time he was a child back in England. Williams may never have encountered these revolutionary tracts, he certainly never mentions them, but the culture he emerged from was deeply informed by their ideas and ambitions.

Indigenous people reported that the most powerful shamans could produce a green leaf in dead of winter, turn a dried snakeskin into a living snake, surround themselves with an aura of flames, make rocks move, trees dance, and water burn. An eyewitness account recorded by one European writer claims an honest gentleman of his acquaintance testified to a healing where the stump of a small tree stuck in an Indigenous man's foot was wrapped in beaver skin, the shaman put his mouth to the beaver skin and using sucking and other charms removed it, spat it into a tray of water, and revealed the foot healed. Other witnesses reported tests reminiscent of Houdini: shamans bound in iron chains and carefully watched, who always broke free. Cotton Mather testified that shamans had the power to quiet dogs.

The shamans were so deeply respected by their people, one reverend in Virginia in 1621 fumed that the only hope for conversion was to slit the throats of every last one of them. One wonders how the ideal represented by Jesus the Prince of Peace, who taught his followers to teach only by example, relates to such a violent fantasy of redemption. What must that reverend have thought about Colonial America's first practitioner of a gender-alternative lifestyle, Thomas Hall?

In 1629 Hall faced the General Court of Virginia. Hearing that

Hall sometimes dressed as a woman he was set upon by several colonists who wanted to find out exactly what was going on underneath his clothes. Hall testified that he had lived as a woman in Plymouth where he did needlework, but earlier had served as a male soldier for the British Army against the French. Upon physical examination it was found that Hall was a hermaphrodite so the court decreed he must wear man's clothes but a woman's cap and apron.

Thomas Morton reported on another shaman who amazed his colonist audience by chanting until a thick cloud arrived out of nowhere. Thunder resounded and a chunk of ice appeared in the bowl of water on a hot summer day. As usual, the devil was given credit for the demonstration. Colonists also reported cases of being bewitched by shamans. Hearing "oho" chanted in the dark outside their settlement, one group of English testified that they became so confused they began fighting with each other, wielding the wrong ends of their tools, they found they could say only "oho" and had lost the power to communicate.

But the shamans could not stop the diseases brought by the Europeans. Because the colonists sent by Sir Walter Raleigh did not get sick, and because they brought no women with them, Thomas Harriot reported that the tribes thought the English an ancient race who had taken bodies again, and they had brought with them English spirits who shot the invisible bullets that killed them with disease. When one Indigenous man, living among the the colonists as a sort of ambassador, told the tribes that the Pilgrims had a cache of these invisible bullets buried in the ground behind their stockade walls, most of the English were outraged, but some found the ruse useful.

Shamans could also practice malevolent magic. They were said to be able to send rattlesnakes to kill their enemies. One shaman was supposed to have by ritual forced the uneasy spirit of a drowned Englishman into the body of an Indigenous woman who became very ill. Another shaman removed it, but told her to relocate far away, for English spirits were difficult to control. Shamans could "shoot bones" into people's bodies, and these embedded spiritual fragments became the source of pain and disease. To have a fragment of foreign bone festering in the body is a good metaphor for the localized pain of a disease. This belief isn't far from Mary Baker Eddy's conviction that she was being killed by the expectations of death thought by her followers.

Souls were especially vulnerable during sleep, and a shaman might steal a fragment of an enemy's soul and attach it to a fly, which he then imprisoned. Whatever he did to the fly would then be reflected in the condition of the victim's body.

Some of the shamanic rituals for war resemble the sympathetic magical practices of ancient Egypt. Egyptian priests would make figures that represented pharaoh's enemies, then with appropriate ritual and prayer crush them underfoot. Indigenous American warriors would choose fire brands out of the bonfire and mock fight them, until every warrior had thus vanquished a symbol of the enemy.

Certainly some of the glamour of a shaman was the result of bravado. In an early interaction between a shaman and a colonist, when the colonist interceded to protect a terrified member of the tribe, the thwarted shaman made terrible threats, promising he'd fly out the chimney and leave the house in ruins behind him. The colonist promptly seized the shaman, tied him up, hung him on a hook, and horsewhipped him. Apparently neither he nor the intended victim suffered any repercussions, but the shaman lost his status with the tribe.

Today many psychics and ghost hunters insist that the presence of skeptics weakens the phenomena. Thoughts are things, they say, and doubt and mockery create a gravity that makes it difficult to encounter the more subtle aspects of experience. Indigenous Americans were sensitive to mockery—war was often the result of an important leader having been laughed at. Many shamans refused to work in the presence of Europeans. Shamans told their tribes that their visions and cures were much less powerful when colonists stood in judgment over them.

Traditions and history were kept by carefully chosen lore keepers of separate male and female lineages. History was also preserved by simple memorials. The grave of a hero would have a stone added to it by every respectful passerby. Where any remarkable event happened, at the place or on the path nearby, they would dig a one-foot-deep round hole, which would be kept clear for generations as the story of what happened there was shared with anyone who noticed the subtle monument.

The two greater gods of the Algonquins had several names. The benevolent god, *Tanto* was his simplest name, was removed from human affairs. The god *Squanto*, or Cheepi, was intimately involved in daily life, and he was feared for his power to bring harm. Death, the cold wind of the northeast, and the underworld belonged to him. The colonists associated Cheepi with Satan, of course. The shaman's job was to learn the ways of Cheepi, to protect the tribe with ritual, to divine the meaning of troubles, and to communicate with and learn from this fearsome deity in dreams and visions. But there were many other gods, some placed the number at thirty-seven, including gods of the directions, of places, of the stars, sun, and moon, of women and of children. Each member of the tribe could have a personal god, a spirit, who would give guidance in dreams.

One English writer preserved an Indigenous man's opinion of fire: "Fire must be a God, or Divine power, that out of a stone will arise a spark and when a poor naked Indian is ready to starve with cold in the House, and especially in the Woods, often saves his life, dresses all our Food for us, and if it be angry will burn the House about us. Yea, a spark fall in the dry wood, burns up the Country" (Massachusetts Historical Society 1810).

Christian writers reported that Cheepi threatened the tribes not to live near the English, and not to learn their language, warning that they would be punished by diseases. But Cheepi was not only a god of fear and harm; he also gave the tribes the gifts of the skills they used to master their environment. He could inspire them to excellence. Much as the Christian god was a god of both fear and love, so was Cheepi, for he loved the people and they loved him. Through his power they were healed and received foreknowledge of important challenges and opportunities in the future. He led them to prey on the hunt, taught them to plant and harvest, and guided even the most simple folk through signs and omens. The very power of plants and animals to grow, and of fruit to ripen was the gift of Cheepi. But Cheepi was also the judge of human behavior, visiting punishment on those who deserved it. Part of a shaman's job was to divine what someone had done to deserve suffering. Cheepi's sacred color was black, so the first Africans in America were frightening apparitions to the Algonquins, who sought to conjure such spirits back to the spirit world.

The colonists were confused by the many creation stories they were told. The Great Hare created the four directions. He made men and women and a deer. Giant spirits tried to eat them, but they were only able to kill the deer. So the Great Hare spread the hairs of the deer over all the land, from which sprang all the wild deer of the American woods. Then the Great Hare took the human beings out of a bag and put them on the land to hunt the deer. Roger Williams reported that the Algonquin creator god first created a man and woman out of stone but displeased with them he broke them, then made a new man and new woman out of a tree. Thomas Harriot reported that the first human created had been a woman, and a god had given her the power to give birth to humanity.

When confronted with Indigenous creation and religious beliefs we enter a chasm of misunderstandings. The history of anthropology is full of stories of tribes who have deliberately misinformed researchers for long periods of time before deciding they had earned the right to hear the real stories. Did the colonists understand the words of these spiritual tales correctly, since they had no command of Indigenous language, only of the stripped-down version they were taught?

When one shaman told a colonist that he had four spirits in him: a crow in his head, a pigeon in his heart, a snake in his loins, and "a man he saw in air" who lived in his entire body, was he to be taken literally, or was this poetic language? The crow is a fine metaphor for the alert and curious human mind. The pigeon describes the human heart alternately peaceful and fretful, and the snake, well, that's rather obvious. The floating man made of air is a common image for the human soul even today. Another shaman reported that he had a hummingbird that would peck at him when he did wrong and sing sweetly when he did right. Under further questioning this shaman admitted that the hummingbird was his metaphor for his conscience.

Thomas Morton, who denied the tribes had anything like religion, and who didn't think much of Puritan religion either, reported that they believed in a creation that had grown evil and had been destroyed by a flood. Roger Williams thought he found parallels between ancient Greek, Hebrew, and the Algonquin language. He relates stories they told him of *Wetucks,* a miracle maker who walked upon the waters, who Williams thought might have been a memory of Jesus. But it's difficult to know whether or not the tribes had learned of the flood from other colonists or from the European fishermen who had been visiting their shores for generations. Were they telling Tom and Roger what they thought they wanted to hear? Finally, it's quite possible that many considered the Christian stories they were being told unbelievable, and so returned nonsense for nonsense, a joke for what appeared to them to be a joke.

Members of a tribe who were not shamans also had prophetic dreams, and the experience of remote viewing was not uncommon, as wives kept watch on their husbands away from the hunt by dreaming, and warriors located the enemy. Dreams could diagnose and cure illnesses. Malevolent spirits could be identified and chased away in a dream. Complete recoveries could occur when a sick person dreamed, or when someone else had a dream about a sick person. Algonquin mothers would ask their children every morning what they had dreamed. Nightmares were considered warnings, and after awakening from a nightmare they would pray to understand how they might correct whatever wrong had occurred. Some spoke of a ball of light that would leave someone as they slept and would return just before they awoke. They believed this to be the soul going out to have a look around on its own. Some said the dark outline of a body could be seen surrounding the globe of light at its center. Light phenomena were also common in areas where someone was about to die or had recently passed away. Today's ghost hunters call them orbs.

Many prophecies of the arrival of the white man were given. Uttamatomakkin, brother-in-law of Pocahontas, traveled with her to London where he told the English that the god *Okeus* had warned the shamans of his tribe of the arrival of people from across the sea. The Mohegans told of one of their chiefs whom as he lay dying warned that light-skinned people would soon arrive from across the ocean. In the 1800s the Narragansett historian Thomas Commuck claimed that his people had heard music in the air many years before the Europeans arrived, recognizing it at last when hymns were sung at the first church services in Plymouth. One prophetic vision of the coming of the white race was said to have begun with the sighting of a white whale; Ahab's Moby Dick may have been a distant echo of a warning about the arrival of Caucasians.

Names held great power among the tribes, a curious reflection of the beliefs of John Dee, and the other sorcerers of Europe, who explored angelic language with the idea that knowing the original and true name of any thing would give power over it. Indigenous people would not give their real names to the colonists. *Pocahontas* was only a nickname; her real name was Matoaka. Indigenous people would also change their names to commemorate important events. A chief who had been friendly with the English but who now planned to attack them would change his name. Those who were kidnapped or who chose to live among the colonists, or to visit their world back home, would change their names to protect themselves against danger and to signify their new purpose.

The greatest of the chiefs among the Carolina Algonquins were mummified. Thomas Harriot carefully described the process by which their bodies were opened and the internal organs removed while preserving the skeletal structure, covered with leather, over which the skin was closed again. The dried organs were carefully placed in baskets at the feet of each mummy. The mummies were laid side by side on a tall platform under which lived a shaman who prayed day and night. Since little was known about ancient Egyptian mummification at the time, no theories about the Algonquins and the pharaohs were hatched.

John Smith wrote of similar practices among the tribes of the Chesapeake, who also had copper chains, pearls, and favorite hatchets stuffed into their mummies, which were carefully wrapped in white furs and woven mats. The humble were simply buried in the ground in a shroud folded with flowers (unless it was winter). Their possessions were laid in and on the grave to rot away.

Widows mourned with what English writers called "Irish-like howlings" and shouts of grief for twenty-four hours, their faces painted black.

Quieter mourning lasted for at least a year. Friends visited to offer consolation. The name of the dead person was no longer used, and if someone within the tribe had the same name, they changed it.

The tribes believed in the immortality of the soul. It's strange to read European writers' dismissive accounts of the Indigenous afterlife as an "imaginary paradise" and the "fictions" of infernal torture for the wicked, when these beliefs were really so like their own. Williams reported that the wicked were doomed to wander helpless as phantoms. Accounts differed. In one, the good went to the top of a great tree. From there they could see the pathway lined by ripened fruit. They followed it to the rising sun, pausing halfway there to get refreshments from a goddess. Finally they came to the house of the Great Hare where they lived a carefree life in the beautiful fields many authors compared to the paradise of Islam. There they lived until they became old and died, to be born again into a woman's womb, to live again a physical life. Pythagoras was mentioned as holding similar beliefs, but it was all dismissed as a fable in favor of the idea of the resurrection of the physical body at the end of days.

THE GUESTS THAT NEVER LEFT

The colonists were the products of what has been called a disease pool, a confluence of maladies from the Far East, the Mideast, Africa, and of course European varieties. Generations of death eventually produced a robust immunity. In America the tribes were protected from these diseases by ice and the oceans. Once the viruses and other parasites arrived, the loss of Indigenous life in many areas reached 90 percent. Entire villages and even tribes were wiped out by illness, and the starvation and war that followed, as colonists and tribes alike tried to control the resources of newly emptied land.

Thomas Morton called the area around Plymouth a second Golgotha because it was strewn with the skulls and bones of the dead. Since virus and other infections can have an influence on the psychology of a human being, could it be that the European drive to colonize these lands might be related somehow to the bugs the colonists brought with them? The colonists were themselves colonized by life-forms that addle human behavior. Perhaps when we consider Indigenous society we get a glimpse of human consciousness free of those microscopic but sometimes lethally powerful influences.

The Holy Bible commanded the colonists to "fill the earth and subdue it." By 1634 the four thousand colonists of the Massachusetts Bay Colony had 1,500 head of cattle, four thousand goats, and "innumerable swine." Courts regularly ordered compensation be paid to tribes whose crops and stores of corn were invaded by livestock, but woe to a member of the tribe who killed a marauding animal. The only solution was building fences, a commitment to concepts of ownership foreign to the Indigenous way of life. Many tribes used the word *eat* to describe possession of land, so that "we have eaten it all" meant something akin to ownership.

By the 1640s native varieties of grasses were being crowded out by European grasses shipped over as fodder and spread by cow dung. The Indigenous grasses did not adapt well to the chewing down by livestock, and the trampling and tearing of the ground by hooves, which removed oxygen from the soil. Before long bluegrass, for example, was considered a native grass, though it was really an import. But the rains brought mud in a way they never had before.

The honeybee was a pleasant import the colonists brought with them, but they also brought the blackfly, the cockroach, the house mouse, and the gray rat. European-style farming greatly increased the populations of worms, caterpillars, maggots, and that considerably cuter but nevertheless relentless pest, the squirrel. Still water created by dams caused more mosquito-spread disease. From this perspective, it's hard not to think of the colonists as the vampire Nosferatu, from the film classic of the same name, arriving in the harbor on a ship teeming with plague-infested vermin.

THE SPANISH DEBACLE

The doom of Indigenous America began when Alonso Álvarez de Pineda followed Cortez, mapping the Gulf of Mexico. In 1521 Pineda became the first European to sail up what would become known as the Mississippi River. He called it *Rio del Espiritu Santo,* the River of the Holy Spirit. Sailing it for a month, he reached twenty miles upriver, making contact with both hostile and peaceful tribes along the way, unknowingly initiating the spread of epidemics. On his way home he landed in what is now Texas where Aztec warriors burned two of his ships and captured him. By then the Spanish had won their war against the Aztec empire and smallpox was ruining what was left of that culture, but Pineda paid the price. His captors flayed him alive then hung his skin as a trophy in a temple.

Six years later Jose Maria Narváez sailed with a fleet of five ships and six hundred men, arriving on the west coast of Florida in spring 1528. He had already lost almost half his men to storms and desertions. Fighting hostile tribes, his expedition marched north searching for gold. Finding none he built and boarded four rafts of which two were wrecked by a storm, killing him and everyone on board. Less than a hundred men were left to go on. They began an overland march to Mexico along which most died of hunger. Only four survived. One of them, a sailor named Corvais, spent eight years walking to Mexico City. A tribe captured him. They forced him by starvation to work as a healer, believing that the strange men who had brought these terrible diseases must somehow be able to cure them.

From 1539 to 1543 Captain Hernando de Soto, an officer of Pizarro the conquistador of Peru, led an expedition in search of silver and gold. They visited Mississippian villages in the Southeast. He hoped to gain submission and peaceful compliance from the tribes by encouraging them to believe that he was an immortal, a sun god. They found countless tribes, five hundred different languages, but no treasure.

To each tribe they read in Spanish the *Requerimento*—first read in 1514 far to the south in what is now Venezuela—it had made its way north all the way to the heartland of what would become the United States. The *Requerimento* was an announcement, in this case delivered by six hundred soldiers, that threatened slavery, "harm and evil," "deaths and damage"; further declaring that the blame would fall on the tribes for disobedience, not on the soldiers or the king. They claimed all the land as the property of Spain. The tribes must have stood dumbfounded as the Spanish wrote down, witnessed, and signed their justification for invasion in a language the locals could not understand.

For many tribes it was not only the first time they saw Europeans, it was also the first time they ever saw a horse, or the shining chain mail and battle lances of European soldiers. The Spanish also brought with them a breed of giant mastiffs bred to kill, called the Canary Island mastiffs, because they exterminated every Indigenous inhabitant of the Canary Islands during the Spanish conquest. These dogs also wore chain mail; the horses had chain mail and metal helmets. No wonder modern Americans have been so fascinated with the idea of aliens arriving in shiny silver ships out of nowhere to claim dominion.

The epic journey of de Soto the sun god began around what is now Tampa, Florida, and continued through Georgia, South Carolina, Tennessee, Alabama, Mississippi, and Arkansas. In some villages he stayed for a month or more. Some of these visits were violent and others peaceful. Some tribal leaders used his presence as leverage for peace treaties with rival tribes. When hostilities broke out de Soto's men usually instigated them. At Mauvila, a fortified Indigenous city in southern Alabama, a major battle occurred. Two hundred Spanish soldiers died, another 150 were severely wounded. Thousands of warriors were killed. Mauvila was burned down, but the Spanish had lost most of their supplies and many horses. Their attacks were so savage that some foot soldiers of the Spanish expedition were horrified by the terrors inflicted by their own cavalry. The tribe's women and children were tied to trees then set on fire. Incidents of rape can be glimpsed in the chronicles, not surprising, since during the conquest of Peru, de Soto himself had organized the gang rape of the sacred virgins of the Inca.

In spring 1541 de Soto demanded two hundred members of the Chickasaw tribe for service as porters to make up for the lost horses. They refused, attacking the Spanish camp at night. The Spaniards lost dozens of men and what was left of their equipment. According to de Soto's records the Chickasaw could have killed them all but showed mercy. By May the expedition reached the Mississippi River. Their crossing was dangerous as warriors patrolled the strong current of the broad river. Soon after, de Soto was the first European to see the Valley of the Vapors, now Hot Springs, Arkansas. Tribes had gathered there for generations to heal in the thermal waters. No weapons were allowed. De Soto stayed only long enough to claim it for Spain.

After a harsh winter de Soto's interpreter died, making communication and trading for food even more difficult. De Soto faced warriors of greater skill and more ferocity as he journeyed west. He decided to head back for the great river. Somewhere on the border of Arkansas and Louisiana he died of fever in a tribal village. His men hid the sun god's corpse in blankets weighed down with sand, and sank it, at night, in the Mississippi River. The survivors headed home by way of Mexico City. Some of the hogs brought along by de Soto escaped to become the ancestors of the razorbacks of the southeastern United States. His expedition spread another series of epidemics across America.

The Spanish may have been more ferocious than other European invaders, but they could also be ironically compassionate. Bartolomé de las Casas first arrived in Cuba as a conquistador but the cruelty he witnessed caused him in 1515 to reject the practices of the Spanish Conquest. He freed the Indigenous people who had been enslaved and returned to Spain to tell the king what he had seen and to suggest more humane and Christian strategies, tragically, one of which involved bringing over African captives to take over slave labor from the tribes.

Casas was sent back to the New World with the title Protector of the Indians. First as a Dominican friar, and then as the first Bishop of Chiapas, he fought for fifty years to give rights to the tribes, the same rights any other subject of the Spanish king expected. Tribal attacks on his attempts at peaceful communities, and Spanish attacks on peaceful Indigenous villages, plagued his efforts. Many authors who praised the civilizing and missionary glory of the Spanish Conquest sought to undermine him, but in 1552 he published his influential *A Short Account of the Destruction of the Indies*. Eventually, the Spaniards in the New World created the first universities where Indigenous people could study, and the first laws to protect them. They intermarried with them, blending cultures to a degree never practiced by English colonists.

The Spanish visited Chesapeake Bay in 1561. The son of a chief agreed to go with them to their world. Don Luis de Velasco, his Indigenous name is uncertain, was treated like an aristocrat in Mexico City, Havana, and Spain. The Dominicans took care of him, the crown paid his way, the viceroy stood for his baptism, and he met the King of Spain. He even received a Jesuit education. In 1570 eight Jesuits traveled with him back to the Chesapeake area where he was to spearhead their mission to bring Catholicism to the tribes. They didn't bring soldiers with them because the Jesuits had experience with how boredom among soldiers inevitably led to drunkenness, rape, and other acts of violence against tribes. Five days after they arrived Don Luis abandoned them. Famine in the area made the Jesuits' isolation all the more precarious. After several months Don Luis led an attack that killed every priest, ending their mission. Don Luis allowed only a servant boy to survive. A year later a supply ship noticed the absence of the Jesuits, and articles of their clothing being worn by Indigenous warriors who admitted to the massacre. The year after that a small Spanish military force arrived to punish the tribe. They took hostages and hearing of the survival of the servant boy they exchanged prisoners for him. From him they learned that Don Luis had betrayed the king of Spain after what they considered so much generosity. Twenty warriors were captured, baptized, and then hanged. But Don Luis escaped, not only from the Spanish, but from the eyes of history.

In what is now North Carolina, the Mississippian culture was again confronted by more Spanish explorers when the Juan Pardo expedition built a base there in 1567 christened Fort San Juan. Eighteen months into the experiment the tribe killed all the colonists and destroyed the fort. Five other supporting forts were burned and 120 soldiers killed, leaving only one survivor. So ended the first European colonization of America. Twenty-one years later Sir Walter Raleigh's Virginia project began, planting the first seed of the culture that would become the thirteen colonies of the United States of America.

TALES OF MANNA-HATTA AND NEW FRANCE

In 1609 Captain Henry Hudson, an Englishman who worked for the Dutch East India Company, and his crew, sailed up the waterway that would become known as the Hudson River. Hudson's pilot jotted down a note in his journal about a place the tribes called *Manna-hata*. His explorations led to the establishment of New Netherlands in 1624 when the first Dutch fur trading outpost was set up on Governor's Island. A year later construction began on Fort Amsterdam on what would become Manhattan Island. The site was bought for about a thousand dollars in today's money value, an amount paid to a tribe who lived in what is now Brooklyn, instead of the people who lived on the land. New York City was born. New Amsterdam was no puritan Boston; this Protestant town was infamous for its taverns full of smugglers.

Today's Wall Street takes its name from the earthen wall on the north border of New Amsterdam, protection against not only the tribes, but also the English. The original wall of Wall Street was built by enslaved African people, as was the settlement, its docks, and roads. A bloody slave rebellion ended in horrific spectacles of torture and execution of rebels. After much Dutch soul searching the Africans were given "half-freedom." They had to pay a yearly tax, and they could be called back to work at any time by the Dutch West India Company. They were allowed to have their own homes, and they created one of the first free Black towns in America. The Dutch West India Company was not interested in the sort of homesteading practiced by the English colonists, instead they competed with the French, developing fur trading outposts on the Hudson, Mohawk, Delaware, and Connecticut rivers. The experiment of New Amsterdam only lasted fifty years.

The tribes of New England called the ships of the colonists giant birds that coughed thunder and lightning. In the 1630s William Wood reported that the Massachusetts tribe thought the first ship they saw was a floating island. They guided their canoes to go pick strawberries on it until the cannon opened fire. When the Dutch arrived their ships puzzled the Indigenous people. They described them as double ships that go both in the air and under water.

The French and Dutch established lucrative fur businesses. By 1628 the Mohawk tribe gained control of the fur trade at Fort Orange, the Dutch colony at New Amsterdam on Manhattan Island. Less than twenty years later a treaty was brokered between the Iroquois and the

Dutch and their tribal allies. It would take thirty more years for the Iroquois to make an alliance with the English. The tribes gained advantages from their alliances with the Europeans. Chiefs who traded with them grew powerful. The English were also useful allies against traditional enemies. The Dutch were played against the English to gain benefits from both.

But the English with their focus on settlements, and their willingness to redefine and argue against any law or deal the Dutch made, eventually took most of the Dutch possessions in North America. They did it by having children in the New World, building houses, clearing fields, and thereby creating a market the Dutch couldn't exploit.

In 1524 Captain Verrazzano, an Italian in the service of the king of France, spent fifteen days exploring the area we now call New England. He reported large families of twenty-five to thirty in each home. He wrote down his first encounter with the Indigenous inhabitants of Manna-hata.

We saw about twenty small boats full of people, who came about our ship, uttering many cries of astonishment, but they would not approach nearer than within fifty paces; stopping, they looked at the structure of our ship, our persons and dress, afterwards they all raised a loud shout together, signifying that they were pleased. By imitating their signs, we inspired them, in some measure with confidence, so that they came near enough for us to toss to them some little bells and glasses, and many toys, which they took and looked at, laughing, and then came on board without fear. Among them were two men more beautiful in form and stature than can possibly be described; one was about forty years old, the other about twenty-four, and they were dressed in the following manner: the oldest has a deer's skin around his body, artificially wrought in damask figures, his head was without covering, his hair was tied back in various knots; around his neck he wore a large chain ornamented with many stones of different colors. The young man was similar in his general appearance. This is the finest-looking tribe, the handsomest in their costumes that we have found in our voyage. They exceed us in size, and they are of a very fair complexion; some of them incline more to a white, and others to a tawny color; their faces are sharp, and their hair long and black, upon the adorning of which they bestow great pains, their eyes are black and sharp, their expression mild and pleasant, greatly resembling the ancients. They live a long life and rarely fall sick: if they are wounded they cure themselves with fire without medicine, their end comes with old age. (Verrazzano 1916)

Like the Dutch, the French were less interested in colonizing America than they were in profiting from the fur trade. Outposts were established in Canada and northeastern America. The power of trading with the French created imbalances among tribes that soon led to conflict. As the French spread epidemics, opportunistic tribal leaders tried to benefit their tribes by gaining new lands. By 1609 the Iroquois League fought a war with the French and France's tribal allies, the Huron. They also moved against the Algonquins and the early English colonies.

In 1634 the French Jesuit Paul le Jeune honestly recorded his attempt to convert an Indigenous man. After telling him that he had left his home and traveled so far for love of him, the Jesuit gave a surprisingly Platonic but moving speech about the beauty and wisdom of the world proving the existence of a divine designer who must watch over every part of it and who judges the dead and keeps the good in happiness for eternity. The Indigenous man responded that the Jesuit didn't know what he was talking about.

In 1684 the Iroquois attacked French trading outposts, which had reached all the way to what is now Illinois. After three years of war, the governor of New France convened a meeting under a flag of truce at Iroquois-occupied Fort Frontenac with fifty hereditary chiefs of the Iroquois League. The truce was a ruse. French forces recaptured the fort, and took captive all fifty Iroquois chiefs, who were sent to Marseilles, France, to be used as galley slaves. A French armada arrived at Irondequoit Bay, devastating the Seneca homeland. In retaliation, the Iroquois became allies of the English, ending French hopes in America.

THE ENGLISH IN THE NEW WORLD

By the mid-1500s hundreds of ships visited the New England coast every year. Castaways and survivors of wrecks had been interacting with the tribes for generations. Colonists were surprised to find Indigenous people wearing European clothes or using a tailored cloth shirt for a canoe sail. The first word spoken by an Indigenous man to the Pilgrims was *welcome*.

In 1569 David Ingram, one of a hundred men John Hawkins left on the shores of the Gulf of Mexico, claimed to have walked in one year with two other sailors all the way to Maine where they were picked up by a ship. His record of the epic journey is a curious blend of observations and hearsay, much of it gathered along the way from Indigenous locals. They told him of tribes with teeth like dogs who were cannibals, and Ingram argued that the English should colonize the New World to help defend the good tribes from their monstrous enemies. One gets the impression that tall tales were being told.

Even the ever-tolerant Roger Williams reported on a zombie tribe that ate the brains of their enemies, but he added that they lived far away, and since they were human beings they might be saved after all. Other such tales of cannibals with three-inch teeth, and Mohawks shouting war cries warning they would suck the blood of their enemies, were quickly discredited and discarded by publishers once the colonists gained more experience with the tribes.

Partly due to prejudices about primitive culture related to their own pagan origins in the blue-painted Picts and Druids of ye olden days, and partly due to the Spanish reports of Aztec religious slaughters, some English writers on Indigenous culture assumed human sacrifice was practiced by all tribes. The *huskanaw* ritual caused much confusion. Adolescent boys were painted white. After a feast and dance, chosen men guided them through gauntlets of men hitting them with bundled sticks while the women mourned and prepared for a funeral. The boys would then lay motionless under a tree. Then they were led away into the woods where the men would teach them the secrets and skills of the tribe. Seeing the apparently lifeless bodies of the boys and hearing the laments of the women, some English observers assumed the boys had been murdered.

Eventually more careful witnesses noticed the boys returned after a period of weeks or months. The famous incident when Pocahontas saved Captain John Smith from having his head bashed in was probably such a ritual, intended to rebirth the Pilgrim as a member of the tribe. The only ritual sacrifices made by the Algonquins were the occasional bonfires of their possessions, as we have seen, most likely intended to restore tribal harmony and the good will of their gods.

The earliest Spanish visitors to the New World reported that the tribes had no religion and no god. The English instead described them as pagans and idolaters, though even the earliest such reports were contradicted by more sensitive writers who insisted such summary dismissals misrepresented the resemblances between Indigenous and European beliefs. Roger Williams and other English writers constantly reminded their readers that all men share basic beliefs about the divine order of the universe and the afterlife. Many English believed the tribes of the New World were the lost tribes of Israel. Didn't they sequester menstruating women, as practiced by the ancient Hebrews?

From their English nobles the colonists expected courtesy and composure, dignity and honesty. A good noble would return a favor done for him and would be good to his word. He would hate lying and rude behavior, and would conduct himself in such a way as to never be laughed at. The colonists were surprised to find these same qualities among the tribal leaders. English writers commented on their civility in one paragraph, while in the next dismissing them as ensnared by the devil in the New World, the godforsaken wilderness.

While the Europeans considered tribes demonic, Indigenous people thought the Europeans animal-like. They had so much body hair and ate a diet of raw foliage, that is, what we call salads. One Indigenous man described the French talking over each other in a crowd as no better than a flock of geese. They were shocked by the bad manners and arguments displayed by colonists in their community meetings, since tribal councils were dignified, thoughtful, and polite. They taught their children not to be boisterous, to hate ingratitude, and to share however little they might have. Even a modest piece of bread would be divided equally among all.

As England became more powerful under the four decades of Queen

Elizabeth I, the Protestants of Europe began to believe the British would lead them into a world where the power of the Catholic church could be broken. America, which many believed had been divinely hidden until this crucial time, was to become a new continent free of the pope, despite the presence of the Spanish in the south and west, and the Catholic colony that would become Maryland. But England was poor and divided. Many loyal to the pope thought the recurrent plagues were punishment for spiritual disobedience.

While a powerful merchant class grew, so did the numbers of the poor and homeless. Many complained that good simple English values were being corrupted by foreign influence. To avoid the fate of the decadent French, gender distinctions were considered so important that the measure of civilization applied to the tribes was based on their strict division between the responsibilities of men and women. Nevertheless, fads inspired by Indigenous American fashions appeared among the poor and rich in England, including scandalous gender bending by wearing items formerly associated only with the opposite sex.

In London, many writers complained, honesty and charity were for fools, communities neglected members who needed help, and the clever were rewarded instead of the virtuous. Still, the English loved the accomplishments of their civilization, the pomp and splendor of their rulers, and saw themselves as "angel Saxons" bringing true religion and improvements in living to the "savages" of the New World. Meanwhile, the hard work demanded by colonization would give England a way to renew the simple virtues, while making wealth available to the unsophisticated.

The Roman historian Tacitus was the most popular ancient writer of the day among the English. His descriptions of the good simple people of Germania and ancient Britannia, liberty loving and valorous, in contrast to the decadence and political scheming of the Imperial Romans, caused traditionalists among the English to compare the tribes of America to their own ancestors, as opposed to their fad-loving contemporaries and the corruptions of the royal court.

The English were particularly interested in Indigenous hairstyles. The Puritans disapproved of the long hair and debauched immorality of the flamboyant cavaliers. During the English Civil War that broke out in 1641, friend or foe could be judged by hair length. European observers noted that grieving Indigenous fathers cut off their hair. Virgin girls wore their hair over their eyes. Captive women were humiliated by having their long hair shorn. The most written-about Indigenous hairdo was worn by males who shaved the right side of their heads and wore their hair long on the other. Few writers pointed out the practicality involved; hunters didn't want their hair interfering with archery. The style led to a fad among young English men who took to wearing one long lock of hair, called a lovelock. Pundits decried the sudden variety of hair fashions for degenerating good plain Englishmen into "Virginians, Frenchmen, and Ruffians!" Indigenous teenage males experimented with their hair with such enthusiasm, one author observed that their hairstyles "would torment the wits of a curious barber."

The colonists wondered that the Indigenous men didn't sport manly beards, they were said to pluck their sparse facial hair, and if one naturally grew a beard he was suspected of having a European father. A few wore artificial beards made of animal fur perhaps to appear more European and therefore up-to-date. Young Indigenous men were especially interested in acquiring European clothes but to the disappointment of the colonists they tended to wear them only when visiting, taking them off to return home. Some among the tribal leaders were given fine red coats to display their allegiance to King James.

The colonists were somewhat perturbed by the tribal habit of painting, dyeing, and tattooing their bodies. Roger Williams learned how to tell them, in their own language, that "the god who made them would not recognize them." The colonists were also much concerned with posture, that of the tribes and their own. The Pilgrim Endicott fretted that he had posed too arrogantly for his portrait as justice of the peace, with his hand on his hip and elbow akimbo. European painters depicted Sir Walter Raleigh and tribal chiefs alike in this pose, which was meant to represent the power and dominance of the aristocracy.

But the English, including comparative free thinkers like Tom Morton, nevertheless considered the New World the devil's playground and thought the tribes hopelessly enthralled by witchcraft. John Smith reported that among their curious self-adornments, men sometimes wore small, bright green live snakes with yellow underbellies (probably *Opheodrys vernalis,* the smooth greensnake) that would curl around their necks and kiss their lips. The snake of Eden must have leapt to mind. The Europeans mistook tribal friendliness for reverence and admiration, but too much friendliness inspired suspicions of treachery.

THE ENGLISH HAD THEIR OWN KIND OF MAGIC

An English minister was said to have converted a tribe by praying successfully for rain when their shamans failed. In 1605 Captain Waymouth used a magnet to move and lift a knife, astonishing his Indigenous guests. English technology, such as clocks, books, and guns, were said to be manitou, and the tribes wondered if the English had been taught by gods. Demonstrating the function of a compass could save a captive's life. Where English medicines and treatments prevailed, sometimes saving the life of a chief or many lives in a village, the tribes considered it a demonstration of spiritual power. When the tribes attacked and destroyed half the colonist plantations in 1622, letters sent home begging for help lamented that the tribes would disbelieve in the Christian god were the English to fail so miserably. When famine and disease followed the attacks, many colonists called it divine retribution caused by unscrupulous private traders who were cheating and abusing the tribes.

The Christians of this era of colonization were not mutually tolerant. Protestants referred to the Catholic church as the Great Whore. The pope was considered antichrist. Roman Catholic missionaries in the New World were called vermin. And Catholics and Protestants referred to each other as atheists. Preachers of either branch of the missionary business who tried to address the tribes were often driven away. Sometimes they were told to wait at specific places and times but no one ever showed up. Christian ministers were sometimes horrified to hear Indigenous people tell them they had themselves crossed over into the spirit world to visit the Christian heaven. One reported he had seen the great gentleman God, the handsome man Jesus, and the saved, like "butterflies of many colors."

The tribes adopted Christianity in their own way. The God of the

Book was added to some Indigenous pantheons. Two of the most powerful chiefs who fought against the colonists during King Philip's War
kept the Sabbath. They considered themselves followers of what they
called the Great God. The English blamed the Catholics, and both
blamed the devil.

Unable to stop the epidemics ravaging their people, some shamans
wanted to convert, especially after colonists told them that the spirit
of Jesus could do the same things for them that their familiar spirits
and traditional gods did: healing, protection from suffering, an end to
nightmares, giving them a smoother path through life. They were told
that their spirit guides were demonic imps and their deity the devil.
The spirit of Jesus, they were promised, was much more powerful. Here
begins American Metaphysical Christianity. The line blurs between
Indigenous and European. Jesus becomes an especially powerful spirit,
the ally of shamans. One spirit is exchanged for another. Jesus must perform the same services as a tribal god: warn of trouble, ward away sickness, give victory in war, end draughts, calm storms, bring prosperity.

Measles, smallpox, typhoid fever, plague, and the common cold had
been wiping out Indigenous villages since the mid-1500s. Sweat lodges,
a traditional healing method, only helped spread the diseases. By the
1600s devastated communities lost their ability to function collectively
and were forced to burn even their tools to keep their fires going. Nature
itself seemed to be working against them as America suffered a cold spell
known as the Little Ice Age. Growing seasons were shorter. Prey and the
wild foods Indigenous people gathered became scarce. The New England
area suffered the worst drought in eight hundred years. Survivors were
forced to band together in new groups. New leaders arose, often using
trade with the colonists to build more power than tribal leaders had
known at any time earlier in their history. Chiefs became kings.

Powhatan, the father of Pocahontas, tried to tell John Smith that
they would both benefit from a loving relationship, and both suffer
from war, but Indigenous people would endure the deprivations of hiding their supplies and sleeping uneasily in hidden places, while colonists
succumbed to exposure and starvation. When native food grew scarce
and the newcomers ignored warnings, attempting to take what they

could by force, several were found dead in their fort with their mouths stuffed full of bread.

English officers faced the challenge of controlling their own men. As John Smith wrote, "Much they blamed us for not converting the Savages, when those they sent us were little better, if not worse." Writers lamented that life in the colonies proved how degenerate and weak the English had become. Punishments were accordingly severe: hanging, burning, being broken on the wheel, shot, or starved to death. The price of English overconfidence is illustrated by an incident during the winter famine of 1609 when Powhatan had a party of English demanding food killed and their leader tortured to death by the women of the tribe. On the other hand, the heads of Indigenous warriors killed in battle were stuck on English stakes, and colonists were known to cut off the hands of Indigenous people they suspected were spies.

The starvation in Jamestown grew so severe incidents of colonial cannibalism were confessed to and punished. Their Pilgrim brethren living by the coast hid their abundant supply of food from their suffering fellow colonists. When supplies finally arrived from England the colonists attacked the weakened tribes, seizing corn, killing the men, and taking women and children hostage. Children were thrown overboard, then shot as they struggled against the waves. Some argued that the chief's wife should be burned alive, but she was run through with a sword instead. As they never killed women and children in war, it's difficult to imagine how the victims viewed these ferocious attacks. The tribes learned what the Europeans taught them and against their own tradition massacred European women and children. Back home in England doubts about the savagery practiced by colonists were met not only by reference to King David's war in the Old Testament but by the more recent examples of slaughter practiced in the English colonization of Ireland. Such cruel acts were said to be merciful since the fear they invoked would hopefully prevent further defiance. When the English Civil War broke out no mercy was shown by either side, as Protestants and Catholics alike justified rape, torture, and slaughter in the name of religion.

Colonists who "went native" were regarded with much suspicion. One Edward Ashley was said to have joined a tribe, to have dressed like them, learned their language, and cohabited with their women. The Pilgrims accused him of cheating them and dealing guns to the tribes. They seized him and sent him back to England. When they heard news that he was lost at sea on a later expedition they celebrated it as divine judgment against him. Another colonist who preferred his Indigenous family to colonial civilization was captured and whipped.

One Indigenous man, who earnestly sought to understand Christianity after witnessing the deaths of so many of his people in a day's battle against the English, and believing it a sign of the power of their god, braved all insults to preach to his tribe. He was poisoned. While many English writers trumpeted his spiritual courage and declared him "the first Indian in heaven," Roger Williams reported that the man died with a heavy heart, deeply conflicted; "Me so big naughty heart, me heart all one stone," the poor man said shortly before he died. Members of a tribe who stayed loyal to the English and their way of life were faced with taunts and death threats. These go-betweens, essential to relations between the tribes and the newcomers, lived difficult lives distrusted by both sides.

By 1677 the English Civil War and the Thirty Years War, which had ruined and rearranged Europe, were objects of curiosity to a new generation hooked on books full of gory details. One of the popular books of the time was written by a Puritan minister in the New World. In it he described the torture inflicted by a tribe on a captured enemy. The captive's fingers were cut where they joined his hands and then torn off. The writer was impressed by the lack of emotion on the victim's face, he showed no sign of agony. Blood spewing, he danced around the fire in a macabre spectacle. Next his toes were torn off. Finally his legs were broken and he was forced to sit, waiting until they cracked open his skull. The writer lingers on the excitement of the torturers and spectators to prove thereby that they were creatures of the devil.

The tribe however experienced this ceremony very differently. For the torturers this was an opportunity to avenge lost loved ones and to express anger against what they perceived to be injustice. The spectators were excited not only because they enjoyed seeing the suffering inflicted on an enemy, they were also reacting to his bravery and his resistance to pain, egging him on. The bleeding victim was not forced to dance: he danced to demonstrate that they could not break his will; he danced to mock their torture of him. For him this was an initiation, a test of strength, a means to achieve an honorable death that would allow him to enter the afterlife fully conscious.

As in Europe, hatred between tribes often won out over common interest. When the Mohegans, made strong by their integration of the shattered Pequots, tried to convince the Narragansetts to join them in a war of attrition against the English to drive them out once and for all by burning their crops, killing their livestock, and ambushing them, the Narragansetts, who had long been insulted for being effeminate because they chose to gain power by trade rather than war, sided with the English.

However the Narragansetts would later reverse their position, and their leader Miantonomi, the Narragansett chief of the Montauk Indians of eastern Long Island, famously counseled united warfare against the colonists in summer 1642: "Our fathers had plenty of deer and skins, our plains were full of deer, as also our woods, and of turkeys, and our coves full of fish and fowl. But these English have gotten our land, they with scythes cut down the grass, and with axes fell the trees; their cows and horses eat the grass, and their hogs spoil our clam banks, and we shall all be starved" (Kiernan 2007). He was captured by a member of his tribe and delivered up to the English, who gave him to the Mohegans for execution by a hatchet to the head in 1643, the same year his friend Roger Williams published *Key into the Language of America*.

By 1660 some chiefs were warning their tribes that the Europeans would not only never be eliminated from their lands but were too dangerous an enemy to make war against. In 1676 a powerful chief named Metacom united the tribes in one last attempt to regain their lost world in what became known as King Philip's War. Metacom received his Macedonian name because it was an easy way for the colonists to remember each tribe had an elder chief, Philip, and a younger chief, to whom of course they always gave the name Alexander. Metacom was the son of Chief Massasoita, who had been Plymouth colony's greatest friend among the tribes, the Wampanoag chief at America's first Thanksgiving.

As early as the late seventeenth century, Indigenous children had been raised as Christians, sometimes with Christian names, and they preached to small congregations. They walked a difficult and narrow path, distrusted by English Christians and despised by members of their own tribes who continued to practice traditional ways. They suffered most during King Philip's War. For example, a minister named John Eliot had translated the Bible into Algonquin and converted many to Christianity. The question Indigenous people Eliot had converted asked him most: "Why have not beasts a soul as man has, seeing they have love, anger, etc. as man has?" These "Praying Indians" were used in propaganda to prove that the "savages desire civilization." Several decades of their loyalty to the English meant little when war broke out. They were rounded up and put in a concentration camp in what is now Deer Island, a peninsula of Boston Harbor. Half of the five hundred prisoners died during the cold winter. The survivors, most weak from hunger and exposure and sick with disease, were released after the colonists realized they would easily win what was left of the war.

Many colonists died and many plantations burned during King Philip's War, eleven towns and 1,200 homes were reduced to ashes, but by then it was too late. Tribes were slaughtered; the survivors, sold into slavery or stripped of property and individual rights, were relocated.

An Indigenous man named John Alderman shot King Philip. He was given the chief's severed hand, which he preserved in rum and showed at taverns for a fee. Metacom's corpse was beheaded and quartered. His head was put on display stuck on a pike on a road at Plymouth for almost twenty-five years. His wife and children were sold into slavery in Bermuda. Cotton Mather took a portion of Metacom's jaw as a macabre collectible. His tribe claimed to have stolen back Metacom's head for proper burial. They insisted the head shown at Plymouth belonged to someone else. Folktales were told for more than two hundred years of King Philip's spirit wandering his old lands.

HONORING THE ANCESTORS

As the United States of America was born and history rolled relentlessly onward, Indigenous beliefs were transformed into folktales, a new tradition of storytelling replaced the old. Some of these tales were propagandistic. The crow who brought the corn kernel and the bean became the dove that fed a white man cranberries so he could defeat an Indigenous shaman in a spiritual battle of endurance. Other stories resemble the lore collected by Harry Hyatt in his monumental compilation *Hoodoo Conjuration Witchcraft Rootwork:* a blend of coded language, for safety's sake, and of the confusion of the disempowered (for example, a poisonous root once used to kill might become a charm that harms the person whose porch it is buried under). Witchcraft practices are a strategy for control that flourishes among people disadvantaged by communal crisis. In these stories anyone practicing traditional ways is now called a witch or a medicine devil. Factional differences are fought out and group boundaries reaffirmed. Wisdom can be found in the fables but only by those with a strong understanding of context, a feeling for metaphor, and a sharp sense of rural humor. When a mother told her children that a white feather floating in the room and then up the chimney was a notorious local witch spying on their conversation, what did she really mean? A joke? A lesson about nosy gossips and the necessity of discretion? Or did she literally think the witch had shape-shifted?

Indigenous gods were transformed into stories about giants; their creation stories now resembled ancient Greek myths about giants throwing islands on shore to create landmark mountains. Cheepi was reduced to a surrogate for the devil, stripped of his powers of healing and wisdom, and of his office of protecting the harmony of the tribe and of nature; he was blamed for any unexplained night terror, used to inspire greater loyalty to the church, and to make children obedient by teaching them fear of the unknown.

By 1830 writers were fondly remembering their Indigenous nannies who told them meteors were spirits, that the winds were spirits singing lullabies, and a chirping cricket the sign that a spirit was near. Not only did they see the deceased relatives of the families they were attached to, but they also related details about what matters had inspired the spirit to visit, sometimes startling family members with details secret or forgotten. These surviving elements of tribal religions were dismissed as quaint superstitions. Christian members of tribes who practiced herbal medicine were called witches because of traditions like picking herbs at midnight, refusing to use metal implements with herbs, choosing the right phase of the moon for harvesting them. To say that herbs must never be gathered during the dog days of summer, or that drying them in the sun gave them extra potency, was to risk the appearance of believing in the old sun god and tribal spirits.

By the mid-1800s stories circulated about talented psychic herbal healers like Dr. Perry. The good doctor was renowned for his healing skills. A respectable white family reported that he healed their daughter of tuberculosis in a matter of days when European doctors had given her up for dead. Doc Perry had a knack for sensing where he might find a rare herb he needed. Walking through the woods he would interrupt a conversation to hike off into the trees, returning with some plant he said he had been looking for. He also showed the uncanny knack of already being on his way to doctor serious cases before having been informed of them. His story dovetailed with the stories of mediums and healers as the spiritualist movement gained momentum in America. Now the traditional shaman was no longer a witch but an honored ancestor of the new religion. No wonder so many of the spirit guides of early spiritualist mediums presented themselves as Indigenous Americans.

Cotton Mather was not far from Indigenous beliefs when he wrote of nature as the "temple of God" and praised the wonders of the sun, stars, moon, of the natural protection and scattering of seeds, and the wonderful variety and interdependence of the animal kingdom, and of even the magnetic power of the lodestone; all were elegant examples of divine creativity. Like a good Platonist, who also had more than a passing interest in the Kabbalah, Mather suggested that by admiring such invisible and inscrutable forces as gravity and magnetism we could be led to worshipping the wisdom of the creator.

While the national flags of Europe featured crosses, the flags of early America featured stars, a rattlesnake, the moon, and an evergreen tree—nature, not religion. Indigenous ideas about sickness, healing, sorcery, and mysterious lights like foxfire and will-o'-the-wisp were adopted by some colonists. For most of American history, academic and popular opinion agreed: the tribes were savage and America was divinely appointed for Manifest Destiny. More recently the opposite perspective has gained ground. Indigenous tribes lived in harmony with nature, and the colonists intended from the first to ruthlessly exploit them both.

In the twenty-first century Water Protectors at Standing Rock made visible the continuing poverty among the Lakota and the continuing disrespect for their lands, their ancestral burial sites, and their rights as American citizens. For the leaders who made it happen the protest was a sacred action, with prayer and ritual every day and night. More than four hundred tribes joined the protest, along with several thousand protestors whose numbers would double on weekends.

Allies who visited the protest included members of the Black Lives Matter movement, Indigenous leaders from the Amazon, military veterans, Catholic and Protestant clergy, rabbis, Buddhist monks, movie stars, rock stars, members of the Rainbow Tribe of the 1960s, and Vermont Senator Bernie Sanders. Through social media and then mass media the world watched as fire hoses were turned on children and old people in the snow. Officers fired pepper spray in the faces of protestors on their knees in prayer.

An unusual detail came up in conversations I had with Water Protectors, Indigenous and otherwise. Most reported the feeling that "the veil" was very thin there. One could "feel the presence of the other side much more easily." Many said it felt as though the ancestors had gathered with the living. All were humbled by the sense of fate and sacredness surrounding the place and the protest. Many who joined the protest were motivated by dreams of messages from the dead or prophetic visions. Reports of telepathy and clairvoyance became so common they were taken for granted. For a moment the eyes of the world were on the Indigenous tragedy at the birth of America, but then politics and a pandemic made it all seem far away again.

We will now take a closer look at some important people in the history of American Metaphysical Religion. Some of them are well known, most all but forgotten. I hope you'll be as amazed as I was by their stories. To tell the tales of all the interesting characters who made significant contributions would require more books than *One Thousand and One Nights,* but here is a careful selection.

6

Thomas Harriot: America's First "Evil" Genius

HE ARRIVES AT THE END of the Renaissance with a mind so modern he was more suited for Silicon Valley than Elizabethan London. Thomas Harriot was the first to assemble and use a telescope in England. Months before Galileo, he was the first human being to accurately map the surface of the moon. He was the first to make a system of binary numbers, to see the value in what would become almost five hundred years later the mathematical foundation of computer science. He has been described as the first modern experimental scientist. He contributed important elements to algebra, geometry, and trigonometry. He invented the symbols we still use for greater than (>) and lesser than (<).

Harriot was the first Englishman to learn an Indigenous Turtle Island language. His *Briefe and True Report of the New Found Land of Virginia* is the earliest record in English of the pristine environment, of Indigenous cultures, and of the moment when it was first exploited. He used his mathematical skills for everything from improving plumbing to refining accounting methods. Finding the most efficient way to stack cannonballs on a ship, he invented what history remembers as Kepler's Conjecture. Harriot began the science of dynamic stability, helping design better ships. He not only refined the navigational techniques of English sailors, he improved the quality of their navigational instruments.

But Harriot was also known for his skills as an astrologer. He explored the mysteries of alchemy. He proved by experiment and careful measurements how rainbows are made by refracted light. He created an alphabet to capture the strange sounds of the language spoken by the Carolina Algonquins, hoping it might someday become a universal alphabet to describe all languages. Instead, it became known as the Devil's Alphabet. For his efforts Harriot was imprisoned, attacked in polemic books, suspected of treason, accused of being a devil worshipper, persecuted as an atheist, and then was all but forgotten by history.

Thomas Harriot was born in 1560. We know nothing about his early life. History first noticed him around two hundred years before the birth of the United States when he studied at Oxford University. There he put on black, the color he wore all his life. At the time only two types of Englishmen had any interest in the New World. In summer, fishermen would land on America's Atlantic shore to dry their ocean catches of cod and other fish. Meanwhile, ambitious English patriots discussed the Spanish who had gained so much wealth and power from their exploitation of the New World, but who had left the northeastern part of the continent relatively unmolested. Upon graduating from Oxford, Harriot was immediately employed by one of the latter, Sir Walter Raleigh.

Raleigh was one of the brightest stars of the court of Queen Elizabeth I. A prolific writer, a poet, a daring sea captain, and a skilled soldier, Raleigh received royal gifts of lands and titles that made him rich. He was captain of the Queen's Bodyguard for a decade. His stylish and opulent clothing was matched only by legendary arrogance made barely tolerable by his wit and charm. On his sea voyages he carried a trunk of books so he could read undisturbed. Of all the nobles of England none was more eager than he to colonize the New World, or as he put it, "I'm after Virginia's maidenhead." Among her gifts to the man she nicknamed "Water," the queen gave Durham House, overlooking the Thames, which would be his favorite home until her death, and the site of many mysterious and wonderful gatherings and experiments.

Raleigh moved Harriot into Durham House where Thomas was often found on the rooftop experimenting with tools of navigation. We can only imagine the looks on the faces of Raleigh's grizzled captains and navigators when confronted with the prospect of being tutored at their craft by a young pup freshly plucked from Oxford. But Harriot made such radical improvements to the instruments and techniques of navigation that he can be partially credited with transforming the English fleet from a pack of feckless corsairs to the most fearsome marauders on the Atlantic.

In 1584 Raleigh sent two of his captains on an expedition to the New World. They arrived in what is now North Carolina. Scouts sent from the Roanoke, a tribe of Carolina Algonquin, approached the English with kindness. They began gift exchanges and rituals to transform the strangers into kin. Their chief, Wingina, had been badly wounded in battle with a rival tribe, so a lesser chief invited the English to visit their village on Roanoke Island. There the rituals continued. Confident members of the tribe welcomed the nervous newcomers, but they trembled with fear when the English demonstrated the firepower of guns. Impressed, the tribe tried to convince the English to join them in an attack on Wingina's enemies, but the English declined to interfere with local politics. Wingina selected two men, Manteo and Wanchese, to travel back to England to learn the ways of their new friends.

When Raleigh introduced Manteo and Wanchese to the royal court of Elizabeth they caused a sensation among the English. Raleigh gave them lodging in Durham House and denied the numerous curiosity seekers access. He put Harriot to the task of learning their language. Manteo was a chief of the Croatoan tribe. He was impressed by London. He could see for himself the level of technology enjoyed by the English. He believed they could be a powerful ally for his tribe. Wanchese, a Roanoke chief, was far less cooperative. He saw the English as a mortal threat, and he was eager to go home to warn his people.

Harriot had already tried to adapt the Hebrew alphabet for universal usage as the alphabet of all languages. Now he devised his own: thirty-six characters, a combination of Greek and Roman letters, algebraic symbols, and invented cyphers. The vocabulary he compiled was destroyed in the Great Fire of London in 1666, but his alphabet survived.

Manteo confided to Harriot that some among the tribes thought the English gods or believed they had been taught by gods. Because only English men came to the New World, and they made no advances toward the Indigenous women, some wondered if they were an old race of half gods not even born from women.

Manteo described tribal war tactics. Chiefs were only as powerful as the number of warriors they could deploy. Sneak attacks and guerrilla strikes at break of day or by moonlight were the most common methods of war. Head-on battle was only risked where there were trees for the warriors to duck behind after firing their arrows. Harriot was reassured that the witch hazel bows and stone-tipped arrows of the tribes would be no threat to the armor of the colonists.

In 1585 Harriot was sent to America while Raleigh sailed in search of the golden city of El Dorado in Guyana. Harriot, fresh from his study of Indigenous culture with Manteo, may have prevailed upon his patron to treat the tribes of Guyana very differently than had the Spanish, who were accustomed to taking whatever they wanted, even out of graves and homes, including forcing Indigenous men into servitude and raping the women. Raleigh ordered every object taken to be paid for, guides and others who served the English were paid, and Indigenous women were to be left unmolested.

Under the command of Raleigh's cousin Sir Richard Grenville and of Sir Ralph Lane, seven ships sailed for the New World. Lane's complaints about Grenville's obnoxious arrogance weren't exaggerated since a contemporary account of Grenville described him downing three or four glasses of wine then crunching the glass with his teeth and swallowing the shards. Though blood ran from his mouth Grenville didn't seem any worse for it. On a ship named *Tiger,* Harriot's crew included John White, a skilled painter, and Joachim Gans, an expert in metallurgy, who joined Manteo and Wanchese for their voyage home. Harriot's superior navigational techniques enabled them to reach warm Caribbean waters in only three weeks.

Wingina and his tribe welcomed the colonists and traded for what they could get of their technology. A small house was built for Harriot that he would fill with the paperwork of his notes and the specimens he gathered. He worked with Gans at what was America's first alchemical laboratory. Gans was the son of David Gans, the Jewish astrologer, historian, and mathematician of the Prague of Emperor Rudolph II. David had worked with Kepler and Tycho Brahe on their astronomical observations. In 1849, a visitor claimed to have found hermetically sealed glass globes full of quicksilver (mercury) at the site of the lab where Harriot and Gans practiced their arts. At the same spot in 1994 archaeologists recovered metallic antimony (used in the separation of silver and copper), slag (the byproduct of smelting), clinkers (the incombustible residue of burned coal), and traces of molten materials. A brass apothecary's weight was found in a ditch alongside glass shards from vessels used by assayers of that time, amid badly burned fragments of Indigenous clay pots. Seeds and nuts from leaf pine and shagbark hickory suggest tests for medicinal properties.

As Harriot gathered specimens, John White painted hauntingly beautiful watercolors of Indigenous people, their villages and ceremonies, as well as butterflies, fish, animals, and plants. Together they collected a treasure trove of information. Among the most marvelous of their specimens was tobacco. English sailors who visited American shores had already taken up smoking tobacco, and there is evidence of shops in London at the time fashioning pipes for that purpose, but it took Harriot and Raleigh to make tobacco all the rage at the English court.

In *Briefe and True Report of the New Found Land of Virginia* Harriot wrote:

> There is an herb which is sowed by itself and is called by the inhabitants *Vppówoc*. In the West Indies it has diverse names, according to the several places and countries where it grows and is used. The Spaniards generally call it Tobacco. The leaves thereof being dried and brought into powder they use to take the fume or smoke thereof by sucking it through pipes made of clay into their stomach and head from whence it purges superfluous phlegm and other gross humors, opens all the pores and passages of the body, by which means the use thereof, not only preserves the body from obstructions but also if any be, so that they have not been of too long continuance, in short time breaks them up, whereby their bodies are notably preserved

in health and know not many grievous diseases with which we in England are oftentimes afflicted. The Vppówoc is of so precious estimation amongst them that they think their gods are marvelously delighted therewith. Whereupon sometimes they make hallowed fires and cast some of the powder therein for a sacrifice. Being in a storm upon the waters, to pacify their gods, they cast some up into the air and into the water. So a weir for fish being newly set up, they cast some therein and into the air. Also after an escape from danger, they cast some into the air likewise, but all done with strange gestures, stamping, sometimes dancing, clapping of hands, holding up of hands, and staring up into the heavens, chattering strange words and noises. (Shirley 1981)

Harriot also learned about Indigenous spiritual beliefs. He says they worshipped many gods but only one great god who has been from all eternity and who had made the others to assist in creating and maintaining the world. The sun, moon, and stars were lesser gods that served the higher order. Harriot must have recognized the resemblance to Platonism. The Indigenous genesis, like ancient Egyptian and biblical creation stories, began with the waters out of which the gods made the world, but the first human being was a woman. They had no idea how long ago this had been. They kept only oral traditions. Harriot reports that they believed in the immortality of the soul. When they died, good people went to live with the gods in eternal bliss, while those who lived badly would burn forever in an enormous pit where the sun set. However, these testimonies are suspect. Harriot wanted to present the tribes as ready for their Protestant makeovers so he exaggerated resemblances to European beliefs. The tribes had probably already heard some Christian doctrine from the European fishermen with whom, as noted, they had interacted for generations. They may have been telling Harriot what he wanted to hear.

The tribes carved and painted black and white four-foot-tall idols with human forms kept in crude temples. Prayer, worship, singing, and offerings were centered around these figures. Their great chiefs were mummified and kept in a temple guarded by a life-size carving of a god. Harriot makes the point that only the most ignorant among the members of a tribe believed that the carvings themselves were the actual gods. Most understood them to be symbols. Their great chiefs were mummified and kept in a temple guarded by a life-size carving of a god.

Harriot also described the activities of what he called conjurors but we would call shamans. They stared up at the heavens in trance. They danced wildly and uttered mysterious declarations. Their strange gestures, herbal concoctions, and rituals were not only used for healing but for remotely viewing the activities of prey and of the enemy. Harriot added that these predictions "often times they find to be true." In one of his less rational moments, or perhaps in an effort to appease public opinion back home, Harriot credited their success to the devil. His descriptions of the activities of these shamans must have reminded some among the English of their own cunning men and women, who were consulted for similar reasons and who used several comparable techniques. In both cultures witchcraft and eclipses were fearsome threats.

Modern studies of Algonquin religious beliefs reveal some similarities to Harriot's descriptions, but some crucial differences. The great god of goodness was not the creator of the other gods. The god who presided over the winter, over the dark, over the pit of suffering was also the patron of the shamans. After all, when suffering was inflicted by a divine being, one had to learn a way around it, a way to appease, one had to acquire the knowledge that could heal and restore order. As mentioned earlier, every morning Algonquin mothers would ask their children if they had dreamed. Not all dreams were important. But certain dreams contained vivid messages. Dreams could reveal ways to heal sickness. They could tell where prey, or the enemy, could be found. They could teach a hunter a new technique. And by paying close attention to dreams, by taking them seriously, the Algonquins believed the quality of the messages would improve, providing guidance through communication with a greater consciousness.

But Harriot was not content with learning the spiritual beliefs of the tribes. He wanted to share his own. As for the Bible, the Indigenous people were "glad to touch it, to hold it to their breasts and heads, and stroke over all their body with it to show their hungry desire of that knowledge." He read to them from it and translated passages into Algonquin. The tribe added the God of the Book to their pantheon but showed no signs of embracing monotheism.

Wingina must have been pleased when the English colonists burned a rival tribe's crops and village after the failure of a local chief to return a stolen silver cup. But then a terrible drought killed many crops, and the diseases brought by the Europeans began to take their toll. Indigenous people sickened and died, but the English remained healthy. Some tribes thought that the English controlled the disease, which they described as invisible bullets, a secret weapon supplied by the English god. When their shamans could not stop the spreading epidemic, some Roanokes, including Wingina, adopted English rituals. They prayed with the English, they sang their psalms, worshipping their god, but to no avail. English *montoac* was not only marvelous but malevolent. Many began to believe that Harriot and the others had been sent to exterminate the tribes, and that more whites would follow to take their lands. Their arrival had roughly coincided with eclipses and a comet. For the tribes these were omens of doom. As an astrologer Harriot concurred, venturing that Providence had made the tribes sicken and die for the benefit of the Christian colonists, who would thereby suffer less opposition. As Harriot wrote, "There could at no time happen any strange sickness, losses, hurts, or any other cross unto them, but that they would impute to us the cause or means thereof for offending or not pleasing us."

Wingina abandoned Roanoke Island, moving his people away. He changed his name to Pemisapan. Sir Ralph Lane was told by enemies of the Roanoke that Pemisapan was planning an attack to destroy the English settlement. Lane was convinced by what was probably a ruse. He called for a parlay with Pemisapan. As they talked peace Lane suddenly ordered an attack. The chief was beheaded. Less than two weeks later, the colony abandoned Roanoke Island, fleeing a powerful storm and amid fears of tribal reprisals. No gold had been found, and there were rumors that the Spanish were on their way to take what they claimed was theirs. In the rush to leave, many of Harriot's specimens were lost at sea, including a necklace intended for Queen Elizabeth, selected from

5,000 pearls, about which Harriot wrote, "the likeness and uniformity in roundness . . . and many excellent colors . . . were very fair and rare." Most of his notes were dropped into the ocean, a priceless record was lost there as the ink bled away in the salt water.

This murder of a chief doomed Raleigh's Roanoke venture. Grenville and company, including Harriot, returned to England leaving only a small group to hold the colony. Wanchese, whose suspicions about the English had proven true, led a raid by his followers wiping out the remaining English in the summer of 1586. John White was declared governor and returned with a larger party of colonists in 1587. They had been there only briefly when White found one of his lieutenants dead, arrows stuck all over his body like quills on a porcupine, his head bashed in. When White called for a peaceful meeting, only members of the tribe maimed in the attack on Pemisapan's camp showed up to remind him of English brutality. White retaliated for the killing of his lieutenant, but he stupidly killed the only Indigenous people still willing to speak with him—Manteo's kinsmen of the Croatoan tribe.

Harriot published his *Briefe and True Report of the New Found Land of Virginia* in 1588, the year the Spanish armada threatened to conquer England. Raleigh was busy leading the British Navy. Only seven copies of the book are known to have survived. It reads like a business plan for prospective investors, an executive summary for potential timeshare owners, but also a legal brief in defense of Raleigh's plans for colonization. Other reports had described the terrible dangers of the New World, the scarcity of food, and the hostility of the tribes. Harriot dismissed these as the complaints of travelers too accustomed to soft English beds. He did not tell how the colonists had to rely on the tribes to avoid starvation in the winter, robbing them of their own meager stores of corn. He downplayed the incidents of poisonous water and food he observed. He mentioned that the violence he witnessed may have been too fierce, but dismissed it as overeagerness caused by the English desire to instill fear and obedience so that future colonists might have an easier time civilizing the uncivilized tribes.

The Spanish since at least 1505 had been publishing sensationalized accounts of cannibalism among the tribes of South America to legitimize their own brutality with lurid stories of naked Indigenous women waylaying explorers only to hit them from behind to carve them up for a feast. Harriot portrayed Indigenous people as sober in drink and diet, intelligent within the limits of their primitive technology. He praised their farming methods for preserving the fertility of the soil and increasing its productivity. He pointed out that the chiefs punished theft, adultery, and other misbehavior with beatings or death depending on the severity of the crime. He suggested they would probably welcome the friendship of the English, and he expected they would embrace the true Protestant religion.

Part 1 of *Briefe and True Report* cataloged profitable products. It began with silk (from grass and worms), hemp, and grapes as wines. He listed sixty plants native to the region or sown by the colonists, nearly forty animals, and a dozen minerals. Two dozen plants were identified only by their Indigenous names because they were entirely unfamiliar. Milkweed was given as the antidote for poisoned arrows.

Harriot was only interested in edible animals. "We have taken and eaten" was a common refrain applied to porpoises, squirrels, swans, turtles (sea and land), oysters, crabs, lobsters, jellyfish, herring, sturgeon, trout, mussels, scallops, partridges, passenger pigeons, cranes, geese, rabbits, muskrats, bears, wolves, deer, and wild turkeys so docile the English could shoot one and the others would not fright. Eight waterfowl unknown to Europeans were mentioned, and seventeen unknown land fowl. It's a bit comical yet disturbingly tragic to read his descriptions of every manner of fish, animals, and birds. He never describes them in any detail. He only pauses to note whether they made for good eating or not. Harriot listed varieties of trees and the commercial uses of them. Now that the vast wealth of species and the great forests are long gone, it's hard to miss the irony that the first European to write a book about them viewed the lush splendor of the New World as nothing more than a massive product aisle.

Raleigh's colony would soon disappear completely. In 1587 Governor John White had left among others, his own granddaughter Virginia Dare, the first English European born in America, while he returned to England for supplies. The war with Spain delayed his return until 1590. He found only empty buildings and no signs of fire or battle. The only clues left behind were the mysterious Roanoke carvings. "Croatoan" carved on a post of the fort and "Cro" carved on a tree. Historians speculate that the survivors may have been absorbed by the Croatoan tribe, but suspect they were killed off by diseases and attacks. Recently an author claimed to have found ruins that may have been left by these survivors of Raleigh's ill-fated colony.

In 1590 Harriot back home in England was lending books to the notorious English magus John Dee. By then Harriot was voraciously reading his way through the three finest libraries in England, those of John Dee, Sir Walter Raleigh, and Raleigh's friend Henry Percy, 9th Earl of Northumberland, known as the Wizard Earl. The earl owned many alchemical manuscripts and books. He had the largest collection in England of the books of Giordano Bruno, who was arguing for a great restoration of knowledge through the blending of Neoplatonic paganism, scientific inquiry, and Christian tradition.

Professor Frances Yates put Harriot at the center of a Pythagorean Hermetic circle some believe Shakespeare referred to as "The School of Night" in his play *Love's Labor's Lost,* where the bard lampoons Raleigh's poetry. Modern scholars suspect Yates was seeing Rosicrucians where there were only Protestants. Harriot appears to have been a basically sound and god-fearing Englishman. He showed no enthusiasm for grand projects of reform, preferring to pursue his own interests and the interests of his patrons.

Raleigh was a hero to the British people after the defeat of the Spanish armada. The queen was not the only one at court who became jealous of his popularity. Her favor to him sharply diminished. Then, in 1592, Raleigh had an affair with Elizabeth Throckmorton, one of the queen's ladies-in-waiting, who became pregnant. They wed in secret. The queen was furious at this impertinence. She had Raleigh called back from his exploration of Panama and upon his return she locked up Sir Walter and his wife in the Tower of London. Raleigh was released only a month later, but Lady Raleigh was left there to taste the harsh cold of December before her release. Husband and wife were devoted to each other.

With Raleigh in the Tower, the Wizard Earl took over as Harriot's patron. The earl was a friend of John Dee, with whom he shared a keen interest in astrology, the occult, and book collecting. But the earl was a wizard by reputation only. Like Dee himself he had discretely gone to the continent to sample Catholic sacraments, and it was no secret that he sympathized with the pope. Because he was born hard of hearing, and with a slight speech impediment, he was not comfortable at the royal court, so he moved Harriot to his country estate, Syon House.

Raleigh had kept Harriot busy with practical matters but the earl allowed him to follow his most esoteric scientific pursuits, treating him like a member of the family, often engaging in deep conversations over dinner, and sometimes joining him in alchemical and other experiments. Harriot designed improvements for the earl's plumbing and while doing so developed mathematical formulas for the velocity and volume of water. His studies of the parabola not only related to projectile weapons, he was interested in creating a parabolic burning mirror. Harriot was one of only two people to see Chapman's *The Iliad,* the first complete English translation of Homer, eighteen years before it was published. One can only imagine the horror Harriot and the earl felt when their idyllic intellectual life was disturbed in 1600 by the news that Giordano Bruno had been burned at the stake as a dangerous heretic.

When the queen died in 1603 Raleigh's fortunes fell further. He was arrested that year. Accused of plotting against the new king he was quickly sentenced to death and suffered a mock execution; or a true execution was halted at the last possible moment. Many plots were hatched against King James, from both Catholic and Protestant extremists.

Raleigh was involved in a scheme to place an English Stuart on the throne, the new king's cousin, Lady Arbella. But Arbella would not allow the kidnapping and killing of not only James but also the royal children. It didn't help Raleigh's case that he was the brightest star in the legend of Queen Elizabeth I's court, and perhaps the most hated Englishman among the Spanish whom James eagerly desired to placate. Fortunately, Sir Henry Percy the 9th Earl of Northumberland had signed the document legitimizing James as king. He rode at the king's right hand when James arrived to take his throne. For the moment Harriot was safe.

Sir Walter Raleigh was accused of running a "School of Atheism" where hell and godhead were laughed at. Harriot's name came up repeatedly in the accusations, first printed in polemic Catholic books, then in evidence given in court cases like that against English dramatist and poet Christopher Marlowe, thought to be a member of the School of Night. Dinner conversations, rumors, and hearsay were the insubstantial substance of most of the accusations against Raleigh. He and friends were said to have believed the tribes of the new world had artifacts and oral history proving the world was older than Adam. Harriot was accused of denying the resurrection of the body, and eternal reward and eternal punishment. Raleigh was said to have dismissed Moses as a "juggler" and to have declared that Harriot could do better. Another member of Raleigh's circle was accused of tearing out pages of the Bible to use for drying tobacco. Harriot's own book was used against him. If the tribes thought Harriot and the other strangers from across the ocean gods, then perhaps Harriot had deliberately misled them.

Harriot was accused of being worse than an atheist. He was accused of devil worship. Didn't he create the Devil's Alphabet? He was reading books on astrology (but also books against astrology). He was reading the pagan hymns of the Neoplatonic emperor Julian, who had hoped to suppress Christianity and restore paganism, whose description of the sun as literally a god must have reminded Harriot of the gods of the Carolina Algonquins. But he was also reading the Catholic fathers. He wrote about the power of the atom, at the time a theory considered atheism. But was he an atheist?

One of the accusations against Harriot was that he denied the biblical creation myth. His notes made plain his preoccupation with the idea that nothing comes out of nothing, that things are not nothing, and therefore how could they have been created by nothing. Harriot was accused of arguing that atoms are infinite, that the creation has always existed and did not suddenly appear a few thousand years ago. But later, partially influenced by his reading of the great Neoplatonist Proclus, Harriot questioned whether *less* or *more* are terms that can be applied to the infinite. Contemplating the indivisible, he wondered whether "all things are made of nothing" and "out of nothing nothing is made" are really contradictions after all. Here he came close to the metaphysics of Hinduism and Buddhism where true reality is nothing to our deluded senses and what we consider reality is nothing but maya or illusion.

In a Sotheby's catalog of 1986 appeared a manuscript dated 1594 purporting to be notes from discussions with Thomas Harriot on theological subjects. If this was indeed Harriot's conversation, he questioned why an all-powerful god would create a war between good and bad angels, and why he would create such an imperfect world and inflict eternal doom on his own ignorant creations. He doubted the miracles of the Bible since no one bears witness to them but the writers of the Bible themselves, and none have occurred in recent history. He wondered why God would allow the Turks to flourish while Christians suffered plague every summer. Since this was the period of Harriot's friendship with Dee, it's tempting to think these are truly notes of a conversation between them. The manuscript included questions about how angels and spirits could see and hear when they lacked the organs for doing so. How could human and angelic intelligences resemble each other? How could one angelic intelligence be evil and another good, on what basis could such assumptions be made? He decided human beings must be incapable of knowing anything about such beings since we can have no experience of them given our limited senses.

When King James anonymously published a book in 1604 that everyone knew he wrote attacking the now widespread use of tobacco, he included a veiled swipe at Raleigh and Harriot for introducing it to English society. The monarch complained about secondhand smoke, he called it passive smoke and warned of dangers to the lungs, calling the odor hateful to the nose. Harriot must have been mortified to be singled out. He was still a heavy smoker, as was Raleigh, who used a long silver pipe in the Tower to help him pass the time.

At first the threats against Harriot were mere gossip. But then in 1605 the earl and Harriot had a guest for dinner: Thomas Percy, a distant relative of the earl. That night, November 4, a rider appeared for a secret meeting with Thomas Percy in the earl's garden; his name was Guy Fawkes. The very next day Fawkes would be arrested strolling out of his hiding place where the explosives he set were ready to blow Parliament and King James sky high. The movie inspired by the ill-fated plot gave the symbol of a Guy Fawkes mask to the Anonymous movement four centuries later; an ironic twist since "Guido" as he liked to be called was trying to give England back to that ultimate authoritarian, the pope. But the immediate aftermath for Harriot and the earl was imprisonment. Most likely they had nothing to do with the plot but the visit from Guy Fawkes was just too suspicious for King James. After all, the Wizard Earl's father and uncle, the two prior earls, had been implicated in plots against their monarchs.

James became frightened that Harriot may have cast his horoscope and the horoscopes of his children. Apparently, for James, a horoscope wasn't only evidence that the earl and Harriot had tried to foretell the end of his reign. The act of casting a horoscope took on the quality of black magic, not just peering into forbidden secrets, but somehow binding the monarch and his family to a particular strand of fate. We still have the list of the king's questions about Harriot's horoscopes, and we still have a letter of true pathos from poor Harriot who spent several weeks in a less pleasant jail than his patrons, and who grew deathly ill there. He wanted to be allowed to quietly pursue his studies; he promised to continue praying every day for the health and glory of King James and the royal family. Soon after, he was released, possibly because Sir Francis Bacon was seeking scholars for his "renewal of the sciences."

The earl adjusted to life in the Tower, where Harriot became known as one of the Wizard Earl's "three magi." Harriot was given a house connected to the Tower. Not only did the earl enjoy tobacco and scientific discussions with Raleigh, Harriot, and other friends, he also took over all of Martin Tower and had an outdoor bowling alley with a roof built. Together they all conducted alchemical experiments. But the privileges the earl and Raleigh enjoyed were a ploy intended to get their confessions. When the ruse failed the privileges were removed one by one.

Harriot created comparative tables of Bible translations for Raleigh, to be used in his defense as his case slowly worked its way through the English courts. Raleigh worked on his *History of the World,* focusing on what makes kings good or bad. Later King James would try to suppress the book he condemned as "saucy," but Raleigh was too smart for him, releasing it anonymously through several publishers directly to the people. Harriot contributed to the sections on geography and chronology of the development of mathematics, but by then he was deeply involved in his experiments in refraction that helped explain rainbows. His theory drew the attention of Kepler who corresponded with him for several years starting in 1606. When Kepler wrote Harriot about the refraction of light and his doubts about the theory of atoms, because of his belief that some mysterious power, perhaps soul, infuses all matter, Harriot invited Kepler to ponder the interior of the atom where mass and motion, soul and energy, unveil an infinity not of boundless cosmos, but an interior infinity.

Kepler and Halley's comet in 1607 turned Harriot's attention to astronomy. In 1609 he bought his first telescope, an invention only a year old. He drew a map of the moon the summer of 1609, months before Galileo did the same, and in winter 1610 he diagrammed sunspot patterns. He and Galileo were the first human beings to see the moons of Jupiter. Harriot was somehow restored to favor at court and he became one of the principal tutors of Prince Henry, the darling of those who longed for the glories of the golden age of Queen Elizabeth. His little sister who shared Elizabeth's name was considered her potential second coming. About Sir Walter Raleigh locked up in the Tower, Prince Henry famously observed, "Only my father could keep such a bird in a cage." Prince Henry died in 1612 at the age of eighteen. Raleigh, Harriot, and Shakespeare found common ground in their grief.

Three years later in 1615 Harriot noticed a small red speck on his nose. At first he didn't trouble about it, but it concerned him as it slowly grew. He continued visiting Raleigh and the earl, sharing his research with them and helping Raleigh develop his plans for regaining his freedom. Somehow in 1617 Raleigh convinced the cash-strapped king to let him go back to Guyana for another crack at discovering El Dorado. After twenty years absence, Raleigh found that the memory of him among the tribes was so positive they wanted to make him their king. But the City of Gold was never found, and the expedition was considered a failure. Worse, he could not resist attacking Spanish ships on his way home. Upon his return to England he was sent back to the Tower, and his death sentence was reaffirmed.

In October 1618 Raleigh was beheaded. When he saw the ax that would behead him, Raleigh commented, "This is a sharp medicine, but it is a physician for all diseases and miseries." Thomas Harriot was there to watch his old patron die. He took cryptic notes on a slip of paper, which has survived. Since Harriot wore black all his life, Raleigh left him his own black finery. Raleigh's head was mummified and Lady Raleigh carried it with her for the rest of her life, not so different after all from the Algonquins and their temple of mummified chiefs.

By then the speck on Harriot's nose had become a serious and painful condition. Still supported by the imprisoned earl, Harriot augmented his income by constructing and selling telescopes. His doctor had been part of a circle studying Hermetic philosophy in Paris, a student of the doctrines of Paracelsus, who became the most renowned physician in England and Europe, and doctor to two kings of England, but he could not heal Harriot's affliction. As he grew more ill and death approached, Harriot read ravenously books of theology modern and ancient, including Libanius's defense of the emperor Julian, and St. Augustine's refutation of Julian's arguments against Christianity. He read the works of Rosicrucian apologists and critics, and the latest scientific volumes. His friends urged him to publish so his discoveries would not be forgotten or claimed by others. But Harriot had suffered too much persecution.

Only one reference to any family associated with Harriot remains, in a list of accounts associated with the expenses of the earl, but historians believe this may have been a convenient reference to Harriot's servants and assistants since no record remains of his ever having had a wife or children.

July 18, 1621, after sixteen years in the Tower, the Wizard Earl was at last released. He had grown so comfortable there they had a hard time dislodging him. Harriot had died sixteen days earlier in London. His patron's final gift was a plaque honoring his excellence in mathematics, philosophy, and theology. His grave is forgotten ground somewhere underneath the Bank of England.

Harriot was considered the most demonic of Raleigh's circle, but no records remain to confirm his alleged heresies, only hearsay. Hostile gossips accused him of scoffing at the idea that something could come from nothing and pointed at the red speck that grew to kill him as an example that it could, and a sign of divine justice inflicted on a man who was sticking his nose where it didn't belong. Harriot left seven thousand pages of notes as unorganized today as the day he died. His manuscript on algebra, *Artis Analyticae Praxis,* was published in Latin ten years after his death by editors who removed whatever they didn't understand—the best parts.

Harriot's influence was subtle. He inspired the metaphors of astronomy in the plays of Christopher Marlowe, especially *Faustus.* He influenced the theories of Descartes. Dodgson (better known as Lewis Carroll of the *Alice in Wonderland* books) studied Hermeticism and Harriot. Until thirty years ago Harriot was all but forgotten by historians and mathematicians. Since then, scholars have begun to reveal his genius, and that melancholy yet marvelous moment he inhabited, at the end of the Renaissance, at the birth of the modern world, at the beginning of the American experiment.

7

The Pagan Pilgrim

I have found the Massachusetts Indian more full of humanity than the Christians.

THOMAS MORTON

THOMAS MORTON WAS THE FIRST MAN banned in Boston; he was the first American foreclosed on by a company and, as mentioned earlier, he was the first American to publish a fart joke and a dick joke. He was also the first American accused of being a traitor. He's the first bad neighbor throwing a wild party in recorded American history. His name was Thomas Morton, but he would have wanted us to call him Tom.

Twelve-year-old Tom must have been terrified when the Spanish armada cut through the waves nearly in sight of England's shore. Like every other Brit, he knew in their wooden bellies the mighty ships carried the terrors of the Inquisition. But the king of Spain deforested the Spanish countryside for nothing. So was born the delusion of invincibility that built the empire on which the sun never set.

Nothing unusual about Tom as a boy. He was middle gentry so he learned to love the bold comedy of the Athenian playwright Aristophanes and the dry wit of the Roman philosopher Cicero. He learned to hunt when the skills included taming and training hawks and falcons. He learned how to use swords and guns, not to mention wine, women, and song. He studied the law and became a lawyer, moving in circles buzzing with the worldly poetry of John Donne.

Tom attended Queen Elizabeth I's Christmas gala. Torch-lit barges

floated in procession on the Thames. Cavalry exercises dazzled spectators in the streets of London. Dramatic tongue-in-cheek proclamations
included a ban on "windy meats." Blustery declarations affectionately
mocked the mysterious potions of alchemists like the queen's own court
wizard John Dee. Sir Francis Bacon gave a stirring speech. The theatrical performances of dance and poetry featured the earliest contributions
of a couple of young writers about to revolutionize European theater:
Ben Jonson and William Shakespeare. Toward the end, the *Masque of
the God of Healing* offered cures by musical charms for such troubles
as lost virginity and old age. Finally a player named Paradox mocked
ancient Athens, modern religious fanatics, and everything in between.
Then they raised a maypole, even though it was Christmas.

But this was also a London where Tom had to dodge the plague
twice; a London where returning war veterans and the poor massed at
centers of power, making the powerful nervous. England's population
was doubling despite years of disastrous crop failures.

Tom was twenty-seven when good Queen Bess, who had reigned all
his life, at long last died. As Tom turned thirty the country was shocked
by Guy Fawkes and the Gunpowder Plot to blow up Parliament, an
event that eventually spawned the English Civil War. At age thirty Tom
couldn't have imagined the adventures, and the enemies, awaiting him
in far-off lands. This quiet and average fellow would become so notorious he was all but written out of American history.

For years Tom rode his lawyer circuit between Devonshire and
London. Well into middle age he met and married a wealthy widow.
But her eldest son was suspicious of his lawyer stepfather and so, even
though his inheritance was legally protected, he took his mother to
court, selling off many of her possessions to demonstrate his power
over her.

Meanwhile, Tom had been granted part ownership of a land patent
for a planting colony in New England. We don't know why he chose to
abandon his practice and his wife to go to America. From his later writings it seems he hoped at first to make his fortune and return to her.
Certainly his absence would make her life with her son at least more
civil. Tom's stepson was destined to become a Puritan, but Tom had no

idea the generation gap ruining his marriage was a hint of a civil war still twenty years away.

When the first Indigenous people abducted from the New World arrived, one of those who became most excited by the prospects for adventure and profit was Sir Ferdinando Gorges, Military Governor of Plymouth, England, The New World captured Ferdinando's imagination. He understood the business possibilities of a vast land of virgin resources. The massive royal land grant he got in the New World was challenged for decades in English courts as a monopoly.

Ferdinando organized a company and sold shares of land patents, a financial product as fuzzy as a subprime mortgage derivative when it came to nailing down land rights in court. Ferdinando sent over John Smith's and many other expeditions. Among his shareholders was a lawyer he sometimes hired: Thomas Morton. In 1622 Tom visited the New World for three months. He returned complaining about intolerant Puritans, but he was eager to go back. He later wrote a bit of horny poesy worthy of American bards like Whitman and Ginsberg: "License my roving hands and let them go before, behind, between, above, below, O my America . . ."

Ferdinando placed Tom in charge of thirty indentured young men. Tom was a creature of the Renaissance. He would fit in better with the culture of the New World, which he described to Parliament as a lawless place where fur traders, a pack of jokers from all over Europe, were teaching Indigenous peoples to fornicate, get drunk, and swear like pirates. They were also using sly hustles like putting a layer of butter over a pound of salt and selling it as a pound of butter; cheating them instead of offering them true religion and civilization. Perhaps Ferdinando had a sense of humor, since he knew Tom would be a thorn in the side of the Puritans. He sent Tom to America on a ship ironically named *Unity*.

Tom was around forty-eight years old when he arrived in New England in June 1624, over 150 years before the birth of America. How fresh it must have looked and smelled in early summer. The air was famous for its sweet fragrance, unspoiled for thousands of years. Later he would write about the beauty of what he called New Canaan.

When they first arrived in Boston harbor they camped on the beach and ate so much of the easily gathered lobster Tom grew tired of the delicacy. Because the tribes burned the underbrush so they could farm and hunt more easily, the surrounding countryside looked like English parks—long grass meadows framed by mature trees. But the beauty of the place hid an ugly secret. Only ten years before, epidemics brought by the Europeans had spread tribe to tribe across the continent killing millions. Nine out of ten Indigenous people died. Between 1616 and 1619 over 100,000 Indigenous people living in what we now call New England died of plague. The beaches were littered with lobster shells, but the woods were littered with human bones.

Tom was fascinated by the hummingbirds of America and enchanted with all the other natural wonders of his new home, a place he later declared "Nature's Masterpiece." He hiked and explored the beaches, the streams, and the hills, all teeming with life. Most of the hunters and fishermen who had helped keep the ecological balance for thousands of years died in the epidemics, causing a misleading overabundance of flora and fauna.

Tom found the local tribes gentle and considerate. He hoped to bring a better life to them, and he would certainly be more tolerant than the Pilgrims who saw the tribes as devil-possessed, barely human creatures. Tom wanted to understand Indigenous culture. He learned the language and believed that some words had the same pronunciation and meaning as their Greek or Latin equivalents, which led him to suggest that the tribes were descendants of ancient Troy. He insisted he didn't trade them guns and metal knives only for profit; he wanted to help them defend themselves from stronger tribes invading to take their lands. He listened to their gossip and their dreams.

Most English thought it ironic that the tribes lived a life of what Europeans thought was poverty amid the abundance of the New World. But Tom, who could not resist imagining all the ways the abundance could be exploited, nevertheless understood that Indigenous people were not to be dismissed, as John Locke dismissed them, for "wasting" the natural resources of the New World. He understood their contentment living simple lives in harmony with nature. He even wondered if the tribal lifestyle made the European idea of wealth wrong. What good were piles of possessions that required constant protection? The tribes lived without want, in communities of mutual trust. Could that be the true definition of wealth?

Tom's idyllic adventure ended when he caught the captain of the *Unity* selling indentured servants into slavery on the colonial plantations, where life was short and brutal and many died their first year. Tom couldn't stop the captain, so with plain talk over ale he sparked a rebellion. The captain and his thugs fled, and America's first utopia was born. Tom declared everyone free. Tom was commander but he insisted everyone call him "mine Host," after Falstaff, Shakespeare's jovial free spirit with a frank sense of humor about life, whose cowardice and hospitality were equally self-serving.

Tom named his new free community Ma-re Mount (pronounced Merry Mount), inspired by the Indigenous name for the area. He was happily aware of all the puns, and in several languages, for example, Latin slang for an erection. Tom's business quickly flourished. Unlike the Pilgrims he was willing to trade guns, and once you had a Ma-re Mount gun you had to come back to Ma-re Mount for powder and bullets. Tom also showed his customers how to maintain and repair their guns, right down to pouring and casting iron replacement screws. Soon the best furs were saved for Ma-re Mount. Not only did the Pilgrims think this an unfair and illegal business advantage, they also considered it treachery since those guns would likely end up being used against them.

Tom adopted aspects of local Indigenous culture. He intended to convert them, but he thought a better way than bullets was giving them salt so they could preserve meat and give up their nomadic lifestyle of hunting. He hoped his experiment in freedom would grow to include all the locals, Indigenous and European, everyone was invited. Anyone, Indigenous or colonist, who joined him Tom called partner. Jamestown, that cannibal village, had required a stockade with cannon and formidable walls. But Ma-re Mount didn't even need a fence.

Tom tried to be a good neighbor to the suspicious Pilgrims. He showed them a way to improve the construction of their houses so their mud huts wouldn't fall apart every year. They spurned his advice. He wasn't one of them. He was condemned as nothing more than an opportunist, his morals corrupted by alcohol and the pagan myths of classical literature he so relished. To the Puritans he was a relic of the rogue generation of their fathers, the royalists.

The royalists or Cavaliers, wore their hair long. They sported dashing beards and mustaches. Their costumes were lavish and romantic. Large codpieces were the fashion equivalent of the tight pants and bulge brigades of 1970s rock. The royalists were unrepentant drunks and fornicators, but they were also students of philosophy, inspired by all cultures of history, not only Christian. Their experiments in alchemy and astrology evolved into modern chemistry and astronomy.

Their opposition, the Puritans, were a younger generation rebelling in every way against their fathers, whom they considered irresponsible, reprehensible, and downright pagan. The Puritans were sober. They forbade dancing. Laughter was not allowed. And they couldn't run or walk too fast, only proceed at a measured pace.

In May 1627 Tom decided to celebrate May Day with the locals. There would be food, drink, a maypole, music, dancing, and hopefully wenching; everyone was invited including Indigenous men and women, a guest list that scandalized the Pilgrims.

Imagine a round green hill that overlooked the Atlantic Ocean. Red gooseberry flowers and white dogwood blossoms decorated the forest bright under the May sun. Indigenous people and Europeans alike helped prepare and raise the maypole. Stripped of bark, the eighty-foot-tall yellow pine practically glowed, decorated with multicolored ribbons flowing in the breeze. A noble set of antlers crowned the top. They served beer they had brewed from their own hops, and they marched with guns and drums in a parade that faintly echoed the cavalry procession at Queen Elizabeth's Christmas gala that Tom had seen as a child so long ago.

Tom and his men composed *The Poem*. Not quite a manifesto, he read it aloud then nailed it to the maypole. Tom must have had to explain the ancient Greek myths he referenced. The widow he loved and left back home in England must still have been on his mind, as were Indigenous widows, who were often seen weeping over the graves of their lost loved ones.

When Tom begins *The Poem* by calling on Oedipus, he's asking the famous solver of the riddle of the Sphinx to solve Tom's riddle. But Tom also knew that Oedipus had cured the plague that was destroying ancient Thebes, so *The Poem* was asking for a healing of the plague-devastated New World.

In *The Poem* America is a widow weeping among graves. But the ancient gods take pity and send a lover strong as the biblical Samson, the European colonists. In the style of Merrie Olde England, it reminds listeners that life is short, so appreciate it while you can. It concludes with a tradition demanded by the Goddess of Love:

> *With proclamation that the first of May*
> *At Ma-re Mount shall be kept hollyday.*

The Poem is a riddle, but it's also a declaration; it's an origin story for the community, but also a prayer and a healing. And since in his explanation Tom mentions Scogan, one of the most famous fools of England, it's also a jest. But *The Poem* is also a justification for invasion. The bereft widow of a fallen culture needed the strong new man divinely sent from across the sea. The maypole wasn't only a billboard for Ma-re Mount, it was a phallic symbol. Tom wasn't a hero for the Indigenous, he was just a friendlier enemy.

Then they sang "The Song," no doubt mostly composed by Tom. They sang in chorus, dancing hand-in-hand around the maypole. "The Song," a celebration of marriage, and of the tonic joys of liquor, concluded by declaring Indigenous lasses welcome day or night. With its drink-and-be-merry lyrics "The Song" would fit right into any Renaissance Faire musical troupe's May Day repertoire.

Everyone shared what they brought to the feast: venison, sturgeon, clams, oysters, lobsters, chestnuts, honey, English biscuits, and Indigenous corn cakes, not to mention wines and brandies. Indigenous people from tribes all over the New England area attended, along with fishermen, trappers, and entrepreneurial sailors. A young servant who became pregnant by her married master in Plymouth ran off with him, but he abandoned her. She came to Ma-re Mount for May Day.

Tom admitted dangerous people attended: pirates, swindlers, outlaws, renegade Indigenous warriors, but they respected him. Tom must have cut a striking figure presiding over Ma-re Mount, on his arm a male falcon it had taken him only two weeks to train. Among all his other firsts, Tom was America's first falconer. He referred to himself using the Algonquin word for chief: *sachem*. Tom Morton at age fifty seemed to have found something greater than the wealth he sought in the New World: a community that looked up to him.

The party lasted for days. Music, dancing, singing! You could hook up, trade, fall in love, run away from an unjust fate, reinvent yourself. You could cross cultural and racial boundaries in ways unimaginable in Plymouth or Salem. Like an early rock concert where race, class and other categories used to separate people dissolved, May Day at Ma-re Mount was the American melting pot boiling hot.

The Pilgrims understood if they didn't do something they'd lose all their servants and allies. Who wanted to hang out in dismal Plymouth? How are you going to keep 'em down on the farm after they've seen Ma-re Mount? Still, the maypole of the familiar woods of England must have inspired a very different feeling from this ominous maypole at the edge of endless and hostile wilderness. An entire wild continent surrounded them but there was not room in the New World for both Plymouth and Ma-re Mount.

In Plymouth, the Pilgrims commented on the kindness of the tribes, but they were terrified of them. The Puritans weren't above using fear of the plague to frighten their Indigenous allies, claiming they could free it from a hiding place where they had put it in the ground (actually their gunpowder stash). They were fighting Satan in the New World. They understood Ma-re Mount was calculated to draw in every freewheeling trader in the territory so they maneuvered for power with the authorities by insisting they represented maximum profit and family values. Ma-re Mount was supposed to have been a law-abiding, self-sufficient plantation but was no more than a pirate's cove.

The Pilgrims denounced the maypole as an idol, comparing it to the Old Testament golden calf. They wrote Tom what may be America's first cease and desist letter. They justified themselves by referencing the ban on illegal trades ordered by King James; after all, selling guns to Indigenous people was illegal. Tom's saucy response was that the king was dead and his ban with him. The English had been trading guns with the tribes for over a hundred years. Plymouth decided they would have to use force. Letters were written to people of influence in the New World and old. Meanwhile Myles Standish planned the attack and drilled his Pilgrim soldiers.

The Pilgrims were understandably nervous about the gun trade. Terror was their policy toward the tribes. They relied on the hostilities between tribes, and lived in fear of the kind of unified attack that, as we have seen, finally happened much too late for the Indigenous cause some forty years later when King Philip's War wiped out half the colonial settlements.

In their letters to authorities back home the Pilgrims created the impression that an army of Indigenous warriors had guns and swords. But the written records by travelers at the time describe tribes who used bows and arrows—a hundred warriors fleeing from a few guns. The Pilgrims accused Tom of providing sixty guns to three different tribes, two of them enemies of Plymouth. The actual number of guns he traded may have been much smaller.

To the Pilgrims Ma-re Mount was "a school of atheism and licentiousness." Tom thought the community, *The Poem,* and "The Song," celebrations of education. Before any Puritan, Tom was the first to convince an Indigenous father to allow his son to be raised by a colonial family, so the boy would be fluent in English and so could read the Bible. He commented that the Pilgrims said uncivilized things about the great universities like Cambridge and Oxford back home in England. To Tom the Pilgrims were low class, "clumsy, anti-intellectual and busily self-righteous, anxious to display bogus purity by bursts of oppression," in John McWilliams (2004) succinct prose.

For all the lasciviousness of Ma-re Mount imagined by the Puritans the truth is probably closer to Tom's own account. Innocent dancing and frolic perhaps but, as Tom later wrote, the Indigenous women were extremely modest. Did the colonists and Indigenous girls get drunk and celebrate May Day fornicating on the grass? Not likely. No doubt some Indigenous women, after the loss of their families and most of their tribe and way of life, turned to the colonists for a future. But intermarriage between Europeans and Indigenous women had occurred for generations before Tom arrived.

Tom and his seven traders were hardly an immediate threat to the Plymouth colony, but the proclamation of Aphrodite to celebrate May Day was broken the very next year. Apparently Tom thought the Pilgrims were riled up enough. It made no difference. The company the Pilgrims worked for claimed legal ownership of Ma-re Mount. Even the English courts were unsure who owned what thanks to years of contradictory royal edicts, Parliamentary procedures, and court judgments.

In June Myles Standish arrested Tom, who probably didn't shirk from using his nickname for Standish to his face: Captain Shrimp. According to Tom, the Pilgrims ambushed him away from Ma-re Mount, but he escaped their cabin, slamming the door contemptuously on his way out. Lightning lit the wetlands as Tom fled home through a storm. He reports that he felt confident out there, like he was part of the wilderness, unlike the inept Pilgrims who wouldn't dare follow him into the elements.

They didn't have to, instead when the storm ended the Pilgrims marched straight to Ma-re Mount, where they said Tom and his assistants had been drinking to steel their confidence and were so drunk their attack was easily foiled. Tom's version is a little different.

When Captain Shrimp arrived, the certainty of bloodshed convinced Tom to negotiate. He would surrender his arms and go with them if they promised not to harm him, or the people or property of Ma-re Mount. The Pilgrims agreed. But, as Tom pointed out, they believed their promise to a sinner meant nothing, so as soon as he opened the door they attacked him. He describes their ferocious violence by comparing them to hungry cannibals. He says only the presence of an old war veteran saved him from being hacked up then and there. The old soldier, horrified by their violence, stopped the frenzied Pilgrims.

When Tom faced judgment by the assembled Puritans, he said Standish was enraged and wanted him dead. But cooler heads prevailed. Tom was too well connected back home. They'd send him to face a trial in London. That would give them plenty of time to deal with Ma-re Mount. After Tom's arrest some of those who lived at Ma-re Mount had sudden religious conversions to the Puritan way. One of Tom's own assistants fell to his knees in front of the Pilgrims and addressed them as if they were holy messengers. This proved to be a good career move. He went on to become a Puritan general and eventually mayor of Boston.

No ships were due to stop at Plymouth that summer so they marooned Tom on New Hampshire's Isles of Shoals from June to September, a place barren as a desert. They sent him a change of clothes, some raisins, sugar, and wine, perhaps so they could claim they provided for him. Tom says the local tribes helped him survive by bringing him supplies, but they did not help him escape. They understood the gravity of the conflict between Ma-re Mount and Plymouth.

While Tom was headed back to England, a Puritan captain named Endicott was on his way to the New World. Endicott didn't wait for his official authority to kick in on May 17. Though there had been no more May Day celebrations, Endicott cut down the maypole and he warned the remaining residents of Ma-re Mount to repent.

Tom reached England before winter. He says the scheming men of London were ready to use poison or false affidavits to defeat him but Tom was much more a threat where he could use his legal skills and royalist connections. Not only did his case never reach trial, the Pilgrims were told to lay off.

By spring 1629 Tom was back in America. But things had changed. The Pilgrims had rechristened Ma-re Mount with the ominous name Mt. Dagon, after the god of the Philistines. Farms had gone to seed, abandoned by colonists who died or went home. The Puritans had bought off Tom's allies with big orders of goods they paid for in cash.

That autumn the Pilgrims summoned their allies and remaining rivals to Salem to sign paperwork granting them a monopoly. Only Tom refused to sign what he called a mousetrap. The Pilgrims complained that the new recruits from England were lazy, they relied too much on servants, and they hadn't planted enough corn. That winter starvation brought fever to Salem; Endicott's wife was one of those who died.

Endicott led a raid on what was left of Ma-re Mount. Tom hid his guns, his powder, and bullets, but the Pilgrims took all his corn. He said he didn't mind. Turning to hunting, he commented in writing on the irony that the Pilgrims starved while the woods around them offered abundant food. When he became their prisoner again, they made him hunt food for them, but they still allowed their poorest to starve, Tom says, though he was more than willing to hunt for them all.

In 1630, with Tom's royalist connections back in England breathing down their necks, the Puritans offered to make a secret deal with Tom so they wouldn't have to undermine their aura of infallibility by the embarrassing public admission they had falsely arrested and imprisoned him. They would let him go but he must keep silent so as not to undermine their authority with "the vulgar people," as they called everyone but themselves.

Parliament was beginning to swing over to the Puritan side as the English Civil War inched nearer. The gun trade was too risky now. Tom would never lead a community again, the most he could do was advise some friends, since he understood the tribes and terrain as well as or better than any other white man.

But later that same year Tom stood somewhere in the Blue Hills watching the Massachusetts Bay Company ships arrive. Governor Winthrop and seven hundred Puritans, with more to follow. The Great Migration of Puritans to America would continue for ten more years. Winthrop had a plan to purify the colonies, to make a holy land.

John Winthrop, author of *A Model of Christian Charity,* twelve years younger than Tom, brought a new legal justification for taking Indigenous lands. So-called natural rights were superseded by the rights of the civilized, and the measure of civilization was cattle breeding. Winthrop unknowingly harkened all the way back to the original Indo-Aryan invasion.

The Indo-Aryans also considered cattle breeding the measure of civilization. Their greatest compliment for a beautiful woman, or a goddess, was "cow eyes." The Indigenous tribes of India, dark-skinned people, they considered savages without rights. As often happens, a few hundred years later the religion of the conquered became the religion of the conqueror, a fate America may yet experience. Captain John Smith had a simpler criteria: the tribes were uncivilized because they did not enjoy "drudgery." *Carking* was Tom's word for what he also called "anxious toil."

A story is told about Winthrop cowering in a menstrual hut after dark, lost only a mile from his house, bellowing hymns for fear of the wilderness. When an Indigenous woman showed up to use the hut for the purpose for which it was built, he kept her out until she gave up and left, grumbling about the crazy white man. Winthrop wasn't in the New World to revel in the beauties of the wilderness. Behind those Pilgrim eyes were highways and strip malls.

August 23, 1630, Massachusetts Bay's first court took its first action by process. It ordered the arrest of Tom Morton. Winthrop spent the two weeks until Tom's arrival looking for evidence against him but found none. They kept Tom at Salem, forcing him to attend their religious services. Rumors that Tom had been stirring up the tribes against the new colonists could not be substantiated. Accusations that he had cheated the tribes were unsupported by any witness. Lawyer Tom argued they had no jurisdiction over him but they ignored him. They charged him with stealing the canoe he took trying to get away from them. The court ordered Tom jailed and sent back to England for trial for his many crimes against the tribes, none of which could be proven, not even the canoe incident. They ordered all his remaining goods seized by the court to be sold to pay for Tom's time in jail and his trip home, and Ma-re Mount was to be burnt to the ground.

Poor Tom was then locked up in the stocks, freshly carved by a carpenter who had been their first prisoner, punished for charging too much. They shipped Tom back to Ma-re Mount so he could watch them confiscate his tools, powder, even his last saucer, then they burned down his dream. The tribes were summoned with the idea that they would celebrate Tom's punishment, or at least be intimidated by Puritan authority. Instead they berated and laughed at the Pilgrims for burning down shelter just before what they knew would be a very cold winter.

The Pilgrims decided to send Tom back to England on a ship that survived by stopping at ports of call. Between the farthest stops the voyagers would be forced to live on a biscuit and a lime a day during the grueling nine-month journey. Tom refused to go. He knew they were trying to kill him. They had to bundle him up and hoist him like baggage onto the ship. He said by the time he arrived in England he looked like Lazarus.

Back in London, Tom's story helped back up Ferdinando as he tried to convince the authorities that the Puritans were acting like an independent country, not a colony of the crown. Ironically, Ferdinando described the Pilgrims as "too free." They were setting up their own church, their own court. It was in the year 1630 that King Charles I, who had granted the charter for the Great Migration of Pilgrims, and who was known to be more religious than his rake father, nevertheless dissolved Parliament. Puritan writings burned in bonfires. Puritan ministers were whipped in the streets.

The year 1633 was a sinister one. The Inquisition silenced Galileo. The Lancashire witch trials ended with ten of the accused executed by hanging. Smallpox and an outbreak of revenge killings ravaged the colonists and the tribes in the New World. Tom was still in London fighting the Puritans in court. He had another year of legal arguments ahead of him.

Tom celebrated May Day 1634 by writing a gloating letter to an infamous gossip back in the New World. He wrote that a new governor was being sent to right all wrongs. Tom would be at his side upon his arrival. The letter, like *The Poem,* references ancient Greek myths. Tom compares himself to Perseus holding up the head of Medusa, the new edict that would turn the Puritans to stone. He especially relishes the approaching comeuppance of "King Winthrop." The new governor was Ferdinando himself, the ambitious seventy-year-old was mustering troops to enforce the king's justice and was having a magnificent ship built to carry them.

But the governor of Puritan Plymouth arrived in London from the New World to defend Pilgrim interests. He warned that the French and the Dutch could attack at any time and England would lose her colonies.

Tom was rebuked, and Ferdinando with him, for overstating the case against the Puritans. But all that changed quickly when a few questions about religious practices were asked. The governor of Puritan Plymouth found himself sentenced to four months in prison. Tom's case had been proven: America's Puritans were political as well as religious separatists.

When Ferdinando launched his grand ship for the voyage to the New World, the vessel, which had been cheaply and hurriedly built because money was running out, fell apart and promptly sank. As England sank with it into an economic depression, a key partner in Ferdinando's New World venture died. Meanwhile the Puritans were building forts to repel the new order they thought would arrive any day from England. One of the forts melted in the rain; they had again ignored Tom's long forgotten good advice about using lyme in their mixture.

Tom was appointed prosecutor for the New England Council against the Puritans. He argued that the Puritans were religious separatists; their politics would certainly follow their religion. Tom spent years arguing what to him must have seemed his own case. He wrote out long legal documents staking his claim against the Puritans and the company behind them that had closed him down. Somewhere during the process someone told him he should write a book.

Tom must have been a happier man in 1637. The Massachusetts Bay Company's rights were declared void. Tom had reworked his legal briefs into a book he called *New English Canaan*. The Puritans claimed it was all slander and lies, but others familiar with the New World praised its accuracy. In it, Tom even grudgingly admitted that the Pilgrims were such hard workers their future wealth was assured. He was right about that. It was also in 1637 that the Puritans sent out their first slave ship, named *Desire*.

By then the Pequot War was raging as the English and Dutch fought alongside their tribal allies. In May of the same year a village of Indigenous children, women, and old men was attacked and burned by Puritan soldiers whose merciless killing so alienated their tribal allies they left the war and went home. Survivors were sold into slavery. The leader of the Mystic Massacre, as it came to be called, later defended it by describing it as God scornfully laughing at the enemy.

New English Canaan was printed in England but made to look like it was printed in Amsterdam, including carefully placed typos, in the hopes it would protect the author and publisher, and the book itself, from censorship and prosecution for such a frank assessment of the New World debacle.

Tom was the first American to publish a fart joke. In fact, he wrote several that would have made Ben Franklin, author of *Fart Proudly,* quite proud indeed. *New English Canaan* begins with the two words *If art,* which with the ornately capitalized *I* reads "I fart." He also noticed the near interchangeability of the *f* and *s* and the *nc* and *r* in the popular font of the time, and so coined a new word for his description of Puritan sanctity: *fartity.* Aristophanes would have been proud.

The first section of *New English Canaan* is a report on the tribes. Tom goes into detail about how they lived, their clothing, utensils, and habits. He compliments the respect given to elders by the young. He claims the tribes have no religious practice. We know now that tribal medicine men drew power from dreams, visions, and rituals. They had plant and animal spirit helpers and served the tribe with healing and divinatory skills. Tom does tell a story about a medicine man healing an Englishman, but the good results mine Host attributes to conjuring tricks and the devil.

Tom claimed the tribes believed in one god above all others who created a man and woman, and who drowned most of humanity for their wickedness. Later studies of Algonquin beliefs in the area suggest Tom was getting told what he wanted to hear by Indigenous people already familiar with Christian dogma. But modern scholars agree with Tom on *Kytan,* the god who makes plants grow, who makes the world fertile, and who looks after the righteous dead, who are fed without having to hunt or labor, living in an eternity of pleasure. Tom wrote that the two sins most despised among the tribes were lying and stealing. Afterlife for the wicked meant wandering in the Northeast in the constant twilight and freezing cold of endless winter.

In section one Tom also describes the robust health of the Indigenous people, musing that it did not save them from the plague and other epidemics brought by colonists from Europe. He describes their sharp senses. He concludes the first section of *New English*

Canaan with a chapter about how content the tribes were as they had little desire for possessions, and for the most part shared and enjoyed the wealth of nature. He described their pleasure at drinking from their cupped hands water bubbling up from natural crystal springs.

In the second section of *New English Canaan* Tom rhymed a long list of all the possible products America had to offer. Every description of vegetation or animal is followed with a sentence about its usefulness and potential for profit. It's not quite as disturbing a shopping list as Thomas Harriot's fifty years earlier.

It's hard to read these lists that describe in detail the flora and fauna we have lost: spruce trees twenty feet around, a mile-long oyster bank, and the seasonal flock of a million passenger pigeons. Tom describes a variety of local waters. One induces sleep, or among the tribes, visionary states. Another, near Ma-re Mount, he recommends for curing melancholy.

In the third section of *New English Canaan* Tom told stories about Puritan violence and unfairness to the Indigenous people. "You may easily perceive," he wrote, "that the uncivilized people are more just than the civilized." Then Tom told the story of the maypole and what he suffered because of it. He referred to himself as "a great monster supposed to be at Ma-re Mount."

In *New English Canaan* Tom admitted that rum, or Kill-Devil as it was known, caused numerous deaths among the tribes, from old women who drank too much at one sitting and expired on the spot, to the warrior Tom described accidentally shooting himself in the chest. Tom confessed he sold alcohol to them, he said because he would have had no trade with them otherwise.

Tom studs his writing with references to Don Quixote and ancient Greek myths. His dry humor can turn a clever phrase but too often his writing reads like the endless sentences of a legal document, leaving the reader wondering about the point of many a paragraph. But one finds moments of writing that are the seeds of what will become the poetry of Whitman and Ginsberg and the prose of Muir and Twain.

Original editions of Tom's book are extremely scarce now since almost all copies were seized and destroyed. Several years ago, an original became available for the first time in twenty-five years, for a mere $137,500. With only one limited edition reprint in two centuries, we came very close to never hearing about Thomas Morton, never hearing his point of view.

In 1641 twenty thousand Puritans suffered America's first economic depression. Then Massachusetts Bay's ironically titled "Body of Liberties" document gave legal legitimacy to slavery and the slave trade began to flourish thanks to the worldwide market for American tobacco.

Soon the original Plymouth colonists were overwhelmed. Not by the new governor from England, who never arrived, or by the tribes, but by competition from the colonists arriving by the boatload. Boston banned the newcomers whose beliefs didn't fit in, who didn't "resemble" them to use their terminology, resulting in flourishing colonies in areas once wild, like the one led by visionary Samuel Gorton whose followers didn't believe in a real hell and who referred to the judges of Boston and Plymouth as "just asses."

By now Ferdinando was out of money and wondering if he was too old to take a boat to America. He couldn't afford to bring an army with him so he proposed a new more modest approach: developing a royalist colony in Maine while letting the Puritans have their way in the south. Ferdinando sent over his twenty-two-year-old nephew, who was a Puritan sympathizer. The new governor, when informed by the Puritans of Tom Morton's reputation, didn't support his uncle's idea that Tom should come to New England to give hope to royalists there.

Tom was in London for the beginning of the English Civil War in 1642. The incident that finally triggered the war was a budget crisis. The royalists had emptied the treasury. They approached Parliament for more money as they had many times before. But this time the Puritans controlled Parliament and they said no. What began as a debate about who really rules, the king or the people, ended in war. Ferdinando forgot all about New England. Well into his seventies he raised a troop and led them in a battle where he lost the gate under his command, and thus the city. They say the old man died imprisoned by the Puritans.

Tom was appointed to wrangle over land grants with his old nemesis Winthrop, but the Puritans were gaining the upper hand, and beheadings were considered a more merciful way to die than being drawn and quartered. So Tom wrote his will while he accumulated the money for his last trip to the New World. He was almost seventy now. On August 23, 1643, exactly thirteen years after the Boston court ordered his arrest, Tom left his niece a list of lands he said he "ought to have."

As 1644 began, Tom was back in the New World. He lived on so little money he was forced to drink only water, never wine. His Puritan neighbors called Tom a serpent. They accused him of being a Jesuit agent. They suspected he had no rights to anything, that he really represented no one, only pretending to be there on a client's business. Captain Shrimp, now a tax collector, was infuriated by Tom's return. That was the year the Puritan parliament back in England outlawed Christmas. Soon after, Boston forbade singing carols, exchanging gifts, or the mention of St. Nicholas.

Tom really was an agent, for royalist friends in Maine, who sent him and others to recruit anyone who wanted to innovate away from the Puritans' smothering laws and customs. Endicott sent spies, and Tom's old enemies concluded he was there to help raise a royalist rebellion against them. Winthrop ordered him arrested again. For ten years the Pilgrims had held on to Tom's gloating letter—now it was exhibit A. Exhibit B was his book, which the Pilgrims considered libel.

Tom was jailed. He sought release as winter approached but they refused, saying they were gathering witnesses. They left him in a cell without bedding or fire through the cold winter. His hands and feet in irons, he withered. He petitioned for mercy again. Perhaps this time his old assistant, now mayor of Boston, would help his old master from Ma-re Mount.

The Pilgrims decided Tom was too expensive to keep, and too "old and crazy" for execution. They fined him what little he had on him and let him go. We don't really know what happened to Tom after that. Winthrop got the final published gloat, claiming Tom died soon after, "poor and despised." They say Tom was buried in an unmarked grave in a cemetery that no longer exists.

By 1646 the Puritans imposed the death penalty for blasphemy by anyone including Indigenous people. By 1648 openly questioning the Puritan strategy, using guns and the Bible to mercilessly convert the tribes, was legally declared blasphemy.

John Smith, Endicott, and Winthrop went on to be enshrined in

American history, and Disney fantasies of Pilgrims and Indigenous people. Ferdinando is remembered as the Father of Maine. But poor Tom was all but forgotten except by a few key American writers. Nathaniel Hawthorne, respectful but not affectionate toward the Pilgrims, wrote a short story called *The Maypole of Merrymount* that includes this memorable line, "jollity and gloom were contending for an empire."

William Carlos Williams thought the Puritans were driven by sexual jealousy. He meticulously examined the historical record on sexuality among the tribes and came to the conclusion that, like women anywhere, some were chaste and some not. While Hawthorne praised the determination of the Pilgrims, Williams despised them for being "shriveled with fear and hate" of the wilderness.

American poet laureate Robert Lowell wrote a play about Ma-re Mount, which he thought a fine example of his view of history as the result of inept fools using bits of ideology to justify actions that cause only damage for everyone involved.

The Wounded Cavalier, a painting by William Shakespeare Burton, captures the demise of Elizabethan England. But I like to think of it as symbolic of that moment in American history when the pagan Pilgrim failed and America's destiny was left in the cold pale hands of the Puritans. The Puritans would win the English Civil War. They beheaded their king. Of course, they were doomed to be as disappointed with their children as their fathers were with them, since the royals were welcomed back only eleven years later. The descendants of Tom Morton's enemies had esoteric interests. A leading Puritan of the following generation, John Butler, commented on the Puritan preoccupation with alchemy. He approved.

Perhaps the Pilgrims were shrewd to eliminate their competition. One can easily imagine Thomas Morton leading pirates and tribal allies against the Pilgrims in an American reflection of the English Civil War. Instead of slaughtering millions of turkeys for Thanksgiving every year, we might have been celebrating May Day with a maypole. There you have it. America's split personality from the very start.

8

The Intelligencers and the Fifth Moon of Jupiter

AS BEFITS A YOUNG REPUBLIC, the history of the earliest origins of American Metaphysical Religion amounts to a long list of extraordinary characters, daring experiments, and unlikely friendships. We'll meet alchemists who persecuted witches, alchemists who were governors, and several alchemists who served as presidents of the first American colleges.

The community of alchemists at home and abroad was in constant touch with each other, eagerly exchanging techniques, results, and useful writing, published and unpublished. At the heart of this vital cosmopolitan movement for cultural evolution were the Intelligencers, as they called themselves, discerning men who were so respected they became gatekeepers. By exchanging letters (sometimes in secret codes), discoveries, and books with fellow seekers of knowledge across continents and oceans, they became the internet hubs of their day. If a valuable discovery was made in a far-off land, news of it would soon be all over the world thanks to the Intelligencers.

Alchemists lived in a world where everything not only had a soul and life but also the desire to evolve. The soul in a lowly chunk of lead longed to become gold. The alchemist could quicken the process. While most alchemists considered themselves sincere Christians, most churches considered such ideas and practices not only scientific but heretic, and unsafe for those concerned about avoiding damnation.

As Jon Butler (1979) wrote: "American colonists had an ambivalent relationship with Christian congregations. After about 1650 even in New England only about one-third of all adults ever belonged to a church. The rate was lower in the middle and southern colonies, and on the eve of the American Revolution only about 15 percent of all of the colonists probably belonged to any church. In 1687 New York Governor Thomas Dongan wrote that settlers there usually expressed no religious sentiment at all or, when they did, entertained wildly unorthodox religious opinions."

Lewis Morris, a politician from New Jersey, wrote in 1702 about his constituents, "Except in two or three towns there is no face of any public worship of any sort but people live mean like Indians" (Butler 1979). The traveling Anglican minister Charles Woodmason reported that in the southern colonies the locals didn't have a Bible among them. They didn't want preachers or churches complicating their lives but they did ask to have their children baptized, just in case.

The British-American colonies, the spawn of England, reflected the mother country's religious diversity. After all, Isaac Newton practiced alchemy. Chaucer, Shakespeare, and Milton littered their creations with astrological references. A small percentage of especially clever or daring nobles had always been fascinated with druids, alchemy, astrology, and the occult. The middle class regularly produced some paragon of independent scholarship like Thomas Taylor, the devoted translator of ancient Neoplatonic philosophical and religious works. Theorists of grand spiritual unities appeared regularly, like Godfrey Higgins who wrote *The Celtic Druids* to prove that the first druids were Buddhists who had traveled all the way to Great Britain, and that Freemasonry originated among the Hashashim, or Order of Assassins, of the Nizari Isma'ili State founded by Hassan-i Sabbah; or General James Furlong whose *The Rivers of Life* includes a room-sized fold-out map that attempts to graph a timeline of every religion and cult in history. These polyglot efforts to envision the entirety of the human experience of religion more than made up for their inaccuracy with their boundless and glorious flights of imagination. They can be enjoyed for their unintentional fictions, as marvelous as the work of Borges, whom in fact they inspired.

As for the poor, they had their cunning folk and fortune-tellers to help them find the things and people they lost, to pick wedding dates, reverse a trend of bad luck, or most of all heal a sickness or injury. To America came nobles with libraries and free-thinking rogue scholars. Witchcraft was strictly prohibited, but occultism was a sport of intellectuals, and homespun cures and traditions were not considered pagan. Almanacs filled with astrology and bits of occult lore were popular back home and abroad. Books on the Kabbalah, the writings of Hermes Trismegistus, the medical and metaphysical works of Paracelsus, were circulated among well-read citizens in England and the colonies. Not that the English and Americans were rejecting Christianity, they simply had a much wider definition of it than we do today. They didn't view the wisdom of the ancients as satanic, nor did they fear astrology. They did not consider experiments in communicating with spirits or foretelling the future punishable offenses against their faith. If anything, by broadening their understanding with the accumulated wisdom and time-honored practices of other cultures, many believed they were becoming better Christians.

But America wasn't immediately fertile soil for alchemy, astrology, and other pagan preoccupations. Religious conformity was a constant force to be reckoned with. Generation after generation of Americans facing this force moved deeper into the wilderness in search of freedom of belief. The American forests were not like the pagan woods of Europe and Great Britain, everywhere haunted by half-forgotten sacred sites and magical natural settings. America was nothing but dangerous wilderness. Wandering in the wilds wasn't mysterious, it was terrifying, and superstition, like smallpox, was epidemic.

FRENCH ALCHEMISTS IN EARLY AMERICA

Alchemists lived in a world where everything had not only a soul but also the will to evolve. These ideas cultivated by the Neoplatonists, reanimated by Marsilio Ficino and the Platonists of the Florentine Renaissance, took full force in the writing and example of Paracelsus, the Swiss genius who foreshadowed what would become pharmaceutical science. He was the Luther of medicine, who coined the term *ylaster,* or star stuff, to describe what matter and hence humans are made of. In his works sympathies and antipathies, attraction and repulsion, the harmonies of correspondences, became laws of spirituality and medicine. Paracelsus thought not only that to understand the book of nature we must walk its pages with our feet, but also that the alchemist must be pure, all the vices must be confronted and conquered before the alchemist could expect to be blessed with success. So these early scientists had something of the medieval knight about them. Only the purest of heart could achieve the grail.

Keep in mind that alchemy has been many things to many people, then as now. A hundred years later a clear line would be drawn between the failures of alchemy and the successes of the new science of chemistry. Not long after, alchemy would find itself alongside palm reading, astrology, and witchcraft as a discredited but romantic art, still capable of inspiring artists, and occasionally sincere practitioners.

General Ethan Allen Hitchcock would argue around the time of Lincoln that alchemy was all metaphor; the true art was a spiritual transmutation, led by the desire to look deeply into the marvels of the divine creation. This became a popular approach for writers from Blavatsky to Manly Hall and beyond. Jung took it even further as he proposed a collective unconscious and made of alchemy something like the language of the arrival of primal religion fresh from the unconscious. The influential twentieth-century historian Mircea Eliade believed alchemy was based on the idea that all matter is living and ensouled. Base metals were not inert, lifeless elements. They were living and could therefore grow. Just as Jesus Christ can turn a soul from shadow to light, Eliade suggested, the alchemists reasoned that the right process could turn lead to gold. To perfect the self would lead to perfecting metals.

Today historians point out that the laboratory and the practice of chemistry were central to alchemy. In seventeenth-century colonial America, alchemy was an intoxicating combination of real chemistry, experimental mysticism, and financial speculation, all at the same time, but the most important was chemistry. In fact, some who have been called alchemists had no interest in a spiritual practice at all. They were chemists before chemistry was a science.

On three ships the first Huguenots, and probably the first alchemists to reach the New World, arrived in 1564, fifty-six years before the *Mayflower*. They were weary of the never-ending war between Protestants and Catholics back home. Near what is now Jacksonville, Florida, with the help of a local tribe, they built triangular Fort Caroline. They were probably the first Protestants to celebrate a Thanksgiving. But Spain had already claimed Florida and most of everything else in America.

When the king of Spain heard about the Huguenot fort he sent an army to erase them and replace them with the Spanish colony, St. Augustine. The Huguenots courageously sailed out to attack the Spanish at sea but a hurricane dashed their ships against the Florida coast. The Spanish quickly took the fort. Survivors were offered conversion to the Catholic faith. Almost every Huguenot refused, so they were executed. Only a few artisans whose skills were needed, and a couple of Catholics who had lived among the Huguenots, were spared, less than ten out of three hundred survived. What was their great sin? They were Protestants. They criticized the Catholic sacraments as obsession with death and the dead.

But in 1568, in the great walled city of La Rochelle in France, the rebellious Huguenots celebrated victory. The Catholic church, eager to absorb, annihilate, or at least expel them had been defeated. The siege was over. The Reformation commenced a new world order. But not for long. In what became known as the St. Bartholomew's Day Massacre in 1572, Catholics killed thousands of Huguenots in Paris. Other massacres of thousands in other towns followed until La Rochelle was under siege again. By 1628 the fortress of the Huguenots was a smoking ruin, and most of the inhabitants were dead, killed by the armies of the Catholic Counter-Reformation.

So much war had created an underground of green men, or leaf men, people who were said to have gone mad. They lived in caves, in the woods, creeping through the leaves with matted hair like fur, refugees from Catholicism who had devolved into wildness. When the Huguenot leaders, or heretics as they had been judged, were marched away to their deaths they were "dressed up in greenery as objects of ridicule." The proud natural philosophers were equated with these alleged madmen.

Many of the survivors fled to the New World, to workshops in the wilderness where they could pursue their arts without fear of Catholic persecution. The Huguenots, like so many after them, were refugees of war who came to America to start new lives and practice religious freedom. In New York and New Amsterdam they became craft workers and especially skilled furniture makers. They sought security in their lives by applying in every way they could the principles of Paracelsus, as described in great detail by Neil Kamil (2005), in his masterpiece of historical scholarship, the thousand-page *Fortress of the Soul: Violence, Metaphysics, and Material Life in the Huguenot's New World, 1517–1751.*

Among the earliest to arrive in America, the Huguenots brought with them Paracelsian medicine and alchemical preoccupations. They wanted to live self-sufficiently, with freedom of belief, relying on their crafts to survive. Their politics and spirituality were local. They had learned from Böhme to think of life as the art of balancing God's wrath and love, called by some communities the masculine and feminine. Until these were in proper ratio our world would be fallen instead of a paradise. The books written by their spiritual leaders, who were often craftsmen, like the great Huguenot artist Bernard Palissy, the father of modern ceramics, were carefully read by reformers in the colonies, including John Winthrop the Younger and later Ben Franklin. The Huguenots assimilated quickly into American Protestant culture, becoming an important ingredient in the melting pot. Paul Revere was the descendent of Huguenots.

SOURCES OF EARLY ROSICRUCIAN AMERICA

The Rosicrucian contribution to culture is shrouded in secrecy and misinformation. The Rosicrucian manifesto called for "Universal and General Reformation of the whole wide world." This idea of an invisible college of spiritually superior human beings benevolently conspiring for the good of humanity to this day catches up novices on the spiritual path, giving them visions of adepts materializing before them like Madame Blavatsky's telepathic masters. On the one hand, scholars like Frances Yates have argued persuasively that a genuine Rosicrucian movement existed, including a variety of secret societies with shared goals.

More recently most scholars have taken the position that the Rosicrucians were more like a literary invention, but based on the experimental practice of alchemy as a quest for breakthroughs in medicine, metallurgy, and what would become chemistry. Telescopes and alembics were holier than sacred relics to these men and women. And women there were in the chemistry labs, mothers and wives; a book that no scholar has been able to find but was referenced by Charles Heckethorn in his dated but once influential *Secret Societies of All Ages and Countries* was titled *Sisters of the Rosy Cross* (1620).

The Rosicrucians had announced in their initial publications that they would stay invisible for a century, but interested parties should publicly declare themselves and if worthy they would be asked to join the order. This invitation triggered a wave of publications, not only from volunteers wishing to be chosen, but also from critics attacking the Rosicrucian order and apologists defending it, even though they were not actual members of it. The most enthusiastic seekers wandered in search of wisdom. Following the example of Paracelsus, they sold their books, their possessions, and their estates to travel in search of wisdom about plants and other methods of healing. They collected recipes from locals and learned the lore of cures. Only then were they ready to buy a furnace and work with the fire that would help them resolve, dissolve, and coagulate, taking matter apart, purifying it, discovering hidden properties. And if they were devoted enough and pure of heart, they would be blessed by the divine with medicines, and other discoveries that would be boons for humanity.

Rosicrucianism was a cultural flowering, both rational and irrational, that arose partly from misinterpretations concerning King James of England giving his daughter Elizabeth in marriage to Frederick the future king of Bohemia. Reformers saw the marriage as an alliance between England and the various German kingdoms opposed to the Catholic church, which was patiently working to reclaim dominion over northern Europe and Great Britain. A prince and princess who fell in love at first sight, the royal couple captured the public's imagination. For them Shakespeare himself presented *Midsummer Night's Dream,* performed for their wedding festivities along with other plays including *Much Ado About Nothing, The Merry Wives of Windsor,* and *Julius Caesar.* The best scientific and esoteric minds in England surrounded them.

The situation was complicated by the death of Henry Frederick, Prince of Wales, the heir to the English throne. Elizabeth's older brother was a passionate Protestant who thought his father a peculiar old fogey. Henry was bright, cultured, an athlete, the very incarnation of what the people hoped a king would be, and he was eager to make war on the Catholic powers. Like his sister he seemed less a Stuart than a Tudor. A swim in the polluted Thames infected him with typhoid fever. Just before his sister's wedding to the German prince who could have united Germany to join England in an alliance strong enough to resist the Spanish and Austrian armies, Prince Henry died. The wedding festivities continued, but despite the best efforts of Shakespeare, and the dazzling theatrical inventions of Inigo Jones, melancholy pervaded the proceedings. Back in Heidelberg Frederick built gardens with mechanical statues that moved and whistled for the amusement of his bride, but these wonders of science horrified local Catholics who condemned the garden as the Gate to Hell. Then Bohemia offered to make Frederick their king. He and Elizabeth considered it a divine duty to accept, much to their misfortune.

Bohemia was already a symbol of the avant-garde and offbeat thanks to the alchemical court of Emperor Rudolf II. Reformers, alchemists, astrologers, inventors like Inigo Jones, Paracelsian doctors, mystics of every stripe, all assembled at the court of Bohemia, where the royal alchemical couple were presiding over the dawn of a new world order. But not for long. Frederick made the mistake of believing he might become emperor when the vision was unwisely dangled before him by rash allies foolishly counting on James. Too expensive. His decision not to support his own daughter was very unpopular with the lords and with the people of England who loved their princess. They had hoped she would be a second coming of Queen Elizabeth. And she too had hoped so, as evidenced by her patient practice of penmanship, which she began as a child, that made her signature a copy of Elizabeth I's majestic scrawl. But without his father-in-law's help, Frederick lost his credibility in the eyes of his German allies, who left him to the tender mercies of the pope's imperial army. In 1620 Frederick's domain was burned, pillaged, and left to the plague. Protestant officials were publicly executed, and their lands and possessions were given to loyal Catholics.

But what of all these reformers of science and education, and the writers promoting imminent utopias? What of the secret societies devoted to the grand project of creating a culture where the best resources could be focused on research colleges instead of war between Christians? What of the alchemists and their dreams of new sciences of health and wealth? With their dream of a Rosicrucian Europe shattered, where could they turn their attention? Europe they knew would be embroiled in war. America beckoned, and authors from Sir Francis Bacon to obscure Rosicrucian apologists began enshrining their visions in the New World. Even if they were as loose and unofficial a band as the Beat poets of the 1950s, these alchemists and aspiring Rosicrucians stamped their image indelibly on America.

Bacon himself has been accused of being the leader of the Rosicrucians. Thanks to Manly Hall's guidance, in his collection I encountered two examples of the mysterious hints that have inspired Bacon and Rosicrucian scholars. The first is a copy of the 1660 edition of *The Anatomy of Melancholy*. On page 62 of the introduction a curious footnote reads, "Joh. Valent. Andreae, Lord Verulam." Andreae was the reputed author of the *Fama* and the *Chemical Marriage,* the books that sparked the Rosicrucian revolution. Francis Bacon was the first and only Lord Verulam in those days. The other hint comes from *Mathematical Magic,* a book by John Wilkins, a friend of Francis Bacon. On page 237 of the edition published in 1680 where ever-burning lamps are discussed, Wilkins makes this provocative statement, "Such a lamp is likewise related to be seen in the sepulcher of Francis Rosicross, as is largely expressed in the confession of that fraternity." Wilkins equates Francis Rosicross to Christian Rosenkreuz, legendary founder of the

Rosicrucians. Were these errors, metaphors, or subtle hints at a deeper involvement by Bacon in Rosicrucian matters? Since Rosicrucians would never talk about being Rosicrucians, the absence of evidence in Bacon's own writing offers no obstacle to the enthusiast. Bacon's own writing certainly shared most of the Rosicrucian goals.

THE COLONIAL COLLEGE OF LIGHT

For John Winthrop the Younger's funeral, American poet Ben Tompson wrote a poem that has much more to do with alchemy than Puritanism.

> *Projections various by fire he made*
> *Where Nature had her common Treasure laid*
> *Some thought the tincture Philosophick lay*
> *Hatched by the Mineral Sun in Winthrop's way,*
> *And clear it shines to me he had a Stone*
> *Grav'd with his Name which he could read lone—*
> *His fruits of toil Hermetically done*
> *Stream to the poor as light doth from the Sun.*
> *The lavish Garb of silks, Rich Plush and Rings,*
> *Physicians Livery, at his feet he flings.*

John Winthrop the Younger, like Lincoln born on February 12, was not only the most popular alchemical physician in colonial America, he was also the first governor of Connecticut colony, and a charter member of the Royal Society. An avid astronomer, his three-and-a-half-foot refractor was one of the first telescopes in America. The son of the three-time governor and founder of Massachusetts Bay Colony, he tried several times in his life to contact the Rosicrucians and he patterned his life after their example.

Winthrop first encountered alchemy and the Rosicrucians when he went to school in London in 1624 just after turning eighteen. Within months he and his roommate and lifelong friend Edward Howes, who later sat in the House of Commons, were skipping classes to conduct alchemical experiments and to search for Rosicrucians. Winthrop was so inspired by the example of Christian Rosenkreutz he tried to use his family connections to imitate the founder of the Rosicrucian order by traveling to Turkey in search of alchemical wisdom. Any well-educated European knew that the teaching of alchemy had been preserved and developed by the Arabs. From them came the copies of alchemical classics long forgotten in Europe. But the Arabian view of alchemy was thought to be somehow tainted by Islam, which was considered inferior to the pure truth of Christianity.

Unable to find passage to Turkey, in 1627 Winthrop took a position as captain's secretary on a ship in the fleet England sent to relieve the siege of the Huguenot fortress La Rochelle. Winthrop hoped that after the battle he might find a boat headed for Turkey. Instead he witnessed the humiliating defeat that left half the English fleet burning, an experience that may explain why as governor he never considered war an appropriate policy. And whenever the king asked him to send soldiers to a war, Winthrop would praise the cause and urge his fellow colonial leaders to send troops, while finding numerous reasons why his own men could not be in attendance.

But Winthrop's trip to La Rochelle wasn't a total loss. He met Cornelius Drebbel, an alchemist, physician, and inventor who had been a court favorite of Henry Frederick, Prince of Wales. Drebbel had built a *camera obscura* (a device that projects its surroundings on a screen), early microscopes, and a submarine that was successfully tested in the Thames. Drebbel mentored Winthrop and left a fond impression. On the flyleaf of a copy of Basil Valentine's alchemical classic *Of Natural and Supernatural Things,* Winthrop wrote: "This was once the book of that famous philosopher and naturalist Cornel Drebbel. He usually carried with him in his pocket and after his death was given me by his son-in-law."

In summer of 1628 Winthrop took a ship to Leghorn, Pisa, Florence, and finally Constantinople. Unsatisfied, he planned to travel to Jerusalem, as Christian Rosenkreutz had done, but rumors of war were everywhere. On the return voyage home the following year in Venice, Winthrop met a Dutch scholar returning from a tour of Turkey, where he had acquired rare Arabic and Persian manuscripts. Two weeks after his son's return to London, Winthrop Sr. became leader of the Puritans. Winthrop Jr. helped his father sell off their property but he still found time for alchemical experimentation. He had become fascinated with John Dee, whom many have credited as being one of the principal inspirations to the Rosicrucian counterculture.

Winthrop began collecting books and manuscripts that had belonged to Dee. He adopted Dee's *Monas Hieroglyphica* as a personal insignia, drawing it next to his signature in alchemical texts. It's an extraordinary image. The symbol invented by John Dee to represent the reformation of the world was an inspiration to the Rosicrucians and was often seen in their books. Now it was the emblem painted on boxes of alchemical supplies imported by the son of the founder of Massachusetts Bay Colony.

In November 1631 cannons and muskets saluted Winthrop Jr.'s arrival in the New World with his bride. Woodward (2010) summarizes the accomplishments that followed. "Over the next half century, Winthrop would found three colonial towns, serve as Bay Colony assistant for nearly two decades, govern the colony of Connecticut for eighteen years, secure that colony a charter from the Restoration court of Charles II, granting it virtual independence, found several New England iron foundries, serve as physician to nearly half the population of Connecticut, and become a founding member of the Royal Society. Alchemical knowledge and philosophies factored, often essentially, into each of these accomplishments."

As soon as he arrived Winthrop set up an alchemical laboratory in his father's house. There was nothing wrong with practicing alchemy in an elite Puritan household. Winthrop assisted his father and others governing Massachusetts Bay Colony. He flourished, but his wife did not. Returning to London in 1634 after her death, he and his college roommate Howes were eager to meet Dr. John Everard, a minister and alchemist, a friend of the Hermetic physician Robert Fludd, and the rumored leading candidate for an actual Rosicrucian. In 1650 Everard would be the first to translate into English the pagan classic *The Divine Pymander of Hermes Mercurius Trismegistus*. But Everard answered Winthrop's questions with poetic generalizations. Winthrop and Howes were unimpressed. Winthrop crossed the ocean again and returned to the colony.

In 1641 Winthrop returned to Europe to raise money for an iron-works in New England, arriving at the same time as Comenius, who impressed him when they met. The great educator and philosopher was celebrated for going beyond the utopias of Bacon and Campanella. Bacon's *New Atlantis* and Campanella's *City of the Sun* were lovely myths but impractical guides to real world challenges. Comenius synthesized the idea of Universal Reformation into some practical suggestions. First, he wanted to establish universal education for men and women. Not everyone would become a scholar, but everyone would know how to read and write and how to do math. Today it's hard to imagine how radical that idea was in the seventeenth century, especially the education of all women, and of the Indigenous people of America and Africa.

Second, Comenius proposed that books be compiled that would contain all the information anyone could need; "the condensed essence of all knowledge" must be given to everyone. Three books would be written collaboratively. *Pansophia,* "All Wisdom," would reveal the metaphysics of the structure of soul and world as designed by deity. *Panhistoria,* "All History," would show how all this unfolds in the specific arts and sciences, in all crafts, and other aspects of life. *Pandogmatica,* "All Dogma," would contain a comprehensive collection of ideas about human life and activity, along with whether they had proven to be true or false. Also, a universal language must be created by collaboration. And finally from all the nations across the globe the best minds must cooperate for the betterment of the world, their organization to be known as the College of Light, where a new generation of innovators would be educated. While none of these suggestions were ever realized they did inspire cooperation and faith in science.

Ironically all of this rational thinking was based on the idea that the end of the world was near. These great intellects of their day were haunted by the fear of imminent doom, though they had no nuclear weapons, and no climate crisis; but they had experienced a deadly pandemic. They believed that just before the end times there would be a great quickening of knowledge. The descendants of Adam would regain the lost language of Paradise just before Jesus returned. Everything would be known, and everything would be understood, by everyone. They hoped by contributing to the process they were bringing the world closer to the Second Coming.

Winthrop left England for Hamburg, the Hague, and Amsterdam, meeting not only with potential investors in his ironworks, but also with alchemists and philosophers. He collected books and manuscripts. The first of his many attempts to desalinate seawater was already in operation, but back then the salt making was more important than the fresh water left behind. By the fall of 1644, he had the ironworks up and running and was ready to move on to a new venture: mining silver.

By 1646 Winthrop was working on the beginnings of what would become New London. He bought seeds from colonial farmers who had shown luck growing English grasses in America. He ordered trees for his orchard, winter wheat, indigo seeds, and livestock. And most importantly, Winthrop was recruiting geniuses for his colonial College of Light.

THE ALCHEMISTS VERSUS THE MOHEGANS

If you're familiar with Uncas, the romantic Mohegan lead in the feature film *Last of the Mohicans,* you might be surprised to learn there really was a Mohegan chief named Uncas. But he wasn't at all like the Uncas in the movie.

Winthrop had his eye on a mountain on Connecticut's frontier where he had found black lead ore. He took the ore with him to England where he got conflicting reports. Important experts declared he had found a silver mine. One dissenting expert insisted he had found no more than graphite. But graphite was rare enough to be a worthwhile commercial venture. The problem with the site was not only that it was outside the jurisdiction of the Massachusetts Bay Colony, but also that it was deep in tribal territory where in 1637 the Pequot War broke out.

The powerful Mohegan tribe led by their great war chief Uncas, along with their tribal allies, had joined forces with the English of Connecticut and Massachusetts colonies, to crush the once powerful

Pequots, who had been weakened by diseases they caught from Europeans. The already dwindling tribe nearly disappeared. Bounties were paid by the English for Pequot heads and hands. The English and the allied tribes divided women and children between them. The surviving warriors disappeared, sometimes joining enemy tribes. Five hundred Pequots huddled in a settlement were all that was left of the tribe. The commissioners of the United Colonies, two representatives each from the four colonies, ordered that all legal rights and even the name of the Pequot tribe be erased. The five hundred survivors were now to pay tribute to Uncas and obey him in all things.

The Winthrop house received their share of the spoils of war. A young Pequot woman was added to their household as a servant. But there had been a mistake. Uncas already had plans for the girl. He wanted to add her to his growing collection of wives. Uncas chose a new chief from the surviving Pequots, an until-then unremarkable man with the mellifluous name Robin Cassacinamon.

Since at the order of the commissioners of the United Colonies all surviving leaders of the Pequot had been executed by the Mohegans, being named a chief must have been a frightening development for Robin. To make matters worse, Uncas ordered him to try to trade with John Winthrop Sr. for the Pequot girl, and if the trade was refused, to volunteer to stay on in service of the Winthrops until he could arrange her escape.

Either the girl was an indispensable servant or she didn't want to marry Uncas because his generous trade for her was refused by John Sr. So Robin did as he was told and arranged for her escape. Uncas rewarded him with the treasure John Sr. refused. The Winthrops could not have been pleased, but fortunately for Robin, he had become friendly with John Jr. The two men found mutual respect and shared goals. Robin told John Jr. about the inner workings of tribal politics. John supported Robin's ambition: the survival of the Pequot tribe and its liberation from the tender mercies of Uncas. Robin returned to his five hundred survivors, and Winthrop decided to establish New London, his alchemical plantation right next to the village of survivors. He would plead their cause to the English and the tribes alike.

The tribes thought Winthrop an English chief, since they considered his father chief of Boston. Also, because his second wife and sister-in-law lived with him along with several wives of colonial dignitaries who had taken ill and were seeking healing, the natives thought Winthrop had many wives, among them a privilege enjoyed only by chiefs. But watching the smoke rising from his laboratory, the sacred smoke that Indigenous people believed connected the worlds of spirit and man, or running long distances carrying messages on behalf of English families begging Winthrop's help to fight disease, or experiencing the healing power of his alchemical recipes, the tribes began to appreciate Winthrop as a shaman. In their culture to be both chief and shaman was to be a great person indeed.

His old friend Howes not only gave Winthrop good advice about dealing with the tribes respectfully, he also sent Winthrop some vocabularies of Indigenous language that were probably the work of Thomas Harriot. Winthrop treated the tribes with not only tolerance but with respect for their traditions. When he bought land from them, he not only satisfied all requirements of colonial and English law, but also tribal law. He added to the contract a description of the ritual enacted and gave the names of those involved. In Winthrop's village, Indigenous people and Europeans were living together with mutual concern and a sense of community.

When thirty of his warriors were wounded, Uncas was surprised by the arrival of Winthrop who treated them effectively. Soon after, Roger Williams, leader of the Rhode Island colony, wrote Winthrop asking for some of his medicinal powder for his sick daughter.

At first Uncas was thrilled to have such a good doctor nearby so he gave Winthrop gifts and participated with the other tribes of New England in the establishment of boundaries for the plantation. This must have been an extraordinary time for Winthrop, inspired by Rosicrucian ambitions he had gone to the heart of the conflict in New England, protected the innocent, and reconciled all tribal factions. In the community he founded, the Indigenous and the English worked and lived together peacefully. The gospel was taught by example, not by force. Pythagorean harmony and hermetic peace seemed to emanate all around him as the colonial leaders and charter members of the Royal Society anxiously awaited news about what he was up to next. It must have seemed possible that Comenius was right and here in America was the first appearance of the society of the Universal Reformation.

Problems began when Winthrop made it clear that the Pequots were now part of his plantation and were no longer subject to Uncas. Uncas showed up suddenly with a large force and attacked the Pequots. Bones were broken, bodies were slashed, and men and women, old and young, were stripped naked and thrown into the cold river of September in Connecticut. The English weren't harmed, but their doors were forced open, and their Indigenous friends who had hoped to hide with them were dragged away. The message was clear. Uncas wanted his five hundred tribute payers back and he wanted Winthrop and the other English to go back home and leave their plantation to the ants and weeds.

Winthrop already had a questionable reputation among colonial leaders thanks to his business partner Robert Childe's imprisonment for challenging the Puritan authorities. When Winthrop sent a friend to carry a petition on behalf of the people of his settlement to the United Colonies the leaders of Connecticut colony weren't too pleased with Winthrop. He had never asked permission to place his alchemical plantation on what they considered their land. Also, he had violated the property rights, human capital, and territory of their proven and loyal ally Uncas. The United Colonies sided with Uncas. Uncas apologized for violently taking matters into his own hands. Winthrop was ordered to return the Pequots to the Mohegans. But Winthrop was able to postpone the inevitable for many months simply by ignoring the order.

In July 1647 Winthrop represented the Pequots at another meeting of the United Colonies. He petitioned for their release from Uncas and for the restoration of their name and status as a legal tribe. He presented a long list of Mohegan bullying that included extortion, intimidation, cutting fishing nets, stealing food, even killing innocent members of other tribes for the fun of it. The Mohegans also refused to honor their gambling debts. So when asked to gamble by a Mohegan the victim was really being singled out for anything from extortion to murder. The surviving Pequots, who had seen their families and friends slaughtered, who were trying to embrace the new culture Winthrop promised, were caught between two worlds.

Again, the commission sided with Uncas. Uncas would pay a fine for the bad behavior of his warriors, a fine he could easily extort from the Pequots when he regained custody of them. He kept the pressure on Winthrop and the Pequots. His brother attacked the Nipmuck tribe, who had sold the land for the graphite mine to Winthrop. Warriors wrecked a canoe at the plantation's fishing outpost and gathered outside the community in a threatening mass before returning to their villages.

Offended by Winthrop's disobedience, in September 1648 the commission sent armed Englishmen with Uncas and his Mohegan warriors to the plantation. The leader of the English observers made a formal declaration, and then the Mohegans were set free to rampage through the town dragging Pequots back into captivity. But the Pequots refused to stay with Uncas. One or a few at a time, they returned to the plantation, until in January 1649 Uncas returned with the English observers and his warriors. The Pequots were beaten and cut, their copper pots, furs, and hemp baskets were destroyed or taken, their shelters knocked down, their clothes ripped off their bodies, old and young alike, and their food supply stolen. The plantation constable's protests were ignored. The surviving Pequots were left shivering and bleeding in the snow. Watching fellow Englishmen stand guard over such cruelty was shocking. As news of the event spread across the colonies public opinion turned against Uncas and the commission.

Three months later, in March 1649 John Winthrop Sr. was gravely ill. He wrote a letter to his son. He thought the commission was wrong, but he wished the constable hadn't tried to interfere. He urged his son to obey the commission. He was worried about his son out there with a recently hostile tribe in the wilderness, disobeying the orders of the commissioners. John Sr. had often warned John Jr. of the dangers of too much knowledge. Now here he was doing his crazy experiments in the middle of a battleground, stirring up every hornet's nest in sight. John Sr.'s last request was that John Jr. give up the Pequots, but he didn't live to see his son's clever solution to what seemed an impossible predicament.

Winthrop found a compromise that everyone could agree upon. The Pequot would be given a safe area of their own, belonging neither to the Mohegans or the English. They could walk to work at the plantation, and live free of Uncas and his bullying. With public sentiment against them, this time the commissioners agreed. Uncas was never able to gain complete control over the Pequots again. Winthrop kept advocating for them until he also won the restoration of their tribal name and legal rights.

Why did he fight so hard for the Pequots? Was it a matter of pure expedience as he claimed before the commission when he argued if they were dependent on the English that they would become an invaluable source of intelligence about the activities and intentions of other tribes? Did he fight for the Pequot because of his friendship with Robin Cassacinamon, whom he named governor of the Pequot, and whom he used often in negotiations with other tribes? Was he putting to work his Rosicrucian principles, proving that Comenius was right, that a new age of wisdom was dawning that would unite all races? Or did he simply do what he had to do to make his potential silver mine viable? Perhaps all these were motivations behind his extraordinary protection of the persecuted tribe.

It cost him. He couldn't find workers willing to mine silver in such a cold and dangerous area. Supporters back in Europe were less enthusiastic when news of the trouble with the Mohegans reached them. Robert Childe went back home to England, and the other alchemists who had promised to join Winthrop's great experiment changed their minds. But Winthrop kept the plantation going. First he made a business out of raising livestock. Then, with numerous blacksmiths joining him, he began supplying hatchets and hoes for merchants in Hartford. In May 1649 Massachusetts colony gave him three thousand acres to build a salt works.

THE ALCHEMICAL DOCTOR
OF CONNECTICUT

New London was more than Winthrop's experiment, he was to act as the agent, the reporter, the eyes and ears of the Royal Society of London who, when he was in London, tutored him to prepare him for the job. For his alchemical project Winthrop now looked for homegrown talent to replace the reluctant Europeans. In this way he became the central intelligencer of the American colonies. He encouraged George Starkey and many other students of alchemy he found at Harvard, or visiting from Bermuda, or newly arrived from England.

Robert Childe continued to send him recipes from England, while recommending people and books, and giving advice about treating the tribes respectfully. Local alchemists sent Winthrop questions, or asked his opinion of recipes or sources, they wrote to thank him for the rare books he sent them. Alchemist Gershom Bulkeley became the minister of New London. William White, an alchemist and expert on ironworks who had moved to Bermuda, returned to New England to work with Winthrop on his alchemical experiments. New London became New England's medical center, the place where sick people went to get better. "Wherever he came," Cotton Mather wrote of Winthrop, "still the diseased flocked about him, as if the healing angel of Bethesda had appeared." Patients arrived from all over the colonies, and even from Europe. Winthrop received heartbreaking letters from sick people from all over the world who had heard about his great talents from friends and relatives. Their conditions can be identified from the descriptions of their suffering. Winthrop usually referred them to physicians in their area; he had more than enough work locally.

Most of Winthrop's medicines involved preparations of antimony and nitre. One of his most famous recipes, widely distributed by his sons after his death, was called *rubila*. Rubila was made of four grains of processed antimony, twenty grains of nitre, a dash of salt of tin, and a mysterious ingredient that turned the concoction ruby red. He also prescribed flowers of sulphur, purest gold, blue vitriol, iron burnt alum, oregano, sarsaparilla, raisins, saffron, horseradish, tobacco ointment, nutmeg, mugwort, sage, pearls, ambergris, and the penis of a seahorse, which was used to treat kidney stones. He devised a system of color-coded packets so his medicines could be identified more easily. To distribute them he organized a network of female healers who dispensed his advice. Winthrop had learned respect for female healers as a young man in England. His cousin Elizabeth was a skilled surgeon who had participated in Winthrop's early alchemical experiments in the 1620s.

In 1650 Winthrop let it be known he was thinking about closing or moving New London, and perhaps even of returning to England. But he seems to have been bluffing. Perhaps contemplating life without Winthrop made officials more cooperative. When Winthrop asked to have the boundaries of the project expanded his request was granted. By 1653 both a gristmill and a sawmill were operational. In 1657, without running for office, Winthrop was elected governor of the colony of Connecticut.

Connecticut was a Puritan colony, part of the new monarchy-free world of Cromwell. But now royalty had been restored. Winthrop's own father-in-law had signed the document ordering the beheading of the new king's royal father. With the least official documentation of all the colonies Connecticut was ripe for a revenge pluck. With a signature Charles II could turn it into a royal colony and replace its government with one of his own selection. In the summer of 1661 Winthrop sailed to England. Within months a new witch hunt broke out in Connecticut. A year of panic followed. Eight witchcraft trials were conducted in eight months. By the time Winthrop returned, three women and one man had died on the gallows. Five had fled Connecticut.

This was, after all, a culture where newlywed couples whose babies arrived prematurely were punished for premarital intercourse with lashes from a whip if they couldn't afford the fine. So intense was the repression of anger, so stifling the community interest that, for example, a young Puritan mother, despairing of ever being worthy of being fit for spiritual grace, spurned the constant "comfort" offered by her betters and threw her newborn down a well, announcing that at least "now she was sure she would be damned, for she had drowned her child," as Winthrop Sr. wrote in his journal.

Puritan culture was not peaceful and joyful. Anxiety and doubt were considered more appropriate for the almost certainly damned. For these Calvinists the relationship with deity was very conditional and humans were hardly ever able to meet the conditions. As schoolmaster and American Puritan minister Thomas Shepard wrote in his journal, "The greatest part of a Christian's grace lies in mourning for the want of it."

When the new charter received the great seal in 1662, Connecticut now included New Haven colony and much of the territory that had been claimed by Rhode Island. The same year, Winthrop became a member of the Royal Society. The Royal Society today is a purely scientific organization but in those early years the writings of Hermes and the Neoplatonists, as well as the alchemists and Rosicrucians, were part of the intellectual climate. While in England, Winthrop was asked to give many presentations about New England flora and fauna.

Winthrop used his new power to release a woman sentenced to die on the gallows after repeated prosecutions. In another case, a cunning woman skilled at healing was accused of witchcraft, including spectral apparitions of herself with a ghostly black dog, and apparently she was psychic, since many witnesses testified her predictions came true. She was a student of the astrology books of William Lilly, about which she publicly boasted. Her accusers seemed more malicious. They maimed her animals and vandalized her property. The court ignored Winthrop's appeal on her behalf and convicted her.

George Bulkeley, the young star among Winthrop's compatriots, handled the next step of her defense. He argued that the rule that two witnesses were necessary to convict meant that two people must have seen the same event at the same time. That weakened the case considerably. As for her spectral apparitions, how could the court know if they were not simply the work of the devil, and not of the alleged witch at all? As for her interest in astrology, Bulkeley reminded the magistrates that their own favorite doctors including the esteemed Winthrop, and William Lilly himself, used the art for healing. As for divination it could only be diabolical if the information provided could come from no natural source. To read the stars intelligently and make informed predictions was simply knowledge of nature, like the farmer's ability to predict the seasons based on natural cycles, not magic. Soon after, the convicted witch was released and Winthrop gave her safe passage out of the colony.

Greater Connecticut didn't last long. One year later Charles II granted his brother the Duke of York a huge grant of land that included

New Haven colony and half of Connecticut. The Dutch were to be kicked off Manhattan, as well. And English warships bearing English soldiers were there to enforce the new order. Not only did Winthrop lose his land grant, many of his powerful allies back home lost their positions to loyal royalists. Winthrop formally renounced all claim to Long Island and other territories that had belonged to Connecticut in a public ceremony attended by an agent of the crown. Then he traveled to New Amsterdam to help negotiate the Dutch surrender. New Amsterdam became New York.

Sir Robert Moray was the privy counselor behind this new colonial government, and he too was an alchemist. Winthrop was pleasantly surprised to find that more land than he expected would be under his jurisdiction. But the king was maneuvering slowly but surely toward new charters. First he would get a thorough reckoning of the situation and resources in the American colonies. Then he would establish his own governors. The people would no longer elect them. Winthrop resorted to his old trick again, keeping as much power as he could by finding good excuses why he couldn't comply with certain orders.

In May 1675 the king ordered Connecticut to surrender all control to the crown. A new government would be appointed. Redcoats were in the harbor ready to enforce the command. As Winthrop lay dying in early April the next year, New England was in flames as King Philip's War threatened to wipe out the colonies. "The blaze of towns was up like torches light, to guide him to his grave," eulogized a Boston poet. Forty-four years after the cannon and muskets had saluted his arrival, they marked his departure. Winthrop spent his last days working on plans for the rebuilding of New England and the restoration of old alliances. The genteel world of his alchemical plantation New London was disappearing and a New World was being born that would result almost exactly one hundred years later in the establishment of the United States of America.

Around that time Gosuinus Erkelens bought a mountain near East Haddam, Connecticut, known to the locals as "Governor's Ring." The president of Yale College, the Reverend Ezra Stiles, explained it was, "the Place to which Gov. Winthrop of New London used to resort with his Servant; and after spending three Weeks in the Woods of this Mountain in roasting ores and assaying Metals and casting gold Rings, he used to return home to New London with plenty of Gold. Hence this is called the Governor Winthrop's Ring to this Day" (Woodward 2010).

WINTHROP'S CHRISTIAN ALCHEMISTS

For Winthrop and his friends Walter Woodward suggested the collective label, "the Christian Alchemists." But, as he pointed out, not all were Christians, and the ones who were belonged to various denominations; a Catholic alchemist was included among them.

The alchemist of Winthrop's flock born into the lowest social status was Gershom Bulkeley, who became the son-in-law of Charles Chauncy, alchemist and president of Harvard College. Gershom was born in Massachusetts in 1636; he worked as a pastor and a minister. At a time in life when his peers would have been unwilling to embark on a new career, Gershom followed his love of Paracelsian medicine into practice as a physician. His healing skills were so in demand he stepped down from his popular pulpit to pursue medicine full time. Bulkeley put together a large library of alchemical works with books by Paracelsus and Sendivogious, including many he hand copied. Not only did Bulkeley's son become an alchemist, so did his daughter Dorothy.

Bulkeley drew the line at astrology, however. The influence of the moon and planetary aspects he dismissed in *Go with Me,* a book he wrote for his eleven-year-old grandson who was considering a future as a doctor. Bulkeley scoffs at a rival physician's thirty-day prognosis astrological chart, pointing out that it doesn't even take into account differences in the lengths of months. Yet he speculates about certain astral influences more subtle and sublime. Advice about laboratory work is abundant, including the crucial importance of clearly labeling dangerous chemicals and keeping them away from children. He left his library to his grandson, who grew up to be an alchemist, physician, and minister himself.

Winthrop's flock also included his investor and partner Robert Childe. Childe was born in England. He's another of those contradictions we find in Europe and the colonies—an alchemist, the object of Rosicrucian rumors, who appears to also have been a strict Presbyterian. He and Winthrop exchanged many letters containing alchemical information, occult speculation, and lists of books being lent or acquired. For example, Childe wrote to Winthrop, "One Vaughn an Ingenuous young man hath written *Anthroposophia*." Childe had plans for a vineyard to be not only a business investment and an experiment in improving the techniques of agriculture, but also for England's pride, since France should not be the only nation to enjoy such praise for wine-making. Winthrop owned eleven copies of the rare volumes of Robert Fludd, probably acquired for him by Childe.

Elias Ashmole was the great antiquarian of his age. In his diary Ashmole relates tantalizing glimpses of his meetings and correspondences with Rosicrucian apologists, alchemists, Kabbalists, astrologers, members of the inner circle of Francis Bacon, fellows of the Royal Society, and early Freemasons. Most of John Dee's library, including his manuscripts, found a home in Ashmole's collection. In *Theatricum Chemicum Britannicum* (1652), Ashmole in his prologue declared that the Earl of Norfolk had been cured of leprosy by a brother R.C., and Queen Elizabeth had been twice saved from smallpox by another. Ashmole was a guardian to astrologers, protecting them from Cromwell. It's extraordinary that he had influence over both Cromwell and King Charles II, who considered Ashmole a favorite. George Lyman Kittredge (1920) writes: "We have still further traces of Childe in 1651. On March 7, Elias Ashmole makes the following entry in his Diary: 'I went to Maidstone with Dr. Child the physician,'" placing Childe at the heart of England's alchemical community.

But perhaps the most dramatic evidence that Childe's interest in the esoteric went far beyond the pale of an average Presbyterian is the dedication in the 1651 English translation of the *Three Books of Occult Philosophy* by Agrippa:

To my most honorable, and no less learned Friend, Robert Childe, Doctor of Physick.

SIR! Great men decline, mighty men may fall, but an honest Philosopher keeps his Station forever. To your self therefore I crave leave to present, what I know you are able to protect; not with sword, but by reason; & not that only, but what by your acceptance you are able to give a lustre to. I see it is not in vain that you have compassed Sea and Land, for thereby you have made a Proselyte, not of another, but of your self, by being converted from vulgar, and irrational incredulities to the rational embracing of the sublime, Hermeticall, and Theomagicall truths. You are skilled in the one as if Hermes had been your Tutor; have insight in the other, as if Agrippa your Master. (Woodward 2010)

The flattery continues, until it is signed by J. F. According to James Ferguson, the early go-to source for most bibliographical questions related to alchemy and Rosicrucianism, J. F. was John French (1616–1657), a physician remembered for his advancement of distillation in chemistry. Tobias Churton and others have argued that James Freake was J. F. Churton also argues that Robert Childe was in a secret society with Samuel Hartlib, Thomas Vaughan, and Elias Ashmole.

Samuel Hartlib was dubbed "hub of the axletree of knowledge." The transplant to England from Poland was a friend of the great educator Comenius and of the poet John Milton of *Paradise Lost* fame. He was probably the best-connected intellectual of his day because he exchanged letters with every kind of expert. Hartlib's friends and correspondents amounted to an Invisible College, and some became founders of the Royal Society, though Hartlib himself was excluded from membership. For his contributions to everything from beekeeping to increasing crop yields, and for collecting medical cures (rational and irrational), Cromwell awarded Hartlib a pension to live on. But when the royals returned, Hartlib found himself abandoned; he died in poverty.

Hartlib spent years discussing a colony of the learned, perhaps in Virginia, but none of the interested parties ever committed to such a terrifying journey across the Atlantic and such an uncertain future on the outer edge of a vast unknown continent. When Hartlib met Winthrop, he was impressed by this brilliant young alchemist from America bearing samples of the richest mineral ore Hartlib had ever seen. But he was one of those who cooled off when the Mohegans demonstrated their disagreement with the plan. What of the fourth member of Churton's proposed Rosicrucian secret society, Thomas Vaughan?

THE ALCHEMICAL MARRIAGE

Thomas Vaughan was involved in a plan by Robert Childe to form an alchemical circle, but Vaughan referred to himself as a member of the Society of Unknown Philosophers. Vaughan, using the pen name Eugenius Philalethes, was the author of *Anthroposophia Theomagica,* a book that weaves magic with mysticism, quotations from Plotinus, from the occultist Agrippa, from the pagan biographer Plutarch, and from Virgil, the pagan poet of ancient Rome, not to mention Hermes Trismegistus and Pythagoras. "I look on this life as the progress of an essence royal: the soul but quits her court to see the country," Vaughan wrote. He also complained: "It is an age of intellectual slaveries: if they meet anything extraordinary, they prune it commonly with distinctions or daub it with false glosses, till it looks like the traditions of Aristotle. His followers are so confident of his principles they seek not to understand what others speak but to make others speak what they understand. It is in Nature as it is in religion: we are still hammering old elements but seek not the America that lies beyond them" (Rudrum 1984).

Vaughan was the twin brother of Henry Vaughan, the physician and metaphysical poet who influenced everyone from Wordsworth and Tennyson to that prophetic master of science fiction, Philip K. Dick. Thomas started out as a minister in his native Wales, with a generous salary including house and lands far above the average expectation for a young man. John Walker wrote about Vaughan's case in *Sufferings of the Clergy* (1714), reporting he was removed from his parish "for Drunkenness, Swearing, Incontinency, being no Preacher, and what was in their Opinion worse than All, for having been in Arms for the King: And perhaps the last Article was the only Proof and Evidence of all the Rest." But Vaughan admitted later in his writing that he "reveled away many years in drinking." The Civil War did far worse than remove preachers from their parishes. Acts of murder and mutilation occurred on both sides of this Christian divide. Vaughan retreated to his experiments and studies at Oxford.

A tragic love story is at the core of Thomas Vaughan's life. He worked closely in his alchemical and initiatory experiments with his wife, Rebecca, his *soror,* or sister in the Great Work. Rebecca was no mere assistant. All the breakthroughs Thomas achieved were either done with her help or by her inspiration. His work after her death merely played out what he had already learned. Her skill was so great he named one of their discoveries *Aqua Rebecca,* because without her help he couldn't reproduce the results.

But in 1658 Rebecca had nightmares about being attacked by a stallion, then she sickened. By April, as she lay dying, Vaughan obsessively chased after a formula he had forgotten from his early days when she first began working with him. Perhaps he thought it would cure her, though he nowhere mentions this. He exults at achieving his goal, just as Rebecca died. In notes first published by A. E. Waite about two hundred years after Vaughan wrote them down, the alchemist at first declares that the grief of so great an impending loss was fuel for his efforts, and that he had been graced with success as a compensation for the loss of his beloved. But later he shared the depth of a sorrow he felt keenly. His notes end with bereft confessions of his yearning for her, his regrets, and a detailed, heartbreakingly fond list of every possession of hers still remaining to him, including a Holy Bible she owned before they met.

The notebook record of their work together he now flipped over and gave a new title page. He invented a monogram out of the initials of her first name, his, and their last name: *T R V.* He used it to sign most of the entries, even the ones made after her death. Just before the first anniversary of her death, Thomas dreamed of Rebecca. She appeared covered in "thin loose silks" of unearthly green; she was taller and her face was shining with an angelic glow. Just before meeting Rebecca in 1651, Tom had written *Lumen de Lumine, or a New Magical Light,* in which he described a goddess of wisdom dressed in green who finally enlightens him. Tom took Rebecca's appearance in the green dress in his dream as a clear message. She had been Beatrice to his Dante, and she would continue to be. Signing his work with their combined insignia was not a sad gesture but an affirmation that husband and wife were still engaged in the Great Work together.

In the months following her death Thomas had dreams about her that brought him premonitions; for example, she appeared in a dream to correctly predict his father's death in June that same year. Haunted by so much death Tom began having nightmares about the murderous stallion. He felt certain his end was near. But at the end of August he had a dream about his wife that left him feeling he now understood what the Bible meant by having a home in eternity.

The melancholy Vaughan then followed the court as an alchemist supported by the king, thanks to his friend Sir Robert Moray, fellow royalist, and his partner in alchemical experimentation, whose accomplishments included being a judge, a soldier, a spy, a mathematician, a statesman, a diplomat, and the first president of the Royal Society. Along with Elias Ashmole, Moray is one of the two earliest recorded Freemasons in English history. Moray, probably assisted by Vaughan, helped Charles II with his own alchemical experiments. When the royal court left London for Oxford to escape the plague in 1665, Vaughan was included in the entourage.

In 1652 Vaughan translated and published the *Fama Fraternitatis Rosae Crucis,* the bedrock document of the Rosicrucian movement, the first English edition since its original appearance in print in Germany almost forty years earlier in 1614. Scholars have argued that Moray gave Vaughan a Scottish manuscript version of the *Fama* that had belonged to Moray's father. This has led to speculation that Moray was a Rosicrucian. But what does that mean exactly? That he was a member of a secret society of almost superhuman adepts? That he was one of the original participants in the benevolent conspiracy of a secret order of Masons? What if he was simply inspired by the Rosicrucian writings? He doesn't mention Rosicrucians anywhere in his letters, but of course a Rosicrucian of that time wouldn't have.

Vaughan may or may not have been a Rosicrucian, but he would have felt right at home with Renaissance Neoplatonists. He thought the spirit to be "a mere enclosure or vestment" for the soul, the "celestial, ethereal part of man." Spirit gives soul the power "whereby we do move, see, feel, taste and smell, and have a commerce with all material objects whatsoever." Vaughan tells us this is what Paracelsus meant by "sidereal man," the part of us connected with the constellations. Vaughan also looks to Plato who described a "thin aerial substance" that acted as the "vestment wherein the Soul wraps herself when she descends." Eliphas Levi had a similar view, but what Vaughan called "spirit," Levi called "the astral body."

In 1664 John Winthrop Jr. wrote to Moray about his discovery of a faint star near the planet Jupiter that he thought might be the fifth moon. Modern astronomers hesitate to credit Winthrop with such a feat of visual acuity but the evidence in the letter is undeniable.

Moray had second sight, said to be common among highlanders; he foresaw his wife's death, but not the death of his friend Vaughan. In 1666 one of their experiments led to Vaughan inhaling mercury fumes, killing him. Moray paid for his friend's funeral.

Moray lived another seven years. Near the end of his life he became a recluse, living like an impoverished person, obsessively pursuing alchemical experiments in a dirty laboratory. For all we know he was having the time of his life unfettered by the court and other responsibilities, or perhaps he was a senile almost ghost, muttering to his old friend Tom Vaughan. Or perhaps he inhaled fumes, too. When Moray died the king ordered him buried in Westminster Abbey.

THE ALCHEMIST STARKEY

In the eighteenth and nineteenth centuries Robert Childe was thought to be the writer behind the highly esteemed books of Eirenaeus Philalethes, a pseudonym that must have been a tribute to Eugenius Philalethes. Some historians have speculated that John Winthrop Jr. might have been the real Eirenaeus. An obscure bit of evidence for Winthrop as Eirenaeus first appeared in Ferguson's *Bibliothecha Chemica* where the usually dependable bibliophile says they are one and the same. In the *Bacstrom Manuscripts* in the Manly P. Hall collection in volume 12, in his notes to the anonymous manuscript *Some Curious Processes* and in his notes to his handwritten copy of Lambsprink's

The Great Work, sea captain and alchemist Sigismund Bacstrom wrote that Winthrop was Eirenaeus. Most likely Bacstrom was reporting an oral tradition, which of course doesn't necessarily make the identification true, but it is an intriguing detail.

The likeliest candidate for the true identity of Eirenaeus may be George Starkey. As William Newman, professor of history of science at Indiana University, shows in his essay in *Alchemy Revisited,* striking similarities of sources and expression can be found between an alchemical work attributed to Eireneaus and letters sent from Starkey to the scientist Robert Boyle.

George Stirk, as Starkey was originally known, was born in Bermuda but educated at Harvard College, where alchemy was a popular pursuit. He settled down in Boston where he practiced Paracelsian medicine professionally. His experiments with the technology of alchemy as it was becoming chemistry were serious enough that he left America for London in search of better materials for building his alchemical ovens. He had just gotten married and changed his name to Starkey. Recently historians have argued that Starkey is America's first important scientist.

Starkey's skills made him popular in Samuel Hartlib's circle of reformers and Paracelsian doctors and alchemists. He was known for being able to produce greater quantities of quality aromatic oils thanks to his secret process. His most famous demonstration or claim to the elixir was the rejuvenation of a withered peach tree. But his influence goes further than that.

William Newman argues that Starkey was probably the most widely read American scientist before Ben Franklin. Starkey's work is said to have been an influence on three of the most influential intellectuals of the age: Isaac Newton; philosopher and physician John Locke; and mathematician and philosopher Gottfried Leibniz. Robert Boyle, a pioneer of scientific method and one of those most responsible for bringing the butterfly of chemistry out of its alchemy cocoon, was impressed when Starkey cured his until then incurable illness. Starkey became Boyle's chemistry tutor. Boyle quotes Eirenaeus Philalethes admiringly in his own works. But he does not appear to have known that Starkey was the author of the Eirenaeus Philalethes books. In fact, critics of the day complained that such a profound author should be distributed by Starkey, a difficult and unpleasant fellow. Recent studies of Starkey's notebooks reveal method and clarity closer to chemistry than alchemy.

Eirenaeus Philalethes wrote elevated prose inspiring to spiritual and political reformers alike—of course, at the time if you were one you were likely to be the other. Eirenaeus wrote in alchemical code, a language of metaphors, the uninitiated reader is left to wonder how to procure such ingredients as "the doves of Diana," "the menstrual blood of our whore," "Gehennical Fire" (hell fire), and "a Fiery Dragon." While possibly easier to obtain, the exact use or meaning of "a hermaphrodite," "a mad dog," and "a chameleon" remain obscure. Gehennical Fire is apparently a universal solvent, but how to store something that dissolves anything it comes into contact with, literally disassembling the building blocks of our material world? And how exactly does the amalgam "fly away seven times"?

Starkey presented himself as the editor and distributor of the secretive Eirenaeus. From 1654 to 1683 over a dozen works were published, including *The Marrow of Alchemy, Secrets Revealed,* and *The Secret of the Immortal Liquor Called Alkahest.* Six of his works have titles that include the illustrious alchemical name of Sir George Ripley; for example *An Exposition upon the First Six Gates of Sir George Ripley's Compound of Alchymie.* After twenty years of study in Italy, where he was a favorite of Pope Innocent VIII, George Ripley went home to Great Britain in 1477, where he wrote *The Compound of Alchymy; or, the Twelve Gates leading to the Discovery of the Philosopher's Stone.* The book was dedicated to King Edward IV and was a favorite of his. Ripley was one of the first to compose poetry on alchemy, and his magnificent scroll and many writings made him famous. His wealth was legendary and made it seem more plausible that he could turn lead to gold.

There are only twenty-three copies of the *Ripley Scroll* in existence. According to London's Science Museum, "the scrolls are believed to be 18th Century copies and variations of a lost, 15th Century original." I was fortunate to have perused the one in the collection of Manly Hall with the great collector himself.

Ripley also has the distinction of being perhaps the first to publish previously unknown manuscripts by the great Raymond Lull, who two hundred years earlier had written groundbreaking works on not only mathematics, statistics, classification, and architecture, but also mysticism and the occult.

Starkey seems to have enjoyed making up details about the life of Eirenaeus. One might wonder about multiple personality disorder until the predicament Starkey was in becomes clear. Starkey in his letters to Boyle writes that he had received offers to use his secrets that could have made him very wealthy. Investors were eager for him to attempt gold and silver making on an industrial scale. But Starkey said that such a life would be like hard labor to him, removing him from what he loved most, studying nature and learning its secrets. Starkey shared his secrets with Boyle, only upon assurance that Boyle would never sell them. The illuminations Starkey had received by grace of what he called the Father of Lights were not for mere vulgar profit. They were to contribute to the reform of the world, the restoration of paradise by divine revelation. It was a delicate situation. Starkey needed Boyle's financial support so he had to show his efforts worthwhile, but if he gave up too many of his trade secrets he wouldn't be useful anymore.

Starkey attributed part of his genius to dreams. One of these dreams was a major contribution to the myth of the adept or initiate who appears to the sincere alchemist. In a letter to Boyle, Starkey writes:

> Behold! I seemed intent on my work, and a man appeared, entering the laboratory, at whose arrival I was stupefied. But he greeted me and said: "May God support your labours." When I heard this, realizing that he had mentioned God, I asked who he was, and he responded that he was my Eugenius; I asked whether there were such creatures. He responded that there were—Finally I asked him what the alkahest of Paracelsus and Helmont was, and he responded that they used salt, sulphur, and an alkalized body, and though this response was more obscure than Paracelsus himself, yet with the response an ineffable light entered my mind, so that I fully understood. Marveling at this, I said to him, "Behold! Your words are veiled, as it were by fog, and yet they are fundamentally true." He said, "This is so necessarily, for the

things said by one's Eugenius are all certain, while those just said by me are the truest of all." (Woodward 2010)

Eugenius is a Greek word, the usual translation is "well born" but good spirit or great spirit, even guardian angel or higher self might be closer to the meaning Starkey intended.

When Starkey turned his writing skills to political pamphleteering and then got caught up in lawsuits, his reputation was hopelessly tarnished. Then in 1665 the great plague arrived in London. George Thomson was a physician and writer on medical matters who rocked the British medical world when he removed the spleen of a dog but kept the poor animal alive for another two years. The old theory of body humors was disproved by that one experiment. When plague came to London, Thomson stayed to do what he could to help patients and to study its symptoms; he even dissected the corpse of a plague victim. He was furious at the Royal College of Physicians for abandoning the population and fleeing to luxurious safety, so he wrote a pamphlet accusing them of dereliction of duty.

English Neoplatonist and public Rosicrucian John Heydon, who practiced law and astrology side by side, responded that same year with a furious pamphlet called *Psonthonphanchia, or a Quintuple Rosiecrucian Scourge for the Due Correction of That Pseudo-chymist and Scurrilous Emperick, Geo. Thomson.* Heydon was well known among royalists and occultists for his powers of prediction. He was supposed to have correctly foretold the end of Cromwell. Whatever powers he had didn't prevent him from being imprisoned in the Tower two years later. Heydon was a notorious plagiarizer of everyone from Thomas Vaughan to Sir Francis Bacon. He can be classified with a certain type of metaphysical writer, colorful characters like L. W. de Laurence, who never hesitated to plagiarize others' works word for word. Elias Ashmole called Heydon "an ignoramus and a cheate."

Thomson lived long enough to read Heydon's pamphlet attack on him thanks to George Starkey. Spending so much time around plague victims, Thomson succumbed. He gave himself up to the medical services of Starkey. Starkey treated him with the dried powder of a toad.

Thomson wore a dried toad around his neck as a booster. The irony was complete when Thomson recovered but Starkey died. Thomson blamed it on the beer Starkey had insisted on having despite his sickness. Thomson suspected that the beer had counteracted the healing power of the toad. George Starkey died at age thirty-seven. If he was Eirenaeus Philalethes most of his works were published posthumously.

THE ALCHEMIST WHO CONDEMNED WITCHES

In his account of the Salem witch trials, Cotton Mather wrote: "And we have now with horror seen the discovery of such a witchcraft! An army of devils is horribly broke in upon the place which is the center, and after a sort, the firstborn of our English settlements. And the houses of the good people there are filled with the doleful shrieks of their children and servants, tormented by invisible hands, with tortures altogether preternatural. After the mischiefs there endeavored, and since in part conquered, the terrible plague of evil angels has made its progress into some other places, where other persons have been in like manner diabolically handled" (Mather 1693).

Mather's conviction that Europeans were bringing God to the country of the Devil was ironic even then, in the aftermath of the epidemics the colonists brought with them that decimated the Indigenous population. Perhaps it's even more ironic now, as the full extent of the destructiveness of the inheritors of this continent has become blatantly obvious. Yet a man so afraid of evil that he could imagine "an army of devils" tormenting simple householders, had no suspicion of the whiff of sulphur in the lab of an alchemist.

In a letter to colonial clergyman John Higginson in 1682, Mather revealed his contradictory morality regarding Christians who approached their faith differently. He refers to the Quakers on board a ship bound for America as "heretics and malignants." So that "the Lord may be glorified and not mocked on the soil of this new country with the heathen worship of these people," Mather suggested they all be sold into slavery. "Much spoil can be made of selling the whole lot to Barbadoes, where slaves fetch good prices in rum and sugar, and we shall not only do the Lord great good by punishing the wicked, but we shall make great good for his Minister and people."

Cotton Mather was a complicated man. He vigorously denounced astrology and all forms of fortune-telling, yet he knew how to cast an astrological chart and argued before the Royal Society that the influences of the stars in the zodiac on planting and harvesting should be measured. He was so eager to prosecute witches in 1689 that he published a bestseller, *Memorable Providences, Relating to Witchcrafts and Possessions.* The book described the symptoms of witchcraft, feeding the frenzy of paranoia, and told the story of Goody Glover, an Irish laundress, or aged mother of a laundress, whose sad distinction was to be the last woman accused of witchcraft in Boston to die at the end of a noose. She was an Irish woman, a widow like many other Catholics sold into slavery by Cromwell in the 1650s during the occupation of Ireland. By 1680 she and her daughter were working as domestics in Boston in the house of John Goodwin. In the summer of 1688, four of the five Goodwin children got sick. The presiding physician's diagnosis was, "nothing but a hellish Witchcraft could be the origin of these maladies." Martha, a thirteen-year-old girl, sealed Glover's fate when she reported they had all become ill after an argument with the miserable old woman who had said rude things to her.

During the court case the frightened Glover refused to speak English, answering questions only in her native Irish. Mather insisted she could speak English perfectly well. Witnesses reported that the old woman seemed distracted and confused. Since the Puritans thought the Catholic church was in service of Satan the widow didn't have a chance. Cotton Mather was MC of the proceedings, full of windy pronouncements and divine revelations, battling Satan in the New World with evidence of evil activities confessed by victims, for instance, the diabolical prank of stealing linen.

Mather reported, "Order was given to search the old woman's house, from whence there were brought into the court, several small Images, or Puppets, or Babies, made of Raggs, and stuff't with Goat's hair, and other such Ingredients." Glover, he continued "acknowledged that her way to torment the Objects of her malice, was by wetting of her Finger with her Spittle, and stroaking of those little images." Such voodoo dolls were a common feature of the witch trials. After Mather visited Glover in her cell, the persecuted Gaelic widow stroked her wet thumb on a smooth stone muttering what may have been curses on Cotton Mather, or Catholic prayers.

Folk magic was a common feature of Puritan life, like burning the tail of a bewitched pig, which then by sympathetic magic caused a burn on the witch's body. Mather wrote that he believed in the power of spells to heal injuries and sickness and knew of many such instances. But most of it appears to be hearsay. One poor witch was identified when a sick boy, supposedly bewitched, provided a few snips of hair to be boiled. Mary Parker happened to show up to ask if she could buy some chickens. But she should have known there were no chickens there as it was common knowledge in the community, though she insisted she did not know. Therefore she must be lying, and the true reason she appeared at the door was the boiling hair drew her.

The widow Glover was found guilty and sentenced to death. They took her from jail to the gallows in a cart, parading her through the streets to be mocked and jeered at. A crowd watched the old woman die then silently dispersed. Her body was left as a warning to other witches. Robert Calef, a Boston merchant who was one of the few who had known her, wrote: "Goody Glover was a despised, crazy, poor old woman, an Irish Catholic who was tried for afflicting the Goodwin children. Her behaviour at her trial was like that of one distracted. They did her cruel. The proof against her was wholly deficient. The jury brought her guilty. She was hung. She died a Catholic" (Calef 1866). In 1988 the Boston City Council established Goody Glover Day, in a strange gesture of reconciliation three hundred years too late.

Near the end of his life Mather wrote: "I am able with little study to write in seven languages. I feast myself with the sweets of all sciences, which the more polite part of mankind ordinarily pretend to. I am entertained with all kinds of histories, ancient and modern. I am no stranger to the curiosities, which, by all sorts of learning, are brought to the curious. These intellectual pleasures are far beyond any sensual ones" (Calef 1866). Like John Winthrop Jr., Mather's birthday was February 12; he died February 13 in Boston, where he had been born.

In his bestseller *Memorable Providences,* Mather had paused in his penned pursuit of witches to describe the qualities of a proper Puritan: "Let us more generally agree to maintain a kind opinion one of another. That charity, without which even our giving our bodies to be burned would profit nothing—it is kind, it is not easily provoked, it thinks no evil, it believes all things, hopes all things" (Mather 1689). The Puritans, you see, were not angry when they executed a witch. Anger was a quality of witches, not of Puritans, who severely condemned extremes of emotion. How could Mather have written such irony with a straight face when he was advocating killing women (and a few men)? How could he consider himself free of thinking evil when he referred to Indigenous Americans as Satan's "most devoted and resembling children" and dismissed Quakers as demonically possessed?

Mather was typical of the contradictions to be found among the Puritans. Another alchemist from Harvard College, William Stoughton, acting governor of the province of Massachusetts Bay, presided over the Salem witch trials when he was chief justice. Mather almost prevented the Salem witch trials. He thought the best way to deal with the afflicted girl was to move her into his house where he and his family could help her and arrive at a better understanding of her predicament. Yet, tragically, Mather gave the Salem witch trials an especially destructive and irrational context when he argued that spectral evidence should be admissible. The girls were now free to unleash the full imagination of their psychotic breakdowns, and the court and community followed them. Yet Mather disapproved of aspects of the trial. His later attempts to cure witches were quiet and private.

Mather lived long enough to become a champion of inoculation at a time when smallpox epidemics were killing off colonists as they had killed off so many Indigenous people, entire tribes disappeared. The battle to allow inoculation was a violent one. Many believed to use science for relief from a god-ordained scourge was akin to witchcraft. Here is a crucial moment in American history and in the history of American Metaphysical Religion. Why did the Mather of the witch trials understand that smallpox inoculation was not a demonic temptation, or the spreading of infection? Why did he consider it not only the answer to prayers, but also the reward of hard labor in laboratories? Why did he have enough faith to use it on his own child? So persuasive was Mather in his argument for inoculation that members of the opposition tossed a grenade into his house. He survived, and inoculation proved itself one family at a time, as people noticed it really worked. Mather was the first American to become a member of the Royal Society. He remains an enigma. He condemned astrology but practiced it. His favorite physician was alchemist John Winthrop Jr., eulogized by Mather as "Hermes Christianus" the Christian Hermes, as good as saying the Christian Pagan or the Pagan Christian.

THE BEST OCCULT LIBRARY IN COLONIAL VIRGINIA

New England wasn't the only American frontier where alchemy and astrology were popular. Tom Teakle was minister to several parishes for more than forty years. He had to take on the extra parishes because so many had been abandoned, and the laziness of many of the remaining ministers was practically proverbial. He arrived in 1652, the year the Commonwealth and Protectorate Governor Richard Bennett replaced Crown Governor Sir William Berkeley. Berkeley was a popular governor during his ten-year first term. He encouraged diversification of crops in Virginia, and as much independence as possible from the crown. On the other hand, he strongly opposed public schools, and his hostility to Puritans and Quakers caused him to help put in place a law to defend the purity of the doctrine of the Church of England.

In 1660, due to the untimely death of Commonwealth and Protectorate Governor Sam Mathews, Berkeley sailed from England, coming out of retirement to be governor again. His seventeen-year second term didn't go as smoothly as his first. He appealed to Charles II for financial aid for Virginia, but the king of England snubbed him in favor of free trade. In 1674 ambitious freeholders on the Virginia frontier were hungry for treaty-protected land that belonged to the Indigenous tribes, with whom Governor Berkeley had always been friendly. He believed their goodwill was a necessary part of the process of growing

Virginia into a viable commonwealth. He had just convinced the chiefs of the Susquehannock tribe that negotiation was better than fighting when a troop of militia disobeyed his orders, attacking the village and killing the chiefs. The Susquehannocks counterattacked in force, burning plantations and killing sixty Virginians.

Berkeley wanted to build fortresses to protect the settlers instead of launching an all-out war. After all, he had fur trade investments that depended on good relations with the tribes. But the frontiersmen grumbled it was just an excuse to raise their taxes. Enter Nathaniel Bacon, who may have been the cousin by marriage of the governor's second wife. Bacon wasn't exactly grateful when Berkeley gave him a place on the governing council. Bacon emerged as the leader of the grumblers itching for a war with the tribes. Berkeley was hard of hearing and showing other signs of age; they thought him too feeble to govern. Bacon demanded a military commission, but Berkeley refused. Bacon led an attack anyway, leading five hundred frontiersmen in a bloody expedition against two tribes that had not been involved in the fighting. Berkeley had Bacon arrested. But Bacon's men went to his rescue, and then they forced Berkeley into a new election that put allies of Bacon in power in the House of Burgesses, America's first congress of local representatives. The vote limited the governor's power and gave more to the frontiersmen.

In July 1675, a few months after the widely mourned death of John Winthrop the Younger, an Indigenous war party attacked an outlying Virginia plantation. Not an unusual event over the last thirty years, but this time the attacks and retaliations continued. Rumors of war spread across the Virginia frontier. July 30, 1676, almost exactly one hundred years before the birth of America, Bacon and his army issued the Declaration of the People of Virginia, accusing Berkeley of unfair taxes, appointing cronies, and failing to protect the locals from attacks by the tribes. The rebel forces and Berkeley's loyal troops battled. Six weeks later Bacon took Jamestown and in a strange demonstration of colonial leadership burned it the ground. For Berkeley it seemed divine justice when about a month later Bacon fell ill with dysentery and shat himself to death.

Berkeley seized the property of several rebels and sentenced twenty-three of them to the noose. By the time the king's one thousand redcoats arrived to put down Bacon's rebellion it was all over. A committee investigated and its report caused Charles II to remove Berkeley from the governorship and order him home. Thirty years later in the colonies the legend spread that the king had commented, "That old fool has put to death more people in that naked country than I did here for the murder of my father."

Teakle managed to navigate the chaos, preserving his health and his wealth. He was notorious for arguing about his salary with the citizens who ran his parishes. He must have won the arguments because he became one of the wealthiest ministers in colonial America. He owned land and eleven enslaved people. Colonel Scarborough and others attacked Teakle's character. But Scarborough was notorious for summoning a tribe by telling them the Great Spirit would speak to them, then shooting them all down. He considered it a good business decision.

Meanwhile, Teakle preached every Sunday, and he was a popular choice for funerals. But we're interested in Teakle because of his library, 317 books, almost as large as the libraries of John Winthrop Jr., and of Increase and Cotton Mather. The 1697 Teakle estate inventory listed all the Anglican and Puritan writers a well-educated Englishman would be expected to know. His library included many books on personal piety. But the occult section was also extensive, especially well stocked with Rosicrucian books, including John Heydon's *The Rosie Crucian Infallible Axiomata; or General Rules to Know All Things Past, Present, and to Come* (1660). It also included Thomas Vaughan's *Magia Adamica; or The Antiquitie of Magic* and the *Descent Thereof from Adam Downwards* (1650). And the Kabbalah was represented with Reuchlin's classic *De Arte Cabalistica* (1517). His copy of the rogue Jesuit Athanasius Kircher's *Magnes Sirede Arte Magnetica* (1641) contained a stew of hermetic alchemical ideas.

Estate inventories of other wealthy early Virginians included books on astrology, alchemy, natural magic, palm reading, and Pythagoras. The most popular occult authors of early Virginia were astrologer physicians, especially Nicholas Culpeper, more famous these days for his *The Complete Herbal,* still considered a standard work of herbalism three hundred years later, and William Salmon, author of the epic three volume *Practical Physick. Shewing the Method of Curing the most Usual Diseases Happening to Humane bodies. As all Sorts of Aches and Pains, Apoplexies, Agues, Bleeding, Fluxes, Gripings, Wind, Shortness of breath, Diseases of the Breast and Lungs, Abortion, Want of Appetite, Loss of the use of Limbs, Cholick, or Belly-ache, Appositions, Thrushes, Quinsies, Deafness, Bubo's, Cachexis, Stone in the Reins, and Stone in the Bladder . . . To which is added, the philosophick Works of Hermes Trismegistus, Kalid Persicus, Geber Arabs, Artesius Longævus, Nicholas Flammel, Roger Bacon, and George Ripley.* Salmon's medical practice was right outside the gate of St. Bartholomew's Hospital in London. His interests included surgery, prophecy, and a technique for indicating specific emotions in portrait painting.

As Darrett Rutman (1984) wrote: "In sound mind and with clear conscience a Virginian could account his poor hunting to the spell of another (1626), could hold that only the horseshoe over his door protected his sick wife from the evil intentions of a neighbor woman who perforce passed under it on her way to saying black prayers at his wife's bedside (1671), could attribute to a witch the death of his pigs and withering of his cotton (1698), and, in court, faced with suits for slander could insist that 'to his thoughts, apprehension or best knowledge' two witches 'had rid him along the Seaside and home to his own house' (again 1698)."

HARVARD COLLEGE OF ALCHEMY

Harvard was a hotbed of alchemy. From its presidents to its graduates, alchemy was everybody's minor. John Allin, one of many alchemist graduates of Harvard, wrote in a letter to a friend that when facing situations where disease could be caught keeping some gold between your teeth and gum does the trick, apparently the perfection of gold would ward off the causes of sickness.

In July 1672 a Harvard graduate who had gone to Cambridge returned to Boston. Leonard Hoar brought with him a letter signed by thirteen influential nonconformist ministers who had helped pay for a new Harvard building. They urged that Hoar be hired as the new president of Harvard College. Charles Chauncy's eighteen-year presidency had ended with his death. While the new building was finished and his quarters and salary were prepared, Hoar earned his bread preaching. In December of that year Hoar became president of Harvard. A friend of Robert Boyle, he planned to add a research center to Harvard's core curriculum of classical study as practiced in Europe.

Hoar's plans for Harvard included in his own words, "A large well-sheltered garden and orchard for students addicted to planting; an ergasterium [factory] for mechanick fancies; and a laboratory chemical" (Woodward 2010). Hoar added that the reading his students were doing was not enough, they needed practical experience. The president of Harvard sent his friend Boyle some local New England berries he had collected describing the process of distillation he used to produce a cure for colic.

But Hoar was an unpopular outsider. The father of his wife, Bridget, had been one of the regicides, the fifty-nine commissioners who voted unanimously to execute King Charles I. For unknown reasons, perhaps loyalty to the homegrown president of Harvard they had expected, students quickly lost their respect for Hoar; they mimicked his gestures and speech. It didn't help his popularity when he ordered a student whipped for blaspheming against the Holy Ghost. Students abandoned the school in protest until only three students were left to graduate in 1673. One of them was Samuel Sewall, a magistrate in the Salem witch trials, the only magistrate who admitted publicly his regret, years later, calling for a day of prayer, fasting, and for reparations. Sewall was one of the few to stand up for Hoar when howls for his resignation arose, but to no avail, in 1675 Hoar was forced to resign. Cotton Mather believed Hoar's grief was so intense it weakened him; tuberculosis quickly killed him.

A decade later, Hoar's alchemical vision of Harvard would come to life again with the help of Charles Morton. Morton was born in Cornwall and educated at Oxford where he had studied the experimental side of natural philosophy. He arrived in New England in 1686, after legal action against him for his dissenting religious views drove him out of England. Morton was nominated president but the position was filled before he arrived. Instead he became Harvard's first vice president and a member of the corporation of the college. He wrote the textbooks of logic and physics for the curriculum; the latter, filled with alchemical information, was almost a practical manual for experimentation. His lectures on philosophy were too popular or too radical, or both; though he gave them only in his rooms, he got into trouble and had to stop. Perhaps his worst fault was his encouragement of the Salem witch trials. But there could be no clearer an illustration of the great chasm between alchemy and witchcraft in early America than the involvement of so many alchemists in the prosecution of witches, though today both activities are labeled occult, and seem to go together in the popular imagination. Morton also dismissed astrology as the work of the devil when it infrequently happened to be right, despite his use of astrological symbols and his own alchemical experiments.

SOCIETY OF THE WOMAN IN THE WILDERNESS AND THE CAMP OF THE SOLITARY

John Jacob Zimmerman was a professor at Heidelberg University who had been a Lutheran minister when his great interest in astrology, biblical prophecy, and mathematics combined as they so often have in a prediction about the day the world would end. Zimmerman convinced forty young scholars to join him as the immodestly named the Chapter of Perfection. They would journey to America to await the end, doing good works until then. Sadly Zimmerman was the Moses of the community in more ways than one. He died just before the ship sailed for the New World, leaving its leadership to the twenty-one-year-old super scholar with a Transylvanian accent, Johannes Kelpius.

Beat poet Kenneth Rexroth may have been waxing poetic when he claimed Kelpius while crossing the Atlantic "proved his powers by stilling the waves in a violent storm." In 1694 at the invitation of William Penn, Kelpius and the other scholars left the continent they thought hopelessly corrupt to settle a commune named Society of the Woman of the Wilderness, the woman in the wilderness of the biblical book of Revelations, a passage much beloved by today's Christian survivalists. Kelpius has been called the first composer in the history of Pennsylvania, and Woman of the Wilderness was the first community with a pipe organ in the colonies.

The founders of Woman in the Wilderness had pooled their

belongings to come to America. They shared property and work equally. The forty scholars built a forty-by-forty-foot meetinghouse with forty rooms they called the Tabernacle. On top they built an astrological observation deck with mounted telescopes. By day they practiced trades including physician, bookbinder, lawyer, clockmaker, teacher, and builder. They grew herbs and vegetables. Astrologers watched the stars looking for signs of the end. They joined together also to study alchemy and the Kabbalah, the writings of Hermes Trismegistus, and of the mystics Meister Eckhart and Jakob Böhme. When one of the forty died or decided to leave he was replaced from the next in a long line of volunteers back home in Germany.

This strange group built around the impending doom of the world continued to practice celibacy in anticipation of the apocalypse even after it didn't occur on the date in question. Kelpius would look to the stars for corrected calculations several times before doubt began to creep in. It must have been a beautiful place, but it becomes less romantic when you discover some including Kelpius himself slept like hermits in caves.

Kelpius died in 1708 of tuberculosis but the community survived until 1740 when, reduced to only seven men, it welcomed Conrad Beissel. Beissel started out as a baker but religious revelation had drawn him to Woman in the Wilderness. He formed a new community with a cloister at center called Camp of the Solitary, better known as Ephrata. Married members lived on surrounding farms, but the men and women in the cloister were celibate. They wore white robes, practiced nonviolence, performed sacred hymns, and were the first vegetarian community in American history, except for communion day when they ate lamb. The resemblance to the Orphics of Ancient Greece is obvious, but almost certainly unintentional.

Beissel was not only spiritual leader, he also played violin, composing music and writing hymns to be performed in four-, five-, six-, and seven-part harmony. He ran Ephrata's singing school, where he devoted himself to applying the principles of alchemy to song. *Chronicon Ephratense,* the chronicle of the cloister's history says of the science of singing: "This science belongs more to the angelic world than to ours." Ephrata historian Julius Sachse (1902) wrote of

Beissel's musical concepts, "this singular system of harmony was an original evolution from the brain of the Magus and has the additional distinction of being the first original treatise on harmony to be published in the Western world." We don't know exactly what Beissel meant when he called the musical notes "letters," when he wrote, "special care must be taken to bring out the distinguishing quality of each letter; and this requires such diligence and costs so much labor that we cannot here describe it." To cultivate what he called an angelic voice the singer would give up meat, milk, cheese, eggs, beans, and honey. Water was acceptable but not when used excessively in cooking, because it can cause food to become an "unnatural delicacy." The music of Ephrata cannot be exactly reproduced since the special training the singers received is lost.

Ephrata imported from Germany one of the earliest printing presses in the colonies, now in the collection of Juniata College in Pennsylvania; the press is still functional. Ephrata also began America's love affair with the font *fraktur,* where calligraphy meets illustrative art.

Despite his relaxing activities Beissel was hot-tempered and the chronicle records his two-hour rants at his singers who could never be pure enough and who never tried hard enough. Most rehearsals ended in tears. But the result was music of such beauty that cultured visitors who had enjoyed the opera houses of Europe said it haunted them more than any other singing they had ever heard.

In Ephrata the telescopes were still trained to the stars, looking for signs of the longed for Second Coming, but no exact dates were offered. Rumors of sexual misconduct were the only possible outcome when local girls began deserting their families to join up. Later Ephrata became a medical center for the wounded soldiers of Washington's Continental Army during the Battle of Brandywine in the American Revolution. But the community slowly died off. When the last celibate died, the married farmers of Ephrata became German Seventh Day Baptists.

Woman of the Wilderness and Ephrata were claimed as pioneer Rosicrucian communities by the early twentieth-century public American Rosicrucian organization AMORC. Here again we run into a blurry definition of Rosicrucianism. Like the term *New Age,* it means many different things, from fraud all the way to truth, depending on the holder of the opinion. Ephrata Cloister had the same preoccupations as Woman in the Wilderness: astrology, sacred music, the writing of the German mystics, and the esoteric interpretation of the Holy Bible. But there is no proof that they were Rosicrucians. Of course, as always, if they were Rosicrucian at that time they were not permitted to mention it. But the most comfortable definition seems to be generalized rather than particular. Perhaps you could say they were an offshoot of Rosicrucian counterculture, the way so-called hippies were an offshoot of the Beat generation. Then these communities would not be the planned results of the precise actions of a secret society, but the collective activity of many individuals willing to contribute whatever they could to the grand project of a better tomorrow.

ALCHEMY IN AMERICA

By 1720 alchemy as a cultural force waned somewhat in the colonies as the proponents of conformity mustered around established churches, and the publishing and import of spiritually controversial books was suppressed. Every generation within every state was reminded that the occult, which now often included alchemy as well as witchcraft, was prohibited. Alchemy was demoted to the world of folklore and fraud. Yet, in 1720 Cotton Mather was still complaining about the locals using occult methods to cure their illnesses. Charles Morton exchanged letters with Benjamin Franklin about the philosophers' stone in 1773. But by 1774 a satirist wrote about a "solemn old fellow" in "homely rustic dress" spouting off about alchemy and astrology while drinking wine in a New Jersey tavern.

In 1785, in Altoona, Pennsylvania, the mysterious *Secret Symbols of the Rosicrucians from the 16th and 17th Centuries* was published. Most of the text is in German. The lavish illustrations combine alchemical symbolism with citations from the Holy Bible, clearly showing the influence of the theosophy of Jakob Böhme. The title page promises to be "A Simple ABC Booklet For Young Students Practising Daily in the School of the Holy Ghost Made clear to the eyes by pictorial figures For the Exercises of the New Year In the Natural and Theological Light by a Brother of the Fraternity of the Rose Cross . . ."

The Reverend Ezra Stiles, president of Yale College from 1778 to 1795, studied alchemy, though he denied it in writing:

> Interspersed among my miscellaneous Writings may perhaps be found things respecting the Rosacrucian Philosophy, which may induce some to imagine that I have more Knowledge of that matter than I really have. I have no Knowledge of it at all; I never saw Transmutation, the aurific Powder, nor the Philosopher's Stone; nor did I ever converse with an Adept knowing him to be such. The only Man that I ever suspected as a real & true Adept was Rabbi Tobias of Poland, but he evaded my Interrogatories & communicated to me nothing. I believe he was only a conjectural speculative Philosopher. I have known 2 or 3 Persons (as Judge Danforth & Rev. Mr. West) who believed the reality of the Philosophers Stone, but neither of them ever obtained it. They are only conjectural & speculative Philosophers and of such, Dr Franklin told me there were several at Philadelphia . . . I never had, or made an experiment with, a Furnace or Alembic in all my Life. I am not versed in the Books of the Adepts; I have seen but few of those authors, & read less, perhaps all the little I have read collectively would not equal a common Octavo Volume. I am infinitely less acquainted with that than any other of the Sciences in the whole Encyclopaedia of Literature. I never absorbed the extracted Sulpher of Gold in Terra: I have no practical knowledge of the Matter: the few Ideas I have about it are only imaginary, conjectural & speculative. (Woodward 2010)

He certainly knew many details of a subject he claimed to know little about.

Another prominent American with an approach to alchemy that didn't involve laboratories was General Ethan Allen Hitchcock, friend of Abraham Lincoln, teacher of Edgar Allan Poe, Robert E. Lee, and every Union general in the Civil War. He redefined the study of alchemy when he published *Remarks Upon Alchemy and the Alchemists* in 1867, arguing that alchemy was more spiritual path than science. Jung took the same approach in his own alchemical studies.

Witchcraft accusations continued into the 1700s, some reaching trial, but never resulting in execution. After the birth of the United States in 1776 alchemists, fortune-tellers, and witches soon disappeared into the backwoods of American culture, becoming curiosities, though their practices never completely died out and would often blossom into new popularity, for example during the late twentieth-century New Age movement.

Generations of historians completely ignored these embarrassing alchemical and astrological roots, instead emphasizing only the mainstream Christian influences on American culture. They carefully sainted certain alchemists proclaiming them early chemists. Only in the last decades have academic authors risen to the challenge of presenting the alchemists of early colonial America in all their contradictory glory.

America itself might be considered an alchemical experiment. To this day Americans are obsessed with the magical cure, the one book that will tell all, the pill that rejuvenates, the gimmick that metaphorically or (even better) really turns lead into gold. Many of our favorite television shows, like *American Idol* or *America's Got Talent* are based on a sort of distillation process. From myriad elements, one pure product emerges refined and ready to make somebody rich. The same distillation process fascinates us in sports as we root for the championship and the MVP. It's why we hold CEOs and billionaires in such high esteem, as if they are rare gold while their workers are common lead. Our comic books, and popular movies based on them, tell stories of misfit scientist heroes who band together, often in secret, to save humanity. Perhaps an argument could be made that the quest of the alchemists, and the goals of Rosicrucian-inspired reformers, shaped American society as much or more than any other cultural influence including denominational Christianity. And like our alchemist founders we're still obsessed with the end of the world. So the next time someone reminds us that America was founded by Christians, we may smile in agreement and say, "Yes, by Christians: alchemist, Kabbalist, Neoplatonist astrologer Christians."

9

The Red Harlot

THE FIRST FEMALE IN AMERICA to address mixed crowds at a public event, Frances Wright was one of the first American feminists and female abolitionists, a champion of worker's rights, and a sharp critic of religious institutions. Frances was the first American to write eloquently of sexual passion as a wonderful pleasure, not a sinful shame. She fought for birth control, divorce, and property rights for women. Her lectures attracted thousands. Jefferson, Lafayette, Monroe, Madison, and Andrew Jackson advised her. Her audacious attempt to cure slavery with an experimental commune scandalized America. When she matured and compromised, no one noticed. Her fame remained a caricature of extremism, until she became a curiosity and then was forgotten in her own lifetime. At the end of her life, estranged from her family, her only friends her lawyer and her carpenter, she died alone.

Walt Whitman saw Frances Wright lecture at the height of her fame, in New York City, where thousands thundered their appreciation of her eloquence as she presented her radical ideas about liberating enslaved people and giving women equal rights. That year a play Frances had originally written only for her friends and family was produced at the Park Theater on Broadway. At Thomas Paine celebrations across America her name was the most toasted. She influenced Whitman's politics. In old age, remembering her, Whitman said he had responded to her more "glowingly" than any other of her gender. He explained, "She was a brilliant woman, of beauty and estate, who was never satisfied unless she was busy doing good—public good, private good. We all loved her: fell down before her: her very appearance seemed to enthrall us—the noblest Roman of them all—a woman of the noblest make-up whose orbit was a great deal larger than theirs—too large to be tolerated for long by them: a most maligned, lied about character—one of the best in history though also one of the least understood" (Traubel 1961).

On the southeast coast of Scotland in 1795, Frances "Fanny" Wright was born. Her father James Wright Jr. adored his wife and children. His career as a merchant suffered from his dedication to spending time with his family, practicing liberal politics, and collecting coins, which included advocating for coin designs featuring good honest work like weaving and mail coaches instead of royal profiles and boring coats of arms. British authorities investigated James in 1794 for printing and distributing Thomas Paine's *The Rights of Man*.

Frances's mother, Camilla, was the niece of Baron Rokeby, vice chancellor of the University of Dublin, and archbishop of Armagh. Camilla's godmother, the bluestocking Elizabeth Robinson Montagu, defended the plays of Shakespeare from the witty attacks of Voltaire. Samuel Johnson nicknamed Montagu "Queen of the Blues," making her possibly the first queen of the blues in history, though she earned the title without having to sing or play guitar. Not long before Frances was born, the queen of England and her six daughters breakfasted with Camilla's godmother.

Frances seemed destined for the comfortable life of a petty aristocrat. Letters from Camilla to her husband record the depth of love these parents felt for their children. With a great-uncle like the Scottish philosopher James Mylne, Frances was assured that her life would not be the empty display of manners and conspicuous consumption practiced by so many of her class, but as a female intellectual all she could hope for was to host a salon, while attending to the responsibilities of a proper wife and mother, with the help of servants and nannies.

When Frances turned two years old, Camilla died in the winter of 1798. Three months later Frances's father died. Frances and her older brother and younger sister became orphans. Her brother they sent to be raised by James Mylne. Loving foster parents took in her sister. But her grandfather and teenage aunt raised Frances.

Major General Duncan Campbell of the Royal Marines had retired into a luxurious life of grand dinner parties with lords and generals, at which ten courses of wine were served. Opulent evenings at the opera interested him more than child rearing. Once when little Frances walked with Duncan through the streets of London, she saw the plight of hundreds of mothers and children in tattered clothes, obviously starving, begging for any pittance. Duncan told her they were begging because they were too lazy to work.

Later, when Duncan refused a beggar at the door, a man asking to work for a little food, Frances announced that she wished she had money to give the poor soul. Duncan told her she was foolish. So, "she asked him why rich people who did not work did not become beggars, he answered that work was shameful." He also informed her that "God intended there should be poor, and there should be rich" (Eckhardt 1984).

In 1803 Frances's uncle William, a military man like his father, was killed in India. He willed half of his property in Bengal, Behar, Orissa, and Benares to his nieces. The other half he willed to his sister. In 1806 Frances and her little sister Camilla were reunited when their young aunt used her new wealth to buy a house on the coast of Devonshire. The sisters became very close and for most of the rest of their lives Frances depended on her sister, named Camilla after their mother, to handle the domestic side of her life.

The twenty-room mansion called the Cottage offered beautiful scenery, including a view of Lyme Bay from the top of a hill. Frances could watch the English Channel flow into the Atlantic. Apricots and peaches ripened in the kitchen garden. Magnolia trees scented the ocean breeze. Frances would read Wordsworth's poetry of the rapture of nature and experience it herself swimming and riding horses. Frances wrote that she was "surrounded at all times by rare and extensive libraries." But this idyllic interlude didn't last long. In 1809 Frances's brother died in a military skirmish with the French, then Major General Duncan Campbell died. By age fourteen Frances had lost her mother, father, brother, and grandfather.

Frances lived in the world Jane Austen wrote about. Women of marriageable age must have only one concern, according to local propriety;

they must compete to marry the finest man available. Frances' conservative aunt demanded conformity to local standards of behavior. Tall, skinny teenage Frances had other ideas. While others politely trotted their horses, she galloped past them. When at high tea an eligible bachelor praised his hounds, she might respond with a recent insight she had regarding a problem of higher mathematics. When polite society chatted about the latest popular novel, she quoted the smoldering poetry of the notorious Lord Byron.

Meanwhile the industrialization of England advanced. Men of wealth and power began to buy enormous areas of land on which to build their noble estates. Frances saw the evictions of families whose ancestors had worked farms on that land before the Norman Conquest. They would become workers in dangerous factories, beggars on the streets of London, or indentured into servitude in the colonies. Lush lawns and gardens, terrain suitable for fox hunting, and opulent mansions replaced the farms. Going to tea or dinner at one of these castles tested Frances's limits. She could not understand how these men could have treated innocent people with such cruelty.

Frances came to think of her aunt as an enemy, or perhaps an example of "the enemy." The domineering woman told the children exactly how much food to eat, how to stand, how to speak. Boys must wear gloves at all times. Her retentive reign of terror predicated on what proper society would think went against the grain of Frances's every instinct.

FALLING IN LOVE WITH AMERICA

In the Cottage library Frances found a book that sparked the most important romance of her life. In her autobiography she described herself at this key moment:

> While still a very young girl, she found by chance among some old books tumbled together in a chest in her aunt's library, a copy of Botta's *History of the American Revolution*. . . . From that moment she awoke, as it were, to a new existence. . . . There existed a country

consecrated to freedom, in which man might wake to the full knowledge and full exercise of his powers. To see that country was, now
at the age of sixteen, her fixed but secret determination—. She had
absolutely devoured the Italian historian and was in the full tide of
ecstasy when a sudden apprehension seized her. Was the whole thing
a romance? What had become of the country and the nation? She
had never heard of either. A panic terror seized upon her. She flew
to examine every atlas in the library. The first was not of recent date
and showed no trace of the United States. She opened with trembling hands another and another. At last she saw "United States"
marked along the Atlantic coastline of North America. (Lane 1972)

In the preface to her *Course of Popular Lectures* (1829) Frances
wrote, "I may observe, however, that from the age of seventeen, when I
first accidentally opened the page of America's national history—from
that moment my attention became riveted on this country, as on the
theater where man might first awake to the full knowledge and the
full exercise of his powers." Soon Frances was reading everything she
could find on this daring experiment in life, liberty, and the pursuit of
happiness.

In 1813 Frances though still underage forced a move to the household of James Mylne. Daughters and sons were equal, and equally
well educated, in the Mylne family. Mylne's colleagues, impressed by
Frances's intellect, since she was not allowed to study at any college,
instead borrowed for her any book she asked for, helping her along in
her career of learning.

Gathering with a circle of like-minded friends of both genders,
Frances began writing Byronic poetry. She also wrote a play and a precocious neoclassical examination of Epicurean philosophy eventually
published as *A Few Days in Athens*. Frances presented it as a translation
of a Greek manuscript discovered in Herculaneum.

While her peers got engaged, Frances decided to move with Camilla
to London. Not only would they pursue a lawsuit against their aunt,
who was unwilling to let go their purse strings, but Frances would get
a better sense of what might be accomplished to do some good in the

world. Instead she got a hard look at the devastation of the poor, as policies of protectionism and industrialization destroyed local economies that had been self-sufficient for generations. Soaring prices and unemployment caused rioting in the streets. Frances decided she must see America for herself because she had no hope for England.

James Mylne was so alarmed by Frances's plan to sail across the Atlantic with Camilla on a trip to see the wondrous republic America, he traveled straight to Liverpool hoping to talk her out of it. But twenty-two-year-old Frances Wright had made up her mind. She was too much for England, perhaps in a country as free, brash, and modern as herself, she could find a destiny more to her liking.

On the way to America, Frances made a science of adjusting diet to support digestion at sea, sharing her know-how with her fellow passengers. Imagine her delight when she found that unlike illiterate British sailors the American crew could read and write. They spoke eagerly and knowledgeably of the history and laws of the United States. In her journal Frances described the voyage as uneventful, but she must have been thrilled with the anticipation of arriving in a republic to her mind like some new Athens, an outpost of a superior civilization.

In the fall of 1818 New York was still a small town. Greenwich Village was a landscape of farms. Though America's economy was struggling, to Frances it seemed no one was too poor and no one too rich. The famous New Yorker exuberance was already in evidence. But a series of hustles and thefts by boardinghouse keepers and servants quickly taught Frances that not every American was a sage.

Walking wherever possible, and taking touristy boat rides, Frances was the original Studs Terkel, interviewing everyone in her path about what was going on in America. Her favorites were the gents from the Carolinas, with their polished manners, and the rugged honest men from the Western frontier. Despite her initial experiences with hustlers, Frances wrote that New York was more honest than other cities. Seeking American citizenship, Frances and Camilla were disappointed to find out that five years of residency were required.

Wealthy and powerful new friends helped make life more gracious for the newcomers. A possible romance with an American banker, son of a famous Irish revolutionary, led to an opportunity for Frances to have the play she'd written for her friends back home in Scotland produced at the ritzy Park Theater on the famous street that even then was known simply as Broadway.

Almost 2,400 people filled the theater on opening night to see this new British production about Swiss freedom fighters. Like Frances's family, most of the lead characters died. The play was credited to "Anonymous"; a female author was out of the question. So Frances sat beside Camilla watching the standing ovation. She had to keep her seat as the audience chanted for the author. She could not share the rave reviews she read proclaiming her play uniquely suited for the American stage because of its passion for freedom. She could not correct the critics who were certain a man had written it.

Despite the exciting premier, the play didn't survive a week before closing down. No secret can last long in New York City. Word got out that a woman had written the play that got a standing ovation. Meddlesome old ladies and conservative old goats were shocked from Boston to Glasgow. Frances searched for a publisher as a new production of the play was prepared for a run in Philadelphia, but no one was in a rush to publish a female playwright.

Frances and Camilla returned to their travels, two young women alone, voyaging thousands of miles. They went north to Montreal and west to Pittsburgh. Frances relished her anecdotal research on Americans. She met wealthy liberal expatriates from Great Britain and simple backwoods mechanics and merchants. She found all of them eager to reflect her own enthusiasm about the republic.

But Frances also saw slavery in America for the first time. She could not accept such brutality and inhumanity in a country devoted to freedom and composed of wilderness.

America's economic depression seemed an easy fix to Frances. If the wealthy had not developed a taste for fancy European fabrics and other products of decadence, if they would be content with their own homespun, the prosperity of the growing country could be immediately restored.

Sick from her travels under difficult conditions, Frances missed the opening night of her play in Philadelphia. Once again the audience responded with a standing ovation. But the play closed that very night. Frances gave away the few copies of her play that she had been able to get printed. She sent some of the copies to Americans she admired, including Founding Father Thomas Jefferson.

Before returning home the sisters visited the future site of Washington, D.C., where Frances relished the muddy roads and the boardinghouses of nailed-together fresh lumber. She knew someday this would be a city of impressive buildings, but she wished it could always retain the innocence of its humble beginning. She foresaw "a sumptuous metropolis, rich in arts, and bankrupt in virtue."

The England that Frances returned to had taken a turn for the worse. While the sisters were touring America, unemployment led to a mass march in Manchester, a protest of over a hundred thousand working people. The swords and guns of their own troops were turned against them. Blood drenched the field. New laws were passed allowing soldiers to search any home or person without a warrant. Political groups were limited to fifty members at any gathering. There would be no revolution in Merrie Olde England.

Meanwhile a frisky new king, George IV, was busy trying to divorce his wife for allegedly having an affair with a servant. Frances told anyone who would listen that America was the hope of humanity. "Truly I am grateful to this nation; the study of their history and institutions, and the consideration of the peace and happiness which they enjoy, has thawed my heart and filled it with hopes which I had not thought it could know again" (Wright 1821). She began to work on a book about her travels.

Frances had faith in the American political system. "The wheel of the people, turns noiseless, and unimpeded, watched by all and suspected by none." But she also criticized America for not living up to its potential. The press used its freedom in shameful ways. Many farmers could only just eke out a living. Slavery was slowly poisoning America. Vital young American girls all became withdrawn sullen wives. Frances blamed exclusion from education and citizenship for the sorry state of America's mothers.

And yet Frances also wrote: "The prejudices still to be found in Europe, though now indeed somewhat antiquated, which would confine the female library to romances, poetry, and belles-lettres, and female conversation to the last new publication, new bonnet, and parasol are entirely unknown here. The women are assuming their place as thinking beings" (Wright 1821).

Then Frances received a letter from Thomas Jefferson praising her play. In her response she didn't mention her Broadway triumph. She mentioned only "chilling disappointments."

Views of Society and Manners in America; A Series of Letters from that Country to a Friend in England, During the Years 1818, 1819, and 1820 By an Englishwoman was published in London in 1821. Frances wrote about Indigenous people she encountered, mail delivery, the famous pirate Jean Lafitte, Niagara Falls, Benedict Arnold, and the history of the federal administration.

"The Americans are very good talkers," she wrote,

and admirable listeners; understand perfectly the exchange of knowledge, for which they employ conversation, and employ it solely. They have a surprising stock of information, but this runs little into the precincts of imagination; facts form the groundwork of their discourse. They are accustomed to rest opinions on the results of experience, rather than on ingenious theories and abstract reasonings—the world, however, is the book which they consider most attentively, and make a general practice of turning over the page of every man's mind that comes across them; they do this very quietly and very civilly, and with the understanding that you are at perfect liberty to do the same by theirs—equally free from effrontery and officiousness—the constant exercise of the reasoning powers gives to their character and manners a mildness, plainness, and unchanging suavity, such as is often remarked in Europe in men devoted to the abstract sciences—wonderfully patient and candid in argument, close reasoners, acute observers and original thinkers.

She claims that one can learn more from an American in half an hour than could be learned from an entire evening with the literary and diplomatic elite of Europe.

The great American novelist James Fenimore Cooper dismissed Frances's book about America as "nauseous flattery." As for British critics, a prominent front-page review claimed to have proof that the author was a "red-hot American" dismissing the book as "a tissue of impertinence, and injustice, and falsehood." The quarterly, which that year had published the review widely credited with having killed the poet Keats, considered *Views of Society and Manners in America* "impudent" and "ridiculous." Only the *Scotsman,* a Scottish journal, praised the book as morally sublime, "deeply felt, and so eloquently described." But the opinions of European critics mattered little to Frances. The book became popular in America, and two heroes of the American Revolution would soon champion her cause.

British philosopher and reformer Jeremy Bentham was an old man when he met Frances. The story was told that Jeremy at age three had begun to study Latin, being dissatisfied with the histories he was already reading in English. His later attempts to codify the laws of England and the United States may have been unsuccessful but he established the trend. In fact, he coined the verb *codify.* All his life he fought for absolute equality for women, abolition of slavery, the repeal of the death penalty, a ban on physical punishment for adults and children, freedom of speech, the right to divorce, and the legality of homosexuality.

Jeremy shared Frances's sentiments about America, and her book supported his own arguments. Jeremy believed the ultimate moral rule to be the greatest happiness for the majority. He didn't respect hereditary power and certainly didn't credit it with superior intelligence. He thought the prisons should be reformed, the ballots blind. He argued that Paul had ruined the religion of Jesus. Jeremy became Frances's mentor. He also sent her to visit friends of his in France, to deliver messages that if intercepted by the British government could have caused him serious trouble. She became acquainted with the elite political intellectuals of France. Then in autumn of 1821 she met Jeremy's friend, the American Revolutionary War hero, the Marquis de Lafayette.

George Washington spoke with tears in his eyes about the contributions to the American Revolution of Lafayette, a man who had shared the rough life of his soldiers, who paid them out of his own pocket, spending his inheritance to support the army Washington gave him, a shrewd tactician and heroic fighter. Good friends, they spoke of more than war. In a letter to the famous healer Mesmer, Washington (1784) wrote, "The Marqs de la Fayette did me the honor of presenting to me your favor of the 16th of June; & of entering into some explanation of the Powers of Magnetism. . ."

Lafayette, the preeminent hero of the French Revolution, dreamed up the tri-color flag of France. The French idolized him. In July 1789 when the troops surrounded the national assembly as the king prepared to dismiss it, Lafayette presented the assembly with the Declaration of the Rights of Man, approved by his friend Thomas Jefferson, author of the Declaration of Independence. Four days later the locals elected Lafayette commander of the Paris militia. He saved many lives from the wrath of the rioters.

Lafayette rescued the royal family twice. Once when rioters broke into Versailles, killing royal guards with pikes and knives, Lafayette saved the queen of France by taking her to a balcony over the central court and kissing her hand. The French understood this generous and sentimental gesture. They shouted long live Lafayette and long live the queen.

But on the next occasion of her rescue by Lafayette, Marie Antoinette sneered at him for being a traitor to his class and refused to be rescued by him, choosing to die by the guillotine instead. Yet because of his respect for the royals, Lafayette was a constant target of radicals who wanted to send him to the guillotine with the queen. When the leaders of the revolution issued warrants for his arrest, Lafayette fled with twenty-two fellow officers, but they were caught in Prussia, and so began Lafayette's five years of prison in Prussia and Austria, an ordeal of deprivation and hunger that damaged his previously robust health.

When Napoleon defeated Austria, the French people demanded the release of Lafayette. Napoleon didn't relish a rival of Lafayette's immense popularity so he negotiated his freedom but exiled him from France. Lafayette snuck in anyway. He wanted to go home to La Grange, his castle on a thousand acres. When Lafayette promised to stay there and keep out of public life Napoleon relented.

By the time Frances met Lafayette, his days of swashbuckling freedom fighting were long over. French realist author Stendhal (1892) wrote this unflattering portrait in his *Memoirs of an Egotist:* "He took each day as it came; a man not overburdened with intelligence—dealt with each heroic situation as it arose, and in between times was solely occupied, in spite of his age, in fumbling at pretty girls' plackets, not occasionally but constantly, and not much caring who saw."

But Lafayette and Frances always insisted their relationship was platonic. When they first met they talked long into the night about their greatest passion, America. According to Frances's letter to her mentor Jeremy, Lafayette described an "army of brothers who had all things in common, our pleasure, our pains, our money, and our poverty—the virtues of that army—their fortitude, their disinterested, and sublime patriotism."

La Grange dazzled Frances, with its park, five towers, moat, menagerie, aviary, and cider presses. La Grange was the creation of Lafayette's beloved wife, Adrienne, who had died in 1807. Adrienne had fought the new bureaucracy of Paris to regain what she could of her ancestral lands and wealth. She had designed La Grange as a tribute and sanctuary for her husband. She made it magical with her sense of decoration. She even wrote the music playing in the background. She was gone but grandchildren, cousins, and dinner guests meant setting the dinner table for thirty. The halls and walls of La Grange were a museum of Lafayette's accomplishments, including flags of historical importance, and paintings of great Frenchmen and Americans who had been his friends and colleagues.

Frances offered to write Lafayette's life story. He had a portrait painted of her that he placed in his study. From the privileged position Lafayette provided, Frances watched the maneuvering of the French political parties in their legislative sessions. Back home in London Lafayette's friends visited Frances, she found herself surrounded by the famous liberal elders of the day.

Frances wrote Lafayette fawning, sycophantic letters in which she claimed to love him more than a daughter could her father, but she was merely imitating his own tone toward her. He was the first to bring up the father and daughter quality of their relationship. While his letters to her seemed to stray into the area of romance, testing her reactions, Frances was careful to stay away from any affection except paternal, she emphasized his importance to her as a mentor and ideal.

Lafayette wrote of her, "to know, to respect, and to love her, will ever be, in my sense, one and the same thing." Their close relationship first caused gossip, then suspicion. Observing the flurries of intellectual conversation Lafayette and Frances enjoyed, the general's family began to fear that she had too much influence over him.

Frances had a simple suggestion to end all such interference. Lafayette could adopt her, or marry her, as he saw fit. Lafayette explained that he had promised his dying wife he would never marry again. How could he adopt her when he already had such devoted children and grandchildren?

When Frances shared with Lafayette her unfinished work about Epicurus, he insisted it be published. Finishing it turned out to be a chore for the impatient Frances, but the book was published in 1822. Jefferson received a copy and gave it a rave review calling it a "treat to me of the highest order." Excerpts from it filled seven pages of his journal. He wrote that "the matter and manner of the dialogue is strictly ancient—the scenery and portraiture of the interlocutors are of higher finish than anything in that line left us by the ancients—if not ancient, it is equal to the best morsels of antiquity" (Bowman 1996).

Frances became Lafayette's agent as he schemed to support the army in Spain who had forced their king to accept shared power with elected officials. But in 1823 the new Bourbon king of France came to his fellow monarch's rescue, and the French army helped crush the rebellion, and then stood by watching in horror as the Spanish royalists took their revenge. Frances dismissed the disaster as the result of supporting a man inadequate to the task. The man in question's last request was to have a lock of his hair snipped off and sent to the Marquis de Lafayette.

In 1824 President Monroe invited Lafayette to return again to the United States. Lafayette considered this his farewell tour. He wanted

Frances to join him and she of course would not go without Camilla. But the family would not allow the sisters to travel with Lafayette, by boat or carriage. Still he loved to have the sisters accompany him to public events and he enjoyed introducing Frances to his powerful friends as the author of his biography.

Reunited in America, immersed in the celebration of Lafayette with artillery salutes, musical flourishes, cheering crowds, and even a visit to the first of many towns named after him, Frances met Thomas Jefferson, Henry Clay, James Madison, James Monroe, and Andrew Jackson. Congress voted Lafayette a gift of $200,000 to help pay back his generous financial support of the American Revolution.

About Frances, Lafayette wrote to Jefferson, "You and I are the two men in the world the esteem of whom she values the most. I wish much, my dear friend, to present these two adopted daughters of mine to Mrs. Randolph and to you; they being orphans from their youth, and preferring American principles to British aristocracy, having an independent, though not very large fortune, have passed the three last years in most intimate connection with my children and myself, and have readily yielded to our joint entreaties to make a second visit to the U.S." (Chinard 1929).

The beauty of Monticello, and the daring of the University of Virginia, America's first institution of higher learning without affiliation to any religious body, charmed Frances. She was moved by the reunion of these heroes of the American Revolution. She described Thomas Jefferson's tall, upright figure, but observing his weakened state she lamented that "the lamp is evidently on the wane nor is it possible to consider the fading of a light so brilliant and pure without a sentiment of deep melancholy."

One female critic at the Jefferson soiree said of Frances, "to ladies she never spoke." The future Frances had as a lecturer became obvious when this critic commented, "the Frenchmen told many instances of her masculine proclivities, on occasion she would harangue men in the public room of a hotel and the like" (Eckhardt 1984).

Frances both charmed and alienated Lafayette's old American friends. One woman in particular set her sights on Frances, outraged by her impudent demands on Lafayette's time and reputation. Mary, or Mindy as she was better known, was George Washington's stepdaughter. She soon convinced Lafayette to distance himself from these two young Scottish sisters traveling scandalously without family, despite his own inappropriate claim to be their protector.

Frances welcomed the opportunity to see the country, becoming the most traveled woman in America, from the frontier outposts of the Midwest to drunken steamboat races on the Mississippi River, all the way to mosquito-infested New Orleans. Frances and Camilla had the foolhardiness and courage to travel alone through the great frontier, astonishing and charming almost everyone they met. But Frances's fond belief that all Americans were well read, and passionate about liberty, required revision. She had seen some rough types along the way, none rougher than the men who practiced the business of slavery.

Reunited with Lafayette in the south, Frances wrote of the dismay she felt watching slaveholders celebrate the marquis. "The enthusiasm, triumphs and rejoices exhibited here before the countenance of the great and good Lafayette have no longer charms for me. They who so sin against the liberty of their country, against those great principles for which their honored guest poured on their soil his treasure and his blood, are not worthy to rejoice in his presence. My soul sickens in the midst of gaiety, and turns almost with disgust from the fairest faces or the most amiable discourse" (Eckhardt 1984).

Could her increasing determination to take action to oppose slavery be in part a response to Frances's rejection by the stepdaughter of George Washington, a woman who owned enslaved people? Or had Frances been influenced by the fervor of a radical social experiment? On the way to New Orleans, Frances had visited the Utopian community of New Harmony, Indiana.

JACOB RAPP AND THE HARMONISTS

Jacob Rapp declared himself a prophet to his thousands of followers in Germany so the Lutheran authorities gave him five days in jail to think it over. Jacob never doubted his calling, but he did decide to transplant himself to America, along with the five hundred families who followed his teachings. The Harmonists had a business: building towns. First they built Harmony, Pennsylvania. Then they built Harmony, Indiana, which they sold. Moving back to Pennsylvania they built the town of Economy.

Jacob was deeply influenced by the great German theosopher and mystic Jakob Böhme. Böhme's extraordinary visions of spiritual dimensions of existence found harmony and geometry throughout the universe, visible and invisible. Jacob Rapp also found inspiration in the works of the great Swedish mystic visionary Emanuel Swedenborg, as we have seen, a curious combination of pioneer scientist and spiritualist author. Böhme's heaven, a shining vision of principles and ratios, seems somewhat remote when compared with Swedenborg's talkative angels and, for the most part, not really all that bad devils.

Since alchemical vessels and bottles have been found in the town of Economy, historians speculate that the Harmonists may have practiced alchemy. Their library included the notorious and spurious magical work *Sixth and Seventh Books of Moses* and *Opus Mago Cabalisticum,* but they resembled Christian mystics more than Hermetic practitioners.

Jacob and the Harmonists expected the apocalypse during their lifetimes. They prized celibacy; even married couples were encouraged to give up the practices that depend on the Adam and Eve world, instead of the Adam world, when he was pure, before the fall. Babies were few and far between. Sundays were for services and singing. No chewing or smoking of tobacco. Harmonists lived five or six in each small house, not necessarily family members, but devoted to living as Christian brothers and sisters.

In 1814 the Harmonists moved to Indiana Territory. That first summer and fall malaria killed over a hundred people. So the Harmonists drained the swamp, then got back to the "hard labor and coarse fare" of building a town in the wilderness. By 1819 the town boasted vineyards, a distillery, a brewery, a winery, and a steam-powered wool carding and spinning factory. The impeccable craftsmanship of the carpentry and masonry was matched by the beautiful symmetry of the architecture. Because they worked in harmony with each other, and with great pride in their work, they outperformed other builders. By the time the Harmonists sold Harmony, Indiana, they had two thousand acres under cultivation. They manufactured peach brandy, whiskey, wine, beer, tinware, rope, wagons, carts, plows, flannel, wool, and cotton. But they didn't like living so near Kentucky slave towns. The Harmonists were strict abolitionists. They all became wealthy when Robert Owen paid them $150,000, the equivalent of many millions today. Robert renamed the town New Harmony.

Robert Owen was an industrialist but also a reformer. A Welshman who ran a model factory in Scotland, he tried to prove that treating worker's decently, paying them well, and providing for their entire lives, instead of working them to death, produced not only superior workers with far fewer issues like violence and alcoholism, but the factory itself could make more money. Sadly, no other industrialists seemed to care. British industrialism rolled on through child labor and matchstick girls with glow-in-the-dark jaws eaten away by phosphorous. Owen had decided to think bigger. He bought the town from the Harmonists so that he could create a model society. Like Plato's Republic, this community was meant to prove the principles of its founder.

It took ten years for the Harmonists to build the beautiful town of Harmony. But Owen's experimental community lasted only two. Owen invited everyone who wanted to try life in a commune devoted to enlightened living to join him, but along with a few idealists he attracted hustlers and freeloaders. A "Constitution of the Preliminary Society" was drawn up. Members invested not just their money but also their household possessions. They would own a piece of an enterprise devoted to reform and equality. Any services they rendered for the community would be paid in points redeemable at the town store, but cash was welcome there, too, for folks disinclined to work.

Soon New Harmony became a cacophony of bickering. Overcrowded, poorly supervised, and unproductive, the town floundered. Within months the shortage of skilled craftsmen and laborers led to breakdowns that were left unrepaired. But Owen soon arrived with reinforcements. He had recruited scientists and educators, and he had raised more funds, so his great experiment was given another opportunity to flourish.

The "New Harmony Community of Equality" was adopted as the town constitution. Happiness would be the result of equal rights and equal duties. All property would be held in common. The constitution mandated cooperation, freedom of speech, kindness and courtesy, preservation of health, and education. What it would not do was provide rules by which these objectives were to be achieved.

America's first anarchist, Josiah Warren was a member of the community. He wrote eloquently of its failure: "It seemed that the difference of opinion, tastes and purposes increased just in proportion to the demand for conformity. Two years were worn out in this way; at the end of which, I believe that not more than three persons had the least hope of success. Most of the experimenters left in despair of all reforms, and conservatism felt itself confirmed. We had tried every conceivable form of organization and government. We had a world in miniature. We had enacted the French revolution over again with despairing hearts instead of corpses as a result—It appeared that it was nature's own inherent law of diversity that had conquered us—our 'united interests' were directly at war with the individualities of persons and circumstances and the instinct of self-preservation" (Warren 1827). To dissolve his New Harmony enterprise, Owen had to spend another $200,000. His fortune never recovered, and his ambitions became less grandiose.

His granddaughter, Constance Faunt Le Roy Runcie, wrote a fantasy book about the Báb, the first prophet of the Bahá'i religion. The wife of an Episcopalian minister, she wrote a nonfiction book about her Christian beliefs. She also composed orchestral music, chamber music, and songs. In 1859 Constance founded the first women's social club east of Mississippi, which she called the Minerva Society of New Harmony, Indiana, named after the Roman goddess of wisdom. She was twenty-three years old at the time. The thirteen charter members did not consider themselves any kind of coven. The club was meant to encourage art and the pursuit of wisdom among women. Near the end of her life, Constance founded the Runcie Club, which is still active in St. Joseph, Missouri.

Unhappily for Frances, she arrived in New Harmony in the first flush of its enthusiasm, before its first constitution. She had heard

Owen address Congress on February 25, 1825. Owen described what he called a New System of Society, a commune where everyone owned an equal share and shared work equally. This experimental community would prove, he promised, that cooperation is superior to competition. To Frances, New Harmony seemed the ideal of America in action.

Two years later Frances would be mired in the failure of her own utopian experiment, Nashoba. Like New Harmony, Nashoba would fail because of naiveté regarding human motivations and the complexities of communities. The Harmonists who had flourished in the town they built were all German immigrants who shared a pious belief system that required constant practice. New Harmony was a melting pot of radicals, crackpots, intellectuals, and opportunists, each with his or her own agenda, but Frances saw only the honeymoon phase of the new community.

THE NASHOBA EXPERIMENT

Frances and Camilla were thrilled when they learned they were eligible to become citizens of the United States of America, despite having spent much of the five eligibility years in Great Britain and France. By the time they said goodbye to Lafayette on his sixty-eighth birthday, as he sailed home from New York harbor on a hot day in July, Frances and Camilla were American citizens.

Now Frances combined the inspiration of New Harmony with her dedication to finding a way to solve the problem of slavery in America in a five-year plan. She would buy or be given enslaved people, who would earn their freedom in five years. While they were earning their freedom, they would receive educations. They would be prepared for life after slavery by learning trades and developing a sense of politics and history. White members of the community, six of them, would supervise and educate. Free and enslaved Black people would do the work. White and Black children would receive the same education.

Frances worked the connections Lafayette had provided to get a chance to pitch her plan to the man who would become the next president of the United States, Andrew Jackson himself. Jackson said he liked the idea. James Monroe approved. James Madison had serious reservations, however. He didn't think the promise of freedom would be enough to motivate enslaved people. He pointed out Spain's policy of offering enslaved people the opportunity to work for their freedom and how few enslaved people took it.

Andrew Jackson suggested Frances buy some recently cleared land in Tennessee on the Wolf River. Jackson had forcibly removed the Chickasaw tribe. Tennessee was the most liberal of the slave states; abolitionist groups were allowed to flourish there. The land was cheap and the population sparse, making local controversy less likely.

Jefferson offered neither public endorsement nor funds but he did encourage Frances. "At the age of eighty-two," he wrote to her, "with one foot in the grave, and the other uplifted to follow it, I do not permit myself to take part in any new enterprises, even for bettering the condition of man, not even in the great one which has been through life that of my greatest anxieties. Every plan should be adopted, every experiment tried, which may do something towards the ultimate object. That which you propose is well worthy of trial" (Eckhardt 1984).

Though Jefferson wondered if "moral urgencies" would be enough to motivate the enslaved people. He also wrote: "You are young, dear Madam, and have powers of mind which may do much in exciting others in this arduous task. I am confident they will be so exerted, and I pray to Heaven for their success, and that you may be rewarded with the blessings which such efforts merit."

No one wanted to invest in her plan except Lafayette who offered her eight thousand dollars. She refused to take it, not wanting to cause him further trouble with his family. In October 1825 Frances used her own money to buy two thousand acres of trees and swamp. She named her raw acreage Nashoba, the Chickasaw word for wolf. She spent more of her own money to buy supplies and enslaved human beings.

Among the founders of Nashoba was Marcus Brutus Winchester, the eldest son of General James Winchester, President Jackson's business partner, and his wife, a free Black woman. They had eight children, the oldest boy they named after Robert Owen, and their second daughter they named after Frances Wright. Marcus's father's gift of 420 acres in 1824 became downtown Memphis. Marcus became a land agent, the county Democratic Party leader, postmaster, and when the town incorporated in 1826, he became the first mayor. He built the jail and the courthouse. His general store where Indigenous people, backwoodsmen, and townspeople mingled gave Frances further education in American frontier society.

Frances was twenty-nine when Nashoba broke ground. In its first year about a hundred acres were cleared, and primitive log structures provided shelter. Frontier life at first agreed with Frances. As Celia Eckhardt (1984) wrote in what remains the only biography of Frances Wright *Fanny Wright: Rebel in America*: "She wrote of forest land still full of bears, wolves, and panthers, and pictured herself galloping her white horse over rough, open country. She slept in log cabins open on all sides, she said, and even in the woods with a bearskin for a bed and a saddle for her pillow. She endured extremes of heat and cold and had never felt better or stronger in her life. She could now ride forty miles a day without fatigue, and she did so often, going between Memphis and Nashoba, greeting the Indians who were her nearest neighbors as they came to sell their furs. She prayed God for a little rain, drank milk from her cow, ate venison from the Indians, and warmed herself at the great fire in her cabin. She closed by saying, 'I begin to cherish life.'"

The land was hard to work, and often flooded. Bad weather made the work harder. Supplies like lime and rocks had to be taken from the earth itself. Despite the hardship, by its first summer Nashoba seemed to be succeeding. Visitors commented that the enslaved people worked with such devoted concentration just seeing them was enough to convince any skeptic that they could match or surpass white men.

In abolitionist newspapers Frances pleaded for stonemasons, carpenters, teachers, and investors to help the great experiment, but her pleas went unanswered. Frances decided in December 1826 that she would write up a new deed for Nashoba. No longer privately owned, it would now be a true commune. That way if anything happened to her the experiment could continue. New rules were written, as well. Six thousand dollars was set as the price of freedom, plus 6 percent interest yearly. No enslaved person could become a trustee, and they would not be involved in making community decisions. Liberated enslaved people would leave the United States. Enslaved people who deserved punishment would be punished according to the old slave system, including flogging, though only in extreme cases. Nashoba's radical experiment in liberation had become a racist atrocity.

Camilla and Robert Dale Owen, son of Robert Owen, were among the trustees. So was James Richardson, an enigmatic man who would care for the sisters through their life-threatening fevers, but who would later destroy the reputations of Nashoba and Frances Wright. Another trustee was George Flower, the only member of the community with farming skills; Nashoba had been his idea at first. Frances and he worked together to realize their dream. Celia Eckhardt suggests that Flower and Frances had a passionate affair when they were alone together on a long trip through the wilderness, in the early days of planning Nashoba. Flower was married with young children. His wife didn't keep secret her disdain for Nashoba and Frances. Mrs. Flower devoted herself to nothing more or less than raising her children. Camilla was eager to see her go. But when she did go, she took her husband, George, with her.

In 1827 Frances visited New Harmony again, hoping to renew her optimism. The dances, the bands, the marches, the organization, all the good intentions had fallen into angry bickering. When Owen suggested everyone return to their beds to contemplate their animosities and mean thoughts the ensuing peace reigned only briefly. Anger ruled the day. So Owen dissolved New Harmony. Unwilling to give up the dream, Robert Dale Owen left New Harmony to join Frances at Nashoba.

Nashoba included mosquito-infested swamp the local tribe had used for hunting only, never for habitation. Could Andrew Jackson, who owned many enslaved people, have suggested the area to Frances because he understood its location would doom her mission? She became ill with fever. Just as Frances began to improve, Camilla was struck by the fever, reinfecting Frances, who spent three months in bed near death. James Richardson took responsibility for nursing the sisters back to health, and both credited his care for their survival. The enslaved people continued to work devotedly, but supplies of rope and other necessities were running out. The school had not yet been built. They still had neither a skilled carpenter nor an expert at farming.

Dale helped Frances make the arduous trip back to Europe. She suffered in a hammock in the back of a wagon bumping over uneven roads all the way to the port of New Orleans. Her ship became grounded on a sandbank. Nevertheless her health began to improve as the ship crossed the Atlantic. On board a hired Scottish servant fed her a steady supply of oatcakes and porridge.

Mary Shelley noticed Frances's arrival, writing, "a woman, young rich and independent, quits the civilization of England for a life of hardship in the forests of America, that by so doing she may contribute to the happiness of her species" (Eckhardt 1984).

Meanwhile back in Nashoba, James Richardson for some reason decided details of his journal deserved to be published in a leading abolitionist newspaper the *Genius of Universal Emancipation*. Two of the excerpts made shocking news. Richardson described two incidents when he whipped enslaved women in the approving presence of Camilla. He also admitted to living outside wedlock with a free Black woman. Accusations flew that Nashoba was a "brothel." Richardson's efforts to defend his position, which culminated in his declaration of atheism, only inflamed the controversy.

Frances and Robert Dale had enjoyed time with Lafayette and his family at La Grange. They toured Paris and the surrounding countryside. Dale assured his sister back home that his relationship with Frances was platonic. He found in her his ideal intellectual companion. But then the news from home arrived; their trip would have to be cut short. Frances couldn't return immediately. The anxiety over the next month began to turn her hair white. A chronic backache tormented her.

Before returning to Nashoba, Frances reached out to Mary Shelley: "If you possess the opinions of your father and the generous feelings of your mother, I feel that I could travel far to see you" (Eckhardt 1984). Mary, the widow of the notorious romantic poet and revolutionary Percy Shelley, was daughter of the English pioneer of feminism Mary Wollstonecraft and of William Godwin, a friend to poets, author of *Political Justice,* who argued for the overthrow of all traditional institutions including government, religion, and private property. Mary had run off with her poet while he was still married to the mother of his children. She had a child with him before she took his name in marriage. Frances must have hoped she would find a kindred soul in Mary, one who might join her in Nashoba.

Frances wrote to Mary, "While we endeavor to undermine the slavery of color existing in the North American Republic, we essay equally to destroy the slavery of mind now reigning there as in other countries." She described Nashoba as "an establishment where affection shall form the only marriage, kind feeling and kind action the only religion, respect for the feelings and liberties of others the only restraint, and union of interest the bond of peace and security" (Eckhardt 1984).

Mary was flattered and wanted to know more, but she wasn't about to abandon Europe. Frances wrote to her passionately hoping to convince her: "I have made the hard earth my bed, the saddle of my horse my pillow, and have staked my life and fortune on an experiment having in view moral liberty and human improvement. Many of course think me mad, and if to be mad mean to be one of a minority, I am so, and very mad indeed, for our minority is very small. Should that few succeed in mastering the first difficulties, weaker spirits, though often not less amiable, may carry forward the good work" (Eckhardt 1984).

Frances traveled south from London. She spent seven days with Mary. The author of *Frankenstein* understood Frances better than most. She wrote of Frances to Robert Dale, "neither so independent or so fearless as you think" (Eckhardt 1984). Mary's son Percy said drily that Frances reminded him of Minerva, the ancient Roman goddess of wisdom and war.

Mrs. Trollope, a friend of Frances, needed somewhere to hide from her creditors so she joined the endless line of visitors in London eager to learn more about Nashoba, which also included Leigh Hunt, who had been a friend of Keats and Shelley. Despite approaching age fifty, Mrs. Trollope liked what she heard enough to pack up her servants and her children with a plan to spend one or two years in the woods. The Trollope troop joined Frances on her voyage home.

Mary Shelley came to see Frances off. Mary asked for a lock of her hair, which she kept near her for the rest of her life. Was tearful Mary reminded of her husband, another tall, thin idealist with curly hair and a way with words? Mary knew that Frances was sailing into a storm of her own.

As the ship crossed the Atlantic, Frances wrote a definitive response on Nashoba she wished to have published. Trollope watched her read portions of the tract to sailors. "Let us correct our views of right and wrong," Frances wrote, "correct our moral lessons, and so correct the practice of rising generations."

On the way to Nashoba, eating beside sailors and working men, Trollope quickly realized that Frances had presented an idealized America quite different from the rude reality. She couldn't keep her clothes clean in this world of tobacco spit and spilled alcohol.

When they arrived in Nashoba, Frances found out that Camilla was now married, and both she and her husband looked alarmingly sickly. James Richardson had already left; he had no apologies for Frances or Nashoba. Food was limited to cornbread, pork, and rice. The farm was a failure. The people Frances meant to help surrendered to futility. The pestilential climate and atmosphere seemed a direct threat to herself and her children, so Trollope borrowed money to make a hasty exit. She commented that Camilla seemed to share her suspicion that the fever may have somewhat deranged Frances.

Trollope quickly relocated to Cincinnati. But the example of Frances wasn't entirely lost on her. In 1832 she published *Domestic Manners of the Americans,* beginning her career as a novelist. Trollope's own antislavery novel influenced Harriet Beecher Stowe, author of *Uncle Tom's Cabin.* Trollope had this to say about America: "How is it that the men of America, who are reckoned good husbands and good fathers, while they themselves enjoy sufficient freedom of spirit to permit their walking forth into the temple of the living God, can leave those they love best on earth, bound in the iron chains of a most tyrannical fanaticism? How can they breathe the balmy air, and not think of the tainted atmosphere so heavily weighing upon breasts still dearer than their own? How can they gaze upon the blossoms of the spring, and not remember the fairer cheeks of their young daughters, waxing pale, as they sit for long sultry hours, immured with hundreds of fellow victims, listening to the roaring vanities of a preacher, canonized by a college of old women?"

When Frances published her *Explanatory Notes, Respecting the Nature and Objects of the Institution of Nashoba, and of the Principles upon Which It Is Founded. Addressed to the Friends of Human Improvement, in All Countrys and of All Nations* she shocked her contemporaries by writing that sexual passion was "the strongest and the noblest of human passions—the best joys of our existence—the best source of human happiness." Virtue is not the province of self-sacrifice and bitter discipline; virtue exists in anyone "in proportion as they are happy, and happy in proportion as they are free—ignorant laws, ignorant prejudices, ignorant codes of morals—condemn one portion of the female sex to vicious excess, another to as vicious restraint, and all to defenseless helplessness and slavery, and generally the whole of the male sex to debasing licentiousness, if not to loathsome brutality."

But praising sexual passion wasn't the most controversial of her points. Frances no longer advocated relocation for enslaved people. She thought the races should mingle. She predicted that once Black Americans received equal educations miscegenation would no longer be controversial. This and her attacks on organized religion only made her all the more notorious. Old allies like James Madison were alienated by her adoption of views at the time almost universally despised. Disappointed, Frances hoped that in the future people would look back in disbelief that her thoughts were ever considered radical.

At this time many of her allies deserted her. The failure of Nashoba cost her half her fortune. The whiff of the scandal haunted her for the rest of her life.

FRANCES WRIGHT SUPERSTAR

Robert Dale returned to what was left of New Harmony, and Frances soon followed. She accepted his invitation to become coeditor of the *New Harmony Gazette*. Frances became the first woman to edit an American newspaper since the colonial days. Her eloquent articles and editorials argued against the death penalty, condemned religious intolerance, demanded rights for women, advocated equality by education, legal rights for married women, simple divorce laws, and access to birth control.

July 4, 1828, Frances as the featured speaker during New Harmony's Independence Day celebration was probably the first woman in American history to address a large mixed-gender crowd at a secular ceremony, or as her critics called it "a promiscuous assembly." The *New Harmony Gazette* became an important source of news neglected by the newspapers who at the time were the mainstream media. When her first lecture in Cincinnati overflowed with a line wrapped around the block, only the *Gazette* reported her triumph. Another newspaper rebutted her ideas with the observation that unhappy marriages don't exist, then reminded the reader of her scandalous defense of miscegenation.

Frances was such a success she toured as a lecturer for several months. She carried notes but seldom consulted them as she spoke. She proposed the creation in every town of a Hall of Science or Temple of Reason, where citizens could see for themselves the fruits of science and of the republic. She suggested correspondence committees create boarding schools, what she called Schools of Industry, to be attached to the Halls of Science, so citizens could become skilled workers and educated participants in democracy. Local leaders lined up to meet her.

Reactions to her lectures were mixed and tended to the extremes of admiration or disgust. According to Trollope in Cincinnati the men cared only about money, and the women only about religion, nevertheless wealthy donors contributed to what they hoped would become the local Cincinnati Temple of Reason, but the chimerical location was never realized.

Then more bad news forced Frances to return to Nashoba. A taskmaster who deserted the farm had stolen supplies. Camilla was now six months pregnant. Did Frances put aside her ambitions to stay with her sister for several months during this anxious time, Camilla's first birth, at risk in the primitive place that was Memphis? Frances left her sister to fend for herself. She took a risky trip over river and prairie, to lecture to bigger crowds, appearing in St. Louis, Louisville, Baltimore, Cincinnati, Boston, Philadelphia, and New York City.

Her fame spread during an especially vicious 1828 presidential campaign between Andrew Jackson and John Quincy Adams. The Great Awakening gave America an evangelical preoccupation with sexual morality. Mrs. Jackson was attacked in the press as an adulteress, and therefore as a threat to society, although the scandal in question was hardly scandalous and had occurred thirty years earlier. In turn Mr. and Mrs. Adams were accused of having had premarital sex. The ladies of the hottest new town on the frontier, Cincinnati, confronted a shopkeeper about his sign depicting a lady in petticoats showing her ankles. He had to have the ankles painted out. Women were scandalized if a man used the word *corset* in their presence. Into this climate of overheated repression Frances delivered lectures praising erotic passion and advocating sexual liberation. She not only ignored the controversies of adultery and premarital sex, she questioned the institution of marriage.

What did Frances think of the evangelical spirit sweeping America, reaching even into New Harmony? "By the sudden combination of three orthodox sects, a revival, as such scenes of distraction are wont to be styled, was opened in houses, churches, and even on the Ohio river. The victims of this odious experiment on human credulity and nervous weakness were invariably women. Helpless age was made a public spectacle, innocent youth driven to raving insanity, mothers and daughters carried lifeless from the presence of the ghostly expounders of damnation; all ranks shared the contagion, until the despair of Calvin's hell itself seemed to have fallen upon every heart" (Waterman 1924).

What her admirers called "noble" her detractors called "masculine." She now carried no notes, only a copy of the Declaration of Independence. The press and the clergy were united in their opposition to her. She was labeled the "female monster," "great Red Harlot of Infidelity," "Priestess of Beelzebub," and "the whore of Babylon." Her supporters organized to provide her protection. She traveled with a bodyguard. Once when a heckler yelled fire and her audience began to stampede Frances stood calmly on stage, soothing the panic like Apollonius of Tyana silencing the riot. When an opponent turned off the gas lines that lit the lecture hall lamps, Frances finished the lecture by candlelight. Earning a thunderous ovation, she was carried out of the venue by her devoted followers.

In January of 1829 Camilla was suffering a terrible labor in Memphis. She was bled three times by the incompetent doctor, and nearly died. She named her newborn son Francis. Frances didn't see her nephew. Instead she commenced a six-lecture series at Masonic Hall in New York City, with an audience of perhaps two thousand each night. The beaten-down liberals of New York found in her words a refuge and hope for their cause. Her lectures there and at the Park Theater brought together what amounted to a political party. Then William Stone noticed her.

Stone edited the *New York Commercial Advertiser*. Though he admired Lafayette and was himself an abolitionist, as Celia Eckhardt (1984) wrote, "Fanny Wright stirred something so deep and powerful in him that he lost his self-control: repeatedly he returned to the attack, with a rage and hatred so little suppressed that it seemed pathological."

Stone admitted, "the sensation of the ludicrous, naturally suggested by its novelty—was entirely superseded." The novelty Stone refers to was perhaps best captured by Samuel Johnson a century earlier: "Sir, a woman's preaching is like a dog's walking on his hind legs. It is not done well; but you are surprised to find it done at all."

Thousands attended Fanny's third lecture at a gothic temple decorated in what was supposed to be Epicurean style. Thousands were turned away. Stone called Frances "the Lioness of the day," but he shuddered at the crowd of women who openly attended the spectacle.

At the fifth lecture a protestor set fire to a barrel of turpentine sending suffocating smoke billowing through the venue. Stone blamed the victim. "It is time we should have done with Miss Wright, her pestilent doctrines, and her deluded followers, who are as much to be pitied, as their priestess is to be despised. She comes amongst us in the character of a bold blasphemer, and a voluptuous preacher of licentiousness. . . . Casting off all restraints, she would break down all the barriers to virtue, and reduce the world to one grand theater of vice and sensuality in its most loathsome form" (Eckhardt 1984).

Other editors argued that she was no more than a curiosity who attracted big crowds because the tickets were free. Many newspapers refused to take ads for her lectures or to print letters or editorials written in her defense. Famous poets lampooned her in verse; cartoonists had their way with her in ugly caricatures.

Undaunted, Frances relocated herself and the *New Harmony Gazette* to New York City. The newspaper got a more modern name: the *Free Enquirer,* printed twice a week. Frances also bought the Ebenezer Baptist church for $7,000 and rechristened it the Hall of Science. Here Frances had her office, printing facilities, and a bookstore. Lectures and debates were held every Sunday and sometimes during the week, at ten cents a ticket.

Finally, Frances asked Camilla to come join her. Camilla was reluctant—she blamed herself for the failure of Nashoba and for the scandal that had so damaged their reputation—but Frances reassured her things would be different in New York City. Frances was planning to start a commune where men and women would live as equals. Camilla was needed to be the housekeeper. Camilla, still sickly and now caring for an infant, hinted that she could use some help getting there. But Frances told her the world was changing right before their eyes, requests for lectures were pouring in from all over America, she couldn't abandon this historic moment that might change the fate of the nation.

April 26, 1829, Frances delivered the first lecture at the Hall of Science. She wondered if it might "mark an era in the moral history of the republic." In a world where women were seldom heard or seen she had found a way to command a stage before an audience of thousands. She became convinced that the people were with her. Trollope wrote Lafayette with her usual dry wit that Frances, "anticipates confidently the regeneration of the whole human race from her present exertions."

Camilla traveled from Nashoba over frontier, and often alone with her child, until she reached Frances. Camilla, happy to see her sister apparently in complete command of her talents, settled into the role she had always played. Yet now she was truly a mother, proud of her child's intelligent eyes. When her son died of a sudden fever Camilla was devastated. Poems of grief were popular in those days. Like many other women of the time Camilla pined away for her lost loved one. The serene optimism of Frances Wright didn't have time to deal with Camilla's grief. In letters Camilla lamented that she just wasn't that important to Frances anymore.

The Hall of Science became headquarters for New York's liberals, and for curiosity seekers. Across the street at the Bible repository the employees saw with dismay the bookstore window featuring Percy Shelley and Thomas Paine. Worse still, the bookstore was a modest success. The *Free Enquirer* published exposés about the consequences of extreme inequality of wealth, and whistle-blower looks at working-class exploitation, like the seamstresses of Philadelphia forced to beg, starve, or practice prostitution.

An assembly Frances inspired in New York City, the National Association for the Protection of Industry, had begun to analyze the conditions of the working class and the poor. Their first report revealed that twelve thousand children in New York City between the ages of five and fifteen had no access to education.

Trollope wrote after a lecture by Frances: "I knew her extraordinary gift of eloquence, her almost unequaled command of words, and the wonderful power of her rich and thrilling voice . . . all my expectations fell far short of the splendor, the brilliance, the overwhelming eloquence of this extraordinary orator—Her tall and majestic figure, the deep and almost solemn expression in her eyes, the simple contour of her finely formed head, unadorned, excepting by its own natural ringlets; her garment of plain white muslin, which hung around her in folds that recalled the drapery of a Grecian statue, all contributed to produce an effect, unlike anything I have ever seen before, or ever expect to see again" (Trollope 1832).

Frances usually walked on stage with a phalanx of women who stood with her throughout her lecture. Imagine a five-foot-ten-inch woman with red curly hair and a Scottish brogue dominating a hall full of astonished listeners, many thrilled by her, and many deeply offended by her unladylike performance and radical ideas. Frances was so eloquent many a bigot admitted to having been inspired by her to reconsider timeworn prejudices.

Frances criticized organized religion as a waste of resources: "Turn your churches into halls of science, and devote your leisure day to the study of your own bodies, the analysis of your own minds, and the examination of the fair material world which extends around you! Examine the expenses of your present religious system. Calculate all that is spent in multiplying churches and salarying their ministers; in clothing and feeding traveling preachers, who fill your streets and highways with trembling fanatics—I say, that Jesus would recommend you to pass the first day of the week rather otherwise than you pass it now, and to seek some other mode of bettering the morals of the community than by constraining each other to look grave on a Sunday, and to consider yourselves more virtuous in proportion to the idleness in which you pass one day in seven" (Wright 1829).

"My friends," she dared to tell audiences, "I am no Christian, in the sense usually attached to the word. I am neither Jew nor Gentile, Mahomedan nor Theist; I am but a member of the human family, and would accept of truth by whomsoever offered—that truth which we can all find, if we will but seek it—in things, not in words; in nature, not in human imagination; in our own hearts, not in temples made with hands" (Wright 1829).

She also said of religion that: "much of our positive misery originates in our idle speculations in matters of faith, and in our blind, our fearful, forgetfulness of facts." In all societies, she believed, priestcraft leads to persecutions. "Your institutions may declare equality of rights, but we shall never possess those rights until you have national schools. Your legislatures may enact prohibitory laws, and laws offensive and defensive, protective or invasive, it matters little which; our liberties will never be secure, for they will never be understood, until you have national schools. Your spiritual teachers may preach damnation and salvation henceforward through all the eternity of existence, and we shall never be wise nor happy, peaceful nor charitable, useful in our generation, nor useful through our descendants, to all generations, until ye open the flood-gates of knowledge, and let her pure waters fertilize all the land" (Wright 1829).

She spoke eloquently as the first feminist lecturer in American history:

However novel it may appear, I shall venture the assertion, that, until women assume the place in society which good sense and good feeling alike, assign to them, human improvement must advance but feebly. It is in vain that we would circumscribe the power of one half of our race, and that half by far the most important and influential. If they exert it not for good, they will for evil; if they advance not knowledge, they will perpetuate ignorance. Let women stand where they may in the scale of improvement, their position decides that of the race. Are they cultivated?—so is society polished and enlightened. Are they ignorant?—so is it gross and insipid. Are they wise?—so is the human condition prosperous. Are they foolish?—so is it unstable and unpromising. Are they free?—so is the human character elevated. Are they enslaved?—so is the whole race degraded." (Wright 1829)

When they banned her in Philadelphia, refusing her a venue, she went to the court to protect her right to free speech, but the case never went to trial. On December 5, 1829, during a lecture at the Hall of Science, Frances had this to say about the plight of working people: "The industrious classes have been called the bone and marrow of the nation; but they are in fact the nation itself. The fruits of their industry are the nation's wealth; their moral integrity and physical health is the nation's strength; their ease and independence is the nation's prosperity; their intellectual intelligence is the nation's hope. Where the producing laborer and useful artisan eat well, sleep well, live comfortably, think correctly, speak fearlessly, and act uprightly, the nation is happy, free, and wise. Has such a nation ever been? No. Can such a nation ever be? Answer, men of industry of the United States! If such can be, it is here. If such is to be, it must be your work" (Wright 1829).

A GHOST IN THE WORLD OF BALZAC

The Working Men's Party candidates in the election of 1830 became known as "the Fanny Wright ticket." Frances gave lectures to support the party's principles and candidates, sharing her staff and resources with the party to launch their newspaper. But her efforts were cut short when she realized Nashoba couldn't go on anymore. The president of Haiti had once promised her when they met on his visit to America that he would help her. Now she would ask him to take the enslaved people of Nashoba and make certain they were provided for. She chose a path to Haiti that allowed her to lecture in areas of America she had never visited before. Some citizens simply waited for her on the road to ask her questions, then invited her to meet their friends. When she was refused a stage by local authorities, she gathered listeners in the fields.

Frances had the paperwork drawn up to free the enslaved people of Nashoba. She traveled with them to Haiti. Frances traveled with a Dr. D'Arusmont. He claimed to be a doctor though he never practiced. At first, he occupied himself with theories of education, establishing a progressive school. He later became a teacher at New Harmony. Then he followed her to New York to run the printing presses for the *Free Enquirer*. Frances took him on the trip because he was familiar with Haiti and the Caribbean.

The president of Haiti was good to his word. He took in the formerly enslaved people of Nashoba and gave them some of his own land, along with the help they would need to learn how to survive as free citizens of their new country. He also wined and dined Frances and D'Arusmont. He surprised her with a small sack of gold coins to repay her expenses. Frances must have relished the quiet walks and lavish tropical meals, a vacation from her work in the political trenches back home. Somewhere in the mood of intoxication she found herself attracted to D'Arusmont and they became lovers.

Upon her return to New York City, editor Stone was ready for her. He wrote a scathing exposé accusing Frances of shady dealing in Haiti, claiming that she pocketed thousands of dollars from what she trumpeted as a moral obligation. Frances responded calmly point by point but won only a partial retraction from Stone. Realizing she was doing more harm than good by having become synonymous with the struggle for workers' rights, Frances left for Europe with D'Arusmont and Camilla. To the chagrin of her friends there, when she arrived she disappeared into an almost complete isolation. No one was to know of her pregnancy. She knew a baby out of wedlock was just the sort of scandal her enemies in America were hoping for. She had her daughter Sylva in secret.

The timing must have frustrated Frances. Fed up with the renewed monarchy, the French Revolution reared its head. The people of Paris elected Lafayette commander again, effectively making him the leader of France. Incapacitated, Frances was reduced to writing short notes in which she advised Lafayette as best she could in flurries of jagged sentences.

Lafayette ignored her advice. He believed promises of a new more enlightened monarchy, the younger generation of royals. He wrapped himself and the new king of France, another member of the Bourbon family, in the tricolor flag, and once again his sentimental gesture moved the masses. As Frances predicted, the new king betrayed Lafayette; the new boss was the same as the old boss. Disappointed, Frances decided she would never write Lafayette's biography, because he had betrayed his lifetime of devotion to freedom with the last act of reaffirming the hereditary monarchy.

When Frances appeared in Paris, making a rare public appearance at Lafayette's reception, James Fennimore Cooper wrote, "She looked haggard and much changed for the worse." The women all shunned her.

A few months later, in Paris, Camilla, who had seemed to have regained her health, swooned into Frances's arms and died. Frances had depended on Camilla all her life. Her grief sealed her isolation as she married D'Arusmont, but Lafayette served as a witness at her wedding ceremony. Mr. and Mrs. D'Arusmont had a second child, but the infant died. From then on Frances used her dead child's birth date as the birth date of Sylva so no would know her daughter was born out of wedlock.

Frances lived a lonely life in France. She avoided her family and her friends. One of her oldest friends, the story is told, also a friend of Lafayette's, asked him for her address. The woman visited unannounced. She found a shabby old apartment building. A bleak, comfortless apartment up four flights of stairs revealed the shocked expression of D'Arusmont, sitting with his son by another marriage in the front room. Asking for Frances the unexpected guest was dismayed to find a disheveled, worn woman, tending to her naked daughter. Frances wanted to know who gave up her address. No, she responded curtly, she wasn't interested in writing anymore, and the very idea of her old fame was painful to her. How Lafayette must have been saddened by this revelation of a transformation no one foresaw.

Husband and wife engaged in lengthy conversations refining each other's theories, and yet becoming ever more obscure and out of touch. Frances developed a detailed counterhistory of the world based on her theories about money and the suppression of women. She could still work up a passion over Polish freedom fighters but the troubles of the poor all around her she ignored.

When the French feminist movement found the heroines who would inherit the mantle of eighteenth-century French feminist author Madeleine d'Arsant de Puisieux, Frances knew nothing about it. Though in conversation and letter writing she was still a feminist she never became involved with them or contributed in any way to their efforts.

Her sense of urgent destiny had rusted into a brittle self-importance. She told the great essayist Thomas Carlyle that he was wrong about his theory that history was made by great men. No one is greater than another, she argued, and yet she portrayed herself as far more important than she had actually been.

How did Frances feel when she was told that her old partner at arms Robert Dale had fallen in love and married a young citizen of New Harmony: nineteen-year-old Mary Jane? She showed no reaction to the news. Mary had seen Frances lecture back home in America, so when she got the chance to travel with her husband to Europe, and to stay for a while with Frances, while Robert took care of family business in England, she had been excited about meeting her heroine. But the household she found was not happy, and the help she tried to provide while being a guest was unwelcome. Seldom was there a day when either Mr. or Mrs. D'Arusmont enjoyed good health. Often, they were both sick. He was an arrogant, irritable control freak, overprotective of his daughter. She was a negligent mother unskilled at even the simplest household task.

Lafayette's daughter-in-law brought the grand old general over for a visit. Lafayette had arranged for D'Arusmont to become superintendent of an experimental garden, but D'Arusmont could not read or write because of worsening problems with his eyes, so he lost the job. If not for their cook, said Mary Jane, the D'Arusmonts wouldn't have seen another living human being. Mary Jane escaped the bleak scene to bravely dare the English Channel off-season to escape into the arms of her loving husband.

The years Frances spent with her aunt had taken place in the world, among the people, that Jane Austen wrote about. Now she lived her life in France among the very people Balzac captured in his coffee-driven stream of books: a new generation of unsentimental people dedicated to the pursuit of money.

When old friend Trollope's humorous sketch of a much less glamorous America became all the rage in Europe, Lafayette asked Frances to come out and fight. Trollope was being used against him politically. Frances could at least bear witness that the suddenly moral Trollope had fled to America to escape her debts. Frances never responded to his request.

In 1832 Jeremy Bentham, Frances's old mentor, died. He gave up his body for a public dissection, inviting his friends, hoping to demonstrate that material things, including one's body, are unworthy of special concern. His skeleton was preserved then dressed in his clothes stuffed with straw. He intended that his mummified head be used to complete his surrogate, but the results of the process were ghastly, so a wax head stuffed with his hair, wearing his hat, completed what Jeremy called his Auto-Icon. The mummified head sat in the cabinet between Jeremy's feet. The Auto-Icon was to be rolled in for any special occasion, on demand. As the "spiritual founder" of University College London, Jeremy's Auto-Icon eventually became the property of the school where it became the object of numerous student pranks. In 1975 students of King's College, London, stole the head and held it for ransom. Another time it was stolen only to turn up in a locker at the train station in Aberdeen, Scotland. When it was found on a soccer field the head was locked away to keep it safe from further mischief. The Auto-Icon anticipates in certain ways the darkly humorous assemblages of Edward Kienholz.

Eventually, Frances returned to London to lecture at Freemason's Hall. The radical press turned out to see her, a Who's Who of forward thinkers from a radius of two hundred miles. Attendance after the first night plummeted. Frances had never faced empty seats before. Then the radical papers criticized her for being too obscure and vague. Where were practical answers to the real problems of the day? Complaining of sickness she went home to Paris, to the comfort of isolation.

A few weeks later Lafayette died. She didn't attend the funeral. She left no writing about the loss. She had no friend to bear witness to her reaction or her thoughts at the loss of her first and greatest champion, the man who had called her daughter.

In 1835, at age forty, Frances returned to America. She claimed to be there on business. She and her husband had left their daughter with neighbors in Paris to travel to New Orleans and then Cincinnati to check up on the brewery business Frances had bankrolled for her stepson. In fact, Andrew Jackson had inspired her. The president was fighting the Second United States Bank. She and the president agreed that the bank was the tool of the rich and powerful, and a sharp golden knife at the throat of the republic. Frances also thought the bank the tool of the Bank of England. Her conspiracy theory included the Rothschild family. If the old powers of Britain and Europe were not able to hold on to America by military force, she argued, then they would bleed it economically and put an end to this dangerous experiment in equality.

America had changed. The president was a violent man, with a history of duels. The country was violent, too. Lynchings tormented the South. An enslaved man was slow roasted alive over green wood in the Deep South. The army fired on protestors. A riot by supporters of slavery lasted three days in New York City. Civil War was still twenty-five years away.

America had not forgotten about Frances Wright while she was in France. When the prosecutor of a blasphemy trial against a preacher who thought women should be able to divorce and to keep their own names and property wanted to sway the jury to understand the danger inherent in such ideas he brought up Frances Wright: "What too did Fanny Wright come here for, but to plant the standard of Infidelity, to raise an insurrection against Christianity, to make an open and gross attack upon our religious faith and our domestic happiness; to open a rendezvous to gather volunteers to enter upon a crusade against religion, marriage, chastity, order, and decency, and the very foundations of civil society?" (Ginzberg 1994).

In spring of 1836 Cincinnati suffered riots. Though asked to give speeches along the way there, even on board the steamboat that took her upriver, Frances refused. But by May she felt moved to speak at the very courthouse where her professional lecturing commenced a mere seven years earlier. She believed she could help calm the town and dispel the extremism. She didn't realize that she was the most notorious woman in America.

Most of her listeners didn't notice that she had reversed many of her old positions. Her two lectures were devoted to supporting Andrew Jackson's choice as his successor, Martin Van Buren. Van Buren had a spotty record on free speech, having been involved in a ban on abolitionist literature delivered by mail. Jackson was one of America's biggest owners of enslaved people, and a friend to the South. Anyway how could the North talk about slavery in the South, Frances argued, when northern industrialists practiced what she called wage slavery? But Frances believed the fight against the Second Bank of the United States superseded all other priorities.

The papers and the authorities didn't notice her new platform. She was banned in Philadelphia again. So she lectured at a country fair to five thousand listeners who braved the heavy rain. When she lectured at an abandoned factory near Laurel Hill Cemetery, Frances and her small phalanx of two women walked onto the rickety stage in the dilapidated building to loud hissing but also cheering. Gentlemen outside urged street brats to hurl stones through the glass windows of the factory. What an eerie scene it must have been as the stubborn lecturer, and her equally stubborn audience of a thousand, sat through the spraying glass and bouncing rocks. The local newspaper chortled that the audience had to suffer the "two-fold pain" of the stoning and the lecture itself. Another newspaper warned, "Fears are entertained that she may not escape personal injury if she persists in her degrading career."

When Frances returned to Cincinnati she found it uneasy after another riot. Abolitionist printing presses had been dragged down the street and thrown into the river. One of Cincinnati's most respectable ladies, Catharine Beecher now set her sights on Frances, establishing a pattern conservative American women have followed ever since. The good Christian lady wrote: "Who can look without disgust and abhorrence upon such an one as Fanny Wright, with her great masculine person, her loud voice, her untasteful attire, going about unprotected, and feeling no need of protection, mingling with men in stormy debate, and standing up with bare-faced impudence, to lecture to a public assembly— There she stands, with brazen front and brawny arms, attacking the safeguards of all that is venerable and sacred in religion, all that is safe and wise in law, all that is pure and lovely in domestic virtue. Her talents only make her the more conspicuous and offensive" (Conners 1999).

But Frances had another adversary in mind. The Second Bank of the United States had to be stopped. Using "promises to pay—they will appropriate American lands, mortgages on American real estate, shares in American internal improvements—the privileged orders of Europe, having drained their own peoples life-blood, may now gorge themselves—with the heart's blood of America" (Eckhardt 1984).

By now Frances and her husband had drifted apart. They had not been sleeping in the same bed. The fiery public defender of the glorious sexual passions now believed husband and wife sharing a bed to be unhealthy. Soon distance settled between them. Though the entire family had returned to America, D'Arusmont and Sylva were always together, and never for very long in any city when Frances arrived.

D'Arusmont had been bickering with Robert Dale over old loans and mortgages Dale owed his wife. Frances chose to write publicly about the trouble. She dismissed her former colleague Dale, even adjusting the facts to aggrandize her own accomplishments, such as describing him as an assistant editor she had hired at the *New Harmony Gazette* when in fact he had hired her as coeditor. Dale forgave her in a public letter, hoping she would come to her senses.

Just before the election, Frances returned to New York in support of Van Buren and the Bank War. The great newspapers of the city ignored her. The minor papers reported the event with sneering prose. "This disgusting exhibition of female impudence has no redeeming excuses. One could very well afford to hear his own opinions of propriety abused by a woman if—from between a pair of pretty lips." The other described Frances as "a great awkward bungle of womanhood, somewhere about six feet in longitude, with a face like a Fury, and her hair cropped like a convict" (Jackson 2019). Pity was owed her husband.

The year 1837 was a rough one for America economically. A $480 lot in New York was only worth fifty bucks. Cotton, nineteen cents in December was suddenly nine cents. Two out of three merchants in New York went bankrupt. Banks in New York, Baltimore, and Philadelphia suspended payments. Twenty thousand people gathered in Philly's Independence Square to protest the banking system. Frances seemed to believe that if she could explain British history to the American electorate they would not make the same mistakes. The banks, she hoped Americans would realize, were nothing more than the new royalty. The old king of France used to appear daily in his golden carriage wearing jewels and priceless fabrics; the new king strolled in a sober suit like any good banker. The banks shared with the royals the goal of hoarding wealth while cheating the workers out of a decent living wage. If Americans could realize that, Frances believed, the republic would be saved.

In Philadelphia her lecture was jeered and heckled until she gave up. She never spoke in Philadelphia again, though she lived there when she wrote and published *Manual of American Principles*. Unfortunately Frances was more useful to the opposition than to the party she hoped to promote. Her name was used to discredit any liberal politician or platform. The *Cincinnati Chronicle,* for example, accused her of "diffusing the worst principles of the French revolution through this land of the Puritan fathers. . . . She has set in motion a train of causes, which will never cease to operate, until that day when God shall come to make inquisition for blood, and to destroy the wicked with the breath of his mouth. Many a happy home has been rendered a moral desert by the trace of her footsteps, many a parent worse than childless, and many a wife more desolate than a widow."

Some called her ugly now. Her deeply furrowed forehead and dowdy dresses mortified her former friends. The monotone of self-importance had crept into her eloquence. She seemed the living embodiment of the consequences of having sacrificed the liberty she had once so fiercely idealized.

In late September 1838 Frances began a series of five lectures at Masonic Hall. There she had first addressed the people of New York nine years earlier. Her first lecture was uneventful except for bad press. At the second the crowd erupted when Frances and thirty women appeared on the platform: hissing, shouting, heckling, hooting, and pounding hundreds of canes. A local newspaper described Frances as a witch from Macbeth because she silenced the crowd with her pointed finger.

The third lecture was broken up by the uproar, more pounded canes and this time shouted obscenities. The papers blamed her again. "Riot and Revolution is the element she creates and breathes in." For the next lecture the mayor stationed police all around the hall, many in plain clothes. When the tumult began inside, police there got the situation under control. After the lecture a bodyguard of fans surrounded her as she walked up Broadway. Small groups of young men insulted and taunted her as she passed.

The fifth lecture, on October 21 was the worst. Five thousand showed up to hear her. Ten thousand gathered outside. After the lecture the crowd outside surged toward her, threatening her, barely restrained by a double line of police. Women leaving the lecture had their bonnets knocked off by bullies who called them whores while yelling every obscenity at them. The flotsam of the mob washed up at Fanny's own doorstep. She must have cowered as the boroughs all around her erupted into riots.

She was now reduced to renting Clinton Hall. Though only a few blocks from the Park Theater where twenty years earlier her play had its triumphant opening night, Clinton Hall was now in a bad neighborhood. She hoped to draw a thousand listeners to the decrepit building. A woman named Elizabeth Oakes Smith left an eyewitness account after ignoring her family's warnings and convincing her husband to brave the heavy fog. "We went upstairs and turned into a very dirty, dimly lighted hall, filled with straight wooden benches, and only three persons in them. The appointed hour had already arrived, and slowly, men, one after another, sauntered in—several women also, some with babes in their arms, and all bring an atrocious odor of tobacco, whisky, and damp clothing. At length there might have been fifty persons, not more, present, and these began to shuffle and call for the speaker. It was all so much more gross and noisy than anything I had ever encountered where a woman was concerned, that I grew quite distressed, and the bad atmosphere nearly made me faint" (Eckhardt 1984). As for the lecturer, Elizabeth found her sound, earnest, and wholesome.

Opposition and controversy she thrived on, but Frances could not face the boredom of curiosity seekers. In March 1839 she surrendered. She announced her retreat to private life. As her ship left New York a newspaper editorial commented, "Let her go home or go to the Devil, so that she never visits us again."

As Celia Eckhardt (1984) wrote, Frances's final years "are both a study in loneliness and a lesson in the perils of isolation." Her return to Europe began auspiciously. In England the *National* appreciated Frances's book *Course of Popular Lectures*: "The work is also invaluable as evidence of the power of a female mind. We especially recommend it to the unprejudiced consideration of all those males, who yet, on the score of intellect, claim a superiority over their more moral sisters, enforcing such superiority by the argument of brutality—muscular power" (Sanders 2004).

In 1844 Frances inherited valuable property and land from a cousin in Scotland. She traveled there to inspect her new wealth. But she seemed to find no relief from this inheritance. A year later she was bedridden with nervous exhaustion in America again, as she turned fifty years old, without her husband or her daughter. They had traveled to Great Britain to try without her knowledge or consent to gain some of her inheritance out of her estranged relatives.

By 1847 she and her husband began a series of lawsuits and financial maneuvers by which he tried to seize control of all his wife's property, though he brought no wealth to their marriage. D'Arusmont was clever and the laws gave wives few rights when it came to property so Frances found herself living on a stipend so meager she had to borrow money to survive.

Through most of the 1840s Frances had worked on her last book, *England the Civilizer* (1848) a pioneering, in some ways gender-based, unconventional history of Great Britain that some leading intellectuals found admirable but that was utterly overshadowed by the publication soon after of Macauley's beloved *History of England*. In her final book Frances revealed that she no longer considered America the glowing ideal of her youth; like any society America was a "complicated system of errors—the most decidedly anarchic and supremely corrupt of any on the face of the globe." Frances had also changed her mind about religion. She now believed that communities require religion, but she didn't consider any of the organized religions widely available to be anything but societies for the enrichment of the few.

In 1850 Frances began divorce proceedings and asked the American court to restore her fortune of $150,000. Her husband responded by circulating a condescending open letter her enemies shared and published. Her husband accused her of falling into mental illness, the natural result of alienation so complete she treated her own husband and daughter as mere appendages. He described his attendance at her lectures as self-sacrifice and claimed to have prevented their daughter from ever hearing her mother speak publicly.

Returning to America, two winters at Nashoba, where a strong wind could blast open the door of her damp cabin, further damaged her health. She began to lose her eyesight. She was preoccupied with the idea that if she could take control of her estate she could win back her daughter. In 1851 she won an important victory in court when the judge decided her husband had abandoned her. But when her daughter came to Memphis, she refused to see her mother without her father in the room. A month later the local sheriff gave Frances a writ informing her that her daughter was trying to take Nashoba from her.

Living at Nashoba, Frances made legal history when a judge granted the petition of the "infirm and aged" complainant to receive $800 from her own property while the court decided. The judge made this poignant statement, "to review the history of two lives—that are closing in suffering and sorrow—a fearful picture—of ambition, disappointed hope, and lost happiness—what demon turned all this love to hate, and their home into hell?" (Eckhardt 1984).

Frances wrote to her daughter again but the five-hour meeting that followed was only an opportunity for Sylva to adamantly refuse any relationship with her mother. So isolated had Frances become her only friends were now her lawyer and the carpenter working on her house. The carpenter was shocked by her way of life. Her possessions amounted to a charcoal furnace, a writing desk, and a table with several chairs. She ate crackers and boiled potato, egg, or beef. She drank only tea or coffee. At first the carpenter had worried that she would oversee his work, but she was more interested in talking about workers' rights. She always invited him to eat at her table. He found her to be a walking encyclopedia and wonderful conversationalist. He said she lamented that her aristocratic upbringing had never taught her the simple skills of housework, which he said, she still had not mastered, being inept at everything from sweeping to cooking. He remembered her prediction that in fifty years America would be covered with railroads built on the backs of the poor, creating more large cities, and more millionaires who would control power at every political level. She was right.

In early 1852 Frances fell on the ice in her front yard in Cincinnati and broke her femur. She spent two months in agony at the Hotel for Invalids, cared for only by a hired maid. Her husband and daughter never visited her. Her lawyer, who brought her the copy of *Uncle Tom's Cabin* she requested, thought she was improving and wrote to her friends at Nashoba that she would return to them, though she would be lame in one leg. She seemed to believe she would recover. She bought Prescott's *History of Mexico,* and a year's subscription to a magazine she liked. She had a dentist visit her twenty times to make her a new set of teeth; she paid in old gold coins.

The death of the first female abolitionist and feminist in America didn't make the news. Frances did not follow her mentor Jeremy Bentham's example; she had no Auto-Icon. She became just another grave at Cincinnati Spring Grove Cemetery, but she did leave a powerful message carved into her tombstone: "I have wedded the cause of human improvement, staked on it my fortune, my reputation and my life." Her estate was still tangled in the courts but upon her death became the property of her estranged daughter, Sylva, as Frances wished. When her father died three years later Sylva battled with her half brother over the estate.

As I researched this chapter in 2015, a collection of Frances Wright's unpublished letters was put up for sale. Nine letters, thirty-two pages in all, in quarto and folio, written as her fame began to spread from 1820 to 1823. Written to a famous Irish exile in New York, the letters praise the free press as "the safety valve of a free Constitution." She writes about the prison systems of England and America. She explains why she favors life imprisonment over the death penalty. She argues for universal education. She comments on Bolivar and the revolutions in South America. She observes that America needs more patriotic songs. She shares Thomas Jefferson's complimentary assessment of her play, and moments from her friendship with Lafayette.

The letters reveal young Frances's excitement about the political upheavals in Europe. "Another revolution!" she wrote. "Naples free and all of Italy in insurrection! How wonderful has been the march of the human mind in these last thirty years—so may it be till the last link of the chains of slavery is broken and the banner of freedom waves over the whole earth!" Frances writes of America: "Is not an hereditary nobility inconsistent with liberty? I will ask more, is it not inconsistent with public virtue? Not only does it lodge authority with the unskillful but with those whose interest it is to abuse it. It does more—it degrades the minds of men, it corrupts their hearts and debases their understanding, leading them to attach honor and to yield respect to something else than talent and virtue." The collection was offered at $28,000. A bookseller in Memphis is offering a small poem Frances wrote for a child during her first theatrical tour of the United States. What would she have made of the asking price of $6,500?

Sylva became a devout Episcopalian Christian. In 1874 the daughter of Frances Wright appeared before Congress to argue against giving women the right to vote. Sylva inherited her mother's unpublished papers. She preserved them for her children but in their hands they disappeared. Still, the grandsons of Frances Wright, Kenneth and William Guthrie, though all but forgotten today, earned a chapter in this book, as they were extraordinary examples of Pagan Christians.

Sylva sent her two sons to get degrees and ordinations at a good American Episcopalian college in Tennessee. Both became ministers of churches in New York City. Both carried on crusades like the grandmother they never met, and each had a toned-down version of her Hall of Science. Kenneth had a Museum of Slavery in his church. He claimed his Neoplatonist translations could save the world. Like his grandmother Frances, elder brother William rubbed shoulders with the famous, from Kahlil Gibran and Martha Graham to Carl Sandburg and Frank Lloyd Wright; he also pioneered the inclusion of Indigenous American and other non-Christian but nevertheless complementary cultural rituals, and of dance, and light shows, in American churches.

At the age of eighty-three, in 1854, Robert Owen, whose New Harmony community inspired Frances Wright's equally spectacular failure Nashoba, became a Spiritualist, thanks to several sessions he had with famous American medium Maria Hayden. Hayden was one of the first mediums to bring to England séances where spirits answered questions with knocks. Owen claimed to have contacted the spirits of Thomas Jefferson and Benjamin Franklin. After his death the famous English medium Emma Hardinge Britten said she received the spiritualist classic *Seven Principles of Spiritualism* from Owen himself. Robert Dale, Owen's son, the longtime ally Frances later dismissed in print after bickering about property rights and loan paybacks, also became a Spiritualist.

One of the most famous of all abolitionists lived in a Spiritualist community for ten years. Born a slave in New York, in 1826 Bell Baumfree walked away to freedom. When she became a Methodist in 1843, she took the name Sojourner Truth. Her memoir *The Narrative of Sojourner Truth: A Northern Slave* was published in 1850 but she became famous after the Ohio Women's Rights Convention in 1851 where she gave her speech "Ain't I a Woman?"

In the summer of 1857, the year the Supreme Court decided enslaved people were property, not human beings with rights under the Constitution, Truth bought one acre on the edge of a village called

Harmonia in Michigan. Harmonia was a Spiritualist utopia, a community devoted to guidance from beyond. She bought a second lot in town a month later. Harmonia provided Truth with a good base for her speaking and lecturing engagements all over the Midwest.

But then Harmonia began to fall part. As the Civil War approached, a utopian Spiritualist community didn't seem to make much sense in a world where everyone was expected to choose a side. Spiritualists didn't get along among themselves especially well anyway. Each one had their own ideas about how things should be and each had authority from their sources on the other side. The Harmonial Institute that had been the purpose of the village went bankrupt in 1860.

In the summer of 1862 a tornado leveled most of the town and killed residents including children, but Sojourner Truth survived and stayed. The family that had financially backed Harmonia saw the writing on the wall and moved away in 1863. Methodists started buying up the properties around Harmonia, methodically driving out their Spiritualist competition. As the last flame of Spiritualism went out, Truth moved to Battle Creek in 1867 where she lived until her death in 1883. Harmonia was left a ghost town. As World War I approached, the area once known as Harmonia became Camp Custer, a training center for troops that remains in use today. On the hill above the military installation the old Spiritualist graveyard behind locked gates is all that is left of Harmonia.

Even the feminists she helped inspire had ambivalent feelings about Frances Wright. Although Susan B. Anthony and Elizabeth Cady Stanton used her portrait as the frontispiece of *History of Woman Suffrage,* Frances soon became a less told story. Nashoba was such a disappointment, and her outspoken atheism was only one of the ways she often inflamed opposition.

What is an atheist like Frances Wright doing in a book about American Metaphysical Religion? Frances Wright's religion was science and her mysticism her romance with the ideal of America. With her confident optimism that science could only bring good things to humanity, she had no presentiment of Chernobyl and other tragedies of science, unlike her friend Mary Shelley. Like the Intelligencers and their inspiration, Paracelsus, Frances believed the ideal itself a call to action that could end all human suffering. Ignorance dictates the fates of individuals and nations, she believed. Like any practitioner of American Metaphysical Religion she believed that knowledge cures all ills.

Once she wrote of how she and D'Arusmont had become husband and wife because of their interest in finding the truth of human society and the cure for injustice and unnecessary suffering, which they believed could be found in the analysis of history. As she discussed this arcane secret she and her partner labored to discover, one can easily imagine them, in the tradition of the alchemist and sorer, or mystical sister, together seeking the philosophers' stone, often in disheveled isolation, chasing the revelation that revolutionizes individual lives and society.

Her science could be mistaken for Daoist alchemy, a theory of Eliphas Levi or Blavatsky, or one can easily imagine the following passage written by Frances (1847) to be an excerpt from that extraordinary documentation of communication from the other side *The Unobstructed Universe:* "We detect then, throughout the whole of things—in the operations of nature, of human society, and in those of our own internal percipient and sentient soul—two master energies. These—while preserving equal forces and acting in conjunction—keep all existences in life, all bodies in place; impart and preserve to each and all their appropriate sphere of action or of movement; and tend, throughout the world of matter, as of mind—to order, harmony, and beauty. Acting in disjunction—i.e., singly, or in opposition—these two principles are transformed into agents of disorder and death; producing variously, violence, inertia, confusion, stagnation, convulsion, decomposition, dissolution" (Wright 1847).

Was she ahead of her time or left behind? Her enthusiasm for the cure-all of science fit better with the Enlightenment than the new world of industrialization. Yet she anticipated many important reforms later adopted by societies worldwide.

10

The Uncivil War

ACCORDING TO THE U.S. CENSUS of 1860, a year before the Civil War, twenty-five percent of Americans listed themselves as Christian. Ten percent described themselves as Spiritualists. When the war between the states broke out at first the populace thought it would be a relatively civil affair, conducted within reason, as European wars were said to be. Spectators had picnics on adjacent hillsides. But the picnics in America looked upon bloody battlefields where brothers killed brothers, and the polite onlookers could not always be guaranteed safety. This was a modern war, especially as waged by the North, with its factories. Yankee armies could bombard longer with bigger bombs. They could make more guns. General Sherman destroyed everything in his path as he marched to the sea in the heart of the Old South. The devastation could be described as industrial.

The terrible bloodshed meant that an unprecedented number of Americans lost someone dear to them. Interest in Spiritualism exploded as devastated people sought solace and reconnection with loved ones. The Spiritualist view of the afterlife was comforting compared to mere doubt or the Christian threat of hell. Christians can only pray for their dead. Spiritualists claimed to be able to connect the bereaved with those who had crossed over, not only comforting grief, but soothing the existential angst of mortality. Even frauds were good at making people believe they had actually communicated with someone on the other side.

During the American Civil War, in the *Richmond Daily Dispatch*, the Confederacy's newspaper of record, Northerners were condemned as demon possessed. Yankees weren't genuine Christians, or real

Americans at all—they were Spiritualists, and therefore debauched. This reputation for immorality among Spiritualists may have arisen from certain cons where fraudulent female mediums would prove they weren't hiding anything, and distract their victims, by wearing transparent or very revealing clothing. Séances, in some circles, were little more than peep shows. With the uncivilized business of industrialism on the one hand, and on the other that unholy and bawdy mischief of women called Spiritualism, Southerners believed they were fighting for the church, for civilization, and for the Bible, which according to their interpretation supported enslaving other human beings.

Lurid tales of half-naked mediums aside, Spiritualism led to strange byways that would have been suitable for an episode of *The Twilight Zone* with an introduction by Rod Serling. Consider, for example, the story of Annie Lord. Her father Dr. Lord lived in Maine. His children grew up in a home where séances were common. One session the spirits instructed him to sit in the circle for ten days, three times a day, with his second daughter, Annie. He wanted to know what would be the result of this experiment. He was told that Annie would become a physical medium, that is, she would display the power to energize or otherwise manipulate physical objects.

At noon, in full daylight, as directed by the spirits, Annie put a guitar under the table. The guitar played itself, producing sounds although no one touched it. Loud knocks followed, in the floor, ceiling, and walls. Annie didn't stop at guitars. At a séance in 1864, in South Malden, Massachusetts, twenty or so participants witnessed Annie make all the instruments play: the music box, trumpets, and small bells on the table, and a drum, cello, violin, banjo, and guitar left lying on the ground. "All the instruments seemed to sound in concert and exact time to our singing," a witness reported. Five hundred miles south, in Virginia, General Grant was using superior numbers to decimate the Confederate army at great loss to his own. In a house in Westbrook, Maine, Annie conducted more séances in full daylight. Witnesses reported hearing singing and music, and seeing fresh flowers manifest out of thin air. She produced nearly forty messages, written communications that appeared on what had been blank sheets of paper locked in a drawer.

But Annie did not have the robust health required to be a successful medium. When she moved away to another town so she could recover, hundreds followed her begging for her help. Annie found herself diagnosing diseases, physical and mental, and prescribing cures, while becoming weaker by the day.

Colonel William Cushman and his wife in Ottawa, Illinois, recognized the condition Annie was in. They rescued her, providing privacy and shelter, uncertain if she would ever return to full health. But Annie grew strong again. Her illness had given her the obscurity she longed for. She eventually married an older man. Mediumship became less important to her, especially in her later years. She lived a long life, while the strange experiences that had briefly made her famous faded into obscurity.

In the North skeptics debated true believers, declaring that only fraud and fakery could be responsible for the strange goings on. What more evidence do you want? The convinced retorted, "The spirits have communicated their presence in undeniable ways." But in the South, both sides of the debate were nothing more than further proof of the spiritual sickness of the North. Only Northerners would commit fraud to enrich themselves at the expense of the bereaved. Only Northerners would dare to communicate with the dead against the explicit prohibitions of the Christian religion.

Spiritualists weren't the only unholy example of Yankee heresies. In the mid-1800s Phineas Parkhurst Quimby, a clockmaker by trade, practiced an unusual healing method that many people claimed cured serious diseases. But he may also have been talking some of his female patients out of their corsets.

Quimby explained that he could sympathize with a patient, even feeling their symptoms. He compared his power of diagnosis to the sense of smell. "To every disease there is an odor [a mental atmosphere]," Quimby wrote, "and every one is affected by it when it comes within his consciousness. Every one knows that he can produce in himself heat or cold by excitement. So likewise he can produce the odor of any disease so that he is affected by it" (Albanese 1990). With the right suggestion, delivered in conversation, Quimby could change the patient's belief. According to Quimby his healings were accomplished by the truth taught by Jesus Christ. There was more to it than simply talking.

Quimby believed the natural state of a spiritually aware incarnate human being must be health. As Quimby saw it the matter the body is made of disintegrates unless a soul is there to give it form and energy. If a soul inhabits its body completely there can be no disease, because health is how the body experiences the immortality of the soul. The soul by its very nature heals the body. But people don't believe it because they're taught otherwise, and so all manner of suffering manifests. Having the courage of his convictions, Quimby affirmed, he could work a miracle.

"Therefore," Catherine Albanese (1990) wrote in her book *Nature Religion in America*, "when illness struck, the magnetic doctor acted as hero-priest, using his or her innate animal magnetism to alter the flow in the invisible fluid—to unblock obstruction—so that a steady supply of the life-force could reach the ailing person." Shamans are said to do the same.

In one example, Quimby asked a man with a diagnosed heart condition to remember when the symptoms first appeared. The man recalled the time he clutched for his wallet, which he normally carried in his breast pocket, but he found it was missing. Realizing the connection between his anxiety about money and his disease, he understood how he was making himself sick. He claimed to have been completely cured.

But Quimby was also known for healing at a distance, which he explained by assuring patients that he could tune in to their true inner selves, of which the body was "nothing but a dense shadow, condensed into what is called matter, or ignorance of God and Wisdom. The priests and doctors conspire together to humbug the people, and they have invented all sorts of stories to frighten man and keep him under their power. The truth shall set you free" (Albanese 1990).

Quimby saw as many as five hundred patients a year. His family showed off testimonials and used them cleverly in advertising "Dr." Quimby's services. But who really wrote the three volumes of Quimby's *Complete Writings*? Quimby himself appears to have been almost illiterate. The most likely candidate is his longtime secretary, the well-educated and cultured Emma Ware. Several personal notes by

Quimby in his own very poor writing, and a note from Emma, survive to witness that he probably wasn't capable of the sophisticated cadence and rhetoric of his essays. Emma wrote a letter as evidence that Quimby cured her, and many others.

Careful scholarship by Professor Gillian Gill has revealed contemporary testimonies that shed a different light on Quimby. Reports, from embarrassed mill girls and shocked wives, of indecent advances and two witnesses to Quimby's fluency in swear words, provide quite a contrast to the kindly old healer his followers remembered fondly. One letter writer tells a story full of pathos about a small boy dying, trying to convince himself Quimby was making him better, trying vainly to think and believe his way free of death's clutches, blaming himself for not believing enough.

Was Quimby a gentle healer or a lecherous hustler? As the history of spiritual leaders in general suggests, he may have been both. Perhaps Quimby healed only psychosomatic conditions that had been mistaken for more serious illnesses, but the fact remains that he personally positively transformed the lives of several thousand people. When he died in 1866, just after the Civil War ended, it seemed probable that only his family and a few friends would remember his practice and theory. But by the turn of the century, he was revered by the New Thought movement as a founding father. Among those healed by Quimby who became his disciples were the founders of Religious Science, Divine Science, and Unity.

Though Emma Ware may have written the essays of Quimby, another of his patients would take Quimby and Ware's ideas and make them her own, and then the world's. When Quimby healed Mary Baker Glover, who would become famous as Mary Baker Eddy, the Quimby family recruited her to write gushing letters of endorsement to the local newspaper. Mary became Quimby's devoted student, taking down notes of his conversations.

The famous New England Transcendentalist and educator Bronson Alcott, the Sage of Apple Slump, was an early admirer of Eddy. Two years before Glover became Eddy, Alcott read her book *Science and Health*. He sent her a letter enthusing that she had put "Christian revelations" into modern language. He recommended her work at meetings with Emerson and friends, and with divinity students at Harvard. In January 1876 he called her a saint. However six months later in his diary he mentioned her "fanaticism," but he remained optimistic that she would grow out of it.

Alcott's nickname, the Sage of Apple Slump, lampooned him for his devoted idealism, but in the Orchard House, his home that became the setting for the classic book *Little Women,* the book's author, his daughter Louisa May Alcott, baked apple slumps that delighted the palates of Thoreau, Emerson, Margaret Fuller, and Thomas Johnson. As we have seen in an earlier chapter Mary Baker Eddy, as extraordinary as she was, may have paled in comparison to several of her relatives, who were less famous, but who took spiritual enthusiasm to what were considered exotic extremes. While Eddy was not famous before or during the war, after the war she exemplified Southern skepticism of Northern spirituality. Only in the North could a woman start her own church claiming that the traditional churches had got it all wrong. Jesus was in reality a man of science.

Just a few years before the Civil War broke out, we are provided a glimpse of a very dysfunctional family's relationship with Spiritualist practices. Victoria Woodhull's father was not only cruel and violent, he also abused her sexually. But then he noticed that she and her sister had a knack for plausibly diagnosing sickness, so around 1850 he put them on the road, augmenting the show with his own old-fashioned mind-reading hustles, and his own recipe for snake oil at two dollars a bottle.

At age fifteen Victoria married a doctor who turned out to be a drug addict and a regular at the local brothels. To support her husband and first child, a son with brain damage probably caused by her drunk husband mishandling the delivery, Victoria turned to the stage, and some said to prostitution. When her husband insisted on redeeming himself at the birth of their second child he showed up drunk again and almost killed their newborn daughter Zulu by forgetting to tie off the cut umbilical cord. Victoria left him. Relatives took care of the children as Victoria rejoined her sister. They traveled together for several years as spiritual healers.

Victoria's second husband, Colonel Blood, a Union army Civil War veteran, inspired her to fight for women's rights. Her reputation and performance as a medium earned her powerful friends. Under the patronage of a titan of industry, Cornelius Vanderbilt, Victoria became the first female stockbroker in America. With her sister she opened a brokerage on Wall Street, and then a muckraking newspaper.

Now financially independent, Victoria took good care of her children. She traveled through nineteenth-century America lecturing on the controversial subject of free love. This was not the free love of the 1960s. Victoria argued that wives should be allowed to leave abusive marriages. Marriage should be an act of love, not economic expediency, or of mere improvement of social standing for the bride's family. She even went so far as to suggest that marriages between the disincarnate and the living would be possible in the future.

A generation later, Ida Craddock would go further than suggesting the possibility. She claimed to have lived it as the wife of an angelic spirit and wrote about her experiences in her books including *Heavenly Bridegrooms* published in 1894 and *Psychic Wedlock* published in 1899. Perhaps Ida's most famous actions as a feminist were her written defenses of Little Egypt's notorious belly dance at the World Fair. Raised Quaker, Ida took to metaphysics like the proverbial duck to water. At one point she declared herself priestess and pastor of the Church of Yoga. When her books *Lunar and Sex Worship* and *The Wedding Night,* among others, were judged obscene Ida went to jail five times, and once to an insane asylum.

Here is an example of her "obscenity," from her book *Psychic Wedlock:* "People who would shrink from drugging themselves with liquor or opium, and who hold that yielding to so-called spirit mediumship is dangerous, will, nevertheless, recklessly abandon their self-control during the sex ecstasy. It is well-established that a child conceived when the father is drunk will be mentally unbalanced, usually to the borders of idiocy. If intoxication—i.e., lack of self-control—at the moment of conception be produced by other means than by alcohol, is it likely that the resulting offspring will not be tainted thereby?" (Craddock 2017). Clearly, Ida was more a prohibitionist than a pornographer.

Victoria Woodhull joined in the rising up of women to demand the right to vote. She became a leader, and discovered she had public-speaking skills. Doors opened for her that she never could have imagined while struggling to survive her childhood. She was the first woman to speak before the Judicial Committee of the United States Congress. Her inspiring speech on the subject of voting rights for women she claimed had been dictated to her by her spirit guide, the ancient Athenian orator Demosthenes. The leaders of the suffrage movement, including Susan B. Anthony and Elizabeth Cady Stanton, were enthusiastic about Woodhull at first. But they were soon taken aback by her political ambitions. In 1872 Victoria Woodhull became the first female presidential candidate in American history. Her announced vice president on the ticket, the great African American abolitionist Frederick Douglass, never acknowledged his nomination.

The U.S. government refused to print her name on the ballot because at age thirty-five she was too young to legally run. After that the invitations to speak at suffrage conventions stopped. When a British leader of the suffrage movement wrote Anthony asking her about Woodhull, Anthony responded, "Both sisters are regarded as lewd and indecent." Anthony and Stanton all but ignored Woodhull when they wrote their history of the movement, despite her significant contributions.

When Victoria used her newspaper to expose the adultery of America's most beloved Christian preacher she found herself ostracized. The preacher happened to be the brother of Harriet Beecher Stowe, the author of *Uncle Tom's Cabin*. If that didn't cause enough trouble, the newspaper then accused a well-known Wall Street trader of intoxicating two teenage girls with alcohol and taking advantage of them. Woodhull and her sister went to jail. The court verdict was not guilty, but the press had ruined them, revealing that Woodhull lived in a house with her lover, her husband, and her ex-husband. Harriet called the woman who denounced her brother an "impudent witch." Famous editorial cartoonist Thomas Nast, known as the father of the American cartoon, drew Victoria as "Mrs. Satan."

First, she was ruined financially, then more charges were trumped up against her. Her spirits abandoned her, she said, her gift seemed to blink off. She was exorcised by Catholic monks as arranged by her mother. Then Victoria divorced her free-thinking husband.

Despised and notorious she fled the United States for the United Kingdom where she married an English lord. Woodhull became a collector of the latest sensation, automobiles. The towns around her estate knew her generosity well. She gave not only donations but services. She also started a school of agriculture that failed quickly. During World War I, in her midseventies, she was a Red Cross volunteer. In her last decade she devoted herself to preserving the English home of George Washington's ancestors. As a noble widow she was known for her dignity. No one remembered, nor could they have scarcely believed, the truth about her scandalous beginnings in America.

In the North even a camera could become something demonic. To make a living William H. Mumler engraved jewelry in Boston, but his hobby was photography. One day he took a self-portrait, or so he reported, and was shocked to find that the developed photograph showed his young cousin sitting in a chair to his right. She had died ten years earlier. Mumler became famous for his portrait of Mary Todd Lincoln with the ghost of her husband Abraham standing behind her with his hands on her shoulders. Mumler became so popular many other photographers became spirit photographers to cash in on the fad.

Then P. T. Barnum took Mumler to court. He was accused of using dirty tricks in the developing process and breaking into victim's houses to steal pictures of dead relatives. He also somehow managed to take spirit photographs of people he had been told were dead but who were actually alive. Mumler could not be proven guilty beyond a shadow of a doubt so he escaped conviction but his career as a spirit photographer came to an end. He continued working as a photographer but only for living subjects.

In the world of American Metaphysical Religion we are often surprised to find that household names had occult connections. For example, Albert Goodwill Spalding and Abner Doubleday, two of the most famous names associated with the early days of baseball, were both heavily involved in the Theosophical Society. Doubleday is still remembered as an inventor of baseball though baseball never appeared in any of his letters or journals. He was honored for having fired the first cannon shot of the Civil War at Fort Sumter in response to the Confederate bombardment. He rode to Gettysburg with Lincoln because the corps of which Doubleday had been forced to take command had retreated but then stood its ground against a superior rebel force, at the cost of being almost annihilated. The sacrifice gave the rest of the Union army the time it needed to deploy.

After the war Doubleday was stationed in San Francisco in 1869 as head of recruiting. But he had bigger plans. He got a patent for a cable-car system and put a business together. His cable-car company was the first in San Francisco. In 1871 he became commanding officer of the African American Twenty-Fourth Infantry regiment in Texas, where he spent his last two years before he retired from service. Spiritualism, the occult, and Theosophy fascinated Doubleday in his later years. A frequent guest of Blavatsky and Olcott he became an early vice president of the Theosophical Society, then became president of what was left of the American branch when Blavatsky and Olcott relocated to India. Doubleday also somehow managed to find the time to translate books by the French expert occultist Eliphas Levi.

A Christie's auction of 2006, of the Stuart and Marilyn R. Kaplan Collection of historic cards and games, included "A Fascinating Manuscript from the Fabled Civil War General on Tarot, Jewish 'Cabalistic' Practice, and Other Aspects of the Occult." According to the catalog, the manuscript includes translations and notes for works by Levi, William Postel, Court de Gebelin, St. Martin, Raymond Lulli, Cagliostro, Papus, T. H. Burgoyne, and Etteille (the first professional tarot reader in history) including highlights from the *Journal of the Theosophical Society,* and the enigmatic and picturesque publication we'll explore in the next chapter, the *Platonist.*

The catalog continues: "Doubleday also discusses Jewish 'cabalistic' aspects, the work of 'Rabbi Abraham,' the Hebrew key, the cabalistic alphabet, and an explanation of the suits (rods, cups, swords, and pentacles), the rods being described as—'the phallus of the Egyptians, or the *yod* of the Hebrews.' Mounted and drawn into the manuscript are various number charts of Mars, the Sun, Mercury, the Moon,

Venus, Saturn, and Jupiter, an 'apocalyptic key' (depicting seven seals of St. John), several hand-drawn diagrams tipped-in, and a group of 78 hand-drawn [traced?] colored woodcuts of tarot cards by 'Farinone Battista in Varallo' captioned in Italian and pasted on 16 pages at the back of the book."

As for Spalding, there is no doubt about his importance to baseball. He's been called the greatest pitcher of the 1870s. He was the first player to gain acceptance for the previously maligned baseball mitt. He founded not only the sporting goods company that still dominates the sport, but also helped organize the National League. He managed and owned teams. In 1900 he was sports commissioner for the Summer Olympics. He wrote the first rulebook for baseball. He even tried to run as a senator for the state of California. He was also an important Theosophist. He lived the last fifteen years of his life at his estate in Point Loma, California, near the Theosophical Society colony known as "White City." Since the 1850s Spalding had opposed allowing men of color, or women of any color, to play baseball. We are left to wonder just how white that city was.

As we have seen, none of this is new in American history. The Indigenous tribes found nothing strange about communicating with their ancestors through dreams or with the help of shamans. The enslaved people brought against their will to the New World came from traditions of ancestor worship where the connection between this world and the next is given constant attention. As we have seen some of the earliest Quakers in America practiced mediumship. But the Civil War brought such loss to every city and town in America that more or less private and secret practices became popular not only on Main Street but on Wall Street, and even in the White House of the Lincolns, where Mary Todd Lincoln sought to alleviate her grief with séances. The Civil War led to a search for meaning that opened the way not only for Spiritualism, but for Theosophy and then for public Rosicrucian groups, in a continuing evolution and elaboration of the central themes of American Metaphysical Religion.

11

The Platonist on the Sunset Strip

ON SUNSET BOULEVARD in West Hollywood, across the street, and about a half a block east of the Whisky a-Go-Go, was a store named Hippocampus. Since it opened in 1967, people have found oddities, curiosities, and treasures. Jimi Hendrix, Jim Morrison, Janis Joplin were very likely to have wandered in when it was new. By the time I was fortunate enough to find a treasure there, more than twenty years after the Summer of Love, the woman who had always run the place had become frail. She stayed home but she was always a phone call away and any important decisions were still hers to make. On a chilly autumn night Tamra Lucid and I wandered in to find a big leatherbound book in the small display area upstairs. I couldn't believe my eyes when I saw the title on the spine: the *Platonist*.

The *Platonist* was a newsprint magazine published in the Midwest in late nineteenth-century America. I turned the thin fragile pages revealing many rare translations by the great rogue scholar Thomas Taylor, a scattering of occult classics, and an announcement about plans for a colony where devoted philosophers could study the religions of the world. Print on demand and online archives have made the contents easily available to anyone. But back then, when the internet was young, the *Platonist* was famously rare. The pages were foxed with age but otherwise in excellent condition for a publication almost 110 years old. To find such an esoteric rarity there on the Sunset Strip seemed an impossible serendipity.

We didn't have much money and didn't think we could afford such a treasure. But I knew there was the chance that they didn't really know what it was. You couldn't yet click over to Abebooks and find the going price. I also knew that sometimes books like this were sold cheaply because their owners wanted them in the hands of people who would appreciate them. So I picked up the book, along with a couple of old Thomas Taylor editions I found nearby, and with trepidation approached the rather severe gay man behind the counter.

I asked him how much the books cost. He had no idea so he called the boss. We watched him talk to her on the phone in the back of the store. He put the phone down and walked over to ask me if I wanted the books because of their decorative leather bindings. I told him we wanted to read them. The telephone conversation ended quickly. He told us we could buy the *Platonist* for $75, all three books for $125. They were worth at least ten times that.

Back home we pored over the pages of learned commentaries, wisdom quotes, and inspiring facts; nearly forgotten history in dense double columns; predominately translations of rare Neoplatonic works. A marvelous compendium of profound and inspiring thought, yes, but what fascinated us most about the *Platonist* was that it provided proof that in a cow town at the heart of the Old West, in the last days of Billy the Kid and Jesse James, some Americans published a newspaper about Plato. We imagined a dusty Western street, an upstairs office in a plank building, and there inside a small room, in the glow of a lamp, a hardy soul, Thomas Johnson, burning the midnight oil, typesetting the sublime communications left by pagan philosophers over a thousand years before. Little did we know how truly popular Plato was in those days.

THE OTHER PLATO

Plato, through his *Dialogues,* his school, and his later successors the Neoplatonists, leads directly to the natural magic of the ceremonial magicians of the Middle Ages, and to the cultural liberation we call the Renaissance. Scratch the surface of the metaphysics of William Blake, Percy Shelley, or for that matter Shakespeare and we find Plato. In the late 1960s New York City's notorious swinger sex club, a popular symbol of the sexual revolution, was called Plato's Retreat. Plato could be called the founding father of the New Age movement of the late twentieth century, since his writings are the definitive pagan influence on Western belief in reincarnation, astrology, Atlantis, and sacred geometry.

The teachers and housewives who formed Plato clubs and met in parlors to discuss ancient Greek philosophy were the children and grandchildren of pioneers, who had built not just a town but hospitals and schools. Upper class to be sure, but the sturdy base of American stock, not the children of great families, or university legacies, there's something 1950s suburban about their earnest desire to use newfound free time well. An elite? Well, perhaps they were trying to develop into one.

THE PLATO CLUB

At its peak the Plato Club of Jacksonville, Illinois, or as it was known then "the Athens of the West," had over four hundred members, but many were spread across the American continent and even overseas, so the largest group at a popular event would be about two hundred, in a town whose population even today numbers less than twenty thousand.

The formal papers presented by members and reprinted in the *Platonist* and other philosophical journals give us a sense of the impact of Platonism on these people who were at the edge of the frontier. The Transcendentalist celebrity Ralph Waldo Emerson who befriended and visited these Platonists of the Midwest thought of them as the ultimate outpost of what he considered true civilization. The idea of a rough farmer reading Plato by firelight in his simple cabin on the prairie captured Emerson's imagination. The admiration was mutual. Thomas Johnson named his sons Ralph Proclus, Franklin Plotinus, and the whimsical Waldo Plato, but there was another Waldo aside from Ralph, Thomas's father, Waldo Johnson.

No one is sure what made Jacksonville such fertile soil for Platonism. Some writers have argued that the first settlers came from cultured places, like Huntsville, Alabama, then known as the Athens of the South. The founding fathers of Jacksonville were all Yale University men, and perhaps they brought Platonism with them. But the man at the heart of nineteenth-century Platonism in the American Midwest and beyond was a doctor in Jacksonville, a town then as now known for its hospitals.

Hiram K. Jones was a conscientious physician with a successful practice. Hiram earned his nicknames by becoming the most popular Platonist in America. He was "the modern Plato," the "Western metaphysical giant," and "the Western wonder." He was America's foremost expert on Plato, according to Emerson himself, though at the Concord School one critic dismissed Jones as a "loose, uncouth thinker."

Hiram was born in the summer of 1818. Mary Shelley's *Frankenstein* was published that year, and the U.S. Congress created an American flag of thirteen red and white stripes and one star to be added for each state; there were twenty stars at the time. Hiram's father's father, an immigrant from England, had served under the command of George Washington in the Revolutionary army. Hiram was a Lincoln man. He felt so strongly about abolition he campaigned for office to fight slavery, but he lost. The underground railroad had a stop at his house.

During the Civil War, Hiram provided medical services to Union soldiers and their families for free. Not only did he shelter runaway enslaved people, but also starving students, including William Jennings Bryan who later became the presidential candidate for the populist wing of the Democratic Party in three elections, though he never won. Illinois College was the place where Hiram's passion for metaphysics began. "When I was a student in Illinois College," he wrote, "there were two other students and myself who got hold of Emerson's writings. Of course we were ridiculed for dabbling in such transcendental nonsense. These writings were then denounced on all sides. We continued to read Emerson. Now within one short lifetime that thought has conquered and subdued all minds" (Anderson 1940).

In 1854 Hiram became superintendent of the Jacksonville Hospital for the Insane only until someone else could be found. After that he returned to his practice, where he doctored generations of loyal patients until a month before his death in 1903 almost five decades later. It took him thirty years to put out a shingle with his name on it. When a new patient hunting for his office on a hot day nearly fainted, Hiram finally put up a sign. He wasn't content with Emerson; he wanted to read the master's sources, which led him to Thomas Taylor, Plato, and the Neoplatonists. By the early 1860s Hiram was reading English translations of Plato. Any friend who showed mere polite interest would find himself listening to passages of Plato read out loud. How did Hiram become the preeminent nineteenth-century American Platonist? He was in Jacksonville at just the right time. The prairie was only a short wagon ride away, but for the prosperous elite of Jacksonville free time was an invitation to culture. Two well-to-do wives and an unmarried well-to-do woman formed a reading club with the intention of getting away from the daily grind that even rich women couldn't avoid on the edge of the prairie. They wanted a regular meeting devoted to spiritual and intellectual enrichment. They thought perhaps they'd read the Holy Bible, but they had heard Hiram K. Jones praise Plato so they asked his opinion. Hiram was always ready to talk about Plato. They all agreed to meet every Saturday morning. That was the humble beginning of the Plato Club in 1866, which influenced American culture for more than thirty years.

Jacksonville's Saturday morning Plato Club quickly attracted local teachers. Mostly female at first, the club soon included the principal of the local high school and other male educators, but women were always in the majority. Dialogues were read out loud and discussed in depth. Jones would then interpret the meaning in passionate rhetoric. His judgment was not to be questioned. The locals considered his opinions worthwhile and happily accepted the benevolent tyranny of their philosopher king. Hiram's talks about Plato drew from the literature and religion of the entire world as he sought to illuminate by comparison. From Dante and Shakespeare to parallels in Hindu, Persian, Chinese, and especially Christian thought. After all, Hiram and his wife were upstanding members of the Congregational Church.

Hiram entranced his listeners with an exotic concoction of civilizations that must have been comforting out there on what had recently been the godless frontier. The Jacksonville Plato Club hosted visiting guest speakers including the Transcendentalist sage Bronson Alcott and Thomas Johnson, publisher of the *Platonist*.

Membership in the Plato Club was open to any religion, gender, or race. Some members merely enjoyed it as a social club, an intellectual amusement, while others moved to Jacksonville specifically to study philosophy. The membership cards featured an illustration of a butterfly, symbol of the soul, with a saying in Greek: "The soul, aye, the immortal." Jones became an in-demand lecturer. Soon Plato Clubs sprang up in other towns, but lacking their own Hiram K. Jones these clubs never achieved the vigor of the original, although a story is told of a society lady who tried to one-up a new acquaintance by asking her if she had ever looked into Plato, but was herself one-upped instead when the acquaintance announced that she had been studying Plato in the original Greek for three years.

Why this attraction for Plato among midwestern dowagers? Women were claiming power in American society. Female mediums delivering lectures in trance could command the attention of large halls filled with men around whom they would otherwise have to be silent. Women were organizing to demand property rights and the vote. Plato was widely respected as the pinnacle of classical philosophy, an exclusive province of men. Women who developed a command of this difficult subject proved their equality with their most sophisticated male peers. But Plato was also teaching them the arts of argument and rhetoric, and a profound philosophy of life. Paul Andersen, the closest thing we have to a biographer of Hiram K. Jones, wrote in 1963, "It was an amateur movement in the sense that none of these people gave their complete time to philosophy and none of them wished to become so involved in the technical issues of philosophy as to disqualify themselves for participation in the solution of immediate and personal problems."

Anderson described this Americanized Platonism: "Jones regarded philosophy as a necessary orientation for the whole business of human living. It gave impetus to vocational pursuits and it enriched the leisure hours. In short, it brought the tangled miscellany of human experience into some semblance of harmony, providing meaning and purpose for all" (1940).

While devoted study of a pagan genius may not seem like a traditional Christian activity, the members of the Plato Club were not rejecting their churches to embrace ancient Greek religion. Some were however willing to view Christianity as one religion among many, and all of them worth studying.

Nearby Quincy, Illinois, was an important partner in the rise of American Platonism. On November 16, 1866, twelve ladies of Quincy were invited to the home of Mrs. Denman, they doubtless did not think of themselves as a coven of thirteen. Their goals involved feminism, education, and self-improvement through philosophy. A name considered for the club was the Embryonic Free and Independent Anti Red Tape Society. A century later that could have been the name of a psychedelic rock band. Instead they settled on the more dignified Friends in Council.

Mrs. Louise Fuller, who was living for a short time in Quincy, but who was from Jacksonville and a member of the Hiram K. Jones circle, was likely the first to suggest he address the new group. Their first organized activity was reading important books. They began with *The History of the Rise and Influence of Rationalism in Europe* by Lecky.

In year two with the membership now up to about seventeen they began to read Plato, helped along by visits from Jones—some a month long. After the first year, enough of them felt so frustrated that they traded Plato in for the Stoic philosopher Epictetus. But soon they were back to Plato, who occupied every meeting for the next year. Mrs. Fuller, back home in Jacksonville, would become editor of the *Journal of the American Akadêmê*. Many members of Friends in Council became members of the Plato Club in Jacksonville, and they joined the Plato Club in Quincy founded by a successful businessman. In 1881, thirty-five years after Friends in Council began, Mrs. Denman died. The clubs lasted only a little while longer.

As his lectures became more popular, Hiram became friends with Emerson, Alcott, and Thoreau. All were visitors to Jacksonville and guests in Hiram's house. In 1879 he helped inspire the self-taught traveling teacher Alcott to realize his dream of an adult summer school: the Concord School. Many of the people who paid to attend came from the Midwest. For four years Jones took up the cause of Plato in a debate with America's leading expert on Hegel and students were spellbound by the clash of ancient Greek and modern German philosophies.

Jones was known for five-hour lectures. Audience members would enjoy an hour, then go out and row on the slow Concord River for an hour, then return to listen to more of the lecture. Jones thought the

Concord School should be moveable and he thought it made sense to move it to the Midwest. But Alcott disagreed. Feeling rejected on behalf of the entire Midwest, Jones never lectured at Concord again, Plato's position was abandoned, and Hegel from then on dominated the suddenly dull philosophy classes of Concord. Jones rallied his friends, and together they started the American Akâdêmê on July 2, 1883. Jones thought they could get four hundred members scattered across the continent, and he believed that many American Platonists would be enough to influence American culture and improve the prospects of the republic, as he wrote to a friend.

Concord was a summer school. The American Akâdêmê was a winter school, ten meetings a year, from September to June. At first the meetings took place in Hiram's study. But as the membership grew, Hiram dedicated a large room in his house to what became known as Akâdêmê Hall. The linoleum floor and simple chairs lining the walls without symbols, paintings, or other decor provided a clean bare space for pondering abstractions. Mrs. Jones would later be fondly remembered for interrupting long-winded controversies with wry comments like, "Come, it is time for terrestrial refreshments."

By May 1884 there were 180 members of the American Akâdêmê. When the last meeting was held in 1892 the membership list was 422, but some members never attended the monthly meetings since they lived across the American continent from Maine to California, and a few members lived in Mexico, France, Australia, and other faraway places. About fifty regulars could be counted on, but that dwindled to thirty in the last few years. The membership included many physicians, college professors, ministers, and an equal number of women.

Akâdêmê members wrestled with the problem of fitting evolution into Plato's vision of the creation and function of the world. They strove to prove the superiority of Plato to Hegel. The speakers never lost sight of the practical advice for living well they had found in Platonism.

As founder of the Jacksonville Microscopic Society, Hiram Jones brought the latest microscopes from Europe, demonstrated them at the college, and allowed other doctors to use them. He became a charter member of the town's Literary Society. He was professor of philosophy at Illinois College from 1886 to 1900. He was president of the Illinois College Board of Trustees for a decade. At the business college he sometimes lectured on anatomy and physiology. He helped maintain a deer park near town and recorded the location of every artesian well in the area, as a public service. But then in 1891 Mrs. Jones died. Hiram never recovered. He was not in the best health himself and already had too many responsibilities as a practicing physician and a professor at Illinois College.

The Akadêmê limped on another year with a watered-down program including classes on Homer and ancient Greek drama. Within two years the Plato Clubs, the American Akadêmê, the *Bibliotheca Platonica* journal, the *Journal of Speculative Philosophy,* and the *Journal of the American Akadêmê* disappeared. Pragmatism and materialism, new American philosophies driven by industrial capitalism and the achievements of science, became the professional standard.

Hiram showed his devotion to Illinois College in his last years by giving generous gifts. In 1895 for a new library and chapel he gave $20,000. The money he was owed for his loan, an annuity, he waived. The building was named Jones Memorial Hall in memory of his wife. He gave another $10,000 in 1902, the year before he died, and in his will bequeathed the college almost forty thousand more, and his library.

Despite reports of his ever-stained vest and his obstinate opposition to the theory of infection by germs, Hiram was remembered as an exemplary physician. According to his obituary in the 1903 *Illinois Medical Journal:* "This Society will cherish the memory of Hiram K. Jones because of his clean, devoted, scholarly, manly and blameless record as a physician. It would urge upon all physicians to follow his example and make intrinsic worth of character with painstaking adherence to the professional ideals, as the true foundation, for success in the practice of medicine" (Pitner et al.). In 1907 Alexander Wilder wrote in a letter to Thomas Johnson that he knew about a scandal that ruined the reputation of Jones at the end of his life. Jones had become engaged to a woman who became involved in a murder. In 1908, the last year of his life, Wilder wrote: "How curious: Jones passing away, the Plato Club is not merely broken, but nonexistent. But so things go" (Wilder 2018).

ALEXANDER WILDER

As a journalist Alexander Wilder supported the abolition of slavery. As an elected official he helped end Boss Tweed's corrupt reign over New York. As a physician Wilder pioneered what would later become known as holistic medicine. As a social activist he was an early feminist, publishing *Plea for the Liberal Education of Women* in 1884. As a book editor he helped Madame Blavatsky complete *Isis Unveiled,* and he left us an explanation for its enigmatic title.

As a young man Wilder was a member of the notorious Oneida cult. Later in life he lectured at the Concord School. The author of a nine-hundred-page history of medicine, and of books on alchemy and theurgy, he somehow found the time to write, edit, and translate articles for dozens of publications, over almost sixty years, on a diverse range of subjects including Platonism, Hermetic studies, and the dynasties of ancient Egypt.

During the Dark Ages, and for some time after, apart from the writing of St. Augustine and the thirteenth-century Franciscan St. Bonaventure, Plato and Platonism all but disappeared. When the leading Platonist of Florence, Italy, Marsilio Ficino, reintroduced Platonism to the West at the beginning of the Renaissance he brought to it the mystical perspective of an Orphic. In fact, he performed the *Orphic Hymns* with appropriate incenses, accoutrements, and astrological timing, playing a lute while singing the words.

At the turn of the nineteenth century, Thomas Taylor (and Floyer Sydenham) sparked a Platonic revival that had Shelley translating Plato's *Banquet* in England and Emerson praising Proclus in America, where Plato became a popular pastime, as we have seen, especially among cultured women in the Old West. Ficino through Taylor cast a long shadow, deeply influencing famous American writers like Thoreau and Edgar Allan Poe. The mystical Plato reigned until the time of Alexander Wilder. As we shall see, Wilder's compatriot Thomas Johnson suffered an early skirmish as a twentieth-century view of Plato formed that would reduce the previously revered Neoplatonists to banishment from the halls of academia. Taylor had thought them the only path to a true understanding of Plato, and the soul. In the twentieth century, with its fetish for the empirical and rational exceeding even that of the eighteenth-century Enlightenment, the Neoplatonists received respect in the work of mystics like Blavatsky and Manly Hall, gathering for the most part only disparaging attention from the arbiters of relevance.

Wilder and Johnson were an unlikely pair of Platonic scholars. Wilder was twenty-eight years older, a New Yorker with political experience. Johnson was a Westerner who never had enough money to keep his beloved journal the *Platonist* going, until he inherited his father's estate, but then he didn't have the time. An attorney, Johnson was never able to make a living as a writer or editor. Wilder was not only an important writer of his time but also an eminent editor. Johnson lived happily in the bosom of his family while Wilder never had children. And yet because of their love of Plato and the Platonic tradition they enjoyed a productive friendship. Together they would face the sudden sunset of a brief but bright Platonic renaissance.

The *Journal of the American Akadêmê,* under the guidance of its editor Alexander Wilder, endeavored to change with the times. The centerpiece of each issue was a print version of the lecture delivered at the most recent gathering. Comments by a selection of members in attendance followed an unwavering pattern. Several experts would carp about details of interpretation or reasoning. Even Wilder himself was not exempt. A certain Dr. Prince in the April 1885 issue grouses that Wilder in his lecture "Life Eternal" "assumes his premises without sufficient inductive reasoning." Inevitably Hiram Jones, referred to as "the President," would step in to deliver in larger paragraphs corrections and diplomacy.

Perhaps in reaction to Theosophy, Buddhism and Brahmanism became important topics but were soon superseded by lectures on Christianity. Among the anachronisms enshrined in the journal are a confident refutation of the scientific idea that the sun and stars are gaseous bodies, and a lament that in America, where liberty is so celebrated, everyone accepts their own opinions instead of first learning how to think by reading Locke, Hegel, and Kant. Perhaps most poignant of all, the president earnestly proclaimed that a golden age of philosophy in the Platonic tradition would soon dawn.

Born in New England in 1823 to a family that left Lancaster, England, in 1638 to settle in Massachusetts Bay Colony, Alexander Wilder grew up on a farm. "I often thought that my father had a dislike for the professions," he wrote,

> He used often to decry professional men as lazy, indisposed to work, etc., and seemed to be determined to make his sons all farmers. Yet my second brother had been disabled while an infant by a young girl lifting him by the arm, and so dislocating his shoulder. There were few surgeons in those days, and though physicians boasted loudly of being a learned body, and invoked special legislation to protect them from competitors, few of them were very expert, and the result was that my brother's dislocation was never reduced. Later, in boyhood, he fell from a ladder and broke his ankles. The family doctor was called but never discovered the trouble, or was able to deal with it, and the result was an additional infirmity. He must therefore be something else than a farmer. A neighbor advised that he study law; but this was contrary to family prejudice, and he became a teacher. (Gunn 1908)

Fifteen-year-old Alexander soon followed his brother and also became a teacher in the one-room schoolhouse where he had been a student. "It was found that several of my brothers could teach in the district schools; so four of us and one sister became teachers, as did also others of our schoolmates. For myself, this was not a very successful employment. The work of instruction was to my liking and I had rare success in communicating what I knew, but the governing was beyond me. Every parent passed judgment on methods, and the children behaved in school according as they were managed at home" (Gunn 1908).

Wilder's father had another plan for Alick, as he called Alexander. He wanted his son to get religion. With the support of his father's zealous friends, Wilder faced a conversion. "It took days to overcome my stubbornness," he wrote, "but the endeavor was successful. I became a Presbyterian of the New School" (Gunn 1908). But to his father's disappointment Wilder didn't want to be a preacher. He wanted to be a doctor. After seeing how doctors had failed his brother and other members of his family, he wanted to find out about medicine for himself. He would be a good doctor, if such a thing were possible.

But Wilder seems to have made a trade with his father instead. If Wilder would be allowed to give up religion, he'd become a farmer, as his father had originally intended. Wilder wrote: "When at seventeen I withdrew from religious associations, I gave up the purpose of going to college, and decided to follow farm work. I worked at home two years" (Gunn 1908). But Wilder wasn't happy farming. So he went to Vermont to learn typesetting, but his employer was a petty tyrant. "I saw the religious boss exhibited in his hatefulness," he wrote. *Slaves, baseness, treachery, unmanly servility* are the words he chose to describe his employment. He added, "My own health succumbed to it" (Gunn 1908).

Then Wilder had an inexplicable experience that set him on a search for wisdom. In Orange, Massachusetts, he got a job as a lumber-jack during timber season. His job was "to cut the dead trees into firewood. One day in April I was felling a tree some fifty or more feet high. The limbs had all decayed and fallen away." Inexperienced, Wilder cut the tree in a way that caught it in a nearby tree. So he had to cut down that tree, too. "As I was striking I felt a voice. It seemed to reach my head at the top." But it hit him right in the gut "with all the force of peremptory command: 'Step back!' I obeyed, going some eight steps. That very instant a limb, about six feet long and several inches in diameter, fell from the top of the tree. It fell along my footsteps, and with such force as to bury itself in the soft earth. If I had failed but a step it would have hit and crushed me" (Gunn 1908).

Wilder's spiritual yearnings now took over from his restless search for a career. "From 1844 to 1851 I drifted from one place and employment to another, part in Massachusetts and part at my father's in New York. My religious experiences consisted in becoming disentangled from the various beliefs and opinions, which for a few years had held me fast, and in the endeavor to learn more of the world of reality. Prompted by a lady who had been one of my teachers in boyhood, I procured and read with interest the philosophical and theological works of Emanuel Swedenborg" (Gunn 1908).

But in this biographical sketch Wilder leaves out perhaps the most disturbing community that entangled him. According to his own affidavit, in winter of 1842, eighteen-year-old Wilder joined the Calvinist Perfectionist community, where he lived in the house of John Noyes, the founder of Oneida.

John Humphrey Noyes is generally credited with being the first American to put *free* in front of love. Free love was then a scandalous but popular subject in America. By the time Wilder arrived, the original community of 87 had grown to 172 and it would nearly double again by 1878. Community members believed that the return of Jesus was not imminent because it had already happened in 70 CE. Therefore a life of perfection was possible. The world had been waiting around for almost 1,800 years for someone to notice that heaven is now.

Everyone worked according to his or her best abilities in the Oneida community. Committees and administrations decided every detail of life. Did Wilder participate in the Oneida practice of Complex Marriage? Everyone in the community was married to everyone else so no one was unavailable. In Oneida postmenopausal seniors were encouraged to teach curious teenagers everything they needed to know about sex. The idea was that the teens would face less risk of pregnancy.

The community also practiced what they called stirpiculture but we call eugenics. Committees chose breeding pairs hoping to create perfect offspring. Parents weren't allowed to bond too closely with their children. What did Wilder think of the practice they called Mutual Criticism, when a committee or the general assembly would criticize members harshly? Victims were expected to be grateful for the good advice. Oneida had branches in New York, New Jersey, Connecticut, Vermont, and Ontario, Canada. Their businesses flourished. From canned fruits and vegetables to animal traps, from silk thread to leather bags and straw hats. But their biggest success was silverware.

In 1879 Noyes was tipped off that he was about to be arrested for statutory rape. He fled Oneida in the night, headed for Ontario where a community factory was in operation. Noyes lived the rest of his life in Niagara Falls, Canada. He wrote letters back to his community suggesting they give up Complex Marriage and follow more traditional customs.

On New Year's Day in 1881 Oneida was dissolved, membership was converted to stock in the successful silverware company. As for Wilder, he didn't last long at Oneida, he also remained celibate except for a brief marriage. What did Wilder think of the founder of Oneida? In an affidavit on Noyes, Wilder testified, "I know him to be a despot—an ambitious self-seeker—and my horror of him is as intense as my horror of a venomous serpent" (Wilder 2017).

After Oneida, Wilder worked at farming and typesetting, while reading medicine with local physicians, until in 1850 Syracuse Medical College gave him a diploma. In 1853 he became an assistant editor at the *Syracuse Star*. A year later he had the same job at the *Syracuse Journal*.

In 1855 when the New York State legislature created the Department of Public Instruction he was appointed clerk in the State Department of Public Institutions at Albany. But he hadn't given up on his dream of becoming a physician. In 1855 Wilder became editor of the *New York Teacher*, the journal of the New York State Teachers Association. He soon left that job to become associate editor of the *American Journal of Education and College Review*, but he only stayed there nine months.

The year 1857 was an important one for Alexander Wilder. He prepared the charter for the teachers' college at Illinois Normal University. The American Institute of Homeopathy released a series of pamphlets written by him. And he moved to New York City to become an editor at the *Evening Post*. The latter job apparently suited him. He spent thirteen years with the *Post*. Political experience and knowledge of financial matters was a side benefit.

Among Wilder's friends was General Ethan Allen Hitchcock, the Revolutionary War hero Ethan Allen's grandson. Hitchcock made his name in 1841 when he investigated fraud complaints in the territory of the Five Civilized Tribes. He found widespread corruption as white agents and traders routinely cheated tribes. His report took five months to compile and was irrefutable, but because negotiations with the Cherokee were underway it was suppressed for over a year, then given to Congress, who ignored it, as did historians for almost a hundred years.

During the Civil War, Hitchcock served in the Department of War as a major general. Wilder met Hitchcock through a mutual friend, a bookseller who arranged the meeting for Wilder, who was a fan of Hitchcock's books, including *Swedenborg a Hermetic Philosopher* (1858), and *The Story of the Red Book of Appin* (1863), where Hitchcock shared his theories about alchemical metaphors in fairy tales. In 1857 Hitchcock had anonymously published *Remarks on Alchemy and the Alchemists*. He argued that alchemical mercury was the human conscience. Until the conscience is awakened the alembic (human being) contains only base metals (ignorance and suffering). Hitchcock wrote that fire and sulphur were alchemical symbols for conscience because conscience burns until what is left is pure. Wilder appears to have based his own 1869 work *Alchemy or the Hermetic Philosophy* on Hitchcock's book. At the beginning of the Civil War, Hitchcock sold his library, to the great regret of Wilder who hated to see such a comprehensive collection scattered.

Around 1864 ex-Mayor Havemeyer, Horace Greeley, and other powerful notables decided New York City needed an Eclectic Medical College. They turned to Wilder to prepare the charter. Just after the Civil War ended in 1865, Wilder pushed the charter through the legislature despite the opposition of traditional doctors. Wilder was the right man in the right place at the right time. A friend of the governor, he knew every member of the legislature personally. They all knew him to be an honest, intelligent scholar, a true man of integrity.

Wilder had a logical answer to every protest the old-school doctors could summon. Besides, after five years of Civil War the United States needed as many doctors as it could get. The college was established. Eclectic medicine was botanically based. Today we'd call it herbal medicine. As for the competition: "Medical Colleges were rare," Wilder wrote, "except those of the dominant school, and these would graduate nobody except with the assurance that he would adhere to the approved practice. Physicians at this time were often illiterate; physiology was almost an unknown science; *materia medica* limited to brief dimensions; and practice consisted of bleeding, the administration of calomel, antimony, and little else" (Wilder 2017b).

Perhaps Wilder's own writing about healing explains eclectic medicine best. "When we are cheerful we are safe from disease; when we are depressed and downhearted we are in danger. An even temperature or well-kept apartment and cleanliness of person are blessings to be prized. When they exist many of the external causes of disease are absent. Our cities are breeding places of disease, because the sunshine is excluded from the houses and the ventilation is defective. Then, too, the poor, who make up the great majority of the population, and, therefore, should be cared for the most, are pressed into dens that a dog or a pig would shudder at, and there live under conditions that make them easily assailable by infection, after which they prove their common human nature by communicating it to those better circumstanced" (Wilder 1891).

Wilder described an experience in his youth that influenced his ideas about medicine. "Being constantly found fault with whether I was right or wrong and overborne by the cruel despotic will of another had depressed me, till the digestive and nervous functions were impaired" (Wilder 1908b). Or as he put it elsewhere, "hopelessness kills" (1905). He turned to Plato's belief that music could cure illness to support his point of view that a life lived in harmony is a healthy life.

Wilder was a keen observer of human behavior. "Individuals parting with cherished possessions," he wrote, "or removed from their home and from habitual scenes of life, or deprived of employment which had engaged attention till it became a habit, are liable to become mentally enfeebled, or to succumb to bodily debility" (1905).

Wilder added, "When a person, one who is more or less dependent, is held back from a cherished purpose because of some abnormal apprehension on the part of others; and so is held back when he may properly do something or pursue some object that he wishes, . . . then such morbid carefulness directly impairs vital energy. All conflict of mind wears and exhausts the powers of the body" (1905).

"There is a killing with kindness as well as with malice," Wilder wrote. "In daily life there are so many injured and even driven to actual death by overmuch anxiety and carefulness, that there is much need also to acquire what we may call the knack of wholesome neglect. Take away from individuals the consciousness of being constantly watched for slips of misconduct or bodily infirmity" (1923). Wilder put it succinctly elsewhere, "There are both an Athens of unblemished fame and an enfeebled, demoralized Atlantis in every human being" (2017b).

However, from 1860 to 1878 Wilder fought against mandatory vaccinations. He insisted that better methods could be achieved to inoculate the masses than what he dismissed as "animal poisons."

Even though Wilder refused to campaign for the office in 1871 he was elected New York City Councilman in a landslide on a ticket promising to end the corruption of the notorious Boss Tweed. Wilder took office on January 1, 1872, but soon learned the new boss was just as tyrannical as the old. So he never held office again. In 1872 Wilder became an editor at *Harper's Weekly*.

Despite refusing the position repeatedly, in 1873 he became professor of physiology and psychology at the Eclectic Medical College of New York. He was also made coeditor of their journal the *Medical Eclectic*. In the biographical note in his monograph *Brethren of the Rosy Cross* (1880), Wilder added that he was "Honorary Member of the Eclectic Medical Societies of Illinois, Michigan, Connecticut and Pennsylvania, Honorary Fellow of the Anthropological Society of Liverpool, Eng."

In the *Transactions of the Eclectic Medical Society of the State of New York,* amid the exchange of cures and medical tips, could be found Wilder's writing about Plotinus and alchemy, illustrating how his esoteric interests could be considered scholarly, and how expert he was at framing respectable contexts and legitimizing them with historical precedents.

Enter Helena Blavatsky, book first. "On a pleasant afternoon, in early autumn," Wilder writes, "I was alone in the house. The bell was rung, and I answered at the door. Colonel Henry S. Olcott was there with an errand to myself. I did not recognize him, as I had never had any occasion to make his acquaintance, but he having had some governmental business with one of my employers several years before, had known me ever since. He had never suspected, however, that I took any interest whatever in unusual subjects; so completely successful had I been in keeping myself unknown even to those who from daily association imagined that they knew me very thoroughly. A long service in journalism, familiar relations with public men, and active participation in political matters, seemed to have shut out from notice an ardent passion for mystic speculation, and the transcendental philosophy" (1908a).

Why had Olcott rung the bell? "He had been referred to me by

Mr. Bouton." Wilder worked for J. W. Bouton as an editor, proofreader (for English and Hebrew), and expert on esoteric subjects. Bouton bought the copyright for Blavatsky's *Isis Unveiled* and refused to return it to the author. Blavatsky wanted to give her book the title *A Skeleton Key to Mysterious Gates*. The mystery of why a book that has so little to do with Egypt should be called *Isis Unveiled* is solved by Wilder: "Mr. Bouton is entitled to that distinction. He was a skillful caterer in the bookselling world to which he belonged, but he had business ability rather than a sense of fitness. He once published the treatise of R. Payne Knight on Ancient Art and added pictures relating solely to Hindu mythology, entirely foreign to the subject. This work of Madam Blavatsky is largely based upon the hypothesis of a prehistoric period of the Aryan people in India, and in such a period the veil or the unveiling of Isis can hardly be said to constitute any part. On the contrary, it is a dramatic representation peculiar to the religion and wisdom of Egypt. Certainly the problems of Egyptian lore are to be considered with other pens than those with which 'Isis Unveiled' was written" (Wilder 1908a).

In 1878 Bouton had committed another publishing gaffe. He released only volume 1 of the two-volume obscurity *Anacalypsis: An Attempt to Draw Aside the Veil of the Saitic Isis, or an Inquiry into the Origin of Languages, Nations and Religions* by Godfrey Higgins, among the books that inspired Borges to write "Tlön, Uqbar, Orbis Tertius." Perhaps Bouton never published the second volume because readers didn't appreciate the way he shrank the size of such a word-stuffed tome, leaving them squinting at tiny print. With both *veil* and *Isis* in its title, *Anacalypsis* seems to have been a possible inspiration for Bouton's christening of Blavatsky's book as *Isis Unveiled*. Also it gave him a chance to adorn the spines of the two volumes with a sexy illustration of Isis nude.

Bouton had started out as a dealer of new and used books. He published more than occult works. His other titles included a handsome quarto reprint of eighteenth-century Anglo-Irish novelist Laurence Sterne's *A Sentimental Journey through France and Italy* (1884) and Thomas Taylor's classic *The Eleusinian and Bacchic Mysteries* (1891) with "Introduction, Notes, Emendations and Glossary by Alexander Wilder M.D." That most treasured remark about Taylor, quoted by Blavatsky, actually came from Wilder: "Tom Taylor may have known far less Greek than his critics; but he knew Plato far better than any of them does."

What was Wilder's first reaction to *Isis Unveiled*? "It was truly a ponderous document." But digging into it Wilder was impressed. He surprised Bouton. "In my report to him, I stated that the manuscript was the product of great research, and that so far as related to current thinking, there was a revolution in it, but I added that I deemed it too long for remunerative publishing." Bouton told Wilder to cut away as much as he could. Wilder wasn't entirely comfortable with his role. "This was a discretionary power that was far from agreeable. It can hardly be fair that a person acting solely in behalf of the publisher should have such authority over the work of an author. Nevertheless, I undertook the task. While abridging the work, I endeavored in every instance to preserve the thought of the author in plain language, removing only such terms and matter as might be regarded as superfluous, and not necessary to the main purpose" (Wilder 1908a).

The results pleased Blavatsky. "At my first visit, her reception was courteous and even friendly. We seemed to become acquainted at once. She spoke of the abridgments, which I had made of her manuscript, extolling what I had done far beyond what it deserved. What had been taken out was 'flapdoodle'" (Wilder 1908a). Blavatsky wrote about *Isis Unveiled*: "Next to Colonel Olcott, it is Professor Wilder who did the most for me. It is he who made the excellent Index, who corrected the Greek, Latin, and Hebrew words, suggested quotations and wrote the greater part of the Introduction 'Before the Veil.' If this was not acknowledged in the work, the fault is not mine, but because it was Dr. Wilder's express wish that his name should not appear except in footnotes. I have never made a secret of it, and every one of my numerous acquaintances in New York knew it." The Neoplatonic paragraphs were his as well. She quoted liberally from his *New Platonism and Alchemy* pamphlet (Blavatsky 1922).

Their first visit had taken some time for Olcott to arrange. "Colonel Olcott was very desirous that I should become acquainted with Madam Blavatsky. He appeared to hold her in high regard closely approaching to veneration, and to consider the opportunity to know her a rare favor for any one. I was hardly able to share his enthusiasm. Having a natural diffidence about making new acquaintances, and acting as a critic upon her manuscript, I hesitated for a long time. Finally, however, these considerations were passed over and I accompanied him to their establishment in Forty-Seventh Street. It was a 'flat,' that un-homelike fashion of abode that now extends over populous cities, superseding the household and family relationship wherever it prevails" (Wilder 1908a).

Wilder was almost sixty years old and not inclined to be impressed by purveyors of exotica. "The dining room," he continues, "was furnished in simple style with no affectation of anything unusual or extraordinary. Perhaps, I ought to add that later in the years following, this condition was quite considerably modified," he quips, referring to the stuffed baboons and oriental furniture and decor that inspired the *New York World* (before it became famous for yellow journalism) to nickname Blavatsky's home the Lamasery.

Wilder describes her workspace: "The study in which Madam Blavatsky lived and worked was arranged after a quaint and very primitive manner. It was a large front room, and being on the side next the street, was well lighted. In the midst of this was her 'den,' a spot fenced off on three sides by temporary partitions, writing desk and shelves for books. She had it as convenient as it was unique. She had but to reach out an arm to get a book, paper or other article that she might desire, that was within the enclosure" (Wilder 1908a).

Wilder lists only a few, among them "Jacolliot's work on India, Bunsen's *Egypt,* Ennemoser's *History of Magic.* The place could not accord with a vivid sense of beauty, except after the ancient Greek conception that beauty is fitness for its purpose, everything certainly being convenient and handy. In this place Madam Blavatsky reigned supreme, gave her orders, issued her judgments, conducted her correspondence, received her visitors and produced the manuscript of her book" (1908a).

And what did Wilder think of Blavatsky herself? "She did not resemble in manner or figure what I had been led to expect. She was tall, but not strapping; her countenance bore the marks and exhibited the characteristics of one who had seen much, thought much, traveled much, and experienced much. Her appearance was certainly impressive, but in no respect was she coarse, awkward, or ill bred. On the other hand she exhibited culture, familiarity with the manners of the most courtly society and genuine courtesy itself. She expressed her opinions with boldness and decision, but not obtrusively. It was easy to perceive that she had not been kept within the circumscribed limitations of a common female education; she knew a vast variety of topics and could discourse freely upon them" (Wilder 1908a).

Blavatsky made Wilder a vice president of the Theosophical Society, but the title was more honorary than active. In a letter from 1877 Wilder wrote that "Blavatsky professes to be a Platonist, & assures me that I am one." The recipient of Wilder's letter, Thomas Moore Johnson, would publish the *Platonist* four years later in collaboration with Wilder.

Wilder gives us a glimpse of Blavatsky's relationship with the perhaps overawed Olcott: "He not unfrequently came under her scorching criticism. He writhed under it, but, except for making some brief expression at the time, he did not appear to cherish resentment" (1908a). Henry Steel Olcott fought for the Union during the Civil War, then rose to the position of special commissioner of the War Department in New York. Next, given the rank of colonel, he was put to work at the Department of the Navy in Washington, D.C. When Lincoln was assassinated Olcott was part of the investigation team. In 1868 he began a law practice. By 1874 he was exploring the séances that were popping up everywhere. He had been horrified by what he had seen on the battlefield during the Civil War. Searching for truth about the meaning of life, he was attracted to these alleged spirit communications. His article about the séances at Eddy Farms was published by the *New York Sun* and then other newspapers. He met Blavatsky the same year. *Isis Unveiled* was published not long after, Blavatsky and Olcott left America for India. Olcott eventually converted to Buddhism and became influential enough to help rekindle interest in Buddhist studies in Sri Lanka, which had been denied its culture during the English occupation. He is still honored as a hero of Sri Lankan cultural revival, with street and place names, and a statue of him that stands at the main rail station in the capital city.

What did Olcott think of Wilder?

Prof. Alexander Wilder, a quaint personality, the type of the very large class of self-educated American yeomanry; men of the forceful quality of the Puritan Fathers; men of brain and thought, intensely independent, very versatile, very honest, very plucky and patriotic. He is not a college bred or city bred man, I fancy, but if one wants sound ideas upon the migration of races and symbols, the esoteric meaning of Greek philosophy, the value of Hebrew or Greek texts, or the merits and demerits of various schools of medicine, he can give them as well as the most finished graduate. A tall, lank man of the Lincoln type, with a noble, dome like head, thin jaws, grey hair, and language filled with quaint Saxon Americanisms. He used to come and talk by the hour with H. P. B., often lying recumbent on the sofa, with—as she used to say—one long leg resting on the chandelier, the other on the mantel piece.—And she, as stout as he was thin, as voluble as he was sententious and epigrammatic, smoking innumerable cigarettes and brilliantly sustaining her share of the conversation.

Olcott continued:

She got him to write out many of his ideas to use in *Isis,* and they will be found there quoted. The hours would slip by without notice until he sometimes found himself too late for the last train to Newark, and would have to stop in town all night. I think that, of all our visitors, he cared about the least of all for H. P. B.'s psychical phenomena: he believed in their scientific possibility and did not doubt her possession of them, but philosophy was his idol, and the wonders of mediumship and adeptship interested him only in the abstract. [HPB's] salon was never dull save, of course, to those who had no knowledge of Eastern literature and understood nothing of Eastern philosophy, and to them time might have dragged heavily when H. P. B. and Wilder were discussing these deeper depths and loftier heights of thought by hours together. (Olcott 1974)

Perhaps Wilder provides a measure of Blavatsky's importance as a feminist when he writes about *Isis Unveiled:* "After the work had been printed and placed on sale, there was discussion in regard to the actual authorship. Many were unwilling to acknowledge that Madam Blavatsky could be sufficiently well-informed or intellectually capable of such a production. True that women like Frances Burney had composed romances of high merit. Miss Farley had conducted successfully the "Lowell Offering." Mary Somerville had written on Physical Science, and Harriet Martineau on Political Economy. The manuscript which I handled I am very sure was in the handwriting of Madam Blavatsky herself. Anybody who was familiar with her, would, upon reading the first volume of *Isis Unveiled,* not have any difficulty in recognizing her as the author" (1908a).

Both Blavatsky and Wilder wrote in run-on sentences that often included long quotes from obscure sources gathered from every corner of the world. Wilder's book *New Platonism and Alchemy* spans centuries, finding common philosophical ground in the works of Pythagoras, Hermes Trismegistus, and Eiranaeus Philalethes. He quotes Aristotle, Plutarch, Iamblichus, Proclus, Apollonius of Tyana, Geber the Arabian, Agrippa, George Ripley, Roger Bacon, Bulwer-Lytton, Goethe, and Hindu stories about Krishna, a Who's Who of Platonically and alchemically inclined intelligentsia, more than enough strange names and long sentences thorny with ancient Greek letters to put off most readers.

While Wilder had no doubt that Blavatsky had authored *Isis Unveiled,* he did have doubts about her. In a letter to Johnson written in 1877, Wilder wrote about Blavatsky and her cohort: "They flattered me very much—almost grossly, & initiated me into their Theosophic Society. I learned no secret, no occult truth, nor any thing which I cared to know; & declined absolutely all public identification with them" (Wilder 2018). He became more suspicious and critical of her as he followed her triumphs and debacles from a distance.

Another doubter of Madame Blavatsky was a rich widow named Elizabeth Thompson. She told Wilder a story about a brazen act of plagiarism by Blavatsky. Wilder doubted her sincerity, and he didn't find her story logical. To Wilder *Isis Unveiled* came from the same stream of consciousness he encountered in his conversations with Blavatsky. But in telling the story Wilder gives us a rare glimpse of the lives of patrons who decided the fates of artists, Spiritualists, and philosophers:

My informant was the late Mrs. Elizabeth Thompson of Boston. Mrs. Thompson was a woman of wealth, abounding with benevolent purposes, but eager for novelties that were more or less visionary, shifting from one pursuit to another, influenced by flattery. For example, she gave the money which enabled a medical college to hold several lecture terms, and then let the enterprise die out. She paid to build a chapel for the sessions of the Summer School of Philosophy at Concord, and then tired of the enterprise. She aided Dr. Newbrough with money to print his new bible *Oahspe,* and employed the artist, Mr. Frank Carpenter, to paint the picture of President Lincoln and his cabinet, which she presented to Congress. The wealth which her husband had bequeathed to her became a bait for all manner of parasites to seek her, and flattery artfully bestowed was often like the magical words: 'Open, sesame,' sure to find the way to her purse. But she quickly dropped one for another.

"For a little time," Wilder continues, "she was attracted to Madam Blavatsky. This was somewhat to be wondered at, for it is hard to conceive that Madam Blavatsky flattered anybody. It might be questioned whether Mrs. Thompson herself was quite sincere. I saw Mrs. Thompson at her own premises, and she asked me my opinion in a manner that impressed me that she was hardly straightforward in her relations with the Theosophical household" (Wilder 1908a). In 1879 after Blavatsky had left New York for India,

Mrs. Thompson had become an inmate of the family of Dr. Newbrough on West 34th Street. He was endeavoring to push the "new Bible" into circulation. I called there one day by invitation, and learning that she had rooms in the house, paid her my respects. In our conversation, Madam Blavatsky was mentioned, and Mrs. Thompson spoke of her in these terms: "If Madam Blavatsky should come in at that door I should kiss her affectionately. At the same time I believe her to be a perfect humbug." She then related the following story: Baron de Palm, a German gentleman, who spent some time in this country, had died in Roosevelt Hospital. He had devoted much attention to arcane subjects, and had written upon them. He was intimate with the party on 47th Street, and made them recipients of his property, but with the assurance that his body should be cremated. There was a woman in the household who seems to have become unfriendly and ready to talk at random. She told Mrs. Thompson that after the death of the Baron she was with Madam Blavatsky while examining the contents of his trunks. One of these, the woman said, was full of manuscripts. Madam Blavatsky looked at a few of the pages, and then hastily closed the trunk, making an effort to divert attention in another direction. Mrs. Thompson apparently believed that this manuscript was the material of the work *Isis Unveiled*. Certainly she endeavored to give me that impression. (Wilder 1908a)

The Oahspe Publishing Association in 1882 published Elizabeth Thompson's *The Figures of Hell; or, the Temple of Bacchus Dedicated to the Licensers and Manufactures of Beer and Whiskey,* an enthusiastic attack on alcohol in which she wrote: "Many who recognize the liquor traffic as a great wrong, defend a license system on the ground that it brings a revenue to the State. This motive greatly enhances the shame and disgrace. A revenue derived from widow's tears and orphan's groans, and drunkard's blood! Is it the business of the State to build poorhouses, lunatic asylums, and prisons, and then authorize a select few to have the exclusive privilege of filling them if they will pay a stipulated sum? Whiskey is one of Satan's whips; beer is his kennel and wine his bait!"

The year 1882 also saw the publication of *Oahspe: A New Bible in the Words of Jehovih and His Angel Ambassadors. A Sacred History of the Dominions of the Higher and Lower Heavens on the Earth for the Past Twenty-Four Thousand Years together with a Synopsis of the Cosmogony of the Universe; the Creation of Planets; the Creation of Man; the Unseen Worlds; the Labor and Glory of Gods and Goddesses in the Etherean Heavens; with the New Commandments of Jehovih to Man of the Present Day.* The dentist Newbrough may have channeled it via automatic writing, but deity and the highest angels were claimed as the actual authors.

Channeled over fifty weeks "every morning half an hour or so before sunrise," as Newbrough wrote, the nine-hundred-page tome preaches service to others as the most important measure of any soul. Angels are no more or less than disembodied human souls after death. Whatever our beliefs, or whether we believe in life after death at all, we will live on. Low angels who indulged their passions, including food derived from animals, enter disorganized lower heavens in the afterlife. Evil angels find their heavens to be hells. But souls who achieve a high degree while embodied rise to the most organized and delightful heavens after death. If this sounds like Spiritualism, it is. In a letter to the editor of the *Banner of Light,* written January 23, 1893, Newbrough wrote, "I discovered, many years ago, in sitting in circles to obtain spiritual manifestations, that my hands could not lie on the table without flying off into these 'tantrums.' Often they would write messages, left or right, backward or forward, nor could I control them in any other way than by withdrawing from the table. Then I went to work in earnest to investigate spiritualism, and I investigated over two hundred mediums, traveling hundreds and hundreds of miles for this purpose. Often I took them to my own house and experimented with them to my heart's content. I found that nearly all of them were subject to this involuntary movement of the hands, or to entrancement. They told me it was angels controlling them."

Newbrough was not only a Spiritualist visionary, he was an inventive dentist. Setting teeth in dental plates was expensive then, but he figured out a much cheaper way to do it. Goodyear Rubber Company owned that market, so they sued him for patent infringement. At dawn on the day of the verdict, the spirits visited Newbrough and told him he would win the case. When he did, he took it as confirmation of his spiritual mission, instead of launching a dental compound company and making a fortune.

Godfrey Higgins, author of *Anacalypsis,* coined the term *Pandeism* to describe a culture, religion, and language he thought had once united the world. Pandeism was neither deism, nor pantheism, rather a way of looking at collections of related gods and heroes, from Pan of Greece to the Pandavas of India, that Higgins argued were the last remains of a collapsed empire. Many of the ideas in *Anacalypsis* reappeared in *Oahspe: A New Bible,* including the word *Pandeism.* The eight-hundred-page Andrew Jackson Davis tome *The Principles of Nature, Her Divine Revelations and a Voice to Mankind* (1847) appears to have provided much of the rest of the content. Davis, a friend of Wilder's, was perhaps the only Spiritualist Wilder wrote about respectfully. Wilder was a friend of Mrs. Davis, and her nephew was the printer Wilder recommended to Johnson for the *Platonist.*

It must have been ironic indeed for Wilder to listen to Eliza's accusation about Madame Blavatsky since he most likely knew that Newbrough had plagiarized Higgins and Davis. It was also in 1879 that Wilder met General Abner Doubleday, as we have seen, a prominent member of Blavatsky's New York circle.

In 1882 Wilder wrote to Johnson about the Theosophists: "They profess to work thaumaturgic wonders; to have the power of prolonging physical life; to become apparent as a wraith or dropped in one place while the unsouled body is asleep in another (Judge professes to have done this); that Mme. B. is not the so-called Russian of that name, but a mediaeval personage whose soul was seeking a new incarnation, & finding her body just unsouled in some skirmish in the Campagna in 1848, got into it, & so is the Man Woman Theosophical Marvel now at Bombay, etc. Very little of all this was ever communicated to me personally; but I get it at second hand from Gen. Doubleday & other" (2018).

In the same letter, Wilder reports that he has in hand Doubleday's translation of *Transcendental Magic* by Eliphas Levi. In a letter written on June 13, Wilder writes that the translation would be published by Bouton. But apparently those plans never came to fruition. When Doubleday died in 1893, Wilder, seventy years old, took on the task of writing an introduction and annotations for the translation. Six years after Wilder's death, the *Word,* a popular Theosophical magazine published it serially over several years. Doubleday also translated Levi's *Fables and Symbols,* but that translation is known only in manuscript.

The New England Transcendentalists were Buddhist, Hermetic, and Christian all at once, but they were devoted Platonists. Thoreau's translation of an ancient Greek Orphic Hymn to Zeus, found among the Orphic fragments in his notebook, is a revision of Orphic verses translated by the Cambridge Platonist Cudworth, who thought Proclus had written them. Emerson wrote, "I hear . . . of the unenvying and exuberant will of the gods, the aquatic gods, the Plain of Truth, the meadow and all the rest of the Platonic rhetoric quotes as household words. . . . I think one would grow handsome who read Proclus much and well." In a lecture at the Concord School, Wilder eulogized Emerson as "This Plato of America," and commented that the difficult inspirations provided by Thomas Taylor were now made readily available in the writing of Emerson. As esoteric scholar Jay Bregman wrote in a personal correspondence of 2021, used by his permission, "Taylor's style is Proclus Englished." Proclus is known for the complexity of his beliefs and his writing, so Emerson was Taylor "Englished."

Yet Thoreau and Emerson were not as ardent Platonists as Alcott, the third of the great Transcendentalist trinity, whom Emerson credited with being able to make the vaguest Platonic concepts seem solid. In 1882 Wilder gave lectures at Alcott's Concord School of Philosophy. As the titles of just a few of Wilder's lectures there prove, he was expert on many subjects. *Functions of the Cerebellum, Relations of Food to Health, The Rosicrucian Brotherhood* (like so many key figures of American Metaphysical Religion he argued that Sir Francis Bacon was a founder of the Rosicrucian movement), *Philosophy in China, Hebrew Scriptures Interpreted Astrologically, The Enigma of Alchemy, The Ethics of the Zoroastrians, Origin of the Universe and Man, Plato on Education, Plea for the Collegiate Education of Women,* and *Should Men Cut Their Hair?* (no). But Wilder was never comfortable among the New England elite of Concord. Looking back, he wrote in a letter to Johnson dated February 24, 1894, that he had felt like a "strange cat in a stranger garret."

THE SAGE OF THE OSAGE

Of the historically notable friends of Alexander Wilder one stands out for the volume of their correspondence: Thomas Moore Johnson, four-time mayor of the small town of Osceola, near the Osage River in the Ozarks about 150 miles from Kansas City. Voters also elected Johnson county prosecutor twice, the second time twenty-four years after the first; after both terms he refused renomination. Johnson was a member of the board of education for a decade before becoming its president for twenty-five years. He was also a director of a bank. Since letters were arriving from Ralph Waldo Emerson, Johnson's transcendental interests were no secret. Eventually he became a beloved local character in the small town, the absent-minded professor.

Johnson's father was a former U.S. senator who served in the Confederate army and who had also been a Confederate senator. Johnson's son Franklin (1949) wrote, "At the outbreak of the Civil War Mrs. Johnson and the children were in Clarksburg, and they remained there through-out the conflict. The family lived in Canada for two or three years after the war, and thereafter in Sedalia, Missouri, until (probably) 1870. The family house had been burned in 1861, along with almost the whole of Osceola, by Jim Lane's raiders from Kansas; and when it seemed safe to return, Judge Johnson bought the residence of Captain Vaughn, on the bank of the Osage river. The Vaughn house had escaped the fire, and a part of it had been the first cabin built in Osceola." The Jayhawkers liberated two hundred enslaved people but executed nine citizens when they burned Johnson's hometown. The attack inspired the backstory for the film *The Outlaw Josey Wales*. Because Mrs. Johnson's papers have not yet been explored by scholars it's possible the timeline will turn out to be different, but it makes sense that a former Confederate senator might want to spend a few years in Canada.

Johnson first encountered the philosophy that would change his life in the spring of 1870 at age nineteen when, while browsing the stacks in the library of the University of Notre Dame, he found a fifty-two-year-old copy of the *Classical Journal* in which he read the "Chaldean Oracles" translated by Thomas Taylor. Works by Porphyry and Plotinus soon followed. He mined every issue of the *Classical Journal* he could find for essays and translations that introduced him to Plato by way of the Neoplatonists.

Around the same time Johnson read a vehemently hostile review of a new edition of Emerson's writing, which inspired him to read the offending essays. In Emerson's essay "Intellect," Johnson read a passage that guided his journey through the great pagan authors of antiquity. "This band of grandees, Hermes, Heraclitus, Empedocles, Plato, Plotinus, Olympiodorus, Proclus, Synesius and the rest, have somewhat so vast in their logic, so primary in their thinking, that it seems antecedent to all the ordinary distinctions of rhetoric and literature, and to be at once poetry and music and dancing and astronomy and mathematics. I am present at the sowing of the seed of the world. With a geometry of sunbeams the soul lays the foundations of nature."

Elsewhere Emerson wrote, "A reading of Iamblichus' *On the Mysteries* would bring about a revival in the Churches." He also wrote, "I read Proclus for my opium." In 1842 he wrote in his journal, "Thou shalt read Homer, Aeschylus, Sophocles, Euripides, Aristophanes, Plato, Proclus, Plotinus, Iamblichus, Porphyry, Aristotle."

Johnson, following Taylor, argued that Neoplatonism was an artificial distinction. Academics had dismissed the Neoplatonists as addled mystics and desperate plagiarists of Christianity. Iamblichus with his mysterious ritual of theurgy was considered the father of the, at best superstitious and at worst heretic, ceremonial magicians of the Middle Ages, a not unreasonable honor given his great influence on them. But as scholarship has progressed, and cultural prejudices have been recognized by academia, a different picture has emerged.

Ceremonial magic had as much to do with science as religion, as human beings attempted to understand the laws of nature and existence. Following Taylor, Johnson argued that the Neoplatonists had access to all the lost writings of Plato and Aristotle, and all the lost work of their commentators, and he pointed to their persistent claim that the most important were never made public. Johnson believed the Neoplatonists were simply Platonists. Studying Plato with their guidance, he thought, led to a much deeper understanding of Platonic philosophy and theology.

In the summer of 1874 the intrepid twenty-three-year-old Johnson, already known as the Sage of the Osage, planned to write a biography of Thomas Taylor. He had already exchanged letters with Bronson Alcott in which Johnson declared his intention to translate and otherwise promote the Neoplatonists. Alcott enthusiastically encouraged him, but Johnson never finished his Thomas Taylor biography. Instead he published much of his research in issues of the *Platonist* ten years later. Johnson became the expert consulted and recommended by American Transcendentalists and Platonists when technical questions about text or definition needed clarification. In 1875 Johnson wrote Alcott to share his plans for a book to be titled *Lives of the Platonists,* but that never came to fruition either, except to provide useful notes for articles he wrote for his periodical.

Johnson visited fellow Neoplatonic enthusiast Alexander Wilder in New Jersey in 1876, during the time Wilder was working with Madame Blavatsky on *Isis Unveiled.* Wilder became one of Johnson's steadiest supporters, his most important collaborator, and Wilder contributed many essays and two translations to the *Platonist.*

On his trip east Johnson also stopped in Concord to meet with Alcott and his daughter, Louisa, the celebrated author who had published *Little Women* seven years earlier. When Johnson finally self-published in 1880 his *Three Treatises of Plotinus,* which included writing never before translated into English, the critics panned him. A St. Louis newspaper wrote: "Doubt remains as to whether Thomas M. Johnson would not be in better business plowing corn and gathering hickory nuts than doing mystic Greek into unintelligible English." Even Wilder disliked the translation, writing to Alcott: "I do not quite like his diction. I do not like a cramped artificial style." Johnson was hurt by the criticism.

The year 1881 was an important one for Thomas Johnson. In February the first issue of the *Platonist* appeared, the same month that prohibition made Kansas a dry state. In May, Mrs. Johnson arrived in the person of his new wife Alice Barr, the daughter of a Presbyterian minister. Johnson's Platonic magazine had a very small subscription base, but it provided rare texts of profound pagan spirituality, from the middle of the Midwest.

The *Platonist*'s eclectic contents also included translations of works on the Kabbalah, tarot, and ceremonial magic by Eliphas Levi, and a translation with notes by Isaac Myer of *On Dreams* by Synesius, the student of Hypatia. In 1881 Johnson also published selections from an English translation of Ibn Tufayl's *Hayy ibn Yaqzan,* a medieval text influenced by Sufism, in which Johnson found Platonic overtones. In a later issue that year he published Alexander Wilder's excerpts from Ibn Bajja about the Islamic perspective on Neoplatonic ideas about the soul.

In 1882 Hiram K. Jones wrote Johnson to tell him he had given away six hundred copies of the first issue of the *Platonist,* but subscriptions were few and far between and scattered all over the continent and even overseas. Jones and Wilder proposed various ways to raise money to keep the *Platonist* going. Johnson proposed a higher subscription price but his friends thought that was a mistake. Since he didn't like any of their ideas, he delayed the second volume.

In 1883 when the American Akadêmê was established in Jacksonville, Hiram Jones promised Johnson fifty new subscribers. Johnson wasn't interested until Jones came up with the idea of publishing all papers by the Akadêmê in the *Platonist*. That way all the members would be likely to subscribe. Johnson received a wave of submissions but subscribers were still scarce, and soon Jones was sending Johnson more money to keep the *Platonist* going. Jones thought it should be turned over to the Akadêmê and renamed *Philosophy*. Johnson could stay on board as editor and director. Johnson refused.

Johnson was on the American Board of Control for the Theosophical Society. Among his jobs was encouraging the creation of more lodges, supervising the lodges already in existence, applying necessary corrections for lodges that may have strayed onto unsanctioned ground, and defending Theosophy from the criticism and slander it suffered from the competition and the disillusioned.

At first the leadership of the Theosophical Society, enthralled by the work of Eliphas Levi, taught practical occultism, including tarot cards. But then the leadership moved away from such controversial subjects to the exotic revelations of Eastern masters. Johnson did everything he possibly could to acquire a pack of tarot cards. He wanted to experiment with them, continuing his research and publishing his discoveries. Eventually he got a pack, what may have been one of the first complete tarot decks in America.

His interest in the tarot was undoubtedly one reason Johnson became involved with the Hermetic Brotherhood of Luxor, which taught not only tarot, but astral travel and scrying with mirrors. As the Hermetic Brotherhood of Luxor's membership swelled with disgruntled Theosophists, in fall 1885 Johnson was appointed president of the American Central Council or the Committee of Seven of the Hermetic Brotherhood of Luxor. A letter to a neophyte signed by Johnson himself provides further proof of his involvement, suggesting that Johnson was not publishing translations of Eliphas Levi in the *Platonist* merely to lure subscribers.

As we shall see in more detail in the following chapter the Hermetic Brotherhood of Luxor is a dense cluster of contradictions. In America the "brotherhood" was predominately female, one of the two main lodges was presided over by a woman, the other, in Osceola, was Thomas Johnson's responsibility. The H.B. of L. claimed to ultimately derive from the ancient Egyptian city of Luxor, yet there was hardly anything at all Egyptian about what they taught. The society admitted that the most recent incarnation of the outer order began in the 1880s, crediting that charismatic enigma Max Theon as its visible founder (the order's highest masters were not visible to the uninitiated), yet the H.B. of L. instructions reflected very little of Max Theon's cosmic philosophy.

Two fellows by the names of Davidson and Burgoyne appear to have cobbled together the order's teachings from books by Eliphas Levi, the self-proclaimed Rosicrucian and highly suspect scholar Hargrave Jennings, and *Comte de Gabalis,* the seventeenth-century "true story" of a conversation with a master who reveals the world of elementals susceptible to ritual, and the secret society of philosophers working to uplift humanity. But they appear to have depended most on the works of Paschal Beverly Randolph and of Emma Hardinge Britten, a leading light of the Spiritualist movement, and a founding member of the Theosophical Society, whom we'll be considering soon.

The author of a shelf full of books on health, sexuality, channeling, and the occult, Randolph ran his own independent publishing company. He wrote two novels, making him one of the first African American novelists published. Burgoyne and Davidson would appear to have taken most of the content of the H.B. of L. program from Randolph's works, especially the materials on sex magic, though they took pains to distance themselves from him, alleging that he had fallen into black magic by using sex magic for material ends, but that was a gross oversimplification of the very complicated life of a man who publicly and enthusiastically endorsed sex, drugs, and the occult before Aleister Crowley was born. Researchers have found Rosicrucians in the Osceola area in those days, mostly remnants and aspirants devoted to Randolph. They may have had some influence on Thomas Johnson's ideas about sex magic.

These days sex magic can be as simple as masturbation with the intention of convincing the universe to provide whatever one desires, perhaps a new car or a better job. Ceremonial sexuality as a form of initiation takes sexual experimentation to another level. But that's not what sex magic meant to the Hermetic Brotherhood of Luxor. Their sex magic was conservative enough to appeal to a devoted Platonist like Thomas Johnson. Sex magic as eugenics claimed to improve the human race. Married couples only need apply. Bachelors were left with their magic mirrors. According to the H.B. of L., children conceived by sex magic would be a step up the spiral of human evolution.

Was Thomas Johnson practicing sex magic? Wilder wrote introductions for *Serpent and Siva Worship* and the notorious *Ancient Art and Mythology,* two books examining the sexual symbolism of world religions. As John Patrick Deveney (1997) wrote, "Wilder was thoroughly convinced of the central role of phallicism in mythology and of the importance of sex in occultism in general." But Wilder favored celibacy over sexual experimentation. The more important H.B. of L. became to Johnson, the less contact he had with Wilder. Johnson's interest in sex magic may have been theoretical rather than practical, but we assume only Mrs. Johnson knows for sure.

It's hard to imagine the four-time mayor and Platonic scholar Johnson, living in his stately home on the Lake of the Ozarks, leading a ceremonial magic lodge, dispensing hashish pills, and teaching tantric sexuality in the tradition of Paschal Beverly Randolph. More likely what Johnson was after was theurgy, the art of self-purification, the epiphany of remembering, the cultivation of cosmic consciousness, or the union with deity, as Iamblichus called it. Theurgy was the way to earn the gift of light, and every member of the Hermetic Brotherhood of Luxor understood that *Lux* was Latin for light.

Johnson promoted Davidson and Burgoyne's periodical the *Occult Magazine,* as well as printing articles by Burgoyne on the Kabbalah and tarot, though Johnson must have known they were mostly rehashed writing by Levi and his student the famous astrologer Paul Christian.

Burgoyne blamed both followers and researchers for making Kabbalah incomprehensible, and thus inaccessible to the average person: "The neglect and disrespect which the Glorious Philosophy of the Kabbalah has suffered, is largely due to the oily vacuity of terms used, and the painfully erudite scholarship, displayed in its exposition. Verily it has been a priest-ridden and scholar-bound system, whose day of deliverance it is hoped is not far from distant" (Putzu 2020).

The HBL mail-order course was accompanied by astral studies with an assigned teacher, letter writing was allowed, too, but the incarnate teacher was only a helper. True initiation would come from the inner dimension where the real masters of the order resided. These practices do not seem so exotic when placed in context. Mediums had popularized the idea of communication with the departed. Many books written by alleged discarnate spirits were published in America. The idea that a magic mirror could be used to scry for information, or that a couple working together could develop extraordinary faculties of sensitivity and magnetism were themes well within the context of widespread American preoccupation with the supernatural, or what promoters preferred to define as a deeper level of the natural, insisting that what they were practicing was a new science. Sex magic and magic mirrors had been ceremonial preoccupations since the days of John Dee and Edward Kelly's Aztec obsidian mirror and angel-appointed wife swap.

But the HBL discouraged interest in Eastern wisdom, which they believed was contaminating and even threatening the survival of Western spirituality. Johnson studied and practiced yoga. He also became one of the first to introduce Sufi ideas to America. Among those whose acquaintance he made by way of the HBL was the scholar and author Carl Henrik Andreas Bjerregaard who had helped bring Inayat Khan to America. Johnson published some of Bjerregaard's work on Sufism in the *Platonist*.

In early 1887 Johnson helped form a probably short-lived Sufi chapter within the Hermetic Brotherhood of Luxor. That year the Theosophical lodge in St. Louis, which had dwindled to a handful of diehards, incubated a shocking event. That lodge had been especially influenced by Johnson and the *Platonist*. One of the diehards became the first famous American convert to Islam, Alexander Russell Webb.

Seven years later Webb lectured for the Theosophical Society in New York on the subject of "Esoteric Islam."

In 1888 one of the Fox sisters, who had sparked the worldwide craze for mediums, confessed to fraud. She recanted a year later, claiming that she had been under pressure from the Christians who had rescued her from poverty and alcoholism, but the reputations of the Fox sisters and of Spiritualism were ruined.

In Philadelphia in that same year Isaac Myer published *Qabbalah: The Philosophical Writings of Solomon Ben Yehuda Ibn Gabirol*. The best book on the subject for many years, Myer's work represented the latest scholarship. He corresponded with rabbis and occultists around the world and translated rare manuscripts. Rumors persist that the book contains several mistakes, such as transposed Sephiroth. Was Myer confused, or did he wish to protect the doctrine from the profane? Myer also wrote books on *Presidential Power over Personal Liberty* (1862), *Scarabs* (1894), and his final book *The Oldest Books in the World* (1900).

Myer had the wealth to publish his own books. The first American edition of *Qabbalah* was an oversized tome, limited to 150 copies, signed by Myer, with fifty engravings of not only Kabbalist diagrams but also of Buddha and of deities of ancient Egypt, Mexico, and India. In this book Myer explored the ways that the Kabbalah agrees with Buddhism, Neoplatonism, Pythagorean astronomy, and the ancient spiritual teachings of Egypt, India, China, and Mexico. For Myer both Neoplatonism and the Kabbalah originated from the ancient universal wisdom of Asia.

Eleven boxes full of papers and manuscripts in the New York Public Library bear witness to Myer's eclectic interests. He writes about the ancient Chinese oracle the I Ching (Yi Jing), "Psychology of Ancient Egypt," "Tibetan Mysticism," "Wonders of Glass Making in All Ages," "Assyrian Musical Instruments," and the rather incongruous "Prostitution."

Thomas Johnson and Myer corresponded. He helped Johnson with his Kabbalah studies. In turn, Johnson could answer any questions Myer might have had about Platonism and the Hermetic writings. They had a lot in common. Not only did they both enjoy esoteric studies, they were both well-respected attorneys. Myer was deeply devoted to the idea of a universal religion, not the secret doctrine within the old traditions, which he also believed in, but a new revelation based on the ancient. Perhaps he inspired Johnson's dream of a cosmic religion to unite America.

Alexander Wilder was Johnson's most important partner in the *Platonist*. Wilder suggested subscribers, provided content, introduced Johnson to a reputable printer, and provided important editorial criticism, for example: "There is one bad feature to those articles. Most of them are 'To be Continued.' I never divide a paper when I can help it. Readers are reluctant to read a long article; but divided ones are commonly omitted. Taylor's barbarous diction, which is germane to no language, will keep most readers away from him; hence every number ought to have one or two papers to attract. I had thought The Banquet, good for that; when lo! the ominous words—'to be continued' cut my hope short" (Wilder 2018).

By 1908 Johnson and Bjerregaard were members of the Order of Sufis, appearing on a list of arcane and Masonic societies, which according to its description taught "the Sufistic and Unitarian Theosophy of the Persians." Perhaps the Sufi group in HBL had splintered off, but that is mere speculation.

The *Platonist* limped along, often delayed, and thereby losing the trust of its few subscribers, until the last issue, number six of the fourth volume, in summer 1888. By then the cattle of Kansas City had been overwhelmed by fields of cotton. Leadbelly was born, and so was Phillip Francis Nowlan, the science-fiction writer who created Buck Rogers. The first Sherlock Holmes stories were published. That year Jack the Ripper terrified London. Women held strikes in the matchstick factories of England. They were organized by Annie Besant, who a year later became a member of the Theosophical Society, and then one of its most popular authors and leaders.

By 1889 Johnson had launched a new publication *Bibliotheca Platonica: An Exponent of the Platonic Philosophy*. In this new publication Johnson followed Wilder's advice. No more articles or translations interrupted with "to be continued." But only four issues made it into print. As Paul Anderson (1963) wrote, "Johnson is less to be criticized for their failure than praised for their existence."

The following record of a Platonic gathering in 1889 appeared in *Bibliotheca Platonica*, giving us an intimate peek at how

nineteenth-century Midwestern Platonism functioned as a social experience. Johnson was president of the central council of the Hermetic
Brotherhood of Luxor by this time, but what we see is more of a wholesome festival than a transgressive occult event.

We note with great pleasure that the holding of an annual
Symposion or festival in celebration of the "birthday" (mundane
descent) of the Divine Plato, revived by the Editor of this journal
in 1888, will probably become a permanent custom. We hope to see
the time when the birthday of Plato will not only be made a national
holiday, but will also be celebrated throughout the civilized world
by Platonists and all others who love Wisdom, and worship in the
temple of truth.

We are indebted to Mrs. Julia P. Stevens for the following report
of the Symposion held at Bloomington, Ill., under the auspices of
the Plato Club of that city. In justice to Mrs. Stevens it should be
said that much of the success of this celebration is due to her inde-
fatigable work and enthusiasm.

In imitation of the nine Muses, nine persons are accustomed to
assemble at stated times for the purpose of making a study of the
works of Plato. Their names are: Miss Sarah E. Raymond, Miss Effie
Henderson, Dr. E. W. Gray, Mrs. Mary A. Marmon, Miss Nellie
Fitzgerald, Miss Clara Ewing, Prof. A. S. McCoy, Mrs. Emelie
S. Maddox, Mrs. Julia P. Stevens. This Club gave a Festival on November
the 7th in commemoration of the Terrestrial Descent of Plato.

They met in a Symposion, with about fifty guests, among whom
were the most cultivated people in the city. Three daily newspapers
kindly lent their aid in presenting to the public the object of the meeting, viz. to attempt to awaken an interest in the Platonic Philosophy.

Music of a very high order was rendered by resident musicians, Prof. Benter, Miss Carrie Crane, Mrs. Eva Mayers Shirley,
Mrs. Lydia Sherman.

Miss Raymond welcomed with cordial greeting, not only the
Philosophers who appeared in response to the invitation, but those
from suburban towns, distant cities, and our own home friends.

She gave likewise a short sketch of the Life of Plato. Mrs. Stevens stated briefly the reasons for fixing the Celebration on the 7th of November, rather than in May, November corresponding to Thargelion the eleventh month of the Attic year, and the time observed by the Florentine Platonists.

Several letters expressive of sympathy and an appreciation of the movement were read from friends deprived of the pleasure of attendance. One says: "Your invitation is both beautiful and original. I like the idea of celebrating Plato's birthday in Illinois.". . .

Rev. George Stevens read a paper by Alexander Wilder, M.D., of New York City, entitled, "Philosophic Morality." Then an anonymous essay was presented on "Euthyphron or Holiness."

Both these papers provoked discussion. Many insisted upon concisely formulated definitions of the two qualities, morality and holiness; and some murmured at not having them shaped into jewels, to be borne away as keepsakes.

Mrs. South, of Jacksonville, Ills., recited a little poem, "Looking Backward," contrasting the socialistic scheme of Edward Bellamy, with Plato's Republic.

At the evening session, although the rain fell in torrents, there were about sixty souls present. The session opened with the following poetical tribute to Plato, which was read by Mrs. Julia P. Stevens:

> *"Immortal Plato! Justly named divine!*
> *What depth of thought, what energy is thine!*
> *Whose God like soul, an ample mirror seems,*
> *Strongly reflecting mind's celestial beams,*
> *Whose periods too redundant roll along,*
> *Grand as the ocean! As the torrent strong.*
> *A few are always found in every age,*
> *'To unfold the wisdom of thy mystic page.'*
> *And now, though hoary centuries have fled,*
> *We wish to honor still, the illustrious dead,*
> *Dead! Did I say? Ah no! He yet inspires*

All lofty souls, with heavenly desires
To mount on Reason's wing, beyond the sky,
Where truly beauteous forms can never die,
Where prophet, saint, and sage in bright array,
Behold the splendors of eternal day." . . .

Mr. Johnson, Editor of the *Bibliotheca Platonica,* read a paper entitled, "Plato and His Writings." Much interest was manifested by various questions, at the conclusion of the reading.

Dr. Hiram K. Jones, of Jacksonville, Illinois, who declared that his "lucid interval" was in the morning, rather than in the evening, delivered a most eloquent extemporaneous discourse on the "Symposion of Plato."

The audience after joining in the song, "Auld Lang Syne," dispersed. The description of the event concludes with the following: "The next day, November 8th, was almost entirely occupied in conversations and discussions on Platonic topics; and I hold in grateful remembrance all the good things uttered both by Mr. Johnson and Dr. Jones. The success of the Symposion was mainly due to the energy of Miss Raymond, who, gifted with appreciation, is the embodiment of generosity, and ever seeks to bring the best of everything to the citizens of Bloomington. The next Celebration will be held on the 7th day of November, 1890, at Jacksonville, Ills."

In 1898 Johnson built a four-room stone building to house his library. His eight-thousand volume collection included a thousand books by or about Plato. His collection of Thomas Taylor editions was probably the finest in America at the time. He was especially proud of his copy of Ficino's translation of Plotinus published in 1492. When archaeologists announced the discovery of the road to Plato's Academy, Johnson wrote an editorial arguing that the Academy should be restored not only as a historical site but also as a functioning school. "There is no good reason why, in due time, the Platonic school should not again flourish on its original site, and again become, as it once was, the nursery of science and wisdom for the whole world" (Johnson 2015).

Louise A. Off in her note "A School of Philosophy" in an 1887 issue of the *Platonist* proposed a new kind of educational institution, a school in California where professors could compare Eastern and Western religious symbolism and practice. Johnson doubted the plan would work. Modern professors, Off sneered, consider philosophies mere examples of the idiosyncrasies of the human mind. She was another true believer in the dawn of an age of enlightenment. "The dust no longer accumulates upon the volumes of Paracelsus, Apollonius of Tyana, and Jacob Böhme," she wrote. "Mankind is suddenly realizing the wonderful virtues of their knowledge." After a discussion of *maya* and *bodhi*, Off proposed Los Angeles as the ideal location. Off never opened her school. In 1934 the Philosophical Research Society established in Los Angeles by Manly Hall fulfilled many of the goals described by Off. The library he founded, and his own writing and practice provide an example of the way different paths can be studied together. His beliefs could be described as Neoplatonic, and he held the Neoplatonists in the highest esteem, but much of what he taught historically and ethically came from or at least agreed with Freemasonry. Yet he called the *Dao De Jing* by Lao Tzu the greatest mystical text, and he revered the doctrine and art of Buddhism.

Johnson had big plans that Alexander Wilder seemed to have endorsed. As Jay Bregman wrote in a personal correspondence shared with his permission, in which QBL stands for Kabbalah: "Recent work has suggested that Thomas Moore Johnson used the QBL ala HBL to work out a 'New Theurgy.' I think both thought of Theurgy and other Occult groups as a possible exoteric 'Big Tent' for their Esoteric Neoplatonism, so to speak. A new 'Cosmic Religion' that could develop a large following for a 'new age,' a religion of the world." Was Johnson having intimations of American Metaphysical Religion?

For Jones, Alcott, and Emerson, philosophy appeared as something like a religious vocation. Johnson, so much younger, lived long enough to see the transformation of philosophy into an industrial age profession. Moore, as Johnson was known by locals, was a lawyer who wanted to be a professor of philosophy. In his journal he admitted reading philosophy books at his law office, which he maintained until 1905. But Johnson longed for a like-minded community. He wrote letters to Alcott and Wilder complaining about the isolation of his life in Osceola. Did he transcend with such gusto because he could not bear the boredom of the quiet hometown he rarely left?

Johnson delivered a few important lectures at key events, for example for the Western Philosophical Association, which became the American Philosophical Association, still the most important organization for philosophers in the United States. His friends, some of them well placed and important, nominated him for academic positions repeatedly, but despite his publishing history he had no teaching credentials. Even credentials may not have helped him since at the time philosophy professors trained in Germany were in demand.

After *Bibliotheca Platonica* failed, Johnson avoided print for over a decade. In 1902 he announced a series of translations to be titled *Platonic Library*. But it took six more years for him to publish his translation of *Exhortation to Philosophy* by Iamblichus, followed a year later by *Opuscula Platonica: The Three Fundamental Ideas of the Human Mind—Hermeias' Platonic Demonstration of the Immortality of the Soul*. Johnson could not resist including a bonus track: Thomas Taylor's *Dissertation on the Platonic Doctrine of Ideas*.

The Three Fundamental Ideas of the Human Mind was a lecture Johnson had given for the Southwest Teachers' Association that was so popular it was reprinted at the association's request in the *Missouri School Journal*. Why did Johnson emerge from his self-imposed literary exile? One friend wrote of his long illness without giving details. But Jay Bregman in his essay "The Neoplatonic Revival in North America" has argued convincingly that Johnson was reacting to what he called "preposterous and fallacious allegations" by Paul Shorey.

As a classical scholar, Shorey had everything Johnson did not, including that coveted German education. Shorey was also one of the first class of students at the American School of Classical Studies in Athens. He had a job at the University of Chicago, and a degree from Harvard. His books were published by universities while Johnson continued to self-publish. Shorey ushered in the next era of scholarship, when philology brought to the study of classical philosophy the perspective of archaeology, rather than the missions of soul and social transformation.

Perhaps most troubling to Johnson was Shorey's argument that the Neoplatonists were not to be trusted when interpreting Plato. According to Shorey, Neoplatonic "sentimentality" had tarnished the reputation of Plato. Shorey took a direct swipe at Johnson when he wrote, "The most conspicuous Platonists have always been those whom Coleridge calls the Plotinists. From Alexandria to Florence, from Concord to Jacksonville and Osceola, they have made Platonism synonymous with mysticism" (Bregman 1990).

The only Platonist from Osceola was Thomas Johnson. Shorey's interpretation of Plato fit right in with America's growing love of utilitarianism. Forget the afterlife in the myth of Er, the true Plato was to be found in his practical approach to examining ethics. Shorey's skeptical view of Neoplatonic claims helped inaugurate decades of academic dismissal of the Neoplatonists.

All too soon modernity swept away Thomas Johnson's Platonic intentions. He had written "the Esoteric doctrine of all religions and philosophies is identical." Academia begged to differ.

On their grave markers, all three of Johnson's sons dropped their middle names; Proclus, Plato, and Plotinus were replaced with the initial *P*. As for Thomas Moore Johnson's grave, after a lifetime of doing everything he could to discover wisdom and share it with others the epitaph carved on his tombstone was his final insight for the world. "Here lies not Thomas M. Johnson but the body used by him. He came Mar. 30, 1851. He departed Mar. 2, 1919."

THE TWILIGHT OF THE PLATONISTS

For a time Johnson, Jones, and Wilder had brought Plato to life in America. In *Plato's Ghost: Spiritualism in the American Renaissance* Cathy Gutierrez (2005) argues convincingly that Platonism deeply informed American Spiritualism. "Spiritualism may be understood as a cultural expression of Neoplatonic Renaissance thinking refurbished for American use. Specifically, the undercurrent of American hermeticism came to its fullest if most populist expression in Spiritualism, with [Andrew Jackson] Davis himself citing the works of such early modern magicians as Cornelius Agrippa, Marsilio Ficino, and Giordano Bruno."

Not only did mediums find reincarnation in Plato's work, they also found the idea of soul mates in his description of how all human souls were split in two so they strive to join again through many lifetimes. In Platonic recollection American Spiritualists found the best description and endorsement of the activities of mediums who claimed to be reacquainting souls with their true histories, explaining suffering as not chaos but the consequences of forgotten mistakes, often in a past life, sometimes in another world.

As Gutierrez (2005) wrote in *Plato's Ghost:* "Reports of Plato clubs were serialized in the *Atlantic Monthly,* magazines wrote multivolume accounts titled 'Plato in History' and the *Yale Review* kept readers current on new translations. In 1869, the *New Englander* sported a densely packed, thirty-two page 'defense' of Plato as a proto monotheist, and in the same year a pamphlet titled 'The Eclectic Philosophy' was circulated with 'An Outline of the Interior Doctrines of the Alchemists of the Middle Ages.' The former endeavors to explain the entire history of Neoplatonism, beginning, oddly, several centuries before Plato and laying claim to a single, united truth known to the ancients and covered loosely under the umbrella of Neoplatonism. From vaunted literary minds to the conspiracy theorists of their day, Americans were awash in Platonic and Neoplatonic writings and thought."

The author of that eclectic pamphlet was none other than Alexander Wilder. Wilder had filled eclectic medical journals, Theosophical magazines, and Platonic periodicals with wry articles, delivering lectures from friends' living rooms and university lecterns with equal enthusiasm, providing so much information on so many different subjects he earned the nickname "The Walking Encyclopedia."

One day before Wilder died in 1908, a passenger on a plane piloted by Orville Wright became the first in history to die in an aviation accident. Nine days after Wilder's death, Henry Ford made the first Model T automobile. Earlier that year the vacuum cleaner had been invented and acquired by a company called Hoover. Wilder's world of Platonic New England Transcendentalists and alchemically inclined Civil War generals who knew Lincoln had disappeared and the industrial world of the twentieth century was just getting underway.

The *New York Herald* of September 20, 1908, remembered Wilder:

Dr. Wilder, Tweed Antagonist, Dead: Journalist Who Put Bible into Six Languages Helped to Overthrow Boss. Dr. Alexander Wilder, who was a member of the Anti-Tweed Board of Aldermen in 1872, and who later became known as a writer upon political, literary and philosophical subjects, died Friday night in his residence, at No. 96 South Eleventh street, Newark, N.J., at the age of eighty-five years. Dr. Wilder had lately been engaged upon a translation of Plato's works, which he intended for distribution among his friends. He had translated the Bible into six languages and had to his credit a great deal of other literary labor. He was a member of that Board of Aldermen which took office January 1, 1872, when it was resisted by the old Board of Aldermen, to dislodge which the courts were called upon. It was at a meeting of the new Board of Aldermen that Abraham Lawrence delivered the speech in which the doom of "Boss" Tweed was forecasted. Dr. Wilder served through the exciting year in which Samuel J. Tilden's civil suit for $6,000,000 brought against Tweed precipitated the investigation, which ended with Tweed's sentence to prison. The so-called "Court House jobs" and other cases of corruption were looked into by the Aldermanic body of which Dr. Wilder was a member, and in which he joined with those Aldermen who were opposed to Tweed and the "Tweed ring."

Dr. Robert Gunn, Wilder's friend for forty years, eulogized him in a thirty-page obituary in the *Metaphysical Magazine*:

He identified himself for a time, together with his brothers, with several religious movements of a revivalist kind, but finally grew out of them and into a sphere of spiritual freedom, and became an outstanding—yet, unfortunately, not well recognized—exponent of Platonism and the Hermetic Philosophy, from the life and religion of Zoroaster the prophet he considered the first philosopher, to the dynasties of ancient Egypt. During the past two years those who knew Dr. Wilder noticed a gradual failing of his physical strength.

He soon rallied from this, however, and continued his writing several hours a day, as had been his custom. In spite of his failing strength his mental powers never lagged, and he kept steadily at his work to the end. I have known him often, after a hard day's work, not to remember if he had eaten anything since an early breakfast, and it usually developed that he had fasted the entire day. Aside from his knowledge of Latin and Greek, which he acquired in his younger days, he mastered by his own efforts, German, French, Hebrew, and Sanskrit, and was able to read and make translations from them all. He was constantly asked to prepare speeches, lectures, essays, and other literary work for physicians, politicians, public men, and others, and he never could say "no." In fact he would take greater pains in writing for others than for himself; and he always delighted in any new theme that required study and careful research. He always worked for the love of it, and never thought of remuneration for what he did. For this reason he was never adequately paid for any of his work, even when others got the credit and large pecuniary rewards for what he did for them.

During his most prosperous days, while connected with the *Evening Post,* he had accumulated a considerable sum of money. At this time he married a cousin, and bought a handsome home on West Thirty-fourth Street, New York City. The union did not prove congenial, though his wife had great admiration for his intellect. He was a close student and constant worker, while she was fond of society and wanted constant excitement. Other interests and pleasures soon occupied her time and she became discontented and irritable. One day, while in a passion, she said to him, "I wish you would go away and never come back." "Do you mean it?" he asked. "Yes," she replied, "I mean every word of it, and you know I do." "Very well," he replied, and left the house. He went to Albany that day, and on his return he wrote her a note, saying if she meant what she said at their last interview to please send his clothes, and he would send for his books in a few days. They never met again, but when he sent for his books he also sent her a transfer of the house and all it contained. I feel that this is a delicate matter to refer to, and yet this sketch would not be complete without it, as it gives some insight to the character of the man, and shows his generous spirit in turning everything over to his wife and leaving himself penniless (Gunn 1908).

The letters of Wilder to Johnson culminate in the melancholy of a cultural twilight. They begin with grand plans for journals, books, and societies but they end in long silences and Wilder's critical comments about Jones, Blavatsky, Burgoyne, and others. Wilder repeatedly and earnestly encourages Johnson to keep the *Platonist* going. But subscribers are too few. The world of eclectic medicine, and of Emerson reinventing Thomas Taylor to inspire Americans, had come to an end, although it would see rebirths in places like the Philosophical Research Society, and movements like the New Age of the 1980s. In many ways Wilder was born too soon, though at the end of his life he might justifiably have felt that he had lived too long.

For the July 1907 issue of the New Hampshire journal the *Rosicrucian Brotherhood* Wilder wrote: "I suppose that the Rosicrucians have existed; I doubt whether there are any now. All of whom I knew that pretended to be such were charlatans."

A biographer could argue that Wilder, and for that matter Johnson, had needlessly complicated their lives pursuing a quixotic quest to save souls and society. While complaining about the gullibility of Spiritualists, like them Wilder attempted to educate common citizens in the mysteries of the soul. In 1877, in one of their early correspondences, Wilder wrote to Johnson, "Ere many years, I think, we shall have our renaissance. I am slowly preparing. I want that or to die." Another Florentine Renaissance was not around the corner. Two world wars loomed ahead. Medicine and philosophy, Wilder's devotions, were becoming industrialized.

In his final years Wilder was sheltered and cared for by a family of brothers and sisters who were all physicians. At the end he was working on a huge two-volume analysis or encyclopedia of symbolism, though he wrote hundreds of pages, he didn't live long enough to finish the first volume, so it was never published. The last medical school of the Eclectics closed in 1939, just as World War II began.

12

Secrets of the Hermetic Brotherhood of Luxor

SEXUALITY CAN DEFINE SPIRITUALITY and vice versa, from the celibacy of Catholic priests and the strict rules of evangelical Christian marriages to transgressive tantric intercourse deliberately breaking taboos, human beings have struggled in vain to find a dependable universal formula for balancing sex and religion. The men and women of the Hermetic Brotherhood of Luxor, a not-so-secret secret society, believed they had found that universal formula. But there was much more to their program of education than instructions for lovers.

In the Hermetic Brotherhood of Luxor we glimpse how these secret societies occurred, assisting and undermining each other, sometimes simultaneously. We also see how the roots of American Metaphysical Religion directly impacted our culture. Max Theon, for example, had little to do with America, yet through the H.B. of L. his influence on American Metaphysical Religion was profound.

We cannot definitively explain the profusion of Hermetic groups at the end of the nineteenth century. First the Hermetic Brotherhood of Luxor, then Anna Kingsford's Hermetic Society in 1884, the legendary Hermetic Order of the Golden Dawn in London in 1888, and in the American Midwest the Hermetic Brotherhood of Light in 1895.

A practical occult order that taught the use of the magic mirror for scrying, the H.B. of L. promised initiates that they would learn how to communicate with secret and even discarnate masters by means of astral travel. Theirs was not a mere correspondence course via U.S. mail.

Students would learn about the astral plane on the astral plane. Why not disembodied masters, when mediums were fascinating the nation with channeled spirits, many of them claiming to be famous historical personalities speaking from beyond the grave?

According to the order itself the H.B. of L. dated all the way back to the ancient Egyptian city of Luxor, and further still, to the primal City of Light, the heaven of archetypes. Yet the order admitted that its most recent incarnation began in Egypt in 1870.

What do we make of Kenneth Mackenzie's claim that he was in contact with six adepts of the Hermetic Brotherhood of Egypt before 1874? Of course, the H.B. of E. may have had nothing to do with the H.B. of L. Mackenzie isn't a reliable scholar, though his *Royal Cyclopedia of Freemasonry* is a feast for the eyes, filled with interesting information and equally interesting misinformation.

Mackenzie began his literary career in his teens by translating authors as diverse as Herodotus and Hans Christian Andersen, but his mentor the astrologer and Rosicrucian enthusiast Frederick Hockley damned him with faint praise, "I have the utmost reluctance even to refer to Mr. Kenneth Mackenzie. I made his acquaintance about 15 or 16 years since. I found him then a very young man who having been educated in Germany possessed a thorough knowledge of German and French and his translations having been highly praised by the press, exceedingly desirous of investigating the Occult Sciences, and when sober one of the most companionable persons I ever met" (Howe 1972).

Apparently Mackenzie was a mean drunk who relished unleashing his eloquence in criticism. Nevertheless at age twenty he was appointed a Member of the Royal Asiatic Society of Great Britain, and a Fellow of the Society of Antiquaries of London. Seven years later Mackenzie traveled to Paris in 1861 to meet with the French magus Eliphas Levi.

Mackenzie was instrumental in the founding of the Hermetic Order of the Golden Dawn. In fact, the cipher manuscripts that were offered as proof of the order's mission having been approved by Anna Sprengel and the German Rosicrucians are in his handwriting.

Then there's Rene Guenon's inexplicably confident remark about the H.B. of L. springing from the Rosicrucians, after Blavatsky emphatically denied any connection between the two orders. In 1875 Blavatsky claimed contact with a Brotherhood of Luxor, masters of the magical arts. Olcott, her compatriot, as we have seen, in the adventure that was the Theosophical Society, believed they were also training him and described one materializing in his room. This was no mere astral projection, the initiate left behind his *keffiyeh* (head cloth), which Olcott cherished.

Did the Theosophical Society find its doctrine of secret masters in the teachings of the Hermetic Brotherhood of Luxor? Blavatsky later condemned the H.B. of L. for swindling gullible truth-seekers. But Blavatsky had good reason to discredit competitors who had seriously eroded her following in America. Theosophists who felt abandoned by Blavatsky's relocation swelled the ranks of the H.B. of L. So much so that Blavatsky felt compelled to temporarily reverse her prohibition against practical occultism. For a select elite she added lessons in astral travel and other occult practices to the curriculum that became known as the Esoteric Section. The Esoteric Section survives to this day in the Theosophical Society.

Members of the Theosophical Society had to rely on Blavatsky and her invisible masters for their miracles and communications, with dim hope of achieving such communication for themselves. But the Hermetic Brotherhood of Luxor offered practical lessons in achieving access to such wisdom. As for the H.B. of L.'s opinion of Blavatsky, they thought she had fallen under the spell of Buddhist masters, initiates of a lower order of enlightenment, nihilists who believed nothing personal survives the death of the body.

Perhaps one of the strangest things about the Hermetic Brotherhood of Luxor is its lack of Egyptian content. As Geoffrey McVey (2005) wrote in his essay "Thebes, Luxor, and Loudsville, Georgia: The Hermetic Brotherhood of Luxor and the Landscapes of 19th-Century Occultisms," "It is significant that, beyond the attachment to Luxor and the occasional reference to Isis, there is nothing especially Egyptian about the teachings and practices of the H.B. of L.; its primary sources include [author of *The Magus,* Francis] Barrett, the French occultist Eliphas Levi, Bulwer-Lytton's *Zanoni,* Rosicrucianism, and the work of

Paschal Beverly Randolph. There are no 'Egyptian rites,' no emphasis on hieroglyphics, and, in fact, very little mention of Egypt at all."

Whereas we have rich documentation of the Hermetic Order of the Golden Dawn, the H.B. of L. remains a confusing collection of mysteries. Yet behind these mysteries were people history has not entirely forgotten.

THE PASSIONS OF PASCHAL

Paschal Beverly Randolph may have been born a free African American, but as a child he was still forced by poverty to beg on the streets of New York City. He taught himself to read and write several languages. He was the only Black man who rode on Lincoln's funeral train, until a racist among the mourners noticed. They dropped Randolph off at the next stop. He traveled across several continents in search of secret knowledge. By 1860 he was a respected writer of wild fiction and even wilder nonfiction: books about sex magic, occult mirrors, the plight of women throughout human history, mediumship, time travel, ESP, erotic potions, and birth control.

Randolph was founder of the first public Rosicrucian order in America. His notorious secret rituals are said to have at one time included gatherings of Black men and white women, where alcohol flowed freely, and hashish provided the incense, at a time when interracial sexual relationships were illegal. His complex amalgam of Kabbalah, Spiritualism, and ceremonial ritual foreshadowed many theories and practices now associated with the New Age.

Freeman B. Dowd, Randolph's successor as Supreme Master of the Fraternitas Rosae Crucis not only practiced sexual occultism, he saw the Theosophical endorsement of celibacy as selfish and delusional. In *Regeneration, Being Part II of the Temple of the Rosy Cross,* he explored the "triple secret of sex: electronic, magnetic, and ethereal." A letter from the 1860s still exists in which Dowd asks Randolph for membership in the Rosicrucian order.

Randolph later admitted that his stories about being taught by Rosicrucians were merely a ruse to gain credibility for his ideas.

Enthusiasts may argue that he was merely covering his tracks, hiding the reality of the order to protect it, and himself. Madame Blavatsky borrowed some of Randolph's concepts but she held him in contempt, in private using the *n*-word to refer to him. She claimed that his alleged suicide in 1875, which may have been murder, was the result of a magical battle between them that he lost when she repelled his attack and he succumbed to his own negativity. Randolph was born a hundred years too early. He would have been right at home in the Haight-Ashbury of the 1960s, or in the New Age movement of the 1980s.

Paschal Beverly Randolph's parentage remains an open question. The uneasy academic consensus is that his mother was free and from Vermont. Rumors circulated in the past about his mother being an enslaved woman from Vermont. K. Paul Johnson's research led him to this perspective, shared in personal correspondence. Randolph could well have been "a triracial north-easterner with multigenerational mixed ancestry." His mother died not long after he was born. He was homeless as a child. The son of a Virginian farmer and an enslaved woman, and therefore legally biracial, he was accepted by neither community. He grew up impoverished in New York City doing menial labor; he worked, for example, as a bootblack. While still a teen he took jobs on ships so he could travel.

In his twenties, in the 1840s, Randolph became a well-known trance medium, and like many Spiritualists of the day his lectures denounced slavery and supported abolition. In 1853 he helped recruit Black soldiers for the Union army. After emancipation Randolph lived in New Orleans where he taught newly liberated enslaved people how to read and write. Randolph also took training in medicine, and maintained a practice of one sort or another most of his life. He fought for birth control when even mentioning it meant risking arrest.

The story has been told that Eliphas Levi initiated him in Paris, but we have no proof that they met. In his *The Great Secret* Levi wrote, "Everything is possible to him who wills only what is true! Rest in Nature, study, know, then dare; dare to will, dare to act and be silent!" Randolph does not appear to have followed Levi's insistence on the magical importance of discretion. In France, Randolph was introduced not only to mesmerism, magic mirrors, and the occult doctrines of

Europe, but also the importance of hashish in clairvoyance. Like John Winthrop Jr., and so many others before him, Randolph went hunting for an actual Rosicrucian. Randolph left his opinion of Hargrave Jennings, of Bulwer-Lytton, and all the other alleged masters he met in Paris and London: "After sounding their depths found the water very shallow and very muddy."

Randolph's Rosicrucian apologists have spread stories about his membership in a secret society of initiates that included Abraham Lincoln. General Ethan Allen Hitchcock is supposed to have introduced Randolph to Lincoln. But these may be folktales rather than facts.

Some researchers have suggested that when Randolph returned to London in the 1870s, he might have initiated Burgoyne and Davidson, who would become the leaders of the H.B. of L. in America. More likely is the possibility that Hargrave Jennings was the source of Davidson's doctrine. Some have suggested that Randolph initiated H.B. of L. founder Max Theon, and others that Max Theon initiated him. But Davidson claimed that Theon had been initiated into the H.B. of L. in England, possibly a nod at Jennings.

Inspired by Richard Payne Knight's notorious book *A Discourse on the Worship of Priapus,* Jennings appears to have been the hub of a community that believed an esoteric approach to sexuality led to not only spiritual attainment but also to the improvement of the human race. Jenning's most famous books were *The Rosicrucians* and *Phallicism.* Randolph called Jennings "the chief Rosicrucian of all England." But how can we know if that was a compliment or a dismissal? Randolph left evidence of both.

Samuel Robinson has argued persuasively that Randolph's Brotherhood of Eulis was not his invention, but rather the source of his program, and further that the Brotherhood of Eulis drew inspiration from the Society of the Dilettanti. The Dilettanti had drawn their inspiration from the Accademia dell'Arcadia. Was this the Rosicrucian secret society under different names at different times and places? Or were these simply generations of like-minded explorers and enthusiasts, inspired by Rosicrucian ideals, what Arthur Versluis has called "ahistorical continuity"?

The pagan revival among Christians found some justification in the Eleusinian Mysteries of Ancient Greece. After all, the sacred object called a *liknon,* displayed in a basket during one of the ceremonies, about which we know almost nothing, is a fertility symbol that was most likely in the form of a phallus. In a world where sex was sin, the idea that it could be holy was attacked as immorality. Jennings wrote a letter in which he referred to Randolph and his book as mischievous. He disapproved. The book should never have been published. Randolph had revealed secrets.

Randolph had a knack for alienating his admirers. A popular Spiritualist, he shocked his followers by denouncing the principles of Spiritualism. When his work for abolition, and then for people who had been enslaved, earned him the respect of average Christians in the communities he worked with, he alienated them by declaring in a lecture that God is electricity, motion, and light, not Jesus. Later in life he would complain bitterly about his abandonment by the Theosophists, the Spiritualists, the abolitionists, and even his Hermetic brethren, often blaming his rejection on his race. Without him the H.B. of L. would have been of an entirely different character, yet his involvement seems to have been minimal, and his rejection by Burgoyne and Davidson final.

Some researchers have argued that when Randolph visited France and Great Britain in the 1860s on his way to Greece, Constantinople, Palestine, and Egypt, he was initiated by Hargrave Jennings. The famous Masonic scholar Mackenzie allegedly initiated Jennings. But was Jennings an actual Rosicrucian? And what did they mean by Rosicrucian? A Masonic order? A telepathic master, or merely a volunteer trying to live up to the calling? Jennings and Mackenzie called themselves Rosicrucians because they were initiated into the Societas Roscruciana in Anglia, founded in the 1860s as an offshoot of Freemasonry's United Grand Lodge of England. But the SRIA, while influenced by the eighteenth-century German Order of the Golden and Rosy Cross, and being itself an influence on the Golden Dawn, was not exactly the product of direct lineage from the originators of the *Fama* and *Confessio.* While Mackenzie and Jennings were wonderful writers, as for historical accuracy, their books were considered fanciful long before modern scholarship.

Was Randolph a Rosicrucian initiated in the 1850s in Germany, as suggested by another Rosicrucian popularizer, R. Swinburne Clymer, Supreme Grand Master of the Fraternitas Rosae Crucis? Clymer is notorious for suspect scholarship, and his assertion seems unlikely given Randolph's own statement, "I studied Rosicrucianism, found it suggestive, and loved its mysticism. So I called myself The Rosicrucian, and gave my thought to the world as Rosicrucian thought and lo, the world greeted with loud applause what it supposed had its origin and birth elsewhere than in the soul of P.B. Randolph. Very nearly all that I have given as Rosicrucianism originated in my own soul" (Randolph 1874). Randolph goes on to explain that, being half Black, he found himself and his ideas ignored by the metaphysical community of the day, but the same ideas once labeled Rosicrucian were successful, and allowed him to overcome the racial prejudice of his peers.

Randolph agreed with the H.B. of L. that sex magic should only be practiced by married couples, and he had just as many warnings about the dire consequences of abusing it, but for Randolph sex magic had many more uses than procreation. As Hugh B. Urban (2006) wrote: "Randolph not only reflects, but in fact epitomizes and exaggerates these claims about the tremendous power and potential evils of sex. Indeed, he developed his own 'science' of sexual magic, in which the moment of orgasm becomes the ultimate spiritual power with the potential to attain virtually any desired end, from health and longevity to mystical insights."

Those who wished to develop clairvoyance, who wanted to enter the path of enlightenment, had to purify themselves. Randolph (1875) wrote, "If your blood is foul with pork fat, rum, disease, etc., don't attempt clairvoyance till you are free from it." Randolph compares the process to a musician tuning up, or an artist preparing paints.

But Randolph became notorious when he was accused of arranging so-called mystical rites where white women could enjoy dalliances with Black men. He found monogamy difficult—at first, because he could not resist the temptations in his path, then because of his terrible jealousy and fear that his young wife would abandon him.

Randolph's death, like his life, was full of contradictions. Fifty years old, married to a girl not yet twenty, father of a newly born son he named Osiris Buddha (who would grow up to become a respected physician), this champion of women's rights and spiritual love had become a depressed alcoholic. Did he shoot himself in the head standing on the sidewalk one morning? The neighbor woman, who claimed he came to her house and committed suicide right in front of her, wrote that while sober he was a sweet man, but drunk he was angry, jealous, and grief-stricken. He had been desperate to raise money, offering to sell the rights to all his books, offering to sell his medical practice, deeply bitter that those who had borrowed freely from his work seemed to be flourishing while he was becoming ever more obscure and poor.

R. Swinburne Clymer wrote of a deathbed confession by a man who had been Randolph's friend. He claimed wild jealousy had caused the temporary insanity that led to his murder of Randolph. But Clymer is not a dependable source.

According to K. Paul Johnson in a personal correspondence used by his permission, "Osiris's daughter or granddaughter married an Italian and all living descendants seem to be in Rome."

GHOST LAND

Emma Hardinge Britten was born Emma Floyd in London, England, in 1823. As a child she astonished people by predicting events that later occurred, and by relaying information from dead loved ones, people she had never even heard of. As a pianist she amused herself by playing songs people were about to request. When her father died, her childhood ended. She helped provide for her family, giving music lessons and finding work as an actress.

Emma wrote: "When quite young, in fact, before I became acquainted with certain parties who sought me out and professed a desire to observe the somnambulistic tendencies for which I was then remarkable. I found my new associates to be ladies and gentlemen, mostly persons of noble rank, and during a period of several years, I, and many other young persons, assisted at their sessions in the quality of somnambulists, or mesmeric subjects—it was one of their leading regulations never to permit the existence of the society to be known or the members thereof named" (Britten 1872). Emma called them the Orphic Circle, but the participants probably had no name for what was more focused social gathering than organized secret society.

Groundbreaking research by Marc Demarest, based on work by Mathiesen, suggests that the Orphic Circle may have been a social circle of occult fellowship and Spiritualist experimentation that included popular occult authors, Lord Bulwer-Lytton, famous astrologers "Zadkiel" and "Raphael," expert on Rosicrucianism Frederick Hockley, and Richard F. Burton, perhaps most famous as the translator of *One Thousand and One Nights*. Another member of the circle, Demarest points out, may have kept Emma as a mistress. Philip Henry Stanhope, an earl, is most remembered for his involvement in the Kaspar Hauser scandal. But he may be the "baffled sensualist" who took advantage of her as a girl that she never names in her autobiography.

Among the luminaries was Charles Dickens. In her next career as an actress, Emma worked with the great novelist, and later referred to him as "my old friend." Another friend of Dickens was Hargrave Jennings, an influential writer on the subject of Rosicrucianism who, when he wasn't busy promoting his books, managed the Covent Garden company where Emma got her first acting credit. Demarest wonders if Jennings was the unnamed fiancée Emma mentioned many years later in her autobiography. They certainly shared the same interests.

From 1838 to 1855 Emma worked as an actress. She never played the starring roles, but in her teens she was promoted as a beauty. When she visited America she did get a leading role in a play on Broadway. She began to write plays. Some may have made it to the stage, but she never had a success.

In February 1856 Emma claimed that the spirit of a sailor from a ship called the *Pacific* communicated with her after the vessel was lost at sea. She began visiting mediums. With the Spiritualists Emma found a new life. She worked as chorale director for Spiritualists in New York, an editor for the *Christian Spiritualist,* and she was tested for ten months as an aspiring medium. In 1857 she began delivering lectures while in trance.

The following summer the important Spiritualist journal the *Banner of Light* published a biographical note about Emma and by the end of the year she was lecturing from the Atlantic to the Mississippi, from Portland, Maine, to New Orleans, so in demand she had to be booked months in advance. European Spiritualist writers took notice.

In 1859 Emma worked to establish the Home for Outcast Women in several cities including Boston and New York. Though some of the leading citizens of Boston were on board the plan failed.

Her lecture circuit now took her to California and Nevada; she even visited mining towns. In a mining town in Nevada, Mark Twain saw her and wrote home about it. This remarkable woman traveled alone, unheard of in those times.

In 1864, during Lincoln's bid for reelection, Emma's skills as a lecturer rallied support for the president on a thirty-two-city tour. Her speech a year later, the day after Lincoln's assassination, was shared far and wide, and praised by journalists as her finest work.

One of the founding members of the Theosophical Society, Emma disapproved of what it became, especially disparaging its appeal to the authority of invisible masters. Emma was the most popular author among the early Theosophists. When she published *Modern American Spiritualism: A Twenty Years' Record of the Communion between Earth and the World of Spirits* in 1870 she became a renowned expert on the phenomena. The book looks at the history of Spiritualism in America by state and region.

In 1870 she married her husband, William. Together they would navigate not only her career as a writer and lecturer but also their own collaboration as healers using "electro-cranial" therapy.

Emma's book *Art Magic, or Mundane Sub-mundane and Super-mundane Spiritism* (1876), published a year before *Isis Unveiled,* covered "Pre-existence of the Soul—Its Descent into Matter," "Extracts from the Vedas," "The History of the Sun God," "Hindoo, Egyptian, Greek and Roman Theology," "Sex Worship," "How Solar and Sex Worship came to be Interblended," "Jewish Cabala," "Spiritism and Magic," "Astral

Light," "Woman as Priestess and Sibyl," "Narcotics," "Thibetian Lama," "Magic Amongst the Mongolians," "The Great Pyramid—Its Probable Use," "The Modes of Divination, both lawful and unlawful, amongst the Jews," "Siberian Schaman," "Salamanders—Sylphs—Gnomes—Fairies," "Witchcraft," "Alchemists—Rosicrucians—Philosopher's Stone," and included chapters on Nostradamus, Agrippa, Swedenborg, Mesmer, and Paracelsus, crystal seeing, stones, charms, amulets, talismans, clairvoyance, and magic mirrors. It also lifted its illustrations from *The Rosicrucians* by Hargrave Jennings.

The similar but more extensive encyclopedic surveys of esoteric tradition, *The Secret Doctrine* and later *The Secret Teachings of All Ages,* and the teachings of the Hermetic Brotherhood of Luxor, the Hermetic Society of the Golden Dawn, the O.T.O., and others, all found a prototype in Emma's work.

Emma and her husband spent 1878 and 1879 as Spiritualist missionaries in Australia and New Zealand. The National Spiritualist Association of Churches in the United States and the Spiritualists' National Union in the United Kingdom still use her bullet points. Among these tenets was a belief in "the Continuous Existence of the Human Soul." When Blavatsky guided the Theosophical Society into an area of Buddhism without belief in personal survival, Emma, joining many other American Theosophists, turned away and gave her support to the Hermetic Brotherhood of Luxor.

Returning to England, Emma at age fifty-eight began a tireless lecture circuit. Within a year, worn down by work and travel, she developed a chronic sore throat, retreating to a friend's house in Paris for rest and recuperation. Yet lecture tours remained her principal activity well into her sixties.

In 1883 Emma published *Nineteenth Century Miracles*. Despite her efforts, which included more advertising than she had ever used before, the sales weren't enough to improve her life. It didn't help that the press ignored her despite the great popularity she had once enjoyed. So she decided to return to America. Her three-year absence had made the American press as disinterested as the press in England. Yet she drew a crowd of perhaps ten thousand to her summer lecture in Lake Pleasant,

New York. The following May she announced her return to England, where she resumed a brutal schedule of lecture tours into 1887. She lectured on a variety of subjects, including her experiences in New Zealand illustrated with "limelight views of the people and country before and after the volcanic eruption."

Late in the fall of 1887, Emma as editor issued the first number of the *Two Worlds,* a journal of Spiritualism and the occult. The journal helped to unite the burgeoning Spiritualist movement and gave an outlet to young writers who later became influential, among them A. E. Waite. Emma didn't shy away from using the journal to promote herself. She published her own novellas in the *Two Worlds.*

But the *Two Worlds* ended in financial scandal and lawsuits. Emma devoted herself to "a fine new magazine," the *Unseen Universe.* Now she had no collaborators, except her sister, a librarian. Despite more novellas, the *Unseen Universe* only lasted a year, leaving chapters of unfinished books.

In 1892 Emma released the second volume of *Ghost Land,* and a novel *The Mystery of No. 9 Stanhope Street.* The book's heroine suffers betrayals, the first by her mother who rents her out as a model to a lecherous artist named Stanhope. Was this fiction really confession? Nearing the end of her life did she feel compelled to record what the earl had really done to her? Yet the character of Stanhope instead closely resembles another Stanhope entirely, the painter of a famous nude, *Temptation of Eve.* While we have no evidence of a relationship, or even contact between that Stanhope and Emma, could she have been his model and mistress, or was this an elaborate ploy to avoid the appearance of an open accusation against the earl? Perhaps the more poignant detail is that, almost age seventy, Emma still wrote and self-promoted to survive.

With the failure of the *Unseen Universe,* Emma turned to autobiography, seeking not only the money she needed, but also hoping to secure her place in the historical record. In 1894 her husband, William, died. Strangely, Emma wrote more about the parrot William had given her than about her husband of twenty-four years.

The first wave of Spiritualism was dying down as the ideal of an international movement faded. Emma planned an encyclopedia of Spiritualism. In 1898 the *Progressive Thinker* republished *Art Magic* and *Ghost Land,* but Emma didn't receive any payment from the reprints. In 1900 *The Autobiography of Emma Hardinge* was published, but she did not live to see it. Her sister the librarian had to edit it for publication and the narrative ends with William's death.

THE SHOP OF MAGICAL MIRRORS

Robert Fryar had a bookstore in the city of Bath. If you wanted to see manuscripts of key writing by Paschal Beverly Randolph in Great Britain, Fryar was your man. He published a notorious series titled *Esoteric Physiology* that included sex magic concepts later found in the teachings of the Hermetic Brotherhood of Luxor.

In Fryar's shop customers could find not just a priceless manuscript on the art of using crystal mirrors to contact spirits and other entities, they could buy a magic mirror. For Emma Hardinge Britten's magazine, the *Two Worlds,* Fryar wrote "The History and Mystery of the Magic Crystal."

Like so many others in the mirror scrying lineage, Fryar worked with a seer, his wife, whom he referred to humbly as "the British Seeress." Before the H.B. of L. he had promoted her in the Spiritualist journals.

Fryar published the Bath Occult Reprint series. One of the books in that series, *The Divine Pymander of Hermes Mercurius Trismegistus,* from the text of Dr. Everard, ed., 1650 (1884), contained the first notice of the existence of the Hermetic Brotherhood of Luxor.

> TO WHOM IT MAY CONCERN, Students of the Occult Science, searchers after truth and Theosophists who may have been disappointed in their expectations of Sublime Wisdom being freely dispensed by the HINDOO MATHATMAS, are cordially invited to send in their names to the Editor of this Work, when, if found suitable, can be admitted, after a short probationary term, as members of an Occult Brotherhood, who do not boast of their knowledge or attainments, but teach freely and without reserve all they find worthy

to receive. N.B. All communications should be addressed "Theosi" c/o Robt. H. Fryar, Bath. CORRECTION. "Correspondents" will please read and address "Theosi" as "THEON."

Inquiring novices received a return letter asking for a photograph and a horoscope. For a small fee a horoscope could be provided for those without one. Those who made it into the Brotherhood, and not everyone did, received mail-order lessons and a mentor by way of pen pal. The name of the order printed on a slip of paper was burned after reading.

But after only two years Fryar became disillusioned. He claimed that the leaders of the H.B. of L. had cheated him. The Theosophical Society's journal *Lucifer* published Fryar's complaint, even naming the H.B. of L.'s leaders: "For the purpose of correcting any prejudicial suspicion or erroneous misrepresentation of myself, arising from the insertion of the note at the end of the 'Bath Occult Reprint Edition' of the *Divine Pymander* as associated with Society of the H.B. of L. known to me only through the names of Peter Davidson and T. H. Burgoyne, alias D'Alton, Dalton, etc, and the supposed adept to be a Hindu of questionable antecedents, I wish it be understood I have no confidence, sympathy, or connection therewith, direct or indirect . . ." So ended Fryar's brief but important sojourn with the Hermetic Brotherhood of Luxor.

THE AMBIGUOUS THEON

Max Theon (the name he took means "supreme god," or perhaps, "god is supreme") was the son of a Warsaw rabbi. His name may have been Maximilian Louis Bimstein, and he may have been born in 1850. His father may have been a leader of the Frankist reformation among the Jews of Warsaw. The Frankists, concerned with sacred sexuality, became notorious for orgiastic rites where ecstasy was a sacrament.

Max traveled the world to learn from Arabic, Hindu, and Jewish masters but Max's first initiation may have been as a Zoharist, an erotically ecstatic sect of Chassidic Jews from whom he seems to have received important ideas about the Kabbalah, and about the integration of sexuality and spirituality.

Recent scholarship argues that Theon's teachings never deviated far from Jewish eschatology, especially Lurianic *Tikkun,* the teachings about how to repair the world taught by the followers of Isaac Luria, the sixteenth-century rabbi and mystic nicknamed the Lion.

In 1873 Carl Kellner, a colleague of Paschal Beverly Randolph, met a young man in Cairo known as Aia Aziz. Later Aziz changed his name to Max Theon. Was Max also a student of Blavatsky's first occult master, Paolos Metamon, the Coptic magus allegedly associated with the Hermetic Brotherhood of Light?

Max's most famous student, Mirra, better known as the Mother, the colleague of widely respected Sri Aurobindo, and with him co-creator of Integral Yoga, claimed that Blavatsky had been Max's student.

In his book *Visions of the Eternal Present,* Max wrote: "In 1870 (and not in 1884, as the Theosophists claimed), an adept of calm, of the ever-existing ancient Order of the H.B. of L., after having received the consent of his fellow-initiates, decided to choose in Great Britain a neophyte who would answer his designs. He landed in Great Britain in 1873. There he discovered a neophyte who satisfied his requirements and he gradually instructed him. Later, the actual neophyte received permission to establish the Exterior Circle of the H.B. of L." Theon was the initiate; his neophyte was Peter Davidson.

But newspapers in London warned of a disreputable psychic healer named Theosi, perhaps explaining the printed correction of the name as Theon in the first notice of the H.B. of L. The address given for the healer matches the address Max Theon later gave in his marriage certificate.

The Ancient and Noble Order of H.B. of L. had a charter signed, "M. Theon, Grand Master pro temp of the Exterior Circle." Among other things the charter proclaimed:

Remember, we teach freely, without reservation, anyone worthy of instruction.

The members engage themselves, to the best of their ability, in a life of moral purity and brotherly love, abstaining from the use of intoxicants except for medicinal purposes, working for the progress of all social reforms beneficial for humanity.

Finally, the members have full freedom of thought and judgment. By no means may one member be disrespectful towards members of other religious beliefs or impose his own convictions on others.

Each member of our ancient and noble Order has to maintain human dignity by living as an example of purity, justice, and good-will. No matter what the circumstances may be, one can become a living center of goodness, radiating virtue, nobility, and truth.

Everything changed for Theon when in 1885 he married the young Irish poet he called Alma, but who was born Mary Ware. Mary was a formidable Scottish medium and lecturer on the occult, as well as founder of the Universal Philosophical Society, all before she met him. She became his seeress, and soon he lost interest in the H.B. of L., though under his guidance a branch in Paris flourished after the demise of the lodges in America. Max and Alma ultimately settled in Algeria.

Alma trance channeled much of the content of their teachings and of their periodical the *Cosmic Review*. They attracted supporters from all over the world. Max took students as he saw fit. He didn't follow the H.B. of L. protocol, and while Davidson and others continued to seek out his advice about the order, Max does not appear to have been active, although when the American branch collapsed he was the one who ordered the lodges closed.

In the tradition of the alchemical soror, or sister, Max and Alma worked together as teachers, writers, and initiators. They called their new order the Movement Cosmic. Alma explored astral dimensions in search of extraordinary information. But in 1908, after twenty-three years of marriage, Alma died. Max became deeply depressed. He stopped publication of their journal the *Cosmic Review,* and ended the Movement Cosmic. Then he suffered terrible injuries in a car accident. World War I completed Max's misery. He lived until 1927, allegedly known among the Algerian locals as a miracle worker, helpful whenever possible, but solitary.

MASTER OF THE MISTLETOE

Peter Davidson is an important but somewhat ignored contributor not only to the Hermetic Brotherhood of Luxor, but also to the O.T.O., and to American Metaphysical Religion. A violin maker born near Findhorn, Scotland, he wrote a popular handbook about violins, which in its last reprinting he stuffed with occult lore unrelated to the instrument.

By the 1870s Davidson was already interested in contacting guardian spirits with magic mirrors and he claimed to be in touch with a Tibetan adept. A student then colleague of Hargrave Jennings, Davidson found his mission when he met Max Theon.

Charged with guiding the Hermetic Brotherhood of Luxor's efforts in America, Davidson and Dalton, under the alias Burgoyne, arrived in late spring 1886. Dalton was already using the pen name Zanoni. Davidson wrote under the pen name Mejnor, Zanoni's spiritual mentor in Bulwer Lytton's novel *Zanoni*.

H.B. of L. had planned a community, or colony as they called it, in California, announced in Burgoyne's lengthy letter in the monthly journal he edited, the *Occult Magazine*. When they realized they would not be able to find support for such an expensive project they focused on Florida, but finally settled on Georgia where the colony was founded, but it became more of a family compound than an active intentional community and agricultural commune. Isolated in the rural American South, his network of pen pals nevertheless made him one of the prime Intelligencers of his time

There, on a gasoline-powered printing press he imported, Davidson published two periodicals, *Mountain Musings,* a daring progressive series of publications for locals, and the *Morning Star,* more traditional and Christian friendly, for the benefit of a wider international audience. As far as Davidson was concerned, both publications served the same ideals as the Hermetic Brotherhood of Luxor, but cloaked in more accessible metaphors.

Davidson was renowned for his herbal formulas. Like John Winthrop Jr., he cooked up an elixir prized in the area. He was also considered the best moonshiner around. He wrote a book that indicated extensive experience with making and using various drugs including a concoction of mistletoe he said could purify the mind and harmonize body and soul. Good ginseng hunters could always find work with him. The elixir of life he distributed would have been recognized by Randolph before him and by Crowley after.

Davidson is probably the source of the Celtic, Druidic, and Irish influences in some of the teaching of the H.B. of L. But the writings of Godfrey Higgins and Blavatsky herself diluted the authority of Druid tradition, theorizing that it came from Buddhist missionaries, rather than being an authentic Western tradition.

In his monograph *Vital Christianity*, Peter Davidson made these remarks based on Revelations 2:17: "The inward and true Self, the Dual-Soul-Germ, the 'I am,' is identical with the Christ, and the nature of such is the great Mystery and final secret which God holds in reserve for those who seek and love Him. 'To him that overcometh will I give to eat of the hidden manna, and will give him a white stone, and the stone a new name written, which no man knoweth saving that he receiveth it'" (Godwin, Chanel, and Deveney 1995).

The prolific Davidson authored *A Homeopathic Pharmacopoeia, Masonic Mysteries Unveiled, The Mistletoe and Its Philosophy, The Book of Light and Life, Scintillations from the Orient, Fragments of Freemasonry, Elementals,* and *The Laws of Magic Mirrors,* and more books and articles, though little of his writing is available online or in print. Davidson was an early champion of what we now call holistic medicine, and a sharp critic of physicians who preferred drastic procedures to herbal and other more subtle medicines.

Davidson also made magic mirrors. His advertisement in the *Occult Magazine* stipulates that the mirrors have the required paranaphthaline-treated surface. What was paranaphthaline? In *On the Heights Himalay* (1896) by A. Van Der Naillen, an occult romance of undependable scholarship, in a ritual presided over by a Brahman, paranaphthaline is a black gum that turns pink when charged with subtle energy by a young couple erotically dancing publicly just before the consummation of their marriage. The scene may have been inspired by an earlier book, Fraser's *Twelve Years in India,* which included a description of an erotic ritual used by a community to charge paranaphthaline gum for use in a magic mirror. Fraser claimed he accurately saw distant and future events in the charged mirror. The passage was important to Paschal Beverly Randolph who quoted it in his book *Eulis.* Davidson later reprinted Fraser's account in the *Theosophist.*

Though his work appeared in the *Theosophist,* Blavatsky warned Olcott to be careful of Davidson. Rumors persisted that after his death Davidson's unsympathetic family and/or locals burned all his manuscripts in a bonfire. But recent research suggests the family preserved his books and his work. Yet the following comment from January 2013 on Sue Young's blog (*Sue Young's Histories*) about Davidson reveals unexplored treasures hidden from scholars. Hopefully they will become available for study some day.

> Peter Davidson is my Great, Great Grandfather . . . Richard Davidson kept all of the books handed down through the years away from family members. Sad to say, but he personally told me that our own family members were stealing antiques, books, and other items from the old house. Twenty-three years before Richard Davidson died he gave me all the old books that had been hidden for over a hundred years. Yes, I have a complete library of Peter Davidson's notes, the books he wrote, and also thousands of rare books that he brought from Scotland. Richard Davidson was a fine man, but Peter Davidson even though he was very smart was a follower of the occult. His books make it clear what he believed. I have visited the original "paradise location" where Peter Davidson settled with his family. I would purchase it from the owner, but I have no desire to do so because the man so many worship was a fraud. The "secret societies" he belonged to were immoral, unethical, and something that even our modern-day society would see as wrong. The only people interested in his work are the "new age" followers in California. . . . So, now you no [*sic*] the truth. Read the facts and stop honoring a man who was a false teacher.

ALIAS BURGOYNE AND THE LIGHT OF EGYPT

In his "The Mysteries of Eros," Thomas Burgoyne disillusions anyone who might imagine the H.B. of L. promoted lascivious or perverted motives and practices: "The awful list of powers and forces set forth in the works of P.B. Randolph as attainable by the use of the sexual force, is a terrible snare. It was this fatal mistake that ruined the unfortunate misguided Randolph himself. . . . It is the way of Voodoo and Black Magic" (Urban 2006). Burgoyne warned his readers that the use of sex magic for selfish goals is forbidden. Ironically. Randolph is dismissed as only half-initiated.

What then is the purpose of sex magic? Burgoyne's candid response: "the evolution of powers in the unborn child and the elaboration of social and domestic bliss in the married state" (Urban 2006). The goal should be procreation. Marriage was the first requirement for full initiation. Bachelors had to content themselves with mere theory. Marriage, the foundation of the next generation, and of every culture, must be approached with an almost supernatural awareness of portents and signs. For example, the wrong astrological pairing could have terrible consequences, as Burgoyne wrote, "Unite a truly saturnine man with a truly saturnine woman, and you will evolve the miserly spleen of Satan in less than a week" (Godwin, Chanel, and Deveney 1995).

In 1886 scandal engulfed the Hermetic Brotherhood of Luxor. A. E. Waite, whose classic works on metaphysical history are still prized by collectors, declared that Burgoyne was a fraud, a name assumed by Dalton, who had done hard time in 1883 on a fraud conviction. Waite claims that it was only after his release from prison that Dalton met Peter Davidson.

A photograph of Burgoyne as Dalton the jailbird in his prison uniform began circulating among American Theosophists. The British branch of the H.B. of L. did not survive the scandal, but Burgoyne did, ending up in Monterey, California, where under the patronage of an admirer he recast the H.B. of L. teachings into the classic metaphysical book *The Light of Egypt*. The author hides behind the pseudonym Zanoni. K. Paul Johnson has shown that Thomas Henry D'Alton's birth register matches the date and place used for Thomas H. Burgoyne's birth chart in the first volume of Brotherhood of Life lesson series *Laws of Occultism*.

But was Burgoyne the sole author of *The Light of Egypt*? Or did he coauthor the book with Sarah Stanley Grimke, Emma Hardinge Britten, or C. C. Zain? Or is he wrongly given any credit for contributing to the book? The second book of the two volume edition of 1900 claims to have been channeled by Burgoyne posthumously.

Remnants of the H.B. of L. in Denver convinced Elbert Benjamine to become C. C. Zain, author of a series of classic handbooks on esoteric practices and founder of the Church of Light, with its twenty-one home-study courses of *Brotherhood of Light* instructions that teach "astrology, alchemy, and tarot." The Church of Light is still active today in Albuquerque, New Mexico, and online. Zain claimed that "The Science of the Stars" section of the book had been written by Emma Hardinge Britten. The rest of the book does resemble Burgoyne's earlier contributions to various magazines, which were strongly influenced by Britten's books *Art Magic* and *Ghost Land*. According to K. Paul Johnson, an expert on this material, the doctrine of those books continues in *The Light of Egypt*.

Emma Hardinge Britten was accused twice of being the real author of *Light of Egypt*. She responded in her journal *Two Worlds,* in the summer of 1889: "A certain American editor of a Theosophical magazine, entitled the *Path,* after venting on this fine work all the abuse, scorn, and display of ignorance and insolence that his malice could dictate, ends by adding that this book is 'by Mrs. Emma Hardinge Britten.' We trust it needs no open disclaimer on our part to assure the gifted author of *The Light of Egypt* that this rude and uncalled-for piece of mendacity could only have been designed by the writer to add injury to insult, and compel the Editor of this journal to express her regret that she has not the smallest claim to stand in a position implying ability far beyond her capacity to attain to."

Emma authored over twenty books on a variety of subjects: *Outline of a Plan for a Self-Sustaining Institution for Homeless and Outcast Females* in 1858, *America and Her Destiny* in 1861, *Modern American*

Spiritualism in 1870, *The Electric Physician* in 1875, *The Chinese Labour Question; or, the Problem of Capital versus Labor* in 1878, and *Nineteenth Century Miracles, or Spirits and Their Work in Every Country on Earth* in 1883.

As K. Paul Johnson has noted, three different sources credit Sarah Stanley Grimké as the ghostwriter or coauthor of *The Light of Egypt*. We'll take a closer look at Grimké in the following pages.

Whoever authored the book, perhaps more than one person, the Theosophical Society provided a particularly catty but accurate review: "Why is it called 'The Light of Egypt' is a mystery which the author does not reveal. 'The Light of Chicago' would seem to be a more appropriate title." Burgoyne was credited with several more books, including *The Language of the Stars* (1892) and *Celestial Dynamics* (1896).

A mystery closes the life of Burgoyne or Dalton. He adopted yet another alias to wed, and manage, the influential and successful spiritual reformer Genevieve Stebbins. The transformation of Burgoyne to Astley is now an established fact, with identical birth dates and identical signatures. Also Astley told a North Carolina newspaper in 1894 that he owned a California ranch. No Astley ever bought one, but Burgoyne did in 1891, possibly with his earnings from *The Light of Egypt*.

Genevieve Stebbins invented Harmonial Gymnastics; in many ways she was the founder of the Westernized yoga for health and happiness tradition that has blossomed several times in the history of American Metaphysical Religion, most notably in the New Age movement of the late twentieth century, and which flourishes to this day. As the author of books like *Society Gymnastics* and *Genevieve Stebbin's System of Physical Training* she was a pioneer of the fitness guru industry.

Her breathing exercises were related to yoga breathing techniques of *pranayama*. Her "one grand surging influx of dynamic life," involved the use of the imagination to feel the body rejuvenated by the nourishment and harmonizing power of the cosmic energy everywhere around us, a constant theme in American Metaphysical Religion. Reading Stebbins it becomes obvious how she helped inspire the simplified but quite similar *Hatha Yoga* written by William Walker Atkinson under his pseudonym Yogi Ramacharaka.

As a child, the great American dancer Ruth St. Denis saw Stebbins and called it "the real birth of my art life." St. Denis wrote that she "glimpsed for the first time the individual possibilities of expression and the dignity and truth of the human body" (Stebbins 1892). Stebbins compared her exercises to movements practiced in temples and sanctuaries, in her own words, "where magnetic power, personal grace and intellectual greatness were the chief objects sought" (1982). Her exercises are "religious training," inspiring "a life-giving, stimulating ecstasy upon the soul." Echoes of the H.B. of L.?

PRESIDENT OF THE HERMETIC BROTHERHOOD OF LUXOR USA

A letter from Burgoyne to someone in the order symbolized by the astrological sigil of the sun may have been addressed to Thomas Johnson as president of the H.B. of L. council in America. It contains the Hermetic ritual, a somewhat cursory and generic recipe, but also recommends prayers to the elements to be found in in Francis Barret's *The Magus,* and in A. E. Waite's 1886 translation of Eliphas Levi's *The Mysteries of Magic.* We can't be certain the letter was for Johnson. Johnson, as editor of the *Platonist,* was the first to publish Burgoyne in America.

According to a document found in the Theosophical Society Archives in Adyar, and reprinted by Godwin, Chanel, and Deveney in *The Hermetic Brotherhood of Luxor: Initiatic and Historical Documents of an Order of Practical Occultism,* as the membership of the H.B. of L. grew in fall 1885, Thomas Johnson was appointed president of the American Central Council or the Committee of Seven. Though president and lodge master, Thomas Johnson does not seem to have contributed significantly to the instructional writing of the order, which belonged mostly to Thomas H. Burgoyne and Peter Davidson, with generous plagiarism from Eliphas Levi and Emma Hardinge Britten.

It's tempting to make something of the fact that Johnson wrote the following letter on Christmas Day, in Osceola, in 1886. Here are some excerpts:

1. The H.B. of L. is an occult organization of great antiquity. It is of Egyptian Origin. This is all I can say on this point. . . . [. . .]

4. Anyone desiring to become a member of the Order may send his application to the President of the Council, stating his age, sex, occupation, etc. He should also send data for horoscope, viz. time and place of birth should be given if known. If unknown, send photograph (which will be returned) and personal description—the fee for horoscope is $1.00, to be remitted with application. The initiation fee is $5.00, and annual due $1.25. Manuscript instructions are sent to Neophytes.

5. The chief qualifications required in an applicant for admission are moral character, and an earnest, genuine desire to know the truth. An inspection of his horoscope determines whether an applicant has any tendency towards the occult.

6. The order is not connected with Masonry.

7. The order has in this country a comparatively large membership, and the number of applicants is rapidly increasing.

8. There are several members in Denver, Col. (Godwin, Chanel, and Deveney 1995)

The H.B. of L. of Denver became less interested in sacred sex and more interested in the study of astrology and New Thought. As the Neoplatonists, and the Theosophists after them, had discovered, there just aren't that many people interested in esoteric systems no matter how profound. But curing illness without a doctor has always been a popular subject and vocation.

JOSEPHINE CABLES AND THE OFFICE OF PUBLIC DEFENDER

In the early 1880s the United States boasted two H.B. of L. lodges: Osceola and Rochester, New York, intriguingly the latter was presided over by a woman, Mrs. Josephine Cables. In 1882 Josephine began publishing the *Occult World,* "a little paper devoted to advanced thought and reform work," according to a biographical note in *Woman of the Century,* which adds, "Mrs. Aldrich is vice-president of the Woman's National Industrial League, vice-president of the Woman's National Liberal Union, and one of the founders of the Woman's National University" (Willard 1893).

Before taking over the Rochester branch of the H.B. of L., Josephine was an important writer and lecturer, and a secretary of the Theosophical Society. In 1889 she married William Farrington Aldrich, a civil engineer, but Aldrich was no common civil engineer, his father was a prominent New York City lawyer and first secretary of the Union Trust Company of New York. One of the founders of the Republican Party, Aldrich Sr. was a popular public speaker for Lincoln and the Union.

In 1882 Aldrich Jr. moved to Alabama where he and his colleagues formed the Montevallo Coal and Transportation Company. He supervised construction, conduct, and community. The aforementioned note in *Woman of the Century* referred to the community as a "model of order, quiet peacefulness and cleanliness." Aldrich was elected to represent Alabama's Fourth District in the United States House of Representatives, serving from 1896 to 1901. He's also listed as an associate of the American branch of the Society for Psychical Research in its June 1901 journal.

The National Cyclopaedia of American Biography (1894) gave this admiring portrait of Mr. and Mrs. Aldrich.

> He soon built up a flourishing town, with stores, school-houses, churches, miners' dwellings, a model farm and private residences, including "Rajah Lodge," his own beautiful home. In 1889 he married Josephine Cables, of Rochester, N. Y., a lady of acknowledged literary ability, wonderful spiritual insight, and possessing a charming personality. Mr. Aldrich was baptized in the faith of his mother, who was a member of the Protestant Episcopal Church. His father was a beloved and upright member of the Society of Friends (Quakers). The son's studies led him to adopt the broad platform of the universal brotherhood of humanity as the common origin and

ultimate end of all religious teachings, and the true and only basis of the future universal church. He could find good in all the creeds, and contributes liberally to the support of each, but has not selected for himself any one sect. He makes a practical application of his rule of life in the conduct of his mining village, where the white and black employees live in perfect harmony, with few regulations save the Golden rule. They need no police; no whiskey is sold; no cruelty to children or animals is permitted. The universal desire to do right for the sake of right, and the evident and immediate rewards attendant upon right doing pervade the place and stimulate and determine the conduct of the whole community. Mr. Aldrich is the personal friend of all his employees, and his gentle dignity and exact judgment win their respect and affection. He made a careful study of the origin and aims of secret societies, of the religions of the east, and of the occult sciences. He is a Knight Templar and a 32d degree Mason, and occupies a high position among the brethren of that ancient and honorable institution. He takes no partisan position in politics, but is ever zealous of the rights of the poor and friendless. With his tenderhearted and sympathetic wife he was the originator and first to advocate the creation of a new office in the courts, that of public defender in contradistinction of the office of public prosecutor, or district attorney; the officer to have all the privileges and be clothed with the same rights before the grand jury and court, his duty being the defense of the poor and unfortunate who have no means of employing the best legal talent.

In other words, William and Josephine helped establish the office of public defender. Rajah Lodge, the Aldridge estate, was a multiturreted thirty-room frame house graced by magnificent gardens, fishponds, and trails designed by a German landscape architect brought from the botanical gardens in Washington, D.C. The Aldrich family name was spelled out on a bank alongside the driveway.

In 1908 William and Josephine built the elaborately decorated Farrington Hall. A two-story brick house with gambrel roof, gabled entrance, and central chimney, Farrington Hall was built of concrete and steel. The interior ceilings were paneled with walnut board. The Italian painter Monetta made of the entire wall of the main room a painted Orphic cave where, as in ancient Greece, the phases of human life were depicted.

Farrington Hall was built as a library, office building, and clubhouse for William F. Aldrich's personal use. The basement was designed to allow Aldrich's mechanically minded eighteen-year-old son Farrington to work on the then newly invented automobile, but just as construction ended, the boy died of typhoid fever after cleaning a coal mine reservoir. His grieving parents named the hall after him.

In 1912, when William and Josephine moved to the comparatively big town of Birmingham, their Rajah Lodge became a boarding house for the miners. It was demolished in 1947. Farrington Hall became the health clinic, offices, and recreation center for the mine operation. A Boy Scout troop once cleaned up some of the landscaping and one of the ponds. The current owner of the property invites tourists with a simulated coal mine in the old company store.

In Mr. and Mrs. Aldrich we find that rare example of an intentional community, successfully applying ideals of reform, inspired by their esoteric studies. Sadly their efforts didn't long survive them, and as we know modern mining little resembles their utopian ideal.

PERSONIFIED UNTHINKABLES

Sarah Stanley Grimké's specialty, as a metaphysical teacher once of some renown, was the connection between personal problems and sickness, and the use of astrology and mystical practices including alchemy to achieve well-being. Although we don't know the exact nature of her relationship with the Hermetic Brotherhood of Luxor, Astro-Philosophical Publications the H.B. of L's press in Denver, Colorado, published her work. As we have seen she may have been the author or coauthor of *The Light of Egypt*.

Sarah Stanley shocked her family when she abandoned orthodox Theism for Transcendentalist Unitarianism. Unitarianism is a denomination devoted to progressive causes, helping the world become a community, encouraging the use of reason in religion, and committed to freedom of belief for all. It was the nineteenth-century version of a Protestant minister's daughter running off to become a hippie in Haight-Ashbury in 1967. Her father, Moses Stanley, wrote to her that he and her mother were "severely, severely disappointed." Moses was pastor of Free Baptist churches in Wisconsin and Maine, a Congregational church in Wisconsin, and Episcopal churches in Indiana and Michigan.

Cyrus Augustus Bartol was to blame. A member of the Transcendentalist Club, minister for Boston's West Church, a founder and teacher at Concord School of Philosophy, for fifty years his lectures on Transcendentalism captivated audiences. Around the time that Mary Baker Eddy and her Christian Science began to be noticed by admirers and detractors in Boston, Bartol published one of four sermons he gave on mental healing, as a pamphlet called "Mind-Cure." "In using the terms *metaphysical* and *Christian science* the new practice disowns the magical or lawless in its belief or procedure," Bartol wrote, "appeals to common experience to attest its claims, and plants itself on the base the Bible builds on, fact and principle in human nature" (Hutchison 1963). Bartol's ideas about healing were an important influence on Sarah's metaphysical writing. She too believed in what Bartol called Mind-Cure. But even more to her father's consternation, as a Unitarian she now believed that Jesus Christ was merely a great man, not the literal son of the one and only God.

In 1836 Angelina Grimké Weld became the only Southern woman to publish an argument against slavery. "An Appeal to the Christian Women of the South" was burned in South Carolina. She and her sister Sarah Moore Grimké were popular speakers at abolitionist events. K. Paul Johnson has called them "the most celebrated abolitionist women of the 19th century." He adds, "The Grimké sisters' spiritual beliefs had inspired their long careers as abolitionist speakers and writers. . . . Later they both developed an interest in Spiritualism, but ended life as Unitarians" (Grimké 2019). As representatives of the American Anti-Slavery Society they were the first women in American history to speak at a state legislature.

This was the family Sarah would marry into. But she was only fifteen when the Civil War ended. By the time she entered Boston College to study philosophy, Angelina Grimké had become very ill, and not long after Sarah Moore Grimké died. So Sarah Stanley never met the women who would loom over her by reputation, and who would be an inspiration to her to speak out her truth.

In 1868 Angelina Grimké Weld read a newspaper article praising Lincoln University's Black student body, especially a formerly enslaved man named Grimké. *Grimké* being an uncommon name, she investigated and discovered that Archibald and his two brothers were her biracial nephews. Their father was Angelina's brother, but their mother was an enslaved woman. After he was widowed, they became his second family. He taught his sons to read and write.

Angelina and Sarah acknowledged the brothers, and their mother, as family. They introduced them to their community and paid for their educations. Archibald met Frederick Douglass, Cyrus Bartol, and Lucy Stone, the first woman in the history of Massachusetts to earn a college degree. Stone became notorious for rewriting the marriage vows and refusing to take her husband's last name. Archibald also met Stephen S. Foster and his wife Abbey Kelly, who were passionate abolitionists and feminists. In 1850 Abbey helped organize the first National Woman's Rights Convention at which she and her husband were featured lecturers. She gave speeches and organized for the American Anti-Slavery Society. She met Stephen on the lecture circuit. They married four years later.

As a young man Stephen had been jailed for debt when studying at the seminary. Shocked at the conditions of the jail, and at being locked up with dangerous criminals, he wrote a letter to the local newspaper from behind bars. His friends bailed him out. The town cleaned up the jail and separated debtors from other prisoners. Instead of becoming a priest he became a militant abolitionist. He was nearly beaten to death by a pro-slavery mob. In him the outrage that Frances Wright had felt about American tolerance of slavery erupted in fiery speeches and dramatic gestures. He interrupted church services to denounce Christians who were not actively fighting slavery. At another convention he called out Elizabeth Cady Stanton, alleging that her dedication to getting women the vote applied only to educated white women. In 1872 the Fosters refused to pay their property taxes. Since Abbey could not vote, they argued with the court that she suffered taxation without representation. Their farm was seized and sold, but their friends bought it back for them.

Archibald attended Harvard University, graduating with a degree in law. This was the man Sarah Stanley would marry. Bartol thought it a splendid idea. At first Moses was shocked and disapproving, but the *free* in Free Baptist didn't just mean freedom from the hierarchies of other churches; it meant a commitment to ending slavery. Eventually Moses accepted the idea that people of different races had a right to fall in love, marry, and have children. Sarah Stanley Grimké and her husband, Archibald, had one child, a daughter named Angelina.

In the spring of 1883 Sarah went to Michigan on a vacation with Angelina, then three years old. Archie, as she called him, wrote a poignant letter to Moses. Sarah had declared that she would not return to Boston. She would raise her daughter on her own. In the letter Archie describes Sarah as having been "unhappy" and "unwell." She had always been sickly even as a child. He blamed her ill health on "the inactive & apathetic life she was living." What drove this apathetic woman to give up her home?

"You know about Mrs. Stuart?" Archie wrote Moses. "Well her theory is that every disease is produced by some fear. If she could make Sarah believe it—it of course will produce some effect proportioned to the current of the belief of the patient. She found the cause and occasion of Sarah's ailments to be grounded in her relations to me" (Grimké 2019). How many such letters have been written by abandoned spouses? That is not only a problem faced by practitioners of American Metaphysical Religion, but in all religions where differing levels of devotion, or changes in spiritual perspective, can produce alienation.

Archie writes that he only met Mrs. Stuart once. But Mrs. Stuart convinced Sarah that Archie was a domineering monster. Archie asks Moses how a husband can be considered domineering when, because of his wife's weakness, he does the dishes, makes the beds, empties chamber pots, sweeps floors, and takes in clothes. Archie reminds his father-in-law that Sarah was sickly before they met. Doctors had told Sarah that she was naturally delicate. But that didn't stop Sarah from blaming all her troubles on Archie's "negative energy." Moses wrote back that his daughter "had never been well since she had the scarlet fever in her 4th year."

In 1887 the *Century* published "Christian Science and Mind Cure" an investigative report debunking Sarah and Mrs. Stuart, among others. Mrs. Stuart bragging to the reporter claimed to have cured a woman who suffered "what the doctors call rheumatism. Mrs. Stuart understood that five years earlier the patient's child had died. That started the onset of the disease. The picture of her dead child was poisoning her health. Mrs. Stuart replaced that picture with the truth: life eternal. The bereaved mother's physical affliction was cured in twenty minutes" (Buckley 1887).

That same year, after four years as a single mother, Sarah wrote to Archie, "Just now I am both physically and mentally unfit to have the care of her at all. She needs that love and sympathy of her own race which I am sure her father still has for her" (Grimké 2019).

In 1900 Astro-Philosophical Publications put out two books, an expanded edition of *The Light of Egypt* and *Esoteric Lessons*. Sarah Stanley Grimké's book *Esoteric Lessons,* published two years after she died, offered no information about its author. The book contained three sections, written at different stages of her life. The first, "Personified Unthinkables," written in 1884, showed the strong influence of the Mind Cure culture in Boston, of Christian Science and its many imitators. Sarah writes, "The problem of Health, then, would be how to cultivate and keep clean and healthy pictures in the mind."

Sarah joined H.B. of L in 1886, the same year she wrote "First Lessons in Reality." Mentalism and Transcendentalism are obvious influences. There she writes, "So that if I would maintain my physical health, I must be able to discern these shades which hang unseemly pictures in my House of consciousness" (Grimké 2019).

But the Hermetic Brotherhood of Luxor inspired the third section: "A Tour Through the Zodiac," written the year that she died. It shows the influence of Neoplatonism, *The Hermetica,* and most likely her collaboration with alias Burgoyne. She writes, "It is man's duty to evolve, not destroy, and his creations must have the wings of the eagle, to bear them aloft above the illusions of matter" (Grimké 2019).

Archie and Angelina did not hear from Sarah for ten years. Then in the fall of 1898 they got a letter from California telling them that Sarah had died. "Your mother, dear Angelina was one of the most wonderful souls that ever came to this planet. When you are old enough to understand I will tell you her wonderful career. . . . Her book *The Light of Egypt* is the most wonderful book of modern times though she says it will be one hundred years before the world will recognize it" (Grimké 2019).

A few weeks later Moses wrote Archie. He explained that Sarah had left for New Zealand. The trip there on a ship exhausted her. Walking down the street she collapsed. After that she knew she could die at any moment. A doctor told her not to risk the return trip to America. If she tried she would be buried at sea. "But she reached home, and was with us a year and a half and went to San Diego to *die of poison*" (Grimké 2019). Moses underlined those last three words but he didn't explain them.

Two months later Moses wrote Archie back: "I did not tell you, I could not—of the last sad scene of her earthly life—a scene that forever hallows the waves of San Diego Bay. By her request, her friends, at the setting of the sun, gathered on the shores, and a few went out in a boat, carrying the urn that contained her ashes, and scattered them over the limp waves. So there is not now a vestige of our dearly beloved one remaining" (Grimké 2019). Moses included a letter he had received from Sarah in New Zealand. She would be so much happier, she says, if she were with her daughter. Despite her absence, she loved Angelina.

Angelina Weld Grimké grew up to become a part of the Harlem Renaissance, one of the first female African American and biracial playwrights with work publicly performed. She was also a poet, a short story writer, a teacher, and a journalist.

When D. W. Griffith's hit film *The Birth of a Nation* glorified the Klan, the NAACP called for artists and writers to counter the propaganda. Angelina wrote a play called *Rachel, or Blessed Are the Barren,* as a protest against lynching. The play was produced in Washington, D.C., and in New York City, with an all-Black cast.

As Maureen Honey (2016) points out in her masterful study *Aphrodite's Daughters,* Angelina's poetry "obsessively returns to moments of longing, regret, and sadness." Honey continues, "her speakers also commune directly with the dead through transcendental mergers with the natural world."

Published in the *Colored American Magazine* in 1900, her short story "Black Is as Black Does: A Dream," is more diary entry than fiction. The protagonist visits the afterlife when she receives a visitation and communication from her discarnate mother in the form of a shining being. Then she sees a Black murder victim made whole on the way to heaven. His white murderer falls into hell. "His skin was white," she wrote, "but his soul was black."

Was Angelina a queer woman? She may have been bisexual but Archie, and her uncle Francis and aunt Charlotte conspired to run off any suitor, male, female, Black, or white. No suitable mate could be found to preserve the family honor. Angelina could have escaped to Harlem where bisexual encounters were possible, but she spent most of her life as a gym teacher residing in the domain of her distinguished father and her preacher uncle.

We know Archie did not approve of his daughter's attraction to women. Perhaps that changed when she cared for him at the end of his life. Passionate letters she wrote to women have survived. After Angelina retired, she became a recluse in an apartment on the Upper West Side. She died in 1958 in a world drastically different from the one she was born in. She had been ten years old when the U.S. Cavalry committed genocide at Wounded Knee. She was twelve when Ellis Island first received immigrants. In 1958 the hula hoop was invented. When Mohawk Airlines hired her, Ruth Carol Taylor became the first African American woman to become a flight attendant. The American satellite *Explorer 1* launched into orbit.

13

Willy Reichel's Psychic Adventure Tour

MOST PEOPLE HAVE HEARD of Mark Twain's classics about Tom Sawyer, Huckleberry Finn, and the *Connecticut Yankee at King Arthur's Court,* written with a conversational humor that revolutionized literature. but few know that he also wrote scathing satires of Spiritualism. In Twain's heaven, harps are handed to new arrivals by spirits who have quickly become bored with the heavenly choir. In Twain's *Christian Science* a fellow with so many broken bones he looks like a hat rack isn't reassured when told his pain is purely imaginary.

Yet earlier in his career, as a reporter, Samuel Clemens had written newspaper articles endorsing mediums he encountered in San Francisco. But then, in grief over his brother's death, he turned to a medium whose inept and fraudulent reading soured Clemens on mediumship for the rest of his life. Ironically, after death Mark Twain enjoyed one of the most prolific of all careers of allegedly channeled celebrities who returned from the beyond. However he, like most of the others, seemed to lack the talent he had when alive.

Spiritual materializations are not unknown in the history of metaphysics. Famously, Eliphas Levi on his trip to the United Kingdom was said to have conjured up the ghost of the pagan sage Apollonius of Tyana. The Neoplatonist and renowned vegetarian Porphyry wrote that an Egyptian priest evoked the guardian spirit of his teacher Plotinus, in Rome at the temple of Isis. Plotinus, it seems, had no ordinary spirit as his guardian, a god appeared instead. But Spiritualism made the phenomena of materialization much more common and much more shocking. Entire books have been written on the different kinds of manifestations, and on the frauds perpetrated by opportunists.

For example, the Davenport brothers in the second half of the nineteenth century had a popular act they toured across America for ten years, and they performed in the United Kingdom as well. Their most famous trick involved tying them down in a large box that also contained musical instruments. The box was closed. The instruments played. When the box was opened the instruments were still in place and the brothers still tied down. Alexander Herrmann, better known as the magician Herrmann the Great, wrote in an article in *Cosmopolitan Magazine* of a performance by the Davenport brothers at which Cornell College students ignited pyrotechnic lights that revealed the Davenports at opposite ends of the stage with musical instruments in their hands. Despite being exposed as frauds repeatedly, they remained a popular act. Houdini was said to have borrowed some of their tricks. But before the Davenport Brothers there was the Psychic Pianist.

THE PSYCHIC PIANIST

Benjamin Henry Jesse Francis Shepard was better known as Jesse Shepherd "the Psychic Pianist." He claimed that many of his musical performances were inspired by his channeling of the spirits of famous composers. Who was this tall, thin, good-looking piano player with a poetic demeanor, large hands, and a beautiful singing voice? Long before free jazz or freestyle hip-hop, Shepard was the first great American musical improviser.

Shepard was born in England but his family immigrated to Illinois when he was six months old. His father's log cabin sheltered fugitive enslaved people as a safe house on the Underground Railroad. At age ten Shepard saw Lincoln and Douglass debate. Lincoln deeply impressed him. He later wrote a book called *Lincoln the Practical Mystic*. At age thirteen, just before and during the early days of the Civil War, Shepard served as a page for General John C. Fremont. His life changed forever when he got access to a piano. He instantly felt a spiritual connection he could never explain. He developed masterful improvisational skills.

Walking along Broadway in New York City in 1868 Shepard passed a lecture hall. He glimpsed a piano through the murmuring audience exiting the hall. About what happened next he wrote, "There was not time for a prelude. With an allegro accompaniment, and chords that produced the effect of a piano duet, I attacked a high C and held it long enough for the people in the street to stop and listen. In less than two minutes people began to rush back into the hall and continued coming until my audience must have been nearly as large as the audience that had left" (Marble 2014).

Shepard toured the world. Initially he had no money, no family, just his innocent faith in the world as a spiritual place where good people were ready to help him. Such an idiosyncratic and naive traveler could have suffered tragedies, but Shepard stayed at the estates of titled patrons. He met leading intellectuals, writers, artists, and politicians. In England he played for the Prince of Wales. In France in the 1860s celebrated novelist Alexander Dumas, author of *The Three Musketeers,* told Shepard, "With your gifts, you will find all doors open before you" (Marble 2014).

Shepard became friends with the poets Walt Whitman, Stephane Mallarmé, and Paul Verlaine, and the architect Claude Bragdon, whom we shall soon hear more about. Mallarmé commented about Shepard that he accomplished "with musical sounds, combinations and melodies what Poe did with the rhythm of the words" (Marble 2014). A friend of the great composer Liszt described Shepard's performance as "truly supernatural," reflecting the maestro's "passion and delicacy." But Shepard's struggles were as extreme as his successes. As Matt Marble (2014) wrote, "His travels and performances had him crossing paths with the highest peaks of wealth, nobility, and celebrity and the lowest ranks of poverty, vulgarity, and anonymity."

In 1871 Shepard played piano for the tsar in St. Petersburg. The tsar's own medium General Jourafsky taught Shepard how to lead a séance. Three years later Shepard returned to America. He met Madame Blavatsky several times, but they did not get along. Shepard's problematic portrait of Blavatsky begins, "Her kinky hair, her wide, almost flat nose, and thick lips, harmonized well with her swarthy skin. Her movements were languid and slow. She never smiled, nor did she ever display a sense of humor" (Marble 2014). He insulted not only her physical appearance, but also the fit, the color, and the style of her dress.

Blavatsky, a skillful pianist herself, later called Shepard a fraud, denying that he ever performed for the tsar. At a once famous séance in Chicago, Shepard performed two vocal parts while playing piano. He also claimed to be conversing with ancient Egyptian spirits. Shepard appreciated the power of theater. His dramatic movements and theatrical lighting added to the impact of his shows. In 1876 Shepard performed at several of California's Spanish missions in what must have been a very picturesque scene.

Baudelaire may never have dyed his hair green, but Shepard wore fashionable wigs, rouge, and he dyed his mustache orange. He was not shy about wearing the fabulous jewelry royalty gave him, including a big ruby surrounded by diamonds. He also sported a fur coat for which many unfortunate squirrels gave up their lives.

Jesse Shepard met Lawrence Tonner in 1885. Tonner, fifteen years younger, became Shepard's loyal secretary and companion. Two years later they moved to San Diego. At the time, San Diego was experiencing a building boom. Railroads had dropped the cost of transcontinental passage from one hundred dollars to one dollar. Aggressive advertising trumpeted the gorgeous weather and cheap building costs in California.

Since San Diego was attractive to writers and artists, as well as metaphysicians and Spiritualists, a developer decided that giving Shepard a house would generate just the kind of publicity needed. Shepard was allowed to design and decorate the house he called the Villa Montezuma. The house still stands, though in need of restoration. It's always in danger of vandalism, and has the reputation of being not only a haunted house but a murder mansion. Those most familiar with the property deny both rumors.

As for the decor, the Pink Room had partially pink walls and an all-pink ceiling. The drapes, the furniture, and the candles were in various shades of pink. In the morning the sun lights up the stained glass window in the east wall of the music room revealing Sappho attended by cupids. Shepherd's bedroom, the Red Room, wasn't bright red. The candles were red, and the embroidered pillows, but the walls did not come right out and say red, they were more subtle. The Blue Room, Tonner's sanctuary, had a corner fireplace, above it a bevel-edged mirror reflected a pale-blue bedcover, pale-blue furniture, and pale-blue candles.

When Shepard decided to write he climbed a narrow staircase to the tower room on the top floor. With windows on all sides the view took in Mexico to the south and the San Diego Bay to the west; in a revolving chair Shepard could see to the horizon in any direction while deciding what to write down next.

When the construction and decor were completed in 1887, Shepard celebrated by inviting the Catholic Young Men's Institute to a reception. For New Year's Eve, Shepard decorated each room with its own kind of flower including roses, lilies, and orange blossoms. After refreshments Shepard played piano and sang selections from the operas of Mozart, Verdi, and Wagner. He concluded with one of his most popular pieces, the "Grand Egyptian March." In a foreshadowing of the famous "Star Spangled Banner" by Jimi Hendrix, Shepard made his piano sound like cannon explosions, marching feet, drums, and clashing swords.

In the spring of 1888 Shepard had a change of heart. He was baptized at Saint Vibiana's Cathedral in Los Angeles. He became a Roman Catholic. After that he sometimes spoke out against mediumship. That fall, Shepard went to Europe to arrange the details for the publication of his book *Thoughts and Essays*. Released in Paris in the spring of 1889 the book included an essay called "La Revolte Idealiste," in which Shepard dismissed materialism. He reminded idealists that they must fight the world of industrialization and war machines. The book made quite a splash in Europe. Shepard received letters from important people who agreed with him.

By the summer of 1889 the San Diego housing boom had busted and prices dropped sharply. That December, a week before Christmas Eve, the house and all the furniture were sold for less than what they were worth. It must have seemed a clear message from fate that the time had come to become a writer in Europe. Along with his transformation from a musician to a writer came new first and last names—the last, his mother's maiden name—Francis Grierson.

Francis and Tonner lived in London, and for a time they returned to France. They traveled for almost twenty years. Francis wrote eight books. The most famous was *The Valley of Shadows*. Francis wrote about being a boy on the prairie, but the book is fiction and the intent is not autobiographical. It's a study of the immigrants whose migrations changed America. The book remains a minor classic. Francis earned extra money contributing poems, articles, and essays to periodicals. But when they could see World War I directly ahead Shepard and Tonner returned to America. In 1920 they like so many others, including Willy Reichel, succumbed to the mystic allure of Los Angeles.

In 1921, encouraged by his friends, Shepard self-published his final book, *Psycho-Phone Messages*. While it may sound like a compilation of telephone pranks it actually contained messages from the illustrious dead, including Thomas Jefferson on the future of American democracy and Abraham Lincoln on the future of Mexico. The book included Shepard's plan for a scientific device that could be a first step to communicating with the other side, anticipating Edison's musings and experiments with a spirit phone.

In a world between world wars Francis found himself a relic of the past. His audiences and readership had evaporated. Idealist writers and psychic pianists had no place in a world of new technology that was about to be unleashed in historically unprecedented destruction.

Shepard didn't approve of the Roaring Twenties. Despite his contributions to popularizing freestyle music he dismissed jazz as "barbaric." He made a little money as a metaphysical lecturer, until his health failed. Tonner became his only support. Faithful Tonner worked part-time in dry cleaning and gave language lessons. Some days they couldn't afford to eat dinner. To keep them going Shepard had to sell most of his remaining treasures. Just before he died, he had been forced to pawn the gold watch King Edward VII had given him.

One Sunday evening in 1927 thirty people or so gathered for a piano recital in a humble house in Los Angeles. The collections after such recitals helped Tonner and Shepard get by. Shepard, now known as

Mr. Grierson, improvised some compositions, then gave a talk about his adventures in France and Italy, laughing with his listeners. He turned to the piano, announcing that he would now play the last piece of the evening's recital. It would be an exploration of Egyptian themes.

The guests listened enthralled to the lengthy improvisation. As the last chord rang out Shepard sat motionless. Was this a dramatic pause? Was he resting after exertion, as he often did? After all, he was almost eighty years old. Everyone sat quietly looking at one another until Tonner investigated. Their friendship spanned over forty years. Shepard's head was bent slightly forward, as if looking at the keys. His hands still rested on the last chord he ever played.

INTRODUCING WILLY REICHEL

Imagine how unspoiled the sky, the beach, and the ocean must have been that summer in the town of Hamilton, in the Bermuda Islands, in 1908, when Willy Reichel signed the preface of his book, *An Occultist's Travels,* a work made more poignant by its descriptions of lost wonders of the natural world irrevocably damaged in less than a hundred years. Equally poignant is the innocence and enthusiasm with which Willy explored the world of the occult. His is not the vantage point of a self-conscious postmodern. Willy is convinced that despite the crowd of frauds harvesting suckers in the fertile field of Spiritualist phenomena, here and there real mediums have manifested experiences inexplicable by the commonly accepted laws of nature as understood by modern science.

Willy had several such experiences to share from his own adventures. He was eager to bring these new wonders to the attention of academia. He believed when credible scientists made the acquaintance of credible mediums a new world of knowledge would dawn.

For ten years Willy had fought for recognition of healing by magnetism. Having had success in his own practice, he insisted scientists should thoroughly investigate the phenomenon. But Willy found that being "an expounder of animal magnetism and occult and spiritualistic science" invited "brutal persecutions on the part of certain representatives of the medical world in Germany, together with the opposition of the clergy."

Seeking to escape the stress of his losing battle over the legitimacy of magnetic healing, Willy wandered the world. "I set out on my travels in order to forget these troubles and to continue my studies. I have traversed France, England, Italy, Africa, America from the Atlantic to the Pacific, Japan, China, the Philippines, and Hawaiian Islands." His wanderings had been foretold. "Experts in chiromancy (or palmistry, as the science is called in England and America) have told me that the lines of my hand showed a predestination for long journeys, especially the well-known chiromancer, Mme. de Thebes in Paris, whom I visited twice" (Reichel 1975).

Willy elaborates: "By the time I was twenty I had travelled through the Riviera, Italy, Austria, Hungary, and Russia. And I have pleasant memories of the time when, in the ruins of Pompeii, I read Bulwer's exciting romances, *The Last Days of Pompeii* and *Zanoni*" (Reichel 1975). The latter he recommends to readers with "transcendental" interests. But it was not in Pompeii that Willy's sense of mission awakened.

Frequent vacations in Monte Carlo, where he wryly notes he could safely travel because he refused to gamble, culminated in an epiphany. "Often have I sat on a bench, high up on the cliffs of Monaco, olive, orange, and lemon trees seeming to smile at me, when I fixed my thoughts upon the mysterious organization of human nature—and again feelings which I believed long buried awoke within me" (Reichel 1975).

Willy immediately traveled to Paris and Nice to consult with mediums there but he was disappointed. He reports he experienced nothing worth repeating. Nevertheless he remained dedicated to his goal of touring the world in search of natural wonders and supernatural revelations.

Willy was a hardy traveler. On board a ship headed for Alexandria, Egypt, in 1902, Willy enjoyed the storm off the coast of Crete that humbled his servant with seasickness. In Egypt, Willy toured the monuments wishing he had a trance medium alongside him to tell him stories of the mysterious ruins. He next traveled back to Paris and from there to Dover and London where he met more highly recommended mediums but experienced nothing worth reporting. His arrival in New York City moved him.

"I had previously visited many harbours: Genoa, Trieste, Marseilles, Naples, Brindisi, Alexandria, Port Said, Dover, Calais, Cherbourg, Kiel, Cronstadt, St. Petersburg, etc., but not one of them compares in magnificence with the harbour of New York. The first sight of it is simply overwhelming!" (Reichel 1975).

In New York City a member of the Swiss Consulate known for his writing in German journals on psychic phenomena took Willy to visit "a medium whose specialty is direct writing on a tablet. I am positive that this is a genuine medium—but the purport of the writing received did not impress me" (Reichel 1975).

His friend from the consulate told Willy to visit Lily Dale. These days with an HBO documentary and nearby highways, Lily Dale is easy to reach, but it wasn't an easy journey for Willy. Leaving New York on the night train he "reached Dunkirk on Lake Erie, from which a small branch road goes to Lily Dale. Violent rains had washed away the embankment of the road, so after waiting nearly six hours at the little station, I determined to take a carriage, in order at least to reach Lily Dale by night" (Reichel 1975).

Lily Dale was born as a summer campground for Spiritualists in the 1870s. The sum of $1,845 bought twenty acres of farmland. Initially christened the Cassadaga Lake Free Association, then the City of Light, shortly before Willy's visit the site became Lily Dale in honor of the water lilies of the lake. In 1915 Lily Dale became even more famous when the house where American Spiritualism was born in 1848, the cottage of the Fox sisters, was moved there. "The Spook House" as it had been known locally in Hydesville, New York, was set for demolition when, in 1915, Spiritualist Ben Bartlett bought it and after having it dismantled into pieces transported it by barge over Lake Erie, 150 miles north to Lily Dale.

Lily Dale medium Flo Cottrell made the cottage a shrine for Spiritualists. But in 1955 a "fire of undetermined origins" burned the cottage to the ground. Back at 1510 Hydesville Road, the site of the original cottage, a replica was built, a cause championed by Spiritualist John Drummond. But it burned down, too, in 1983.

Lily Dale is the most famous example of a Spiritualist community in America, but there were others. Let's take a look at several of them. Temple Heights Spiritualist Camp in Northport, Maine, was founded in 1882, according to the *New York Times* (1998), by Dr. Benjamin Colson. Colson cured the gravely ill daughter of the governor of Maine with a combination of herbalism and spiritual healing. The grateful governor gave him a hundred acres and four thousand dollars to realize his dream of a community for Spiritualists. A year later the new community purchased a farm half a mile from Saturday Cove for a tent ground, and to sell lots for cottages. A new wharf was built so guests intimidated by the wilderness could arrive on a steamboat. In a grove of evergreens on the shore of the Atlantic Ocean meetings were held that lasted a week. The grove itself was a distant echo of the sacred trees the tribe indigenous to the area revered as shrines of their ancestors. Later Temple Heights built a simple chapel to shelter the program of services. Visitors multiplied until a lodge was built in 1927 that had to be expanded to twice its original size in 1960. Eventually the old cottages were sold for summer homes. Now the lodge and chalet are all that remain but the community is still a destination for visitors from as far away as New Zealand.

Fraser's Grove Camp in Vicksburg, Michigan, influenced seekers in the Midwest for around four decades. Vicksburg was known for the beautiful water lilies that bloomed on Sunset Lake. Jeannette Fraser had a twenty-seven-acre farm in the woods just outside town. She believed in the Spiritualist movement. Around her farm a community grew. The humble first meeting at what became known as Fraser's Grove took place in 1884. Before too long, over a thousand people were visiting the campgrounds on summer weekends to enjoy not only séances, weddings, and funerals, but also music, dancing, and ice cream. No smoking or drinking, by order of Jeannette.

As the twentieth century began, Fraser's Grove became so popular the Pennsylvania railroad set up a station there. Séances cost thirty cents each, but there was a ten-cent fee to enter the campground. Chicken dinner cost another quarter. A medium with a megaphone on a stage out front fired up the arriving guests, channeling carnivalesque evangelical messages from the spirits. Traces of Fraser Grove–like activities could be found in Vicksburg into the 1940s but the community no longer exists.

After a visit to Fraser's Grove, the founders of Camp Chesterfield organized their own official Spiritualist community in 1891. Home to the Indiana Association of Spiritualists to this day, the quiet town offers readings by mediums, psychic healing, classes in spirituality, and a seminary. Over the years Camp Chesterfield's reputation suffered. In 1925 fourteen mediums were arrested after an investigative reporter turned evidence over to the police. In 1960 a Spiritualist attempted to use infrared film to capture spirit activity, instead he captured the tricks of the medium and her accomplice. In 2002 the *Skeptical Inquirer* published more evidence of fraud by mediums, the result of their sting operation. Then there's the story of M. Lamar Keene, to whom we'll return in a little while. Camp Chesterfield continues to flourish. As mediums have always said, mediums are like lawyers or doctors, there are a few good ones, plenty of mediocre examples, and a percentage of outright frauds.

Lily Dale was partially responsible for the creation of Southern Cassadaga Spiritualist Camp on thirty-five acres near Lake Helen in Florida between Daytona Beach and Orlando in 1894. Like a Disney World set, the grand old oak trees covered with Spanish moss cast shadows on tin roofs. Claiming to be the Psychic Capitol of the World and the Metaphysical Mecca, Southern Cassadaga Spiritualist Camp attracts thousands of visitors. Like Lily Dale, the population is made up of Spiritualists. Now fifty-seven acres and fifty-five homes, with several parks, including Fairy Trail, the community has a website that carefully explains that Spiritualists do not worship Satan, they are not witches, and they do in fact worship God whom they call the Infinite Intelligence. The online directory categorizes residents as healers, mediums, and teachers, but services overlap, as some healers, for example, offer communication with the dead. Click on a name for more info and you'll find that most provide a photo and brief introduction, and are available not only in person, but by telephone, only a few are online.

Florida's Spiritualist community began with a boy baptized in a freezing cold lake in Minnesota. Not long after, his late uncle manifested to him to announce that someday George Colby would become known for his psychic abilities. Not only that, he would be the founder of an important spiritual community in the South. In his teens, despite the beatings administered by his outraged Baptist parents, George performed healings and gave readings. When he'd had enough parental abuse, he ran off to become a wandering medium, leading séances in parlors or meeting alone with the sick or bereaved. He became well known for relaying accurate details about dead relatives. At a séance in Iowa an Indigenous American spirit with the Stoic name Seneca introduced himself. He became George's most important guide. Seneca told George his trip to the South was about to begin, but first he must meet with certain people whose help he would need. Names and locations were supplied.

Marion Skidmore, who would become known as Mother of the Camp, had come down from Lily Dale to explore the possibility of a sunny winter retreat in warm Florida for the Spiritualist community. George and the folks from Lily Dale started the camp in 1894. George named the place *Cassadaga,* a Seneca Indian word for "rocky waters". George didn't stay for long when he visited, but he didn't stay away for long either. He would return to lecture, consult, and tend his citrus trees. When he became too ill to continue his circuit, as he was still a traveling medium, George moved into a house provided for him by the residents of Cassadaga, who took care of him until his death not long after. As recent scholarship has shown, the women of Cassadaga were not only pioneers of the Spiritualist movement, but also in the fight for women's rights.

What impressed Willy most about Lily Dale was not the mediums, whom he found performed much better when in group sittings than face to face. What impressed Willy was the fact that Lily Dale existed at all. "The liberty of Spiritualism here is entirely different from what it is in Europe. Charmingly situated on Cassadaga Lake, N. Y., the little wooden houses of the mediums stretch in various directions; perhaps fifty of all descriptions live here together. Before each house is a sign, stating the kind of power the occupant possesses, and no one disturbs them in the exercise of their calling; on the contrary strangers come here from all quarters, seeking the mediums which seem to them best suited to their purpose" (Reichel 1975).

Willy's own experience was pleasant, but by his standards unimpressive. "I can say that I was most kindly received, perhaps partly because my name was not unknown there, as I have contributed a great deal for several years to American publications. So I visited many trance, speech, and materialization mediums. True, I did not obtain much . . ." (Reichel 1975).

Yet his disappointing experience would be a marvel to any of us. "I have seen at the séances of the mediums Winans and A. Nermann, within two hours, in the presence of perhaps thirty people, probably twelve different materialized phantoms, large and small, Indians, Englishmen, and Americans, each of whom appealed to some one present to prove himself a relative or friend. I, too, was summoned, but I could not recognize the being in question as the person he alleged himself to be" (Reichel 1975).

Were these apparitions an elaborate theatrical ruse to which Willy and thousands of others fell victim? His further adventures will leave us wondering if he is a liar, or if some inexplicable phenomenon has all but disappeared from human experience.

In Lily Dale, Willy got a tip to visit a medium in Chicago. "Miss Bangs possesses a very peculiar power as a medium, which I had never witnessed before. A letter is written to some intelligence from whom one desires to receive a communication, a few empty sheets are enclosed for a reply, then the envelope is sealed with one's own seal and put between two slates on a table in the bright sunshine. Miss Bangs, after placing an inkstand and a penholder on the slate, sits down opposite with folded arms. The noise of writing is now distinctly heard, then rapping, and then the slate may be taken. My letter lay exactly as I had left it, with the seal uninjured. I opened it, and all the empty pages were filled with writing in ink, and all this was done at noon, in broad daylight! In spite of all skepticism, I could discover no fraud there" (Reichel 1975).

CALIFORNIA DREAMS

Next came a dreary journey to California. "Nothing but endless prairies—enough to drive one to despair!" Arriving in San Francisco before the devastating quake he quickly moved on to Los Angeles, a farther ride of eighteen hours. Willy loved L.A. "Still a comparatively new city, at the junction of the Southern Pacific and the Santa Fe railroads.

On this account its growth has been incredibly rapid, even for American conditions. All kinds of tropical plants—only the dates and bananas do not ripen—grow there in unexpected magnificence, which is increased by countless hummingbirds. Situated at the foot of the Sierra Nevada, three quarters of an hour distant from the ocean it possesses a climate superior to that of the Riviera, for I could not endure the heat there in April, while in Los Angeles, after noon, there is a sea breeze from the ocean which renders the nights cool" (Reichel 1975).

At a newly formed Spiritualist camp nearby, Willy saw "probably eight phantoms within an hour who all appeared in white veils," which puzzled Willy because "in Lily Dale, they showed themselves in the clothes they wore in life. It is not clear to me why the spirits in Los Angeles appeared in one way and those in Lily Dale in another" (Reichel 1975). Later in the book Willy will venture a guess, but his roundabout approach seems rather perfunctory. The book doesn't seem to have warranted a rewrite. Willy is fine with statements made early on that he explains away as the book proceeds. More like a contemporary travel and psychic adventure handbook than a serious work of nonfiction, there's an almost nostalgic quality to *An Occultist's Travels,* with its long-gone addresses of mediums and quotes from then current journals, like newspaper cuttings stuck in a scrapbook.

Willy marveled at the beauties of California. The Sequoia redwoods astounded him; he compared them to the pyramid of Cheops. Not long after, Los Angeles became Willy's home for five years. But first he traveled on a fateful boat trip to San Francisco. "Whales and flying fish were our constant companions."

Willy met many mediums on this trip to San Francisco, all recommended by experts and friends, but no one impressed him until he met Mr. Miller. "Mr. Miller must be described more fully, since my experiences with him surpassed everything that I had previously known, at least in his character as a materialization medium" (Reichel 1975).

We don't know much about Mr. Miller. The *San Francisco Call* (vol. 87, no. 81) of May 30, 1902, contains a small classified ad under the category Spiritualism: "C.V. Miller world's famous materializing medium, spirits speak face to face; séance. Tue., Fri., Sun. 50 cents."

Another ad just beneath advertises Miller's Decoration Day 2 p.m. matinee, also half a dollar. Miller was said to have been born in France not America. According to Willy, Miller had a day job: "Mr. Miller then owned a business in Japanese art wares and old pictures at 568 Geary Street" (Reichel 1975). Willy compliments Miller's "modest bearing."

Willy describes extraordinary events at their first meeting: "I mentioned neither my name, nor my occupation, because he did not ask for them. On Thursday, October 1st, 1903, I went to him and found there twenty-five persons, both men and women. His so-called cabinet was a bow-window of three sections, with a curtain of black material, facing directly upon the street." Most mediums had cabinets of one kind or another, like *torii,* the spirit gates of Shinto, intended to mark the threshold between the sacred space of the spirits and the realm of daily life. "When I entered, the curtain was drawn back, and I investigated everything in the most thorough manner. To come in from the outside was utterly impossible, as Bush Street is well frequented and fully lighted by lamps, so that any attempt to enter from without would be impracticable on account of the pedestrians constantly passing" (Reichel 1975). This is the stage upon which these extraordinary events or fictions would unfold: a bay window in the house of a gallery owner.

Willy continues, "Miller first requested everyone present to search this bow-window thoroughly, and he really made so pleasant, simple and frank an impression that harmony, which is a principal matter in such séances, was not difficult to establish" (Reichel 1975). But Willy's adventure with the dead was about to become much more personal.

Willy describes what Miller did next: "After the appearance of the second phantom he said suddenly: 'Here is a Spirit, who calls himself So-and-so'—he mentioned a name known to me—'and says that Moppel, a dog that is still alive, remembers you vividly, and is faithfully guarding your home.' Now for the explanation. At my temporary home in Southern California, I had a very faithful white Alaska dog, which I had left there, and to which I had given the name of Moppel. Besides, it is a German dog-name, and Miller does not understand a word of German! No one in this séance knew me, or was aware of that" (Reichel 1975).

This detail impressed Willy, though it never occurred to him apparently that he might not be so hard to identify with his German accent and other easily recognizable characteristics. Perhaps it's possible that a mutual acquaintance knew this detail about Willy's life in Los Angeles. But then what to make of this: "The spirit, who said this, was, as I have said, known to me by name and seemed to be very familiar with my private affairs" (Reichel 1975).

What happened next, however, cannot be easily explained. What it describes must be dismissed as a lie or accepted as a legitimate mystery in need of scientific investigation, the message to which Willy dedicated his life's work. "After a number of spirits had first mentioned their names, they summoned several of those present and talked with them. Some of those asked for were not present, upon which the spirits withdrew with words of regret. Mr. Miller then stated that he would retire into the cabinet, because then the phantoms have more power, and from it they would go to those present. And so it was. Scarcely four minutes had elapsed, when the curtain opened entirely and Mr. Miller was seen asleep, with six fully developed phantoms in white robes beside him, who all clasped hands. Gradually the different phantoms came out of the cabinet, went to those present, and talked eagerly with them; two spoke German. As I heard later, they were conversing with Germans" (Reichel 1975).

Now comes the really mysterious part: "Suddenly I heard distinctly, loudly, and clearly a name which I knew very well, from a phantom who wished to speak to me of private matters, concerning which I must keep silent. Another phantom came close to me, bowed, and I recognized it; his name, which he then uttered, corresponded" (Reichel 1975). Our instinct as postmoderns is to dismiss this as pure fiction, a money grab by a guy with a vivid imagination. Yet thousands of such experiences were reported, often under strict conditions.

Willy closes his account of the strange event: "Almost at the same moment that the last phantom withdrew from our circle, Mr. Miller came out of the cabinet. There was ample light during the whole séance. The following phenomenon was also extremely interesting: a white ball, which looked like muslin, hovered a short time in front of the curtain, then sank before the eyes of all, and in scarcely two minutes a new spirit figure formed itself. The dematerializations principally took place in full view, in front of the curtain. I can only say that during many years I have seen a great deal, but nothing like this, and I only regret that Germany does not possess such a medium. Unfortunately I was obliged to go away, but I hoped at no distant time to see Mr. Miller again" (Reichel 1975).

From his adventures with the dead, Willy returned to appreciation of the beauties of life in Southern California. "In December, 1903, I spent some time in San Diego, the last city this side of the Mexican frontier; the Coronado Hotel there, built on Coronado Beach, is probably the most aristocratic place on the coast of Southern California." But his journeys always return to the metaphysical: "Near San Diego (a carriage drive of an hour and a half) at Point Loma, the Theosophists have built a wonderful monastery, from which one has a magnificent view of the wide ocean, San Diego Bay, and the Mexican mountains. In winter, after the heat has somewhat diminished, everything grows here in tropical glory of colour. The wonderful begonias and the superb bougainvilleas with their thousands of yellowish red and blue flowers here twine around almost every one of the little houses, which, of course, on account of the frequent earthquakes, are built of wood, as they are nearly everywhere in California. In this institution Theosophy is taught according to the ideas of Mme. Blavatsky. Point Loma Homestead is the name of the monastery, in which any one who is seeking rest and recuperation can find accommodation at the rate of three dollars a day" (Reichel 1975).

The founder of Point Loma Homestead was Katherine Tingley. During the Spanish-American War she was a relief worker and a field hospital nurse. She not only founded what she called Lomaland but also hospitals and schools in Cuba, two homes for orphans, and the International Brotherhood League. As president of the Theosophical Society she used her authority to relocate the organization's international headquarters from chilly and expensive New York City to sunny Southern California.

In January Willy traveled to the San Gabriel Canyon, where he encountered gold miners. Their life was hard, "digging in sandbanks, hills, mountains." Their justice didn't depend on law enforcement. "Strict laws prevail in these mountains. Every thief is pursued and shot without mercy. The gold miner, who lives in a tent, to which everyone has easy access, spends the day in his mine, and his tent is usually filled with stores of provisions, which are brought on horses from long distances. Anyone can take from them, but he must leave a note there, stating who he is, and what he has carried away, or 'to horse,'—the search for him begins, and woe betide him!" (Reichel 1975).

Again he waxes poetic about the area around Los Angeles: "The climate of Southern California in winter is about the same as I found in Sicily, only the magnificent floral display is greater in California. As soon as the first rain begins to fall in December or January, after an interval of nearly seven months, everything commences to grow with wonderful luxuriance" (Reichel 1975).

Willy is enchanted by "Santa Catalina Island, a romantic isle in the sea, like Helgoland or Capri. Rowboats, with a glass bottom, permit a view of the floor of the sea, which displays a fairy-like splendour in its plant formations, amid which swim throngs of goldfish and other species. Only on the Lake of Garda in 1896, and later on the road along the Mediterranean, between Nice and Villa Franca, have I seen anything like it. I brought cones seventeen inches long from the pine trees on the snow-clad mountains and adorned my room with them" (Reichel 1975).

But Willy was not impressed by the desperate seeking healing in L.A., and the throng of questionable people who ministered to them. "From December until the end of March Los Angeles is crowded with invalids and people who wish to escape the cold weather of the eastern states. With these strangers a number of mediums usually arrive, and so now came a 'Count Gabriel Dizara,' who calls himself 'Anglo-Hindu Palmist and Medium, Member of the Ancient Order of Occult Scientists, Psychical Research Society of America, and President of the Balfour Institute of Science in New York.' He boasts of knowing the secrets of the Lama priests, and will allow himself to be buried six days, like some Hindu fakirs" (Reichel 1975).

Like many transplants to Los Angeles, Willy soon found the unrelenting heat and infrequent rain intolerable. Immigrants would echo his sentiments for generations and still do. "I had hoped gradually to acclimatize myself to Southern California, but I had now been a year and a half in this climate and suffered no less than at first in this half-tropical region. It is true, as acquaintances consoled me by saying, that one can make snowballs, gather roses, and take a sea bath on the same day; but one cannot be always 'in the car'" (Reichel 1975).

Nevertheless, Willy's wanderlust took him south of the border to Mexico City. "A really charming city, thoroughly clean, and built with much architectural magnificence in the new portion. Everything there is nearly one-half cheaper than in the United States; the climate, too, is much more agreeable than in Southern California; yet it lies at a height of nearly 7,500 feet, so that it is never too hot and never too cool" (Reichel 1975).

As Willy left his luxury hotel behind, the wonders he encountered multiplied. "In order to see a genuine tropical landscape, I resolved to go to Vera Cruz, on the Gulf of Mexico, along which road one can most readily become acquainted with the tropics. I did not regret it. Orizaba, Jalapa, and Puebla were recommended to me. I had already seen the beauties of the tropics in Southern Egypt and Nubia, and shall never forget the brilliant starry sky arching above the ruins of the Temple of Ammon of the Pharaohs in Karnak, opposite ancient Thebes, or a wonderful tropical night in Assouan in the Libyan desert, but there one finds no vegetation except palms and cacti. On this route, however, I was to see tropical forests in their full indescribable majesty" (Reichel 1975).

THE MARVELOUS MR. MILLER

As was his way, Willy returned from terrestrial wonders to Spiritualist adventures, visiting San Francisco and the astounding medium Miller again. The results were even more spectacular and inexplicable. "I saw, by an amply sufficient light, while Miller was standing before the curtain, a fully developed spirit come out from behind it, go about nine feet, to a lady sitting beside me, embrace and kiss her—it was his mother—and then watched Mr. Miller who—not in a trance—slowly followed him, as he took him by the hand and led him back to the curtain, where he dematerialized before it" (Reichel 1975).

But that was only the beginning of the marvels Willy claimed to have experienced:

I also saw eight times a gentleman well known to me in life, ten feet away from the medium, first approaching and sinking in front of me as a little floating flame, develop in perhaps a minute and a half, till he stood in his full figure directly before my eyes. He then held long conversations with me, drew back himself to the curtain, where I followed, and dematerialized himself before my eyes, still talking until his head at last vanished.

This spirit, in his voice and his whole manner of speech, was absolutely unmistakable; but as he developed himself in white robes, I asked him if he would be able, that is, if he could remember in what dress he was laid in the coffin, and to materialize in this for a still more positive proof of identity. He promised to do so, and came the next day to a séance in a dress-coat, exactly as I had seen him in the coffin, his face without any covering. (Reichel 1975)

What are we to make of these alleged phenomena? "I saw with my own eyes little revolving flames, white, blue, and a wonderful light-blue, from which voices spoke to me, giving their full names, and those of friends and relatives; some sank and quickly developed, but others had not yet attained this ability" (Reichel 1975).

What happened next leaves us again with an apparent choice between calling Willy a liar, admitting unknown phenomena, or concocting some scheme of hypnosis, theatrical effects, perhaps even telepathy, to explain it all away—hypotheses Willy himself considered, often by quoting authors from the many Spiritualist and Theosophical journals he enjoyed reading. "I saw my nephew Helmuth, who died in Berlin, August 1, 1898, as a child four years old, float with his fair hair out of the cabinet, calling constantly: 'Uncle, do you see me?' I saw him hovering about in the room a long time and then disappearing through the ceiling. Who, having had such an experience fall to his lot even once, which makes all further proofs superfluous, could still doubt the truth of Spiritualism? I saw and heard these things several times" (Reichel 1975).

The wonders continued. "At a private séance, standing directly behind Miller, who was not in a trance, I saw bright flames floating from every direction, from which voices addressed me in the most touching manner.

I saw at a public séance, for at least twelve minutes, a spirit, fully materialized, sit among us and talk with us. I saw at least a dozen spirits develop before those attending the séance, usually two or three yards from the medium who, meanwhile, was talking unconcernedly several times; and heard rappings, which sometimes echoed like cannon; also other tests, for instance bringing back a watch that had been lost six years, I will mention only incidentally, as the materialization was so amazing, that all the rest recedes into the background by comparison" (Reichel 1975).

Are we to believe that a watch lost six years ago far away from California materialized at the séance? Can we believe it? Apparently Willy could. His book lacks the smooth veneer and tactical layout of a hustle. His claims are too far-fetched, too numerous, and his narrative too haphazard. It reads like the feverish outpouring of a man encountering something inexplicable.

Miller's chief spirit control Betsy orchestrated another bizarre event. "Mr. Miller was sitting in the cabinet, in a trance, and Betsy summoned me into the cabinet in order to convince myself that Miller was sleeping in it. She called me 'the German gentleman.' The séance this time consisted of twenty-seven persons. She said to me: 'We will now dematerialize our medium and remove him to the second story, and you and another gentleman and two ladies must get the key to the second story and bring the medium down again'" (Reichel 1975).

Teleportation of a human being was hardly your average Spiritualist phenomenon. "I will mention that the whole house belongs to Mr. Miller, and the séances were held on the ground floor, while the second story, as Miller is not married, is kept securely locked, since thieving is not rare in California. Betsy also requested us to join hands and sing, in order to obtain perfect calmness of soul, and the greatest harmony, because her purpose was extremely difficult. I again carefully examined everything, convinced myself that it would have been utterly impossible for Miller to get out of the cabinet, since twenty-seven persons were sitting directly in front of it and there was abundant light, while the back of the cabinet faced directly upon the street. Even if a window should be opened—there was no door—any draught of air, and besides, it was stormy, rainy weather, it would have been instantly noticed by us" (Reichel 1975).

Now that Willy has set the stage, Betsy becomes master of ceremonies: "After about four minutes, Betsy's voice was heard, asking that we four persons should now go. I had the housekeeper, who was sitting in the circle, give me the key, and we went to the second story, where I unlocked the door, and really found Mr. Miller, breathing heavily, sitting in a chair. I took the medium, who was still in a trance, by the hand and led him back into our circle, where he awoke without any recollection of what had happened; only his heart gave him pain" (Reichel 1975).

Sometimes the supernatural became especially entertaining: "I have experienced many other things with Miller; for instance, once, two spirits materialized who said that they had been Egyptian dancing girls; they wound up themselves a musical clock standing beside me, and danced, that is, made the dancing movements, similar to those I had seen the dancing dervishes perform in Cairo in January, 1902, after which they dematerialized before my eyes" (Reichel 1975).

The dead were not the only guests at Miller's séances. "Another time beings appeared, shining radiantly from within outward—words of description fail me—they said that they had never lived upon this earth, but were 'Spirits of the Sun,' and allowed me to touch them, in order to convince me that, out of love for mankind, they had adapted themselves for this moment to the earthly sphere" (Reichel 1975).

Lest we think that Mr. Miller's house was rigged for these performances, Willy assures us to the contrary:

Mr. Miller visited me in April, 1904, in Los Angeles, where I was then residing, about five hundred miles from San Francisco. On his arrival I examined him, as well as his two pieces of hand-luggage, and built a cabinet myself in my own private dwelling; but again, as at the first séance, behind my chair five feet away from the medium—the same spirit that I have previously fully described, developed himself in shining robes. Then a female spirit came out of the cabinet, went through the door into the entry, about thirty feet away, and blessed the house. Other spirits, with whose works I had occupied myself years ago, appeared and greeted me in the most cordial manner. The most striking thing with Miller is that all these

spirits instantly mentioned their names—Christian and surnames—
and with an accuracy which I never before experienced. In a word,
these séances in my own residence presented the same phenomena as
those in San Francisco. In everything I am writing down here I am
perfectly aware of the full significance of my words. (Reichel 1975)

Willy speculates about the fourth dimension. Perhaps that is how
science will explain the wonders he is witnessing. Unfortunately, information about Miller is sparse. Most of it depends on Willy's reports.
However according to Willy, "Miller has had a great deal written about
him in the American professional press, as well as in the daily papers"
(Reichel 1975).

Willy traveled to the World's Fair in St. Louis in summer of 1904.
But he didn't bother to write about his experiences there. On the way he
stopped at the Grand Canyon. On his way back he visited Yellowstone.
He thought the geysers something out of Dante's *Inferno*.

Despite his experiences, Willy can't bring himself to state categorically that survival of death is a fact. Willy explains one source of his
continuing doubts: "It has often happened to me, as it probably has to
every trained experimenter in this province, with mediums through
whom I spoke to spiritual beings and also saw them fully materialized
and believed I recognized them as the persons they announced themselves to be, that afterwards they said something which again awakened
doubts of their identity in my mind" (Reichel 1975).

Willy is all too aware of the opposition and ridicule he invites but
he considers it "a moral cowardice to withhold my testimony." As for
those who categorically deny the reality of Spiritualist phenomena,
Willy has no respect for their skepticism. "I do not understand how a
man can be so presumptuous as to believe that he knows all the laws of
Nature" (Reichel 1975).

But Willy's book and his adventures were far from over. His malaise
was a calm before the storm. In the August 1904 issue of *Revue Spirite,* a
Spiritist journal published in Paris, Willy wrote of his favorite medium
Mr. Miller: "In January, 1905, 1 heard from San Francisco that a letter had come from Valence-sur-Khone to Mr. Miller, from a gentleman,

J. Debrus, requesting him to give twelve séances for de Rochas, him-self, and several friends, because I had remarked that Miller would visit France again in 1905. My wish was fulfilled insofar as Colonel Count de Rochas desired to see Mr. Miller. So, full of good cheer, I went to San Francisco to try what was to be done, and with the intention of eventually accompanying Mr. Miller to Paris."

But Mr. Miller was not enthusiastic about the prospect of being tested in Europe. "I did not find Mr. Miller in the best state of mind, as certain recent psychical excitements had made him somewhat nervous. His con-trols told me that he could not go to Paris under four or five months, and on account of the sudden change of atmosphere, and other conditions in France, I must not expect such wonderful séances as in California; but perhaps M. de Rochas might be persuaded to come here" (Reichel 1904).

Lt. Col. Eugène Auguste Albert de Rochas d'Aiglun, officer of the Legion of Honor, expert on a wide range of ancient technologies, including fortification, water clocks, and temple machinery, researched the influence of music on human emotions, while earning awards for his translations from ancient Greek. Though he published a very long list of scientific articles, he is most remembered for his research into the paranormal. He documented the phenomenon of "externalization of sensibility" that causes some hypnotized people to display sensitivity to pinches and other stimuli at a distance. Stewart and Betty White explored the same territory, considering it evidence of the soul outside of body. Rochas was also among the first to explore past-life regression.

Willy arranged a visit by Professor van der Naillen, a friend of Rochas. A séance that very evening produced "two fully materialized phantoms," van der Naillen "was permitted to touch them, and other things induced him to give me his support in every way, in order to per-suade de Rochas, in the interest of occultism and humanity, to accept my invitation. In order to lead the latter investigator to do this, that is, to be able to send him a report which might induce him to undertake this long journey, we were obliged to forward to him a report of a test séance under absolutely conclusive and unobjectionable conditions, with signatures from persons of scientific reputation" (Reichel 1904).

It's hard to imagine any enthusiasm in Miller's response to this new challenge: "Do with me as you please." After all, Miller was either a fraud in danger of detection, or a man with a talent so rare it could revolutionize several fields of science and modify every religion; a heavy responsibility for a skill that depended on indefinable atmospheres.

Willy provides a detailed description of Miller's test:

Professor van der Naillen called in as a third, Dr. Rem., a universally esteemed German physician, and we agreed what tests we must require. I first bought a new black shirt, black under vest and trousers, then ordered a new suit for Miller, and had these articles sent directly to the Palace Hotel, where I was living, so that Miller did not see them before the séance. I then hired at the Palace Hotel— it is the most aristocratic one in San Francisco—a second room, whose selection I left to Professor van der Naillen, and had the cabinet constructed of black material by an upholsterer. On the 2nd of February this test séance took place. Besides Dr. Benz and his wife, Dr. Burgess, Professor Braunwalder, Professor of Electricity at the School of Engineering in San Francisco, Mr. Charles Dawbarn, the Californian philosopher, the Turkish consul, and other prominent persons who had accepted our invitation were present.

When Mr. Miller arrived,

we took him to my room, where before our eyes, he undressed entirely and put on the articles of clothing already mentioned. Then we went into the séance room, where Professor van der Naillen and Dr. Benz bound the medium with strong ropes, previously purchased, by his arms, hands, chest, neck, and feet, three or four times to a chair, and sewed the ends fast to the carpeted floor. The room was about forty feet above the street. During the whole séance Miller was not in a trance and the cabinet was almost always open. In spite of these difficult conditions, nine phantoms gradually materialized sometimes ten or twelve feet from the medium. Betsy, the principal control spirit, went away so far that Mr. Miller called: 'Betsy, come back, I am suffering terribly.' (Reichel 1904)

Mr. Miller passed his test with flying colors. "I received later from Professor van der Naillen a very long and full report in the French language, which, with a letter of introduction from myself to de Rochas, I sent to Paris to be forwarded. There was not one in this séance of sixteen persons, among whom were several avowed skeptics, who did not become convinced of the genuineness of the phenomena by this sitting under such conditions" (Reichel 1904).

Willy reports another of Mr. Miller's miracles.

At a séance, held three days later, at Mr. Miller's house something occurred so interesting that I would not like to pass it over. The sitting took place at noon. Before it began, and while Mr. Miller was standing in front of the cabinet, I heard Betsy's voice whisper: "Go out into the sun with the professor a moment." I took Mr. Miller by the arm and went with him into the street, which was reached directly from the room by merely opening a door, after which we immediately returned. At the moment we entered the dark room, I and all present saw Mr. Miller completely strewn with a shining, white, glittering mass like snow that entirely covered his dark cheviot suit. I have witnessed this singular occurrence several times; even when he had not previously been in the sun, even for a moment, his clothing, as soon as the room was darkened, gradually appeared covered with snow. This is evidently the white element of magnetism which the phantoms use in their development, as distinguished from the blue, which is effective in healing operations. (Reichel 1975)

The white magnetism apparently explains the sartorial variations among spirits. "It is more difficult for phantoms to appear in the garments which they wore in life, because they must take these materials from those present, while, so they told me, they could find the 'white magnetism' in the atmosphere. In the séances at Miller's I almost always felt, just before the appearance of the phantoms, the well-known almost icy breath of air, which has been so often described in test sittings" (Reichel 1975).

But de Rochas disappointed Willy. He had been severely ill and could not take a journey to California, though he admitted he was tempted, he also confessed that results outside of France itself, and the strict controls of French scientists, would never be taken seriously. But de Rochas was ready to put his money where his mouth was. He suggested several suitable locations, and a suitable group of scientists, and offered to set up Willy and Mr. Miller in something like a research compound, and at his own expense.

Meanwhile back home in Los Angeles, Willy's love/hate relationship with the new city swung back to love as summer gave way to winter: "Eleven palm trees of different kinds stand in my garden, among orange, lemon, peach, banana, and fig trees, which latter produce black figs almost as large as my hand. The lemon trees are already bearing new blossoms, although the old fruit is not yet fully ripe. The magnificent bougainvillea, with its thousands of lilac blossoms and the yellow begonia are twining up to the roof of my house, and in the so-called winter season." Willy can't help gloating a little: "Zero weather and snow in Berlin. While reading this, I do not feel much longing for the low-lying plains of North Germany" (Reichel 1975).

Willy had a favorite spot in Los Angeles. "The best place is Ocean Park—Yesterday, April 24, I went by electric car through fields of grain ready for harvesting, past Hollywood, a French colony, and along the spurs of the Sierra Madre of Southern California to Ocean Park to enjoy the sea air and the magnificent flowers, which extend directly to the ocean. Here I fed the pelicans, which, with the sea gulls, people the ocean and reminded me of Egypt" (Reichel 1975).

There Willy found another supernatural wonder. "A sign on a cottage by the shore attracted me: 'Madge, the Romany Gypsy Queen, palmist and clairvoyant and crystal-gazer.' The latter particularly interested me. Palmists and clairvoyants, of whom in this country there are several in every city, I had visited by dozens, and found three-quarters of them ignorant people, who had their wisdom from worthless books; but every visit costs a dollar, and they often earn an immense amount of money, for the otherwise smart American is superstitious. Extremes meet" (Reichel 1975). Before returning to the crystal gazer, Willy reports that in California mediums could get a license simply by paying thirty dollars a month. He adds sardonically: "in Germany they always stand with one foot in jail."

"A crystal-gazer," he writes, sharing one of his most picturesque experiences,

> was something new to me; I knew of the existence of such people from occult literature, but up to this time I had had no personal experiences in this province. Mrs. M. Ingalls—this is her real name—placed a flat crystal cube with octagonal cutting, "a Chinese" one, she said, upon the palm of my left hand, which it nearly covered, and then told me actually almost my entire life. I was not a little surprised. She saw, so she explained this gazing, symbolically in this cube pictures come and go, whose interpretation was the outcome of her experience.
>
> The first thing she saw were medical instruments and her first statement was that I must be a physician. True, I was not in the ordinary sense, but for nearly twelve years I made cures with excellent success. She then, with wonderful accuracy, told me my thoughts, my character, my disappointments, and my struggles; all this in a little cottage, directly on the shore of the great ocean, whose waves almost washed the walls of the little wooden house. (Reichel 1975)

While most of what Reichel had to say about Americans was complimentary, the temperance movement inspired Willy to describe less praiseworthy American characteristics. "In my opinion the United States has a tolerably large dark side in their temperance movement. I am no drinker, though I do not at all despise a glass of wine, but what the temperance people have accomplished here is almost incomprehensible to German ideas. In the states of Maine, Iowa, Kansas, North Dakota, the sale of alcohol is prohibited. Now in Los Angeles beer can be had only when a whole meal is ordered. And what beer! Germans would refuse it. In social gatherings one almost always receives only ice water at lunch or dinner. In the Luxor Hotel, at Luxor, in Egypt, I witnessed for the first time this sight, which is positively comical to Germans" (Reichel 1975).

Here and there Willy lets the attentive reader know that there's more to him than meets the eye. He's not some uncultured adventurer on the fringes of metaphysical phenomena, but a gentleman well read in the esoteric. The Indian "Vedanta Society," he writes, "has established a mission here, as well as in San Francisco, a mission which has a very agreeable representative and teacher in Mr. Swami Sachchidananda. . . . He preaches a sort of pantheism in the meaning of Spinoza, combined with mystic ideas, such as we find in Xenophanes, Plato, Eckhart, Theophrastus Paracelsus, Giordano Bruno, Böhme, and others" (Reichel 1975). I have not been able to find a reference to this swami. Swami Sachchidanand and Swami Satchidananda were born after the publication of Willy's book.

Willy reveals that his study of the esoteric included star reading; "astrology, which I studied through its best representatives, as George Wilde and Alan Leo in England, and especially Albert Biniepf in Hamburg" (Reichel 1975). He shares that his experience with astrology left him wondering about predestination.

Willy embarked next on a tour of the West Coast. He describes Mt. Shasta, and the town of Tacoma beautifully situated on the ocean near Mt. Rainier, but his greatest praise is saved for Alaska. "The Yosemite is beautiful; the Yellowstone is wonderful; the Grand Canyon of Arizona is colossal, and Alaska, with its fjords and mountains, glaciers, and rivers, possibilities and distances, is all of these. It is not only colossal, but wonderful and beautiful as well" (Reichel 1975).

Returning refreshed to his preoccupation with the supernatural, Willy visited Miller again with the usual spectacular results:

A former patient, the widow of a Grand Duke of a South German reigning House, who had died about eight weeks before, also came, embraced me with great delight, gave her full name, and showed the same mannerisms, which to one familiar with occultism, is the most difficult thing in such cases. A short time after death it is more possible; but when the spirit has progressed further in its development, that is, has especially developed the principle of love, it has, according to my experience, to struggle to forget the mire of earth more and more in order to progress, and then the identity is difficult to prove, because the personality has vanished, and only the individuality has remained, which, however, usually has to develop in a totally different direction from what the sphere of earth permits. . . . I also attended a "trumpet sitting." I heard the trumpets flying about in all the corners of the room, heard voices speak through them, saw everywhere little flames from which words were spoken; but as the room, meanwhile, was kept perfectly dark, I will not describe this séance as at all conclusive. (Reichel 1975)

But not all the séances were positive experiences: "This time an unhappy spirit—the control Betsy said she had been too much occupied to be able to prevent it—stole into his séances. It was a female black spirit that went about the circle of fourteen persons, striking and spitting upon nearly all of them, and continually using abusive language. She touched me on the left leg and said in English: 'You want to go to Europe with this medium—I'll fix you.'" That is, she'll prevent the manifestations Willy explains. "Betsy told me afterward that this spirit had given a minister of the Episcopal church two hundred thousand dollars, because he had promised her that, after her death, she should see Christ. As this had not followed, she was so furious that she injured Spiritualism wherever she could. Whole companies of Jesuit spirits were doing the same, and in Europe Spiritualism would have advanced much further if such spirits, whose influences and thoughts hung like a wall over Europe, did not so eagerly oppose Spiritualism" (Reichel 1975). It's quite an image, an invisible army of deceased Jesuits impinging their will on Europe to prevent Spiritualists from proving life after death.

For Willy death is the ultimate healing and homecoming. Reincarnation may separate loved ones for lifetimes, but lifetimes are merely a blink of the eye viewed from beyond. Of course, having been so bitterly persecuted for it he must write to defend the honor of animal magnetism and magnetic healing. Here is the heart of his defense, and perhaps the purpose of his book:

Surgeon General von Stuckrad personally expressed to me the following opinion, which I will add in his honor and the interest of the cause: "After repeated treatment by Professor Willy Reichel, I have reached the conviction that by the direct contact through laying the palms of the hands on various parts of the body there passes from Professor Reichel to the patients an invigorating, extremely beneficial influence, which may be compared to an agreeable and strengthening current affecting the nervous system; under the palm of the hand a feeling of increased warmth instantly developed in me, and quickly spread, radiating in every direction, whether the application of the hands was on the back laterally from the spine, or in the pit of the stomach, in the region of the heart. The direct effect of the magnetic treatment consisted in the undoubted feeling of warmth, strengthening, and invigoration, combined with the comfort of repeated, very deep inspiration." (Reichel 1975)

On a visit to gold mines in fierce desert Willy describes something like cosmic consciousness. Impressed by the vast universe of stars above him he feels, as many have before him, consoled and more certain than ever that life goes on beyond death. "In the desert of Nevada, as formerly in the Libyan wilderness in Egypt, I suffered the magnificence of nature at sunset to exert its influence upon my spirit" (Reichel 1975).

Willy's many Spiritualist adventures in San Francisco abruptly came to a temporary halt. "On April 18 the frightful catastrophe at San Francisco occurred. I also felt a short shock at Los Angeles on the 19th, just as I was cutting a palm tree in the garden; in the early morning, at five o'clock, black clouds with ashes had been seen to draw over Los Angeles, a thing which seldom occurs in the almost constantly cloudless sky" (Reichel 1975). The Great Earthquake and the fire that followed devastated San Francisco.

The media was not to be trusted, even when seeking information about the biggest stories. "The newspapers in the Eastern States published many stupid errors, which I afterward found copied into the German papers, such as that Santa Catalina Island, in the Pacific Ocean, had disappeared, and that the port of Los Angeles had been overwhelmed by a tidal wave" (Reichel 1975).

Willy decided to view the tragedy firsthand, and to check up on his friends in the devastated city. "On May 16 I took my passage on a steamer of the Pacific Coast Steamship Co., in order to go from Los Angeles to San Francisco. . . .On May 17, at four in the afternoon, we reached the Bay of San Francisco. The Cliff House, which is seen soon after passing the Golden Gate, is still standing, and the seals still sun themselves on the cliffs in front, while the azure heavens are mirrored just as ever in the lightly curling waves of this noble bay. Oakland, Berkeley, Alameda, etc., are seen as before, lying like pearls in the sunshine on the slopes of the ridges, and at last our steamer rounds the last promontory and San Francisco is in sight—or at least the place where it once stood!" (Reichel 1975).

One would think that since the book is about the occult Willy might immediately address the question of whether Mr. Miller in any way saw it coming? Did he even survive? But Willy is in no rush to reveal the results of what may have been the most important test Miller ever faced. "It is a frightful sight from a distance a heap of ruins, which is still partly smoking, four weeks after the catastrophe. Even the pier, to which our steamer makes fast, is half burnt away, and the *Spokane* in which I went to Alaska in 1905, lies at the pier, converted into a hotel, for not one is left in San Francisco" (Reichel 1975).

Willy was impressed by the country's response to this disaster at a distant port. "The help afforded by the United States filled me with admiration and respect. Hallway trains poured in uninterruptedly from all quarters to Oakland with provisions, for there were about 400,000 people to be taken—I myself stood in the so-called bread-line, where thousands took their places every day to receive meat, potatoes, milk, and crackers free of cost, for nobody had any money, the banks dared not open their vaults for four weeks, in order to allow them to cool, and there were no longer any stores in existence where people could buy anything" (Reichel 1975).

The following summer Willy traveled back east to visit Niagara Falls and Lily Dale, among other places. In Lily Dale he reports his experience with a medium named Keeler.

Keeler takes two slates, and after the sitter has wiped them himself with a wet sponge, he places one upon the other and asks the sitter to write questions for the spirits on small pieces of paper, fold them up so that Keeler can see nothing of what has been written, and then lay them on the edge of the slates. Then Keeler himself takes the pencil in his hand and writes—in my case correctly—the names of the spirits to whom the questions have been addressed (I had written five, of which he could not himself have thought). He explained to me that he is clairaudient; his control tells him these names, and these spirits are now present, though invisible. Then he tied the two slates together, and gave them into my hand, so that he held them by two corners and I by the two others, in full noon sunlight, about a foot above the table. Then I heard marvelously rapid writing, and raps, whereupon Mr. Keeler handed me the slates with the remark that the sitting (which cost two dollars) was at an end. I went out with the slates, untied the knots in the park, and found five separate messages, written backward and forward, with the signatures of those to whom I had addressed the questions. (Reichel 1975)

Back in New York City, Willy had more fascinating experiences with mediums of various kinds.

On October 16, I visited for the first time the celebrated clairvoyant, Mrs. May Pepper, of Brooklyn, who is pastor of the First Spiritualist Church there. I found 38 ladies and four men, so closely packed together in a basement room that an apple could not have fallen to the ground between them. Her Tuesday and Friday sittings are so frequented that her sister, who sits at the entrance as cashier (50 cents each person) simply closes the door when there are no more chairs vacant, and many people are thus turned away.

Each visitor lays a closed envelope, containing the questions to which answers are desired, on a small table, which is so heaped with them that many of them fall to the ground as soon as Mrs. Pepper, at the beginning of the séance, begins to feel among them to find the one she wants. She usually tears off a little piece, the size of a thumbnail, puts this into her mouth and then tells fluently what is in the letter, gives the names of living and deceased persons, which are not written in the letter, but who are connected with the contents of the letter or with the writer. She tears the veil from the past and present with such striking certainty that in the cases of some twenty persons whose letters she handled in my presence, she only made one single mistake or misconception. As a psychometric clairvoyant she is quite astounding, that is an unquestionable fact. (Reichel 1975)

Willy claims it was mere chance that he was in "New York when Mr. Miller returned from Europe. He made a great sensation in France and Germany. After having recovered from the shock to his nerves caused by the news of the destruction by earthquake of his property and business in San Francisco, Miller went to Paris, where he gave the series of séances, which caused great public excitement in France, and attracted the attention of persons in Europe interested in psychics. Miller also went to Munich, Germany, and convinced the scientists in that country of his wonderful powers. Articles in *Die Uebersinnliche Welt*, Berlin, by Dr. Walter Bormann, and in *Psychische Studien*, Leipzig, October, 1906, by Colonel Peters, sounded the enthusiastic praises of Miller" (Reichel 1975).

Despite Miller's apparent success Willy failed in his ultimate goal. "I have, however, to regret that Mr. Miller failed to become personally acquainted with Colonel de Rochas. Had the two met in séances in the sense in which de Rochas wrote to me, then the scientific world would have heard of it. As it is, the world of Spiritualism has been informed that my observations relating to Mr. Miller, as published in Germany, France, and America, were correct; but the world of science, which does not concern itself with Spiritualism, did not hear of these evidences" (Reichel 1975).

The intent of Willy's book is to preserve the evidence he believed he had found, hopefully to help someday inspire science to seriously consider the mysteries of mediumship and magnetism. Willy never tells us whether the spirits warned Miller about the earthquake. Perhaps it was enough that Betsy reversed her opposition to Miller traveling to Europe and sent him out of town at the right time.

Willy next provides an unusual blend of channeled material and classical philosophy:

I once asked the phantom, who called himself Dr. Benton, as to my former incarnations; he answered that he would ask "my soul," and tell me next time. I replied that this could soon be done; my soul was here. His answer was, no; that was an error; my soul was not here, but in the "spheres"; it was connected with my body by a cord, like a balloon, so that I, for instance, as my soul was developed, could not be drowned. This of course sounds very mystical, if not downright absurd. But the Alexandrian Neoplatonists, such as Plotinus and his teacher, Ammonius Saccas, asserted something similar. According to Plotinus, man has a double soul, a double Ego: the higher, which lives entirely in the supersensible world, and the lesser one, which is bound up with the body and its activities. Saccas says on this point that the soul is partly on earth and thinks by means of the senses, and partly in the supersensible world without mediated thoughts. This, moreover, is a very ancient idea. Whether it can be accepted as plausible in view of what I have set forth above, and in the present condition of our knowledge, I must leave the reader, who has followed me so far, to decide according to his own judgment. (Reichel 1975)

Willy now introduces us to yet another of his discoveries in the New World:

Madame Seera calls herself Clairvoyant, Astrologist, and Palmist, and she possesses these talents in such a degree that she surpasses Madame de Thebes, of Paris. She looked at me and told me things which I had to admit were true, to my great astonishment. Then she asked me to allow her to take an impression of my hands, for I had lines which are very rare, and promised to send me gratis a complete chart. I have not found these lines of my hand mentioned, even in the important work on palmistry. I received the chart by post, very lengthily and carefully drawn out, and must acknowledge that no one has ever yet read my life so correctly as Madame Seera. According to statements in her prospectus, she has read the hands of President Roosevelt, Governor Deneen of Illinois, President Harrison, J. Pierpont Morgan, John D. Rockefeller, Mme. Sarah Bernhardt, and many other celebrated personages. She claims to know nothing of Spiritism. I have had a good deal to do with palmistry, or chiromancy, and have visited dozens of so-called palmists, mostly ignorant persons; Madame Seera and Madame de Thebes prove that palmistry is true, but few understand it. (Reichel 1975)

Willy next quotes at length from Proverbs, Exodus, Isaiah, and Job to prove that "palmistry is in perfect harmony with the Bible."
Returning to Madame Seera, Willy shares her PR apparently verbatim.

Madame Seera gives the following remarkable account of the temple in which she studied: "Close to the ancient city of Benares, situated upon a beautiful hill, in the midst of solitude and loneliness, is a cave temple, which has been owned and protected by the Joshi Priests, who have practiced palmistry in all the generations from 1000 B.C. to the present day. In this temple, musty with years and mysticism, are hidden invaluable books on palmistry, written on silver and gold plates. There are three maps of the hand on human skin, written in a bright red colour, which age and sun cannot obliterate. They are supposed to have been written on human skin for preservation, as they have been preserved in the same manner as the mummies. They are finely illustrated, containing great information on palmistry, which has been a perfected science with the Hindus from time immemorial. The dates of two of these hands are unknown, but one shows 1000 B.C." (Reichel 1975)

We're not sure if we're listening to Willy or Seera as the story continues: "This cave is the most sacred and holy spot to the Hindus, the great men of India, who have astonished the world with their psychic power, having gained their knowledge at this temple. Not only the Hindus themselves, but the most celebrated palmists in Europe, such as the well-known Cheiro and others, have perfected their knowledge in this temple" (Reichel 1975).

Now Willy himself vouches for her talents: "Madame Seera gives an honest and truthful delineation of future events. Many have already come true. For instance, she gives the following as having already come to pass." Willy provides a list of allegedly genuine forecasts of future events: "Roosevelt's nomination, accidents in July and October, his miraculous escape from death, and his overwhelming victory were fore-cast through a horoscope published in the *Chicago Inter-Ocean* newspa-per." The list continues: "The great danger which threatened the Czar of Russia; the great disasters on land and sea, were forecast in a horo-scope cast for Alexis, heir to the Imperial throne of Russia, by request for the *Chicago Evening American* and published August 27, 1904. The accident to King Edward VII of England, which occurred November 15, 1906, was forecast by Madame Seera in an astrological horoscope, pub-lished June 16, 1905, in the *Chicago Inter-Ocean*. The great disaster of San Francisco was also forecast by Mme. Seera on February 4, 1906, in the *Evening Post*" (Reichel 1975).

Could this be the same Madame Seera who starred in a sordid exposé of the criminal side of Spiritualism? In 1911, in volume 26 of the *Hamptons* magazine, Madame Seera was featured in Roy McCardell's article "Dealers in Destinies: Tricks of Seers, Soothsayers, and Second Sighters." McCardell writes: "Madame Seera, blonde, unkempt, stand-ing beneath the gaslight of the poorly furnished back parlor of her second-class boarding house, brushes back an unkempt yellow lock and looks at an elderly gentleman with thin, gray hair, and a lean and anx-ious expression, clad in garb of deepest black."

As McCardell tells the story Seera's ads say $2, her client gives her $5, but she tells him that her "angel child" spirit control Baby Ruth likes spirit candy so $10 would probably make for a better experience. When the $10 is paid she kicks herself for not having asked for $20 while slip-ping the tenner into her stocking. This Madame Seera, "or Madame Vashti or whatever highfalutin' name she calls herself," as McCardell puts it, has none of the skill or charm reported by Willy.

In a sofa chair Seera's body shakes and shivers with the arrival of Baby Ruth. "Dood Evenin'," she announces in a lisping falsetto, "I's little Baby Ruth. I's come from the most booful land, everything white and gold, where everyone is happy. I's so happy, but I's hungry, too. I wants some spirit candy." Baby Ruth, supposedly in control of Seera's body, got up and sat on the lap of the intended. McCardell adds, "If the 'come-on' is an old gentleman who permits this familiarity, further advances may be made." It's a sordid kinky scene McCardell paints. If

Baby Ruth can't hit a home run she goes away pouting to be replaced by Mohawk, a curious name for a Sioux warrior who was supposed to have died in the massacre of Wounded Knee. McCardell wonders at Mohawk's primitive communication skills yet considerable knowledge of Wall Street. But Mohawk won't commit too easily. Better come back next week when he's had a chance to confer with his elders about whether you should buy or sell.

The mediums, McCardell writes, are in cahoots with the stockbrokers. They get a kick back for every share sold. The cops get a piece so they don't break up a beautiful thing. The mediums he compares to Freemasons, in that they look out for each other. Often, he says, a medium will complain that the atmosphere is disturbed, an excuse reported by Willy, but really a ruse that allows the medium enough time to dig up information from church records, public records, visits to neighbors and even undertakers for information about the recently departed and their surviving relatives, but mostly from other mediums. Mediums, he writes, then recommend the "boob" sending all the juicy information along with the new customer.

At times McCardell seems to be writing about Willy's book, or at least the genre. While neither Willy nor Mr. Miller appear, Keeler the slate medium doesn't escape scrutiny. He apparently concocted the will of a dead man whose Spiritualist relatives were outraged when the court rejected it.

What do we make of Willy's enthusiastic endorsement of Madame Seera? Was Willy merely a fool or a fraud? McCardell provides no evidence for his allegations against Madame Seera. What if he was merely providing salacious slander for the audience of a magazine that appealed to men who liked to think of themselves as modern? Or was this Madame Seera an imposter? Or perhaps, as happened with other famous seers, Madame Seera began with talent and ended with a hustle.

Miller's reputation was not entirely spotless either. In the 1988 *Letters to Hereward Carrington from Famous Psychical Researchers* is found this note from the famous magician Harry Kellar in 1911: "C.V. Miller was a celebrated materializing medium several times exposed in fraud. I knew him well."

In 1910 the U.K. journal *Light* published a letter in which Willy figured prominently.

We had the pleasure of a visit on February 1 from Professor Willy Reichel, the well-known occultist and traveler; who told that he was awaiting the arrival of Mr. Charles Bailey, the medium of apports, from Melbourne, Australia, in order to introduce him to Colonel de Rochas and a committee of scientific men sitting at the School of Medicine, Grenoble, France, so that his genuineness might be scientifically proved, and the progress of mankind thereby advanced. Professor Reichel had assumed all the expenses, which were considerable, because Bailey never travels without a companion.

We cannot, of course, anticipate the report of Colonel de Rochas and the committee, but we regret to learn from Professor Reichel that Bailey resorted to artifices at the sittings, which is all the more deplorable, because, judging from the published reports of his test séances in Australia, genuine phenomena have occurred in his presence. As soon as the report appears we shall return to the subject.

On Tuesday last, Bailey called at this office to receive the money left for him by Professor Reichel for his return passage to Australia, and said that the committee at Grenoble had had as much success as they deserved. In a letter to Professor Reichel, Bailey threatens legal proceedings, although the Professor had paid all the expenses connected with his journey to Grenoble (amounting to over 200 pounds).

In a letter which we have received from Colonel de Rochas, that gentleman informs us that the two birds which were produced at the recent sitting as being brought from India were purchased in Grenoble by Bailey—they were identified by the bird-seller, who also identified Bailey as the purchaser, and that at a subsequent meeting Bailey refused to submit to a test search and to give further sittings.

Professor Reichel assures us that he is confident that the phenomena produced through Bailey at Mr. Stanford's circles in Melbourne were genuine, and that this bitter experience is another illustration of the fact that even otherwise reliable mediums sometimes "help out" the phenomena when their powers become weak.

As president of the National Association of Spiritualists in New Zealand I believe it is my duty to acquaint the public with the result of Bailey's visit to France. I have persistently contended that at the séances held in Wellington last year Bailey was not "proved" fraudulent; that here was no evidence worthy of credence, and in the face of fierce denunciation I held to this. In the public press I have given as my opinion that Bailey was no angel—he was known to be erratic, I will not say eccentric, in his everyday life.

When he left New Zealand I wrote to Professor Reichel and urged him to take every precaution so that Spiritualists might have the truth, even if Bailey had to stand down. The result is before us. And yet I cannot believe that for so many years, under the stringent conditions imposed upon Bailey at Melbourne and elsewhere, he hoodwinked those who sat with him. The Italian medium, Eusapia Palladino, tried to use a little artifice among the scientists she was sitting with, but this was discovered and the tests were made much more stringent. For thirteen years the London Society of Psychical Research shelved her, yet she went on astounding and convincing one scientific skeptic after another. And now the above society endorses her surprising manifestations of power as genuine. It may be so yet with Bailey. (Nation 1910)

The letter continues to say that the author, W. C. Nation, can't defend Bailey but he reminds his readers that Christianity, and every other institution, are not dismissed outright because of their prominent frauds.

This wasn't Bailey's only brush with disrepute. In the May issue of the *Open Court* appeared "The Ghost of a Living Person" which revealed that "A Melbourne medium, Charles Bailey, claimed to be controlled by the late Rev. W. H. Withrow while that gentleman was actually living in Toronto" (Carus 1909). The article was written by Paul Carus, a German American philosopher much influenced by Spinoza. A prolific author, Carus worked to blend not only religion and science, but Christianity and Buddhism, receiving criticism for not adhering to the rules. Before the wave of recent books about Satanism an American edition of Carus's *The History of the Devil* added an intimidating note to the shelves of many a spiritual rebel in the late 1970s and 1980s. The black, red, and white cover featured Baphomet as the title character. Though often chosen as a frightening representation of Satan, goat-headed Baphomet is a symbolical illustration by Eliphas Levi, which has more to do with Pan than the devil.

In the list near the end of his book of all the things Willy likes about America he includes "the very influential position of women." A striking feature of Willy's occult travelogue is his open-mindedness about the relevance of female sources of knowledge. Like the Theosophists to whom he refers, female authority in matters of wisdom was comfortable for Willy. But this liberal atmosphere was about to change radically. By the 1920s Houdini and other magicians, along with journalists, were attacking Spiritualism not only as a fraud but also as a negative social force undermining the masculine prerogative.

As Fred Nadis (2005) wrote in "If Not Spirits What Is It?":

The efforts of Houdini and other stage magicians to either replicate Spiritualist effects or unmask them also had a misogynistic aspect, in keeping with fears of the "effeminization" of daily life in the progressive era. Mediums tended to be women, and their workplaces often were their home parlors, the only place of power that society accorded them. The press depicted the typical Spiritualist society member as female, past her prime and laughable. An 1893 cartoon featuring Maskelyne [a prominent rival of Houdini] shows him in one corner strangling a serpent labeled "humbug" with the subtitle: *He is rough on Spiritualists.* Further down some matronly women surround the conjurer above the caption: *The Ladies of the Spiritualistic Societies Will Persist in Claiming Him as One of Their Own.* One of the matrons says, "Why should you not own that you are a medium?" As in this cartoon, journalists tended to treat stage magicians as virile, top-hatted gentlemen while depicting Spiritualists as matronly, superstitious women—or effeminate men—prone to "intuitions" and to romantic but wrong-headed views of the world.

We don't know what became of Willy Reichel. If he lived to see World War I it must have been very difficult for someone who loved to travel and experience other cultures, and who understood the treasures of nature and culture that were being destroyed.

In his introductory notes for the 1975 Running Press reprint of Willy's book, Colin Wilson wrote: "If all Reichel says is true then spiritualism is very important. It should have forced science to completely reverse its foundations. Instead, for the most part, scientists sat tight and insisted that the occult explosion was all a lot of nonsense and would soon blow over."

Wilson denied that *An Occultist's Travels* is "a collection of inexplicable absurdities." But his half-hearted introduction raises more questions than it answers. Wilson points out that it should be easy enough for some researcher to look up the newspapers Willy mentions, but no one ever did. Wilson's endorsement rings hollow as he wonders about the connection between mediumship and hysteria. Reichel never appeared in Wilson's own works on the occult.

But Reichel's value is not only in the evidence he wishes he could provide for the reality of the mysterious phenomena he described. His travelogue of turn-of-the-century America reveals not only a lost world of occult enigmas but also lost natural beauty. His book is stark proof of the enormity of the impact of our ever-growing population and unbridled industrialization. Wonders that had existed for thousands of years disappeared in mere decades. Reichel witnessed history—from the San Francisco earthquake to the European colonies in China, he provided a quirky diary of a journey through a world that was changing more rapidly than anyone could imagine, with two world wars just ahead.

14

Pagan Christianity of the Early Twentieth Century

THEY WERE THE GRANDSONS of Frances Wright, "the Red Harlot." Their good Episcopalian mother tried to protect them from the fearsome inheritance of her infamous mother. But they expressed aspects of their grandmother's revolutionary spirit in their own ways.

Christianity remains the most acceptable, best known, and officially sanctioned religion in America. Yet, as we have seen, American Metaphysical Religion has intersected, and in many ways transformed, Christian belief and practice. The brothers Guthrie are an example of the tension in this dichotomy. Both were Episcopalian ministers in New York City, but both had deep interest in non-Christian culture, including European paganism.

The elder brother, William, integrated Indigenous American, Hindu, pagan, and other spiritual traditions in his liturgies and services at an iconic church in New York City. He also pioneered color concert lighting. He presented events with Kahlil Gibran and Isadora Duncan, in a church where Allen Ginsberg and Patti Smith would later perform.

The younger brother, Kenneth, self-published many books about Neoplatonism and also the first translation into English of the Mayan *Popul Vuh*. But neither brother considered themselves anything but Christian, although in earlier eras of Protestant and Catholic governance they would have certainly been persecuted as heretics if not outright pagans.

A THRILL AND A THROB

According to the Interstate Lecture Bureau Company brochure about William, "Mr. Guthrie is a man of splendid appearance, magnificent physique, and extraordinary physical vigor which makes him drive his speech like a steam engine. He never does anything meekly, or perhaps even mildly, and does all forcibly." A quote from the *New York Times* praises his "fascinating lecture on William Blake" and he seems to have left the *Memphis Appeal* with a case of the vapors: "He is not only a profound scholar, but he is strikingly original. Moreover, his personal magnetism is extraordinary," or as William himself wrote about an ideal religious service, "a-thrill and a throb with spiritual conviction" (Alofsin 2019).

William was born in Scotland in 1868. As we have seen, his grandmother was perhaps the first famous feminist and female abolitionist in America. In 1886 the eighteen-year-old William began studying at University of the South, the Episcopal college and seminary in Sewanee, Tennessee. He edited the undergrad literary magazine. In 1891 he got his master's degree, and two years later he was ordained to the priesthood. That year he also married Anna Stuart, a fellow student at Sewanee. Anna had been born in New Orleans in 1869. They would have two daughters, Anna and Phoebe. William taught comparative literature at Sewanee, and then moved to Ohio to teach at the University of Cincinnati and the University of Chicago, serving as assistant rector at nearby churches.

In *Modern Poet Prophets: Essays Critical and Interpretive* (1897) William lingers on Shelley's epic poem *Prometheus Unbound,* and ponders deeply the poetry of Walt Whitman, lamenting that in his earlier writing he dismissed Whitman as someone who had "lost his wits, and never gone in search of them." But now William's respect for Whitman was so great he even compiled a concordance for *Leaves of Grass.* As Tisa L. Wenger (2006) writes in her essay "The Practice of Dance for the Future of Christianity: 'Eurhythmic Worship' in New York's Roaring Twenties," William considered Whitman "'a religious teacher,' a bearer of the 'vital core' of Quakerism's Inner Light, and a poet-prophet who revealed 'the mystic secret of religion.'"

William may have been influenced by Richard Maurice Bucke. A Canadian, Bucke's most influential book, *Cosmic Consciousness*, was published in Philadelphia in 1901, in a limited edition of five hundred oversized books printed on rag paper. As superintendent of an insane asylum Bucke experienced aspects of human consciousness and behavior outside the norm. His biggest inspiration was his friendship with Walt Whitman. They spent the summer of 1880 together at Bucke's home in London, Ontario. Whitman, but also Shakespeare, Balzac, and Dante, among others, led Bucke to the idea of a higher consciousness.

Bucke believed that alleged human powers that seem to flicker infrequently in the long view of history would one day become natural human faculties. He believed that in the future humanity will develop cosmic consciousness. But some human beings might develop different faculties, such as the power to heal, true psychic awareness, or the ability to communicate with the dead. He believed that these would eventually become senses as natural as sight. Bucke (1901) wrote, "This consciousness shows the cosmos to consist not of dead matter governed by unconscious, rigid, and unintending law; it shows it on the contrary as entirely immaterial, entirely spiritual and entirely alive."

Alan Watts, the popular Buddhist, referenced "cosmic consciousness" in his influential 1962 book, *The Joyous Cosmology*, sparking the fascination with cosmic consciousness among hippies, which blossomed into wider awareness with the New Age. Cosmic consciousness has become so popular it has been categorized by writers within their own agendas, not to mention being dismissed by some scientists as a symptom of brain disorder. However, this state of consciousness has been described throughout history, and all over the world, from yogis to Buddhist masters, from the Platonists of ancient Greece to the ancient Chinese *Secret of the Golden Flower.*

Bucke viewed Whitman as his ultimate example of cosmic consciousness. He believed that Whitman's masterpiece *Leaves of Grass* captured it better than any other literature. With only five hundred available copies, we don't know whether William Guthrie read *Cosmic Consciousness* or not, but he certainly agreed with Bucke's enthusiasm for Whitman.

From 1903 to 1908 William served as rector of a church in sunny Alameda, California. But in 1908 he returned to the University of the South to teach literature. He hired Frank Lloyd Wright to build him a home in Tennessee. But then William decided against teaching and building, at least in Tennessee. He had a new career: rector of St. Mark's Church in New York City.

St. Mark's in the Bowery Church was built in 1799 on what had been the farm of the last Dutch governor-general in America. The second church built in New York City, and the oldest in continuous operation, it had once been the place of worship for Manhattan's wealthy white Protestants. But as the rich folk moved to the north of the island the parish became a neighborhood of immigrants. The newly arrived Jewish, Russian Orthodox, and Italian Catholic families had little use for an Episcopalian church. In 1911 the vestry invited William to become rector. His first response to St. Mark's was a remark about the surrounding buildings, which were in "shocking condition . . . tenanted by Industrial Workers of the World, Bolshevist presses and other nuisances." He talked the vestry into buying the buildings. He wanted writers and artists to move in. "In a spiritual account of this downtown parish," William wrote, "one should not forget the constant pressure exerted by a neighborhood wholly alien." Since rent was affordable in the area, writers and artists began moving in. Three years later William wrote Frank Lloyd Wright this candid appraisal of his opportunity and predicament: "To do anything in St. Mark's meant to become an ecclesiastical outlaw. I couldn't be elected to a rat-hole anywhere else" (Wegner 2006).

In 1915 William celebrated the first of many annual "Indian Day" events at St. Mark's. Wenger (2006) writes: "These special services involved prayers and responsive readings drawn from translations of various Indigenous American myths, holy songs, and secret traditions, chiefly from the *Hako* of the Pawnees." Underlining the importance of American tribes for his work, William purchased sculptures of two chiefs, titled *Aspiration* and *Inspiration,* to flank the church doors, thereby framing the entrance to the physical space of the church with an artist's rendering of native figures." These sculptures were the last works of Solon Burglum, installed posthumously. Solon, who trained in Paris, founded the American School of Sculpture in New York City.

At the St. Nicholastide festivals between 1915 and 1920, William staged "The Ritual Dance of the Zuni Corn-Maidens" based on actual Zuni ritual. In May 1924 a Mohawk dancer led the congregation outdoors where five young women danced in "flowing Grecian costumes" to the beat of his tom-tom drum. This William called "the ceremonial sacred dance of the Planting of the Seven Varieties of Corn."

William's books of poetry and literary studies earned him an honorary doctorate from Sewanee in 1915. His literary interests strayed into many areas unusual for a minister of any Christian denomination. *Uncle Sam and Old World Conquerors* (1915) boasts a character with the racist epithet Sambo Hilarious, hailed on page 1 as "the dark Osiris." A year later William's interest in ancient Egyptian religion produced *The Gospel of Osiris,* which includes this invocation that must have been rather surprising to less eclectic Episcopalians:

> *As a lion he croucheth,*
> *To spring and roar in glory*
> *Upon Bakha, the mount of sunrise,*
> *Between twin turquoise sycamores:*
> *Hail Heru! the lion of God.*

Leaves of the Greater Bible (1917) includes Shelley's *Ode to the Skylark,* Ankhenaten's *Hymn to Aton,* selections from the Buddhist classic *Dhammapada,* and a paraphrased Navaho blessing, but the Neoplatonists and even Plato himself are notably absent from this collection of gospel friendly spiritual classics, except for a footnote about three Hymns to Zeus that William refers to as "the so-called Orphic (neo-Platonic?)." In May 1917 William's "Service of Patriotic Dedication" featured the names of men killed in World War I.

In 1918 William installed in the churchyard *The Little Lady of the Dew,* a fountain that apparently featured a nude sculpture by Solon Borglum. The fountain may still be there, but if so the nude was removed, leaving only corrosion like a shadow. Those who insisted on seeing something sinful in this chaste beauty inspired by the "Venus in the garden of the Palace of the Popes in Avignon" William dismissed as "filthy minded."

While *The Religion of Old Glory* (1919) is firmly in the tradition of American Metaphysical Religion books fetishizing the flag and other symbols, it avoids the preoccupation with secret societies or mystical initiates by embracing a wide-ranging, mostly free association of a variety of mythological traditions including the Homeric, Hindu, and Hopi. At times the writing is reminiscent of Joseph Campbell.

In 1921 William wrote that afternoon services at St. Mark's would feature consideration of "Vedantism, Parseeism, Bahaism, Buddhism, Taoism, Confucianism, Shintoism, ancient Roman religion, ancient Greek religion, Chaldean religion, Egyptian religion, Mithraism, etc." (Wegner 2006).

Though William respected the spirituality of other cultures, he was quite clear about the superiority of his own. He liked to include Shakespeare in his liturgies as what he called a "racial scripture"—"the most important thing we can do for the preservation of our race character. When America is being submerged with foreigners and their ways tend to supplant our way, it is our duty to see that they become acquainted with our ways so that they may be preserved as racially superior" (Wegner 2006). Despite his appreciation for other cultures, William was a racist. He spoke candidly of "Americanizing our incoming Polish citizenship." When he granted the petition of a group of Polish Catholics to use as their church one of the buildings owned by the vestry he insisted they use the Episcopal Prayer Book.

Despite believing in the superiority of Christianity, William did not support missions. He called them "Caeserism in disguise . . . pioneering for trade, creating demands for wares, disturbing the religions of the countries where we went. This scaring or bullying or bribing the world into attempting to 'Westernize,' 'Europeanize,' 'Americanize,' doesn't look to me like the work of Christ" (Wegner 2006). He thought the best result of Christian missions to foreign nations was the growing interest Christian nations were finding in other faiths. By finding spirituality in another religion, Americans "might be Christianized via the Buddha and Lao-Tse."

BARE LEGS, BARE KNEES, AND BARE HIPS

William was influenced by, and helped influence, the American Pageantry movement, which from 1910 to 1917 was so popular historians call it a craze. Historical occasions, or heroic persons, were usually the themes of these dramatic public rituals as celebrations of art, democracy, and spectacle. Entire communities would join together to create something between a modern parade and living theater. Gifted public speakers told the appropriate stirring stories for the occasion. Local businesses, politicians, clubs, and social service organizations promoted themselves, popular performers strutted their stuff, culminating in a costumed carnival parade. The American Pageant Association and the Drama League of America were instrumental in the promotion of the pageants. William spoke at the first Drama League convention. He reminded his listeners "crowds can be managed in both ways, upward and downward" (Glassberg 1990). Pageants could elevate the taste of the masses. He used the principles of pageantry in his church.

At Sarah Farmer's Greenacre community in Maine, William met Mountfort Mills, a practicing Bahá'i. At Greenacre, liberal Christians mingled with Hindus and New Thought leaders in search of a universal religion. Abdu'l-Baha, son of Bahaullah the founding prophet of the Bahá'i faith, directed Mills to join William's church. William confirmed the Bahá'i, who became a member of the vestry of St. Mark's, and one of William's most loyal allies during his rebellion against Bishop Manning, which began with a scandal.

As Wenger (2006) wrote: "The 1922 version of the service began with hymns, Guthrie's recitation of a poem by Henry Adams titled 'Prayer to the Virgin of Chartres,' and a choir performance of an 'anthem on the Annunciation,' composed by the rector himself. The danced portion of the service was titled 'Ritual Dance of the Della Robbia Annunciation.' It featured five Barnard College dance students, young women draped in flowing white robes and illuminated by blue spotlights. Their performance concluded with a pose drawn from the fifteenth-century Italian sculptor Andrea dell Robbia's rendition of the Annunciation, depicted on a plaque hanging behind the dancers."

The trouble started when in 1922 William invited Isadora Duncan to speak at St. Mark's, but Bishop Manning, ultimate authority for the Episcopalians of New York City, ordered William to cancel the engagement. The goal of this dancing was, as William's daughter Phoebe described it in a letter to Ruth St. Denis, the teacher of Martha Graham, "a real sense of religious worship." But local newspapers saw it differently. To them dancing girls in church were dancing girls in church. Headlines sensationalized the story: "Women Faint in Jam in Mystic Service," "Girls Dance under Spotlight at Church." Bishop Manning was "shocked and scandalized." After all, what sort of preacher titles his sermon "The Necessity of Paganism?" William and his vestry were called to the office.

William's troubles with Manning went back to an earlier scuffle. In 1921, his thirteenth year as rector of Trinity Church, the wealthy Episcopalian capital of lower Manhattan, Manning was elected Bishop of New York. Wishing to demonstrate why he thought Manning a bad choice, William organized his parish to provide food and shelter for several hundred homeless men. He suggested they attend Sunday services at Trinity, and that they demand that Trinity follow the good example of St. Mark's. Manning pleaded inadequate facilities. Guthrie accused Trinity of being "lined up with the capitalists instead of with the house of God" (Glassberg 1990). But three years later, one of the leading protestors William sent to Trinity returned to protest at St. Mark's. Apparently William had less interest in the difficult challenge of curing homelessness than he had in challenging Manning.

Who knows where the tension between William and Bishop Manning actually began? Manning went to school at the University of the South in Sewanee; he and William became fellow students in 1888. William was two years ahead of him but they were both undergraduates in 1888 and 1889.

Manning is remembered for organizing a successful battle to block Bertrand Russell's opportunity to teach at the City University of New York. The great British philosopher was denounced as an atheist and an apologist for free love. During the Great Depression Manning put a different wrinkle on William's commitment to spirituality and art, by training local men from the neighborhood to work as artisans for the church.

Manning listened as William described the dancer's full-length robes and personally guaranteed that even their bare feet would be covered. William insisted that St. Mark's needed these innovations to survive, and he believed that Christianity itself must evolve in his direction or lose its relevance to the modern world. William was frank about his reasons for flirting with socialism in his sermons—"people who had never entered the church came often to blaspheme, and in the course of a few months had been sweetened and persuaded to consider the claims of religion" (Glassberg 1990). Like art and dance, a concern for the poor was a way to attract people who otherwise wouldn't be interested in the church. Manning wasn't impressed; he ordered William and his vestry to cease all such nonsense at once. William, supported by his vestry, refused. The only punishment at Manning's disposal was his refusal to visit St. Mark's therefore making it impossible for new members of the church to be received. But St. Mark's wasn't getting new members anyway. However a large audience of appreciative counterculture types could be counted on. William's rebellion against Manning lasted eight years.

This brings us to an interesting moment. We have little information about the relationship of the Guthrie brothers. They didn't reference each other's work in their own numerous publications. Yet Kenneth was a member of the vestry of St. Mark's. On this occasion we get a glimpse of what may have been a cause, or a symptom, of a possibly strained relationship. Kenneth commented, "There is nothing in bare legs, bare knees and bare hips except notoriety" (Wegner 2006). He seems to have projected quite a different scenario than the artistic display emceed by his brother, which he obviously didn't attend. Kenneth, and many others, believed that even a fully clothed young woman dancing in church might as well be a naked pagan. Many churches throughout history have banned dancing and music entirely, considering them expressions of sexuality. Two decades of dance fever had swept up America and Christian crusaders were up in arms about modern dance. Critics refused to accept William's rationale that dance has almost always been a part of sacred ritual.

The *New York Times* reported on one of Guthrie's rituals in 1923. It envisioned crowds of women in religious ecstasy trying to reach an inner sanctum obscured by clouds of incense. Fainting women had to be carried out. A Catholic critic described the "semi-vaudeville" of "barefoot girls," comparing them to the holy rollers and snake dancers of rural Christianity.

No matter how much William argued that the dancing at his church was slow and graceful, not crude, ecstatic, vulgar, or frenzied, reporters preferred to depict their own lurid scenes from their own lurid imaginations. William responded, "The movements of the participants only faintly suggested flesh beneath the long white silken flowing robes, that same suggestion which one receives from Fra Angelico angels moving in the fields of God" (Wegner 2006).

William's daughter Phoebe was a dancer. When Isadora Duncan died in 1927, William held a memorial service, eulogizing her as a genius. William and Phoebe exchanged letters with Ruth St. Denis, and in 1930 Martha Graham performed at St. Mark's the "Adoration Scene" from a fifteenth-century British miracle play called *The Chester Mysteries*.

To William dance was beauty, and the essence of religion. He wrote passionately in defense of dance as a spiritual art form. "The dance is the most inevitable form of expression; it is the human body speaking. The body cannot be denied. An intelligent religion will idealize it. To attempt to ignore it brings disaster. What the world needs is not a frantic faith that will suppress and condemn any normal functioning of the body, for this ends in all sorts of abnormalities" (Wegner 2006).

William derived some of these ideas from the work of G. Stanley Hall, the psychologist who in some ways laid the framework for the masculine sports culture so beloved by many Americans. Hall believed that the nerve force of white men was being drained by the overstimulation of modern society. The cure was sports, a play "savagery" that gives a man the vitality of primitive masculinity. William and Hall, however, believed the result would be a culture of refined men, instead of bullies wearing logos.

Music was as important to William as dance. He compared the well-known melodies of classic hymns to jigs, replacing them with music by

Beethoven and Chopin, among other great composers. In his introduction to Platt's *The Forgotten Books of Eden* (1927), the most popular collection of apocryphal and pseudepigraphal literature until the explosion of gnostic publications in the late twentieth century, William makes this statement that will be dear to the hearts of all musicians suffering in a world that ignores copyrights. "An American Indian's Song is his very own. No other man can sing it without his explicit permission. It is impregnate with his aura. It is not in our sense, however, property. It is believed to invest magically the singer with the mood whence it proceeded, and must, therefore, merge in some way the performer's identity with that of the originator's. To sing another's song is an invasion of his personality, a sort of spiritual piracy involving sacrilege." As for the power of music, he remarks: "When last year in Arcady and Andritzena, I induced primitive shepherds to sing and play for me lustily all sorts of occasional songs and rituals, they refused to do a burial chant, most positively. For to perform one would surely cause a death in the house."

According to the *Message of the East,* a monthly issued by the Vedanta Centre, in 1919: "On the invitation of the rector, Rev. Wm. Norman Guthrie, Swami Paramananda spoke at St. Mark's in-the-Bouwerie, New York, on Sunday, February 9. At the regular Vesper Service which preceded the swami's address, Dr. Guthrie read some Persian poems and prayers in order to lead his hearers gradually Eastward to 'the great land of mystery' as he put it, 'whence the Occident has drawn so much of its inspiration.'"

Then distinguished young Lebanese poet, Kahlil Gibran, read some of his own poems publicly. "After Mr. Gibran concluded," Dr. Guthrie writes in a letter telling of the afternoon,

Swami Paramananda, the founder of the Vedanta Centre of Boston, arose and calmly spoke on the genius of mystic poetry in India, captivating all, even those who may have come with some degree of prejudice against his special message. He struck and held the universal note in an Oriental way, which had been struck in the Church in an Occidental way. The Swami winsomely and sagaciously indicated the great preciousness of the permeating sense of unity, of identity. His uses of typical Indian chants imparted a mystic solemnity to the meeting; and one felt that he had closed the program with a truly Catholic benediction, under the beautiful Della Robbia Annunciation, before which nine candles were lit, in a manner that will make the afternoon ever memorable to all those who had the good fortune to participate. Many of the audience could not leave for half an hour or more, talking in groups and expressing their joy at the rare quality of the occasion, and hoping that at some early opportunity the thrilling experience might be renewed. Hopes were expressed that Swami Paramananda might open up a branch at St. Mark's. (Vedanta Centre 1919)

Paramananda was a student of the sage Ramakrishna.

In 1919 Kahlil Gibran was appointed to the St. Mark's Arts Committee. He read from his yet-to-be-published masterpiece *The Prophet,* his voice echoing in the small church. Other important writers were welcomed as guest speakers. Sunday afternoon stars included multiple Pulitzer Prize–winning poet and Lincoln biographer Carl Sandburg, modernist poet and pediatrician William Carlos Williams, and Pulitzer Prize–winning playwright and poet Edna St. Vincent Millay, one of many outspoken feminists William welcomed to his church.

William might be considered a pioneer of the light shows that became so famous in the 1960s, and then again in the rave and festival cultures. In the June 1922 issue of *Popular Mechanics* (vol. 37, no. 6) a short article titled "Unusual Lighting Effects Produced in Church" reported, "Guthrie, rector, conceived the idea of delivering 'prismatic sermons,' meaning the use of varicolored lights in synchronism with the sermon. Realization of this unusual undertaking required rather elaborate electrical equipment. Fixtures, having lamps of red, blue, green, and amber color, were uniformly distributed throughout the interior, each lamp being so wired that either of the various tints, or a diffusion of two or more of them could be obtained from the switchboard. Clear lamps and spotlights, with special shields that conceal them from the congregation, are also installed in sufficient numbers to provide proper illumination for reading purposes. Favorable comment on the innovation has been plentiful, and it is thought that the same, or a similar course will be followed in other places of worship." Handsome six-foot-tall plus William must have been that much more charismatic in a spotlight.

In March 1923 William's "Sun-God Service" was an ancient Egyptian call-and-response ritual that included these verses: "Hail to thee, beautiful God of every day! Beautiful is thy rising in the horizon of the sky" and "Thou art beautiful to behold, great glistening high above the whole earth–Thou art Ra, the Sun-God." The *New York Times* reported, "green, blue, red, and amber shades played here and there in the church." William in a white spotlight "addressed the ancient god." How did William justify such pagan extravagance? "All these religions must be regarded as preparatory and auxiliary to the highest and most inclusive religion, and therefore capable of contributing to a yet imperfect Christianity . . . so that Christianity may ultimately become the religion of a united world" (Wegner 2006).

In July 1923 William opened the Body and Soul Clinic where physical and spiritual healing would be combined. Dr. Edward Cowles, a psychiatrist practicing in Manhattan, was director of the clinic and its six physicians. William and his group of ministers attended to the souls of the patients. Two thousand people were treated in the first three months. Most suffered nervous disorders. The clinic claimed 90 percent of the patients were healed. Treatment began with a physical examination, followed by an interview to establish mental health issues, and then the ministers provided spiritual advice and meditations. Phobias may have been the principal illness treated, but many children, too poor for other doctors, received their first medical attention at the clinic. In 1932 the vestry, in the throes of the Great Depression, disappointed William, ordering him to close the clinic. The clinic stayed open anyway, forcing the vestry to lock the church doors.

Wanting to generate more income for his church in a neighborhood rapidly declining, in 1930 William had to choose between launching a million-dollar endowment campaign during the Great Depression or constructing an apartment building on church land. Getting his friend Frank Lloyd Wright on the job wouldn't be easy. William pointed out that Wright was arrogant in meetings and had less experience with skyscrapers than many equally pedigreed New York City architects. Wright agreed with William's list of his faults but insisted he alone could really bring a great building to life. Wright provided some of his more impressive achievements as evidence of his superior art. Guthrie wanted a simple sketch for $150. Wright wanted $7,500 to provide finished plans right down to the cost breakdowns.

William wrote to Wright: "You always play solitaire. That's our difficulty.... Only genius condescending to magic can save us—coercing, bamboozling them with pictures. That you can't give them.... All they want is a picture that 'gets' them. They need an idol—an outside.... And you want to develop a perfectly realizable organic plan. O dear theorist—you talk as a Moses just back from Sinai. What they want is a Peter Pan" (Hoffman 1998).

On Christmas day Wright began drawing St. Mark Towers, a skyscraper apartment block: three octagonal towers with alternating vertical and horizontal facades, with cantilevered floors and hung exteriors of copper and glass, two fourteen stories and one eighteen stories high. "I believe the relationship between the old church and the modern prismatic building," Wright wrote, "would be extremely agreeable." Wide open windows on the city. Copper fins would reflect light in ever-changing patterns while slowly turning a pleasing green. Residents would stroll through a leafy park on their way home to light-filled duplex apartments with double-height windows. "The building increases substantially in area from floor to floor," Wright explained, "as the structure rises—in order that the glass frontage of each story may drip clear of the one below, the building, thus, cleaning itself" (Wright 2010). He would build the towers one at a time, the first would finance the second, and so on, until the old stone church would be surrounded by three towers of light.

A real estate lawyer blocked the towers. Since so much of the architecture had no precedent, accurate cost projections based on similar buildings were impossible. Wright lamented, "When I first started my day-dreaming, it was because I believed so deeply in beauty." Guthrie wrote back to Wright: "The more I think of the tower, the more convinced I am that it should not be in the city at all, but in a grove of trees full of brown thrashers or mockingbirds. Being open to a friendly world is one thing, and being in our style world, in which one seeks refuge is another. . . . You ridicule the cave, but I suspect that in Manhattan each has to have a cave in which he can escape sight and sound and the new detective systems by which privacy is abolished, and one dreams of a primal cave." Wright's response: "You yourself do not know yet what the thing is all about. You've been poisoned by the New York atmosphere" (2010). A modified version of the design was eventually built in Bartlesville, Oklahoma, as the Price Tower.

Later William asked Wright to design a "colossal interfaith cathedral," actually nine large cathedrals and several smaller chapels, a monument to religious toleration, but also a shopping mall of spiritual traditions. Wright knew it wouldn't be built but he drew up some plans anyway. The huge structure, part pyramid, part beehive, had a hexagonal base and reached into the sky twice the height of the Eiffel Tower in Paris. This "temple of temples" was designed to uplift the spirits of a million people at a time.

Wright could never think of William "otherwise than in a fervor over some quest, spiritual or aesthetic." He reported being lectured by William on the philosophy and functions of ancient Greek temples. William told Wright that his mission was "reconstruction of religious expression to make religion again sincerely possible." Song, dance, sounds, color, processions were the new rituals of his church. He once wrote Wright, "I've planned out so many new rituals my choirmaster is having a picnic" (Hoffman 1998). William never built any of the designs he commissioned from Wright, but the designs were usually adapted and used in future projects.

In 1932 most of the vestry members changed their mind about William. They accused him of mismanagement and demanded that he clear any future expenses before planning his events. A month later William called for the election of a new vestry. He nominated his own supporters, and since he decided who could vote, not surprisingly they won. Eventually New York Supreme Court ruled that as rector William was within his rights. But the last five years of services weren't as extravagant or as popular.

In the mid-1930s Phoebe took the St. Mark's dance group on a tour of Protestant churches and the old Chautauqua circuit. The seeds Guthrie and Phoebe planted grew until in 1955 the Sacred Dance Guild proved that Protestant and Catholic churches had arrived at the realization that dance had a place in their services.

In the "Private Lives" section of the June 28, 1937, issue of *Life* magazine (which contains a surprising amount of female nudity) William's distinguished profile appears alongside W. C. Fields. Fields lost a court case for not paying a doctor. The judge ruled whiskey, not the doctor, caused his bad health. There's also a story about Leni Riefenstahl at a party in Berlin. Goebbels accused her of having non-Aryan grandparents.

William's *Life* magazine entry reads: "The Rev. Dr. William Norman Guthrie plans to retire as rector of Manhattan's Episcopal Church of St. Mark's-in-the-Bouwerie before September. In his 26 years he has made his church a centre of controversy by sponsoring eurythmic dances, inviting in unorthodox lecturers like Helen Menken and the late Amy Lowell. In 1924, Bishop Manning cut his church off from Episcopal visitation." Austrian occultist and innovator of arts and sciences Rudolf Steiner invented Eurythmy as a form of sacred dance intended to heal body and soul.

Helen Menken was one of the great ladies of Broadway. After her illustrious career as an actress and producer she became a popular performer on radio. Cofounder and trustee of the American Shakespeare Festival Theater and Academy, Menken was also Humphrey Bogart's first wife. Their marriage only lasted a year and a half—apparently the young Bogart was a mean drunk. In 1927 Menken starred in the American version of *The Captive,* a hit play in Paris, about a woman leaving her abusive husband for another woman. The lesbian theme attracted the wrong kind of attention. When Basil Rathbone forcefully embraced Menken in their steamy scene together the police shut down the show. At night court Menken, wearing handcuffs, found herself standing shoulder to shoulder with Mae West, who had been busted for her production *Sex*. But we are left wondering what was so unorthodox about Helen's lectures.

Cigar chain-smoking queer woman Amy Lowell, American poet and champion of free verse, was on the cover of the March 2, 1925, issue of *Time* magazine, just a few months before she died. The following year she posthumously won the Pulitzer Prize for Poetry. In a letter dated October 21, 1924, Lowell wrote to William to inform him that she could not accept his most recent invitation to lecture because she was preparing for a lecture series in England. She admitted she neither desired nor needed the Christianity of churches but "others do need it." Guthrie should not limit his expression of his theories "within the four walls of a church." She felt she couldn't be the one to help him develop his theories. She admired him, but she didn't agree with him.

William's support of women wasn't superficial. "Later, having cast out from our world of ideals and divine symbols the woman," he wrote, "the Protestant reformers left woman without an adequate spiritual expression, and naturally compelled the unconscious feminization of Christ to meet this need. If we have suffered from an effeminate Christ, it has been because the faithful have not been allowed to express their ideal of womanhood in a normal way by the cult of the Mother of Jesus." Bold language from a Protestant. He sounds like a Catholic convert in that paragraph. But here he sounds like a nineteenth-century American Neoplatonist: "Whatever is beautiful is good. Seize all beauty, the handiwork of God, and find a way to use it for the advantage of the spirit" (Wegner 2006).

In 1937 William finally left St. Mark's. He died December 9, 1944; the Battle of the Bulge began one week later. It must have been depressing for a man who had labored so mightily for communication between cultures and the refinement of religion to see the world at war.

His wife Anna Guthrie died in 1959, the same month that saw the premier of *Plan 9 from Outer Space*. Elvis was in the army. A new world of pop culture was beginning to evolve into the international juggernaut it is today. It would take almost three decades for William's spirit to return to St. Mark's. The eclectic cultural tradition William began was reborn when Allen Ginsberg and friends asked if they could use the church as a place to share their writing, after they lost their local bar in the 1960s.

The church welcomed Allen and his friends by creating the

Poetry Project, which has taught and showcased poets ever since. Sam Shepherd produced his first two plays at St. Mark's. *Mind Garage's Electric Liturgy,* which claims to be the first rock mass ever written, was performed at St. Mark's in 1969. Patti Smith's first public performance took place at St. Mark's in 1971. In 1982 Robert Christgau, Richard Hell, Legs McNeil, and Billy Altman held their "A Tribute to Lester Bangs" at St. Mark's, a memorial for the celebrated rock critic.

Soon after the Poetry Project got off the ground, St. Mark's introduced Danspace, to train choreographers and dancers, while providing a space for performance. St. Mark's doesn't have pews anymore; they would get in the way of the large, open dance floor.

THE LONELIEST NEOPLATONIST

What of William's younger brother Kenneth? Though they had much in common their relationship appears to have been strained, since they never mention each other's works, though they explored similar themes in their writing. As we shall see, Kenneth may have printed snarky remarks regarding his glamorous older brother.

If you prefer Castile soap, you have probably at one time or another used Dr. Bronner's and been bemused by the bottle label with its curious patchwork of urgent messages about everything from Thomas Paine to true faith and religion. That style of communication, packed with information in small print, was also practiced by Dr. Kenneth Sylvan Guthrie, who used it as a sales pitch for his publications on obscure topics.

With a sense of humor bordering on recklessness, occasionally a touch salacious in his overtures to female readers, Kenneth's advertisements provide a striking contrast to his low-profile career as rector of All Saint's Church in New York City. Unfortunately, his vestry and the members of his church never recorded their feelings about their rector's literary hawking of his books on Neoplatonism, the mysteries of Mithras, and Zoroaster.

Kenneth lived during a time of rapid change, in many ways like our own, a resemblance he captures in the first paragraph of *Regeneration: The Gate of Heaven* (1897):

It is hard to realize that during the last hundred years more progress has been made in the arts of civilization than during the many
thousand years since the first anthropoid appeared on the earth.
The marvels of the steam engine, the telegraph, and the printing-
machine are so familiar to the rising generation that they seem
nothing extraordinary. When the thousands of years of the life
of mankind within the light of history, within which so little real
advance was made in scientific research, are considered, it seems little short of a miracle that within a century science should have suddenly arisen, that connection should have been established between
the most remote corners of the globe, and that race, nation, and class
distinctions should suddenly begin to crumble, leaving each man, in
the words of Shelley:

> *Sceptreless, free, uncircumscribed, but man:*
> *Equal, unclassed, tribeless, and nationless,*
> *Exempt from awe, worship, and degree, the king*
> *Over himself; just, gentle, wise: but man.*

Such sentiments may be the reason Kenneth was deposed in 1899,
and that wasn't the only time. Kenneth always reacted by becoming
more devoted to his esoteric studies and practice. Perhaps in reaction to
being deposed he began a journal called the *Prophet* and a secret society
known as Brotherhood of the Eternal Covenant, which involved astrologically timed prayers and the familiar tantric eugenics of the Hermetic
Brotherhood of Luxor. According to Guthrie the Brotherhood taught
regenerative angelic initiation.

For the most part Kenneth's passion for Neoplatonism failed to
inspire the response he hoped for. He published *Numenius of Apamea:
The Father of Neoplatonism* in 1917, the year the last tsar of Russia abdi-
cated his throne, and World War I horrified people all over the world
with the destructiveness of tanks, trench warfare, and poison gas. On
the copyright page the author provided his bio as nothing more than
an academic resume. But eight years later in his introduction to his
translation of Proclus, Guthrie gave a much more detailed biography.

The first paragraph is one line providing his place and date of birth. The next long paragraph he devoted to "his maternal grandmother, Frances Wright of Dundee." He lists her literary achievements, refers to Nashoba, where "she educated slaves, and freed them in Haiti." He considers her "the real pioneer of the Woman's Rights movement, and is so recognized in *Appleton's Encyclopedia*."

Kenneth writes about his grandfather, "Casimir Silvain Phiquepal d'Arusmont, a noble French emigre. . . . He was a philosopher and scientist, and invented the since then so popular tonic sol-fa system. The married pair then went to Paris where was born their daughter Frances Sylva. But Frances Wright returned to the United States to her lecturing, and published her still continually reprinted *A Few Days in Athens*."

Now Kenneth presents his academic credentials, which are formidable. "Being born too late in his family's fortunes to be given an education, he earned one, taking his M.A. in 1890 in Theology at Sewanee; his Ph.D. in 1893 at Tulane; A.M. Harvard, 1894; M.D., with three gold medals, 1904; Marburg and Jena, 1911; Ph.D., Columbia, 1915; Professor in Extension, Sewanee, in 1912."

Kenneth next turns his family into a sales pitch. Frances Sylva, mother of the Guthrie brothers, converted to Catholicism in the cathedral of Notre Dame. She made certain her sons would become ministers, but in the Episcopalian church, because she considered it the most liberal. Thanks to his mother, Kenneth wrote four books suitable for less adventurous Christian readers.

His grandmother Frances had married a man who studied the Neoplatonists, and so, "his grandfather's philosophical and educational interests resulted in his monumental opening to the world in translations of Plotinus, Numenius, Pythagoras and Zoroaster."

Frances Wright's inspired "literary taste produced" three books. "Her quest for truth originated" four more. "Her crusades against abuses continued in" two more books. "Her sociologic ideals matured in his *Complete Progressive Education, A Romance of Two Centuries*, etc." Kenneth resorts to a fatigued etcetera at the end of the list of books inspired by his family tree.

The biography ends with a melancholy confession. "But the very unusual breadth of his conflicting interests checkmated his career, so far as worldly advancement. Little understood or recognized, he had to find consolation in earning his living honestly by teaching a language to children, by pouring out his religious experiences to the few who visited his semi-deserted East Side church, and in putting the accumulated results of his studies in such shape that, to the greater glory of God, they may be of service to humanity, if possible through his children."

This sentimental introduction lacks Kenneth Guthrie's usual optimistic fervor. His candor is surprising; he doesn't hide his nostalgia, sadness, or bitterness. His appeal to his grandparents, and his listless list of works is weak tea compared to the boisterous hard sell of his appeal to the browsing reader in the front and back pages of his self-published books. But readers are left wondering why Kenneth didn't mention his older brother, William, a controversial yet respected minister, and a popular lecturer and author.

Despite his many publications, Kenneth has for the most part escaped the historical record, at least compared to his better-documented brother William. A few references in church records give glimpses of his course. "Rev. Kenneth Sylvan Guthrie, PhD, Priest, has been deposed by the Bishop of Pennsylvania for causes not affecting his moral character." What those causes were remains mysterious but it may have had something to do with Kenneth's visit to the commune of Hiram Butler.

Kenneth traveled to California to spend close to a month on Butler's commune. He respected Butler. He put in writing his recollection of weeping and being consoled by Butler, whom he considered gifted. Unfortunately, the commune did not live up to Butler, at least in Kenneth's estimation. Disappointed, he returned to the East Coast where he practiced Butler's regenerative philosophy for the rest of his life, never calling it by name in his work. Butler's theory of regeneration included the practice of seminal retention, so Kenneth is another example of the American fascination with mixing metaphysics with sexuality.

In 1900 Kenneth published *Regeneration Applied*. In the preface he apologizes to the subscribers of the *Prophet,* complaining that he had to do all the work himself, including the typesetting; "it has been a weary wait," he wrote, "wearier than for the subscribers." Then he brushes off potential requests for refunds asking that any dissatisfied customers pray for him. The book covers much of the same territory as the famous Yogi Ramacharaka books, but whereas those are succinct and intended for practical application, Kenneth's book is wordy, providing a brisk but bewildering collection of details most readers would find daunting.

In his book *In the Presence of God* (1904) Guthrie writes with prophetic pathos: "The road is hard and steep. The hills grow bolder, as it were, and O, the level reaches are so rare! Always another valley, and never the summit yet! Forests to the right, and forests to the left, and never yet one glimpse of that white Temple far above. The stones, oh, how they hurt! Mud, mud at every step, and yet at every splash I must proceed, while still the light of day will last." He wrote that at age thirty-five but it described the career as an author he was doomed to lead another thirty-four years. His work never won the popularity or the academic acceptance he hoped for.

Kenneth authored the first English translation of the *Popul Vuh,* the famous Mayan *Book of the People,* which appeared in the American Theosophical Society magazine the *Word* in serial form from 1906 to 1907. Unfortunately, his translation suffers from its florid scriptural language. By then both the *Prophet* journal and the Brotherhood secret society were no more.

Kenneth was a priest in New Jersey when he was deposed again in 1908, perhaps in reaction to his work on Mayan religion, more evidence of his religious extremism. Kenneth taught German and French for one term at South Brooklyn Evening High School in 1909–10, and in other high schools for three more years. Then, as the Bishop's Diary, 1912–1913 section of the *Journal of the Proceedings of the Annual Convention, Episcopal Church, Diocese of Harrisburg* notes, the day after Christmas the bishop "received notice that the sentence upon Kenneth Sylvan Guthrie had been terminated by the Bishop of Pennsylvania." Was this related to the issues that caused him to be deposed in 1891? In the *Journal of the One Hundred and Thirty-First Convention of the Diocese of New York A.D. 1914,* Kenneth is listed as a warden of his brother William's church. A year later he became rector of All Saint's Church.

In 1919 Kenneth published *A Romance of Two Centuries: A Tale of the Year 2025* featuring a narrator who is reanimated by scientists. Clothing designers take note, here is Kenneth's description of the fashions of 2025: "The loose trousers were buttoned on to a vest, to which were also buttoned soft collars and cuffs, and the artist's cravat. The outer coat was double-breasted, each flap being buttoned under the opposite arm . . . starch had disappeared, as both ruinous to materials, and wasteful of human labor. Pressing, also was tabooed, as were pleats, ruffles, and flounces."

In the kitchen of the future, men were expected to cook alongside women. Sickness is regarded as disreputable incompetence, proof of negligence and lack of judgment. Kenneth describes "a life-card, which I was to retain permanently, which bore all permanent identification data. My photograph was affixed." Names of the future, which would include information like birth dates, would be based on the code invented by Sir Francis Bacon. Banks were abolished because in the past "if the bank failed, the manager only had to hang up a sign that payments were suspended, and policemen drove the unfortunate depositors out in the street to whistle for their money, till they got tired." In 2025 churches have gone the way of banks, not because religion no longer exists, but because like banks, churches tended to serve their own interests instead of the public good.

Kenneth was another in the long line of American Metaphysical Religion oriented independent scholars who believed that Sir Francis Bacon not only authored the Shakespeare plays, but he included in them messages to be decoded for the future. Kenneth also wrote an odd little book on Rosicrucianism: *Rosicrucian Mysteries: Playlets.*

Perhaps Kenneth's most successful work has turned out to be his *Pythagoras: Source Book and Library* (1920), about which David Fideler wrote, "Guthrie's edition contained his own translations of ancient Greek writings in addition to edited versions of writings initially translated by Thomas Taylor." In 1986 Fideler edited and published with his Phanes Press a popular and respected expanded edition under the title *The Pythagorean Sourcebook and Library.*

In 1921 *The Living Church* printed an investigation of the slave gallery in what was by then a "venerable but little known Church," reporting that Episcopalians had been expected to convert or maintain the Christian faith of their slaves. The articles were based on interviews with Kenneth. In 1924 the 100th anniversary of the church, under Kenneth's leadership his congregation presented a pageant remembering the slave gallery. Sometime in the 1930s Kenneth opened an Abraham Lincoln Museum, with an iron shackle and a bill of sale from the days when the church had been a slave market.

Kenneth also directed the Netherlands Art Museum of All Saint's, commemorating the early Dutch colony in New York. He preserved the original organ of the church, the only remaining window in New York dating to colonial times, and the only surviving "three Decker chancel," a piece of furniture that provided a reading desk for the church's clerk, a high pulpit for the rector, and a small altar.

One of Kenneth's books was inspired by a dream a stranger had. Kenneth wrote:

> How was I led to resurrect Proclus? On the 21st of May 1924 I was visited by a California miner, Mr. Emil Verch, who though ignorant of Greek, and of even who Proclus was, had visions of a sage giving that name lecturing and demonstrating theorems in an unknown tongue. When I had explained who Proclus was he besought me to restore these inaccessible treasures to humanity by an English edition. I showed him the ponderousness of the undertaking; which indeed I was fortunately in a position to carry out so far as texts went; but as I have to earn my living would he supply the money? Willingly, if he had had the means; but he was working as a sailor just then. Still, wouldn't I do something for Proclus, anyway? As my whole life has been devoted to just this, making accessible to the public the neglected treasures of Neo-platonism, I tightened my already tight belt by one notch and gathered in one volume everything that was not ponderous or already in print, so as to give the reader a master-key to the situation. (Guthrie 1925)

In 2013 Kenneth's pebble-grained cloth-boards bound typewritten manuscript of *Angelic Mysteries of the Nine Heavens: A Drama of Interior*

Initiation (1926) was offered for sale at $1,250. The ink and pencil corrections and annotations are in the author's own hand. *Angelic Mysteries* is not a John Dee–style exposition of angelic arcana, instead Kenneth offers an allegorical poetic dialogue, of awkward rhythms and rhymes, teaching a blend of spiritual beliefs and practices drawn from many different religions, and combined into a practical course on self-enlightenment and healing that can only be described as American Metaphysical Religion. Kenneth himself describes it as "embodying Dionysius the Areopagite's nine-fold celestial hierarchy, a vision of judgment and heaven, an evocation of the historic lawgivers, the reincarnatory career of a famous soul, a passage through hell, purgatory & heaven and the mystery of the twenty-four elders."

Kenneth's books were published by his own Platonist Press, a name perhaps inspired by Thomas Johnson's earlier periodical the *Platonist*. The press also published several books by Thomas Kip Turvey Jr., including *The Conservation of Your Vitality: Explained Physically, Mentally, Spiritually* (1926) a thirty-page booklet, and the sixty-four-page *Temple Doors Revealed: An Anthology of Advanced Experimental Religion* (1929).

In personal correspondence of 2021 used by his permission, Matt Marble writes:

> Using the name "Thomas Kip Turvey Jr.," I was able to track down a library bound copy of *Temple Doors Revealed*—the "esoteric" and "advanced" writings of Guthrie's experimental religion—one of the few books that is not available online or readily sourced elsewhere. I am certain that Thomas Kip Turvey Jr. is a pseudonym, and (as far as I can tell) so are the following names: Henry Howard Linton and Nathan Dranald Palleyn (there's no trace of them anywhere but in Guthrie's writings). In "Temple Doors Revealed" I found one reference to the Turvey family. Mr. Thomas Turvey (Sr.) was a piano teacher and personal friend ostensibly to Guthrie—there is no mention of Turvey Jr. or Turvey-Jr-as-author's relation to Turvey Sr.—so odd! Why the use of pseudonyms I wonder? An attempt to evade his own name for sales? It's really strange how he does that but then writes explicitly, autobiographically "a la Guthrie."

In this very book, allegedly authored by Turvey Jr., there is also the most extensive autobiography of Guthrie I have found, with detailed reflections on his spiritual experiences/influences and family. For example, he was a member of the Scottish Rite (Mason of the 32nd degree). He was a member of the Theosophical Society— friends with Harold Percival editor of the Theosophical journal *The Word,* Harold also wrote the metaphysical classic *Thinking and Destiny*—but rejected their invitation for him to join the Theosophical Society's Esoteric Section. He rejected them because he felt his own esoteric perspective to be "under appreciated." Percival also listed the personal encounters he had with diverse world faith leaders, including Jainist Virchand R. Gandhi, Swamis Saradananda and Abhedananda, as well as leaders in Martinism, Buddhism, and Quietism. He also documented his drug-induced religious experiences (e.g., chloroform, ether, laughing gas), and actively recruited others to submit their own experiential entheogenic reports.

In his one volume *Plotinus: Rearranged Chronologically Complete Translation with Concordance, and Studies, Showing Origin Development and Influence* Kenneth inexplicably includes a page of ads that undermine the dignity of the work he considers so worthy of respect. Here is an example.

SPICY SITUATIONS, and
Dr. Kenneth Guthrie's REMEDIES

The Board of Education's Examiner had just turned down the blushing Miss Teacher Candidate, Weeping, she wailed. Is there no hope at all for me? Oh, yes, purred he. Try again next year! What could I study in the meanwhile? Dr. Guthrie's "TEACHERS PROBLEMS & HOW TO SOLVE THEM. $1.25." Value and Limits of the History of Education, and "The Mother-Tongue Method of Teaching Modern Languages," each 30 cents. Will that pass me? Really, Miss you are too pretty to teach school. Get his Progressive Complete Education, or Marriages as the Supreme School of Life, $1.25. And if I pass examination on it? Then I will marry you. "Thanks, kind sir!"

Like today's hard-sell network marketers of self-help spirituality, Kenneth knew he had to appeal to the personal predicaments and identifications of his potential readers. The dense page full of type is divided by eye-catching headlines. Apparently teachers were still a good market for the Platonically inclined, as they had been during the glory days of the Plato Club. Next up are pessimists who can learn to become optimists, though the example given is a theological student who meets with a bishop who recommends Kenneth as the "wizard" who can "send you Zoroaster teacher of purity and angels," followed by a list that includes Plotinus, Proclus, Pythagoras, Apollonius, and other luminaries of the Platonic tradition.

The next headline: "This is what occurred at the Masonic Club after last night's Lodge-Meeting." The Master Mason recommends to a new recruit several books by Guthrie including *The Modernized Mithraic Mysteries,* and books on the Rosicrucians and Shakespeare. Next comes this surreal headline: "Savanarola's Ghost met Giordano Bruno's, still reeling from the fire's agony." Strangely Savanarola, who burned books in the Bonfire of the Vanities, comforts Bruno, offering him several mystical publications by Guthrie.

The last headline, "A Fundamentalist-Modernist Fracas," tells the story of a recent railroad wreck where "the renowned Fundamentalist Rev. U. Cheatem" wound up "cheek to jowl" with "the Modernist Rev. I. Catchem of St. Shark's-in-the-Mill-pond." The latter could be a reference to Kenneth's brother William and his church St. Mark's of the Bowery. Cheatem and Catchem exchange secrets for managing their flocks. For Fundamentalists Guthrie suggests his *Romance of Two Centuries* to keep the flock distracted, and *Of the Presence of God* is among the titles suggested for Modernists, who by cribbing notes can make themselves popular experts.

The ad concludes: "Pray? That was the only point where Fundamentalist and Modernist agreed: Let us prey on the PLATONIST PRESS, Teocalli, 1177 Warburton Ave. No. Yonkers, NY."

What was Kenneth hoping to accomplish with these lampoons? He complained bitterly about being ignored by academia yet he indulged in jokes that had the whiff of snake oil. Despite his comedic interludes

Kenneth was a serious author. For example, in *Teacher's Problems* Kenneth provided a "Calendar of Famous Men, for Object Teaching." For each month he gave twenty-eight names.

April was the month of writers and dramatists and May the month of soldiers. June was for wealthy men and July for pioneers. August belonged to the philosophers, including Plato and Hypatia, with Pythagoras on August 1 and Plotinus on the seventh, but Kant, Darwin, and Nietzsche made the list, too.

September was the month of artists, which included composers and musicians. October was for inventors, and November for philanthropists and teachers. December was the month of poets from Homer to *The Ramayana*. January was for statesmen, from Moses to Queen Elizabeth I. February was the month of religious leaders as diverse as the Buddha, Zoroaster, Jakob Böhme, and Mary Baker Eddy. March was the month of scientists. Plutarch, who taught history through character study, may have inspired Guthrie's system. To Plutarch belonged August 4.

For leap years Kenneth provided six intercalary days devoted to prominent women, including Aspasia, the courtesan wife of Pericles of Athens. According to Plato, Aspasia taught Socrates eloquence.

In *Teacher's Problems* Kenneth printed an advertisement for his four volume (or sometimes one wide volume) translation of Plotinus the beginning of which follows.

What Are the Special Merits
of the Guthrie Plotinus?

1. It is the only complete one, and will always be the cheapest. It is the famous edition of which Stephen McKenna said, "1 congratulate you; you have gotten ahead of me."

2. It is the best for the student, as it has a 60-page concordance, and has the first explanation of Plotinic philosophy's origin, development, and destiny. Only Dr. Guthrie could do this, because it was he who dug out Plotinus's master Numenius. Also, his version is representative of contemporary language and ideas, and is not merely taming puzzles into modem dialect.

3. It is the best for him who wishes to understand Plotinus, because it is the only edition that unscrambles, chronologically, Plotinus's 4 progressive stages of development from Porphyry's frightful hodgepodge of 9 medleys. Other translators who perpetuate this disorder after Dr. Guthrie's discovery seem to be keeping the subject hazy purposely, not for the reader's benefit.

Reader, Do You Need an
Introduction to This Plotinus?

Then send for the free booklet "Names to Conjure With" which explains why he is of interest to all religious people; also why PROCLUS, now accessible in Master Key form at $3.00 is of permanent, universal importance . . .

Note that Kenneth misspells MacKenna's name. MacKenna's translation of Plotinus has become a classic. In *Ulysses,* James Joyce gives librarian Richard Best this remark: "Mallarmé, don't you know, has written those wonderful prose poems Stephen MacKenna used to read to me in Paris." MacKenna's work was much beloved by his peers, while Kenneth's languished in comparative obscurity. MacKenna's version of Plotinus, *On the Beautiful,* captures the poetic intensity of Plotinus. Kenneth's translation is a rocky road of labor for the reader, without the beauty of diction that gives MacKenna such elegance.

Academia never took a shine to Kenneth's reorganization of Plotinus, though modern scholars agree that Porphyry's arrangement, while perhaps not quite a "frightful hodgepodge," is out of chronological order. As for his production being unappreciated, that was something Kenneth could count on. Nevertheless he has not gone completely unnoticed. In the fifth book of his *Adepts of the Eastern Esoteric Tradition: Venerated Teachers of the Jains, Sikhs, and Parsis,* that connoisseur of the esoteric, Manly Hall, described Guthrie as a "brilliant but eccentric scholar."

In the *Catalog of Copyright Entries: Musical Compositions for 1938* Kenneth is listed as composer of a song with the dubious title "American Loyalty Hymn." Music and art were more than hobbies to him. As Matt Marble (2014) writes, "There are also some pieces with single-tone chanting and pretty far-out organ harmonies shifting around that single-tone chant drone. I was also wide-eyed to note that in his 'Angelic Mysteries' there is included tone-color music. Also found a great article in which he speaks solely of music, calling it 'the audible God.' The uncredited illustrations in his books are probably examples of his artistry."

In the book *The Philosophy of Music: What Music Can Do for You,* published in 1944 by Harriet Ayer Seymour, an early advocate of music therapy, she writes about her visit to Kenneth's church, which she describes as "well known for the practical nature of its spiritual life." Addressing the "four hundred people, cultivated men and women" in attendance, Harriet mentioned musical meditation as a form of therapy. Kenneth insisted that they give it a try. Harriet led the gathered flock as they improvised softly, repeating the two-word lyric, "Infinite Goodness."

Marble's in-depth research on Kenneth and his books has revealed a disturbing side of Kenneth's self-expression, "I was surprised to find numerous instances of explicit anti-Hindu or Indophobic commentary, which he also connected to an allergy and distaste toward Theosophy" (Marble 2021).

Nashoba continued to cause trouble for her descendants, as it had for Frances Wright as factions of the family fought over the property. The Guthrie brothers were well acquainted with the accusation that their mother was not the daughter of Frances Wright, but of her sister.

As for Kenneth's strange relationship with his brother, given their similar interests one might have expected them to get along, to support each other gladly. Instead they did not cooperate. They didn't trust each other. William was the more popular sibling, in the family and out in the world. But there must have been more to it than that. The papers of Frances Wright were inherited by William alone, and William wasn't willing to share them with Kenneth. Kenneth groused that he was the only one in the family with any actual interest in the papers. Kenneth's suspicion that William would steal his metaphysical discoveries borders on paranoia.

Kenneth was only twenty years old the year Hiram K. Jones died and the Plato Club faded away. Thomas Johnson had given up on his second periodical *Bibliotheca Platonica*. Guthrie was a lonely torch-bearer, with no journals to publish in, and no powerful friends to lift him out of poverty and obscurity. His feats of translation would have been welcomed with open arms by Emerson, Jones, the Concord School, the Plato Club, the American Akadêmê, but all that was gone. He could have at least been the Thomas Taylor of America; perhaps he hoped his books would eventually make him that. But no American Shelleys or Blakes followed to take the Neoplatonic vision to new horizons of poetic glory. The irony could not have escaped him.

Perhaps Kenneth was a man born fifty years too late. By the early 1920s Edgar Cayce was beginning to achieve renown, and the Ouija board became everyone's favorite parlor game. Platonism was passé. Kenneth died in 1940, the year France fell to the Nazis and the Battle of Britain began. He had lived long enough to see the destruction of an earlier epoch's fond hope for a civilized future informed by classical philosophy and the ancient mysteries. A few days before spring, after giving benediction at Keyport Baptist Church, as he walked home, a car driven by Abraham Pleasant, a twenty-three-year-old football player, ran him over in an accident on Route 36.

While William Guthrie's legacy remains a vital part of New York City's Lower East Side, until recently historians have largely ignored both brothers. Too Christian to thrill pagans and the theosophically inclined, too pagan to be remembered fondly by Christians, they are nevertheless good examples of American Metaphysical Religion's impact on American Christianity and culture. Happily, Matt Marble is working on a book about Kenneth, "I will be focusing on the active imagination of heaven and clairvoyant methodology and will feature his visual maps/illustrations, music, poetry, and fiction (*Votive Garlands,* his large collection of poetry, is surprisingly engaging to read). He may have failed at heaven, finances, Episcopalianism, and universal brotherhood, but what a persistently inspired/inspiring imagination!"

15

Scandalous Psychic Adventures
of the Roaring Twenties

AN ANCIENT CHINESE DIALECT spoken by a barely literate psychic was only one of the inexplicable happenings. The events described in the following pages didn't occur in the nineteenth century in some rural town. They happened in 1927 in New York City. Dr. Neville Whymant, linguistics professor at both London University and Oxford, formerly of Tokyo University and Peking University, didn't know what he was getting into when in October 1926 Judge William Cannon invited him to his posh Park Avenue home for a dinner party. A discussion of psychic phenomena was part of the evening's agenda. Grown accustomed to peculiar American preoccupations, Whymant and his wife agreed to attend. He had fallen into a trap set by the judge's wife.

Psychic Adventures in New York is a slim fifty-page book published in London by Morley and Mitchell in 1931. Whymant begins by explaining that he has no agenda, no belief to sell. In fact, he didn't want to write the book at all. But he was asked so many times to explain every detail of what happened to him, and no one else being willing to step up to the author's chair, he finally accepted the responsibility of reporting the mysterious event he witnessed. I'm fortunate to own a copy with Whymant's inscription to his sister. In neat but tiny handwriting in ink Whymant wrote:

> To my sister Grace,
>> Who was so sweet and faithful a
>> companion during my troubled days

in India: who cheered my lonely
hours and to whom I owe a depth
of affection I can never repay

FROM NEVILLE

WITH ALL HIS LOVE

LONDON, SEPTEMBER 18, 1931

A. Neville J. Whymant is best known as the author of *Colloquial Northern Chinese, A Mongolian Grammar,* and *A China Manual.* He also wrote *The Psychology of the Chinese Coolie and Chinese Coolie Songs,* an acceptable title at that time, but shockingly racist. The doctor was in America studying Indigenous dialects, to add to his familiarity with thirty living and dead languages. Hearing that he was one of the world's authorities on obscure dialects, Mrs. Cannon set her sights on getting the doctor to her next séance. It seems a spirit speaking Chinese had been showing up and she wanted to know what he was saying.

The medium the Chinese spirit spoke through was George Valiantine. Few mediums have experienced such a rise to international fame and such a crushing fall to obscurity and poverty. Like many other mediums George was a fraud who seemed to occasionally produce real phenomena, or a real medium who resorted to fraud. Dr. Whymant was about to become part of one of the most stubborn mysteries of American Metaphysical Religion. Just how did a barely literate American like George channel an ancient Chinese dialect?

When the situation was explained to the doctor he responded that he had no interest in talking to ghosts or any other Spiritualist activity. He and the Mrs. had tried séances out ten years before and found the activity boring and useless. They remained skeptical. Mrs. Cannon apologized for not warning him in advance, but she was afraid he would have politely refused the invitation. Whymant decided to stay.

H. Dennis Bradley (1931), Valiantine's most devoted booster, observed of George in his book *And After:* "He is a man of instinctive good manners but it is essential to state that he is semi-illiterate. He possesses no scholastic education whatever, beyond the ordinary simplicities; he is ill versed in general conversation and ideas. I mention these facts because many of the communications which have been made in the direct voice under his mediumship have been brilliant in their expressions and culture."

Whymant (1931) was more blunt: "Before the sitting began I had a talk with Valiantine, who struck me as a typical example of the simpler kind of country American citizen. His speech was far from polished, he seemed to lack imagination, and his interests were of a very commonplace order. He was almost untraveled, and exhibited no desire to see or know anything of countries other than his own. Occasionally he made amusing (and obviously unrehearsed) blunders in speech and misconception, and above all he seemed always to be natural. It was as if he were incapable of any form of acting at all. He was, in that company, a fish out of water, and although somewhat bewildered at it all, he seemed quite prepared to accept the position and make the best of it."

Whymant and company entered a small dining room. They were invited to look around and examine everything to see for themselves that nothing was out of the ordinary. "There was no appearance or suspicion of trickery," he wrote, "but I mention these things to show that I was alert from the beginning, and that within the limits imposed upon us I was prepared to apply all the tests possible to whatever phenomena might appear" (Whymant 1931).

The lights were shut off. The Lord's Prayer was recited. The gramophone played sacred music to provide an atmosphere of calm harmony. Unlike most mediums, especially modern, spirits did not speak through Valiantine. They spoke through an aluminum trumpet daubed with phosphorescent paint so its movements could be seen in the dark.

The first voice, a doctor, seemed to bellow from beneath the floor a brogue so loud Whymant thought he felt the vibrations of it. Next came an Indigenous American called Blackfoot after his tribe. He was said to be the keeper of the spirit door. Here is the melting pot of American Metaphysical Religion in action. The tribes who had been decimated and cheated out of their land were now gatekeepers to the afterlife, a constant theme in American mediumship from its beginnings. Whispers to séance regulars followed, private conversations with lost loved ones. Then a rich singing voice louder than the doctor's spoke fluent Italian in a conversation with Whymant that ended with an obscure Sicilian dialect Whymant could identify but not understand.

Then the séance took a surprising turn. Next was heard "the sound of an old wheezy flute not too skillfully played." Whymant was reminded of street musicians he had heard on his visits to China. Then the doctor was surprised to hear from the trumpet an ancient Chinese dialect. "Greeting," the spirit said, "O son of learning and reader of strange books! This unworthy servant bows humbly before such excellence" (Whymant 1931).

"Peace be upon thee, O illustrious one," Whymant responded. "This uncultured menial ventures to ask thy name and illustrious style." At first Whymant had trouble understanding what was being said:

the next sound seemed to be a hollow repetition of a Chinese name—K'ung fu tzu—the name by which Confucius was canonized. I was not quite sure that I had heard aright, but I did recognize the sound for some variety of Chinese speech and so I asked, in Chinese, for another opportunity of hearing what had been said before. This time without any hesitation at all came the name K'ung fu tzu. Now, I thought, was my opportunity. Chinese I had long regarded as my own special research area, and he would be a wise man, medium or other, who would attempt to trick me on such soil. If this tremulous voice were that of the old ethicist who had personally edited the Chinese Classics, then I had an abundance of questions to ask him. More even than any classical scholar could have to ask of Plato or Socrates should they venture to put in an appearance in a twentieth-century classroom. For if Homer and his followers nodded, at least they had a language far easier than that of Confucius and his successors, and the loose ends in the Chinese Classics had defied the efforts of twenty-five centuries of commentators.

Whymant continued,

The voice, as I have said, was tremulous. It was very difficult to discover what was said next, and I had to keep calling for a repetition.

Then it burst upon me that I was listening to Chinese of a purity and delicacy not now spoken in any part of China. As the voice went on I realized that the style of Chinese used was identical with that of the Chinese Classics, edited by Confucius two thousand five hundred years ago. Only among the scholars of archaic Chinese could one now hear that accent and style, and then only when they intoned some passage from the ancient books. In other words, the Chinese to which we were now listening was as dead colloquially as Sanskrit or Latin, and had been so for even a greater length of time. If this was a hoax, it was a particularly clever one, far beyond the scope of any of the sinologues now living. I was determined to test the matter to the full limit permitted, and so my next remark took the form of a question intended to prove the identity of the communicator. (Whymant 1931)

Whymant explained:

All Chinese who attain any eminence in public or private life have an abundance of names bestowed upon them at different periods. Confucius was no exception, and I asked for details of his life and "style" (the name by which a man is known as soon as he achieves individuality in early manhood), for particulars of his preoccupations on this earth, and set some posers of the type with which all students of Chinese have wrestled in their studies of the Confucian Canon. All my questions were answered at once, without any pause or fumbling; in fact, the answers came so swiftly upon the question that all too often I had to ask the voice to repeat its answer, as I had been unable to follow. The voice grew stronger with the passing of the moments, so that although the early part of the conversation was to some extent lost or doubtful, the succeeding phrases were quite clear so far as I was able to understand them. Although I had given much study to the classics—even to the length of knowing whole sections of them by heart—I found it extremely difficult to follow a voice speaking in that style. Another remarkable thing about this communicator was that, sensing my difficulty, he gradually assimilated his speech to my own, all the time, however, keeping his own accent and intonation so distinct that it was obvious to the other sitters (none of whom understood Chinese) that there were two distinct voices and that an actual conversation was going on. (Whymant 1931)

Remembering that the *Shih King,* the Classic of Poetry of Confucius, included several poems that had baffled both Chinese and Western scholars, the doctor asked: "This stupid one would know the correct reading of the verse in *Shih King.* It has been hidden from understanding for long centuries, and men look upon it with eyes that are blind. The passage begins thus: *Ts'ai ts'ai chüan êrh* . . . the first line of the third ode of the first book of *Chou Nan*" (Whymant 1931). But Whymant couldn't remember the other fourteen lines. The voice recited the rest accurately, then made sense out of the part that had baffled so many scholars.

Whymant continued his exploration, switching to the Analects of Confucius: "'Shall I ask of one passage in the Master's own writing? In *Lun Yu, Hsia Pien* there is a passage, which is wrongly written. Should it not read thus: . . . ?' But before I could get out even the details of the passage in question, the 'voice' took up my sentence and carried it through to the end. 'You were going to ask me about the two characters which end the last two phrases: you are quite right. The copyists were in error. The character which is written *se* should be *i,* and the character which is written *yen* is an error for *fou*.'" Whymant admitted, "again, all the winds had been taken out of my sails!" (Whymant 1931).

Whymant pondered the idea that some sort of telepathy had been involved, as if a medium could get into his brain and pick out the ancient Chinese dialect and literature there, and then use them fluently. But even if one were to go to such lengths for a telepathic explanation, Whymant dismissed the possibility since he had never considered the elegant solution the voice provided to that linguistic mystery.

Confucius became weaker in voice and more banal in message ending his portion of the séance with this advice to Whymant: "I go, my son, but I shall return. . . . Wouldst thou hear the melody of eternity?

Keep then thy ears alert" (Whymant 1931). Next up was a voice that claimed to be Whymant's father-in-law, speaking the specific accent of Somerset. This especially impressed Whymant because everyone at the séance mistakenly thought his wife was American.

Whymant attended another eleven séances. Not only did Confucius return but also other languages were heard. A different voice spoke an obscure French dialect that the doctor recognized as Labourdin Basque. Whymant wrote: "Altogether fourteen foreign languages were used in the course of the twelve sittings I attended. They included Chinese, Hindi, Persian, Basque, Sanskrit, Arabic, Portuguese, Italian, Yiddish (spoken with great fluency when a Yiddish and Hebrew-speaking Jew was a member of the circle), German, and modern Greek" (Whymant 1931).

Whymant wrote that at one of these séances Valiantine was having a conversation with the person beside him in American English while the trumpet was producing foreign languages. That meant that not only was telepathy not a satisfactory explanation, neither was ventriloquism though "voices seemed to come from the far corners of the room, out of the very wall against which the back of one's chair was pressed, from the ceiling, and from the floor" (Whymant 1931).

Another strange event was the appearance of the spirit of Abdu'l-Baha, the second leader and son of the founder of the Bahá'í faith, who had died five years earlier. A friend of the holy man's daughter was at the séance. The voice spoke "in a Levantine dialect of which I had the sketchiest knowledge. I could not understand much of what was said, but I translated the more elementary parts of what was quite a long speech. I must frankly admit that I did not even understand the purport of my English rendering, as it had much to do with the practice of the Bahá'í faith, of which I knew very little. But I was assured at the end of the evening that the long awaited message had been delivered" (Whymant 1931).

Four months later the *New York Herald Tribune* carried a lengthy report on the English professor's strange experience that even included a respected translation of the poem in question, and the translation given by the alleged spirit of Confucius.

Whymant concluded that he had no conclusions. He was left with one overwhelming question: "There was no doubt that somebody or something had been speaking most excellent Chinese there that evening, better Chinese than I, with all my training and experience in China, could speak. Whence came it, and for what purpose?" (Whymant 1931).

MR. X

Valiantine had spent most of his life as a small manufacturer in Williamsport, New York. At age forty-three, after hearing inexplicable knocks on his hotel room door, he consulted a Spiritualist who took him to a séance. Communications with mysterious knocks and raps led to a message from George's late brother-in-law. Working with his brother-in-law as his spirit guide, George became a medium.

In 1923 he entered a competition *Scientific American* sponsored offering $2,500 for verifiable physical phenomena by any medium. He called himself Mr. X. Mr. X was the first medium tested. Famous magician and skeptic Harry Houdini was a member of the committee. The SA committee heard voices that seemed to be high in the air. But an electric apparatus they had secretly attached to George's chair showed no weight in the chair for almost fifteen seconds. They couldn't explain how being out of the chair for a few seconds could have produced voices conversing at length above them, but Mr. X didn't win the prize.

A year later, at his Ramsey, New Jersey, home, retired lawyer and financier Joseph de Wyckoff introduced Valiantine to Irish writer H. Dennis Bradley, a wealthy businessman. Bradley was on his first visit to America, and he was not a believer in Spiritualism.

A copy exists of Bradley's book *Not for Fools* that he inscribed to the artist Louis Wain four years earlier in 1920. Wain was a household name around the turn of the century famed for his humorous anthropomorphic cats. *Not for Fools* collects opinion pieces published in the advertisement columns of newspapers criticizing the bureaucracy of World War I. By then Wain's popularity was beginning to wane, and his charming quirkiness was only four years away from the violent outbursts that led him to spend the rest of his life in institutions. Of course, given the ruthless treatment this innocent artist received from so many business partners, he may have welcomed his refuge in a sheltered world of fantasy. Events of 1924 also challenged Bradley's sense of reality.

As Bradley wrote later, after twenty minutes of singing hymns, "it was fortunate that our expressions could not be seen, for my nose was tilted in scorn and my lip curled in unrestrained contempt. I wondered at intelligent people submitting to such infantile forms of amusement. I wondered how a shrewd mind like that of my host could be induced to waste his time on such silly exploits" (Bradley 1924).

At the first séance George's wrists were bound by luminous bands so any movement would be clearly visible in the dark. Bradley sensed a presence in the room he thought was another person. He later wrote: "I was called by my name, and the voice, which sounded about three feet away on my right, was full of emotion." He heard his first name whispered repeated twice, and then his sister, Annie, who had died ten years before, identified herself. "Then we talked, not in whispers, but in clear, audible tones, and the notes of our voices were pitched as if we might have been speaking on earth. And that which we said to each other were things of wondrous joy. Every word was heard by the other three men in the room" (Bradley 1924).

For fifteen minutes Bradley and his sister discussed details of family life. "She said sayings in her own characteristic manner. Every syllable was perfectly enunciated and every little peculiarity of intonation was reproduced. Any suggestion of ventriloquism is ridiculous," Bradley continued. "No man living could imitate the clear and gentle voice which spoke, and, beyond this, no man living could talk in Annie's characteristic way, with her individual enunciation, her own choice of words, and her knowledge of the many things which she and I alone could have known" (Bradley 1924).

The next night the séance was attended by Joe de Wyckoff's cook and butler. Annie returned: "Her tones were clear and bell-like, her notes were sympathetic and understanding, and were radiant. How can I describe the indescribable?" More secrets only his sister knew were communicated. Then the cook was addressed by her late husband. They shared a conversation in fluent Spanish. Bradley wrote, "Doubt took flight when faced by an unchallengeable fact and the mind understood in a flash that what had hitherto appeared to be impossible was possible." He declared it the "most staggering event of my life" (Whymant 1931).

Bradley was also amazed as Valiantine's trumpet "floated in the air and careened around the room." In later reports of séances Bradley wrote, "Valiantine, the medium, often speaks and can be spoken to at the same moment that the spirits are speaking." Materializations and mysterious lights were described. A hand surrounded by astral light rested on Bradley's hand for a second. "Luminous lights floated about the room" (Whymant 1931).

George showed his financier friend Joe pages of writing he claimed were produced out of nowhere, by no human hand. The message was about a mission to Guyana. Guyana's history of mediumship goes back to the Indigenous culture, as it usually does. French Guiana in particular received further influence through the popularity of the French father of Spiritism Allen Kardec, author of the popular Spiritualist classics *The Spirit's Book* and *The Medium's Book* but most of George's Guyana messages were probably a get-rich-quick scheme.

Nevertheless Joe de Wyckoff was a businessman with an eye for detail. He noticed the similarity in handwriting between George and the spirits urging the Guyana adventure. So he took the samples to a handwriting expert. They were identical. George stubbornly insisted he had not hand-written the message about Guyana. Joe proposed a test. George would be tied to a chair at a séance and if writing showed up on paper he would be vindicated. The séance was a failure. Joe turned his back on George. Back home Bradley heard the disturbing news in a cable from Joe.

Bradley consulted the famous English medium Gladys Osborne Leonard. Gladys was the daughter of an entrepreneur who made a fortune in the yacht business. When her father lost his wealth she became a singer and theatrical actress. Singing at a Spiritualist church, without having much interest in or knowledge of their beliefs, she was told her guides were busy planning what would become her "great spiritual work."

Gladys's mother was ill but not gravely. Gladys wrote down the strange experience she had: "I looked up and saw in front of me, but about five feet above the level of my body, a large, circular patch of light. In this light I saw my mother quite distinctly. Her face looked several years younger than I had seen it a few hours before. She gazed down on me for a moment, seeming to convey to me an intense feeling of relief and a sense of safety and well-being. Then the vision faded. I was wide awake all the time, quite conscious of my surroundings" (Whymant 1931). She found out the next morning that her mother had died at that moment. That sent her back to the Spiritualists.

The Society for Psychical Research conducted hundreds of tests on Gladys. They concluded that she was impeccably trustworthy, and under strict conditions had provided credible evidence of the survival of personality after death. For fifty years Gladys conducted her practice as a medium. Theories have been proposed to explain away her record. One of her favorite demonstrations, for example, was to pick out a person's favorite book from their bookshelves. Later analysis showed that she was only 35 percent successful. On the other hand, try to pick out a stranger's favorite book with a success rate of one out of three. Her most famous case involved Sir Oliver Lodge and his son who had died in the war. Lodge was so convinced his son was communicating to him he wrote the bestseller *Raymond,* named after him. Raymond also communicated to his father through Valiantine's trumpet, and Lodge wrote the foreword to Whymant's *Psychic Adventures in New York.* When Bradley consulted Gladys his sister appeared again. She repeated enough of the conversation she had with Bradley during the Valiantine séance to convince him he had cross-evidence of life after death.

Visiting Europe, Joe de Wyckoff told Bradley he thought George Valiantine a fraud. But Bradley insisted otherwise. His results had been too impressive to ignore, and they had been corroborated by a second medium totally unconnected. So Joe invited George to join them in England. Over a five-week period fifty prominent people attended George's séances in Bradley's home where over a hundred different voices spoke a large variety of languages including obscure Cardiganshire Welsh, which Caradoc Evans, a Welsh novelist, being present, verified;

not only that, but he was convinced he had spoken to his own deceased father.

But again, in April 1924 Joe believed he had caught George in a cheat. Sensing movement in the dark at the end of a séance, Joe struck a match and there was George fiddling with the trumpet. Not only that, but the trumpet was warm just where a hand would be placed, and the mouthpiece was moist. But that didn't disturb Bradley. He reported that those phenomena were common, even on trumpets seen flying around the room. He theorized it was ectoplasmic manifestation.

Tests by the Society for Psychical Research the following spring produced nothing deemed worthy of further study. But their research officer Dr. Woolley back at Bradley's house heard eleven distinct voices he could not explain by rational means. He also reported a luminous trumpet moving in the air that he considered a supernatural phenomenon. In broad daylight he heard faint voices from inside the trumpet though the medium's lips never moved. Investigators often brought unknown guests to the séances without advance notice, yet the voices provided details like names, relationships, personality traits, and events. Most left believing they had spoken to friends and relatives from beyond the grave.

Bradley himself wrote about a séance in 1925 where he claimed he heard a prophecy that came true. Fourteen years before World War II one of Valiantine's spirit guides, the doctor speaking in a Scottish brogue, "gave a very grave warning about the secret preparations of Japan and Germany for war in the air, although any forecast is problematic, yet he insists on the point that the next war will be comparatively soon and that it will be the most terrible that human civilization has had to endure" (Bradley 1925). Having recently been released from prison, Hitler would publish *Mein Kampf* a few months later.

The Marquis Centurione Scotto of Genoa visited the Bradleys in 1927 for a séance with Valiantine. The marquis and his wife were stunned to hear their late son speaking in fluent Italian providing convincing details. When they returned to Italy they became mediums themselves.

That same year Valiantine was tested in London again. Countess

Ahlefeldt-Laurvig provided an ancient Chinese shell for a séance in the apartment of Lord Charles Hope. The circular folds of the shell tapered to a small mouthpiece. In China these shells were used as horns. The guests tried but they couldn't make any sound with it. During the séance the shell horn was blown; the notes even matched the melody known in China.

Having received no information that impressed him, Hope remained skeptical, but reported quite a list of inexplicable events. While most of the information the spirits provided was worthless, there were moments of accuracy, too. Not only was Japanese spoken to the satisfaction of a Japanese guest, but real Chinese characters were written down, though how the medium managed it in the dark room with his limited literacy Hope did not know. An expert in Chinese calligraphy told Hope he couldn't have done it. A conversation in old-fashioned German, and the floating trumpet, completed the bafflement.

On March 25, 1927, the mysterious voices were recorded. A telephone cable was set up to connect Hope's apartment to Columbia Gramophone Company's recording house. Hope, Bradley, and his wife heard three distinct voices that spoke in English, one in an Indigenous American dialect, one in Hindustani, another in Italian, and two in Chinese. The last, claiming to be Confucius, Whymant said sounded to him like the voice he had heard back in New York.

Whymant was invited to hear the recording by the Society for Psychical Research. He could only interpret a few sentences because the voice was faint and the recording distorted. But he recognized enough of the intonations to gather the general meaning. The Society for Psychical Research dismissed Whymant as unscientific. They focused on the lack of strict controls in the initial sittings in America. One SPR writer speculated that Valiantine had picked up enough Chinese from local immigrants to fool the doctor into fooling himself. Unable to exactly make out what the voice was saying she argued that the doctor's subconscious filled in the startling details he reported. Here is a remarkable example of the irrationality of the rational: to allege that an internationally acclaimed linguist would fool himself into mistaking broken Chinese for a conversation with Confucius.

Over the next two years Bradley conducted over one hundred experiments he declared 95 percent successful. In April 1929, mere months before the infamous Wall Street crash, Valiantine and the Bradleys traveled to Germany for séances with the Berlin Occult Society, who were put off by the lack of strict controls, and two members claimed to have seen the medium moving when he was supposed to be still.

A month later, in Genoa, Italy, Valiantine's séance with the marquis and the psychical researcher Ernesto Bozzano was strictly controlled. He was tied to a chair by ropes with sealed knots, the doors were locked, and an adhesive bandage was stuck on his mouth. The results were the opposite of what had occurred in Germany; everyone was impressed, at first, but as the séances continued one guest claimed he felt Valiantine lean forward to speak into the trumpet. Another caught Mrs. Bradley touching him on the back of the head. The indignant accused refused to stay another moment. Later the accusers were less certain. One apologized to Mrs. Bradley.

Here's what Bradley himself had to say about it: "The Marquis Centurione Scotto, Mr. Rossi and Madame Rossi, unknown before to me or to Valiantine, visit me in England in 1927. The marquis, to his astonishment, speaks to his son in Italian. The marquis and Mrs. Rossi then develop voice mediumship entirely from, and because of, their meeting and initiation with Valiantine. Valiantine then, in 1929, visits them in Italy and is accused of being a fraud. The poet is right when he declares, 'It is a mad world'" (Bradley 1929).

In 1931 Valiantine was accused of fraud again. He was attempting to fingerprint three late English notables including the recently deceased Sir Arthur Conan Doyle. The ectoplasmic prints made on wax and smoked paper would be compared with an actual print of Doyle's thumb. Valiantine had managed this feat before and Bradley had written about it in *The Wisdom of the Gods*. The print provided turned out to be a match for Valiantine's big toe. When confronted with the evidence, George sobbed and insisted. "I cannot understand it."

The experts who examined him reported he used his big toe, middle finger, and elbow for the various prints, and that the chemical used was found all over his body. Could he have been so stupid as to believe his big-toe print could be mistaken for Doyle's actual fingerprint, or anyone else's? Some Spiritualists have claimed that this was typical of the pranks played by spirits drawn to such ostentatious demonstrations. Bradley turned his back on the medium he had so righteously defended, but he was careful to say that George's fraud did not invalidate the voice phenomena.

Bradley blamed the debacle on the sudden wealth and fame Valiantine had found. He had become conceited and arrogant. Yet, Bradley wrote, "his reason for attempting these imprint frauds will remain incomprehensible. He received no money from me, and for him to imagine that in the presence of imprint experts he could commit palpable fraud and escape detection was a sign of sheer lunacy" (1929).

Not long after, Surgeon-Admiral Nimmo had two sittings with Valiantine by daylight. He reported hearing voices from the trumpet that gave him intelligent communications he considered evidence of survival after death. Another observing doctor also reported hearing the voices but his observation of the medium showed no signs of movement of his lips, hands, or feet. George was not manually responsible for whatever was happening.

Were Valiantine and the Bradleys coconspirators in an elaborate fraud? How then to explain the inexplicable events that occurred, such as the Confucian experience of Neville Whymant?

Valiantine's fate is a mystery. All we know is that he died without the fame or wealth his mediumship had given him. Mrs. Eileen E. McAlpine (2007), who knew Whymant at the end of his life, wrote that a few days before his death he told her of a "brief black-out when he saw two old friends of his, holding out their hands to receive him. They were Mr. F. T. Cheng, the pre-Mao ambassador to the UK and Lionel Giles—keeper of oriental books at the British Museum. They were great friends of his in life. I subsequently had a sitting with F. Jordan Gill, Neville told me, through him, that they had indeed been the first friends who greeted him after he died."

HOUDINI VERSUS THE WITCH OF LIME STREET

Valiantine wasn't the only famous medium to produce evidence in Chinese. Dr. Whymant was also called in to verify automatic writing by Mina Crandon, better known as Margery the Medium, or the Witch of Lime Street. In total darkness she had written two columns of Chinese. Try to write a few words with ink and brush in the dark, not an easy task even for a skilled calligrapher, seemingly impossible for Margery, who didn't know Chinese, and who had no experience with Chinese calligraphy.

Margery was already married and a mother when she met Dr. Crandon when he took out her appendix. As a teenager she had played in professional bands and orchestras and had been good at sports. World War I brought them together again at the New England Naval Hospital where he was a top doctor and she was a civilian volunteer ambulance driver. She divorced her first husband and married the aristocratic Boston physician who loved reading the writings of Lincoln. But he was an older man, and his day job as a surgeon had understandably left him preoccupied with mortality. Some say Margery at first treated mediumship as an amusement to distract and reassure her husband, who was fascinated by telekinesis and séances.

Impressed by his wife's displays of powers, including typical magician tricks like making a dove appear, he wrote to Sir Arthur Conan Doyle, who was impressed enough to put the matter in front of his friends at the Society of Psychical Research in America. As the wife of a respected doctor, a charming and refined woman, without need for more money than she already had, Margery quickly became popular.

Lascivious rumors about Margery multiplied. Were they true? Mediums who met in private with strange men aroused and outraged regular folks. Margery was said to have greeted her clients in a sheer dressing gown, bedroom slippers, and silk stockings, supposedly intended as transparency. Nothing could be hidden since everything could be seen. Margery's dark blonde hair, worn bobbed, set off her sparkling blue eyes.

The Roaring Twenties must have been roaring indeed if the

allegations are true that her husband not only helped her commit fraud but allowed her to enjoy affairs with an occasional client. That may also have been their favorite method for silencing important critics. A simple case of you keep my secret and I'll keep yours. Was it mere rumor or fact that Margery conducted séances in the nude, allegedly the better to manifest the mysterious ectoplasm, not only from her mouth, but from her most scandalous region?

Like Valiantine, Margery was seriously considered for the *Scientific American* prize in 1924, for telekinetic phenomena demonstrated under strict control. The committee reported effects produced in a sealed glass jar, with electric bells under a lid, and on a scale. The committee member most convinced was later said to have been romantically involved with her. A. Malcolm Bird, an officer of the American Society for Psychical Research, and the one who had first proposed the *Scientific American* contest, leaked a story that the committee was leaning toward verifying her. A headline declared that another of the judges, Harry Houdini had been stumped. Bird confided to Houdini that he considered Margery 50 to 60 percent genuine. Researchers were well aware of the strange brew of fraud and evidence mediums provided.

Houdini didn't take kindly to the rumor that he had found Margery genuine since he had so far been absent from the proceedings. He personally supervised the next round of tests, which quickly degenerated into accusations. Houdini built an elaborate box that would prevent Margery from committing any clever fraud. Margery was game. The bell the spirits were asked to ring rang though she was supposedly immobilized. When the lights were turned on everyone could see the top of the box had been forced open. Houdini claimed Margery was responsible. She said her late brother Walter, her spirit guide, had done it because he was infuriated by Houdini.

There's no way around it, this was a kinky scene. Margery in nothing but a sheer dress, sitting in a restraining contraption with her legs spread. Houdini ankle to ankle with her, his leg on the inside of her thigh pressed against her bare skin, holding her hands or wrists. He said his suspicions were aroused (among other things?) when he felt Margery's muscles move whenever anything happened. When the spirits were asked to ring the bell five times, Houdini felt Margery move her leg five times coincidentally with each ring. Later he wrote that he thought she might have believed he would play along with her.

At the next séance, back in the repaired isolation box, Margery was asked again to ring a bell. Walter complained that the bell could not be rung because Houdini had rigged it. When the bell was examined a small eraser was found pushed in far enough to stop the bell from ringing. Houdini denied putting the eraser there. Was this a clever ruse by Margery or her husband to neutralize the relentless Houdini? When Dr. Crandon found a ruler hidden inside the box Houdini had prepared for Margery he was furious. He accused Houdini of deliberate sabotage and threatened to end the experiments if Houdini didn't leave never to return.

Despite promising Houdini that he would debunk Margery, in 1924 Bird published three articles about her in *Scientific American,* portraying her in a positive light. Houdini began demonstrating some of her tricks during his performances. He wrote a pamphlet against her, also published in 1924, that gave the secrets of her stunts. Despite his exposés, Margery was still a popular medium for the middle class and the elite.

"Margery Genuine Says Conan Doyle, He Scorns Houdini," a *Boston Herald* headline declared. Doyle even defended Margery from the pioneer parapsychologist J. B. Rhine's accusations of fraud, going so far as to buy an ad in Boston newspapers that stated, "J.B. Rhine is a monumental ass." Rhine was deeply disappointed by his experience with Margery, which he called, "premeditated and brazen trickery." The experience set him on a different path of research into the paranormal that resulted in his famous parapsychology program at Duke University, where research on ESP replaced studying mediums as a national preoccupation. By 1935 Rhine was inspiring headlines like this from the March 25 *Halifax Daily Courier,* "Biologist's Claim for Telepathy. Series of 100,000 Experiments. Special Pack of Cards Used in Tests."

In 1925 Bird, far from denouncing Margery as he had promised Houdini he would, published a book about her. He was convinced her powers were genuine proof of life after death. The Society for Psychical

Research in London tested Margery, too, and reported that their famous fraud-proof table had been twice levitated six inches off the ground, not in the dark, but in bright light. One scientist reported playing a game of checkers with Margery's deceased brother Walter.

When *Scientific American* said they wanted to conduct another investigation, Margery agreed. Three professors conducted the experiment. One of them, Dr. Wood, an enthusiastic debunker of mediums, noticed the silhouette of a rod moving over the luminous checkerboard on the table across from Margery. Moving side to side it lifted an object. Wood touched it with his fingertip following it right up to Margery's mouth. He figured she was holding the stick in her teeth. Warned that touching the ectoplasm might kill the medium, Doc Wood gave it a good pinch. Margery didn't react. He reported it felt like a knitting needle wrapped in soft leather. As Wood dictated to the stenographer. Margery shrieked then fainted. Wood was never allowed to set foot near her again.

In 1928 Margery and Valiantine were tested side by side by the American Society for Psychical Research. They were also tested together on separate continents. In one experiment involving dates, they both wrote 3-5-10, though Margery was in Boston and Valiantine was in Venice, Italy. The *Margery Mediumship,* the voluminous notes of this series of experiments published by the ASPR, reached over one thousand pages. Margery would sign copies for friends and clients. Enough inexplicable events occurred to exhaust the imagination of the most skilled debunker. Utterly improbable coincidences abounded.

But in 1930 Bird turned in a report denouncing Margery as a fraud. He confessed she had asked him to be her accomplice. Crestfallen, he resigned from the society and disappeared. Like Valiantine, Margery's reputation was damaged most by a fingerprint stunt. She claimed to have produced Walter's fingerprint from the great beyond, but the print in wax turned out to be her dentist's and he admitted to teaching her how to do the trick. Less popular but still in demand, Margery continued her practice with fewer and fewer followers. She sought solace in alcohol. Soon she looked old before her time. Her slim figure turned stout and her casual disarray once considered erotic was now described as dumpy. After a long illness her husband died in 1939. Margery became depressed. At one of her last séances she ran off to the roof where she threatened suicide.

Houdini claimed that one of his spies had been told by Margery that she respected the magician for not being duped by her. She claimed to have become a medium only to save her marriage when her husband had become bored with her. According to the spy, Crandon became so infatuated with her mediumship and her hundreds of thousands of followers, he would brutalize her to force her to invent new and better wonders.

The most lurid accusations against Margery included ectoplasmic manifestations from the most sensitive and private area of her body. She refused requests to be examined more closely. Demands that she wear tights during the séance she also refused. Speculations that her husband had surgically altered her to enable her trickery take this trend to its inevitable extreme. Did Margery really perform séances in the nude? Or are these rumors another example of the sexualized slander of mediums, a common experience among the first generations of women who found in mediumship a way to have power in the world from which they had been otherwise excluded.

Some have accused Margery's husband of acquiring animal parts through hospital labs; for example, writers have speculated that the ectoplasm in photographs of Margery were sewn together tracheas or strands of animal lung tissue. But neither Margery nor her husband left any indication of what their motivations might have been. This is the case with almost every famous medium, amid all the obvious fraud there remain inexplicable moments witnessed by many.

A story is told that a psychic researcher asked Margery on her deathbed to confess for posterity how she had fooled so many. He couldn't hear her muffled response. When he asked her to repeat it, she said clearly, with a twinkle in her eyes: "I said you can go to hell. All you psychic researchers can go to hell. Why don't you guess? You'll all be guessing for the rest of your lives" (Polidoro 2000). Those were her last words. She died in 1941 at age fifty-three.

In 1959 American novelist William Gresham published his nonfiction book *Houdini: The Man Who Walked through Walls* in which he wrote about Houdini and his assistant Jim: "Years later, when the Self-Liberator was dead, Jim Collins was asked about the mysterious ruler. Collins smiled wryly. 'I chucked it in the box meself. The boss told me to do it. He wanted to fix her good.'"

Houdini died of acute appendicitis on Halloween eve 1926. A diseased appendix began the relationship between Dr. Crandon and Margery, and ended their conflict with their nemesis Houdini. The great magician's widow Bess announced a $10,000 reward for any medium who could deliver the ten-word, coded message Houdini and she had decided on as his final challenge. Three years later Arthur Ford the pastor of the First Spiritualist Church of New York became world famous when Bess declared, after thousands of failures, that he had delivered Houdini's message at a séance in her home.

It began when Houdini's mother, the spirit the magician had been most eager to contact, who was supposed to provide a medium a word to prove her survival of death, showed up at one of Arthur's séances. She gave him the word *forgive* and told him to write Bess. Bess must have been impressed when this stranger delivered the word Houdini had vainly hoped for. However, eleven months before, Bess had revealed the word in a newspaper interview.

Bess asked Ford to conduct a séance in her home. At that séance a spirit claiming to be Houdini revealed the code, which used each word to provide a letter spelling out *believe.* The message started with a word that didn't need to be unlocked by a code: *Rosabelle,* a short ditty that Bess sang for Houdini at their first show together. The lyrics were etched inside her wedding ring: "Rosabelle, sweet Rosabelle, I love you more than I can tell. Over me you cast a spell. I love you my sweet Rosabelle." Rosabelle was Houdini's pet name for her.

The full message was, "Rosabelle, sweet Rosabelle, believe! Spare no time or money to undo the attitude of doubt I had on earth. Teach the truth to those who've lost the faith, my sweetheart. Tell the world there is no death." The very same day in an interview with the *New York Times* Bess said, "They are the exact words left for me by Harry, and I am absolutely convinced that my husband talked to me and that there is life beyond the grave."

Two days later a New York newspaper accused the widow of being in cahoots with Arthur Ford. The reporter claimed to have witnesses to Ford telling him that he had paid Bess for the secret. But Ford had witnesses who swore he had been somewhere else at the time. Did Ford brag to a reporter immediately after arranging the hustle that would make him famous? Bess vehemently denied it. She wrote the paper's famous columnist Walter Winchell a letter defending Ford and herself.

But when it came time to pay Ford his $10,000 reward she refused claiming that Spiritualists had convinced her to retract it to preserve the purity of the proof. Due to the bad press, Ford was suspected of chicanery and was ostracized from Spiritualist circles. But no proof of fraud was found. A reporter suggested that Bess had accidentally leaked the details to the press. Perhaps she leaked the message, but would she have explained the complicated code? The controversy was discussed in every newspaper. As men and women in every town and farm had to give their opinion, too, Spiritualism found itself more popular than ever. Crowds of fifty thousand showed up for events in Lily Dale.

A friend of Houdini's argued that a clever reader could figure out how to use the code from a book published the year before that Bess had coauthored: *Houdini: His Life-Story*. By 1930 Bess was telling reporters she had never gotten Houdini's message from a medium. She added that she had given up on contacting him. Nevertheless she held séances on the anniversary of his death for seven more years.

Skeptics argue that Bess knew Ford had tricked her. Believers suggest that she quickly learned from the hostile reactions of her social circle, and the press, that if she became a Spiritualist they would all write her off as a mentally impaired old woman. By reminding the world once a year of her husband Houdini, each séance brought the eye of the public back to Bess. A recent biography of Houdini suggests that Bess was infatuated with Ford, twenty years her junior, and that as lovers they hatched a scheme she quickly regretted.

Ford was injured in the car accident that killed his sister not long after the Houdini publicity. He became addicted to morphine and alcohol for the chronic pain he suffered the rest of his life. Ford became famous again years later when in 1967 he convinced Bishop Pike on national television in Canada that Pike's late son communicated from beyond the grave. But after Ford's death in Florida four years later, startling evidence of fraud was discovered. Ford owned bound volumes of poetry he liked to read from before each séance. But those weren't poems he was reading. The books actually contained a collection of cut out obituaries and newspaper articles. He was a man who did his research. Just imagine the stunning readings he could have done with access to the internet.

The Zen koan-like effects of these narratives of outrageous fraud mixed with moments of seemingly impossible serendipity may say more about the observer than the subjects of observation. Rationalists will dismiss the inexplicable as the self-hypnosis of the credulous, guaranteed by the human capacity to delude ourselves, which seems as unlimited as our imaginations. Spiritualists will dismiss evidence of fraud as inevitable human frailty that doesn't diminish actual evidence. No amount of hearsay will convince a skeptic who has not had the experience personally. No logic will dissuade the believer who has.

America is the country where communication with the dead was attempted among the Indigenous tribes, from the earliest colonial days and has been pursued ever since. While France and other European countries, especially England, conducted their own experiments in mediumship and the practice existed already in Asian cultures and among most Indigenous tribes, America can be viewed as the field for an extensive experiment of the dead speaking to the living. An experiment that evolved new techniques from primitive knocking to direct-voice archaic Chinese, from ectoplasmic phantasms to floating trumpets, from shouted prophecies to quietly prescribed cures, there are many colors in the full spectrum of mediumship in America.

16

American Metaphysical Religion in the Twentieth Century

ALONG OUR JOURNEY we have already visited the twentieth century, from the last of the nineteenth-century Platonists to the Spiritualists of the Roaring Twenties. Now our tour turns to a consideration of seven major themes. The Reincarnation Renaissance, the Tarot Renaissance, the Astrology Renaissance, the art of the Southwestern Transcendentalists, the midcentury cosmic jazz of Vincent Lopez, the private interests of two very different writers J. D. Salinger and William Safire, and the mystical fascism of Nazi Germany and their American admirers the Silver Legion, which had connections to the I AM movement, and the Violet Flame. This will give us context for a following chapter that provides an overview of American Metaphysical Religion in the early twenty-first century. But first, let us consider the fate of mediumship in the twentieth century.

Mediumship remained popular throughout the twentieth century. Some mediums became world famous, such as Edgar Cayce. But one of the most successful and inexplicable experiments in mediumship has fallen into obscurity. Big game hunter and bestselling author Stewart Edward White wrote adventure novels popular with generations of American boys. Several of them were made into movies, and a TV series by Disney. During their long and very happy marriage and travels, White and his beloved wife Betty (not the Golden Girl) discreetly explored mediumship. They were tenaciously focused on experiencing, and finding a way to describe, what she called the higher frequency of life beyond death.

441

Stewart has a grove of redwood trees and a California golden trout named after him. Teddy Roosevelt said Stewart had the best aim of anyone who had ever shot a gun on his range. But Betty convinced Stewart to shoot big game with a camera rather than a gun. During their world travels she collected seeds, introducing many new plants to Santa Barbara. These extremely wealthy people had no need for book royalties, no desire for power, and no love of fame, yet they succeeded as few had before them, and with dignity.

It all started with a few friends laughing over a Ouija board at a party. The board indicated it wanted to communicate with Betty. Betty thought they were playing tricks on her, but she eventually gave in. The board repeated over and over again that she should get a pen. When she eventually did, a long series of run-on sentences carried a message that convinced the Whites they had to explore further. Eventually Betty became a voice medium. But she was unlike most mediums. She wasn't conveying messages from dead relatives. Betty received special training that involved exploring, describing, and adapting to life on the other side. This universe, the Invisibles as they called themselves told her, is obstructed. But the universe that is our true home is unobstructed. Not that these are separate universes. They are one. For low frequencies there is obstruction. Higher frequencies experience the freedom to be anywhere and everywhere. The obstructed universe is an educational illusion, a laboratory of exaggerated consequences, a place in which spirits mature by experimenting and learning, a kind of nest for our fledgling souls.

Emerson's masterpiece *Nature,* published in 1836, includes his succinct description of a mystical state: "I became a transparent eyeball; I am nothing. I see all: the currents of the Universal Being circulate through me." Over fifteen hundred years earlier Plotinus wrote: "There, however, everybody is pure, and each inhabitant is, as it were, an eye. Nothing likewise is there canceled or fictitious, but before one can speak to another, the latter knows what the former intended to say." The Whites experimented with and described in great detail similar states of consciousness.

While Stewart was public as the author of the bestselling books about his adventures with Betty, they always kept her identity secret. But then Betty died, just prior to the beginning of World War II. Stewart experienced her presence and love in such an overwhelming way he declared he needed no further proof of the truth of her continuing existence. The book they had been working on was rushed into print. In the afterword Stewart admitted that the medium who had received the teachings of the Invisibles was actually his wife. Another bestseller, the book gave hope to many readers.

But then something amazing happened that required Stewart to write another book as quickly as possible. He began receiving letters from friends and strangers, believers and skeptics who reported playful intrusions by Betty, in dreams, synchronicities, and other unmistakable nudges. Stewart admitted that he did not want to try to reach Betty through a medium. He was afraid the subtle assurance he had received might be disrupted by doubt if the messages from beyond were disappointing.

A man with many friends, Stewart traveled from one to the next to avoid being at home with only memories. Most of the world was at war two years before Pearl Harbor. No matter how many experts he hired to stop the withering of Betty's beautiful garden of exotic plants gathered during their travels it was as if the plants didn't want to be there anymore if they weren't being cared for by Betty. The last stop on Stewart's tour of mourning was with a couple that had been great friends of theirs. They had helped the Whites navigate the world of both psychic channeling and anonymous book publishing. "Joan and Darby" had authored the bestseller *Our Unseen Guest*.

Unbeknown to Stewart, Joan had recently had an experience that had puzzled her. She had been compelled to take the wrong bus, which led her to a store she had no intention of visiting, in which she found a Chinese red lacquer box carved with swallows. When told the last one had been sold, she insisted the salesperson look through the stockroom. He found one left behind, which Joan eagerly purchased. On the way home she came to her senses and wondered why on earth she had bought the box, when she already had other Chinese carved lacquer boxes and no room for a new one.

Since Joan was a medium, she thought it might be good for Stewart to have a session. She promised not to channel Betty after Stewart made that stipulation. But the moment Joan went into trance Betty barged in. "Betty began," Stewart (1941) wrote in *The Unobstructed Universe* published that same year, "talking to me quietly, fluently, with assured and intimate knowledge of our common experience and living. There was no 'fishing' and no fumbling. That part of it became almost ridiculous, it was so easy for her where with usual 'psychical research' it has been so difficult. Here, in this first evening, she literally poured out a succession of these authentications. She mentioned not one, but dozens, of small events out of our past, of trivial facts in our mutual experience or surroundings, none of which could by any possibility be within Joan's knowledge."

Stewart heard the story about the Chinese box when Betty told him to pay back Joan. Betty explained it was a gift for her younger sister; the carving of the birds was the important part. When Stewart presented the box to his sister-in-law, she explained through tears that when they were children Betty would help her climb into a tree where they watched a nest of fledgling swallows.

Stewart reported only one miss in the two-hour session. But the miss turned out to be a most important hit. Something that Betty had deliberately chosen because she knew Stewart had forgotten about it. It involved a fancy pair of blue slippers. Stewart had no memory of blue slippers. He found no blue slippers among his or Betty's belongings. Her maid didn't remember them either. Then the nurse who had been taking care of Betty near the end of her life reconnected with Stewart. He asked her about the blue slippers. She laughed, explaining that Betty when she was in the hospital had asked Stewart to bring her slippers. He had brought her fancy boudoir stiletto slippers decorated with fluffy blue feathers. Betty and the nurse had laughed about it. Stewart was obviously in shock, about to become a widower, he had no memory of the blue slippers. Betty not only knew about them, she knew that he had forgotten. She explained that the mystery of the blue slippers ruled out telepathy.

Betty's poetic sensitivity to beauty and her wholesome, humorous, and sometimes sublime advice about living a good life, were eagerly read by a nation at war and in mourning that found hope in the revelation that the mysterious Betty was none other than the wife of the beloved writer. Stewart could have built a metaphysical empire from the attention he received.

Leslie Kimmell, Stewart's secretary at the end of his life, said he was a quiet man with a sense of humor, a good listener, with a horror of meddling in other people's affairs. He amused himself by reading, seeing movies, gardening, dictating letters giving advice to seekers who were encouraged to think it out for themselves. Two cairn terriers followed him around, one chosen from beyond by Betty, with whom they often seemed to be interacting, chasing invisible toys and barking at an invisible something about four foot eleven.

Kimmel recalled that Stewart spent an hour a day meditating in Betty's blue room, where he not only felt her presence but also received instruction. Private interviews were granted to people seeking help only after Stewart felt more secure in the support he believed Betty and the Invisibles gave him. The many requests for a school or organization of some kind were "gently but determinedly discouraged." He didn't want to convert anyone. He often said, "every fellow has to find his own way" (White 1948).

Carl Jung, in a letter to a friend, confessed that he thought Betty not only an archetype but an actual spirit. *Who's Who,* impressed by her communications, declined to include a date of death in her entry.

On the other end of the spectrum we have a medium who exemplifies the ambiguity of American Metaphysical Religion, Morris Lamar Keene, who practiced in his hometown of Tampa, Florida, but also at Camp Chesterfield.

Keene was known as the Prince of Spiritualists, but in 1976, at age forty, he published *The Psychic Mafia*. He admitted that he had been a fraud his entire career. His tricks weren't clever, and neither were his clients. Keene had this to say about them, "The true-believer syndrome merits study by science. What is it that compels a person, past all reason, to believe the unbelievable? How can an otherwise sane individual become so enamored of a fantasy, an imposture, that even after it's exposed in the bright light of day he still clings to it—indeed, clings to it all the harder?"

Keene alleged that many of his fellow mediums were as crooked as he was. They shared information about clients. They worked together to create the illusion of communication with the afterlife. The book was a success, but one evening as Keene walked on his lawn at home in Tampa a shot was fired at him. His colleagues did not appreciate his candor.

Keene changed his name. He moved away. He got a warehouse job. But at the end of a workday in 1979, as he left his office, a car drove up, and shots were fired. This time Keene was hit. He had a long stay in the hospital. After that, he changed his name again, living quietly until his death in 1996.

Most astoundingly, while he confessed to fraud, Keene never renounced his Spiritualist beliefs. In *The Psychic Mafia* he declared, "Life after death? I believe in it. I believe that human beings maintain their individuality after death. I believe that we go on to higher and better expressions of ourselves than those which we are now expressing. I believe that evolution, growth, is the whole thing: mankind evolves, it doesn't regress. I believe that, in spite of all I've seen and experienced. Extrasensory perception and psychic phenomena? I believe that the individual can have his or her own private psychic experience—that there is such a thing as ESP. But when it comes to paying a medium to do it for you—beware!" (Keene 1976).

Of course, Keene's advice was ignored. Mediumship became ever more popular in the twentieth century and continues to flourish in the twenty-first, appearing on television shows, in hit movies, inspiring YouTube channels, and readings by Zoom and every other form of social media and online communication.

THE REINCARNATION RENAISSANCE

Although there have been traditions in the West, such as Gnostic Christianity, that believed in reincarnation, the vast majority of Westerners for many generations accepted the idea of one life per customer. In the America of 1850, hardly anyone could be found who believed in reincarnation, except for exploited workers still practicing the religions of their homelands. According to a Pew poll published in 2018 roughly 33 percent of Americans believe in reincarnation. How did reincarnation become so popular in America?

In 1919, when eighteen-year-old Manly Palmer Hall became minister of the Church of the People, at Trinity Auditorium in downtown Los Angeles, his first lecture was on the subject of reincarnation. Madame Blavatsky and the Theosophical Society had made it a popular subject for debate among esoterics since the end of the nineteenth century. Hall went on to write a popular book called *Reincarnation: The Cycle of Necessity*.

In the late 1930s and early 1940s the beginning of Edgar Cayce's popularity brought attention to reincarnation as many of his psychic readings included past lives as explanations for current predicaments. Belief in reincarnation in America got a big boost in the 1950s with the popularization of the case of Bridey Murphy. Morey Bernstein was a businessman in Pueblo, Colorado, whose hobby was hypnotism. Morey's specialty was regression but he had an idea for an interesting experiment. A housewife named Virginia Tighe agreed to be his subject. He returned her to childhood, and then regressed her before birth, curious if she might report from the afterlife. That's how he met Bridey Murphy, a nineteenth-century Irish woman, Virginia's past life.

The *Denver Post* covered the story in 1954. That led to Morey's book getting published by Doubleday two years later. Film rights were sold before the book hit the shelves. When it became a bestseller, a reincarnation craze inspired cocktails, cartoons, comedy, movies, and Come as You Were parties. Paramount rushed the movie version of *The Search for Bridey Murphy* the same year.

While neither the author or the publisher had bothered to confirm the facts about Bridey's life, the reporters sent to Ireland to validate, or hopefully expose, the story found no evidence to support her existence. They did find factual errors. Bridey mentioned attending St. Theresa's Church, but it did not exist in those days. Still, how did Virginia correctly name a church in the area at all? On the other hand, Bridey's geographic descriptions, and certain other details, including the name of a grocer she recalled, were accurate.

Then an American newspaper claimed that Virginia had an Irish aunt who told her stories about Ireland. Not only that, but as a girl Virginia had a crush on a neighbor boy who lived across the street. The boy's mother was Irish. Her unmarried sister Margaret Murphy also lived there. Bridey Murphy, they argued, had never resided in Ireland, only in Virginia's confused memories.

The book continued to sell well, but the public moved on to another fad. The investigative journalism that discredited *The Search for Bridey Murphy* may itself have been suspect. As Colin Wilson (2013) wrote in his book *The Supernatural,* "To begin with, the newspaper that did the exposé was the one that had failed to gain the serial rights on Bernstein's book, which had gone to a rival. It emerged that Virginia had never met her 'Irish aunt' until she was eighteen, and that she was certainly never in love with Mrs. Corkell's son—who turned out to be the editor of the Sunday edition of the newspaper that denounced her."

Whatever the truth behind *The Search for Bridey Murphy,* it blazed a path for other successful books about hypnotic subjects producing historically verifiable details about past lives, including *Died 1513, Born 1929; Second Time Round; Lives to Remember;* and *The Cathars and Reincarnation.*

As for Virginia, she regretted getting hypnotized in the first place. She was not a believer in reincarnation but thousands of readers held her up as proof of it. In 1966 Virginia accepted an invitation to appear on the television show *To Tell the Truth,* but she had no taste for fame. Later in life she commented ironically, "Well, the older I get the more I want to believe in it."

Morey enjoyed his success with the book. He didn't set himself up as the world's most famous regression therapist, even though the field grew exponentially, steadily becoming more acceptable and more organized. He did not succumb to the desire for continued fame by becoming a guru or attempting to replicate his experience. He went back to business. His great success allowed him to become known as a philanthropist.

Professor Ian Stevenson researched reincarnation in Nepal, India, and Lebanon, finding startling cases, including a deaf and dumb boy who was born a few days after a neighbor had drowned. As soon as he could walk the boy began visiting the dead neighbor's family. He mimed how he had drowned. He correctly showed them where he had drowned. He claimed to be the children's father. The University of Virginia published several volumes of Stevenson's research in the 1970s.

In 1997 Stevenson published *Reincarnation and Biology*. Two volumes, 2,000 pages, it reported 225 cases of children whose past life memories matched their physical anomalies, including details confirmed by autopsy records. For example, a child born in India with boneless stubs for fingers on one hand, recalled losing the fingers of that hand in a machine accident in his past life. Another child had a birthmark on the back and the front of his head that resembled an entry and exit wound. The child remembered being shot in the head in his past life, and Stevenson found a murder that matched the details the child reported. Another child reported thirty statements about her past life. Stevenson verified twenty-seven, and the other three were not complete misses. For example, she said her father had been bald. He was not, but her uncle was. A nickname she wrongly gave to one relative, belonged to another.

Reincarnation stories have become perennial, returning every generation. In the 2000s America was fascinated by the story of a boy who remembered being a World War II pilot. The story goes that a boy named James began having nightmares after visiting a museum where he saw WW2 fighter planes. His vivid dreams of getting shot down by the Japanese near the end of the war left him screaming in the night. His parents worried deeply about him, but they were told that such night terrors are normal for children.

The strange thing was that the boy had always loved airplanes. Most of his toys were airplanes and airplane models. At age two he knew the names of different kinds of WW2 fighter planes. The obsession on a certain kind of toy is not an unusual experience during childhood.

The boy's father claimed to have resisted the possibility of reincarnation, as a good Christian and an oil industry executive, he insisted that there must be some rational explanation for his son's detailed accounts. Much of it could be explained away as the boy's high intelligence and memory for facts about his favorite planes, but some of it involved more unlikely coincidences. A pilot named James took off from a ship and was shot down, as in the nightmares. They asked for the name of a friend he had then. They found a record of someone by that name in the right place at the right time, but he wasn't around anymore. So they contacted his surviving sister who allegedly confirmed more details the boy provided. She said he knew things only she and her brother had known.

In 2009 the Leiningers's book *Soul Survivor* was published, with the help of mass media coverage and television appearances, becoming a *New York Times* bestseller. But there are troubling aspects to the story. At the beginning, when the nightmares began happening several times a week, a book about children with past life trauma led to a communication with a popular author who specialized in regression therapy for children. James was to be told that these were not nightmares, they were his memories. The therapist had no doubt that this was a case of reincarnation caused by a traumatic death.

As his father researched ever more deeply into the history his son might be remembering, ostensibly to prove it mere imagination, was there no coaching at all, even unconscious? Since planes had become their mutual obsession is it likely that he didn't discuss details with James? The therapist encouraged the Leiningers to write their book. She even wrote the foreword for it, bringing attention to her own books and practice. How dependable are the motives of the participants in this enterprise if they are to be our proof?

Stevenson's work continues at the department he founded—the Division of Perceptual Studies (DOPS), a unit of the Psychiatry and Neurobehavioral Sciences program at the University of Virginia. Stevenson's successor Dr. Jim Tucker's book *Return to Life: Extraordinary Cases of Children Who Remember Past Lives* was a *New York Times* bestseller in 2015. Tucker revealed another startling case. Ryan, a kid from the Midwest, claimed to be the reincarnation of a movie extra who became a successful Hollywood agent. Tucker (2013) writes about their search for a person that might match Ryan's descriptions. "It had seemed unlikely that an extra with no lines would have danced on Broadway, had a big house with a swimming pool, and traveled the world on big boats. But Marty Martyn did."

Ryan got a lot right about Marty's life: his mother's curly brown hair, his two sisters, his brief career dancing in Broadway reviews, a sister who became a successful dancer. He described correctly how much Marty liked to relax at the beach with his girlfriends, watching surfers and getting sunburned. According to Ryan, the beautiful house with the swimming pool in Beverly Hills had the words *rock* or *mount* in the address. Marty lived on Roxbury. The English geographic term *-bury* derives from *bergaz,* a Germanic word for mountain.

THE TAROT RENAISSANCE AND THE SCHOOL OF AGELESS WISDOM

In the chapter "The Platonist on the Sunset Strip" we saw how difficult it was for a wealthy and well-connected collector like Thomas Moore Johnson to acquire a pack of tarot cards. This often maligned magical device used to read the past, the present, and the future had been considered the tool of criminals for centuries. A good Christian would never have a deck like that in the house. But as we have seen in the twenty-first century there are Christian versions of oracular card decks.

The kind of difficulty Thomas Johnson faced when he tried to acquire a tarot deck eased around 1918 when pirated editions of British occult historian A. E. Waite's *The Pictorial Key to the Tarot: Being Fragments of a Secret Tradition Under the Veil of Divination,* and its accompanying tarot deck illustrated by Pamela Colman Smith, became available in America thanks to L. W. de Laurence. De Laurence pirated many important occult works of the early twentieth century often replacing the author's name with his own, and even mimicking unusual bindings, such as the red pebbled covers of A. E. Waite's two-volume work on Paracelsus. De Laurence also published spell books and grimoires such as *The Sixth Book of Moses.* These books became so popular in Haiti, and the cause of so much trouble, that to this day de Laurence editions cannot be imported into the country.

Paul Foster Case, as we shall see later in this chapter, offered a tarot deck through his organization BOTA as early as 1931. C. C. Zain, who we met in the Secrets of the Hermetic Brotherhood of Light chapter also made an Egyptian deck and an informative book available from 1936. But both the Case and Zain decks were only available to members. Very few people even had the opportunity to hear of these organizations.

The Rider deck can be seen in the classic noir book and movie *Nightmare Alley* (1947), but tarot decks were not something one could find easily especially outside big cities. In 1959 University Books printed the first version of the Rider deck available nationwide. This was the deck beloved by hippies in the 1960s.

The first popular book about the tarot in America was by Eden Gray. Gray was born Priscilla Pardridge, a Chicago debutante. She became a successful actress on Broadway. Photos of her from the Roaring Twenties survive scantily clad as the artist's model "Angelica" in *The Firebrand*. The play attracted the attention of the authorities. The photograph of a scene where the dashing leading man in tights stands with his left leg between the bare feet and thighs of Angelica, his nether regions pressed against her breasts as she gazes up into his eyes, suggests why the production was asked to change certain "actions." During World War II she served as a Woman's Army Corps laboratory technician. She had a background in Ernest Holmes's The Science of Mind movement, earning a doctorate of divinity degree at the First Church of Religious Science in New York, the city where in the 1950s Gray opened Inspiration House Publishing, an occult bookstore and publisher. In 1960 she self-published her classic *Tarot Revealed: A Modern Guide to Reading the Tarot Cards*. In 1969 it was reissued by a major publisher and became a bestseller. Late into her life she gave tarot readings at her home and for charity events. At age ninety-six she attended the 1997 International Tarot Congress costumed as the sunflower in the Rider-Waite-Smith tarot card The World. She was delighted to discover how revered she and her book had become.

Stuart R. Kaplan is another of the many who helped make the tarot popular. He wrote some of the most influential books about the cards, including the four volume *Encyclopedia of the Tarot*. As a collector, writer, and publisher he made what was once rare available at local bookshops. He was in the toy business. At the Nuremberg Toy Fair in 1968 he browsed looking for something to import or knock off.

He found a pack of tarot cards he liked so much he made a deal to distribute them. The stores that took them were soon calling for more, but they also relayed a common complaint. Why was there no instruction book? Kaplan wrote *Tarot Cards for Fun and Fortune Telling* and started U.S. Games Systems, Inc. As of 2021 they have almost four hundred different tarot and other oracle card decks in print.

Kaplan was born on April 1 in 1933 so he chose the Fool card from the Rider-Waite deck as his company logo. The Rider-Waite-Smith deck is what most people think of when they think of tarot cards. Stuart had a lot to do with that. He researched Smith, collected her art and her publications, wrote a biography of her, and released the lavish *Pamela Colman Smith Commemorative Set* in 2009, which includes over a hundred illustrations of art she made that was unrelated to tarot. But before Kaplan there was Paul Foster Case, one of the people most responsible for making possible a wider acceptance and better understanding of the tarot.

Occasionally when doing research at the Philosophical Research Society Library, I'd find things I wanted copies of for myself. I was allowed to use the copy machine in the shipping room. My most prized copies are of Manly Hall's typed notes from a course on the tarot he took as a teen in Los Angeles that was taught by Paul Foster Case. MPH had written his initials in diluted ink or watercolor at the top of the first page. He spoke fondly of Case and respected his scholarship. Hall went on to publish lectures and books on the tarot, and he issued the Knapp-Hall tarot deck. Knapp had also provided the color illustrations of Hall's magnum opus *The Secret Teachings of All Ages*.

The son of a deacon who was the town librarian, Paul Foster Case had always been interested in the occult. Even before he could read, he pored over the few esoteric books he could find. He read them before he could understand what he was reading. Like many metaphysicians he was also a musician. He played the organ well enough to make himself a career out of it. He accompanied silent movies. He liked that he could play for a few hours, a few days a week, and make enough money to get by. He played parties, too. At a charity performance he met Claude Bragdon.

Bragdon was a highly respected architect. He built important buildings in Rochester, New York, including two churches, the Central Railroad terminal, and the Rochester Chamber of Commerce. He wrote six books, including *More Lives Than One, Architecture and Democracy, Four-Dimensional Vistas,* and his lyrical classic *The Beautiful Necessity: Seven Essays on Theosophy and Architecture.* The first edition has graceful, embossed gold-ink scrollwork on its black cover. Bragdon advocates for what he considers the most organic architectural style, gothic. By the 1930s his architectural flavor had fallen out of favor. But he was an influence on the inventor of the geodesic dome, Buckminster Fuller.

Since Bragdon could read Russian, and had an interest in the fourth dimension, a friend gave him a copy of Ouspensky's *Tertium Organum.* Ouspensky had studied with Gurdjieff for ten years. In this book he denies the reality of space and time. Aristotle's axiom that A = A, the basis for our concept of reality, Ouspensky refutes by pointing out that A = A + not A. Bragdon liked the book so much he translated it into English, wrote an introduction, and published it himself. The book was popular enough that the prestigious publisher Knopf printed the second edition. Ouspensky didn't know about any of this. As royalties accumulated Bragdon went on an expedition to find Ouspensky. He found him in Constantinople, and Ouspensky enjoyed the delightful surprise of receiving his royalties.

This was the man that Paul Foster Case met in 1900 at the charity performance. Case was sixteen years old. Claude Bragdon was thirty-four. They became good friends. When Bragdon asked Case where he thought playing cards came from the boy was intrigued. Doing research in his father's library he found references to "The Game of Man," and so his lifelong interest in tarot cards began.

In 1907 Case's summer read was *The Secret of Mental Magic* by William Walker Atkinson. The book inspired Case to write the author. Atkinson was a successful lawyer in Chicago when stress ruined his health. He lost almost everything. In search of healing, he found it in the New Thought movement. Reinvigorated by positive thinking he embarked on a new career. Many of his monthly lessons for student subscribers became books that have never gone out of print. Atkinson wrote and self-published them in his own name and a host of pseudonyms including Yogi Ramacharaka, Swami Bhakti Vishita, Swami Panchadasi, Theron Q. Dumont, Magus Incognito, probably Swami A. P. Mukerji, and perhaps the Three Initiates. He could be compared to the Portuguese literary genius Fernando Pessoa, as they were both many writers in one person, and they both shared an interest in the esoteric. However Atkinson's pseudonyms sound more like each other than not, unlike Pessoa's carefully articulated collection of personas, each with their own personal astrological birth charts.

Atkinson's works contain genuine wisdom, conveying an insightful understanding of religions he for the most part never experienced in person. The series of books on yoga by his pseudonym Yogi Ramacharaka are widely regarded as classics. Atkinson advised his readers on the geography of the afterlife, the breathing exercises and asanas of hatha yoga, and the use of self-hypnosis for healing and prosperity. Many of his books, written over a hundred years ago, are still popular today, and though he never visited India, his yoga books remain widely read and respected there. Like many American metaphysical teachers Atkinson wound up in Los Angeles. None of his neighbors in a quiet suburb of the city knew that he was famous for books he had written masquerading as three initiates, three swamis, a yogi, and a magus.

Cases's biographer claims that proof of Case's contributions to the metaphysical classic *The Kybalion: A Study of the Hermetic Philosophy of Ancient Egypt and Greece* can be found among his papers. There is no definitive proof that Atkinson wrote the book alone, but he is the most obvious choice, as it is in his style, and was published by his publishing company. On the other hand, perhaps Case made some contributions that Atkinson thought worthy of anonymous acknowledgment.

Case met a stranger who walked up to him on the streets of Chicago—not the Dr. Fludd of Rosicrucian fame, although this Dr. Fludd was a prominent physician, too. Fludd explained that he had been sent by another, who "is my teacher as well as yours." The man knew more than Case's name. He knew all about him, even his thoughts. Case wondered if the man had telepathic powers. Fludd told Case that he could continue in his career as a musician, or he could devote himself to humanity. After that meeting Case put all his effort into his esoteric studies. He began to write a series of lessons. He cleared up deliberate or accidental errors in the tarot. He arrived with a splash in 1916 when he published the immediately influential *The Secret Doctrine of the Tarot*, in a series of articles in the *Word*, a Theosophical magazine.

In 1918 Case became involved with Chicago's Thoth-Hermes Lodge of the Rosicrucian Order of the Alpha et Omega (A.O.), the organization MacGregor Mathers founded after the demise of the Hermetic Order of the Golden Dawn. Case moved up the ladder of initiations quickly until he introduced discussion of sexuality into his lodge's curriculum. Nothing too exciting, the writing in question had more to do with kundalini than the erotic, but in 1921 MacGregor's widow Moina Mathers took exception. She warned Case that she had seen others try to discuss these matters and always the results were bad. Case disagreed. Moina ordered him to resign. He felt a great relief when he did.

In 1922 Case decided to start his own school. At first, he named it the School of Ageless Wisdom. When he moved to Los Angeles it became the Builders of the Adytum. *Adytum* is Latin for "Inner Shrine." Case described BOTA as a "direct offshoot of the Golden Dawn." But he did choose to make a crucial difference. Case had a colleague with a deep interest in the Enochian magical practices of the Golden Dawn. When he fell ill and died, Case thought Enochian magic was to blame so he would not allow it in his curriculum.

BOTA was and remains most famous for their tarot decks that individuals can color for themselves. Instructions are provided for proper coloration but people have always felt comfortable about coloring them to suit their own fancies. The deck is based on the Rider tarot, but Case claims to have made corrections by removing intentional blinds. Like the Rider deck, a woman illustrated the cards, Jessie Burns Parke who was known for her portraits. Her work is in many collections including the Philadelphia Museum of Art.

There's a story that Case once suffered the delusion that all his fellow passengers on a bus were evil, but that's not unusual in New York City. Case blamed the incident on his getting overheated from too much yoga, especially pranayama. With his wife, Harriet, and his secretary Ann Davies, he created a durable mystery school through correspondence courses. He authored seventeen books. Most of them were about the tarot, but his popular pamphlet *The Great Seal of the United States: Its History, Symbolism and Message for the New Age* (1935) is a cult classic among students of America's destiny.

In 1954 Case went on vacation to Mexico with Harriet where he died without warning. Ann Davies took over BOTA, helping it flourish. With five thousand members in study groups on four continents, BOTA continues to function as a mystery school in the twenty-first century.

Mary K. Greer is another author and lecturer who has contributed greatly to the rising popularity of the tarot, and among her sources of inspiration was BOTA. Greer was kind enough to allow me to share this paragraph from a 2021 personal communication. "I have extensively researched playing card divination and have copies of most of the old books on the subject. The oldest evidence is primarily found in genre paintings that I've collected online and through 18th–19th century prints that I've purchased. The first to write about tarot fortune-telling were late 18th century French Freemasons in an encyclopedia volume (*Le Monde Primitif*) to which Ben Franklin and John Adams subscribed. I tend to follow Jung's theory of archetypes as almost every culture has myths or folklore that can be correlated with the tarot trumps. In fact, I've been to Egypt twice looking for any correlations I could find to tarot. I've also done three tarot-focused trips to Northern Italy and met with tarot scholars there to see what evidence I could find."

Growing up as a midcentury army kid, Greer never lived any place for long. Every time her family moved Greer would head to the nearest library to look up the words *witch, gypsy,* and *magic,* but she found little information. She did check out the books about ghosts, dreams, and yoga. In high school she and her friends experimented with a Ouija board. Like many of her generation, Greer first saw tarot cards in action, and found further metaphysical inspiration, from the goth soap opera *Dark Shadows.*

The day after New Year's Day in 1967, California elected Ronald Reagan governor. In January of that year the Doors released their first record. It included their hit song "Light My Fire," a song that set the tone for a year when 159 American cities burned as riots broke out protesting institutionalized racism and poverty. For hippies it was the

Summer of Love. Jimi Hendrix and Janis Joplin were introduced to the world when they played the Monterey Pop Festival. Thousands of kids from all over America dropped out, hitchhiked, and experimented with drugs and alternative spirituality in San Francisco, or wherever they could find like-minded conspirators for a psychedelic future. At the end of the year, during that strange week between Christmas and New Year's Eve, Mary Greer encountered the tarot when her friend Nancy showed her a surprising Christmas present: Eden Gray's *Tarot Revealed*. Greer returned to college in Tampa, Florida. She asked around about a place in the area that might carry tarot cards. She was told about an odd store across town with the word *metaphysical* in its name. Borrowing a car she found the store, which had several tarot decks in stock. She bought the classic Rider-Waite-Smith deck.

Now she had the cards but she could only find a couple of books on the subject, and they didn't go into the depth she desired. So she continued to read the cards, experimenting with her friends. She was already picturing herself as an eventual crone sharing her wisdom in a book about the tarot.

A year later Greer was applying to her tarot readings what she learned from reading Jung and Joseph Campbell as an English major studying "Archetypal Criticism." After graduation in 1969 she began studying astrology. In 1970 she moved to London. Her relationship with a manager of the Atlantis Bookshop opened a world of resources, including many new friends with similar interests. She took astrology classes at the Theosophical Society. But she still couldn't find a class or a teacher on the subject of tarot cards.

Greer returned to Florida in 1973. She continued studying astrology and attended old-fashioned Spiritualist churches where she learned skills like psychometry. Even so, she had remained a solitary practitioner on her own path. Then she joined a chapter of BOTA. With her own experience, augmented by what she learned from the Builders, Greer began teaching a noncredit tarot course at the University of Central Florida. The small class was a success. The following semester a newspaper in Orlando ran a story about the teacher of a tarot class and Greer found herself instructing sixty students.

In 1976 Greer moved to California where she taught tarot as an academic subject at the New College of California. She also taught Women's Studies including classes in moon mysteries and goddess traditions. She became an ordained priestess in the Fellowship of Isis. All while continuing to pursue a Ph.D. she never completed because her career as a metaphysical teacher demanded more attention.

In 1979 while on sabbatical in Mexico with her future husband, the legendary vagabond writer and photographer Ed Buryn, with his encouragement, Greer decided to write her first book on the tarot: *Tarot for Your Self: A Workbook for Personal Transformation.* Since then Greer has written eight more books on tarot, aromatherapy, and her groundbreaking history *Women of the Golden Dawn: Rebels and Priestesses,* published in 1995. Her most recent book *Pamela Colman Smith: The Untold Story; A Biography of the Artist of the Waite-Smith Tarot* was cowritten with Stuart Kaplan, Elizabeth Foley O'Connor, and Melinda Boyd Parsons and published in 2018. The third edition of her book *Tarot Constellations* followed in 2021 with a new title *Birth Cards: Archetypal Tarot.* Greer's books, workshops, and lectures have been inspiring seekers for decades, greatly contributing to the popularity and availability of the cards that have fascinated her since she was a child.

As for the tarot itself, it has evolved into an art medium that explores social justice, as in the Indigenous LandBackTarot & Oracle of Colonization; fine art, such as Tarot Dali and the Tarot of Claude Monet; and history and literature, such as the American Renaissance Tarot. The tarot's tantalizing blend of psychological symbology and meaningful imagery has proven so evocative that on tarot message boards posters complain they are addicted to collecting decks. According to U.S. Games Systems sales of tarot cards tripled during the pandemic, as they had during the financial crash of 2008. Quite a contrast to 140 years earlier when Thomas Moore Johnson couldn't find a single deck for sale in the United States.

In a private communication in 2021, used with his permission, I asked Adam McLean for an estimate of how many different kinds of tarots exist now. Adam is a Scottish writer specializing in alchemy and symbolism, he was editor of the *Hermetic Journal* from 1978 to 1992, and is publisher of the much beloved *Magnum Opus Hermetic Sourceworks,* which makes available hand-bound leather limited editions of rare and important primary texts of the Western tradition. He is also a leading expert on surrealist artists. His surrealism website documents over one hundred of them, rescuing many from obscurity. In 2004 McLean began collecting tarot decks. Here is his response to my request for a rough estimate, provided with the understanding that "I may be entirely wrong."

"I have no clear figure," he continues, "I collected 2,700, up to around 2015 but there were many missing from my collection, perhaps as many as a further 1,000 items. Since 2015 there has been a massive explosion in the production of tarots due to the easier and less expensive ways of printing as well as the use of funding systems such as kickstarter. I suspect there may be as many as 7,000 to 8,000 tarots produced since the beginning of the 20th century, with an exponential growth curve at present." However, as of 2022, cities in thirteen states continue to ban or restrict tarot readings.

THE ASTROLOGY RENAISSANCE

Around 250 CE the great Neoplatonist philosopher Plotinus foreshadowed Jung's idea that the planets don't rule our fates, they indicate spectrums of circumstances. "The stars are like letters that inscribe themselves at every moment in the sky," Plotinus wrote. "Everything in the world is full of signs. All events are coordinated. All things depend on each other. Everything breathes together" (Plotinus 1937).

Astrology is a science for poets, metaphor sneaking around with mathematics. Like the Bible, astrology can drive you crazy if you surrender free will and become addicted to constant guidance. Astrology is a conversation with the heavens. A map of shifting possibilities, not an infallible oracle. There is no doom in astrology. Only the spectrum of choices. Your good choice may be someone else's bad choice. Hard aspects can have happy results. Happy aspects can disappoint, and sometimes harm, by causing excess or false optimism.

Astrology is as ambiguous as mediumship. Just as we are left dumb-founded by the miracles and frauds of a psychic, we harbor deep doubt about an alleged science that isn't scientific. Just how do the planets sup-posedly influence our lives? How can something so far off emanate such power, and in such particular ways? Why do different systems of astrol-ogy all seem to work, though they contradict each other significantly? The placement of planets in a birth chart might be in completely differ-ent houses depending on what house system is used, Placidus, Koch, or Whole Sign. Then there are the astronomical issues, such as precession, that render the old ways obsolete, yet they still work for so many. Are these alleged maps of outer space really maps of inner space? As above so below, they say.

In America, as we have seen, astrology dates back to the earliest days of colonization. Robber barons, military generals, and presidents have consulted with astrologers. Rumors were heard in the metaphysical community that Trump consulted an astrologer and a psychic during his presidency. But the popularity of astrology in the early twenty-first century has reached new levels. New astrology books appear daily. The astrologers of YouTube upload predictions, some weekly, others monthly. People are less ashamed to admit the subject interests them.

This astrological renaissance began with Alan Leo, a British astrolo-ger, author, and publisher well known as the father of modern astrology, but its flowering into a significant culture owes much to the astrologers of the latter half of the twentieth century, including Stephen Arroyo, Lois Rodden, Robert Hand, Liz Greene, Linda Goodman, Rob Brezney, Tracy Marks, Stephen Forrest, Joyce Jillson, Eric Francis Coppolino, and many others. In their books they combined depth psychology with astrology to create new approaches more like psychotherapy than fortune-telling. Jim Maynard's *Celestial Guide and Astrological Week at a Glance Engagement Calendar* and Lewellyn's *Daily Planetary Guide* allowed students of astrology to see the aspects for each day, while providing space for notes. Once astrologers had a small collection of such calendars they had a useful tool for looking back at how certain aspects may coincide with repeated patterns or themes, in areas such as health, relationships, or evolution of the soul. The pioneer of this approach sometimes called Spiritual or Evolutionary Astrology was an artist named Dane Rudhyar.

Dane Rudhyar was born in Paris, France, as Daniel Chenneviere. A health crisis he suffered as a child left him with time to apply his high intelligence to the study of music. His parents were strict. He graduated the Sorbonne at age sixteen and studied at the Paris Conservatoire. As a composer he specialized in short pieces of dissonant harmony. The music is less pleasing than Satie, yet resembles his work. Both have a sonorous sense of unexpected harmony, but Satie is after beauty, while Rudhyar seeks to transcend the rules of music.

A trip to America in 1916 changed his life, when the New York Metropolitan Opera performed his compositions. While he was in New York City, Rudhyar met one of the first Zen teachers in America, Sasaki Roshi, beginning his lifelong interest in Eastern culture. Rudhyar did most of his music composing in his teens and after age seventy. Astrology and his spiritual interests dominated everything in between. He took the name Dane Rudhyar, his last name being a combination of Hindu words, especially Rudra, the ancient Vedic god of the hunt, the deity who removes obstacles at their root.

Rudhyar moved to Los Angeles where, as a young composer influenced by radicals like Debussy and Scriabin, he didn't make enough money to survive, so he worked as an extra in Hollywood movies. He played a secret service agent in one film, but his most illustrious role was Jesus Christ in Cecil B. DeMille's 1923 silent epic *The Ten Commandments,* but he's only shown from behind, healing the lepers.

Rudhyar didn't write about astrology exclusively. He wrote books about music, beginning in 1913 with *Claude Debussy and His Work.* In 1928 he wrote *Rebirth of Hindu Music* and in 1982 *The Magic of Tone and the Art of Music.* Publishing books over a seventy-year period is only one of his accomplishments. He was both a painter and a composer specializing in dissonant harmony. His most famous pieces were scored for piano, including a series in the mid-1920s called *Pentagram.*

In the summer of 1938, as America's recovery from the Great Recession of 1937 staggered, and Hitler prepared to annex western Czechoslovakia, a little over a year before the Nazis would start World

War II, a small group of artists met to declare a manifesto proclaiming their intention "to carry painting beyond the appearance of the physical world through new concepts of space, color, light and design, to imaginative realms that are idealistic and spiritual." They were inspired by Theosophy and Zen. Raymond Jonson and Emil Bisttram officially founded the Transcendental Painting Group at a gathering of painters at Bisttram's home in Taos, New Mexico, that included Dane Rudhyar, one of the main writers of their manifesto.

In his books and articles Rudhyar wrote about the New Age, further popularizing the phrase, predicting that the Age of Aquarius would not arrive until the 2060s, although he had high hopes for the hippies, at first. He had learned the term *New Age* from the woman many believe invented it, his friend Alice Bailey. Alice, born in England, had become a leader of the Theosophical Society's Krotona Temple in Hollywood, California. But she later broke with them as they were skeptical of her claim that she was channeling a Tibetan master without Blavatsky's permission. Bailey's *Esoteric Astrology* and her applications of the Seven Rays to all areas of life, have remained influential, especially her book *White Magic*.

Rudhyar wrote hundreds of articles and more than forty books about astrology and spirituality. His first book on astrology, *The Astrology of Personality: A Reformulation of Astrological Concepts and Ideals, in Terms of Contemporary Psychology and Philosophy,* was published by Alice Bailey's Lucis Trust in 1936. It established his reputation. Rather than attempting to predict the future, or find lost items, he argued astrology should be used for gaining insight into the human psyche and individual personalities. In addition, the stars do not impel us, they do not rule our fates, they are signs, we are all linked in a great synchronicity, as Plotinus said, "all breathing together."

A resident of San Francisco in the sixties and seventies, Rudhyar became a popular lecturer among the hippies. The first wave of hippies, the idealists and intellectual rebels, he thought a possible sign of the New Age. He also cast an astrological chart for Elvis Presley, giving him a comprehensive reading the king was said to have consulted often.

Rudhyar contributed to American Metaphysical Religion's library of books encouraging American exceptionalism *The Astrology of*

America's Destiny: A Birth Chart for the United States of America, published by Random House in 1974. He was rather pessimistic in the short term but optimistic about our time in ways that haven't rung true yet. When the 1980s mass market commercialization of the New Age arrived Rudhyar reached a wide audience and was viewed with great respect by the astrological community. He died in San Francisco at age ninety in 1985.

How did Rudhyar become interested in astrology? In 1930 he had married Marla Contento, secretary to a Theosophist who introduced Rudhyar to Marc Edmund Jones. Jones introduced Rudhyar to astrology, sharing mimeographed lessons with him. Jones was friends with Israel Regardie, Aleister Crowley's former secretary, who published once-secret Golden Dawn documents and rituals. Jones was also friends with Corinne Heline.

Jones, like Rudhyar, had a job in early Hollywood. He has forty-nine writing credits for films from 1913–1939, but most of them between 1913 and 1915. He would have had more credits if ghostwriters were allowed them. He went on to write twenty books about astrology, becoming a popular lecturer across the nation. He attended some of the earliest workshops on Zen in America, conducted by the great Japanese Buddhist scholar D. T. Suzuki.

Jones founded the Sabian Assembly in 1923 with the help of Manly Hall and his Church of the People. One of the Sabian lesson sets, still offered by the Assembly, includes the study of Ibn Gabirol, Plotinus, Plato, Aristotle, *Grimm's Fairy Tales,* Blavatsky's *The Secret Doctrine,* and *One Thousand and One Nights.* Other lesson sets cover astrology, the Kabbalah, and the Bible.

In 1925 Jones conducted an experiment with a psychic named Elsie Wheeler. Jones would drive to Balboa Park in San Diego where he would write down Wheeler's visual symbols for each of the 360 degrees of the zodiac. Because Wheeler was disabled they would remain in the car, but Jones reported that the view of lawns and trees near the Pacific Ocean helped Wheeler receive the visions more easily.

Jones was ordained as a Presbyterian minister in 1934. He shared the symbols with Dane Rudhyar who was so impressed he asked Jones for permission to publish the material with Rudhyar's own notes. Jones allowed it and *The Astrology of Personality* became one of Rudhyar's most successful books. In 1938 Jones became a student at Columbia University where he excelled. He was editor of the *Teachers College Student Forum* and president of the Philosophy Club, earning his Ph.D. in 1948.

Meanwhile the Sabian Symbols had become increasingly popular among astrologers. Jones released his own book *The Sabian Symbols in Astrology* in 1953. As the New Age took flight more books were released about the symbols, as well as new books about other ways of symbolizing each degree of the zodiac.

The year Jones was born, 1888, George Eastman registered the trademark for Kodak. In the fall of that year Jack the Ripper was in the news. That was the year Blavatsky published *The Secret Doctrine*. Jones lived to the age of ninety-one. He died in 1980, the year the *Star Wars* saga's second episode *The Empire Strikes Back* played movie theaters worldwide. CNN began broadcasting that year. Sally Ride became America's first female astronaut.

In 1974 Richard Tarnas arrived at Esalen in Big Sur, California, the famous retreat center and landmark of the Human Potential Movement. There he studied psychotherapy with Stanislav Grof, the founder of Transpersonal Psychology. Among his other teachers were a Who's Who of famous authors: James Hillman, Elizabeth Kübler-Ross, Joseph Campbell, Huston Smith, and Gregory Bateson. In 2006 Tarnas published *Cosmos and Psyche,* a different kind of astrology book. By examining patterns in history Tarnas revealed a correlation between certain astrological aspects and recurring trends. For example, a crisis that causes widespread panic is more likely to happen when Saturn conjuncts Pluto as in 2020. When Jupiter conjuncts Uranus people tend to be in the mood to protest, to declare the right to freedom and equality, and to demand a share of the future. Tarnas (2006) demonstrated the new respect for astrology when he wrote: "Yet perhaps those stars will have been there all along, hidden by the bright dawn of our modernity. And our Ulysses will be but awakening to a very ancient cosmos whose vast intelligence, beauty, and mystery we have been slowly preparing ourselves to know."

As the 2020s dawned Richard's daughter Becca Tarnas, Ph.D., emerged as a popular astrologer in her own right. As editor of *Archai: The Journal of Archetypal Cosmology* she curates in-depth explorations of the frontier where astrology and Jung found agreement.

In the last days of 2020, the *New York Times* editorial page published an opinion piece by a popular astrologer. Astrological predictions and psychological profiles continue to multiply across social media platforms. There are millions of unique #astrology posts on Instagram on any given day.

THE COSMIC JAZZ OF VINCENT LOPEZ

We have seen metaphysics and music combine to entrance Quaker girls in the early American colonies. They heard strange music in the air that mysteriously transformed them into spirit mediums. Mediums who played musical instruments provided an atmosphere not unlike a modern music concert, often with an undercurrent of repressed libido, moments of shared space in total darkness, weird lighting, drums struck in midair, or trumpets blaring while resting on a table.

We have seen how important music was to metaphysicians like Kenneth Guthrie, Corinne Heline, and Dane Rudhyar. American jazz, blues, and rock music have trafficked with the occult ever since Robert Johnson had a hellhound on his trail after selling his soul to the Devil at a crossroads at midnight. Rock star Stevie Nicks has long denied practicing witchcraft, but in 1998 a high school student in Huntsville, Alabama, was not allowed to sing "Landslide" at a graduation ceremony in a church. The minister explained that "the leader of Fleetwood Mac is a witch and a Satan worshipper." From the strictly Christian perspective rock has always been the devil's music.

Michael Ventura (1985) wrote, in an essay titled "Hear That Long Snake Moan," from his book *Shadow Dancing in the U.S.A.,* "Every history of jazz goes back to the slave celebrations in a field that came to be called Congo Square, in what was then the center of New Orleans. (Interestingly, the Oumas Indians once used the field for their corn feasts and considered it holy ground.) On Sundays, slaves from all over the city arrived, watched over by white police and an encircling throng of white spectators."

New Orlean's Queen of Voodoo Marie Laveau attended Catholic Mass in St. Louis Cathedral regularly, but many eyewitnesses reported seeing her dance in Congo Square. In the one place left them to congregate, enslaved people invented what would become jazz and rock and roll.

In the 1960s Jimi Hendrix sang about the chakras in his song "Bold as Love." Neil Young in an interview with *Forbes* in 2006 said, "I think I found peace in paganism." Alice Cooper famously got his stage name from a Ouija board. Marilyn Manson has an honorary priesthood in the Church of Satan. The band Coven's singer Jinx Dawson posed nude on a ritual altar on the inside of their first record, titled *Witchcraft Destroys Minds & Reaps Souls* (1969). Few rock stars have resisted the allure of the esoteric. Alice Bailey's occult classic *A Treatise on White Magic* circulated around the Warhol Factory crowd. In that book Lou Reed found the title of one of the more famous Velvet Underground songs: "White Light, White Heat." The drummer of iconic metal band Tool published a book called *The Wickedest Books in the World: Confessions of an Aleister Crowley Bibliophile.* Elvis Presley owned a signed copy of Manly Hall's *The Secret Teachings of All Ages.*

Although there is not much that Jimi Hendrix and Portuguese American bandleader, pianist, and Broadway marquee sensation Vincent Lopez, had in common, it could be argued that Lopez, the inventor of what he called cosmic jazz, anticipated Hendrix's blend of the cosmic, mystical, and musical.

Lopez was famous during the Swing Era. When radio was introduced to New Jersey the programmers chose Lopez to play a radio residency. Both Lopez and radio became hits. That was the beginning of his successful career. Lopez would have his own TV show on CBS. His music was on the soundtrack for *The Wizard of Oz.* Liberace was a devoted fan.

Lopez disappointed his father who wanted him to become a Catholic priest. But at the age of fifteen the call of music was too much for Lopez so he escaped the monastery where his father had sent him. Lopez used numerology, astrology, and séances to guide his daily decisions and to manipulate his musicians.

Lopez didn't hide his potentially controversial interests. A Capricorn, one of his jazz compositions was called "Capricorn." He had a column in a San Francisco periodical where he told fortunes. In the early 1930s he published *Vincent Lopez Modern Piano Method*. Lopez said about jazz (1933) that it must be "Fast and furious fun. How much wiser the jazz makers! They too sometimes make ugly music, but they do it with comic attentions, which makes all the difference in the world. In the last analysis, the quintessence of jazz is fun, or humor, ranging from horseplay to the exuberant outbursts of animal spirits in great men." Some amazing musicians and future bandleaders passed through his band including Xavier Cugat, Glenn Miller, Artie Shaw, Jimmy Dorsey, and Tommy Dorsey.

By the early 1940s he had become Prophet Lopez. He added a mystical flair to his shows by giving predictions. A newspaper lists his eight successful predictions for 1941, including the German invasion of Russia and Nazi leader Rudolf Hess's flight to the United Kingdom. However, his predictions for 1942 missed badly, especially "Germany will break up," and "Japan will become the ally of the United States," although both those predictions eventually came true. Another big miss was his prediction that Hess would die in 1942, he lived until 1987. But Lopez correctly predicted that the Nazi war machine would lose its war in the extreme cold of Russian winter.

In 1944 he published not only *What's Ahead? A Musician's Prophecies of World Events,* but also *Vincent Lopez's Musical Horoscope and Personal Number Guide,* which contained "a Musical Horoscope Suite." In *Lopez Speaking: An Autobiography* published in 1960, between reminiscences of Jimmy Durante and W. C. Fields, Vincent wrote that his lifelong fascination with numbers began when he read Shakespeare and found a reference to Pythagoras.

Years after his stardom a reporter found Lopez playing in the elegant lounge of a luxury hotel. Lopez granted him an interview. He claimed to still be receiving a thousand letters a month. He mentioned that he thought numerology should be called "human engineering." In 1960 Lopez was given a star on the Hollywood Walk of Fame at 6609 Hollywood Boulevard. Fortunately, he was still alive to enjoy the honor, though we do not know if he was pleased by the numerology of the address.

THE SOUTHWESTERN TRANSCENDENTALISTS

Mabel Gansen Evans Dodge Sterne Luhan, with her Louise Brooks hairdo, and her reinvention of the salon, was a friend to artists. She could be temperamental and domineering or sweet and kind, depending on the situation. Her unhappy trust fund parents provided wealth, but otherwise only neglect. In her autobiography *Intimate Memories* published in 1933, Luhan writes about bisexual experiences she had in her youth, giving details of her encounters with women. She married young but she did not learn to enjoy being a wife, or for that matter a mother. When her husband died in a hunting accident she took her son on a trip to Europe. In Paris she met her next husband, a wealthy architect from Boston. In Florence, Italy, they took up residence in an estate built for the Medicis. She hosted a salon that included Italian aristocrats and influential writers and art collectors, Gertrude Stein and her brother Leo, as well as other writers and artists.

Luhan had never been in love with her second husband. When her son became an independent teenager she took him to New York City. Her friend Lincoln Steffens, the great investigative journalist, encouraged her to start another salon. At her home on Fifth Avenue she hosted Wednesday Evenings. Luhan helped define the avant-garde, presenting anarchist author Emma Goldman, and evenings on Freud, Free Love, but also Theosophy, and the other popular esoteric topics of the day.

As she explored the world of avant-garde art in America she accepted invitations to write for art, literary, and political journals. Her job as a widely read syndicated advice columnist didn't last long, but it does preserve a glimpse of her interest in the healing tradition of positive thinking called the Mind Cure.

Luhan married a third husband, the artist Maurice Stern. She had heard about New Mexico from Gertrude Stein's brother Leo. She sent Maurice to investigate a possible visit or move there. It took a few weeks but Stern wrote back "Save the Indians, their art, culture, reveal it to the world!"

Upon arrival in Santa Fe, Luhan was disappointed. But Taos felt like coming home. She began visiting the Taos Pueblo where she met

Tony Luhan, a local Indigenous American. Soon Maurice was on his way back to the East Coast. It took a few years, but she wound up marrying Tony. Tony built the adobe structure that became the center of Southwestern Transcendentalism, first as four rooms, ultimately as seventeen rooms, on twelve acres, with a view of the Sacred Mountain.

Visitors included Aldous Huxley, Martha Graham, Georgia O'Keeffe, D. H. Lawrence, and Ansel Adams. She reached out personally to Lawrence, telling him that only he could capture the truth about the place. His visits over several years were always productive, though he didn't write the Taos novel that Mabel Luhan had hoped for. "I think New Mexico," Lawrence wrote, "was the greatest experience from the outside world that I have ever had. It certainly changed me forever" (Torgovnick 1998).

In 1932 Luhan published *Lorenzo in Taos,* her memoir of D. H. Lawrence's visits. She had been sending parts of the manuscript of an autobiography she was writing to Lawrence. He was reading them as he approached his death. He responded that she must publish these revelations masquerading as confessions. She published the first volume *Intimate Memories* in 1933. Two years later she released *European Experiences,* the following year *Movers and Shakers,* and the year after that *Edge of Taos Desert.*

After decades helping artists with patronage, good advice, her own writing, and as a host, Mabel Luhan died in 1962. She was buried in Kit Carson Cemetery. Not only does her historic adobe still stand but visitors can rent a room.

Taos was not only the setting for Mabel Luhan's southwestern salon, it was also the town where the Transcendental Painting Group was born. Dane Rudhyar and his colleagues emphasized the spiritual aspect of modern art. They inspired artists everywhere, but especially at the Colony of Sven-Ska. Here, too, the artists studied the metaphysical, the mystical, and the psychic, with a special affinity for the writings of Helena Blavatsky. The influence of the Transcendental Painters on the Colony of Sven-Ska is one example, chosen from many, of the quiet circulation of metaphysical concepts that appear repeatedly in American history as sources of inspiration for evolving artists, writers, and communities.

As Ann Japenga wrote in "The Lost Colony of Sven-Ska: Christina Lillian and the Cathedral City Artists" published by the website California Desert Art in 2016, "The Sven-Ska women were fully immersed in small town life—decorating tables for Women's Club luncheons, giving neighbors rides to the market—at the same time they were quietly probing philosophy, the occult, mysticism, Theosophy and how it all related to art."

Born in 1888, her parents named her Emma. Her childhood in small Kansas towns settled by Swedish immigrants left her longing for the freedom and glamor of Hollywood. Since she was good at making clothes for her siblings she decided to have a career as a designer for movie stars, a goal she achieved. She became friends with Greta Garbo, and other famous actresses. The name Emma didn't seem to fit this tall, elegant woman who was often compared to Katherine Hepburn, so she took the name Christina Lillian.

In the 1920s she explored the Arizona desert, on a mission to befriend Apaches, attempting acts of kindness similar to the local services that would later be practiced by the members of Sven-Ska. The Apache didn't trust her much, refusing her offers to chauffeur them in her 1927 Studebaker.

Still looking for inspiration, in the 1930s Christina studied with the renowned teacher of abstract expressionism, Hans Hoffman. Then Mabel Dodge Luhan invited Christina to a residency at her salon in Taos. Christina lived in the adobe house with fellow guests, painter Georgia O'Keeffe and writer D. H. Lawrence and his wife, Frieda. Christina was inspired by Luhan's example. She became an artist. She called her creations of salvaged tin her Taos Tintypes. But another ambition had been aroused by her residency. She wanted to start her own art colony. Helping other artists became her mission. She moved first to Palm Springs, and then to Cathedral City where she bought a house next door to the modernist painter Agnes Pelton, who had been a member of the Transcendental Painting Group in Santa Fe. Famous astrologer Dane Rudhyar and other members of the group visited Agnes and became friendly with Christina. Many artists, writers, and intellectuals stopped over for a stay in Cathedral City.

What attracted Christina to a blue-collar town known for its working-class bars and brothels? As Ann Japenga has pointed out the rent was cheap and the views of the local mountain ranges spectacular. The colony was productive, not only artistically, but in their community. They would help found the Palm Springs Art Museum and the Desert Art Center.

Christina had no desire to marry. She didn't relish the idea of a husband telling her what to do. She described family life as raising a carnival. Some have suggested that since Agnes, Christina, and the other members of the colony were rather butch, preferring pants to skirts, and practical hair to hairdos, they were queer women. But we have no definitive evidence.

Agnes Pelton has become the best-known member of Sven-Ska. Born in 1881 to American parents in Stuttgart, Germany, she moved with her family to the United States in 1888, and later attended Pratt Institute in Brooklyn. Her influences included Blavatsky, Jung, and the agni yoga of heretic Theosophist Helena Roerich and her artist husband, Nicholas. After joining the colony her home became Cathedral City's first venue for viewing art.

Agnes left the East Coast behind for good in the early 1930s for a move to California. Unlike most of the settlers headed for as close as they could get to the famous beaches, Agnes found a home in Cathedral City. There she had a studio with a meditation room, her shelves of esoteric books, and the mountains looming over the desert. "The vibration of this light, the spaciousness of these skies enthralled me," she wrote. "I knew there was a spirit in nature as in everything else, but here in the desert it was an especially bright spirit" (Aberth 2019).

When Pelton died in 1962 few in the art world knew enough about her to mourn. She had never achieved even regional fame, surviving by painting desert landscapes popular with tourists. Her abstract work did not receive attention until *Agnes Pelton: Desert Transcendentalist* opened at the Phoenix Art Museum in 2019.

"Pelton possessed a strong will to remain true to her vision despite poverty and marginalization," art historian Susan L. Aberth writes in an essay in the *Desert Transcendentalist* exhibition catalog. "It is time to realize that she was not alone in her quest to capture the esoteric in a more abstract idiom, but part of a trajectory of women artists who will undoubtedly become better known and eventually be given their proper art historical due."

In 1986 a now legendary exhibition at the Los Angeles County Museum of Art called *The Spiritual in Art: Abstract Painting 1890–1985* challenged prevailing histories of modernism by tracing the origins of Western abstract art to the esoteric traditions that American Metaphysical Religion has always drawn upon. The book includes etchings from the works of Robert Fludd, provided by Manly Hall and the Philosophical Research Society library.

The catalog also records that "at Manual Arts High School in Los Angeles in 1928–1930 Jackson Pollock's first art teacher, Frederick Schwankovsky, was a Theosophist and devotee of Krishnamurti (he drove Pollock to Ojai to hear him), and other mystics such as Manly P. Hall." Schwankovsky introduced Pollock to "the concept of poured and dripped painting."

More recent esoteric exhibitions include *Blessed Be: Mysticism, Spirituality, and the Occult in Contemporary Arts* in 2019 at Museum of Contemporary Art in Tucson, Arizona, and *Supernatural America: The Paranormal in American Art* in 2021 curated by the Minneapolis Institute of Art.

THE PRIVATE INTERESTS OF SALINGER AND SAFIRE

From Walt Whitman's familiarity with the Kabbalah and Anaïs Nin's fascination with alchemy to Sylvia Plath's Ouija board, American Metaphysical Religion has been an inspiration to many American writers. Here we will take a brief look at two very different writers. The author of the famous and infamous *The Catcher in the Rye* and President Richard Nixon's speech writer William Safire.

J. D. Salinger was famous for his reclusiveness, and for his famous book made infamous by the man found reading it just after he murdered John Lennon. Salinger is most often written about as the patron saint of adolescent rebellion and longing for meaning, but he was also the American Hermann Hesse. Like Hesse, Salinger found inspiration in the spirituality of the East.

Salinger survived D-Day on Utah Beach and the Battle of the Bulge. In the first ten weeks of deployment his unit lost thousands. The carnage he witnessed was capped off by his experiences at the liberation of the concentration camp Dachau. He would never mention the name of the camp.

Seeking relief from the trauma he suffered as a soldier in World War II Salinger practiced first Zen then Vedanta philosophy. Like Joseph Campbell he studied at the Ramakrishna-Vivekananda Center in Manhattan. Salinger explored the works of Edgar Cayce, the beliefs and practices of Christian Science, and Dianetics, the precursor of Scientology.

"Teddy," the final short story in Salinger's classic collection *Nine Stories* introduced his readers to the Vedanta concepts of nonattachment and reincarnation. At one point in the story ten-year-old Teddy explains that he incarnated again because in a past life, "I met a lady, and I sort of stopped meditating."

The last work Salinger published, "Hapworth 16, 1924," made up most of the June 1965 issue of the *New Yorker* magazine. The story refers to past lives as "appearances." Readers received instructions in yoga breathing exercises. The careful reader can follow hints offering insight into tantric sexual practices.

Salinger's family later revealed how difficult it was for them to have to adapt to each new path the great writer decided to explore. It was not enough that Salinger do the breathing exercises. Wife and children must also participate in the great experiment.

Conservative icon William Safire had the dubious distinction of being asked to write a speech that Nixon would give if our astronauts were stranded on the moon. He's better known as a syndicated columnist on politics for the *New York Times,* and for his column in the *New York Times Magazine* on the subject of word derivations and other interesting quirks of language.

Safire's bookplate appears on a copy of an obscure set of two ponderous volumes that we have already met earlier, *Anacalypsis* by Godfrey Higgins. Safire's copy of the 1927 limited edition was available for sale online in early 2020. The volumes boast not only Safire's bookplate, and the ownership signature of his father, but each volume also contained folded wax paper in which many four-leaf clovers were preserved, but there is no way to know if they belonged to the Safires.

Higgins, who first authored *The Celtic Druids,* spent twenty years on the research that went into *Anacalypsis,* but he didn't live long enough to finish the last chapter. Though the work was printed in very limited runs it has beguiled and influenced many readers with its lengthy rants against the Catholic church interspersed with fanciful word derivations and comparisons. He argued that the original true religion, preserved throughout history by secret societies, was what he called *pandeism,* the belief that it takes a village of deities to make a creation. It's not one god in all things; it's a divine family working together to make it all happen.

FROM THE SILVER LEGION TO THE VIOLET FLAME

For the generations who grew up from the 1950s through the 1990s, the occult and New Age communities were assumed to be liberal. Scientific atheists and monotheist traditionalists, along with corporate industrial culture, seemed to be arrayed against what they dismissed, and still dismiss, as hippies. All the streams of American Metaphysical Religion met in the communities and practices of the so-called hippies. The lunatic fringe were overwhelmingly on the liberal side, as were supporters of causes such as ecology, feminism, gay rights, organic food, racial equality, and sexual liberation.

In the 1960s and 1970s, for example, the naked witch in films, books, magazines, and music iconography was not only a symbol of the exploitation of liberated female sexuality, but also of feminism and of goddess spirituality. Much of the youthful interest in the occult those decades and the next were connected to popular music. Iconic musicians modeled these interests for their fans. David Bowie talked about the Tibetan Book of the Dead by a pool at a hotel he passed through on his American tour. Patti Smith told her fans to read Rumi. Jimi Hendrix talked about astrology. Jimmy Page popularized Aleister Crowley. Stevie Nicks sang about "an old Welsh witch" named Rhiannon.

For these generations recent developments may be shocking, and perhaps hard to fathom. Neofascism and neo-paganism have found much common ground. The flag of rebellious cool, in the possession of progressives since the 1950s, seems to be in danger of being captured by the Far Right. In the pagan and occult worlds today fascist and racist groups actively recruit. Of course, the idea that American Metaphysical Religion is intrinsically liberal was never realistic; it coexists comfortably with all forms of politics in America, from the mainstream to the most extreme.

Right-wing politics is no stranger to the occult. Julius Evola, the radical traditionalist and fascist intellectual who admired the Waffen S.S., is only the tip of the iceberg. History shows us that fascism flourishes in the fertilizer of conspirituality (the combination of conspiracy theories and the wellness movement). Both communities believe that thought and willpower can change reality. Both fetishize purity, lineage, hidden histories, covert conspiracies, and suppressed secrets.

To provide context for our exploration of the authoritarian side of American Metaphysical Religion we must explore the last time New Age sentiments met right-wing politics, Nazi Germany. While Nazi police put astrologers out of business, Himmler had his own personal astrologer and he hired astrologers to find Mussolini. Goebbels believed Nostradamus had predicted the success of the Nazis, so he spread the prophecies in Europe, Russia, and America. Hitler hired Germany's most famous dowser to detect death rays projected at the Reich Chancellery. A government team researched a technique for finding enemy submarines that used a map of the Atlantic and a pendulum, a metal cube dangling on a string.

Hitler and Himmler, and other Nazi leaders, were devoted to natural healing methods such as homeopathy and Paracelsian medicine. Many ate organic vegetarian diets. They were against vaccinations. Nazis founded the Paracelsus Institute for research into the paranormal, and the Institute for Occult Warfare. The Nazis were environmentalist and holistic. They promoted organic farming and Rudolf Steiner's biodynamic agricultural techniques. There was a biodynamic farm in Auschwitz. Making individuals and societies whole again was a Nazi preoccupation. Communion with Nature, with a capital *N,* and respect for it, reached epic proportions, as what had once been pagan rituals, such as the festivals of the solstices and equinoxes, became occasions for civic celebrations. As Erich Fromm (1957) wrote, "the power that impressed Hitler more than history, god, or fate was nature. Contrary to the tendency of the last four hundred years to dominate nature, Hitler insisted that one can and should dominate man but never nature."

Madame Blavatsky's fascination with Aryan civilization made Theosophy popular with the Nazis. Jesus and the Buddha received make-overs as blonds in contemporary depictions. Himmler cherished his copy of the Bhagavad Gita and took it everywhere he went. Inspired by the Hindu warrior caste, he encouraged SS officers to practice yoga. They also studied the mystical runes. Himmler funded an expedition to Tibet to find out what kind of magic the Dalai Lama might be willing to share, as a fellow Aryan, and to look for a lost tribe of uncontaminated blue-eyed blonds. An avid reader of occult books, Hitler underlined this sentence in his copy of Ernst Schertel's *Magic: History, Theory, Practice* (1923): "The man with the greatest force of imagination commands the world and creates realities according to his will instead of being the slave of an unsubstantial, bodiless empiricism." A similar idea has long been dear to the hearts of generations of positive thinkers in America.

In the late 1970s in Italy a political alliance called *Terza Posizione,* or Third Position, sparked a movement that became the International Third Position in Europe and the United States. This new anticorporate right-wing voice of populism opposed to globalism and imperialism has become more attractive to younger generations whose social contract was not sealed with an electric guitar. In defense of ecology, and a pre-Christian cultural heritage, the Third Position rejects capitalism and socialism. The Third Position claims to be neither right nor left, but its ultranationalism speaks for itself.

Ironically, agreement can be found between the social justice wing of the left and the racist wing of the right in that both are disapproving of syncretism, which is, as the Oxford dictionary tells us, "the amalgamation or attempted amalgamation of different religions, cultures, or schools of thought." Both wings agree that spiritual seekers should stick to the traditions of their dominant DNA. But that can be problematic for the multi-ethnic, and then for one out of three Americans there's the question of reincarnation.

The blurred borders between pagan and occult belief systems, loosely organized political organizations like the Third Position, and militias, are evident in the tattoos of the participants. White nationalists who aren't Christian tend to be pagan. One group, for example, fetishizes black metal music, male virility, survivalism, and fitness workouts. Anticorporate conservationists, they endorse the sustainability catch phrase popular in the 1970s, "small is beautiful." Loosely based on Norse religious practices their rituals include animal sacrifices, which they post on social media, along with photos of weapons, and quotes from Julius Evola. They say they believe that racism is less effective than tribalism, but one member received a two-year sentence for an act of arson committed against an African American church in Virginia.

However, the occult left is also flourishing. Political sentiments are shared alongside tarot readings and horoscopes on Instagram. When Marianne Williamson ran for president, she had a few moments on the national stage when she said things the audience was excited to hear from a candidate. Many people believed they knew exactly what she meant by "dark psychic force."

For some Americans just before WW2 Hitler appeared to be just the leader needed to stop communism. The Russian Revolution had left many countries nervous about the pent-up anger and ambition of the working class. The American fascist movement known as the Silver Legion of America also called themselves the Christian Party and the Foundation for Christian Economics. The Silver Shirts, as they were nicknamed because they wore Nazi knock-off military tunics made of shiny gray and blue fabric, was the invention of William Pelley, who has the distinction of being one of the few American spiritual leaders whose face appeared on a wanted poster. A Hollywood screenwriter, Pelley's metaphysical career began with Spiritualism.

One night in his bungalow in the Sierra Madre Mountains near Pasadena, California, Pelley had an out-of-body experience he called "Seven Minutes in Eternity," that included a talk with God and Jesus.

They directed him to save America. Pelley's mystical experience bears more than a passing resemblance to the plot of the metaphysical classic *Dweller in Two Worlds* by "Phylos the Thibetan," a book that described life in Atlantis with wireless phones, television, and antigravity aircraft. Lemuria and Mt. Shasta myths elaborated in this book remain credible in some circles to this day.

Pelley blended Spiritualism, Theosophy, and Rosicrucianism into a new doctrine that he taught at the college and press he founded, both named Galahad. Pelley's magazine, the *New Liberator,* mixed his essays on the occult with messages he channeled from ascended masters. Then his Spiritualism took on a political dimension. He believed Hitler's rise proved a prophecy the spirits had shown him in 1929. It also meant that he would rise like Hitler to his destiny as American führer. Catholics, Jews, and communists, he taught, are the "dark souls" representing the powers of evil.

A congressional committee described the Silver Legion as, of all the Nazi copycat organizations, "probably the largest, best financed, and best publicized." A report in the *Associated Press Dispatch* of February 8, 1940, reveals Pelley's ambition in his own words. "With a trace of wistfulness, William Dudley Pelley, leader of the Silver Shirts, told the Dies committee today that if his organization had succeeded in its purposes, he would be in charge of the government now. And in that case, he continued, he 'probably' would have put into effect something resembling Adolf Hitler's policies with respect to the Jews, although he said he does not endorse Hitler's exact methods."

Like the führer he revered, Pelley traveled far and wide, holding rallies to build membership in the Silver Legion. At its peak, in 1935, the legion boasted fifteen thousand Silver Shirts. The membership shrank as Pelley had to fight a series of court cases. After the bombing of Pearl Harbor, Pelley disbanded his legion. But it was too late for him to avoid consequences for his politics. Less than a year later he was charged with twelve counts of treason and sedition.

In 1950, fighting prosecution for securities fraud, he published *Star Guest,* an introduction to his new philosophy, inspired by aliens and UFOs, which he called Soulcraft. In 1954 he published twelve volumes of *Soulcraft Scripts: A Post-graduate Education in the Eternal Verities.* Here we find answers to enigmas such as "Why Souls in the Higher Realms Are Reluctant to Give Evidence of Their Spiritual Survival," "How Occupancy of Organic Bodies Expands Spirit's Realization of Itself," and "What the Phenomenon of Americanism Means in the Cosmic Blue-print."

Pelley and the Silver Shirts remind us again that right-wing infatuation with the occult, and its translation into political action, is nothing new in American Metaphysical Religion. Pelley was an inspiration to someone more subtle and more successful, Guy Ballard.

Guy Ballard dabbled in mining and prospecting, but he had more experience as a medium. His wife, Edna, worked as an assistant in a Spiritualist bookshop. They had attended lectures at the Theosophical Society but Guy was the proud owner of a silver shirt. Edna was enthusiastic about Pelley, so much so that she had modeled her opinions and writing after his. In 1930 the Ballards were living in the town of Mt. Shasta, California. Guy liked to hike on Mt. Shasta. During one of those hikes, he claims as he approached a spring for a drink of water he encountered a young man who gave him an elixir in the form of a "creamy liquid." This was no ordinary man—Ballard could feel an electric charge in his presence. The stranger identified himself as the Count of Saint Germain.

Ballard provided details of his meetings with St. Germain and other ascended masters in books he wrote under the pen name Godfré Ray King. He, Edna, and their son Edona, declared themselves the only "accredited messengers" of St. Germain. The ascended master gave Edna the nickname Little Dynamite.

In most photos and illustrations the Ballards are dressed all in white. According to a book by a former follower of Ballard, at meetings with Pelley and his top cronies, Guy had channeled St. Germain, whose plan for a new America was more in line with the fascist ideal closely aligned with Pelley's point of view. St. Germain flattered all with juicy past lives filled with glorious achievements. Not only that, but they were always pleased to be told that they were old friends of St. Germain, returned to help him realize the plan for a "New Government," as they called it. As for their own past lives, it turned out that Guy had been both Richard the Lionheart and George Washington. Edna had an equally illustrious past as not only Joan of Arc and Queen Elizabeth I but also Benjamin Franklin.

When the Silver Shirts began to fall apart in the late 1930s, St. Germain proved to be a good recruiter for disillusioned members, many of whom joined the "I AM" Activity, as it became known. The Silver Shirts could never have become as popular as "I Am." By 1938 the Ballards had a million followers.

In his book *Psychic Dictatorship in America,* disgruntled former follower Gerald Bryan (1940) detailed many of the practices taught by the Ballards. "I AM-ers, when they want quick action over some entity or other evil, frequently use the words 'Blast! Blast! Blast!' For instance, one stopped with her companion in front of a downtown shop window. On display was a black gown with red trimmings! These are hated colors among the I AM-ers—the color of the black magician and the communist! All she did was to stop at the window for a second, looked at the gown; then, to the amazement of her companion, uttered very vehemently the words 'Blast! Blast! Blast!' in an aspirate voice, and passed on, evidently feeling a duty had been performed."

Bryan (1940) describes the mixture of influences on the Ballards so typical of American Metaphysical Religion. "They imbibed a little of Christian Science, read a bit of the Walter Method C.S., branched over to the Unity School at Kansas City, linked up with the Ancient and Mystical Order Rosae Crucis (A.M.O.R.C.), joined the Order of Christian Mystics, studied under Pelley the Silver Shirter, sat at the feet of some of the Swamis, read a little of Theosophy, looked into the magic of Yogi Philosophy and Oriental Mysticism."

The Ballards taught that "decrees" must be repeated regularly to drive away sickness, poverty, and the swarms of entities waiting everywhere to devour the careless. If members became doubtful, pointing out that ordinary Christians and even atheists of their acquaintance seemed to be healthier and richer, they were told if the decrees weren't working it must be because the believer was not true enough. In the *I AM Decree Book* the Ballards provided seventy-one decrees.

A rather chilling example of a decree is especially relevant to the subject of this book. "I call the Angels of Blue Lightning, the Legions of Light to stand guard over your America; My America; that every person who tries to bring destructive conditions, qualities or activities into

America, SHALL CEASE TO EXIST IN HIS HUMAN FORM!"
This prayer was often directed at FDR and the New Deal administration, but one can hear similar expressions of vitriol in the second decade
of the twenty-first century from politically motivated preachers like
Greg Locke and Paula White.

Apparently, Guy's ambition, like his mission, was inspired by Pelley.
Guy wanted to become president of the United States. Pelley had once
run for president, but he was a marginal candidate who received very few
votes. In the administration of the Ballards the ascended masters would
rule America. Who wouldn't want St. Germain as the power behind the
presidential desk? Some found comfort in the rumor that America was
St. Germain's special project. In channeled messages St. Germain not only
approved of Pelley's political ambition he also helped fill out the details.

At the close of 1939, just a couple of months after Hitler's invasion
of Poland, in a huge Spanish Colonial Revival mansion in Los Feliz,
California, on Vermont near Griffith Park, Guy journeyed to the great
beyond again, but this time he didn't come back, at least, not in his
body. He suffered gruesomely at the end, even undergoing surgery in his
home, but to no avail. For years he had claimed that his body enjoyed
"Immortal Endurance." Despite his appearance, which had been older
than his sixty-one years, his followers believed him and continued to
believe even after his death. Guy had not died. He had ascended. His
body never suffered pain or disease, though he suffered for more than
three months, according to the official death certificate filed at the
Bureau of Vital Statistics in Los Angeles.

The *Los Angeles Times* wrote about him, "attracting a huge following across the nation—[he] preached that through 'thought octaves' he
could defend himself against all enemies, all evils—traveled in expensive
fashion and owned four canary-colored high-priced automobiles—used
a suite of rooms at the most expensive downtown hotel."

According to the *Times,* Edna had this to say to their followers,
who responded with cheers and applause, "Our Blessed Daddy will
come back, and there will be a big temple in Los Angeles where he will
some day appear in all his Ascended Master Radiance, wielding infinitely more Power of the Light Rays than before his Ascension." The

photos of him she sold she claimed had been charged with the energy of her disincarnate husband.

In 1940 a federal grand jury in Los Angeles indicted twenty-four leaders of the I AM movement on sixteen counts of misuse of the mails, and one count of conspiracy. But that didn't stop Edna. She outlived Guy by over thirty years. She continued the work they had begun together. He continued to collaborate by means of his messages from beyond. Eventually Edna, too, became an ascended master.

What the Ballards began went on without them. Though it never regained its early mass appeal, three hundred loosely affiliated groups continue to this day in the United States, Latin America, Europe, India, and Africa. The Saint Germain Foundation conducts summer programs near Mt. Shasta that include a teen week, a patriotic play, and a colorful pageant dramatizing the life of Jesus.

In 1958, with the foundation of Summit Lighthouse, the mantle of messengers of St. Germain was claimed by Elizabeth Clare Prophet, and her husband Mark. Conveniently, the disincarnate Edna Ballard dictated a message through Mark that approved the transfer of power. Like the Ballards, the Prophets claimed to be in touch with the invisible masters of Theosophy who had guided the work of Madame Blavatsky. Prophet's mother had been raised Catholic, but her involvement with the I AM Activity, Christian Science, and Theosophy had greater influence on her daughter Elizabeth.

In 1975 Prophet started the Church Universal and Triumphant. Her lectures became popular, and her star rose with the arrival of what in the 1980s would become known as the New Age. Prophet achieved fame at a level the Ballards could only have dreamt of. She appeared on the news show *Nightline,* and on talk shows including *Donahue* and *Larry King Live.*

Guru Ma, as her disciples called her, got some bad press in the 1980s. Gregory Mull, who developed multiple sclerosis while fighting Prophet in the press and in the courts, sued the church leaders for $253 million, alleging fraud, involuntary servitude, and emotional harm. He threw in some salacious details. While still married to Mark Prophet, he alleged Elizabeth had an affair with a kitchen worker. She married the man the same year her husband died. In the past Mull had credited Prophet with saving him from homosexuality.

Elizabeth ignored advice to settle. She became convinced that Mull was possessed by evil entities trying to stop her divinely appointed mission as the only one permitted to speak for the ascended masters. She believed that Mull must be punished to the full extent of the law, to teach his soul a lesson about truth and justice. She compared her difficulties with the court case to Jesus on Golgotha. She seemed to believe certain passages written in the Bible referred to her struggle.

According to an *LA Times* article about the lawsuit, church practices included "rapid-fire prayer called 'decreeing,' tithe to the church, practice celibacy if single and avoid oral sex. Church literature endorses certain colors, and members of the church have appeared in court wearing purple, yellow and other favored hues." According to the lawsuit, Prophet had adopted the blue lightning of the Ballards, but now these attacks against enemies were visualized not as bolts but as bombs.

The jury found against the church leaders. Penalties amounted to over a million dollars. Elizabeth didn't have that kind of money. The Malibu beach mansion and the 12,000-acre ranch in Montana near Yellowstone Park didn't belong to her, they belonged to the church. Her many helpers were mostly volunteers. Elizabeth took a salary of only thirty thousand dollars a year. She feared that her possessions might be taken from her if she couldn't pay up. She tried to raise the money from her followers, asking for a thousand dollars from each. It had worked before. That's how she had paid for the ranch. But the donations she received this time seemed to be subtracted from donations to the church. She couldn't risk that, so she tried another approach. She appealed the case. But she lost again. Mull didn't live long enough to collect. His daughter got the money.

Despite the assistance of the ascended masters, Prophet had been defeated by the forces of evil. Pessimism and presentiments of doom then crept into her once relentlessly uplifting orations. In the summer of 1987, she organized a campaign of prayers meant to block the Harmonic Convergence, history's first synchronized worldwide peace meditation. She felt that its declaration of a New Age represented an effort by the forces of evil to draw away people and ensnare them, when only her church could save them.

In 1987 Prophet claimed to have foreseen an imminent nuclear strike by the Soviet Union. That was the year the United States and the U.S.S.R signed a treaty limiting medium- and shorter-range nuclear missiles, and an American president asked a general secretary of the Communist Party of the Soviet Union to tear down the Berlin Wall. Many members of Elizabeth's flock followed Elizabeth to Montana. Bomb shelters were built. Prophet came back to California to speak at big events, but lived in Montana the rest of her life.

Embroiled in a custody dispute over her youngest child, her organization spending much more than it was taking in, Prophet began forgetting things, like the name of the person in the portrait at her lectures, Jesus. Diagnosed with Alzheimer's in 1998, she retired from public life. She died eleven years later. The daughter she chose to become the next leader of her organization turned down the potentially lucrative honor. Prophet placed her children in positions of power, such as on the board of directors, but they had all moved on. One wrote a fascinating book about what it was like to be Guru Ma's daughter.

The organization Guru Ma founded keeps her books in print, including *Violet Flame: Alchemy for Personal Change, The Lost Years of Jesus: Documentary Evidence of Jesus' 17-Year Journey to the East,* and *The Great White Brotherhood in the Culture, History and Religion of America,* which contains lectures delivered by Prophet at an I AM Activity meeting held at Mt. Shasta in 1975. One of them includes a singalong to Helios and Vesta, the ancient Greek god of the sun and the Roman goddess of home and hearth. Vesta was credited as the songwriter. The book also included chapters dictated by Pallas Athena, Goddess of Wisdom, and Jesus Christ. Curiously, it doesn't have much to say about American history.

17

Prayer Wheel for the
Bodhi Tree Bookstore

LOS ANGELES IS INFAMOUS for surrendering architectural treasures to developers. In Boston you can still eat cornbread and chowder at a restaurant Benjamin Franklin liked. But L.A. is one long recitation of mostly forgotten places. The subject of lost shops could fill volumes. Tower Records on the Sunset Strip was an essential part of the Southern California music scene for decades, but the shopper could also find metaphysical books. The building is still there, a hollow travesty of its former self, with an empty parking lot. Just down the street Schwab's Pharmacy was a Hollywood legend, replaced by an ugly shopping center.

Until the end of the 1980s, Patty's African Museum was a barrage of the fantastic. Just around the block from the Bodhi Tree Bookstore, her shop was a stucco bungalow with a Spanish tile roof, converted into what could have been a museum of African arts and crafts. Masks, sculptures, and carvings crowded the rooms, looming over browsing shoppers. A few regulars, a few celebrities, serious collectors, and the curious made up Patty's clientele. Decorating the walls and counters, snapshots of Patty proved she could smile, but only in Africa, standing beside her real friends.

Ten-foot-tall hornbill guardian birds of carved teak dominated the entrance to Patty's shop, ironically chained with heavy shackles so they couldn't be stolen at night. Something as rare and wonderful as a Bakuba kingmaker mask could easily be missed among all the treasures. If it fell and cracked a little, Patty would sell it cheap, practically giving it to someone she liked. In one room glass cases of antique and contemporary beads from all over Africa and the Middle East looked like a miniature model of the outdoor markets of Marrakech. Patty herself, a weathered gray tree stump of a woman, infamously unpleasant to customers and sometimes downright rude, knew exactly where everything came from and what it meant and what it was used for. The parolees who worked in the store would recommend a specific talisman for your trouble, if you showed appropriate respect to Patty.

But perhaps of all the lost places of Los Angeles, the Bodhi Tree Bookstore at 8585 Melrose Avenue casts the longest shadow. The flag over the Bodhi Tree flapped in the breeze like a Tibetan wind horse, or the unfurled banner of the king of Gondor in the *Lord of the Rings*. Many homes have known the ubiquitous Bodhi Tree bookmarks, with the quaint tree logo and the slogan, "Books to Illuminate the Heart and Mind." The first popular New Age bookstore in Los Angeles, Bodhi Tree became the prototype for not only New Age shops that opened all over America, and the world, but also for a more enlightened way of doing business. How many bookstores can boast of having received a constant stream of thank you notes from people whose lives were changed for the better?

In the beginning the Bodhi Tree was just a couple of rooms, where some hippies did carpenter work while other hippies shopped. Posters on telephone poles, next to posters for rock concerts and lost dogs, were the store's first promotion. Only a few pictures of gurus were on the wall then. Eventually there would be dozens. Not long after, punks arrived, mostly because Bodhi Tree was the only place to find poetry by William Burroughs, Patti Smith, and Bukowski, unless you drove west of Sepulveda, over to the huge hippie haven of Papa Bach's bookstore, across the street from the art house movie theater the Nuart, and only a few wanted to drive that far.

Around the time of the U.S. Bicentennial in 1976, a neighbor named Carl who lived down the block gave Bodhi Tree its very own bodhi tree (*Ficus religiosa*), a sapling he had grown from a seed in a simple pot. It stayed in the pot till it was six feet tall. During the great remodel of 1983 the bodhi tree of West Hollywood at long last got some ground for its roots in the small yard behind the store. A fitting tribute to the tree under which Buddha gained enlightenment, the tree grew to become a forty-foot-tall, fig-bearing landmark. But the tree was not the only mascot of the Bodhi Tree Bookstore.

Reminiscing former regulars ask each other how many Bodhi Tree cats they knew. Did they know them well enough to get a head bump greeting? Would they stroll out to welcome you, or accompany you to the door? What about the cat who liked to curl up next to the shelves of books on witchcraft in the used branch? Or Bear, the big ginger cat who started the feline tradition when the Bodhi Tree first opened? Some knew them all. One by one the feline guardians were buried under the fig tree. Their photos went up on the store walls, in places of honor, alongside the masters of Eastern and Western spirituality. The used branch had its own feline lineage: adorable Chubby, delicate Little Girl, and noble Tara. On the final day an employee took home round little Lucia, the last in a long line of Bodhi Tree cats.

Marianne Williamson had this to say about the store, "I started lecturing in 1983 before words like *higher consciousness, new spirituality* or any of that was mainstreamed. In a way things were more pure back then, and there were only a handful of serious teachers and places you could go to for significant spiritual information. In LA, the Bodhi Tree has been our high temple. It was the place, the only place. And it has always worn its power and influence with grace. Phil and Stan have been role models for me, like the coolest, most humble high priests. They've been a gift to more than just LA; those two have truly blessed the world" (Williamson 2011).

L.A.'s most famous occult rocket scientist is Jet Propulsion Lab's Jack Parsons, whose colorful life inspired the TV series *Strange Angel*. But the principal founders of the Bodhi Tree, Stan and Phil, were a couple of rocket scientists themselves—aerospace engineers to be exact. They had worked on weapons of thermonuclear war, figuring out how to cause ever more carnage. They weren't the only young engineers in the 1960s who wanted to do something more positive for humanity. Very few achieved that goal as well as Stan and Phil did.

They presided over the Bodhi Tree with the keenly aware gaze and paternal calm of experienced meditators; they were not your average bosses. They started the Bodhi Tree for $18,000, leasing the two-bedroom bungalow. Back then in Southern California it was easier to meet Krishnamurti than to find his books. A frustrating search, after some conversations with the man who refused to be the Theosophical messiah, led directly to the idea of opening a bookstore. Traditional bookstores weren't carrying the kinds of books Stan, Phil, and their friends, and most of their generation, wanted to read. This bookstore would fix that. The humble ideal they had in mind was the Library of Alexandria, except you could buy the books.

The songs on the radio the year the Bodhi Tree opened almost tell its story. The Beatles broke up that year. "The Long and Winding Road" must have played on a transistor radio when they were building the shelves and painting the walls in the modest Bodhi Tree 1.0. "Let It Be" had been on the radio for a few months already, along with Simon and Garfunkel's "Bridge Over Troubled Water." Sly and the Family Stone had a hit with "Everybody Is a Star," a song title to put a smile on the face of any Platonist, Paracelsian, or Thelemite.

The melancholy melodrama that was *Love Story,* and George C. Scott chewing up the scenery, making a mockery of the mincing but nevertheless formidable Patton, were blockbuster movies that year. *MASH* was a big-screen hit before it became a beloved TV show. The merchandising trends triggered by Woodstock showed future protectors of the status quo how to not only co-opt but also how to profit from counterculture.

On July 10, 1970, at 2 p.m., a time chosen by an astrologer, the Bodhi Tree opened with an inventory of two thousand books. Bodhi Tree's first Christmas, George Harrison's "My Sweet Lord" was number one. But Janis Joplin had just died that October. Jimi Hendrix had died only a few weeks before that. Brian Jones had died the summer before. Jim Morrison would die the following summer. The times were changing. Soon the clean mellow sound of Laurel Canyon folk pop, the introspection of James Taylor, Joni Mitchell, and Carole King, would rule the airwaves. People were turning inward in search of answers to suddenly pressing questions about the meaning of life, the laws of good health, and the history of human spirituality. By 1976 the Bodhi Tree's business had doubled, then redoubled, and so on, so rapidly that they bought the building they were renting.

In 1978 the small bookcase of used books was replaced by the stucco cottage next door that became the used book branch. It had a few shelves on the porch outside the old wooden door, offering free books at all hours. The aromatic delights of the herbs room drew in the browsing shopper. Shelves full of big glass jars, with a silver scoop in each, offered the common and the rare, always fresh and organic, and special teas—the yogi blend was always popular. The catnip was legendary among humans and felines.

Across from the table of discounted damaged merchandise and the adjacent cash register stood two tall but narrow cases of collectible books. If you kept walking you'd have to choose which way to walk around the bench where heaping boxes of books were often sold as soon as they could be priced. The psychology section was undoubtedly the best place in town to buy used books by Jung. You never knew when you might find vintage Theosophical Society pamphlets, or an obscure first edition of an occult classic. All religions were represented with special attention to the Near and Far East. The astrology section was an education, and browsing was encouraged by the ever-present free tea.

One year a manager of the used branch visited Tibet. He returned renewed and ready to tell stories of his adventures to any customer who would listen. Many working there seemed to have pilgrimaged to India at least once. If they liked you, they'd call you when they knew they were getting a box of treasures, which they sold at impressively fair prices. Books that would cost a fortune today were easily affordable, and available for layaway. Many great book collections originated from that store.

The used branch had a spiritual mission to get the right books in the right hands. Once they got used to a shopper's taste, they would make suggestions. You could be sure that anyone who worked there would at some point involve you in a fascinating conversation about anything from the way thunderstorms clear the ether to an ancient herbal remedy. Sometimes they told you their own stories, how they arrived as counterculture casualties, and in the encouraging refuge provided by Stan and Phil, they blossomed into authors, artists, and teachers.

In 1983 Shirley MacLaine took the New Age mainstream when she published the autobiographical *Out on a Limb,* where she told the story of how her spiritual path began at the Bodhi Tree. Tourists began asking to see the shelf from which the book fell into MacLaine's hands. By 1987 *Out on a Limb* was adapted for television. The miniseries made an even bigger splash than the book. Esoteric historian and philosopher Gary Lachman worked at the Bodhi Tree while earning his degree in philosophy, part of his transition from punk rock bassist and member of the band Blondie to respected intellectual. He recalls, in personal correspondence from 2021, "I managed the new book branch in the evenings—it was open until 11:00 p.m.—and worked in the used book branch on the weekends, where I was one of the buyers. I didn't help Shirley MacLaine, but I was in the shop when she came once. You must know that it became famous overnight when she mentioned it in her book and in those TV films. It had been around for fifteen years or so before that, but after she started her quest it was packed most evenings and weekends."

Once and future California governor Jerry Brown spent weekend hours intently reading, often bringing along his then girlfriend the famous singer Linda Ronstadt. Donovan played a song on his acoustic guitar when he dropped by. Deepak Chopra spent two hours perusing the shelves with Michael Jackson, who wore a disguise. Timothy Leary popped in unexpectedly one October 31 to sign "Happy Halloween" in copies of his books.

The Bodhi Tree new branch became a cornucopia of imported and domestic handcrafted art, exquisite gift cards, crystals, jewelry, chimes, dream catchers, statues, oils, and an antique glass case full of every possible deck of tarot cards available at the time. A chime rang when you opened the door and stepped into an olfactory overload of alluring aromas including the scents of new books, fragrant soaps, scented candles, and incense. Gary Lachman remembers, "it reeked of incense, although none was lit. People would ask what we were burning and we'd say we weren't burning anything: the scent was coming from the boxes of incense in the storage area. There was so much of it we didn't need to light any. It clung to one's clothes."

Obscure magazines on spiritual topics from all over the world filled long shelves. Small independent publishers were assured the attention they deserved, not only by the staff, but also on the new arrivals table that everyone loved to circle upon first entering. The store sparkled with crystals, from the tiniest and most affordable to grand mineral specimens. Artisans and craftsmen filled the glass cases and shelves with handmade charms, jewelry, sacred decor, and decorative treasures, much of it handmade. In this way Bodhi Tree nurtured hundreds of artisans.

Like a wishing well, the Bodhi Tree wouldn't judge you. You could find Christian books on angels, and *The Satanic Bible;* the latest translation of the Flower Ornament Sutra, or the most obscure Sufi poetry imported from publishers in India. Once in the Bodhi Tree Used Branch a big set of dull colored flimsy hardcover books filled a box on the new arrivals bench: transcriptions of the Stalinist Show Trials of the 1950s translated into English, and as always affordable.

At times, on weekends in the early afternoon and late evening, the Bodhi Tree could take on the atmosphere of a club, as flirty singles offered unsolicited comments on book choices, took hold of hands to read palms, or played the inevitable game of guess your zodiac sign. The carefully chosen books and art were so abundant shoppers felt they were entering a temple of every spirituality that was ever written about, with that characteristic dense atmosphere of serenity and concentrated inspiration one expects from sacred places. The musical selections complemented the mood of discovery, and showcased new artists, often first listens of musicians who became legendary, like synth pioneer Kitaro, or pianist composer George Winston.

At the height of its success Bodhi Tree had a hundred employees. They were making close to two thousand transactions a day, with a cash flow of roughly $5 million a year. By 1990 so many people hoping to open their own versions of Bodhi Tree Bookstore were writing for advice that a photocopied manual was put together, called *How to Open a Metaphysical Bookstore.* In 1994 they bought the storefront next door and put it to use as a meeting room, a lecture hall, and a center for book signings.

Bodhi Tree's international influence is shown in this reminisce by Gary Lachman (from personal correspondence), "Sometime in the early 90s, I hosted Colin Wilson and his wife while I was housesitting for Stan Madson, one of the owners, who had a fantastic place in Laurel Canyon. I called it a 'Zen castle,' three floors in the Hollywood hills, with a large terrace garden and jacuzzi. Wilson came to the secondhand shop and bought something like $500.00 worth of books to be shipped back to Cornwall."

In 1996 Leon Chaitow became the first naturopath/osteopath appointed as a consultant by the British government. He was author/editor of over seventy books. He trained a multitude of students in the healing arts. He was founding editor of the Medline indexed *Journal of Bodywork & Movement Therapies*. His daughter Sasha, caretaker of his legacy, is a renowned esoteric scholar and artist with an art gallery called ICON on the island of Corfu. She was founder of the Phoenix Rising Academy, an online school for the study of Western Esotericism aimed at making it available outside formal academia. In 2022 she taught an updated version of her Introduction to Western Esotericism Course: From the Ancients to the Renaissance, sponsored by Treadwell's Books of London. She recalls memories that illustrate the international influence of the Bodhi Tree.

"My memories are from childhood and fragmented," Sasha writes in personal correspondence of 2021:

> My dad used to wax lyrical about the Bodhi Tree, and in the early '80s when he started teaching in the U.S., he used to bring armloads of books back with him. When we traveled there as a family in '86 and '88, he was doing a lecture tour of the U.S. and my mum and I came for the ride, we spent the whole summer traveling around. I know that we visited LA and the Bodhi Tree both times, and that he had someone really important recognize him as we were browsing there, which led to some new lecture invitations, but I really can't remember more than that. And then when I started Phoenix Rising, he took some flyers with him and had them agree to hand them out with any book sales. But I really don't have more detail than that,

nor do I remember names of people involved. Only that I have fond memories, which were fueled by my dad's affection for the place, the people he met there, and the fact that I think to his eyes it was a paradise to see the alternative medicine material sit alongside so much other mind-blowing stuff.

Three American esoteric publishers have been most influential on American Metaphysical Religion: Llewellyn, Weiser, and Inner Traditions. Llewellyn was born in 1901 in Portland, Oregon, when Llewellyn George began publishing astrology books. Llewellyn was born in Wales the year Dickens published *Great Expectations*. He died in Los Angeles the year the first *Godzilla* film premiered in Tokyo. Not just a publisher, but also himself an author, his first bestseller was *The Llewellyn Moon Sign Book and Gardening Guide for 1906*. In 1910 he published his classic *A to Z Horoscope Maker and Delineator*.

Weiser Antiquarian Books is the oldest occult bookstore in America. The first Samuel Weiser Bookstore was started on Book Row in New York City in 1926. Weiser began publishing in the 1950s under the name Occult Research Press. The familiar publisher's mark of an Egyptian ankh at the bottom of the spine of a book gleamed on many a bookshelf as the New Age movement grew from Bermuda Triangle and Pyramid Power paperbacks in the 1970s to the mainstreaming of the esoteric in the 1980s and 1990s.

Speaking of Pyramid Power, a book of that title was the first big hit for Inner Traditions. *Time* magazine covered the phenomenon in 1973. No author is credited for the article, which begins with a glimpse of American Metaphysical Religion, Hollywood-style, "Gloria Swanson sleeps with a miniature pyramid under her bed because, she says, it makes 'every cell in my body tingle.' James Coburn, after he meditates inside his pyramid tent, puts his cat and her kittens to bed over a nest of tiny pyramids, on the theory that the kittens may grow up in a unique way."

Inner Traditions could perhaps be described as the Bodhi Tree of esoteric book publishers. Ehud Sperling, a first-generation Sabra, whose parents moved to Washington Heights when he was four years old, started Inner Traditions in 1975. With a stylish vest and epic fro, Sperling was a radical in the 1960s. The revolutionary's life was revolutionized in 1970 when he asked for a job at his favorite bookstore, Samuel Weiser's Inc. Specialist in the Occult, Orientalia, and Metaphysics. Not only did he learn the book trade, he had access to the legendary collection of esoteric volumes in the basement. Like Stan and Phil, Ehud had received training in mathematics and science, but his experiences in the 1960s had proven to him that there's more to life than what can be measured. Inner Traditions continues to publish dozens of books a year, many of them ingenious delights for specialists.

Jon Graham, acquisitions editor for Inner Traditions, remembers, in personal correspondence, how the Bodhi Tree did what it could to help the fledgling publisher. "I met the owners, Stan and Phil at the LA Festival of Books when it was still held on the UCLA campus. They used to buy our overstock and ship our supplies back for us after the book fair ended. When they stopped going to the book fair, they still did this for us but I would have to deliver the books to their store on Melrose."

When Borders and Barnes & Noble started carrying larger inventories of discounted esoteric books, Stan and Phil could see the Bodhi Tree's days were numbered. West Hollywood's shortsighted decision to bow to local pressure and install permit-only parking made matters worse. Pulling up to have the car parked by a valet for free, but only for purchases of over fifty dollars, was a far cry from serendipitously finding a spot on the street or being lucky to get one of the spaces between the store branches, especially the one under the carport, one of the most coveted parking spots in Los Angeles on a hot summer day.

Jon Graham recalls, "The ecology of that neighborhood was completely changed because a wealthy developer was buying up all the available properties, and the people who shopped at Bodhi Tree had less and less motivation to make the trek to a neighborhood they could no longer afford to live in. Stan told me that he and Phil decided the end was in sight when they learned that the place across the street that had been a tea house was going to be rented as a retail space to some designer clothing store for some astronomical monthly sum (if I recall correctly, Phil said it was something like $60,000)."

After the economic crash of 2008, for many book buying became a luxury. The new digital formats, instantly downloadable for pennies on the dollar, or for free, were the final nails in the coffin of the Bodhi Tree. Even before the pandemic, one out of every two spiritual books bought in the United States was sold by Amazon. The pandemic closed many bookstores permanently, giving online retailers even more of the esoteric book business. But the Bodhi Tree didn't last long enough to face that challenge. It barely made it into the 2010s.

What was once a lower middle-class neighborhood of butcher shops and gas stations, around the corner from a lumberyard, is now home to boutiques offering $500 handbags and $10,000 bathtubs. To keep the Bodhi Tree open two extra months Stan and Phil had to pay forty thousand dollars in property taxes. The land and buildings that cost them $650,000 were assessed at 2.7 million.

As soon as word got out that the store was going to be sold, the many regulars, a few having gone there for over forty years, returned to peruse the shelves one last time. Conversations were overheard about the first time people had visited; the significant other they had met; the friend who bought a magazine with an article about a diet that cured a serious illness, or the life-changing books they found. One fellow claimed his own bookshelves and benches in his living room were almost identical copies of the ones at Bodhi Tree.

The store slowly became depleted of stock as a series of progressively steeper discounts thinned the inventory. It felt like visiting an elderly relative you know is dying, someone you remember in all their wise and vibrant joy, now gaunt and disinterested. Stan and Phil themselves used the word *transitioning* about the end of their store, a term used by hospice professionals.

But there was much more to the Bodhi Tree than its wonderful stock and staff, including the cats. Much more than the bathrooms, like bathrooms in a comfortable home not a store, old-fashioned but always kept stocked and clean, with a box of incense next to a bowl of sand.

Bodhi Tree was a place of serendipity. For many it was our first choice for gift buying. Not only was the selection marvelous, but the store had a strange way of fitting people with the right gift at the right time. If you were sensitive, you didn't have to ask for help. As you explored you would be drawn to the perfect present. The book someone most needed to read. The work of art they would cherish all their lives. The incense that became their signature scent. The oracle they would rely on. The candle that would light their way. A favorite necklace or ring. The Bodhi Tree lived up to the famous esoteric saying, "when the student is ready the teacher will appear."

Some teachers you meet only once. Some teachers you never even learn their name. I never knew the name of my Zen roshi. He didn't wear traditional robes. He had no temple. He haunted the Buddhist nook of the Bodhi Tree. He could be found only by serendipity. I overheard him speaking to another of his students. At the time I was deeply absorbed with technical aspects of Tibetan Buddhism, specifically drops and the other structures of the subtle bodies. I had not yet made the connection between the yogic bindu and drops. When his student left, I decided to approach him. I asked him if he could help me understand these Tibetan mysteries. He said, "If there is no mind there are no drops."

I met him several times. I tried to make appointments to see him but he refused. He would be there if I needed him. Our meetings always consisted of me posing detailed questions and his deflecting them with koans and non sequiturs. He became short-tempered with me. Irritation crept into his voice when he asked me why I was so fascinated with the finger that I never looked at the moon. But he could also be witty in a way that would ring in my consciousness for weeks.

Deep in my studies, reflections on his skepticism would stop me. Then it happened. That is, nothing happened. There it all was, shining now, made up of everything. Instead of facing the world through the blinders of all my training, I was simple and everything around me beamed with the same simplicity, and I felt a tragic yet joyous love for all my fellow travelers in each fleeting moment of time.

He was there in the windowless corner of colorful mostly Buddhist banners and carvings, bent over staring at a book's full-page reproduction of a painting of Daruma by Shunso. Two masters dubiously eyeing each other, one in brush strokes the other in a plaid shirt. He hadn't seen me in a while. Had probably given up on me. I thanked him for helping me realize a spring day. The serenity and warmth the words conveyed made him smile. We were no longer teacher and student. We were more like two children not too awestruck to giggle at the miracle and mystery that is being. A distraught-looking young woman appeared to demand his attention and I left smiling, knowing she was in good hands. Though I returned to the Bodhi Tree many times, I never saw him again.

Words are dangerous, slippery, magnetic, filled with prejudices. A word can be a violent tool in the wrong hands. Words tell only a fraction of the miracle and mystery of life. Words often confuse and cause conflict. The emotional charges of words can differ so greatly between cultures and individuals that even when the same definition is held, the real meaning can be quite opposite. I have a friend who is a master of the African American martial art Kia Asilia A Vita Sanaa. He tells me most of his African American students find it almost impossible to use the word *master* even when it is a term of respect. Though they earnestly want to honor him, they refuse to address him as master.

What the Zen teacher taught me was to trust a deeper awareness of being. Away from words we listen more deeply. Words are the past and the future intruding on the present. They are useful, but they can be deceitful and dangerous when they take over. People have struggled to name and describe this awakening to the present. Bucke called it cosmic consciousness. Generations of metaphysicians talked about the Higher Self, or over-self, others used the Sanskrit word *atman*. Suchness, thusness, Zen, all emphasize that the mystery is far greater than a brain anchored consciousness can conceive, at least as currently underutilized by inhabitants of human bodies. But what is brain when there is no mind?

Through riots, earthquakes, wildfires, floods, serial killers, AIDS, the Bodhi Tree Bookstore was the calm at the eye of the storm that is Los Angeles, a spiritual oasis in the desert of Hollywood. For anyone wanting to dismiss L.A. as a plastic place of shallow people Bodhi Tree was a reminder that looks can be deceiving.

The bookstore was up for sale until the bitter end, with the hope that some visionary with deep pockets would step in, add an online dimension to the Bodhi Tree, and continue the mission. Ultimately the brand name, customer database, and other intellectual property passed to a new owner, but the store itself, at its iconic location, was doomed.

I went to Bodhi Tree a few days before it closed, to buy one last gift. I doubted I would find anything. Only leftovers remained. I was buying a gift for someone I love deeply, whom I had been buying gifts for at Bodhi Tree since we were kids. The store had never failed me. And it didn't this last time. I found a beautiful print of Green Tara that, according to the price tag, had been there for seven years. Perhaps other shoppers had mistaken it for one of the gurus on the wall, which were not for sale. The Buddha of Enlightened Activity seemed the perfect parting present from a lost shrine of American Metaphysical Religion.

The corner the Bodhi Tree had occupied has become the sleek glass home of the L.A. office of PrettyLittleThing.com, a fashion retailer based in Manchester, U.K. This time the Library of Alexandria didn't burn, it succumbed to gentrification, the economy of scale, and the search engine. When the developer's construction crew cut down the fig tree, they didn't know they were on sacred ground, disturbing the bones of beloved cats.

18

American Metaphysical Religion in the Early Twenty-First Century

IN THIS CHAPTER we will take a broad view of American Metaphysical Religion in the early twenty-first century by considering seven themes that have emerged strongly in the first two decades of the new millennium: Apocalyptic Politics, Digital Sigils, Electronic Mediumship, Psychedelic Salvation, Evoking Queer Power, Evolving Female Power, and the Sekhmet Revival, one example among many of ancient deities who have gained a place in popular culture, but also among sincere devotees. Of course, all of these themes have their roots in the twentieth century, but they are strongly defining early twenty-first-century spirituality in America.

The business of spirituality is worth billions of dollars. As many works document, including Carolyn Chen's bestseller *Work Pray Code: When Work Becomes Religion in Silicon Valley*, wealthy executives spend big money for retreats, workshops, and sessions that promise to equip them with the most effective beliefs and practices culled from all around the world. They learn mindfulness to align their spirituality with their work. But which takes precedence in their decisions? Spiritual tourism has become an industry. Factories make votive figures of not so long ago nearly forgotten deities like Model T Fords on the old assembly lines. What happens when everything sacred is turned into banal products intended to add an exotic touch to the decor? That twentieth-century question will receive a twenty-first-century answer. Here at the beginning of the second decade of the new millennium the answer that seems to be brewing is if the sacred can become banal, the banal can become sacred. The imminence of the sacred is everywhere. The plastic good luck charm can be as inspiring as the old-fashioned do-it-yourself talisman. Because if the plastic good luck charm is all the soul and the gods have to work with, then it will have to do. The more suppressed the sacred the more certain its return.

APOCALYPTIC POLITICS

As Gertrude Stein wrote about Americans in her book *Picasso* (1939), "they do not need religion or mysticism not to believe in reality as all the world knows it, not even when they see it." But the line between religion and politics has always been blurry, even in America where the law demands separation of church and state, but presidents end their speeches with "God Bless the United States of America" and every dollar says, "In God We Trust." Political crusades driven by religious zeal are a constant theme in politics all over the world. America is not the only nation that has spent millions of dollars investigating the military possibilities of telepathy, remote viewing, astral travel, and astrological prediction.

Exceptionalism has always been a seductive political force in the United States, and all nations have their own forms of it, but the militant exceptionalism of the early twenty-first century owes much to story-telling. Did Manly Hall intend that an inspiring tall tale he told about the Fourth of July in his book *The Secret Destiny of America* would proliferate among American exceptionalists as proof of divine providence on their side of a culture war?

The story goes that on July 4, 1776, when the Second Continental Congress faced the moment when they must sign the Declaration of Independence, fear overcame them. They knew this meant war with England, the greatest military power of their time. They knew how little real unity existed between the states. They were more likely to hang separately, then to hang together. But then a tall, fiery-eyed, slender man, dressed in a dark robe on a summer's day, seemed to appear out of nowhere. He told them that if they had to spill blood for freedom then so be it. What he had to say to the Founding Fathers inspired them so much they vied for the right to sign first. He was never seen again. Among occultists some whisper that the mysterious stranger was the Count de St. Germain. Among Christians an angel of the lord had brought inspiration from heaven.

The story is more popular than ever today. But it's actually a work of fiction by a once very popular American writer named George Lippard. Titled "The Fourth of July, 1776" and published in 1847 by the newspaper the *Philadelphia Saturday Courrier,* it received a more permanent binding in a posthumous collection of Lippard's Revolutionary War fiction entitled *Washington and his Generals: Or Legends of the Revolution.*

Ever since the uncomfortable convergence of QAnon and New Age, and the advent of digital sigils and the chaos magick of meme warfare, the political side of American Metaphysical Religion has taken on a sinister quality that is contrary to decades of progressive tradition. But as we have seen this is far from the first time that metaphysics has taken a turn toward fascism in America. Both right and left attack each other as fascists. But things were different not too long ago.

"People who really responded to the classics usually joined organizations, learned how to meditate, did yoga and changed the way they related to themselves, their bodies, their families, and all that became the New Age," said Phil Thompson, one of the founders of the Bodhi Tree Bookstore, in an interview with *Whole Life Times.* "A lot of those people are now in corporate positions and government (notably Gov. Jerry Brown), so I always think that has an influence. All the letters and email we've gotten, people say, 'You changed my life.' These new concepts took them out of traditional religion, government, and rationality, made them question things. It's been a progressive wave pushing people to look at their lives and the implications" (Lewis 2011).

The idea is that spirituality, whether encountered in organized religion or on the frontiers of experimentation, is a civilizing force in societies. However, we know from the violent histories of the most popular religions that this is not necessarily so. In the 2020s the alternate reality known as QAnon displayed the dangerous potential of the shadow side of American Metaphysical Religion as the Alt Right pushed its way to the forefront.

The innocent cartoon Pepe the Frog on the notorious website 4chan became a hypersigil for racists who believed that the right meme posted at the right time can have magical power. Posting to seek guidance from coincidences in post numbers on message boards is a kind of omen reading. Just add *pareidolia,* the human tendency to see patterns where there really aren't any, and to many who had fallen down the rabbit hole the president and other celebrities seemed to be sending secret messages.

The much maligned Illuminati reared their fearsome heads again, alongside such timeworn classics as the Hollywood Satanists, the neo-liberal Ivy League elite, and the inevitable Reptilians. Conspirituality, the unholy marriage of conspiracy theories and the wellness movement, is nothing new. History has shown how conspiracy theories catalyze metaphysics, sometimes giving it political aspirations.

Racist punk and metal bands have existed for decades and have always been overt about their beliefs. In the twenty-first century neofolk music movement, and its defiantly dismal relative Martial Industrial, fascist elements masquerade as apolitical music scenes while lyrics and interviews make clear the racism. These musicians readily discuss and recommend the fascist mysticism of Julius Evola. Opposing them at the most grass roots level several artists in today's neofolk underground intentionally create antifascist music. The blog *A Blaze Ansuz* covers their work and the Left/Folk organization puts out compilations of their music, proudly declaring themselves "politically unambiguous."

Since pagans believe that the purity of nature must be preserved, then why not the purity of races? Questions like this are used by racists to recruit people to the cause of eco-fascism, the belief that the only way to protect the integrity of nature is by authoritarian government. This approach has been successful enough that *Teen Vogue* published an article in April 2020, titled "Eco-fascism: What It Is, Why It's Wrong, and How to Fight It."

A subculture of self-proclaimed half-alien Starseed souls concoct heady brews of UFOs and shamanism. Memes and online workshops spread not only the idea that the more sensitive among us might be related to extraterrestrials, but in some cases also QAnon-related political conspiracies. One Starseed became famous at the storming of Congress in 2021, while wearing face paint, fur, and a horned headdress. A navy veteran and yoga practitioner, while behind bars he petitioned the court for organic food as a religious right, and received it. Eventually he complained that he had been duped by Trump. About five months later the *New York Times* ran an article with the headline, "QAnon Now as Popular in U.S. as Some Major Religions, Poll Suggests." Why is Q popular among what used to be the liberal progressive core of the New Age movement?

As Jules Evan wrote in his Medium essay "Starseeds: Nazis in Space?": "This is not so different from other religious narratives, like Platonism or Sufism, which also tell us we don't really belong on Earth, we're cosmic beings, and that's why we feel homesick. What's different about the starseed gospel is, this isn't necessarily true for all humans. You're special, you're a starseed, you're not like everyone else!" When the ancient Orphics inscribed on leaves of gold: "I am a child of earth and of starry heaven but my race is of heaven," they were describing the origin and the exile of every soul, from the truth about self, not from a distant planet. Having said that, we cannot dismiss the possibility of alien DNA in human beings, because we cannot dismiss the probability that aliens exist, or the likelihood that they may have interacted in various ways with the human race.

Among the many victims of the pandemic that began the 2020s were yoga studios. The number of physical fitness businesses in America shrank by almost one-fourth in 2020. The online followings of yoga teachers who adopted QAnon vocabulary and conspiracy theories grew rapidly. In some cases they were able to survive the closure of studios by monetizing their online traffic. Isolation and the search for meaning, for some semblance of a sense of control, created ideal conditions for conspirituality in the metaphysical and yoga cultures, where the most eager members are often vulnerable novices who attend classes and workshops to find a sense of community. They've been taught that this world isn't exactly real, and they've learned to collect explanations of why things are so. But they have not yet developed discernment.

According to a poll by OmniPollSM in 2013, 41 percent of American adults, 54 percent of Protestants, and 77 percent of Evangelicals believed we were in the end times. I was unable to find a poll for 2020 but the numbers were undoubtedly higher. It's put a strange twist on U.S. politics that millions of voters are rooting for the apocalypse. QAnon has taken the place of the book of Revelations as the authority on the timing of Judgment Day.

When Christians endorse QAnon, have they left Christianity for American Metaphysical Religion? When praying for angels to strike enemies or proselytizing for prosperity many American Christians are pagans wearing crosses. As Jean Baudrillard (1983) wrote in his book *In the Shadow of the Silent Majorities,* "They were and have remained pagans, in their way, never haunted by the Supreme Authority, but surviving on the small change of images, superstition and the devil."

QAnon shows us what can happen when spiritual seekers cast aside all dogma to pursue truth in the online world, where they encounter what Gary Lachman has called "a cascade of trapdoors." Highly educated, conventionally successful mature adults have fallen through these trapdoors into irrationality and delusion. An ornament on a Christmas tree became a secret message from the president about his effort to rid the world of Satanic overlords. They were able to disbelieve a pandemic that killed millions worldwide. Among those whose desperation was evident in the breakdown of their sanity were supporters of OccupyWallStreet, Anonymous, and Standing Rock. Seduced by hoaxes and propaganda they found new hope and community in a web of misinformation. Many writers have reported the great kindness and warmth shown by QAnon converts to each other, and to newcomers, a hospitality and camaraderie reminiscent of charismatic churches. But in this case the good news is not the gospel, it's apophenia.

Apophenia is a compulsion for meaning. In the search for messages from the divine, or guidance from nature, human beings have interpreted bird flight, dreams, organs of sacrificed animals, tea leaves, coincidences, tortoise shells cracked in fire, illustrated cards, constellations, planetary motions, comets, eclipses, random encounters with creatures in the wild, overheard snippets of conversations, randomly opened pages, dice, sticks, and clouds.

If everything has a soul, even a rock, then we are surrounded by potential messengers, as the Algonquins believed before the arrival of Europeans. That can be a mindful and compassionate way of life, but the problem begins when neurosis tries to banish all doubts. Then the search for meaning turns compulsive. Suddenly messages are everywhere all the time. What a relief this development is at first. The sense of having broken through to a more enlightened relationship with life is deeply comforting and energizing. God or spirit is talking directly to the true believer, through traffic lights, a song on the radio, or the hand gesture of a president—what Baudrillard called "the pagan imminence of images."

QAnon appears to be a variation of the Apocalyptic Jubilee theme also found in the monotheistic religions. The remnant, the faithful who have survived, are used by God to build a new and better order. We may wonder how well-educated people with families and careers could have fallen into such irrational beliefs, but this is not an unusual phenomena in the history of American spirituality.

In 2005 evangelical Christian broadcaster Harold Camping predicted that the Day of Reckoning had arrived. He preached that there would be five months of fire, brimstone, and plagues. Millions would die every day until the world ended on October 21, 2011. His followers behaved accordingly. They did what they could to warn their disbelieving friends and families. They supported each other during a time of imminent catastrophe and wrapped up their affairs wherever possible. Camping had made the same prediction for 1994. In fact, three of them. September 6, September 29, and October 2. Something terrible did happen in 2011, to Harold. He suffered a stroke and had to retire from radio. He had been a popular preacher but when October 21 came and went, he was ridiculed by the media as the leader of a failed doomsday cult. Of course, Christianity is the ultimate in organized apocalyptic religion, but the same cognitive dissonance can be found along many less organized spiritual paths.

On Christmas Eve, in a suburb of Chicago in 1954, the Seekers, also known as the Brotherhood of the Seven Rays, gathered outside the humble home of their leader, an earnest older woman named Mrs. Dorothy Martin. Dorothy had briefly been one of the earliest Scientologists but her interest in the occult was born when she attended several lectures on Theosophy fifteen years earlier. Dorothy was most influenced by the *Oahspe Bible* of the community that called itself the I AM Activity.

Dorothy claimed she was channeling, through automatic writing, what she called the Guardians. These spiritually advanced extraterrestrials from the planet Clarion warned Dorothy that a cataclysmic flood would end the world soon. But if the faithful gathered on the given date they would be rescued by UFOs come down from the sky. Christmas Eve was the fourth such date. Earlier misses were explained away. Some detail must have been overlooked. Perhaps someone neglected to remove all metal from their clothing. Or the aliens might be testing the Seekers to make certain that on the real departure day all would go smoothly.

The Seekers were organized by Charles Laughead, a physician at Michigan State who was asked to resign because of his annoying habit of preaching the Clarion gospel to his students. Charles sold his possessions in preparation for his escape to outer space. That Christmas evening he stood with several incognito scientists who were there to study cognitive dissonance. They wrote a book about what they witnessed called *When Prophecy Fails*. The reporters present far outnumbered the Seekers. Newspapers had been ridiculing the cult for months. It was a popular story in 1954. A few hours after they were supposed to arrive, Dorothy channeled a message that somewhat relieved the tension as far as the Seekers were concerned. The Seekers, according to the aliens, "had spread so much light that God had saved the world from destruction."

As the group fell apart Dorothy moved on. In 1961 she became Sister Thedra and revealed that she was now channeling Jesus Christ, whose real name was Esu Sananda Kumara, an associate of the 144,000 Kumaras from Venus, 144,000 souls of light who hold the vibration of Christ until its return after 2012. In 1965 Dorothy founded the Association of Sananda and Sanat Kumara. She quietly shared almost three decades of channeled messages, mostly through the U.S. mail.

Dorothy lived in Mt. Shasta, California, then in Sedona, Arizona. In her nineties she passed away peacefully in her bed after automatic writing final messages to her small but faithful flock.

American poet and Santee Dakota activist John Trudell is not known as a metaphysical teacher, though he said his poetry was given to him line by line from the afterlife by his disincarnate wife. He was also a believer in the power of prayer: "When we think" he explained once at the kitchen table, "we project electromagnetic energy out into the universe. Praying is active. When we pray we're thinking. When we pray we're projecting electromagnetic energy out into the universe. We are flowing with the universe. When we hope, we're not projecting that energy anymore, because there's no thinking connected to it. We're just waiting for the world to deliver to us. When we're praying we're participating with the universe" (Lucid 2011).

John also had this to say about America's fascination with the Day of Reckoning: "Apocalyptic propaganda is the basis of Western religion. It's a control mechanism by instilling fear. You instill the fear so people won't think clearly. Everything is there to disrupt the creative intelligence so it doesn't flow with clarity and coherence. So fearing the apocalyptic is just a mining tool they've been using since they came up with the concept of the male dominator god" (Lucid 2011).

DIGITAL SIGILS

Sigils are meant to change reality. If they work they redirect wealth and power, they protect and curse. Closely related to amulets, usually written on paper or parchment, and often destroyed to complete the ritual, few have survived. Sigils are where Kabbalah and astrology meet. The right words written the right way during the right astrological aspect could bring healing or victory, secret knowledge, or adoration. In the late seventeenth century sigils were treasured instruments of sacred knowledge and power. Not long after they would be consigned to curio cases.

The surge of interest in sigils driven by the political ambitions of the denizens of 4Chan and 8Chan evolved into a more generalized interest by a much wider spectrum of people, most with more mundane goals. Tutorials on the creation of sigils can be found on TikTok and YouTube. Chaos magick books are available on Amazon and as PDFs online.

Creating a sigil can be a complex process or a simple one. Traditionalists contend that to do it right one must first undergo purification of diet and celibacy. Appropriate meditation and mental preparation provide the proper focus. The time of creation must be chosen astrologically according to not only the day but the minute most potent for the realization of the sigil's purpose. The sigil might be created by connecting the angles of the astrological aspects of the hour, along with the appropriate symbols of angels or demons with powers appropriate to achieving the goal.

For most sigil creators in the early twenty-first century the process is much simpler. Write down the intention. Take away all vowels and any repeated consonants. The remaining letters are then positioned into an arrangement that feels right to the sigil maker. The sigil is inert until charged. The most popular way to charge it is by maintaining intent focus while masturbating or participating in some other form of sexual activity leading to orgasm. Singing, prayer, meditation, holding a yoga posture, or repeating a mantra are among the many other ways to charge a sigil.

But technology has made sigil creation even easier in the digital age. Meant to be a worldwide art project involving the projection of sigils in public spaces, Sigil Engine did not achieve its original purpose. It became instead home base for sigil makers. From going live at the end of 2020 to three weeks into February 2021 the Sigil Engine had created 300,000 sigils for users all over the world.

The use of technology for divination can be found on numerous online Yi Jing (I Ching), tarot, and oracle sites, where users can throw the Chinese coins or yarrow sticks digitally, shuffle and draw tarot cards, and otherwise engage with software as a way to predict the future or solve a predicament. Some tarot decks exist only online. *Technomancy* is a popular theme in science fiction, but it's a good word for this use of technology as an oracle or a tool of magic.

The Sigil Engine experience begins with a black screen and a pause. Darragh Mason, a co-creator of the site, describes it as "a prayer or a moment of reverence to the goddess Babalon" in "the great expansive void from which all things spring." By logging how long it takes between keystrokes, and mysteriously correlating that measurement with a Thelemic holy text authored by Aleister Crowley, a unique sigil is drawn electronically. A circle can be drawn around the sigil, a technique for keeping out demons found in the mid seventeenth-century grimoire *The Lesser Key of Solomon*. They acknowledge that their creation is considered an abomination by purists who believe that careful attention to each detail of creation over time is what gives a sigil its transformative power.

Austin Osman Spare, the British artist, surrealist, writer, and occultist, who in the mid-twentieth century revived interest in sigils, described them as a "lodging of a desire or wish at subconscious levels without the conscious mind being involved or aware." Such a well-placed wish allegedly has a better chance of coming true than throwing a penny into a well. Among the successes reported by users of Sigil Engine have been a longed-for pregnancy and a remodeled home. The future may include downloading the sigil to your 3D printer.

Among the more metaphysically inclined early adopters of Bitcoin and other cryptocurrencies, especially Burning Man participants, the idea is common that Bitcoin itself is a form of magical sigil created with the intent of eliminating fiat currencies and the political manipulation attached to them. Crypto art and collectibles, also known as nonfungible tokens or NFT, have made the news as prices soar. In 2018 a cryptocurrency named Sigil was introduced.

Music is another means of creating sigils. By using correlations between tarot cards, Hebrew letters, and musical notes Paul Foster Case and other synthesizers of esoteric doctrines provided ritual-oriented musicians with a foundation for experimentation. Genesis P-Orridge and his band Psychic TV considered each of their songs a unique sigil.

In 2017 esoteric electronic composer Kim Cascone's Silent Records, an indie label and hub for electronic music, released the compilation *Tulpamancers,* twelve tracks of musical tulpamancy. In a *Psychology*

Today article from 2016 called "Daring to Hear Voices," Samuel Paul Veissière wrote, "The new subculture of Tulpamancy has garnered a lot of online attention of late. Tulpas, a concept borrowed from Tibetan Buddhism, are sentient imaginary friends conjured through 'thoughtform' visualization. Tulpamancers are people who conjure Tulpas, and experience their imaginary companions as semi-permanent, non-threatening auditory 'hallucinations.'" But Tulpas can also function as sigils, for instance by the creation of a musical sigil for an astrological aspect with the intent of bringing out the best qualities of the aspect on all future occasions.

Of course, the most dramatic use of sigils so far in the twenty-first century involved the impact of memes such as Pepe the Frog. As we have seen, believers in QAnon used 4chan and other other online platforms to stoke the feeling that something magical was about to happen, and that anything was possible. Sending memes into the world to change the minds of voters proved itself to be an especially powerful kind of ritual involving digital sigils. Perhaps Jean Houston was prescient when she wrote in her memoir *A Mythic Life* (1996) that "we live in self-created chaos to hasten our own meeting with ourselves." We will be seeing more of Jean in the upcoming section on the Sekhmet revival.

ELECTRONIC MEDIUMSHIP

After the invention of the telephone in 1876, a class of mediums emerged called "phone voyants" who claimed they could hear the voices of the dead crackling through telephone wires. They had some substantial backing in that belief from none other than telephone inventor Alexander Graham Bell. Bell, like so many other great minds of the era, was fascinated by Spiritualism and was known to attend séances. He even made a pact with his younger brother, Edward, that the first to die would attempt to contact the other. Tragically, Edward died in 1867 at the age of nineteen. But instead of passively waiting around for his brother's signal, Bell set out to create electronic spirit communication so that even those without the talent for mediumship could reach loved ones in the world beyond. Bell's assistant, Thomas Watson, was completely on board with this project, being a practicing medium who approached electricity as an occult force. But nothing came of it.

In 1920 Americans reeling from the horrors of World War I embraced Spiritualism again. Experiments with Ouija boards and séances became popular party games. Then *American Magazine* proclaimed the revelatory announcement from Thomas Edison that he had been working on a scientific breakthrough, a "spirit phone" for communication between this world and the next. Every newspaper and magazine in America, and many around the world, ran stories about the incredible invention as if Edison had already achieved it. The hoopla died down. The spirit phone never saw the light of day.

After Edison's death, the search for the spirit phone resumed as researchers looked through his archives for a prototype, or at least a schematic, but none were to be found. Some have argued that Edison was pranking reporters, the invention had been a hoax lampooning Spiritualism. Edison was proudly agnostic and made no secret of his contempt for mediums. Nevertheless he told the *American Magazine*, "I have been at work for some time building an apparatus to see if it is possible for personalities which have left this Earth to communicate with us."

A group of Spiritualists claimed that Edison reached out to them during a séance in 1941. Edison's spirit allegedly shared the plans for building the spirit phone he had spent the last decade of his life working on. The group followed the entity's instructions, but when assembled, the machine didn't work.

The debate about whether the spirit phone was a hoax or a genuine Edison project ended in 2015 when a French journalist named Philippe Baudouin browsing in a Parisian thrift shop found an extremely rare copy of Edison's published diary. A chapter was devoted to Edison's ideas about life after death, including his plans for a spirit phone.

The ambiguity of Spiritualism continues into the 2020s with the saga of the SoulPhone. Would you invest in a device, designed by great scientists in the afterlife, that would allow for text communications with the dead? The first step to this ultimate Ouija board was accomplished with the creation of the Soul/Switch, a simple switch amiable to manipulation by the disincarnate. Sounds like a hustle from the heyday of Spiritualism? But this project is led by Dr. Gary Schwartz, former professor at Harvard and Yale, now a senior professor at the University of Arizona in psychology, medicine, neurology, and psychiatry. He was director of the Yale Psychophysiology Center, and codirector of the Yale Behavioral Medicine Clinic. He currently directs research at University of Arizona's Laboratory for Advances in Consciousness and Health.

The SoulPhone is no home-cooked scheme of entrepreneurial Spiritualism. This project is science taking Spiritualism very seriously. Interviews and research studies revealed statistical trends that gave Dr. Schwartz confidence that communication from the afterlife is not only possible, but also not uncommon. That's how a scientist found himself conversing with Nikola Tesla and other discarnate geniuses who volunteered to be "Hypothesized Postmaterial Collaborators," so as to spearhead an invention that will prove once and for all that communication with the beyond is possible.

Dr. Schwartz has written popular books including *The Sacred Promise: How Science Is Discovering Spirit's Collaboration with Us in Our Daily Lives,* with a foreword by celebrity psychic John Edward, and *Super Synchronicity: Where Science and Spirit Meet.* The SoulPhone website tells us, "Dr. Schwartz's work has been the subject of documentaries and profiles on Discovery, HBO, the SciFi Channel, Arts & Entertainment, Fox, and others. His research was featured in the documentary *The Life After Death Project* and has been described in various magazines and newspapers including *USA Today,* the *London Times,* the *New York Times,* the *LA Times,* and others."

The plan was to make Soul/Switch available for sessions as early as 2021. At this primitive stage of development the Soul/Switch can only provide yes or no answers. A more sophisticated step toward SoulPhone is under construction. It is meant to establish a form of communication with the beyond similar to texting short sentences. For some readers these devices will seem highly improbable. Other readers may eagerly anticipate that moment when science and the afterlife will connect in a way that changes how people view life on planet Earth. But all may agree that it must have taken courage for a well-established Ivy League academic to follow his research, and Edison, into such uncharted territory.

PSYCHEDELIC SALVATION

Mystics are no strangers to the bottle and the pipe. The incense of the ancient Orphic mysteries intoxicated the faithful. Madame Blavatsky had a predilection for smoking hashish. The pill form was preferred by the Hermetic Brotherhood of Luxor. Christian monks invented champagne. Paschal Beverly Randolph wrote candidly about his use of narcotics, as did Aleister Crowley. Alongside the illusion that American Metaphysical Religion is intrinsically liberal is the similar belief that the use of psychedelics, and other intoxicants, makes people more compassionate and wise. In fact, right-wing politics has long been a part of the history of drug use, especially among the social elites.

For example, in 2021 venture capitalists were betting big on the therapeutic uses of LSD, ecstasy, shrooms, DMT, ketamine, and increasingly more powerful and legal marijuana. Two of the biggest investors in therapeutic psychedelics are right-wing billionaires. As drugs become legalized, the drugs that had once been available only to researchers soon became the drugs of the artists who sparked the musical and sexual renaissance of the 1960s and 1970s. Then they became anyone's drugs. As of June 2022, in thirty-seven states in America drugs once characteristic of counterculture can be purchased in a shop or administered by a trained technician at a storefront in a convenient mall.

Most twentieth-century drug enthusiasts believed that if uptight conservatives smoked a joint, or took an acid trip, they'd be converted into progressives. Small studies seem to support this idea, such as the one done by Psychedelic Research Group at Imperial College London that found a significant and enduring decrease in authoritarian attitudes among those they gave shrooms. But that infamous alleged hippie scheme to dose all the reservoirs with LSD may not have unleashed utopia. Abundant circumstantial evidence can be found in news stories about, for example, members of a notorious twenty-first-century racist terrorist organization who were arrested for possession of opium, cannabis, and shrooms. The founder of a leading American Nazi website, as a teenager used LSD, shrooms, marijuana, and cocaine. The founder of one of the most notorious havens for white supremacy online got the idea while taking shrooms. Like paganism and the occult, these drugs expose and amplify human nature, but they don't necessarily convert realists into idealists, or conservatives into liberals. They are not the philosophers' stone of politics turning lead to gold.

Timothy Leary was perhaps as responsible as anyone for the promulgation of the idea that psychedelics inspire progressive politics by increasing empathy and understanding of self and others. His famous mantra "tune in, turn on, drop out" inspired many to do just that. The idea was to find oneself in harmony with the world, to face the shadow, and share the light. But many hippies gave up liberal politics as they grew older. In his later books, instead of promising a personal and collective renaissance, Leary counseled his followers to avoid the people he once hoped to convert, comparing them to genetically programmed breeding robots.

The Psychedelic Experience: A Manual Based on The Tibetan Book of the Dead, published in 1962, was coauthored by a trio of counterculture superstars who believed they had found in the sketchy Evans-Wentz translation of what is really a class of books not one uniform edition, a blueprint for a plan to help their readers get the most, and avoid the worst, during LSD trips. The trio included Leary, a Harvard professor about to become a notorious psychedelic guru and political activist, his fellow researcher at Harvard, Ralph Metzner, and Richard Alpert, better known as Ram Dass.

While visits to India and Hindu spiritual beliefs and practices were key to the path of Ram Dass, at times his writing echoes the American nature religion of John Muir, Emerson, and Thoreau. For example, "When you go out into the woods, and you look at trees, you see all these different trees. And some of them are bent, and some of them are straight, and some of them are evergreens, and some of them are whatever. And you look at the tree and you allow it. You see why it is the way it is. You sort of understand that it didn't get enough light, and so it turned that way. And you don't get all emotional about it. You just allow it. You appreciate the tree. The minute you get near humans, you lose all that. And you are constantly saying 'You are too this, or I'm too this.' That judgment mind comes in. And so I practice turning people into trees. Which means appreciating them just the way they are" (Ram Dass n.d.).

The New York Public Library preserves an exchange of letters between Timothy Leary and Robert Anton Wilson. They discussed the occult, including Aleister Crowley and Gurdjieff's self-observation techniques. Leary was doing time in Folsom Prison, only one of the thirty-six times he was arrested in the 1960s and 1970s.

Robert Anton Wilson was a self-made expert on the esoteric, a novelist, and a cultural hoaxer. His blend of satire with religion reinvented, while mocking, American Metaphysical Religion. In his works such as the *Illuminati Trilogy* the border between politics and conspiracy theories became blurry, as did the line between fiction and nonfiction. While Wilson's fiction wasn't as serious about masquerading as journalism as, for example, the books of Carlos Castaneda, they could easily be misunderstood by being taken literally. At the heart of Wilson's approach is the idea of reality tunnels, the way our beliefs shape our experiences. To choose our own reality tunnels, instead of having them forced on us by others, and to be able to switch between several, was an important part of the liberation Wilson tried to teach.

Castaneda's books are classified as nonfiction, but they might be considered masterpieces of magical realism. His first three books were written as research notes for his doctorate in anthropology from UCLA. His first book, published by UCLA in 1968, was *The Teachings of Don Juan: A Yaqui Way of Knowledge*. The book tells the story of an encounter between a scholar and a shaman. At the peak of its popularity the mass market paperback edition sold sixteen thousand copies a week. As tripping hippies earnestly discussed the mescaline lessons of the mysterious Yaqui medicine man Don Juan, Castaneda became a millionaire.

Many intrepid souls traveled to Mexico to find Don Juan but without success. Castaneda encouraged the idea that Don Juan was a real human being who deliberately made himself unavailable. When *Time* magazine gave him the cover for a feature article titled "Magic and Reality," rumors began spreading that Castaneda had sent somebody else to masquerade as him for the photo shoot. It's hard to be certain if the picture is genuine because there are so few pictures of Castaneda. Sales of the books bought Castaneda an Audi and an apartment house in Westwood Village, an expensive neighborhood near UCLA. There he lived with the women who became known as his witches. They served him to the end, even when the suffering of his last illness made them question the powers he had claimed.

In the 1990s Carlos and his witches emerged to introduce a repackaging of his philosophy under the brand name Tensegrity. Buckminster Fuller coined the term *tensegrity* in the 1960s, as a contraction of tensional integrity. Also known as floating compression, tensional integrity happens when isolated parts become a system under compression in a network of tension. The most famous example is Kurilpa Bridge, a pedestrian and bicycle bridge over the Brisbane River in Brisbane, Queensland, Australia. Casteneda taught Tensegrity students modernized versions of techniques, including hand motions called magical passes, allegedly practiced by tribal shamans before the Spanish Conquest.

One of his followers, who became romantically involved with him reported Castaneda's strange theory that the first lover of any woman thereafter receives energy from any other man with whom she makes love. Castaneda, of course, knew how to break the connections that make such parasitic energy transfers possible. But another follower told about the time she got sick and how Castaneda said he would come over and visit her. She preferred that he did not. The next day a big crow tapped at her window demanding attention, knocking over plants until she came outside. For the next month she fed the crow grapes. It gave her something to look forward to every day while she healed. She wondered if Castaneda had visited her after all. In one of his books he tells the story of how, as part of his shaman training, he had learned how to transform into a crow.

Castaneda wrote nine books about Don Juan, the last in 1993. After that he wrote two books about Tensegrity, replacing Don Juan in his titles with "Shamans of Ancient Mexico." His final book, *The Active Side of Infinity*, released after his death, returned to the subject of his experiences with Don Juan. On the book cover the *New York Times* enthused that "we are incredibly fortunate to have Carlos Castaneda's books." Deepak Chopra wrote, "His insights paved the way for the future evolution of human consciousness."

As scholars learned more about Yaqui religious culture, and the practices of Yaqui shamans, it became clear that what Castaneda had taught was not Yaqui culture, but a collection of various beliefs, Indigenous and otherwise that included plagiarism. When Castaneda died in 1998, five of his female friends, including his three remaining female devotees, disappeared. All that remained of the only witch presumed to have been found was a faded fragment of pink shorts and sun-baked bone in Death Valley, California. Researchers, professional and amateur, have yet to find Don Juan. But Robert Mashall's new biography of Castaneda, to be published in spring 2023 by UCLA, addresses not only UCLA's reluctance to admit enabling an academic fraud, among other things, but also a portrait of what can only be described as a cult leader.

In 1994 Portuguese filmmaker Edgar Pera made a movie inspired by dada. *Manual of Evasion* starred Robert Anton Wilson and Terence McKenna. Their images and voices are woven through a trippy exploration of time. Wilson advocates "astonishment" as the only technique that allows us to avoid having time stolen from us by the extraterrestrial influences that condemn us to the mundane tasks of the unexamined life. "Forward! To the new order of the trans-temporal dream!" McKenna exults. He calls for the end to the "reign of the constipated nitwits and their bloodsucking stooges." He believed revolutions and art go together, but nitwits and stooges can have their own revolutions and arts.

As an expert on psychedelics and plant allies, McKenna combined the botanical knowledge of a Paracelsus with the zeal for universal reformation of a Rosicrucian. Inspired by *The Rosicrucian Enlightenment*, a book by the controversial British scholar Frances Yates, McKenna starred in a film called *The Alchemical Dream: Rebirth of the Great Work,* which was filmed in Prague in the 1990s. McKenna played the role of John Dee. The film tells the story of the alchemical renaissance in Europe, and the fate of the Winter King and the Queen of Hearts, Frederick and Elizabeth of Bohemia, and the destruction of their realm.

McKenna made famous the idea of the Archaic Revival, the return of the shaman. He was hopeful that by using ancient spiritual technologies, and the new discoveries of science, people could achieve a better existence individually and collectively. Electronic music festivals and Burning Man have been held up as examples of the Archaic Revival. But as the storming of Congress proved, the politics of a shaman are not necessarily progressive. As Terence's brother Dennis McKenna has said, "Psychedelics can be used for good or ill, but the moral dimension comes from the human heart. Psychedelics will not turn sociopaths or psychopaths into peace/love flower children!" (Mignano 2021).

Dennis McKenna conducted postdoctoral research at the Department of Neurology of Stanford University School of Medicine, and in the Laboratory of Clinical Pharmacology at the National Institute of Mental Health. An adjunct professor in the Department of Spirituality and Healing at the University of Minnesota, Dennis taught graduate courses in Botanical Medicines and Ethnopharmacology, as well as an annual intensive in Hawaii. For University of Arizona he taught field courses in Equador, and for Albany College of Pharmacy and Health Sciences, and University of Kansas, courses in the Andes and the Amazon. But let us consider his contribution to the reinvention of the business of cosmetics.

In the days before they were acquired by Estée Lauder, a company named Aveda revolutionized the world of hair and skin products. The brand name is a contraction of Ayurveda. The founder, Austrian American Horst Rechelbacher, was inspired by a trip to India. He wanted his products to have a healing dimension, not just physically but spiritually. When he started his company, in Minnesota in 1975, he could not have imagined the extent of his eventual success: spas, schools, salons, copycat brands. Horst became a legend as he championed organic products and sustainable ecological practices.

In 1993 Dennis McKenna moved to Minnesota to work at the headquarters of the Aveda Corporation as Senior Research Pharmacognosist. His expertise helped make Aveda a beloved brand. Thanks to Aveda, and other similar innovators, the humble shampoo became an elixir. Retired now, Dennis serves as an advisor on "Eco-Initiatives, Permaculture and Mission" to Soltara Healing Center in Costa Rica, where access to Indigenous healers meets a swimming pool with an ocean view. Soltara offers the genuine experience of a Shipibo ayahuasca ceremony conducted by master healers without the discomfort of a visit to the Peruvian jungle.

EVOKING QUEER POWER

Freedom of religion and the freedom to love and marry as we choose are deeply related. While furthering gay rights, some queer activists did important work toward the acceptance and accessibility of pagan and other forms of unconventional spirituality. In this chapter we will consider two of the most notable. Arthur Evans, the activist and scholar, and the controversial queer witch Z. Budapest.

Near the end of his life, Arthur Evans was told that he could undergo treatment that would debilitate him, or he must expect to die very soon. Arthur chose to face death. "He spent his last year pursuing his pleasures," he wrote in his own obituary, "translating ancient Greek, playing chess with his best friend, going to the Castro Theater, dining out, writing letters to the editor and visiting with friends. He remained chipper to the end, often joking about his situation" (Laird 2011).

For gay rights activists, pagan revivalists, and fans of Dionysus and *The Bacchae* of Euripides, Arthur Evans was practically a saint. He was a primary moving force in the liberation of queer and pagan spirituality. As founder, he wrote the statement of purpose and most of the constitution of the Gay Activists Alliance (GAA). His book *Witchcraft and Gay Counterculture* inspired the creation of the Radical Faeries, whose appropriation of Indigenous culture was one aspect of their rebellion against rules. Like the hippies of the 1960s, these rebels wore Indigenous clothing to symbolize their rejection of the corporate status quo's stifling conformity. They embraced the sacredness of nature, which included their own natures. When AIDS began killing members of his community, Arthur became active in several San Francisco groups that later became ACT UP/SF, fighting to save lives while President Reagan and the media refused to talk about the growing pandemic, which inspired the slogan Silence=Death.

Arthur's father dropped out of elementary school to work on an assembly line; a drinker with a violent streak, he broke furniture and beat his wife and children. Arthur found liberation when he attended City College in the 1960s. He began postgraduate work for a Ph.D. in ancient Greek philosophy at Columbia University. His advisor Paul Kristeller had studied under Martin Heidegger until he had to flee Germany when the Nazis killed his parents during the Holocaust.

Arthur read the poetry of Allen Ginsberg, which he credited as a major influence on the formation of his values. He also joined many antiwar protests including those at Columbia in April and May of 1968, and the riot in Chicago at the Democratic National Convention. But he was closeted, and lonely. He had no gay friends. That changed when he moved to the Village. He became a leader of New York City's emerging gay liberation movement in the late 1960s and early 1970s. There's a black-and-white picture of him protesting antigay policies outside the New York City Board of Education. Young Arthur smiles, longhaired, bearded, and bespectacled. He carries a sign that says, "Was Socrates a Lousy Teacher???"

An early member of the Gay Liberation Front, he split to establish the Gay Activists Alliance in 1969. Arthur writes in his obit, "Acting on the principle that the personal is the political, GAA held homophobes who were in positions of authority personally accountable for the consequences of their public policies. Accordingly, Robinson, Evans, and Owles developed the tactic of 'zaps.' These were militant (but nonviolent) face-to-face confrontations with outspoken homophobes in government, business, and the media." Evans was often arrested in such actions, participating in disruptions of local business offices, political headquarters, local TV shows, and the Metropolitan Opera.

"In effect," Evans continued, "GAA created a new model of gay activism, highly theatrical while also eminently practical and focused. It forced the media and the political establishment to take gay concerns seriously as a struggle for justice. Previously the media treated gay life as a peripheral freak show. The new gay activism inspired gay people to act unapologetically from a position of gay pride."

Arthur appeared on the Dick Cavett show in 1970, along with two other GAA activists, the first openly gay people to appear on national television. That year Arthur and two friends formed the Weird Sisters Partnership. They bought forty acres of forest on a mountain in remote northeastern Washington State. In summer they pitched tents and camped out. They named their wilderness paradise away from prying eyes New Sodom.

In New York Arthur had begun researching the history of counter-culture. During cold winter months in Seattle he finished his work. In 1973 he published excerpts in the gay journals *Out* and *Fag Rag*.

In 1974 the New Sodom interlude ended and Arthur moved to San Francisco. He lived the rest of his life in an apartment at the corner of Haight and Ashbury Streets. The following year Arthur organized a pagan group in San Francisco called the Faery Circle. He wrote in his obit that it "combined countercultural consciousness, gay sensibility, and ceremonial playfulness."

His research came to fruition in 1976 when Arthur "gave a series of public lectures at 32 Page St., an early San Francisco gay community center, entitled 'Faeries,' on his research on the historical origins of the gay counterculture. In 1978 he published this material in his ground-breaking book *Witchcraft and the Gay Counterculture*. It demonstrated that many of the people accused of 'witchcraft' and 'heresy' in the Middle Ages and Renaissance were actually persecuted because of their sexuality and adherence to ancient pagan practices" (Laird 2011). Arthur then focused his research on *The Bacchae* of Euripides. The Greek god Dionysus tricks the heterosexual warrior prince into cross-dressing, which ends tragically when the prince is murdered by his mother who is crazed by the god. Arthur translated the play himself and in 1984 he directed a production at the Valencia Rose Cabaret in San Francisco. The translation was published as *The God of Ecstasy* by St. Martin's Press in 1988, with Arthur's extensive introduction on the cultural influence of Dionysus and the historical importance of the play.

In *The God of Ecstasy,* Arthur (1988) wrote, "The established concept of how human beings must behave—butch, competitive, violent men dominating passive, feminine women—is not necessitated by the order of the cosmos, but is a lopsided and arbitrary re-enforcement of certain human capabilities."

His next project began with a grant from the San Francisco Arts Commission in 1988. Arthur devoted himself to nine years of research. *The Critique of Patriarchal Reason,* published in 1997, is in Arthur's own words "a monumental overview of Western philosophy from antiquity to the present. It shows how misogyny and homophobia have influenced the supposedly objective fields of formal logic, higher mathematics, and physical science" (Laird 2011). Along the way this extremely erudite yet enjoyable book provides an illuminating analysis of the life, ideas, and influence of Wittgenstein, while exploring Kant, Descartes, Chaung Tzu, Quine, Occam of Occam's Razor fame, and many others.

Arthur argues that science, because of its fetishizing of reason, has imposed its rules on not only its own domain but all Western experience of reality, falsely discrediting other human abilities. Patriarchal reason has infected everything from art to politics. Vine Deloria Jr. described the same problem in a more poetic way: "Not only did secular scientists rout the Christian fundamentalists, they placed themselves in the posture of knowing more, on the basis of their own very short-term investigations, than the collective remembrances of the rest of humankind" (Deloria 1997).

Arthur's sharp wit and readiness to criticize led to his coining of the term *Castro Clones.* He observed that the ideal represented by muscular hypermasculine gay males had created harmful hierarchies in the community. He regularly punctured with wry comments the pomposity of the perpetual perfection on display.

Near the end of his life, he was widely criticized for scathing editorials he wrote in favor of keeping the homeless from sleeping on the sidewalks of his neighborhood. He responded that safety of the community is the number one priority of activism. When Arthur moved there Haight-Ashbury had already descended into a territory of predators and prey drawn there by a myth that had been made hollow by not only Altamont and Manson, but also by opportunists. He had lived through the gentrification of the neighborhood, and many ups and downs along the way. But for the first time he did not feel safe walking to the store or crossing the street. The unsanitary conditions and public drug use, he argued, were public health disasters waiting to happen.

Two months after his death the LGBT Community Center's National History Archive invited veterans of GAA and GLF to gather in Manhattan to celebrate Arthur's life. Hal Offen, Arthur's best friend and his immediate successor as GAA Delegate at Large, reminisced about the early gay liberation movement, which he called "Arthur's major legacy. There were few people as responsible as Arthur for launching the Gay Movement." He recalled meeting Arthur at a demonstration against a company that refused to sell gay people life insurance. Hal mentioned the Buggery, the Volkswagen repair shop in San Francisco that he owned with Arthur.

Arthur's spirituality wasn't a significant part of the event, until two excerpts of his poetry were read. "To Mystery" and "Affirmation of Unity," from his poem "The Cosmic Rosary," which he wrote in Latin then translated into English.

Queer paganism's second wave flourishes in the new millennium with groups like the Brotherhood of the Phoenix, Circle of Dionysos, and Ekklesia Antinuou.

In 1975 an undercover policewoman entered a small store on Lincoln Boulevard not too far from Venice Beach called "The Feminist Wicca." The owner of the store sat alone with her cards. The officer listened to the reading then she arrested Z. Budapest for breaking a city law against fortune-telling. Her lawyers referred to it as the first witch trial since Salem. After the media covered what they described as weird news crowds of pagans protested at the court. Z was found guilty.

The case went all the way to the Supreme Court of California where the judges considered the merit of the argument that Dianic Wicca is a religion protected by the Constitution. Z's lawyers argued that a tarot reading is "an example of women spiritually consoling women within the context of their religion." Nine years of appeals followed until the verdict was reversed. The laws that made fortune-telling illegal in California were nullified.

Zsuzsanna Budapest was born in Hungary in 1940. As a child she lived in bunkers, surviving the war machines of Germany and Russia. Her mother, Masika Szilagyi, was a practicing witch as well as a medium, but she made her living after the war as a sculptress of the Fates, and of the Triple Goddess. Masika raised her daughter in the craft.

In 1959 Z moved to Chicago to study at the University of Chicago, and with Second City, but her first job in the entertainment business was Color Girl for the Ed Sullivan Show. The cameramen adjusted color on their cameras while focusing on her face. She studied at the American Academy of Dramatic Arts in Manhattan. One marriage and two children later, like many women in the 1960s, Z realized she was lost.

In 1970 she moved to Los Angeles. She worked at the Women's Center. She organized the Take Back the Night movement in Southern California. As she examined the reasons for the frustrating lack of progress toward equality, she came to understand that mainstream religions were holding back women's liberation. Z believed that women needed to find their own spiritual paths. Returning to the Goddess path taught to her by her mother, Z meticulously researched pagan traditions, focusing especially on the ancient Greek goddess Artemis and her Roman counterpart Diana. In 1975 Z published *The Feminist Book of Lights and Shadows* the first guide for women to their almost forgotten spiritual heritage, republished in 1989 as *The Holy Book of Women's Mysteries*. "Pleasure is worship," Z wrote, "because it replenishes the soul."

At first Dianic witches kept to themselves. But eventually they accepted an invitation to join a popular pagan festival. They were going to introduce something a little different: a circle for women only. The event didn't go over well. Husbands retrieved their wives from the circle with gusto, causing injuries. The Radical Faeries came to the rescue. They had excluded women for years, though that changed in the early nineties, but they agreed with Z that women should have the right to their own public circle. Z called them the "guardians." The Radical Fairies surrounded the Dianic circle protecting them with their own bodies. But the touching scene must also have been awkward. If the Guardians faced the women they would be male observers intruding on their privacy. Turning their backs, the event became a symbolic reenactment of a shunning.

In 2011 Z caused further controversy when she offered a public ritual for "genetic women only." A silent meditation in protest took place outside the event. Some of the women attending found it intimidating. Here at the cutting edge of awakening spirituality, gender issues are being worked out as communities weigh their opinions and their options.

A few years later Z got into trouble with her own community for initiating a man into the Dianic mysteries. Z explained that he had only received the initiation appropriate to a male priest. Those who disapproved of Z's gender exclusion were unhappy that the honoree accepted the honor, but he explained he was trying to build bridges, in the hope of a more inclusive future for the pagan community.

Z has published over a dozen books and hundreds of articles. She has led countless classes and given hundreds of lectures. On YouTube in 2013 Z shared an ancient spell to still the winds. She tells us about using the spell with a group on a Malibu hilltop on a rainy night. She assures us that fifteen minutes is long enough to wait for Mother Nature to respond. She finishes with a prayer that is all inclusive.

Starhawk, the well-known ecofeminist neo-pagan teacher, and author of thirteen books, trained with Z. Budapest. In 1979 Starhawk's book *The Spiral Dance: A Rebirth of the Ancient Religion of the Great Goddess* became a bestseller. One of the most influential books in the early Goddess movement it had tenth and twentieth anniversary editions. As cofounder of the coven Reclaiming, in 1979 Starhawk combined Goddess spirituality with feminist activism. She is a Jewish woman who travels to Palestine to work for peace. She's also devoted to spreading the word about permaculture, which she refers to as systems of regeneration. As for her stance on gender and sexuality, Starhawk identifies as bisexual. She has avoided the controversies that embroiled her teacher, but she has not entirely avoided controversy. In 2016 she attended the Standing Rock protest. There the friction she has experienced with Indigenous activists in the past surfaced again as they revealed that her protest and ceremony did not strictly obey the rules of the camp, or Lakota laws of hospitality, and that they happened without permission from the elders.

Millennial witches like Gabriela Herstik bring intersectional awareness to the craft. Much of her magic involves healing the damage caused by the rejection and judgment inflicted on women, as well as queer and transgender people. Self-love is not enough, self-lust is required to awaken true individuality.

However challenging the process of evolving equality, liberty, and the pursuit of happiness, we have come a long way from the world Holly Woodlawn used to tell me about. Holly Woodlawn was a Warhol superstar and a groundbreaking transgender legend. I knew her as a friend, musical collaborator, and neighbor. Holly for the most part hid her mystical side. When we met she was glad to have found someone to read her birth chart, and to talk to her about other esoteric subjects. According to Holly the inspiration for her transformation was a movie she saw as a child. Lana Turner starred as Samarra the High Priestess of Astarte in the film *The Prodigal*. Holly wanted to be Samarra. I spoke with Holly many times about her love of Astarte, Isis, and another of her favorite goddesses Sekhmet.

Holly rolled the *r* in *Santeria* when she talked about her experiences with it. She felt sorry for the chickens. She said she seldom discussed such matters around the Warhol crowd or the other countercultural elites with whom she had enjoyed friendships. Spirituality was considered a wacky California thing, she explained. But once she moved to Los Angeles where she met others with such interests, who didn't care who disapproved of them, she felt more comfortable revealing her beliefs. While Holly was never overt about her spirituality, her ability to cheer up and inspire people who were suffering is fondly remembered by her friends.

Madeleine Carlyle in her article "The Pain and Pride of a Generation Changing How America Sees Gender" published by *Time* magazine in June, 2022, explores how a new generation encounters difficult issues that previous generations have struggled to solve. Some use *Two Spirit* to describe themselves, a term some scholars worry is an over simplification that does not reflect the nuanced meanings of many Indigenous words in many different Indigenous languages. The creation of an Indigenous lesbian and gay international gathering in Winnipeg in 1990, the term *Two Spirit* was formally chosen as a phrase that all tribes could use. Some argue that Two Spirit was actually coined by Will Roscoe, author of *The Zuni Man-Woman* (1992) and *Changing Ones: Third and Fourth Genders in Native North America (1998)*. Will was not Indigenous, but he was a Radical Faerie.

EVOLVING FEMALE POWER

Even before the eighteenth century some women found ways to participate in European Freemasonry, often invited by the men who respected them: husbands, fathers, brothers. But the original charter of the first Masonic authority in the United Kingdom used the word *men* in its eligibility requirements and women therefore cannot be equal members. French Masonic authorities, as we shall see, were less inclined to exclude women. They created co-Masonry so women could participate to some degree. But in America women and the men who respected them pioneered a more female-friendly Freemasonry. Still the goal of female equality remained as elusive in Masonry as in society in general.

Rob Morris was an American poet. Except for his marriage to his wife, Charlotte, his early years were devoted to becoming a school teacher. Rob taught at the Sylvan Academy for boys in Oxford, Mississippi. There, just before spring in 1846, a former Masonic grand master and high priest of Mississippi initiated Morris, who at twenty-seven years old was having a good Saturn return.

Impressed by Freemasonry, Morris soon came to believe that a way must be found for female relatives of Masons to benefit from its wisdom, community, and culture. In 1849 teaching at Eureka Masonic College in

Mississippi, a place known as The Little Red Brick School Building, he began writing the Rosary of the Eastern Star, the first ritual for the Order of the Eastern Star, a Masonic order women could join. The idea was met with not only encouragement but collaboration. Morris organized a Supreme Constellation in 1855 with the power to charter chapters.

In 1866, because of his plans to travel, Morris turned over leadership of the Order to his friend Robert McCoy, one of the most important publishers of Masonic books. Other such experiments followed including McCoy's similar Order of the Amaranth, the Ladies' Oriental Shrine of North America, Chicago's the Order of the White Shrine of Jerusalem, and the Prince Hall Order of the Eastern Star in 1874, the first entry into Freemasonry for African American women. Today the Prince Hall Order has over 300,000 members.

Morris spent years doing research in what was then called the Holy Land. He became a popular lecturer in Europe where the future king Edward VII was said to have attended, sitting beside the most humble workers. Morris was a prolific author of Masonic books and a publisher of Masonic periodicals. He also wrote over four hundred poems. In 1884 more than half a million Master Masons around the world voted that he should receive the laurel wreath of a Poet Laureate of Masonry. The only other Freemason so honored was Scotland's national poet Robert Burns in 1796. Morris died in 1888. Today the Order of the Eastern Star has over one million members belonging to over 7,500 chapters worldwide.

In 2018 guidance the United Grand Lodge of England stated that a Freemason who transitions from male to female is still a Freemason, and transgender men are welcome to apply. Officially outsiders in the English speaking world of Freemasonry, some women find that actual practice may differ from statements issued by distant authorities. For example, in English and Spanish speaking Masonic and Rosicrucian chapters of southern California where women are welcome as equals. As of 2010 the Grand Orient de France officially recognizes female inclusive orders all over the world, and empowers them to initiate women into Freemasonry. But the Grand Lodge of England declares all such orders and chapters "irregular." Membership is grounds for expulsion from Masonry.

In the early days of Spiritualism, to speak with authority women had to represent male voices. Aristotle, Caesar, and other famous men were commonly channeled by female mediums. Their important messages to humanity usually amounted to sales pitches for Spiritualism. Apparently, whatever their backgrounds, all the historical celebrities who communicated from the beyond had been converted to Spiritualism. Becoming a spirit would necessitate that, one supposes.

When Dorothy Jane Roberts channeled Seth, she brought to the world of Spiritualism an interest in modern politics and cutting-edge science. Seth and Jane brought a new perspective. Some content, of course, was traditional. For example, Seth's ideas about masses of repressed, angry, or suffering people invoking natural disasters. A flood, for example, can represent the release of pent-up hostility or criminality in a community. Christianity is no stranger to this kind of thinking. But Seth and Jane also introduced more radical ideas. Reincarnation is true, but the lives do not happen one after the other. They all happen at once. In fact, some souls incarnate more than one body at the same time. While you read this book, another version of you may have an entirely different life somewhere on this planet.

The Seth books became bestsellers in the 1970s. The mass market purple paperback of *Seth Speaks,* with a creepy photo of Jane in trance resembling a ghost or a stoned beatnik, could be found in many homes. People were talking about channeling. Through the Seth books, Jane had great influence on several generations of New Age writers and teachers.

The core of the Seth books, that "you create your own reality," was a powerful restatement of the bedrock concept of New Thought and American Metaphysical Religion. Among those who have referred to Seth as a source of inspiration have been Louise Hay, the popular author on the influence of thought and feeling on health and healing; bestselling author and presidential candidate Marianne Williamson; Richard Bach, author of *Jonathan Livingston Seagull* and other massive bestsellers in the 1970s; Shakti Gawain, whose *Creative Visualization: Use the Power of Your Imagination to Create What You Want in Life* has been a bestseller in the metaphysical genre for forty years; and celebrity author of *Quantum Healing,* Deepak Chopra.

Jane's husband Robert Butts was her devoted partner in these explorations. They were avid readers. Among the influences on Jane were the Tibetan Book of the Dead and the Don Juan books by Carlos Castaneda, but it all started, once again, with a Ouija board.

Her husband Robert took as much of the workload off Jane as he could. He gave the books their characteristic format, making frequent notes about details of time and place that some readers thought added context to the material, but others found intrusive and distracting. Robert was listed as coauthor on four of the eight Seth books.

Like her predecessors Jane claimed to have channeled several famous men of history, the painters Rembrandt and Paul Cézanne, and William James who reported from the other side that "each environment is formed by people's belief in it."

As Jane worked to emerge as an author separate from Seth, she found her own books did not achieve the popularity of the Seth books. Not only was Seth the star of the show in the public imagination, but he did not even refer to Jane by her name, or as a woman. He gave her a man's name: Ruburt.

Judy Zebra Knight is a well-known spiritual teacher. If success is measured by money earned, she is one of the most successful. *Time* magazine once called her "probably the most celebrated of all current channelers." She made her fame by channeling a distinctly male 35,000-year-old spirit named Ramtha. Ramtha claims to have been a great Lemurian warrior who led an army of a million in a war against Atlantis, as the two lost civilizations clashed. Shirley MacLaine's exciting first meeting with Ramtha culminated in their agreement that when Ramtha had been incarnate, she had been his brother. Among Ramtha's several thousand followers were other celebrities, including TV star Linda Evans, distinguished actor Richard Chamberlain, and New Age music legend Yanni.

Ramtha advised his followers to invest in Knight's project, a horse-breeding ranch in Yelm, Washington. Many Ramtha enthusiasts relocated to Yelm, where Ramtha's School of Enlightenment allegedly uses unorthodox teaching methods that may include blindfolded running, wine drinking, and dancing to rock music. The school has been accused of brainwashing by disgruntled former students alleging dangerous practices.

Knight built a French chateau with beautiful gardens in Yelm, and repurposed a barn into a small but charming auditorium. She got her horse ranch, too. When necessary, she has defended her copyrights in court. A woman by the name of Julie Ravel reported that Ramtha showed up in her crystal shop in Berlin to declare her his new channel. Ravel became popular as Ramtha's voice in Germany, but Knight sued. She won her case. The Austrian Supreme Court ruled that only Knight had the right to represent Ramtha.

In 2011 Ramtha allegedly pontificated, "Fuck God's chosen people! I think they have earned enough cash to have paid their way out of the goddamned gas chambers by now." In 2012 the *Seattle Times* reported, "State Democratic Party Will Donate Money from JZ Knight after Offensive Comments." Knight had been a longtime donor but suddenly she found her money unwelcome. In 2014 *Alternet* news site carried a story headlined, "Ramtha, New Age Cult Leader, Unleashes Drunken, Racist, Homophobic Rants to Large Following." In the records of a court case can be found the accusation that Ramtha had said HIV is nature's way of "getting rid of" homosexuals. People were equally shocked by Ramtha insisting that because of reincarnation murder and other violent crimes are unimportant.

Videos of Ramtha rants were posted on YouTube by Virginia Coverdale, a former follower who had started a website called Enlighten Me Free, an online support community for former students of the Ramtha School of Enlightenment. Knight spent five years and a million dollars suing Coverdale into bankruptcy. That should have been the end of it, but Knight argued that the Federal court must recognize Coverdale's debt to Knight's lawyers as nondischargeable. Coverdale would have had to pay off the debt for the rest of her life.

In 2017 the Federal court rejected the argument, comparing it to indentured servitude. The judge wrote, "JZK attempted to use its superior financial resources to intimidate its dissident ex-students by its lawsuit." He added: "While JZK attempts to portray Coverdale's primary purpose as an attempt to expose and discredit J.Z. Knight and RSE, that is a bit of the pot calling the kettle black. There is more evidence that JZK used the lawsuit and the damages award as an attempt to dissuade Coverdale and other ex-RSE members from speaking out about RSE and J.Z. Knight's statements, teachings and behaviors."

On election night 2020 Knight tweeted that the president of the United States should declare martial law and invalidate all votes, along with other QAnon messages. She had been a member of Trump's reelection committee. Knight exemplifies how the male spirit can serve the empowerment of the female channel. There is a woman leading her community, but in a sense her job is representing a man. It is the male spirit who gets most of the credit for the wisdom that improved her followers' lives.

In contrast, we may consider Marianne Williamson. She got her start at the Philosophical Research Society, where she not only worked in the office, but also gave some of her earliest lectures. Her lectures and writing on *A Course in Miracles* catapulted her to worldwide fame.

A Course in Miracles was written by Helen Schucman. From 1965 to 1972 Schucman wrote down what she considered messages from Jesus. She was not in a trance. She compared the process to having a dream or vision, but also to inner dictation. During those years Schucman was a tenured associate professor of medical psychology at the Columbia University College of Physicians and Surgeons at the Columbia-Presbyterian Medical Center in New York City. With the help of William Thetford, her colleague at the medical center, Schucman organized the writing into a book published anonymously in 1976. Schucman didn't want anyone to know she had authored *A Course in Miracles* until after her death. Her wishes were respected. The book begins with the sentence: "This is a course in miracles. Please take notes." Marianne Williamson has described *A Course in Miracles* as "a self-study program in spiritual psychotherapy." According to her, the book changed her life dramatically, and she has witnessed it change the lives of many others, as perhaps the most important modern teacher of its concepts.

In the 1980s Williamson founded Project Angel Food, a charity that provided necessities for victims of AIDS at a time when the president and many other Americans refused to talk about the disease. Williamson visited many deathbeds, bringing comfort to people marginalized out of existence. Her lectures at a church in Hollywood gave inspiration to the desperate. Some activists have blamed her for turning the attention of so many dying men to spirituality instead of activism, but her lectures became an important hub of connectivity for the gay community during the crisis and its aftermath.

Williamson has authored four *New York Times* bestsellers. She became known as Oprah's spiritual advisor. When Williamson ran for president in 2019 her beliefs inspired insults from the media. They called her "Secretary of Crystals," "bonkers," "wacko," "joke," "hokey," "scary," and "dangerous." But her reference to a "dark psychic force of collectivized hatred" resonated with many voters. Her appearance in the primary debates may have provoked a flicker of recognition among those who practice American Metaphysical Religion without ever having heard of it.

THE SEKHMET REVIVAL

The word *occult* can attract or repulse. Less fascinating than the occult, the term *metaphysical* at least has a somewhat more neutral association. Occult continues to be a word charged with negative connotations. For most Christians it is almost synonymous with Satanism. Occultism often conjures images of practices dedicated to material ends, such as seduction or money attraction. The term *occult* certainly misrepresents the diversity of beliefs and ethics found in American Metaphysical Religion. However, at what point does the term *metaphysical* become nothing more than a label for everything that doesn't fit into the major religions of the world? In fact, to fundamentalists of all faiths any religion but their own might as well be the occult.

To illustrate the awkwardness of both words, consider how to categorize sports fans who, in the season following Kobe Bryant's death, eagerly reported the recurrence of the numbers 8 and 24 as the Los Angeles Lakers played their way to a championship in a pandemic bubble. Of course, those were the numbers Kobe wore on his jerseys. Fans found mystical significance in the scores of games, or statistics added or subtracted from each other, points scored by a particular player, even the championship being the franchise's seventeenth (1+7=8). These were understood as signs that Kobe was sending to let people know he was helping the Lakers win another title from the other side. Fans with such beliefs included Christians and agnostics. Are sports superstitions occult? Are they metaphysical?

Hemingway wrote, "A big Austrian trench mortar bomb, of the type that used to be called ash cans, exploded in the darkness. I died then. I felt my soul or something coming right out of my body, like you'd pull a silk handkerchief out of a pocket by one corner. It flew around and then came back and went in again and I wasn't dead anymore" (Montgomery 2005). But that doesn't make Hemingway a Spiritualist.

How, for example, do we categorize the revival of ancient Egyptian religion in America inspired by sacred literature like *Awakening Osiris,* Normandi Ellis's classic rendition of the Egyptian Book of the Dead first published in 1988 by the small but influential Phanes Press. Ellis has published fourteen books bringing to life for her readers many aspects of ancient Egyptian spirituality and the nuanced meanings of hieroglyphics. She is also a Spiritualist minister in Camp Chesterfield, a clairvoyant medium certified by the Indiana Association of Spiritualists, and earned her Ph.D. with a dissertation that investigates belief in the existence of angels across Western, Eastern, and Silk Road traditions, including Yazidi beliefs about the Peacock Angel. In personal correspondence about her research used with her permission she writes, "I discovered primarily that angels are a state of consciousness."

The ancient Egyptian revival is also the result of organized communities such as the Fellowship of Isis, and the Isis Oasis Sanctuary founded by Olivia Robertson, an Irish aristocrat who authored five books and the liturgy of the Fellowship. Her cousin was Robert Graves, author of *I, Claudius* and *The White Goddess.* The Fellowship ordains priests and maintains a lineage. With dedicated buildings in fourteen countries and robust online resources they claim to have 24,000 members in 2021.

Among the prominent members of the Isis Oasis Sanctuary was Serena Toxicat, founder and priestess of the Oakland Temple of Bast. She was an author, poet, model, musician, fashion designer, painter, burlesque performer, and a renowned protector of cats, big and small. Many people seeking to encounter the sacred found inspiration in Serena's work, at the events she organized, and from the examples she gave of her generosity, kindness, and grace. She surrounded herself with a world of colorful sacred images, making of herself something of a living sacred statue of a cat.

The Sekhmet revival was also inspired by the work of women who have created workshops and handbooks for self-transformation based on Egyptian mythology, for example, Nicki Skully who was ordained as a priestess of Hathor by Olivia Robertson. Skully was the wife of Rock Skully, who managed The Grateful Dead. Nicki Skully visited Egypt with the Dead when they played live at the Giza pyramid complex in 1978. Her book *Sekhmet: Transformation in the Belly of the Goddess* incorporates shamanic and alchemical approaches.

Devoted to reconstructing ancient Egyptian religion as accurately as possible, Tamara Suida, a professional Egyptologist, founded Kemetic Orthodoxy in 1988 and has reigned as pharaoh for several decades. As a college student, Suida was a follower of Wiccan rituals. During a Wiccan initiation rite, she experienced a powerful connection with what she later understood to be several ancient Egyptian deities. As an initiate of Haitian voodoo, but also a scholar who has written books and academic papers about Haiti and ancient Egypt, she brings a rare combination of personal experience and academic scholarship to her leadership. By 1994 Kemetic Orthodoxy was recognized as a religion by the U.S. government. Normandi Ellis, Olivia Robertson, Serena Toxicat, Nicki Skully, and Tamara Suida have contributed greatly to the rising popularity of ancient Egyptian spirituality, each in a unique way.

As late as the mid-twentieth century, encountering the name or image of Sekhmet anywhere was a serious challenge requiring trips to specific museums or access to expensive tomes of Egyptology. Her image could be glimpsed in the background of a handful of Hollywood costume dramas and horror films, a goddess that had been forgotten two thousand years.

Sekhmet since then has become more present across the globe. For example, Thea Wirsching has done groundbreaking research on Edgar Allan Poe's Hermetic influences. She's also an initiated priestess of Sekhmet. She related to me that in 2021 at a statuary shop in San Gabriel, California, she approached the Cambodian manager. "I asked the guy if he took commissions, ancient Egyptian themed, he took one look at me and said, 'the Lion?' He scrolled through his phone to show me a Sekhmet in progress. He has them made in China." How did this reemergence of a goddess lost for centuries happen?

Even now scholars know little about Sekhmet. She has the solar disk on her head; she is considered a sun goddess. We know some of her priests wore red linen robes and were the ancient Egyptian equivalent of physicians. Her name was added to that of other goddesses to indicate they were the same, or aspects of each other, or sisters, or to increase their power. She was especially associated with Hathor, the ancient Egyptian goddess of love, music, dance, beauty, and motherhood. Sekhmet was sometimes represented as a form of Hathor. But Sekhmet alone protected the pharaoh, riding with him into battle, and at his death guiding him to the afterlife. Above all, she protected the balance that is required for life. That's what we know about Sekhmet, except for a couple of fragmented myths we'll look at later in this section, and her numerous epithets such as "At Whose Sight Everyone Lives," "Before Whom Evil Trembles" and "More Divine Than the Gods."

As we consider the beginning of the revival, its earliest appearance in the history of American metaphysics may be in 1915 when H. Spencer Lewis, the first Imperator of the Ancient Mystical Order Rosy Cross (AMORC) in America, placed a small statuette of Sekhmet on his desk where it stayed for many years. But it would take decades for more appearances.

Most likely the revival began in earnest because of the work of Robert Masters. The near fifty-year epic love story of the adventurers Jean Houston and Robert Masters has yet to be told. As the *Oregonian* newspaper said in their obituary for him, "The couples' shared passion for charting, understanding, developing and teaching of human and extended human capacities, fueled their lifelong adventure toward improving the quality of life for peoples of all ages, cultures and geographic locations. Together, they were among the principal founders of the human potential movement."

Masters was a WW2 navy veteran. He served in the Pacific, and then after the war assisted his father, a colonel, in the distribution of supplies to war-ravaged France and Germany. Masters took advantage of the opportunity. He met and informally studied with Jean Paul Sartre and Simone de Beauvoir, the lifelong soul partners at the heart of France's intellectual culture. In Germany he researched the work of Martin Heidegger, one of the great philosophers of the twentieth century, becoming one of the first to translate his classic *Being and Time*.

Going back to Missouri to teach philosophy must have been dull work after his wartime adventures so Masters got a job as a newspaper editor in Houston, then in Shreveport, Louisiana, where he and Elvis Presley became pals. Masters couldn't resist the opportunity when he was asked to become editor of the Library of Sex Research for the Julian Press. He moved to New York City in 1962, where the government was doing LSD research. Soon Masters was involved. Jean Houston was one of the volunteers. The daughter of a writer who wrote jokes for Bob Hope and George Burns she had attended Barnard College but was already driven by the desire to explore human nature. They were married in 1965. Between them Houston and Masters authored and coauthored nearly fifty books and more than a hundred papers and articles.

In his paper "Consciousness and Extraordinary Phenomena," published in 1974 in the book *Psychic Exploration: A Challenge to Science,* coedited by Edgar Mitchell, the Apollo 14 astronaut who walked on the moon, Masters described an experiment he conducted. Not content with debate over Jung's ideas about archetypes, Masters wanted direct experience. With the help of Michele Carrier, an artist who volunteered to be his research subject, Masters hoped to explore what Jung had theorized about. The results surprised him. They had not set out to meet Sekhmet. The subject was instructed to draw images from the subconscious. Masters (1974) writes about what happened next.

"It was doubtless because of [her] interest in a particular statue of the goddess that she found herself, while in trance, in a temple of Sekhmet on the occasion of our first working together. . . . The first trance, however, proved so exciting to [the subject] that she expressed a strong wish to return to the temple. . . . She already had had considerable trance experience and felt that the imagery of the Sekhmet temple was different from any she had encountered in the past, whether images of trance, dreams, meditation, or drug states. Everything was more vivid, more beautiful, more 'real,' and as a student of Jung's psychology, she felt that she possibly had entered into a world of archetypes." Carrier returned many times to that world, bringing back with her detailed descriptions and dozens of drawings.

In "Consciousness and Extraordinary Phenomena" Masters (1974) wrote about two cases "in which extraordinary phenomena appear to have been elicited within the context of altered states of consciousness (trance) in a laboratory setting." Of course, the question arises, what exactly is a laboratory setting when exploring altered states of consciousness?

One example he gives is Carrier's Sekhmet experience, and this is how he summarizes it, "the research subject, over a period of more than half a year, experienced herself as receiving training in 'magic' from an Egyptian deity, the goddess Sekhmet. Her experiences are related in terms of the possible activation of an archetype, and it is suggested that those experiences are analogous to ones described by such historical visionary mystics as Swedenborg and Ibn Arabi" (Masters 1974).

In the other experiment another subject "was given prolonged and elaborate training as a trance subject, including experiencing of trances of several days duration. The subject then was able to demonstrate telepathic functioning repeatedly, as have a few other subjects who were participants in a similar training program" (Masters 1974). This appearance of Sekhmet in the work of Robert Masters was the first mention of the Sekhmet revival in print, but certainly not the last.

From a completely different angle, as an academic with an interest in archaeology and ancient Egyptian culture, Philippe Germond published *Sekhmet et la protection du monde* in 1981, a translation of a series of invocations of Sekhmet from the temple of Horus at Edfu, including a summary and contemplation of Sekhmet's traits. Germond focused on the dual nature of Sekhmet. On the one hand she protects the order of the universe, the good pharaoh, the honest citizen; she's a friend to the poor and the oppressed. On the other hand she could visit pestilence and other catastrophes on people found unjust. The only right way was to appease her on a yearly and daily basis. Amulets, invocations, offerings, gifts, and prayers not only show respect but also remind everyone of Ma'at, the truth about the laws of existence that underlie genuine morality, the force of balance and justice that orders the universe. Those who ignore Ma'at experience the destructive side of Sekhmet: disease, war, famine, and natural disasters.

Sekhmet was in the news again when in 1986 an almost eight-foot-tall, two-ton Egyptian granite sculpture of the goddess, 3,300 years old and most recently owned by John Lennon and Yoko Ono, sold for over $740,000 at a Sotheby's auction. In 1993 Yoko unveiled one of several works titled "Bastet," ninety-nine bronze cats painted blue with fluorescent yellow eyes, or nine black cat figurines with glowing golden eyes, all identical. They were based on the famous statue of the goddess Bast, the sister of Sekhmet. In 2000 a *New York Times* article about Yoko mentions a three-thousand-year-old bronze of Sekhmet from Karnak staring out Yoko's window.

Is it possible that Masters was responsible for the interest John and Yoko had in Sekhmet? John was a fan of *Mind Games: The Guide to Inner Space,* a book Houston and Masters wrote together. He even recognized Masters in a restaurant and told him that reading the book had inspired him to write the hit song "Mind Games."

In 1988 Masters published the paperback that let the cat out of the bag: *The Goddess Sekhmet: Psycho-Spiritual Exercises of the Fifth Way.* Beloved mostly for its list of the names of Sekhmet, but a direct inspiration to practice and devotion for others, especially those who were initiated by Papa Bob, as Masters was known by his students. Masters did an interview with the *Monthly Aspectarian,* a Chicago zine that later became *Conscious Community* magazine, where he admitted that he used psychedelics when he wrote the book. However, he later denied that.

In *The Goddess Sekhmet* Masters describes being overtaken by the deity. He claims that witnesses confirmed that his features had taken on her likeness during the strange experience. This began a series of channeling experiments that resulted in the publication of the book. Masters believed he had received the mission to revive the Sekhmet religion and reestablish her mysteries. He promised more books of revealed secrets. More books have been written about Sekhmet, but none by him. He went on to repackage his wisdom and visualization exercises in less controversial formats.

A second edition of *The Goddess Sekhmet* was published in 2002 with a forward by Kenneth Grant, the British poet and Thelemite, whose popular writing about the darker corners of ceremonial magic opened new fields of study and practice for the ceremonially inclined. "It does not surprise me," Grant writes, "that there has been a call for a new edition of this fascinating book. Dr. Masters describes it as a 'scriptural work,' thus claiming for it a higher than mortal authority—a means by which a Nonhuman Being 'manifests to humans in a way suited to the present consciousness of humans.' The reader is warned in no uncertain terms to be prepared 'to risk transformation,' or to set aside the book. As one who has had experience in these matters, I endorse and underline this warning."

Masters introduced the 2002 reprint with an update about his experience since the paperback had appeared on bookshelves in 1988. "Since the publication of the first edition of this book there has occurred a worldwide movement among those dedicated to the revival, in one form or another, of the magic and religion of the Goddess Sekhmet. I have had many hundreds of letters from readers describing how they have been 'seized' by Her, and had their lives very powerfully and beneficially transformed as a result."

Masters approached the religion of Sekhmet as a hierarchy demanding personal instruction, but readers took inspiration as they found it, often ignoring not only the complicated visualization exercises in the book, but also the warning that initiation could only be given in person. The goddess herself seemed to ignore these rules as many worshippers have reported Sekhmet's entrance into their lives without the Masters book being involved at all. Dreams appear to be the most common first contact with Sekhmet. One devotee told me that he first heard the name Sekhmet in a dream. It took him years to find out what the word meant. At first sight of an image of her his agnostic attitude about religion gave way to devotion. For many, a random encounter with her image, whether as a statue in a museum or a character in a comic book, becomes transformative. Quite a few claim to have seen statues of her move and speak. Most experience epiphany and recognition when discovering her image. As Olivia Ciaccia wrote in "Seeking Sekhmet: The veneration of Sekhmet Statues in contemporary museums," "Despite their seemingly secular location within numerous museums across the globe, ancient statues of the Egyptian goddess Sekhmet have become focal points of contemporary spiritual pilgrimages . . ."

Of course, deities old and new are popping up all over the place, from 4chan mascot Kek's success as an election consultant to white supremacists worshipping Odin and MS-13 revering Santa Muerte. For some, this is proof of the end times and the return of the Golden Calf, but these experiences can also be understood as a spiritual renewal. People are showing the courage to explore humanity's religious heritage in a wider sense. Their thirst for healing and meaning is so strong they must go where they can find it. Some are surprised to find themselves devoted to unexpected symbols of the divine, but for the first time in their lives they have the religious experiences, the spiritual life, they could find nowhere else.

Sekhmet is perhaps the most interesting of these returns. Unlike most of the others, Sekhmet was never famous in the educated circles of the Renaissance, the Enlightenment, or any other era after her long importance in ancient Egypt. It seems the boys' clubs of scholarship up until this point were not comfortable with a feline goddess of justice.

In the Masters book Sekhmet, who is called "The Adorable One," is quoted as saying, "Images of me please me most." In the last twenty years Sekhmet's appearances in all media have multiplied like litters of kittens. Let's take a look at some of the places from which she watches us.

The Mercury Cafe in Denver is a well-known musical and metaphysical venue and organic restaurant that got its start in 1975 in Indian Hills, Colorado. A move to Denver, and several relocations there, led to the site downtown where this community center has flourished for thirty years. A brightly colored, enthroned Sekhmet looks down protectively upon the audience from the balcony stage left. No one is sure how long it has been there.

Some thirty years after the Masters book, Sekhmet can be encountered as a character in the Marvel comic universe where she is among the gods of Wakanda, but also an enemy of the Avengers. Sekhmet can also be found in the card game Immortal Battleground, in the computer game *Freespace 2* as a Vasudan heavy bomber, and in the video game *Assassin's*

Creed: Origins. She's a character in the *Ronin Warriors,* a Japanese anime series. An underground female rapper in New Orleans goes by the name Aisha Sekhmet. A death metal band from Belgium named themselves Sekhmet. Enthusiasts can purchase images of the goddess Sekhmet as art prints, pens, T-shirts, necklaces, phone cases, stickers, accent pillows, wall stickers, and mugs. She's also a popular subject for tattoo art. The Surly Brewing Company makes a pomegranate red beer called Sekhmet's Rampage. Sekhmet Ventures of California is not the same company as Sekhmet Pharmaventures of Mumbai, India. On Ebay and Amazon, but also smaller sites, and in a few brick-and-mortar stores, alleged artifacts of Sekhmet, in most cases amateurish re-creations, can be bought at a wide range of prices. But there are also beautifully fashioned statues for sale, and many artist renditions depicting the goddess as cute and sexy, serenely beautiful, or majestically wrathful. On social media there are memes involving cute cats named Sekhmet. Near-Earth asteroid 5381, which currently poses no threat, is named Sekhmet. As of June 2022 Sekhmet has over four million Google search results.

There have been over twenty books about Sekhmet published in the last twenty years. The curious can encounter TikTok and YouTube videos, and active Facebook groups. The Goddess Temple of Orange County, California, features an eight-foot-tall statue of Sekhmet. A modest temple of Sekhmet exists in the desert of Nevada. Workshops, conferences, and a lineage of ordained priests and priestesses have been established. However, the self-initiated command equal respect in the Sekhmet community.

To the Egyptologist, Sekhmet is an ancient deity who protected the pharaoh, and who avenged insults to her divine father, Ra, the king of the gods. Sekhmet was the guardian of Ma'at, the balance that makes life possible. Scholars regard her worship as the antiquated invention of an extinct culture. Perhaps the original origin of this Goddess was in areas of Africa where tribes coexisted with lion prides. Observing the social dynamics of the dominant species may have inspired leadership by female warriors. Ancient Kush had a lion temple, like ancient Egypt. The Kushite war god Apedemak, often depicted as a man with the head of a lion, or with three lion heads, looks much like Sekhmet. Apedemak was said to have been the companion of Queen Amanirenas in her war against Rome.

After defeating Cleopatra and Antony in his conquest of Egypt, Augustus decided to conquer Kush. Hearing of this through her spy network Amanirenas launched a surprise attack that liberated three Egyptian cities from Roman control and killed many Roman soldiers. The statues of Augustus that had recently gone on display were destroyed; the head of one was embedded in the steps of the queen's palace so those who entered could walk on him. Furious, Augustus invaded Kush selling thousands into slavery and destroying temples. He declared victory and began gathering taxes. But Amanirenas counterattacked with speed and shock tactics, like Alexander fighting at the front of her army. She is said to have used elephants against the Romans. They heard the stories of how this queen stood with a sword in each hand as she fed Roman captives to her weened lion cubs. In one of these battles she lost an eye, but as soon as she was able she returned to the war. In the end Augustus left Kush. If Sekhmet was not so much more ancient than Amanirenas we might suspect that this queen inspired the legends of this goddess, but it is more likely that both are offshoots of a far earlier perhaps even neolithic culture's lion totem.

For some American feminists the invincible goddess of justice is a world heritage and a promise of power. In the riot grrrl subculture of punk rock, Sekhmet appeared in tattoos and online handles such as Sekmet380, used by a riot grrrl who started the first riot grrrl group on AOL near the beginning of social media. On YouTube and TikTok women of color can be found sharing their efforts to reclaim their power with the help of Sekhmet—which brings up the problem of appropriation. Among Sekhmet worshippers there are people of color who believe that Caucasians have no right to appropriate the gods of their ancestors. Ptahmassu Nofra-Uaa, the world's leading maker of sacred icons for ancient Egyptian deities, a Caucasian himself, responds to this exclusion with the observation that divine beings call whom they will. If there are divine beings, then they are able to do as they wish, without regard for human preferences.

In the hearts of her new worshippers Sekhmet is a powerful and merciful goddess, supportive and encouraging, whom they turn to for healing, protection, consolation, and guidance, to surrender their troubles, and for victory in their struggles. This growing community illustrates the freedom felt by some Americans, and non-Americans, to encounter the divine in the form that moves them most.

Do these Sekhmet enthusiasts belong in the occult category? Certainly to most evangelical and liturgical Christians their practices would be considered occult. Classical occultists, students of the well-established mystical arts, of the sort that might own Agrippa's *Three Books of Occult Philosophy*, may not feel comfortable occupying the same category as revivalists of an ancient Egyptian war goddess.

In fact, some occultists warn that Sekhmet is a dangerous *egregore*, which they define, roughly speaking, as "a thoughtform created by a collective, a thoughtform that takes on a life of its own". Interested only in the continuation of its own existence and the magnification of its power an egregore can cleverly manipulate not just individuals but entire cultures. From this point of view to reawaken an ancient Egyptian goddess known for her apocalyptic rage might have unwelcome consequences.

After all, the most famous myth about Sekhmet involves her near eradication of the human race. Ra grows old. Humanity doesn't respect him anymore. They lose respect for the balance that is required for beings to exist. They grow selfish, crude, and cruel. His priests ridiculed, his temple poor and empty, Ra decides he must demonstrate who is boss. And so the Eye of Ra incarnates as his daughter Hathor, a goddess of love, who transforms into the invincible protector of Ma'at called Sekhmet. Normally her idea of a good time is wandering in the desert beyond the edges of the fields. But on this day her job is to kill the unjust, but only the unjust. She can use plague, a drought, war, volcanoes, anything massively destructive to take away the unjust and teach the rest a lesson.

Unfortunately, no human being is entirely just. We are only human. Sekhmet finding no one worthy of mercy released her rage in a frenzy of killing that would have ended the human experiment if Ra, or possibly Thoth, had not thought of adding red pomegranate juice to a crescent-shaped pool of beer. That shimmering crescent of red could not but attract the bloodthirsty lioness Sekhmet had become. This part of the story has fascinated the vampire subculture who perhaps misunderstand the nature of this sun goddess. There she drank, her tail slowly swishing, until the beer took away her rage and made her amorous. Every year the people would celebrate the holiday with music, intoxication, and uninhibited sexuality, followed by a morning of prayers.

Recently scholars have pointed out the until now unmentioned but rather obvious implications of a female, blood, and a moon-shaped pool. Or is this tale merely a philosophical contemplation of natural disasters? Why aren't the righteous saved from such tragedies? Because human beings are imperfect creatures.

In ancient Memphis, the city with polished white walls on the Nile delta, Sekhmet was worshipped as part of a triad. The most famous trinity of course is Catholic: the Father, the Son, and the Holy Ghost. We are left to wonder if the Father was a widower. The trinity of Memphis appears rather wholesome in comparison. Sekhmet as a goddess of justice, of war, but also of love, fertility, and healing is the protective complement to her loving husband Ptah. When the first small mound of land appeared from the endless waters there was Ptah. The earliest inscriptions from Memphis are from a granite slab over 2,700 years old. The slab preserves writing from lost papyrus scrolls dating to probably around 2400 BCE. The first inscription refers to Ptah.

Ptah created the gods by imagining them in his heart, which is called "divine knowledge," then he gave them form with his words, "divine utterance," and brought them to life with his breath, "divine energy." Ptah next created human beings, wild creatures, cities, temples, and religious ceremonies. Sekhmet and Ptah have a lion-headed son, Nefertum, known as He Who Is Beautiful, and Water Lily of the Sun, a god of healing symbolized by a young man or a blue lotus. A strong mother with a good sense of right and wrong and the muscle to back it up. A creative father in a loving marriage. A child who represents the beauty and healing possible in this world. A trio a bit healthier perhaps than a judgmental dad, a martyr son, and a ghosted mom.

Among UFO researchers, both egregores and Sekhmet appear as metaphors for encounters with aliens. In ancient Egypt Sekhmet was associated with the star Sirius. Skeptics may invalidate the Sekhmet revival as simply the result of the increased availability of books and images made possible by the internet. Together with her picturesque appearance, that explains the phenomena. But it does not explain why so many of the devotees of this goddess encountered her first in a dream, having neither heard of her nor seen her image. Sekhmet devotees ignore all glib dismissals of their goddess. For some she is one among many deities, and each to their own, and the more the merrier. For a few she is the only divine being. For them she is the one symbol of the divine that generates the resonance necessary for true reverence.

In 2022 the British Museum's *Feminine Power: the Divine to the Demonic* exhibit featured an ancient statue of Sekhmet. To the billions of patriarchal monotheists inhabiting our planet she can only be considered demonic. But to those who have chosen or been chosen she symbolizes the power and beauty of a justice that all other gods are said to tremble before. We have many perspectives from which to view the Sekhmet revival: as a religious reaction, as an expression of sociological forces, as a source of artistic inspiration, as a Jungian archetype, as the result of hubris and appropriation. Yet Sekhmet's growing popularity is undeniable. So it has always been along the byways of American Metaphysical Religion, salvation is found in unexpected places.

And so our tour comes to an end, but America's great experiment of religious reinvention continues. Despite long-standing anxiety about the alleged evil of esoteric spirituality, and about individualism leading to isolationism (the origin of dismissive labels such as *religious bricolage* or *religion à la carte*) most Americans whose spiritual paths fit the definition of American Metaphysical Religion turn to the deities of their choice, or that have chosen them, for strength, wisdom, and comfort during challenging times. They find others of like mind, in person and online, to achieve a sense of belonging in the effort to become better human beings and to improve their communities and the world. Practices and beliefs differ but most human beings want to live meaningful lives. At the heart of religious freedom we may yet find that diversity of beliefs and practices is not only nothing to fear but something to celebrate.

Esoteric Architecture of Washington, D.C.

An earlier version of this chapter was commissioned by Greg Kaminsky for *Occult of Personality*.

LONG BEFORE DAN BROWN'S ENIGMATIC BESTSELLER *The Lost Symbol* popularized the idea that Masonic emblems reveal a conspiracy involving the history and design of Washington, D.C., generations of writers have speculated on the subject. Various Christian authors have developed an extensive mythology around the idea that a Satanic pentagram marks the original D.C. city plan. Meanwhile some Masonic authors celebrate possible influence and ubiquitous symbols without regard for objectivity.

In his influential, but also much maligned, *The Secret Destiny of America,* when Manly Palmer Hall wrote that America could become a new more enlightened Atlantis, he mentioned the "democracy" of ten kings, and praised the idea of one world government in a world of free trade. Taken out of context, in today's zeitgeist, he seems to be advocating an elitist neocon agenda. But in fact, writing in 1944 with the world at war, he was trying to inspire Americans to a vision of a better way of life in a world of cooperation. MPH was always free with metaphors. Without connection to universities, in the days before the internet, he depended on a limited pool of questionable scholarship.

In 1989 a book titled *The Temple and the Lodge* claimed that George Washington interfered with the design, but no proof beyond speculation was offered to support the thesis. The authors also failed to explain the letters between Washington, L'Enfant, and Jefferson, indicating that Jefferson was the one consulting L'Enfant about the details of D.C., not Washington. Jefferson was not a Freemason.

David Ovason, the dean of this school that brings new meaning to the word *speculative* in Speculative Masonry, is honest throughout his work about the fact that most of the conclusions to be drawn, from the apparently obvious to the obscure, cannot be verified.

For example, consider the many zodiac sculptures in D.C. studied by Ovason. They could have all been designed in advance by a secret society, then they were created over generations as not just a message but also a series of magical acts. But then Freemasons being the studious types they are, we can safely assume most Freemason architects working in D.C. would study the work of the Masons who built zodiacs in the city before them, continuing and commenting on their themes. Of course, some of the zodiacs may have been built by people who had nothing to do with Freemasonry. Nevertheless, they may have decided to study the zodiacs of D.C., to which they would add their own designs. Perhaps a Mason or two decided to ignore tradition and create something fresh? Ovason has shown great patience in exploring these confusing nuances and possibilities.

Unfortunately, most of the popular authorities on the subject have no surveying experience, and much of their work is riddled with elementary errors spelled out in brutal detail by DCsymbols.com. For example, Ovason, who paints a truly lovely picture of sunset in D.C. in August lining up with Pennsylvania Avenue, comes out on the wrong side of a protractor.

Perhaps the most extreme example of the trend is Marie Bauer Hall, whose booklet *Foundations Unearthed* documented the beginning of her lifelong preoccupation with Bruton Vault in Williamsburg, Virginia. I knew Marie and worked with her when her husband Manly Hall asked me to help make her ideas more accessible to people. Many times I heard her tell the story of the worldwide reformation that would have been sparked by her discovery, but the vested interests and the power elite obstructed her and then removed the contents of the vault to hide the truth from the people. Had the people been given the chance, they would have been transformed, she insisted, to begin a true new age of enlightenment and equality. Marie described this with such passion she would sometimes become enraged or shed tears at the urgent need to get the contents of that vault to the people as their birthright.

"What's in the vault?" I asked Marie. The original Shakespeare manuscripts, and the original of the Constitution of the United States, along with documents that would reveal that Sir Francis Bacon, working with the Rosicrucians and the Freemasons, designed America to free humanity from tyranny. A theory her husband also held, but he drew the line at blaming the Rockefellers.

Marie was quite convinced that the American people and the world would be awestruck and inspired by the genius and self-sacrifice of Bacon and his enlightened coconspirators. We could renew America, Marie believed, if we uncovered the truth about the intentions of our founders.

Here we are, arguably at the heart of American Exceptionalism, the belief that America unlike any other nation was born to a great destiny ordained by the only true god. Students of history know that ancient Egypt, ancient Athens, ancient Rome, and the capitals of every empire since men first noticed the stars, included design elements oriented to heavenly bodies, and edifying symbols intended to prove that the destiny of that culture differed from all others by divine sanction. We might say that the surprise would be if D.C. lacked these symbolic embellishments.

But what of the first surveyors and designers of D.C., did they have the conscious intention of dedicating the city, or were they even more ambitious? Can a city be an invocation, a communication with the gods, a prayer in brick and mortar? Beyond the calendar of Stonehenge or the astronomical orientation of the Great Pyramid, could it be possible to build a city to receive the wisdom, the protection, and the guidance of the divine? Reading the stars, and by the law of correspondence, using materials associated with certain planets, and the right hour of the right day of the week, to invoke the desired, has long been a human preoccupation. Could a capital city be made into a gigantic talisman?

The first designers of D.C. had esoteric interests, but were they initiates serving secret societies? George Washington, well known as a Freemason, hired the talent, picked key sites and building designs, but didn't live to see the completion of the city that would be named after him. In his letters, he expressed more interest in comfortable rooms than symbols.

One of the surveyors Washington hired was African American astronomer Benjamin Banneker, whose father had been an enslaved man. Banneker studied advanced mathematics and astronomy using borrowed books and instruments. Many nights he would wrap himself in a warm cloak to recline under a pear tree observing the stars until dawn.

Just shy of sixty years old, Banneker worked with surveyor Andrew Ellicott, taking the first measurements for the design of the federal city. In his journal Banneker records the full solar eclipse he witnessed in the field. He published six annual *Farmers' Almanacs* between 1792 and 1797, compiling cures and treatments, lists of tides, astronomical data, including eclipses, all calculations his own. In Banneker's almanac appears an illustration of the sign Virgo as a woman holding a five-petal flower. We have no evidence to connect Banneker with Freemasonry, though his funeral monument is an obelisk.

Ovason, in his popular books, shows the recurrence of the sign Virgo and symbols of Virgo, not just this five-petal flower, or pentagram, but Mercury, lord of the zodiac sign Virgo. In his view, D.C. is a series of monuments to Hermetic Christianity; the Virgo/Pisces orientation of the city he believes invokes the Mary/Jesus evolution of the genders.

In the horoscope for April 21, 1791, the day the foundation stone for Washington, D.C., was laid, Jupiter was rising at 23 degrees Virgo. October 13, 1792, the day the stone for the White House was laid, the moon conjunct north node was at 23 degrees Virgo. Ovason (2008) writes: "On September 18, 1793, when President George Washington in his role as Grand Master laid the foundation stone for the Capitol the Sun was in 24 degrees of Virgo, and thus reflected the Virgoan nature of the new city. When the cornerstone for the Washington Monument was laid July 4, 1848, the moon went into Virgo; more importantly, the north node was at 25 Virgo." Ovason explains, "According to medieval Arab astrologers this degree had a particular importance: it marked that point in the zodiac where the Moon was thought to promote the greatest happiness and well-being."

But how can we be sure that alleged monuments of Virgo are not images of Columbia? Before Uncle Sam, Americans symbolized our country as Columbia. Samuel Johnson seems to have coined the word but Columbia first became a significant symbol in America in 1776 in a poem written by Phillis Wheatley, the second African American poet and first African American woman published in America, an enslaved woman. In the nineteenth century, Columbia became a common symbol of the United States. Before the "Star Spangled Banner" became our official anthem in 1931, "Hail Columbia" was the unofficial; these days it's only played for the vice president.

While Columbia has been shown bearing a sword, she was often depicted with a stalk of wheat or a five-petal flower in hand. Could some of the sculptors be honoring Ceres, who along with other Greco-Roman deities adorns allegorical sculptures all over D.C., dedicating America to science (Minerva) and commerce (Mercury), to agriculture at home (Ceres), and dominion over the seas (Neptune). They preferred the Roman names of these deities, not the ancient Greek, though Athens practiced an early form of democracy and Rome became an empire.

Various symbols have been found in the design of D.C., including the pentagram, pyramid, cross, cross-section of the inside of the Great Pyramid, and the Masonic compass and square. But none of the symbols are rendered with complete accuracy. No proof of any such plan has ever been found. Contrast the incomplete symbols of D.C. with the impeccably Masonic design of Sandusky, Ohio.

Major L'Enfant the city planner, hired and fired by Washington, was initiated as an Entered Apprentice, but he never bothered with achieving any of the higher degrees, nor do we have evidence that he attended Masonic meetings. In short, he never became a full member. As befits a man whose father was a court painter for the Bourbon kings of France, L'Enfant's plan was based on André LeNotre's Versailles but also Christopher Wren's unrealized plans for London.

After Washington fired the perfectionist and cantankerous L'Enfant, Andrew Ellicott, the head surveyor took over, expanding on L'Enfant's ideas with an imagination more given to the monumental. Ellicott not only surveyed and helped design D.C. (and Erie, Pennsylvania) but also mapped for the first time areas west of Appalachia; he also taught surveying to Lewis of Lewis and Clark fame. Even so illustrious an intellectual as Francis Fukuyama falls into the swamp when writing about Ellicott for the *American Interest* in 2007, declaring that Ellicott was a Freemason, when we have no evidence that he was.

Still, a Masonic obelisk was a key part of the original design for D.C. And how can any scholar underestimate the influence of Royal Arch Masonry, which first reached America in the lodge George Washington attended?

Yet it would not require membership in Freemasonry for a builder or sculptor to adopt Masonic symbols. In 1760 *Hiram; or, The Grand Master-Key to the Door of Both Ancient and Modern Free-Masonry* was published in London, revealing details of Masonic ceremonies, symbols, and even secret names and handshakes. In America Masonry attracted poor craftsmen, country cousins, and wealthy landowners alike. As the poor and the powerful traveled west, Masonry with its alleged connections to Moses and ancient Egypt provided a sense of comfort. Biblical quotes freely mixed with Masonic ideas in hymns, and Freemasons had the reputation of being upright, moral types, the creators of not only buildings and towns, but of a new world of high moral standards for all.

But then in 1826 William Morgan threatened to publish a book revealing Masonic secrets. False arrest escalated to arson at the printer's shop, then the determined Mr. Morgan disappeared without a trace, inspiring a wave of angry paranoia not seen since the Rosicrucian scare of eighteenth-century Paris. Local Masons were accused of murdering Morgan. Soon an anti-Masonic party gained popularity in U.S. politics. Americans were disgusted with corruption in the halls of power and they blamed Freemasonry. Morgan's beautiful widow, Lucinda, later became one of the wives of Joseph Smith, whose Church of the Latter-Day Saints reflects strong Masonic influence.

Among the mystics and occultists I met thanks to Manly Hall, and among the spiritualists I met on my own explorations, I often heard the phrase "capping the pyramid" as a shorthand description of some mysterious fate for the United States: America's esoteric destiny. The dollar bill has the most familiar symbol of the uncapped pyramid, although it is capped by the all-seeing eye. The Scottish Rite House of the Temple in D.C., with its thirteen-step unfinished pyramid on top, is the most monumental version of the theme.

Several psychics assured me that many ancient Egyptians were reincarnating as Americans to achieve the culmination of a plan that began in the days of the pharaohs. In his writing on America's secret destiny, Manly Hall presented an idealized interpretation of the pharaoh Akhenaten as "the first democrat." While most scholars would disagree with Hall's rosy portrait of the pharaoh, there's no denying his observation that here was the first great ruler in history to insist on being depicted with his arms around his wife and children.

But what possible connection could Akhenaten have with America? Like an overtone of music or an unexpected word in a poem, some tantalizing almost fact always seems to pop up when the researcher is ready to refuse the idea once and for all as obviously ridiculous. For example, Akhenaten's temple to his queen Nefertiti was oriented to the setting of the star Spica. Washington, D.C., is also oriented to Spica, the brightest star in the constellation Virgo.

Veteran provocateur Robert Hieronimus, in his popular book on the Great Seal of the United States, suggested that capping the pyramid means crowning the multitudinous forms of matter with the all-seeing eye of the divine eternal monad thereby uniting the opposites to create an enlightened citizenry and society. He ascribed such talismanic power to the Great Seal of the United States that he wrote if given appropriate attention, like an ultimate alchemical emblem of the Great Secret, it would inspire an evolved citizenry and society. According to Hieronimus, when the Freemason FDR lifted the Great Seal from the obscurity of government use to the ubiquitous dollar bill, America was given the opportunity to evolve into a spiritual nation.

The history of corruption in D.C., our bellicose foreign policy and perpetually dysfunctional Congress and federal institutions, our all too often predatory capitalism, not to mention the notorious predicament of the poor there, would seem to contradict the notion that the city embodies a greater wisdom. But then the United States has only two and a half centuries of history.

While no one has proven beyond a doubt that a secret society shaped the architecture of Washington, D.C., we can be inspired by so many individual efforts to remind us of what America was meant to be, and perhaps still can be. Ironically, while our culture, media, and until recently academia, have ignored the importance of the esoteric history of American Metaphysical Religion, Washington, D.C., itself pays homage to a nation, as Catherine Albanese has written, "awash in a sea of metaphysics."

Bibliography

Aberth, Susan L. 2019. "Women, Modern Art, and the Esoteric: Agnes Pelton in Context." In *Agnes Pelton: Desert Transcendentalist,* edited by Gilbert Vicario. Phoenix, N. Mex.: Phoenix Art Museum. Exhibition catalog.

Abler, Thomas S. 1980. "Iroquois Cannibalism: Fact Not Fiction." *Journal of Ethnohistory* 27 (4): 309–16.

Abzug, Robert. 1986. "The Power and Danger of Empathy." *Reviews in American History* 12 (4): 495–97.

Adler, Margot. 1986: *Drawing Down the Moon: Witches, Druids, Goddess-Worshippers and Other Pagans in America* Today. Boston: Beacon.

Ahlstrom, Sydney. 2004. *A Religious History of the American People.* New Haven, Conn.: Yale University Press.

Akkerman, Nadine. 2022. *Elizabeth Stuart: Queen of Hearts.* Oxford: Oxford University Press.

Albanese, Catherine L. 1988. "Religion and the American Experience: A Century After." *Church History* 57 (3): 337–51.

———. 1990. *Nature Religion in America: From the Algonkian Indians to the New Age.* Chicago: University of Chicago Press.

———. 1999. *America: Religions and Religion.* Belmont, Calif.: Wadsworth.

———. 2007a. "Introduction: Awash in a Sea of Metaphysics." *Journal of the American Academy of Religion* 75 (3): 582–88.

———. 2007b. *A Republic of Mind and Spirit: A Cultural History of American Metaphysical Religion.* New Haven, Conn.: Yale University Press.

Aldrid, Lisa. 2000. "Plastic Shamans and Astroturf Sun Dances: New Age Commercialization of Native American Spirituality." *American Indian Quarterly* 24 (3): 329–352.

Alimurung, Gendi. 2010. "Farewell to the Bodhi Tree Bookstore." *LA Weekly,* February 11, 2010.

———. 2012. "Bodhi Tree Bookstore's Final Hours." *LA Weekly,* January 12, 2012.

Alofsin, Anthony. 2019. *Wright and New York: The Making of America's Architect.* New Haven: Yale University Press.

American Society for Psychical Research. 1933. *Margery Mediumship.* Vol. 2 of *Proceedings of the American Society for Psychical Research.* New York: American Society for Psychical Research.

Anderson, Paul. 1940. "Hiram K. Jones and Philosophy in Jacksonville." *Journal of the Illinois State Historical Society* 33 (4): 478–520.

———. 1963. *Platonism in the Midwest.* New York: Temple University Publications.

Anonymous. 1996. "George Valiantine." *NAS Newsletter,* February–March 1996.

Anonymous. n.d. "The True Story Behind the Aquarian Gospel." *Dokument* (website). Accessed April 27, 2022.

Asprem, Egil, and Julian Struge, eds. 2020. *New Approaches to the Study of Esotericism.* Leiden, Netherlands: Brill.

Baudrillard, Jean. 1983. *In the Shadow of the Silent Majorities.* Los Angeles: Semiotext(e).

Bederman, Gail. 2005. "Revisiting Nashoba: Slavery, Utopia, and Frances Wright in America, 1818–1826." *American Literary History* 17 (30): 438–59.

Bednarowski, Mary Ferrell. 1984. *American Religion: A Cultural Perspective.* Victoria BC: Pearson College.

———. 1989. *New Religions and the Theological Imagination in America.* Bloomington: Indiana University Press.

———. 1999. *The Religious Imagination of American Women.* Bloomington: Indiana University Press.

Beekman, Scott. 2005. *William Dudley Pelley: A Life in Right-Wing Extremism and the Occult.* Syracuse, N.Y.: Syracuse University Press.

Beery, Janet, and Jacqueline Stedall, eds. 2008. *Thomas Harriot's Doctrine of Triangular Numbers: The "Magisteria Magna."* Zurich: European Mathematical Society.

Bellah, Robert N., Richard Madsen, William M. Sullivan, Amy Swidler, and Steven M. Tipton. 1985. *Habits of the Heart: Individualism and Commitment in American Life.* Berkeley: University of California Press.

Bender, Courtney. 2007. "American Reincarnations: What the Many Lives of Past Lives Tell Us about Contemporary Spiritual Practice." *Journal of the American Academy of Religion* 75 (3): 589–614.

———. 2010. *The New Metaphysicals: Spirituality and the American Religious Imagination.* Chicago: University of Chicago Press.

Bennet, Bridgett. 2007. *Transatlantic Spiritualism and Nineteenth-Century American Literature*. New York: Palgrave MacMillan.

Bennett, Chris. 2018. *Liber 420: Cannabis, Magickal Herbs, and the Occult*. Walterville, Ore.: Keneh Press.

Berger, Helen. 1999. *A Community of Witches: Contemporary Neo-Paganism and Witchcraft in the United States*. Columbia: University of South Carolina Press.

Bishop, Meade. 1861. *Old Churches, Ministers and Families of Virginia American Philosophy and Religion*. Philadephia: J. B. Lippincott.

Blavatsky, H. P. 1922. *Theories about Reincarnation and Spirits and My Books*. Point Loma, CA: Theosophical Publishing Co.

Bloom, Harold. 1992. *The American Religion*. New York: Simon & Schuster.

Blum, Deborah. 2006. *Ghost Hunters: William James and the Search for Scientific Proof of Life After Death*. New York: Penguin.

Bogdan, Henrik, and Martin P. Starr. 2012. *Aleister Crowley and Western Esotericism*. Oxford, UK: Oxford University Press.

Boke, C., J. Koopmans, and J. Perez. 2020. *The Key to the Hermetic Sanctum*. Auckland, New Zealand: Rubedo Press.

Bowen, Patrick D. 2011. "Abdul Hamid Suleiman and the Origins of the Moorish Science Temple." *Journal of Race, Ethnicity, and Religion* 2 (13): 1–54.

———. 2014. "Magicians, Muslims, and Metaphysicians: The American Esoteric Avant-Garde in Missouri, 1880–1889." *Theosophical History* 17 (2): 48–70.

———. 2015. "Islamophilic Masonry." In *White American Muslims before 1975*, 115–38. Vol. 1 in *A History of Conversion to Islam in the United States*. Leiden, Netherlands: Brill.

———. 2020. "'The real pure Yog': Yoga in the Early Theosophical Society and the Hermetic Brotherhood of Luxor." In *Imagining the East: The Early Theosophical Society*, edited by Tim Rudbog and Eric Sand. Oxford, UK: Oxford University Press.

Bowman, Rebecca. 1996. "Frances Wright," Monticello Research Report. Monticello.org. October 1996.

Bradbrook, M. C. 1936. *The School of Night*. Cambridge, UK: Cambridge University Press.

Brading, David. 1993. *The First America: The Spanish Monarchy, Creole Patriots and the Liberal State*. Cambridge, UK: Cambridge University Press.

Bradley, H. Dennis. 1925. *The Wisdom of the Gods*. London: T. W. Laurie.

———. 1931. *And After*. London: T. W. Laurie.

———. 1937. *Towards the Stars*. Rev. ed. London: T. W. Laurie.

Bragdon, Kathleen. 1996. *Native People of Southern New England 1500–1650.* Norman: University of Oklahoma Press.

Brasas, Juan A. Hererro. 2010. *Walt Whitman's Mystical Ethics of Comradeship: Homosexuality and the Marginality of Friendship at the Crossroads of Modernity.* Albany: State University of New York Press.

Braude, Anne. 2001. *Radical Spirits: Spiritualism and Women's Rights in Nineteenth-Century America.* Bloomington: Indiana University Press.

Bregman, Jay. 1990. "The Neoplatonic Revival in North America." In *The Heritage of Platonism,* special issue, *Hermathena* 149 (Winter): 99–119.

———. 1991. "Thomas M. Johnson the Platonist." *Dionysus* 15: 98–99.

———. 2000. "Alcott and the Concord Summer School." In *Alexandria 5: The Journal of Western Cosmological Traditions,* edited by David Fideler. Grand Rapids, Mich.: Phanes Press.

Bregman, Jay, and Melanie Mineo, eds. 2008. *Platonic Traditions in American Thought.* New Orleans, La.: University Press of the South.

Britten, Emma Hardinge. 1872. "Annie Lord Chamberlain: A Biographical Sketch." *Western Star,* December 1872.

Brown, Walter Lee. 1997. *A Life of Albert Pike.* Fayetteville: University of Arkansas Press.

Bruno, Cheryl, Nicholas S. Literski, and Joe Steve Swick III. 2002. *Method Infinite: Freemasonry and the Mormon Restoration.* Sandy, Ut.: Greg Kofford Books Inc.

Bryan, Gerald. 1940. *Psychic Dictatorship in America.* Los Angeles: Truth Research Publications.

Bryan, William Jennings. 1925. *Memoirs of William Jennings Bryan: By Himself and His Wife.* Philadelphia: John C. Winston.

Buchanan, Susy. 2014. "Ramtha Riled." *Intelligence Report,* no. 154 (Summer).

Bucke, Richard Maurice. 1901. *Cosmic Consciousness: A Study in the Evolution of the Human Mind.* Philadelphia: Innes and Sons.

Buckley, James Monroe. 1887. "Christian Science and Mind Cure." *The Century* 34.

Budapest, Z. 1975. *The Feminist Book of Lights and Shadows.* Venice, Calif.: Luna Publications.

———. 2014. *My Dark Sordid Past as a Heterosexual.* Santa Cruz, Calif.: Women's Spirituality Forum.

Bullock, Steven. 1998. *Revolutionary Brotherhood: Freemasonry and the Transformation of the American Social Order, 1730–1840.* Chapel Hill: University of North Carolina Press.

Burton, Dan, and David Grandy. 2003. *Magic, Mystery, and Science: The Occult in Western Civilization.* Bloomington: Indiana University Press.

Butler, Jon. 1979. "Magic, Astrology, and the Early American Religious Heritage 1600–1700." *American Historical Review* 84 (2): 317–46.

———. 1992. *Awash in a Sea of Faith: Christianizing the American People.* Cambridge, Mass.: Harvard University Press.

———. 2007. *New World Faiths: Religion in Colonial America.* Oxford, UK: Oxford University Press.

Calef, Robert. 1866. *More Wonders of the Invisible World.* Roxbury, Mass: W. E. Woodward.

Carnes, Mark C. 1991. *Secret Rituals and Manhood in Victorian America.* New Haven: Yale University Press.

Carr, Jessica. 2020. "Redefining Kabbalah: Combinative American Religion at the Kabbalah Centre." *Shofar* 38 (1): 78–108.

Carus, Paul. 1909. "The Ghost of the Living Person." *The Open Court* 1909 (4).

Chajes, Julie, and Boaz Huss, eds. 2016. *Theosophical Appropriations: Esotericism, Kabbalah, and the Transformation of Traditions.* Beer Sheva, Israel: Ben-Gurion University of the Negev Press.

Chen, Carolyn. 2022. *Work Pray Code.* Princeton University Press.

Chéroux, Clément. 2005. *The Perfect Medium: Photography and the Occult.* New Haven, Conn.: Yale University Press.

Chinard, Gilbert (ed.). 1929. *The Letters of Lafayette and Jefferson.* Baltimore: Johns Hopkins Press.

Chireau, Yvonne P. 2006. *Black Magic: Religion and the African American Conjuring Tradition.* Berkeley: University of California Press.

Churton, Tobias. 2009. *The Invisible History of the Rosicrucians.* Rochester, Vt.: Inner Traditions.

Ciaccia, Olivia. 2021. "Seeking Sekhmet: The veneration of Sekhmet Statues in contemporary museums." *The Pomegranate: International Journal of Pagan Studies.* Vol. 23, No. 1–2.

Clayton, Lawrence A., Vernon James Knight Jr., and Edward C. Moore, eds. 1993. *The de Soto Chronicles: The Expedition of Hernando de Soto to North America in 1539–1543.* 2 vols. Tuscaloosa: University of Alabama Press.

Clucas, Stephen. 2009. "Thomas Harriot's A brief and true report: knowledge-making and the Roanoke voyage." In *European Visions, American Voices,* edited by Kim Sloan, 17–23. London: British Museum Press.

Coleman, William Emmette. 1893. "Critical Historical Review of the Theosophical Society [An Expose of Madame Blavatsky]." *Religio-Philosophical Journal,* September 16, 1893, 264–66.

Conners, Robert J. 1999. "Frances Wright: First Female Civic Rhetor in America." *College English.* Vol. 62, No. 1. National Council of Teachers of English.

Conrad, Bryce. 1990. *Refiguring America: A Study of William Carlos Williams' In the American Grain.* Urbana: University of Illinois Press.

Coulthard, Cheryl. 2019. "Frances Wright's Nashoba: Seeking a Utopian Solution to the Problem of Slavery." *Communal Societies* 39 (2). Communal Studies Association.

Cox, Robert. 2003. *Body and Soul: A Sympathetic History of American Spiritualism.* Charlottesville: University of Virginia Press.

Craddock, Ida. 2017. "Psychic Wedlock" in *Ida Craddock Collection.* CreateSpace (website).

Crane, Clare. 1970. "Jesse Shepard and the Villa Montezuma." *San Diego Historical Society Quarterly* 16 (3).

Cronon, William. 1983. *Changes in the Land: Indians, Colonists, and the Ecology of New England.* New York: Hill and Wang.

Cunningham, Elizabeth. 2013. *Remarkable Women of Taos.* Taos, N.Mex.: Nighthawk Press.

Davis. Jack L. 1970. "Roger Williams among the Narragansett Indians." *New England Quarterly* 43 (4): 593–604.

Davis, William. 1996. "Musical Therapy: The First Handbook of Music Therapy Clinical Practice." *Journal of Music Therapy* 33 (1): 34–46.

Deloria, Vine Jr. 1975. *God Is Red: A Native View of Religion.* Delta.

———. 1997. *Red Earth, White Lies: Native Americans and the Myth of Scientific Fact.* Fulcrum.

———. 1998. *For This Land: Writings on Religion in America.* Routledge.

———. 2006. *The World We Used to Live In: Remembering the Powers of the Medicine Men.* Fulcrum.

———. 2012. *The Metaphysics of Modern Existence.* Fulcrum.

Demarest, Marc. 2009. "Revising Mathiesen: Updating Richard Mathiesen's Work on Emma Hardinge Britten." Emma Hardinge Britten Archive (website). Revision 3, October 2009.

———. 2011. "Hypotheses On the Orphic Circle." Emma Hardinge Britten Archive (website). Revision 5, June 2011.

Demos, John. 1982. *Entertaining Satan: Witchcraft and the Culture of Early New England.* New York: Oxford University Press.

Dempsey, Jack. 2000. *Thomas Morton of "Merrymount": The Life and Renaissance of an Early American Poet.* Stoneham, Mass.: Digital Scanning.

Deslippe, Philip. 2018. "The Swami Circuit: Mapping the Terrain of Early American Yoga." *Journal of Yoga Studies* 1 (1): 5–44.

Deveney, John Patrick. 1997. *Paschal Beverly Randolph: A Nineteenth-Century Black American Spiritualist, Rosicrucian and Sex Magician.* Albany: State University of New York Press.

———. 2021. "Kenneth Sylvan Guthrie and Sexual Regeneration." In *The Occult Nineteenth Century: Roots, Developments, and Impact on the Modern World,* edited by Lukas Pokorny and Franz Winter. Cham, Switzerland: Palgrave Macmillan.

Dickson, Donald, ed. 2001. *Thomas and Rebecca Vaughn's Aqua Vitae: Non Vitis.* Tempe: Arizona Center for Medieval and Renaissance Studies.

Doss, Erika. 2019. "Agnes Pelton's Spiritual Modernism." In *Agnes Pelton: Desert Transcendentalist,* edited by Gilbert Vicario. Phoenix, N.Mex.: Phoenix Art Museum. Exhibition catalog.

Drury, Nevill. 2011. *Stealing Fire from Heaven: The Rise of Modern Western Magic.* New York: Oxford University Press.

Duncan, David. 1997. *Hernando de Soto: A Savage Quest in the Americas.* Norman: University of Oklahoma Press.

Duncan, Ian. 2011. "On 10th Street: Towers That Never Were." *New York Times,* July 7, 2011.

Dunn, Richard. 1994. *Astrology in Harriot's Time.* Thomas Harriot Seminar #14. Durham, UK: Durham University History Education Project.

Eckhardt, Celia. 1984. *Fanny Wright: Rebel in America.* Cambridge, Mass.: Harvard University Press.

Eldon G. Ernst. 2001. "The Emergence of California in American Religious Historiography." *Religion and American Culture: A Journal of Interpretation* 11 (1): 31–52. University of California Press.

Elliot, Helen. 1939. "Frances Wright's Experiment with Negro Emancipation." *Indiana Magazine of History* 35 (2): 141–57.

Ellwood, Robert S. 1994. *The Sixties Spiritual Awakening.* New Brunswick, N.J.: Rutgers University Press.

Evans, Arthur. 1978. *Witchcraft and the Gay Counterculture: A Radical View of Western Civilization and Some of the People It Has Tried to Destroy.* Boston: Fag Rag Books.

———. 1988. *The God of Ecstasy: Sex Roles and the Madness of Dionysus.* New York: St. Martin's Press.

———. 1997. *Critique of Patriarchal Reason.* San Francisco: White Crane Press.

———. 2018. *Evans Symposium: Witchcraft and the Gay Counterculture and Moon Lady Rising.* New York: White Crane Books.

Festinger, Leon. 1964. *When Prophecies Fail.* New York: Harper Collins.

Finklestein, Katherine E. "Northport Journal; the Very Determined Meet the Dearly Departed." *New York Times,* April 25, 1999.

Finley, Lana. 2015. "Paschal Beverly Randolph in the African American Community." In *Esotericism in African American Religious Experience,* 37–51. Leiden: Brill.

Fisher, Marc. 1988. "Dr. Buzzard's Voodoo Cure." *Washington Post,* December 11, 1988.

Flexner, James. 1972. *George Washington: Anguish & Farewell (1793–1799), Volume IV.* Boston: Little Brown.

Forbes, Jack D. 2008. *Columbus and Other Cannibals.* New York: Seven Stories Press.

Ford, Arthur. 1958. *Nothing So Strange.* New York: Harper and Row.

Fox, Robert, ed. 2000. *Thomas Harriot: An Elizabethan Man of Science.* Aldershot: Ashgate.

Fromm, Erich. 1957. "The Authoritarian Personality." *Deutsche Universitätszeitung, Band 12* (9).

Fryer, Paul, ed. 2012. *Women in the Arts in the Belle Epoque: Essays on Influential Artists, Writers and Performers.* Jefferson, N.C.: McFarland.

Gabriel, Mary. 1998. *Notorious Victoria: The Life of Victoria Woodhull, Uncensored.* Chapel Hill, N.C.: Algonquin Books.

Gallagher, Eugene V., and W. Michael Ashcraft, eds. 2006. *African Diaspora Traditions and Other American Innovations.* Vol. 5 of *New and Alternative Religions in America.* Westport, Conn.: Greenwood Press.

Gardetta, Dave. 2011. "Finding Closure: Bodhi Tree, the bookstore that enlightened New Age L.A. readies for its final exit." *LA Mag,* July 1, 2011.

Garland, Hamlin. 1962. "Centennial tributes and a Checklist of the Hamlin Garland papers." Edited by Lloyd A. Arvidson. Los Angeles: University of Southern California Library.

Gatti, H. 1993. *The Natural Philosophy of Thomas Harriot.* Oxford, UK: Oxford University Press.

Gaustad, Edwin S. 2005. *Roger Williams.* New York: Oxford University Press.

Gilbert, Bennett, ed. 1986. *Alchemy: A Comprehensive Bibliography of the Manly P. Hall Collection.* Los Angeles: Philosophical Research Society.

Gill, Gillian. 1998. *Mary Baker Eddy.* Reading, Mass.: Perseus Books.

Ginzberg, Lori D. 1994. "'The Hearts of Your Readers will Shudder': Fanny Wright, Infidelity, and American Freethought" *American Quarterly.* Vol. 46, No. 2. The Johns Hopkins.

Glassberg, David. 1990. *American Historical Pageantry: The Uses of Tradition in the Early Twentieth Century.* Chapel Hill: University of North Carolina Press.

Godbeer, Richard. 1992. *The Devil's Dominion: Magic and Religion in Early New England*. New York: Cambridge.

Godwin, Joscelyn. 1991. "Hargrave Jennings." *Hermetic Journal* (1991): 49–77.

———. 1994. *The Theosophical Enlightenment*. Albany: State University of New York Press.

———. 2001. "The Survival of the Personality According to Modern Esoteric Teachings." In *Ésotérisme, gnoses & imaginaire symbolique. Mélanges offerts à Antoine Faivre*. edited by R. Caron, J. Godwin, W. J. Hanegraaff, J.-L. Vieillard-Baron. Leuven, Belgium: Peeters Publishers.

———. 2015. *Upstate Cauldron: Eccentric Spiritual Movements in Early New York State*. Albany: State University of New York Press.

Godwin, Joscelyn, Cristian Chanel, and John P. Deveney. 1995. *The Hermetic Brotherhood of Luxor: Initiatic and Historical Documents of an Order of Practical Occultism*. York Beach, Me.: Weiser.

Goodrick-Clarke, Nicholas. 2008. *The Western Esoteric Traditions: A Historical Introduction*. New York: Oxford University Press.

Gordon-Bramer, Julia. 2015. *Fixed Stars Govern a Life: Decoding Sylvia Plath*. Nacogdoches, Tex.: Stephen F. Austin University Press.

Grant, Kenneth. 2002. Foreword to *The Goddess Sekhmet: Psycho-Spiritual Exercises of the Fifth Way*, by Robert Masters. Ashland, Ore.: White Cloud Press.

Greenberg, Herbert. 1937. "The Authenticity of the Library of John Winthrop the Younger." *American Literature* 8 (4): 448–52.

Greenfield, Allen. 1992. *Notes on P.B. Randolph and the Hermetic Brotherhood of Light*. Eulis Lodge: LAShTAL journal.

———. 1998. "Hermetic Brotherhood Revisited: Thoughts on the Antiquity & Continuity of the Hermetic Brotherhood of Light." *Scarlet Letter* 5 (2).

Greengrass, Mark, Michael Leslie, and Timothy Raylor, eds. 2002. *Samuel Hartlib and Universal Reformation: Studies in Intellectual Communication*. Cambridge, UK: Cambridge University Press.

Greer, Mary K. 2015. "Origins of Cartomancy (Playing Card Divination)." *Mary K. Greer's Tarot Blog*. Last updated February 1, 2015.

Grimké, Sarah Stanley. 2019. *Sarah Stanley Grimké Collected Works*. Edited by K. Paul Johnson and Patrick D. Bowen. n.p.: Independently published.

Guenon, Rene. 2003. *Theosophy: History of a Pseudo-Religion*. Hillsdale, N.Y.: Sophia Perennis.

Gunn, Robert A. 1908. "Alexander Wilder, M.D., F.A.S.," *The Metaphysical Magazine* 23 (5), November 1908.

Guthrie Jr., John J., Phillip Charles Lucas, and Gary Monroe, eds. 2000. *Cassadaga: The South's Oldest Spiritualist Community.* Gainesville: University Press of Florida.

Guthrie, Kenneth. 1917. *Teacher's Problems and How to Solve Them.* Grantwood, NJ: Comparative Literature Press.

———.1918. *Plotinos Complete Works. In Chronological Order, Grouped in Four Periods; With Biography by Porphyry, Eunapius, & Suidas, Commentary by Porphyry, Illustrations by Jamblichus & Ammonius, Studies in Sources, Development, Influence; Index of Subjects, Thoughts and Words.* London: George Bell and Sons.

———. 1925. *Proclus's Life, Hymns & Works.* Yonkers, N.Y.: The Platonist Press.

Guthrie, William Norman. 1916. *The Gospel of Osiris: Being an Epic Cento and Paraphrase of Ancient Fragments.* Manhattan: Brentano's.

———. 1919. *The Religion of Old Glory.* New York: George H. Doran Co.

Gutierrez, Cathy, ed. 2005a. *The Occult in Nineteenth Century America.* Aurora, Colo.: Davies Group.

———. 2005b. *Plato's Ghost: Spiritualism in the American Renaissance.* New York: Oxford University Press.

Hall, Manly P. 1944. *The Secret Destiny of America.* Los Angeles: Philosophical Research Society.

———. 1973. *America's Assignment with Destiny.* Los Angeles: Philosophical Research Society.

———. 1986. *The Rosicrucians and Magister Christoph Schlegel: Hermetic Roots of America.* Los Angeles: Philosophical Research Society.

———. 2019. *The Secret History of America: Classic Writings on Our Nation's Unknown Past and Inner Purpose.* New York: St. Martin's Essentials.

Hallowell, Ronan. 2017. "Dancing Together: The Lakota Sun Dance and Ethical Intercultural Exchange." In *IK: Other Ways of Knowing,* vol. 3, issue 1.

Hammer, Olaf. 2000. *Claiming Knowledge: Strategies of Epistemology from Theosophy to the New Age.* Leiden, Netherlands: Brill.

Hanegraaff, Wouter J. 1997. *New Age Religion and Western Culture: Esotericism in the Mirror of Secular Thought.* Albany: State University of New York Press.

———. 2014. *Esotericism and the Academy: Rejected Knowledge in Western Culture.* Cambridge, UK: Cambridge University Press.

———. 2015. "The Globalization of Esotericism." *Correspondences* 3 (1): 55–91.

Harper, George Mills. 1967. "Toward the Holy Land: Platonism in the Middle West." *South Atlantic Bulletin* 32 (2): 1–6.

Hawthorne, Nathaniel. 1837. "The Maypole of Merry Mount." In *Twice-Told Tales*. Boston: American Stationer's.

Heartney, Eleanor. 2022. "Across the U.S., Museums Are Exploring Spiritualism and the Occult as Powerful, Unsung Forces in Art History." *Artnet* (website), February 21, 2022.

Heath, Pamela, and Jon Klimo. 2010. *Handbook to the Afterlife*. Berkeley, Calif.: North Atlantic Books.

Hedesan, Georgiana, and Tim Rudbøg, eds. 2021. *Innovation in Esotericism from the Renaissance to the Present*. Cham, Switzerland: Palgrave Macmillan.

Heimbichner, Craig, and Adam Parfrey. 2021. *Ritual America: Secret Brotherhoods and Their Influence on American Society*. Port Townsend, Wash.: Feral House.

Helborn, Thomas Scott. 1864. "Spiritualism: Musical and Other Manifestations in Boston, U.S.A." *Spiritual Magazine* 5 (10): 471–77. Reprinted in *Christian Spiritualist*, 1873.

Hibben, Paxton. 1929. *The Peerless Leader William Jennings Bryan*. New York: Farrar and Rinehart.

Hieronimus, Robert. 2005. *Founding Fathers, Secret Societies: Freemasons, Illuminati, Rosicrucians, and the Decoding of the Great Seal*. Rochester, Vt.: Destiny Books.

Hieronimus, Robert, and Laura Cortner. 2008. *United Symbolism of America: Deciphering Hidden Meanings in America's Most Familiar Art, Architecture, and Logos*. Pompton Plains, N.J.: New Page Books.

Hoffman, Donald. 1998. *Frank Lloyd Wright, Louis Sullivan and the Skyscraper*. New York: Dover.

Honey, Maureen. 2016. *Aphrodite's Daughters: Three Modernist Poets of the Harlem Renaissance*. New Brunswick, N.J.: Rutgers University Press.

hooks, bell. 2018. *All About Love: New Visions*. New York: William Morrow.

Horowitz, Mitch. 2009. *Occult America: The Secret History of How Mysticism Shaped Our Nation*. New York: Bantam Books.

Houdini, Harry. 1924. *Houdini Exposes the Tricks Used by the Boston Medium "Margery" to Win the $2500 Prize Offered By the Scientific American. Also a Complete Exposure of Argamasilla the Famous Spaniard Who Baffled Noted Scientists of Europe and America with His Claim of X-Ray Vision*. New York: Adams Press.

Howe, Ellic. 1972. "Fringe Masonry in England 1870–85." *The Skirret* (website).

Hudson, Charles, ed. 1994. *The Forgotten Centuries: Indians and Europeans in the American South 1521–1704*. Athens: University of Georgia Press.

Hudson, Charles. 1997. *Knights of Spain, Warriors of the Sun: Hernando De Soto and the South's Ancient Chiefdoms.* Athens: University of Georgia Press.

Huss, Boaz. 2020a. *Mystifying Kabbalah: Academic Scholarship, National Theology, and New Age Spirituality.* Oxford Studies in Western Esotericism. New York: Oxford University Press.

———. 2020b. "The Qabbalah of the Hebrews and the Ancient Wisdom-Religion of Asia: Isaac Myer and the Kabbalah in America." In *Kabbalah in America Ancient Lore in the New World,* edited by Brian Ogren. Leiden, Netherlands: Brill.

Hutcheson, Cory Thomas. 2021. *New World Witchery: A Trove of North American Folk Magic.* Woodbury, Minn.: Llewellyn Publications.

Hutchison, William R. 1963. "To Heaven in a Swing: The Transcendentalism of Cyrus Bartol." *Harvard Theological Review* 56 (4): 275–95.

Hutton, Ronald. 2021. *The Triumph of the Moon: A History of Modern Pagan Witchcraft.* Oxford, UK: Oxford University Press.

Imy, Kate. 2016. "Fascist Yogis: Martial Bodies and Imperial Impotence." *Journal of British Studies* 55 (2): 320–43.

Jackson, Holly. 2019. *American Radicals: How Nineteenth-Century Protest Shaped the Nation.* New York: Crown Publishing.

Jaher, David. 2015. *The Witch of Lime Street: Séance, Seduction, and Houdini in the Spirit World.* New York: Crown Publishing.

James, William. 1936. *The Varieties of Religious Experience.* New York: Modern Library.

Japenga, Ann. 2016. "The Lost Colony of Sven-Ska: Christina Lillian and the Cathedral City Artists." *California Desert Art* (website). Accessed April 27, 2022.

———. 2019. "Lost Farm: The Rediscovered Homestead of Agnes Pelton." *California Desert Art* (website), September 7, 2019.

Jenkins, Philip. 2000. *Mystics and Messiahs: Cults and New Religions in American History.* Oxford, UK: Oxford University Press.

Johansen, Bruce. 1998. *Debating Democracy: Native American Legacy of Freedom.* Santa Fe: New Mexico: Clear Light.

Johnson, Franklin P. 1949. *The Thomas Moore Johnson Collection.* Columbia: University of Missouri.

Johnson, K. Paul. 1998. *Edgar Cayce in Context: The Readings; Truth and Fiction.* Albany: State University of New York Press.

———. 1999. *The Masters Revealed: Madame Blavatsky and the Myth of the Great White Lodge.* Albany: State University of New York.

———. 2012. "The Early Theosophical Society and the Hermetic Brotherhood of Luxor." Paper presented at Esoteric Traditions in the Ancient and Modern World Conference, Alexandria, Egypt, July 12–24, 2012. Available online at YouTube channel esoterictraditions.

———. 2021. *The Duped Conspirator: Colonel Olcott in the Hodgson Report.* Independently published.

Johnson, Thomas Moore, ed. 1881-1888. *The Platonist* journal. Vols 3. St. Louis, Mo. 1889.

———. 1889. *Bibliotheca Platonica: An Exponent of the Platonic Philosophy* 1 (2).

———. 2015.*Collected Works of Thomas Moore Johnson: The Great American Platonist.* Frome, Somerset: Prometheus Trust.

Judge, William Q. 1892–1893. "Faces of Friends." *The Path* 7.

Kamil, Neil. 2005. *Fortress of the Soul: Violence, Metaphysics, and Material Life in the Huguenots' New World, 1517–1751.* Baltimore, Md.: Johns Hopkins University Press.

Karlsen, Carol. 1987. *The Devil in the Shape of a Woman: Witchcraft in Colonial New England.* New York: W. W. Norton.

Kastrup, Bernardo. 2016. *More Than Allegory: On Religious Myth, Truth and Belief.* Winchester, UK: IFF Books.

Keene, Lamar. 1976. *The Psychic Mafia.* New York: St. Martin's Press.

Kerr, Howard. 1972. *Mediums and Spirit Rappers and Roaring Radicals: Spiritualism in American Literature 1850–1900.* Urbana: University of Illinois.

Kiernan, Ben. 2007. *Blood and Soil: A World History of Genocide and Extermination.* New Haven: Yale University Press.

Kittredge, George. 1920. *Dr. Robert Child the Remonstrant.* Cambridge: Publications of the Colonial Society of Massachusetts.

Kramer, Hans Martin, and Julian Stube. 2021. *Theosophy across Boundaries: Transcultural and Interdisciplinary Perspectives on a Modern Esoteric Movement.* Albany: State University of New York.

Kupperman, Karen. 1980. *Settling with the Indians: The Meeting of English and Indian Cultures in America 1580–1640.* Totowa, N.J.: Rowman and Littlefield.

———. 2000. *Indians and English: Facing Off in Early America.* Ithaca, N.Y.: Cornell University Press.

Lachman, Gary. 2012. *Madame Blavatsky: The Mother of Modern Spirituality.* New York: Tarcher.

———. 2018. *Dark Star Rising: Magick and Power in the Age of Trump.* New York: Tarcher.

Laird, Cynthia. 2011. "Gay Pioneer Arthur Evans Dies." *Bay Area Reporter,* September 14, 2011.

Lane, Margaret. 1972. *Frances Wright and the Great Experiment*. Manchester, UK: Manchester University Press.

Laycock, Joseph. 2013. "Yoga for the New Woman and the New Man: The Role of Pierre Bernard and Blanche DeVries in the Creation of Modern Postural Yoga." *Religion and American Culture* 23 (1):103–36.

Leary, Timothy. 1977. *Exo-Psychology: A Manual on the Use of the Nervous System According to the Instructions of the Manufacturers*. Los Angeles: Starseed/Peace Press.

Leary, Timothy, Ralph Metzner, and Richard Albert. 1964. *The Psychedelic Experience*. New York: University Books.

Leonard, John. 1990. "The Mission: For Historic St. Mark's in the Bowery Crusades and Good Works are a Way of Worship." *New York Magazine,* December 24, 1990.

Lepore, Jill. 1998. *The Name of War: King Philip's War and the Origins of American Identity*. New York: Knopf.

Lewis, Abigail. 2011. "Farewell to the Bodhi Tree Bookstore." *Whole Life Times,* December 2011.

Lopez, Vincent. 1933. *Vincent Lopez Modern Piano Method*. New York: M. M. Cole Publishing.

Los Angeles Herald. 1904. "Founder and Seer of New Sect Would Build Holy City by Sea," October 7, 1904.

Lowell, Robert. 1965. *The Old Glory*. New York: Farrar, Straus & Giroux.

Lucid, Tamra. 2011. "Interview with Poet Activist John Trudell" *Newtopia Magazine* (Medium website), December 14, 2011.

———. 2021. *Making the Ordinary Extraordinary: My Seven Years in Occult L.A. with Manly Palmer Hall*. Rochester, Vt.: Inner Traditions.

MacGee, Glenn Alexander, ed. 2016. *The Cambridge Handbook of Western Mysticism and Esotericism*. Cambridge, UK: Cambridge University Press.

MacLaine, Shirley. 1983. *Out on a Limb*. New York: Bantam.

Magee, Tamlin. 2021. "Trying to Change Reality with a Magickal Algorithm." *Vice,* February 22, 2021.

Manseau, Peter. 2017. *The Apparitionists: A Tale of Phantoms, Fraud, Photography, and the Man Who Captured Lincoln's Ghost*. Boston: Houghton Mifflin Harcourt.

Marble, Matt. 2014. "The Illusioned Ear: Disembodied Sound & The Musical Séances of Francis Grierson." *Ear Wave Event* 1 (Spring). Available at Ear Wave Event online.

———. 2021. *Buddhist Bubblegum: Esotericism in the Creative Process of Arthur Russell*. New York: CoolGrove Press.

———. 2021. Personal Correspondence.

Marsh, Sarahbelle Alyson. 2011. "Rolfing: Structural Integration as American Metaphysical Religiosity." Master's thesis, University of Colorado.

Massachusetts Historical Society. (1794) 1810. *Collections of the Massachusetts Historical Society, For the Year 1794. Vol. III.* Boston: Munroe and Francis.

Masters, Robert. 1974. "Consciousness and Extraordinary Phenomena." In *Psychic Exploration: A Challenge to Science,* edited by Edgar Mitchell and John White. New York: G. P. Putnam's Sons.

———. (1988) 2002. *The Goddess Sekhmet: Psycho-Spiritual Exercises of the Fifth Way.* Reprint, Ashland, Ore.: White Cloud Press.

Mather, Cotton. 1689. *Memorable Providences.* Boston: R. P.

———. 1693. *Wonders of the Invisible World.* London: John Dunton at the Raven in the Poultry.

McAdams, Elizabeth, and Raymond Bayless. 1981. *The Case for Life After Death: Parapsychologists Look at Survival Evidence.* Lanham, Md.: Rowman and Littlefield.

McAlpine, Eileen. 2007. "George Valiantine." *The Voice Box* (website). Accessed April 29, 2022.

McClanan, Anne, and Eliot Morrison. 2012. "Alchemy, Magic and Science: An Analysis of the Ripley Scroll, Mellon MS 41." Undergraduate paper, Portland State University.

McKenna, Terence. 1991. *The Archaic Revival.* New York: Harper Collins.

McLoughlin, William G. 1978. *Revivals, Awakenings, and Reform.* Chicago History of American Religion. Chicago: University of Chicago Press.

McMillion, Scott. 1998. "Prophet Family Struggles with Problems Right at Home." *Bozeman Daily Chronicle,* March 14, 1998.

McTeer, J. F. 1970. *High Sheriff of the Low Country.* Beaufort, S.C.: Beaufort Book Company.

McVey, Geoffrey. 2005. "Thebes, Luxor, and Loudsville, Georgia: The Hermetic Brotherhood of Luxor and the Landscapes of 19th-Century Occultisms." In *The Occult in Nineteenth-Century America,* edited by Cathy Gutierrez. Aurora, Colo.: Davies Group.

McWilliams, John. 2004. *New England's Crises and Cultural Memory: Literature, Politics, History, Religion, 1620–1860.* Cambridge: UK: Cambridge University Press.

Mead, Sydney. 1963. *The Lively Experiment: The Shaping of Christianity in America.* New York: Harper and Row.

Meares, Hadley. 2021. "The Witches of Westwood and Carlos Castaneda's Sinister Legacy." *LAist* (online), September 2, 2021.

Medhurst, R. G., ed. 1972. *Crookes and the Spirit World: The important investigations by Sir William Crookes OM.FRS in the field of psychical research.* New York: Taplinger.

Meier, Alison. 2020. "Agnes Pelton: The Forgotten Woman Modernist Inspired by Nature's Unseen Forces." *Art and Object* (website), March 13, 2020.

Melton, J. Gordon. 1991. *Religious Leaders of America: A Biographical Guide to Founders and Leaders of Religious Bodies, Churches, and Spiritual Groups in North America.* Detroit, Mich.: Gale Research.

———. 1992. *Perspectives on the New Age.* Albany: State University of New York.

Midorikawa, Emily. 2021. *Out of the Shadows: Six Visionary Victorian Women in Search of a Public Voice.* Berkeley, Calif.: Counterpoint.

Mignano, Mitch. 2021. "The Faux Shamanism of Jake 'Angeli' Chansley." *Lucid News* (online), February 12, 2021.

Miller, Tirzah. 2000. *Desire and Duty at Oneida: Tirzah Miller's Intimate Memoir.* Bloomington: Indiana University Press.

Mills, James F. 2011. "Bodhi Tree, Silver Spoon to be Missed in the New Year." *Patch* (website), December 31, 2011.

Milton, Giles. 2000. *Big Chief Elizabeth: The Adventures and Fate of the First English Colonists in America.* New York: Farrar, Straus and Giroux.

Montgomery, Paul. 2005. "Paul Hemingway and Guy Hickok in Italy: The Brooklyn Eagle Articles." *The Hemingway Review* 25 (1), Fall 2005.

Moore, R. Laurence. 1986. *Religious Outsiders and the Making of Americans.* Oxford, UK: Oxford University Press.

Moore, Sue. 2017. "Spiritualist Camp in Vicksburg Was a Big Attraction." *South County News,* November 7, 2017.

Morell, Michael. 2010. *Empathy and Democracy: Feeling, Thinking, and Deliberation.* University Park: Pennsylvania State University Press.

Morton, Thomas. 2000. *New English Canaan.* Edited with notes by Jack Dempsey. Stoneham, Mass.: Digital Scanning.

Murillo, Phillippe. 2011. "A Renewal of the American Metaphysical Religion: An Analysis of Christ Church Unity, Orlando, Florida, USA." Paper presented at the CESNUR International Conference, Changing Gods. Between Religion and Everyday Life, University of Torino, Torino, Italy, September 9–11, 2010. Reprinted in *Research and Analyses* 24 (February 2011) at *Religioscope* (website).

Nadis, Fred. 2005. "'If Not Spirits What Is It?'—Turn of the Century Magicians and the Anti-Spiritualistic Performance." In *The Occult in Nineteenth-Century America,* edited by Cathy Gutierrez. Aurora, Colo.: Davies Group.

Nagy, Ron, and Joyce Lajudice. 2010. *The Spirits of Lily Dale*. Lakeville, Minn.: Galde Press.

Nartonis, David. 2007. "Metaphysics: A 'third stream' of U.S. Religion." *The Christian Science Monitor,* February 6, 2007.

Nation, W. C. Letter to the editor. 1910. *Light: A Journal of Psychical, Occult, and Mystical Research*. London: Eclectic Publishing Co.

National Cyclopaedia of American Biography. 1894. s.v. "Aldrich, William Farrington." 5:65–66. New York: James T. White.

Nelson, Steffie. 2016. "A Bodhi Tree Grows in Los Angeles." *Bodhi Tree Journal,* November 11, 2016.

Newman, William. 1994. *Gehennical Fire: The Lives of George Starkey, an American Alchemist in the Scientific Revolution*. Cambridge, Mass.: Harvard University Press.

———. 2005. *Promethean Ambitions: Alchemy and the Quest to Perfect Nature*. Chicago: University of Chicago Press.

Newman, William, and Anthony Grafton, eds. 2006. *Secrets of Nature: Astrology and Alchemy in Early Modern Europe*. Cambridge, Mass.: MIT Press.

Newman, William, and Lawrence Principe. 2002. *Alchemy Tried in the Fire: Starkey, Boyle, and the Fate of the Helmontian Chymistry*. Chicago: University of Chicago Press.

———. 2005. *George Starkey: Alchemical Laboratory Notebooks and Correspondence*. Chicago: University of Chicago Press.

Newport, John P. 1997. *The New Age Movement and the Biblical Worldview: Conflict and Dialogue*. Grand Rapids, Mich.: W. B. Eerdmans Publishing.

Nichols, Mark. 1991. *Investigating Gunpowder Plot*. Manchester, UK: Manchester University Press.

Oberg, Michael Leroy. 2009. "Lost Colonists and Lost Tribes." In *European Visions, American Voices,* edited by Kim Sloan, 101–5. London: British Museum Press.

Ogren, Brian. 2020. *Kabbalah in America: Ancient Lore in the New World*. Leiden, Netherlands: Brill.

———. 2021. *Kabbalah and the Founding of America: The Early Influence of Jewish Thought in the New World*. New York: New York University Press.

Olcott, Henry Steel. *Old Diary Leaves Vol 1*. Adyar: Theosophical Publishing House.

Ovason, David. 2008. *Secret Architecture of Our Nation's Capital: The Masons and the Building of Washington, D.C*. New York: Harper Collins.

Owens, Elizabeth. 2001. *Cassadaga Florida: Yesterday and Today*. Rev. ed. San Diego: Pisces Press.

Paglia, Camille. 2003. "Cults and Cosmic Consciousness: Religious Vision in the American 1960s." *Arion* 10 (3): 57–111.

Partridge, Christopher. 2005. *The Re-enchantment of the West.* New York: Bloomsbury.

Perry, Mark. 2002. *Lift Up Thy Voice: The Grimké Family's Journey from Slaveholders to Civil Rights Leader.* New York: Penguin.

Pike, Albert. *Morals and Dogma.* Charleston, 1871.

Pike, Sarah. 2001. *Earthly bodies, Magical Selves: Contemporary Pagans and the Search for Community.* Berkeley: University of California Press.

———. 2004. *New Age and Pagan Religions in America.* New York: Columbia University Press.

———. 2017. *For the Wild: Ritual and Commitment in Radical Eco-Activism.* University of California Press.

Pitner, T. J., C. E. Black, and F. P. Norbury. 1903. "Obituary: Hiram K. Jones." *Illinois Medical Journal* 5: 173–74.

Plagens, Peter. 1974. *Sunshine Muse: Art on the West Coast 1945–1970.* New York: Praeger Publishers.

Plaisance, Christopher. 2013. "The Transvaluation of 'Soul' and 'Spirit': Platonism and Paulism in H.P. Blavatsky's *Isis Unveiled.*" *Pomegranate: The International Journal of Pagan Studies* 15 (1–2): 250–72.

Plotinus. (1924) 1937. *Plotinus: The Enneads,* translated by Stephen MacKenna. London: The Medici Society.

Pochmann, Henry. 1948. *New England Transcendentalism and St. Louis Hegelianism.* New York: Haskell House.

Podmore, Frank. 1963. *Mediums of the 19th Century.* New York: University Books.

Polidoro, Massimo. 2000. "Houdini v. The Blond Witch of Lime Street: A Historical Lesson in Skepticism." CICAP (website), December 12, 2000.

———. 2001. *Final Séance: The Strange Friendship between Houdini and Conan Doyle.* Amherst, N.Y.: Prometheus.

Prevots, Naima. 1990. *American Pageantry: A Movement for Art and Democracy.* Ann Arbor, Mich.: Umi Research Press.

Priestley, Lee. 1988. *Shalam: Utopia on the Rio Grande.* El Paso, Tex.: Western Press.

Prince, Walter Franklin. 1926. "A Review of the Margery Case." *American Journal of Psychology* 37 (3): 431–41.

———. 1930. "The Case Against Margery." *Scientific American* 148 (5): 261–63.

Principe, Lawrence, and William Newman. 2006. "Some Problems with the Historiography of Alchemy." In *Secrets of Nature: Astrology and Alchemy in Early Modern Europe,* edited by William Newman, and Anthony Grafton, 385–432. Cambridge, Mass.: MIT Press.

Prophet, Erin. 2010. *Prophet's Daughter: My Life with Elizabeth Clare Prophet Inside the Church Universal and Triumphant.* Guilford, Conn.: Lyons Press.

Putzu, Vadim. 2020. "Kabbalah in the Ozarks: Thomas Moore Johnson, the Platonist, and the Hermetic Brotherhood of Luxor." In *Kabbalah in America: Ancient Lore in the New World,* by Brian Ogren. Leiden, Netherlands: Brill.

———. 2021. "Heretical Orthodoxy: Eastern and Western Esotericism in Thomas Moore Johnson's 'Platonism.'" In *Esoteric Transfers and Constructions: Judaism, Christianity, and Islam,* edited by Mark Sedgwick and Francesco Piraino, 273–96. Cham, Switzerland: Palgrave Macmillan.

Raboteau, Albert J. 2004. *Slave Religion: The Invisible Institution in the Antebellum South.* Oxford: Oxford University Press, 2004.

Ram Dass. N.d. "On Judging Yourself Less Harshly." *Ram Dass Love Serve Remember Foundation* (website).

Ramirez, Juan. 2000. *The Beehive Metaphor: From Gaudi to Le Corbusier.* London: Reaktion.

Randi, James. 1995. *An Encyclopedia of Claims, Frauds, and Hoaxes of the Occult and Supernatural.* New York: St. Martin's Press.

Randolph, P.B. 1874. *Eulis.* Toledo, OH: Randolph Publishing Co.

———. 1875. Seership! The Magnetic Mirror. Toledo, Ohio: Randolph and Co.

Randolph, P. B., and Maria de Maglovska. 2012. *Magia Sexualis: Sexual Practices for Magical Power.* Rochester, Vt.: Inner Traditions.

Razzeto, Thomas. 2007. "Houdini's Afterlife Experiment—Did It Work?" *Infinitely Mystical* (website). Accessed May 9, 2022.

Reeds, Karen. 2009. "Don't Eat, Don't Touch: Roanoke Colonists, Natural Knowledge, and Dangerous Plants of North America." In *European Visions American Voices,* edited by Kim Sloan, 51–57. London: British Museum Press.

Reichel, Willy. 1904. "Matérialisations." *Revue Spirite.*

———. 1975. *An Occultist's Travels.* Forward by Colin Wilson. Philadelphia: Running Press. First published 1908 by R. F. Fenno (New York).Rhine, J. B., and Louisa E. Rhine. 1927. "One Evening's Observation on the Margery Mediumship." *Journal of Abnormal and Social Psychology* 21 (4): 401–21.

Richardson, Mark. 1928. *Teleplasmic Thumbprints: Experiments in thought transference; Account of experiments made in the Margery mediumship during the years 1927 and 1928.* New York: American Society for Psychical Research.

Richardson, Mark Wyman, and Charles Stanton Hill. 1925. *Margery, Harvard, Veritas: A Study in Psychics.* Boston: Blanchard Printing.

Robinson, Samuel. 2019. "Beverly Randolph and the Forgotten Eleusinian Rosicrucians of England." *Pansophers* (website), February 25, 2019.

Rocks, David. 1996. "Mrs. May Banks Stacey." *Theosophical History* 4 (4): 144–50.

Ross, Steven A. 2010. *And Nothing Happened: Have Greed, Ego and Vested Interests Kept New and Potentially Safer and More Effective Medical and Health Technologies from the Public.* N.p.: Less Complicated.

———. 2019. *A Grand Design of Dreams: Contemplating Divine Revelation.* Paradise Valley, Ariz.: Theosis Press.

———. 2021. *Manly P. Hall's Unpublished Pages of the Secret Teachings of All Ages.* N.p.: Less Complicated.

Rothenberg, Celia B. 2013. "American Metaphysical Judaism: Rabbi and Shaman Gershon Winkler." *Nova Religio* 17 (2): 24–39.

Rubies, Joan-Pau. 2009. "Texts, Images, and the Perception of 'Savages' in Early Modern Europe: What We Can Learn from White and Harriot." In *European Visions, American Voices,* edited by Kim Sloan, 120–30. London: British Museum Press.

Rudrum, Alan, ed. 1984. *The Works of Thomas Vaughn.* Oxford, UK: Oxford University Press.

Rutman, Darrett. 1984. *A Place in Time: Middlesex County Virginia 1650–1750.* 1984. New York: W. W. Norton.

Sachse, Julius Friedrich. 1895. *The German Pietists of Pennsylvania: 1694–1708.* Philadelphia: Printed for the author.

———. 1902. *The Music of the Ephrata Cloister.* Lancaster, Pa.: Pennsylvania-German Society.

Sager, Mike. 2020. *Shaman: The Mysterious Life and Impeccable Death of Carlos Castaneda.* New York: NeoText.

Saint Germain Foundation. 2003. *The History of the "I AM" Activity and Saint Germain Foundation.* Schaumburg, Ill.: Saint Germain Press.

Salisbury, Neal. 1982. *Manitou and Providence Indians, Europeans, and the Making of New England.* New York: Oxford University Press.

Salomonsen, Jone. 2002. *Enchanted Feminism: Ritual, Gender and Divinity Among the Reclaiming Witches of San Francisco.* New York: Routledge.

Sanders, Mike, ed. 2004. *Women & Radicalism in the Nineteenth Century.* 4 vols. New York: Routledge.

Satterstrom, Frederick. 2004. *Alchemy and Alchemical Knowledge in Seventeenth-Century New England.* Honor's Degree thesis, Harvard University.

Scarborough, Samuel. 2001. "The Influence of Egypt on the Modern Western Mystery Tradition: The Hermetic Brotherhood of Luxor." *Journal of the Western Mystery Tradition* 1 (Autumnal Equinox).

Schaff, Phillip. 1961. *America: A Sketch of Its Political, Social, and Religious Character.* Cambridge, Mass.: Harvard University Press.

Seabrook, William. 1941. *Doctor Wood: Wood as a Debunker of Scientific Cranks and Frauds and His War with the Mediums*. New York: Harcourt, Brace.

Sexton, Jared Yates. 2020. "Commentary: The Confederacy, QAnon and the Cult of the Shining City." *100 Days in Appalachia* (website), August 6, 2020.

Shafton, Anthony. 2002. *Dream Singers: The African American Way with Dreams*. New York: John Wiley and Sons.

Shirley, James W., ed. 1974. *Thomas Harriot: Renaissance Scientist*. Oxford, UK: Clarendon Press.

Shirley, James W. 1981. *A Sourcebook for the Study of Thomas Harriot*. New York: Arno Press.

———. 1983. *Thomas Harriot: A Biography*. Oxford, UK: Clarendon Press.

Singleton, Mark. 2010. *Yoga Body: The Origins of Modern Posture Practice*. New York: Oxford University Press.

Stahlman, William D. 1956. "Astrology in Colonial America: An Extended Query." *William and Mary Quarterly* 13 (4): 551–63.

Stavish, Mark. 2018. *Pietism, Pow-Wow, and the Magical Revival: Institute for Hermetic Studies Monograph Series*. N.p.: CreateSpace.

Stebbins, Genevieve. 1892. *Dynamic Breathing and Harmonic Gymnastics: A Complete System of Psychical, Aesthetic and Physical Culture*. New York: Edgar S. Werner.

Steiger, Brad. 1976. "A Visit from Sekhmet: An Archetype Comes to Call." In *Gods of Aquarius: UFOs and the Transformation of Man*. New York: Harcourt Brace.

Stein, Gertrude. 1939. *Picasso*. London, UK: B.T. Batsdorf.

Stendhal. 1949. *Memoirs of an Egotist*. Translated by T. W. Earp. London: Turnstile Press.

Sterne, Richard. 1970. "Puritans at Merry Mount: Variations on a Theme." *American Quarterly* 22 (4): 846–58.

Stevens, Henry. 1900. *Life of Thomas Hariot and Hariot's brief and true Report of Virginia*. London: Chiswick Press.

Stevenson, David, ed. 2007. *Letters of Sir Robert Moray to the Earl of Kincardine, 1657–73*. Burlington, Vt.: Ashgate.

Stryz, Jan. 1999. "The Alchemy of the Voice at Ephrata Cloister." *Esoterica* 1: 133–59.

Stuart, Nancy. 2005. *The Reluctant Spiritualist: The Life of Maggie Fox*. Orlando, Fla.: Harcourt.

Sutcliffe, Jamie. 2015. "What We Do Is Secret: The Relevance Today of Arthur Evans's Witchcraft and the Gay Counterculture." *Frieze* (online magazine), February 15, 2017.

Sydney, Chapman. 2011. "A Victorian Occultist and Publisher: Robert H. Fryar of Bath." *The Road: A Journal of History, Myth and Legend,* no. 4 (June): 3–11.

Szonyi, Gyorgy. 2004. *John Dee's Occultism: Magical Exaltation through Powerful Signs.* Albany: State University of New York Press.

Tanner-Kennedy, Dana. 2020. "Gertrude Stein and the Metaphysical Avant-Garde." *Religions* 11 (4): 152.

Tarnas, Richard. 2006. *Cosmos and Psyche.* New York: Penguin.

Thomas, Keith. 1973. *Religion and the Decline of Magic.* London: Penguin University Books.

Thompson, Robert Farris. 1984. *Flash of the Spirit: African & Afro-American Art & Philosophy.* New York: Vintage.

———. 2011. *Aesthetic of the Cool: Afro-Atlantic Art and Music.* New York: Periscope.

Thorpe, Kimberly. 2009. "A court case forced a Santeria priest to reveal some of his religion's secrets. Its ritual of animal sacrifice, he revealed on his own." *Dallas Observer,* Oct. 22.

Time. 1973. "Modern Living: Pyramid Power." October 8, 1973.

Tooker, Elisabeth. 1979. *Native American Spirituality of the Eastern Woodlands: The Classics of Western Spirituality.* Mahwah, N.J.: Paulist Press.

Torgovnick, Marianna. 1998. *Primitive Passions: Men, Women, and the Quest for Ecstasy.* University of Chicago Press.

Traubel, Horace. 1961. *With Walt Whitman in Camden.* New York: Rowman and Littlefield.

Travis, Molly Abel. 1993. "Frances Wright: The Other Woman of Early American Feminism." *Women's Studies* 22 (3): 389–97.

Trollope, Frances Milton. 1832. *Domestic Manners of the Americans.* London: Whittaker, Treacher & Co.

Tucker, Jim B. 2013. *Return to Life: Extraordinary Cases of Children Who Remember Past Lives.* New York: St. Martin's Press.

Twombly, Robert. 1987. *Frank Lloyd Wright: His Life and His Architecture.* New York: Wiley.

Tymn, Michael. 2008. *The Articulate Dead.* Lakeville, Minn.: Galde Press.

Upton, Charles. 2001. *The System of Antichrist: Truth and Falsehood in Postmodernism and the New Age.* Hillsdale, N.Y.: Sophia Perennis.

Urban, Hugh. 2006. *Magia Sexualis: Sex, Magic, and Liberation in Modern Western Esotericism.* Berkeley: University of California Press.

———. 2021. *Secrecy: Silence, Power, and Religion.* Chicago: University of Chicago Press.

Valiantine, George, medium, and Neville Whymant, recorder. 1926. *Records of sittings:* Photostat of holograph ms, 15 leaves. New York. In Hamlin

Garland papers, Collection no. 0200, Special Collections, USC Libraries, University of Southern California.

Vaughn, Thomas. 1919. *The Works of Thomas Vaughn: Eugenius Philalethes.* London: Theosophical Society Press.

Vedanta Centre. 1919. "Report." *Message of the East* 8 (3): 72.

Veissière, Samuel Paul. 2016. "Daring to Hear Voices." *Psychology Today* (online), April 15, 2016.

Ventura, Michael. 1985. *Shadow Dancing in the U.S.A.* Los Angeles: J. P. Tarcher.

Verrazzano, Giovanni da. 1916. *Verrazzano's Voyage. 1524. Captain John de Verrazzano to His Most Serene Majesty, the King of France Writes.* Albany: The University of the State of New York.

Versluis, Arthur. 2001. *Esoteric Origins of the American Renaissance.* New York: Oxford University Press.

———. 2014. *American Gurus: From Transcendentalism to New Age Religion.* New York: Oxford University Press.

Von Martels, Z. R. W. M., ed. 1990. *Alchemy Revisited: Proceedings of the International Conference on the History of Alchemy at the University of Groningen April 17–19, 1989.* Leiden, Netherlands: Brill Academic Publishers.

Waite, A. E. 1923. *A New Encyclopedia of Freemasonry and of Cognate Instituted Mysteries: Their Rites, Literature and History.* London: Rider.

Wallace, Amy. 2013. *Sorcerer's Apprentice: My Life with Carlos Castaneda.* Berkeley, Calif.: North Atlantic Books.

Wasserman, James. 2008. *The Secrets of Masonic Washington: A Guidebook to Signs, Symbols, and Ceremonies at the Origin of America's Capital.* Rochester, Vt.: Destiny Books.

Watanabe, Teresa. 2010. "Booksellers Step Out from beneath the Bodhi Tree." *Los Angeles Times,* January 18, 2010.

Waterman, William Randall. 1924. "Frances Wright." *Studies in History, Economics and Public Law,* vol. CXV. Columbia University.

Weeks, Andrew. 1997. *Paracelsus: Speculative Theory and the Crisis of the Early Reformation.* Albany: State University of New York Press.

Wenger, Tisa L. 2006. "The Practice of Dance for the Future of Christianity: 'Eurhythmic Worship' in New York's Roaring Twenties." In *Practicing Protestantism: Histories of Christian Life in America, 1630–1965,* edited by Laurie F. Maffly-Kipp, Leigh E. Schmidt, and Mark Valeri. Baltimore, Md.: John Hopkins University Press.

White, Christopher, and Mark Silk. 2022. *The Future of Metaphysical Religion in America: Boundaries of Religious Freedom: Regulating Religion in Diverse Societies.* New York: Springer.

White, Stewart Edward. 1941. *The Unobstructed Universe.* New York: E. P. Dutton.
———. 1984. *The Job of Living.* Kirksville, Mo.: Hickman Systems Pub.
Whymant, Neville. 1931. *Psychic Adventures in New York.* London: Morley and Mitchell.
Wicker, Christine. 2004. *Lily Dale: The True Story of a Town That Talks to the Dead.* San Francisco: Harper Collins.
Wilbur, C. Keith. 1996. *The New England Indians: An Illustrated Sourcebook.* Old Saybrook, Conn.: Globe Pequot Press.
Wilcox, Ella Wheeler. 1918. *The Worlds and I.* New York: George H. Doran.
Wilcox, Melissa M. 2002. "When Sheila's a Lesbian: Religious Individualism Among Lesbian, Gay, Bisexual, and Transgender Christians." *Sociology of Religion* 63 (4): 497–513.
Wilder, Alexander. 1869. *New Platonism and Alchemy.* Albany, N.Y.: Weed, Parsons.
———. 1891. "Observations on Sanitary Science." *Medical Tribune* 8 (10), October 15, 1891.
———. 1905. "Not Uncommon Cause of Disease and Death." *Eclectic Medical Journal* 65, 1905.
———. 1908a. "How 'Isis Unveiled' Was Written." *The Word* 7 (2): 77–87.
———. 1908b. "Taking Cold and Kindred Ills." *The Metaphysical Magazine* 11 (2).
———. 1923. "How Disease is Desseminated." *The Metaphysical Magazine* 20 (2).
———. 2016. *The Later Platonists and Other Miscellaneous Writings of Alexander Wilder,* edited by Mark R. Jaqua. McLure, Ohio: Canine Endeavors.
———. 2017a. *Eclectic Medicine and Other Writings of Alexander Wilder,* edited by Mark R. Jaqua. McLure, Ohio: Canine Endeavors.
———. 2017b. *The Undying Soul and Other Writings of Alexander Wilder,* edited by Mark R. Jaqua. McLure, Ohio: Canine Endeavors.
———. 2018. *Letters to the Sage: Selected Correspondence of Thomas Moore Johnson,* edited by K. Paul Johnson and Patrick Bowen, vol. 2, *Alexander Wilder, the Platonist.* Forest Grove, Ore.: Typhon Press.
Wildermuth, Rhyd. 2021. "A Plague of Gods: Cultural Appropriation and the Resurgent Left Sacred." *A Beautiful Resistance* (website), June 3, 2021.
Wilkinson, Ronald. 1963. "The Alchemical Library of John Winthrop Jr. (1606–1676) and His Descendants in Colonial America." *Ambix* 11 (1): 33–51.
Willard, Frances Elizabeth. 1893. *A Woman of the Century: Fourteen Hundred-Seventy Biographical Sketches Accompanied by Portraits of Leading American Women in All Walks of Life.* Buffalo, N.Y.: Moulton.
Williams, Roger. 1643. *A Key into the Language of America.* London: Gregory Dexter.

Williams, William Carlos. 1925. *In the American Grain*. New York: Boni.

Williamson, Marianne. 2011. In "Literary Luminaries Acknowledge the Bodhi Tree." *Whole Life Times* (website). December, 2011.

Wilson, Brandon. 2021. "A Forgotten Father of the New Age: Manly P. Hall and His Impact on American Metaphysical Religion." Masters dissertation, Rice University.

Wilson, Cecile. 2014. "Is AMORC Rosicrucian?" *Aries* 14 (1): 73–94.

Wilson, Colin. 2013. *The Supernatural*. London: Watkins Publishing.

Wilson, Robert, and Robert Shea. 1983. *Illuminatus! Trilogy*. New York: Dell.

Wilstach, Nancy. "Scouts Create Garden at Aldrich Coal Mine Museum." *Birmingham News,* August 27, 2008.

Wirsching, Thea. 2021. *The American Renaissance Tarot*. Atglen, Pa.: Red Feather.

Woodward, Walter. 2010. *Prospero's America: John Winthrop Jr., Alchemy, and the Creation of New England Culture, 1606–1676*. Chapel Hill: University of North Carolina Press.

Wright, Frances. 1829. *Course of Popular Lectures as Delivered by Frances Wright*. New York: Hall of Science.

———. 1847. "An Exposition of the Mission of England: Addressed to the Peoples of Europe." *The Reasoner,* 3 (54): 321.

———. 1963. *Views of Society and Manners in America*. Edited by Paul Baker. Cambridge, Mass.: Harvard University Press.

Wright, Frances. 2014. "An important collection of nine autograph letters signed to Dr. William James MacNeven." Stevenson, Md.: Luxury Catalogs.

Wright, Frank Lloyd. 2010. *The Essential Frank Lloyd Wright: Critical Writings on Architecture,* edited by Bruce Brooks Pfeiffer. Princeton, N.J.: Princeton University Press.

Young, Jason R. 2011. *Rituals of Resistance: African Atlantic Religion in Kongo and the Lowcountry South in the Era of Slavery*. Baton Rouge, La.: LSU Press.

Young, Sue. 2009. "Peter Davidson 1837–1915." *Sue Young Histories* (blog). April 28, 2009.

Zain, C. C. 1962. *Mundane Astrology: Interpreting Astrological Phenomena for Cities, Nations & Groups*. Los Angeles: Church of Light.

Zakian, Michael. 1995. *Agnes Pelton: Poet of Nature*. Palm Desert, Calif.: Palm Springs Desert Museum. Exhibition catalog.

Zárate, Arthur Shiwa. 2019. "The American Sufis: Self-Help, Sufism, and Metaphysical Religion in Postcolonial Egypt." *Comparative Studies in Society and History* 61 (4): 864–93.

Index